The Cultural Context of Aging

The Cultural Context of Aging

WORLDWIDE PERSPECTIVES

Second Edition

EDITED BY

Jay Sokolovsky

BERGIN & GARVEY
Westport, Connecticut • London

Library of Congress Cataloging-in-Publication Data

The cultural context of aging : worldwide perspectives / edited by Jay
  Sokolovsky.—2nd ed.
      p. cm.
    Includes bibliographical references and index.
      ISBN 0–89789–452–9 (alk. paper).—ISBN 0–89789–453–7 (pbk. :
    alk. paper)
      1. Aged—Cross-cultural studies. 2. Aging—Cross-cultural
    studies. I. Sokolovsky, Jay.
    HQ1061.C79   1997
    305.26—DC21   96–37124

British Library Cataloguing in Publication Data is available.

Library of Congress Catalog Card Number: 96–37124
ISBN: 0–89789–452–9
      0–89789–453–7 (pbk.)

First published in 1997

Bergin & Garvey, 88 Post Road West, Westport, CT 06881
An imprint of Greenwood Publishing Group, Inc.

Printed in the United States of America

The paper used in this book complies with the
Permanent Paper Standard issued by the National
Information Standards Organization (Z39.48–1984).

10 9 8 7 6 5 4 3 2 1

Copyright Acknowledgments

Grateful acknowledgment is given for permission to use:

Excerpt from *Being an Anthropologist: Fieldwork in Eleven Cultures* by
George D. Spindler, copyright © 1970 by Holt, Rinehart and Winston,
Inc., reprinted by permission of the publisher.

Every reasonable effort has been made to trace the owners of copyright
materials in this book, but in some instances this has proven impossible.
The author and publisher will be glad to receive information leading to
more complete ackowledgments in subsequent printings of the book,
and in the meantime extend their apologies for any omissions.

To granddaughter Josephine, who calls me goofy,
grandson Alex, who likes to beat on a toy drum,
and daughter Rebecca, who is oh, so far away.

Contents

Preface

When I first taught a course on the anthropology of aging in the fall of 1976, there was a mere scattering of substantial writings available for students. However, at that time a large number of young anthropologists were engaged in or about to begin research on aging in diverse societies around the world. This included a wave of graduate students who were ethnographically studying the environments in which North Americans lived their elder years. These scholars have been joined by persons in many other disciplines who have forged an emphasis in "qualitative gerontology." This expanded second edition reflects the rapidly growing body of research undertaken not only by anthropologists but by scholars in other social and behavioral sciences. Suggestions of how this body of work can be used with this text can be found in *Teaching About Aging: Interdisciplinary and Cross-Cultural Perspectives*, 2nd edition (Shenk and Sokolovsky forthcoming).

Curiously, the process of getting all these works together took on a special poignancy as some of the authors began to confront several of the issues discussed in their writings. In my own case, the interaction with my first two grandchildren born over the course of working on this book has substantially altered the view of where I now sit within the span of life. Much more difficult issues were encountered by other authors in caring for either aging spouses or elderly parents. One potential contributor had to withdraw his chapter as he attempted to assist his 96-year-old mother who lived more than 2,000 miles away from him. Another personally confronted the experience of widowhood in the middle of writing a chapter about that situation in another culture.

A SPECIAL NOTE TO STUDENTS

Besides including eight more chapters than the previous edition, I have attempted to enhance the usefulness of the book's introductions in various ways. First, these sections have been expanded to not only give a background for the chapters they introduce, but also to provide some discussion of related topics not otherwise covered. Second, I have included short "boxed" sections which highlight important issues. Third, in the body of the text I have cited references most appropriate for undergraduates, while placing more advanced sources in endnotes. Finally, each introduction ends with a Key Resources section, which points students to important research centers, Internet sites, databases, bibliographies, special issues of journals, and a host of other print materials. *Note: Updates for these resources can be found at my web page, http://bayflash. stpt.usf.edu/faculty/jsokolov.*

I have chosen the Internet sites for their ability to give students rapid access to supplementary materials with some substance. In a few cases these sites actually provide working papers and databases from ongoing research projects related to the topic of specific chapters. Students, please be advised that by the time this book is published in the summer of 1997 some of the World Wide Web sites listed may have moved their location. If you have a problem linking to them you can search the World Wide Web for the center or research project mentioned. Frankly, you have run out of excuses in terms of finding materials about aging in just about any region of the world.

ACKNOWLEDGMENTS

There are many people who made this book possible. I wish to thank Ann Terrell, who helped me type and organize the long bibliography and accomplish many of the copyediting tasks. I also want to thank students in my Spring 1996 Anthropology of Aging class, who made many thoughtful comments on the manuscripts which eventually emerged as this book's chapters. From this class I want to especially thank Jennifer Salmon, Cheryl O'Neil, Nelson Mongovi, Rebecca Browning, Suzanne Reynolds-Scanlon, and Jan Nicols, who took the time to seriously critique some of these chapters. A special thanks also goes to my graduate assistant, Eric Chrisp, who labored in helping me physically organize the manuscript, double-checked the web sites, and contributed some insightful comments on my writing. Finally, I want to express my gratitude and deep appreciation to Maria Vesperi for her invaluable editing help with my own contributions to this work and putting up with the long hours of trying to get everything right.

Jay Sokolovsky
St. Petersburg, Florida
E-mail: jsokolov@bayflash.stpt.usf.edu

Starting Points: A Global, Cross-Cultural View of Aging

Jay Sokolovsky

We do not have elders because we have a human gift and modern capacity
for keeping the weak alive; instead, we are human because we have elders.

David Gutmann

A unique aspect of the evolution of the human species, compared to other primates, is that we alone have a distinct, significant postreproductive phase of life. As the intriguing quote from clinical psychologist David Gutmann implies, aging need not be thought of only in the catastrophic terms of abandonment and loss but also in terms of the crucial roles that elders play in their kinship and community groups throughout the range of human societies. This "strong face of aging," as Gutmann terms it, derives from the function of elders in our species' early history, as a vital link in the transmission of our socially learned systems of belief and behavior which imbue children with the essence of humanity.[1]

As the twentieth century draws to a close, the United Nations is making plans to celebrate, in 1999, the "International Year of Older Persons."[2] This will, it is hoped, consolidate almost two decades of global effort to appraise the needs and potential of the aged. Western thinking about aging itself also seems to be maturing, with the creation of a whole new stage of late adulthood, identified not with death but with productive engagement with life. To cite just one example, in 1991 the Commonwealth Fund of New York financed a five-year study on the productive activities of Americans over age 55. Their survey found that elders not only provide significant direct cash contributions to their families, but also substantially augment the nurturing and care of grandchildren. The economic value of this child-minding is being estimated at almost $20 billion per year (Bass and Caro forthcoming).[3]

Although the evolutionary legacy of aging also includes a powerful biological dimension of senescence, or decline in functioning, a global perspective on aging yields a wondrous array of social responses to the physical imperatives of growing old.[4] It will be the purpose of this book to employ such a worldwide view to explore two broad, interrelated facets of elderhood: (1) how older adults function as social actors in the setting of diverse societies and (2) how the cultural context in which people grow old creates a varied reality of what aging means.

THE CULTURAL CONTEXT OF AGING

These issues will be examined by considering the fabric of values, perceptions, human relationships and socially engineered behavior which clothes people as they pass through the older adult years. Such varied patterns of created ideology, social organization and the ways people produce and distribute valued objects constitute the cultural systems into which all humans grow. Each cultural system creates a perceptual lens composed of potent symbols through which a particular version of reality is developed. For example, over twenty years ago, J. Scott Francher suggested that in the United States the symbolic themes represented in the glorification of the youthful, competitively self-reliant and action-oriented ''Pepsi Generation'' presented a set of core values contradictory and harmful to the self-esteem of the old (1973). The continuation of this advertising sentiment through the Nike Corporation's ''Just Do It'' campaign in the 1990s reflects key elements of American culture which have not been ignored by the elderly. As I write this, older adults in the United States are harnessing elements of cultural ideals such as independence and personal initiative in the process of reshaping the very meaning of middle and old age.

This change is motivated by a momentous demographic occurrence—middle age is finally catching up to the ''me'' generation. As a business writer for the *New York Times* put it in 1996:

The generation that once refused to trust anyone over 30 is turning 50 . . . a member of the baby-boom generation is marking a 50th birthday every seven to eight seconds every day for the next 18 years. That's more than 10,000 people who were born from 1946 through 1964 crossing over daily into the mature market. (Elliot 1996)

This population watershed will influence a wide range of economic activities, from the marketing of types of soups (more low fat); the production of cars (bigger, more comfortable); and the way health care is managed (increase in preventative health care, rehabilitation and self-medication).

Set in the postmodern cultural age, new images of aging are being created where ''elderhood has been constructed as a marketable lifestyle that connects the commodified values of youth with bodycare techniques for masking the appearance of age'' (Katz 1995:70).[5] Some gerontological writers see the postmodern lifecourse as characterized by a blurring of traditional age divisions and the integration of formerly segregated periods of life. This attempt to recast the life span in fantasy images of timelessness draws from fountain-of-youth movies such as *Cocoon*, self-help books such as Dr. Deepak Chopra's *Ageless Body, Timeless Mind* (1993) and reports about very long-living peoples in distant lands (Conrad 1992; Cole 1992).[6]

Yet, people are not just passive recipients of culture. They craft lifestyles within broad patterns of values and ideal behavior. In Chapter 17, Japanese anthropologist Yohko Tsuji provides an excellent view of this process as she explores how American values are put into action in creating a sense of community in a small-town senior center. Another important example is to be found in the day-to-day realities of Southeast Asian ethnic cultures, as discussed in Chapter 14 by Barbara Yee. We will see that the ethnic mix of the American social landscape greatly complicates any simple analysis of ''American'' culture.

Culture exists in relation to the contextual framework in which human actors find themselves. Such ''background'' factors can be relevant at various levels of analysis. On the personal level, this might involve looking at how childlessness or poor health affects the chances for aging well or the nature of support in one's later years (Rubinstein 1987). On a societal scale, one could examine how, for example, differential access to wealth and status (class variation) or even the structural differences between communities in the same society alter culturally-based premises about how one grows old. In Chapter 5, Christine Fry and the team involved in Project AGE (Age, Generation and Experience) show how intercommunity variation interacts with cultural systems to influence how people define successful aging.

Situational factors can be strong enough to completely reverse patterns of respect and support linked to cultural traditions. As Anthony Glascock demonstrates in Chapter 3, ''death hastening'' of the aged can take place in societies which, in general, claim to revere old people. Yet the decision to quicken the demise of an elderly person is vitally connected to situational conditions, such as very low levels of functioning by an elder or a lack of close kin. Such factors can completely reverse culturally mandated patterns of respect and support. Similarly, in Chapter 12, my own research shows how the clash of ethnic cultures and contextual realities in the United States can dramatically transform the traditional meaning of ''filial devotion'' toward the elderly in some Asian groups.

In this volume the cultural context of aging is to be understood as the way in which traditions have meaning in the situational framework of personal lives and societal functioning. By exploring aging in this fashion, we can discover how social groups construct shared expectations about aging that interweave notions of time, life cycle, intergenerational relations, dependency and death. It is this cultural context of aging which gives rise to the exciting diversity of experience, perception and achievement during the last phases of the human life cycle. Such divergence in the nonphysical manifestations of old age is to be seen both within and across the multitude of world societies. Even among very small-scale societal types such as hunters and gatherers or tribal horticultural peoples, a wide variation exists in how older people are evaluated and treated. Some such societies regard their older citizens as revered personages to be carried on one's back as communities move over the landscape, while others see them as excess baggage to be left to the elements when they can no longer keep up. To see this, students can compare the positive situation of the Ju/'hoansi (Rosenberg, Chapter 2) or Mbuti (Turnbull 1965) people of Africa with the much less favored position of the Siriono of eastern Bolivia (Holmberg 1969) or the Chipewyan Indians of northern Canada (Sharp 1981).

THE ANTHROPOLOGICAL ENCOUNTER WITH AGING AND THE AGED

Typically, cultural anthropologists have chosen to study such human variation by establishing themselves for long-term stays in locales where people carry out their everyday lives. The prolonged, very personal encounter of an anthropologist with persons under study can provide a special insight into how people confront and deal with the cultural context life has dealt them. In this volume, most of the authors use the experience of real people to illuminate how aging is actually lived in such places as rural Kenya, a tiny South Seas island, U.S. urban ethnic enclaves or a New York City women's shelter.

While gerontological research as an anthropological specialty spans barely three decades, studies conducted earlier in this century can provide revealing, yet tantalizingly incomplete, glimpses of the elderly in non-Western cultural settings (see especially Warner 1937; Arensberg and Kimball 1940; Hart and Pilling 1961; Spencer 1965; Turnbull 1965). For example, in 1928 anthropologist C. W. Hart encountered the cultural context of frail old age among a preliterate people called the Tiwi, who generally accorded the healthy elderly high levels of support. As seen in these diary passages from his early fieldwork, the severe physical and cognitive decline of a particular Tiwi woman set in motion a dramatic ritual for dealing with this situation.

After a few weeks on the islands I also became aware that [the Tiwi] were often uneasy with me because I had no kinship linkage to them. This was shown in many ways, among others in their dissatisfaction with the negative reply they always got to their question, "What clan does he belong to?" Around the Mission, to answer it by saying, "White men have no clans," was at least a possible answer, but among the pagan bands like the Malauila and Munupula such an answer was incomprehensible—to them everybody must have a clan, just as everybody must have an age. If I had a clan I would be inside the kinship system, everybody would know how to act toward me, I would know how to act toward everybody else, and life would be easier and smoother for all.

How to get myself into the clan and kinship system was quite a problem. Even Mariano, [Hart's native guide], while admitting the desirability, saw no way of getting me in. There did not seem much hope and then suddenly the problem was solved entirely by a lucky accident. I was in a camp where there was an old woman who had been making herself a terrible nuisance. Toothless, almost blind, withered, and stumbling around, she was physically quite revolting and mentally rather senile. She kept hanging round me asking for tobacco, whining, wheedling, snivelling, until I got thoroughly fed up with her. As I had by now learned the Tiwi equivalents of "Go to hell" and "Get lost," I rather enjoyed being rude to her and telling her where she ought to go. Listening to my swearing in Tiwi, the rest of the camp thought it a great joke and no doubt egged her on so that they could listen to my attempts to get rid of her. This had been going on for some time when one day the old hag used a new approach. "Oh, my son," she said, "please give me tobacco." Unthinkingly I replied, "Oh, my mother, go jump in the ocean." Immediately a howl of delight arose from everybody within earshot and they all gathered round me patting me on the shoulder and calling me by a kinship term. She was my mother and I was her son. This gave a handle to everybody else to address me by a kinship term. Her other sons from then on called me brother, her brothers called me "sister's son"; and so on. I was now in the kinship system; my clan was Jabijabui (a bird) because my mother was Jabijabui.

From then on the change in the atmosphere between me and the tribe at large was remarkable. Strangers were now told that I was Jabijabui and that my mother was the old so-and-so and when told this, stern old men would relax, smile and say 'then you are my brother' (or my son, or my sister's son, or whatever category was appropriate) and I would struggle to respond properly by addressing them by the proper term.

How seriously they took my presence in their kinship system is something I never will be sure about. However, toward the end of my time on the islands an incident occurred that surprised me because it suggested that some of them had been taking my presence in the kinship system much more seriously than I had thought. I was approached by a group of about eight or nine senior men all of whom I knew. They were all senior members of the Jabijabui clan and they had decided among themselves that the time had come to get rid of the decrepit old woman who had first called me son and whom I now called mother. As I knew, they said, it was Tiwi custom, when an old woman became too feeble to look after herself, to "cover her up." This could only be done by her sons and her brothers and all of them had to agree beforehand, since once it was done they did not want any dissension among the brothers or clansmen, as that might lead to a feud. My "mother" was now completely blind, she was constantly falling over logs or into fires, and they, her senior clansmen, were in agreement that she would be better out of the way. Did I agree? I already knew about "covering up." The Tiwi, like many other hunting and gathering peoples, sometimes got rid of their ancient and decrepit females. The method was to dig a hole in the ground in some lonely place, put the old woman in the hole and fill it in with earth until only her head was showing. Everybody went away for a day or two and then went back to the hole to discover to their surprise, that the old woman was dead, having been too feeble to raise her arms from the earth. Nobody had "killed" her, her death in Tiwi eyes was a natural one. She had been alive when her relatives last saw her. I had never seen it done, though I knew it was the custom, so I asked my brothers if it was necessary for me to attend the "covering up." They said no and they would do it, but only after they had my agreement. Of course I agreed, and a week or two later we heard in our camp that my "mother" was dead, and we all wailed and put on the trimmings of mourning. (Hart 1970:149–154)

AGING AND THE ANTHROPOLOGICAL PARADIGM

This brief encounter with aging among the Tiwi can help introduce students to the way in which an anthropological approach can help us understand the last phase of adulthood in cross-cultural context. Such an anthropological paradigm has a dual lens: an internal focus (called an *emic* perspective) which seeks to comprehend the "native's" view of why certain behaviors are performed or images about the world are held; and an external, comparative focus (called an *etic* perspective) which uses the world's societies as a natural laboratory to separate the universal from the particular. From combining both perspectives to study aging and the aged there has emerged in the last decade an important new specialty variously referred to as "comparative sociocultural gerontology," "ethnogerontology," or "anthropology of aging." Despite the early seminal book by Leo Simmons, *The Role of the Aged in Primitive Society* (1945), and articles by such luminaries as Gregory Bateson (1950), and Margaret Mead (1951, 1967), concern for a worldwide, cross-cultural analysis of aging has developed slowly.

It was not until the publication of the volume *Aging and Modernization*, edited by Cowgill and Holmes in 1972, that knowledge from modern ethnographic studies was employed to test gerontological theory. Here, detailed studies of fourteen different societies were compared to examine the impact of industrialization, urbanization and Westernization on the status of the aged. As will be seen in Part III, the theoretical propositions developed in *Aging and Modernization* and in Cowgill's later works (1974, 1986) have served as a most controversial stimulus to subsequent work on aging done around the world. The maturing of an anthropological specialty in aging has unfolded through gerontologically focused ethnographies and edited books, texts and special issues of journals.[7] Importantly, three recent works, *Age and Anthropological Theory* (Kertzer and Keith 1984), *New Methods for Old Age Research* (Fry and Keith 1986), and *Old Age in Global Perspective* (Albert and Cattell 1994) have finally brought to bear the distinct realm of anthropological methods and theory on questions of aging and the aged.[8]

Over the past two decades a multidisciplinary movement, sometimes referred to as "Qualitative Gerontology," has also been seeking to establish qualitative modes of analysis as an equal partner to more quantitative methods (Gubrium and Sankar 1990). Outside of anthropology one of its strongest advocates is sociologist Jaber Gubrium, who, in an editorial in *The Gerontologist*, argues that qualitative approaches should not be viewed solely as a second-class precursor to more "powerful" statistical analysis (1992). According to Gubrium, good qualitative research is scientific in striving to generate theoretically informed findings. Such work attempts to represent the "native complexity" of behavior and how that complexity is organized (Rubinstein 1992, 1995b; Abel and Sankar 1995).[9] Most of the chapters in this volume follow this approach and seek to deeply enter the world of meaning by viewing how the lives of real people intersect with the reality of cultural settings. For example: In Part I Harriet Rosenberg shows how harsh complaints of mistreatment can be part of a positive system of elder care; in Part V Dena Shenk finds that the quest for independence among older rural women in the United States and Denmark is based on fundamentally different perceptions of their social support systems; and in Part VI, Charlotte Ikels' work in urban China demonstrates how symptoms Westerners associate with Alzheimer's disease can be interpreted elsewhere as part of normal aging.

THE "NATIVE" VIEW OF AGING

The *emic* component of the anthropological paradigm which seeks to behold the world through the eyes of the people being studied is grounded in the methods of modern cultural anthropology. Hart's research on the Tiwi was a classic example of the investigative strategy called ethnographic fieldwork. The aim of this approach is to gather data about a culture by actually living for a prolonged period with the people one is trying to comprehend. The holistic construction of cultural systems is learned through direct observation, participating in daily life and recording in the native language the meanings of things, persons and actions. This generalized process of "participant observation" was exemplified by Hart's experience. The Tiwi incorporated Hart into their kinship system and made use of him in a difficult decision, just as he used his designation as "son" and clan member to study their society on an intimate basis.

Participant observation is critical in developing an *emic* understanding of old age and even in learning appropriate questions to ask (Keith 1986, 1988). This applies as much to studying aging in small villages in the South Pacific as it does to research in an American nursing home, the African-American community, or among urban Japanese households. We will see in Part IV that Jane Peterson, in trying to understand Seattle's black aged, entered into the midst of their cultural world by working as a nurse for a church group that provided important services to the elderly. In my own work on skid row, I found that asking seemingly straightforward questions without a clear understanding of the lifestyle of long-term homelessness resulted in almost worthless data and frequent hostility. It was necessary not only to learn the colorful argot of the streets—such as "carrying the banner" (sleeping outdoors)—and to travel with men on their daily rounds, but also to work in a soup kitchen which fed many of the aged I studied.

Several of the authors in this volume have had long-term research connections—upwards of two decades—to the people they write about. We shall see the advantages of this approach in the chapters in Part I by Rosenberg and Cattell and later on with my work in Mexico (Part III) and Henderson's in Tampa, Florida (Part IV). Such temporal perspectives provide a unique opportunity to scrutinize how well the implications of gerontological theory stand up to longitudinal testing within whole communities. This is an indispensable way to examine the roles of aged citizens and the support directed toward elderly people within the context of sweeping global changes.

Returning to an examination of the Tiwi in their own cultural context, we can begin by noting that they are a foraging, seminomadic, small-scale society where kin-based groups (clans) named after mythological ancestors control key elements of the life cycle. How one enters adulthood, whom one marries, and the consequences of frailty in old age are largely determined by the cluster of elder males who have membership in a given clan. The Tiwi represent one of the few actual cases of gerontocracy—rule by the eldest group of males—and an exaggerated case of what has been called "gerontogamy." This latter term denotes a case in which a society not only practices polygyny (men can have more than one spouse at the same time) but where the older adult males have greater access than the younger men to the youngest women. Typically, Tiwi men above middle age already have several wives, including very young teen-agers, while a man marrying for the first time after age 25 might be wed to a 45-year-old widow.

While not controlling material wealth as might be the case in an agrarian tribal society, groups of elder males cautiously dole out esoteric wisdom to younger persons. Without this knowledge they cannot relate to spiritual forces or function as culturally competent adults. Regarded with a mixture of fear and reverence, the oldest males sit at the top of a generational pyramid, authorita-tively dominating society by the exclusive possession of key cultural knowledge. These elders, as a group, also dominate the dramatic life-cycle rituals which mark the transition from status to status as one goes from birth to death. Unlike the Western linear view of the life cycle, which sees death as a discontinuity from life, the Tiwi have a cyclical, mythologically linked notion of time and the passage of life forms through it. From this perspective, ancestors can have a powerful influence on the fate of the living and can be reborn in a future generation. As Judith Barker shows in Chapter 21, dealing with another Pacific Island people, an *emic* understanding of belief systems is necessary to compre-hend the radical change in behavior which can accompany the shift from healthy old age to severe senescence.

While females among the Tiwi had fewer formal bases of power, one must not assume from the very limited segment of Hart's research that women in old age are a totally repressed lot. Subsequent work among the Tiwi by Jane Good-ale (1971) shows the impressive amount of *de facto* power women could ac-cumulate by middle age, especially through their ability to control conflict in the community. Recent ethnographic studies (see especially Kerns and Brown 1992) and Chapter 4 in this volume have demonstrated how, even in "male chauvinist" cultural contexts, older women can acquire an importance and power far beyond the normative societal constraints placed on females.

THE COMPARATIVE VIEW OF AGING

How are we to apply the second, transcultural part of the anthropological paradigm? The treatment of the frail and possibly demented older woman in Hart's narrative must not only be examined through an emic understanding of the process of "covering up" but also by applying an etic comparative per-spective. One way of doing this is to translate the insider's "folk" view into comparable categories, such as "abandoning" or "forsaking," that can be used to construct theories and test hypotheses. The broadest such research design, called "holocultural analysis," makes use of the major anthropological data bank, the Human Relations Area Files (HRAF), which house ethnographic data representing over 1,000 societies. The intent of this approach is to statistically measure "the relationship between two or more theoretically defined and operationalized variables in a world sample of human societies" (Rohner et al. 1978:128). In this way it is hoped that we may eventually comprehend what aspects of aging are universal, as opposed to those factors that are largely shaped by a specific sociocultural system.

As demonstrated by Anthony Glascock in Part I, carefully defining types of "death-hastening" behaviors allows us to make powerful use of the holocultural method. Using this approach, Glascock's research demonstrates that counter to what one might expect, about half of his worldwide sample act out variants of behavior that lead to the death of older citizens. As the case of Hart's Tiwi "mother" exemplifies, this is seldom a simple matter and is usually predicated on severe physical and cognitive decline and the redefinition of the person from a functional to a nonfunctional individual.

Leo Simmons was the first to apply the holocultural method to the subject of aging. His 1945 study examined the interrelation of 109 sociocultural traits grouped under habitat and economy, political and social organization and religious beliefs and ritual. Despite some serious methodological flaws, Simmons's book and subsequent summary articles remained the main font of anthropological knowledge on the elderly for over 25 years (1946, 1952, 1959, 1960). One reason was his attempt to go beyond numbers and treat his data as an elaborate cross-cultural analysis from which hypotheses could be extracted.

One of the significant problems with cross-cultural research, however, is the difficulty of gaining consistency in methods used to study qualitatively the intricate cultural phenomena observed in the societies being contrasted. An attempt at confronting this issue directly is Project AGE. As discussed by Fry and her colleagues in Part I, their cross-cultural comparison of the aged in two American communities with elder residents of Hong Kong, Botswana and rural Ireland combines long-term fieldwork with a precise and consistent research protocol. The methodologies employed in this project were developed in the early 1980s by a working group of anthropologists and other scholars concerned with cross-cultural gerontology. The book which resulted from this collaboration, *New Methods for Old Age Research* (Fry and Keith 1986), constitutes the most important guide available for conducting research on aging in different cultural contexts.

CROSS-NATIONAL VERSUS CROSS-CULTURAL

It is important to distinguish *cross-national* from *cross-cultural* studies in gerontological research (Fry 1988).[10] The first type of study takes as the unit of analysis the nation-state and compares whole countries by measuring, through survey questionnaires, a large array of primarily demographic, interactional and health-related variables (Andrews et al. 1986, 1992; Altergott 1988).[11] One of the first (and arguably the best) of such efforts was *Old People in Three Industrial Societies*, based on work carried out in the early 1960s in England, Denmark and the United States (Shanas et al. 1968). A significant contribution of the study lies in its demonstration of the similar impact of industrialization in all these countries whereby bureaucratic structures of care were created to link retired status to a separate category of person called "old." The authors show that in each country the majority of persons over 60 reject this designation and the concomitant attempt by the social order to keep them "at arm's length from the social structure" (p. 425). Yet they also found that a large majority (75 percent) of those 65 years old or older live within close proximity to at least one child, and, of those aged with children, fully 80 percent claimed to have seen their offspring during the prior week. What such structural data reveals, however, is merely the potential for social integration. It does not tell us about differential cultural meaning or the reality of how an older person connects with a kinship network or other system of support.

Another interesting example is a massive World Health Organization (WHO) cross-national survey conducted in eleven countries during the 1980s. In a re-examination of the data on loneliness from this project, Marja Jylha and Jukka Jokela found that the statistics such studies typically produce are of little use without making a serious attempt to connect this data to cultural context (1990). Surprisingly, correlations in six of the study countries showed the result that expressed loneliness was most prevalent where living alone was rare and community bonds were strongest. Using the two most divergent research sites, the industrial town of Tampere, Finland (lowest loneliness) and rural Greece (highest loneliness), the authors show how studying the complex connections among family, community and ideology can explain the variation in loneliness in old age.

As in the research by Jylha and Jokela, *cross-cultural* studies of the aged tend to focus on small-scale societies or individual communities of industrial states. This perspective permits comparisons to be made between the complex interwoven wholes of cultural systems. One approach centers on highly controlled comparisons, where the social units under study are similar except for one or two features. A classic example is S. F. Nadel's (1952) study of two African tribal societies, the Korongo and the Mesakin. While alike in terms of environment and economic, political and kinship organization, each society differed in the degree of intergenerational conflict and the attitude of males toward aging. The key difference seemed to lie in the greater number of age distinctions recognized by the Korongo and the smoother transition into old age characteristic of this society. As a consequence, there was not only a greater congruence between social and physical aging among the Korongo but also an easier and more cheerful acceptance of old age itself.

Alternatively, the more typical approach to cross-cultural studies has been to maximize the difference between the societies being contrasted. In certain instances, researchers have searched the available literature to see what could be learned about a specific aspect of aging such as intergenerational relations, age as a basis of social organization, widowhood and general aspects of female aging.[12]

Whichever approach is taken, cross-cultural research on aging is important in at least three ways. First, it may suggest general hypotheses about the aging experience that can be tested by employing larger samples or conducting longitudinal studies. By using a relatively small number of cases, it is possible to retain a picture of the qualitative nature of sociocultural variables and thereby avoid overly simple theoretical models. A good example of this is found in Chapter 8 where Hiroko Akiyama, Toni Antonucci and Ruth Cambell contribute to theories of exchange and reciprocity through the cultural comparison of intergenerational support between women in Japan and the United States.

Second, intercultural comparisons can help us to understand in a detailed fashion how aging in the United States varies from that experienced in other places. Such analysis can suggest alternative strategies for developing diverse environments in which to grow old. This is brought home very clearly by Dena Shenk, who in Chapter 16 shows how differently rural elderly women in Denmark and the United States perceive and use available informal help from relatives and more formal aid from social service agencies.

A third use of global information is to create a cultural laboratory. This allows us to look at societies that have developed models and found potential solutions under demographic conditions which other societies will face in the future. A particularly good example of this is found in Chapter 11, where Bruce Zelkovitz explores policy initiatives toward the "aging enterprise" in the world's most aged society, Sweden. Here he contrasts Swedish and American ideologies related to state intervention in the life of the elderly. Sweden is proposed as a possible model of the way in which complex industrial nations might actively facilitate the integration of their older citizens as active, healthy and productive members of society. The last several decades have, in fact, seen a flowering of numerous cultural transplants in areas such as residential design, service delivery and long-term care. For example, the "Day Hospital" model was developed within the British health system as an alternative to traditional nursing homes. It was used as the archetype for the creation of the very successful "On Lok" community-based, long-term care system in the United States (see Chapter 12 for more information about On Lok). In another part of the world, Japan is about to initiate a national caregiving insurance system based on German and British models (see Chapter 10).

At present the United States is in a unique position to gain from a world perspective on aging. Unlike Western Europe or Japan, it still has a decade or more during which the percentage of aged and the growth rate of older citizens will be modest compared to other nations. Led by 76 million baby boomers reaching traditional retirement age, after 2010 the U S. rate of aging will begin to accelerate. Two decades later, there will be twice as many U.S. citizens over age 65 than in 1997 and about 8.4 million over age 85, up from 4 million today (U.S. Bureau of the Census 1997).[13]

However, one must be extremely cautious about blindly borrowing programs, residential designs or policy initiatives wholecloth, without accounting for cultural differences. A dramatic illustration comes from the research of Lawrence Cohen in urban India. He chronicles the rise of Western-based gerontological programs, legitimized by the lament over impoverished older citizens and the disruption of the traditional morals of the joint family (1992b). In studying the development of new residential settings for the elderly in urban India—called *Nava Nir* Homes—Cohen found his Western-based assumptions about aging were the diametric opposite of how life in the homes was perceived by the residents:

I was enthralled by the independence of Nava Nir residents and the openness of the institution. . . . Social life within was not characterized by the redundancy and dehumanization found in more total institutions. Yet for the Calcutta residents whom I interviewed, the *Nava Nirs* were unauthentic, even pathetic environments precisely because of the perceived lack of a total environment of care and dependence. The ''independence'' of residents pointed to the fact that they had no one to offer them proper service, or *seva* (1992b: 150).

On the surface, many of these residences seemed to create the ''fantasy home of Western gerontological literature'' by promoting independence, openness to the outside world and limited institutional control. Yet, Cohen found that the lack of enveloping support within the joint family created a loss of selfhood, and the autonomy so cherished in the United States only signified to those living in *Nava Nir* homes the glaring indifference of relatives.[14]

MYTHS OF AGING IN EXOTIC PLACES

In taking a global approach to the cultural contexts of aging, it is tempting to present a number of wildly diverse, exotic tableaus of growing old in a Chinese city or in a tiny encampment of foraging people in Botswana. Such a perspective would miss the important lessons to be learned by considering variety in light of common issues which bind the aged in all human groups. It has helped us learn that the Tiwi, a tiny, culturally homogeneous non-Western society living in a benign climate, have not escaped confrontation with the physical and emotional burdens of senility or what we call euthanasia. In sum, while the literature on aging in non-Western contexts contains a good deal of romanticized nonsense, there are several generalizations that are relevant to a realistic consideration of aging in an international perspective. For example:

1. A single cultural system may provide highly successful solutions for some problems of aging but fare miserably with regard to others (Beall and Goldstein 1981). A unidimensional evaluation of the aged based primarily on the concept of ''status'' is simply inadequate for understanding the multidimensional phenomena of aging, even in the smallest of human societies.

2. Not all non-Western, nonindustrial cultural systems provide a better milieu for aging and intergenerational relations than is found in the modern industrial West. Those who yearn for the ''world we lost,'' or even former President Reagan's small-town America, should think again. While this volume contains various examples of cultural contexts for aging which many North Americans might care to emulate (see especially Rosenberg, Zelkovitz this volume), the ethnographic and historic literature also contain numerous cases of ''traditional'' societies whose attitudes and treatment of the aged, healthy or frail, provide little to envy (Maxwell, Silverman and Maxwell 1982; and Chapter 3 this volume).

3. Social change does not automatically reduce the quality of life of the elderly. It is worth noting that under certain conditions, massive societal change, referred to as modernization, can have a positive impact on the lives of the aged (Foner 1984b; Chapter 9 this volume).

4. A single cultural system may offer vastly different opportunities for successful aging based on gender, class, or rural/urban variation (Halperin 1984, 1987; Kerns and Brown 1992; Chapter 4 this volume). All too often, descriptions of aging in non-Western societies are based on cultural ideals or an exclusively male perspective and have skewed the reality of how intracultural distinctions can alter the meaning of aging within the same societal setting.

5. The potential security and quality of life of the aged is maximized when cultures facilitate (a) both community and kin roles for the elderly, and (b) these arenas of interaction are mutually supportive rather than constructed as separate entities (Chapters 9 and 12 this volume).

6. Until quite recently, there was widespread belief (even in the scientific community) that there were geriatric utopias where old people existed but the normal aging process did not. Isolated mountain valleys in Ecuador, Pakistan, and especially the Caucasus region of the former Soviet Union were thought to contain villages with very long-living people (130–150 years of age) who were free of ''old people's diseases'' such as memory loss. Despite the long-standing quest for the ''fountain of youth'' (and cute yogurt commercials), careful studies have now shown that even the most idyllic spots in the world contain roughly the same share of centenarians and a similar incidence of dementing diseases as that found in the United States (Rubin 1983; Palmore 1984; Beall 1987).

These six propositions represent a core of ideas which I believe can transcend cultural boundaries. They are linked to the gerontological topics around which this book is organized. While these themes do not exhaust the range of important aging studies, it is hoped that the following 26 chapters will illuminate how the experience of becoming and being old is made meaningful in the cultural context of aging.

In several places throughout this text I have also included "boxed" materials briefly illustrating some key issues facing the elderly. Box 1, set below, describes the Evergreen Project, an ongoing effort which provides a compelling example of how an anthropology of aging can be put to use. It also represents a multidisciplinary approach to comprehending and making use of the aged's perception of their local environment to redesign parts of a center city area.

BOX 1. THE EVERGREEN PROJECT: ETHNOGRAPHY OF AGING IN ACTION

The Evergreen Project is creating a shared vision of healthy urban environments for older adults through applied anthropological research. With funding from the Retirement Research Foundation and numerous local sources, including hospital, municipal and university support, this ongoing project seeks to understand the quality of the day-to-day environments of older adults in Bloomington (IN), a small Midwestern city and the home of Indiana University. Using ethnography, humanities projects, intergenerational interviewing, focus groups and quantitative surveys, five important "design principles" of healthy environments were derived. These are: neighborliness; an environment for growth, learning, and autonomy; a positive image; diverse and affordable housing options; and an intergenerational retirement community.

Using these design principles as a premise, neighborhood "charrettes" or design workshops have been convened with a school of Architecture and Planning to involve elders in the actual creation of new environments. Neighborhood charrettes empower potential residents of new housing options to exercise choice and control in their lives and build community as people work together for the common good. The second phase of the project, underway in 1997, is applying the knowledge accumulated thus far to guide development of a innovative "aging in place" plan blending housing and health care. Two building blocks of this community-based effort include (1) a Senior Health Cooperative, employing the notions of rigorous illness prevention, nurse-run clinics and service credit exchange and (2) a Senior Housing Resource Center, promoting home sharing, residence modification and reverse equity mortgages.

The project's ethnographic work has shown that the image of the neighborhood, fixed in memory, becomes a cradle of individual and community meaning and pride. Witnessing the real lives of elders through their undiminished voices gives compelling evidence of their needs. One of these elders powerfully described the relationship between his overt "behavior" and his reliance on meaningful human interactions. "You know why I like to come to the bank, and never use the ATM? It's one more human contact. . . . Without relationships I'm a dead man."

For more information about this project contact: Dr. Phil Stafford, The Evergreen Institute on Elder Environments, P.O. Box 1149, Bloomington, IN 47402. Phone: (812) 336-9263. Check updates and resources through their web site, http:// slis-lab-v.lib.indiana.edu/townsq/evergreen.html. See also the Fall 1996 issue of

continued

CRIT37, the Journal of the American Institute of Architecture Students.
This box was written by Phil Silverman.

KEY RESOURCES

Center

United Nations Programme on Aging, Officer-in-charge Dr. Alexandre Sidorenko, rm
dc2–1358, 2 United Nations Plaza, New York, NY 10017. Phone (212) 963–
0500; FAX (212) 963–3062. This center coordinates the activities of member
states in the area of aging. They also publish the *Bulletin on Aging*, focusing on
demographic and economic aspects of global aging. Their web site (http://
www.un.org/dpcsd/dspd/iyop.htm) is small but includes such things as the ''International Plan of Action on Ageing'' and a report of the World Summit for
Social Development.

Organizations

The Association for Anthropology and Gerontology (AAGE). This professional society
has an interdisciplinary membership with an interest in cross-cultural and qualitative studies of aging. They produce a quarterly newsletter, teaching guide, bibliography and a membership directory. AAGE also has an annual cash award for
student papers, ''The Margaret Clark Award.'' There is also a special low student
rate. For information contact: AAGE Treasurer, Melissa Talamantes, Department
of Family Practice, University of Texas Health Science Center, 7703 Floyd Curl
Drive, San Antonio, TX 78284–7795. Phone (210) 270–3930; e-mail Talaman-
tes@uthscsa.edu.
International Federation on Ageing was founded in 1973 to provide a worldwide forum
for governmental and other organizations which address issues touching the lives
of elderly persons. They have recently expanded their former newsletter *Ageing
International* into a semi-annual journal. They have a small web site at http://
www.zorin.com/inia/.

Grants

The National Guide to Funding on Aging. This guide includes facts on more than 1,000
grant makers, foundations, state and federal programs and voluntary organizations. Contact: The Foundation Center, 79 Fifth Ave., New York, NY 10003, 1–
800–424–9836.

Internet Resources

Jay Sokolovsky has his own web page, The Cultural Context of Aging, at http://
bayflash.stpt.usf.edu/faculty/jsokolov. This site will provide supplemental materials including course outlines using this book, new bibliography, web sites and
other resources.

Joyce Post of the Philadelphia Geriatric Center maintains a list of "Internet and E-Mail Resources on Aging" at the World Wide Web site: http://www.aoa.dhhs.gov/aoa/pages/jpostst.html.

She also writes a column on such resources in *The Gerontologist*. At the end of each part I will include key Internet sites. For example:

(1) http://www.aoa.dhhs.gov/aoa/webres/. This site from the U.S. Administration on Aging includes over 175 direct connections to Internet information sources. It is particularly strong on government agencies and organizations providing community services.

(2) http://www.iog.wayne.edu. This site at the Institute of Gerontology at Wayne State University can connect you to many other university and research sites on aging.

(3) http://www.aoa.dhhs.gov/aoa/webres/int-indx.htm. A site providing links internationally to institutions doing gerontological research. For instance, students can search here to supplement their readings on China, Sweden and Japan.

(4) http://www2.ageinfo.org/naicweb/bibinfo.html. A database managed by the National Aging Information Center. It contains references to program- and policy-related projects on aging, seldom referenced in any other resource. For instance, after reading Neil Henderson's article on ethnic-based Alzheimer's support groups, students can search here for other projects seeking to help ethnic families cope with dementia.

(5) http://WWW.aarp.org. AARP is developing the *Internet Resource Guide to Aging, version 2.1,* which can be accessed from their web site. It will include an international section which will have country-specific information such as on national journals, a compilation of declarations of rights for older people being developed around the globe, and "Coalition '99," AARP's efforts to work with others around the world to celebrate the International Year of Older Persons in 1999.

(6) http://www-lib.usc.edu/info/gero/ at the University of Southern California Gerontology Library. This is the place to look for graduate student dissertations on aging.

Print Resources

Guide to International Informational Sources

Directory of Library, Clearinghouse, and Bibliographic Data Bases in Social Gerontology Around the World, 2nd ed., 1996. Washington, DC: American Association of Retired Persons.

Guide to Research

Nusberg, C. and J. Sokolovsky, eds. 1994. *The International Directory of Research and Researchers in Comparative Gerontology*, 3rd ed., Washington, DC: American Association of Retired Persons. Available in print or computer disk format. Information and publication references for over 300 recently completed or ongoing projects in comparative gerontology around the world.

Guide to Policy

International Database of National Policies on Aging. New York: United Nations Programme on Aging. Available 1998/1999.

Newsletter

Global Aging Report. An informative publication of AARP. It includes both short research summaries and information about local level programs and activities for and by the elderly worldwide. For further information, contact the AARP International Activities Department, 601 E St. NW, Washington, DC 20049.

Journals

Journal of Cross-Cultural Gerontology; *Journal of Aging Studies*; *Bold*; *Ageing International*; *The Gerontologist*; *Journal of Gerontology*; *Ageing and Society*; *Journal of Aging and Identity.*

Bibliographies

(1) Schweitzer, M. 1991. *Anthropology of Aging: A Partially Annotated Bibliography.* Westport, CT: Greenwood Press. The most comprehensive guide in print to bibliographic references dealing with cross-cultural and bibliographic works.

(2) Cattell, M., G. Harper and J. Salmon, eds. 1997. *Anthropology of Aging: A Compendium of Bibliographies from the Association for Anthropology and Gerontology Newsletter, 1989–1996.* Providence, PA: Association for Anthropology and Gerontology. For ordering information contact AAGE Treasurer, Melissa Talamantes, Department of Family Practice, University of Texas Health Science Center, 7703 Floyd Curl Drive, San Antonio, TX 78284–7795. Phone (210) 270–3930; e-mail Talamantes@uthscsa.edu.

Other Print Resources

Albert, S. M. and M. G. Cattell. 1994. *Old Age in Global Perspective.* New York: G. K. Hall. A sophisticated summary and analysis of crucial issues related to the cross-cultural, global study of aging.

Bagnell, P. and P. Spencer Soper, eds. 1989. *Perceptions of Aging in Literature: A Cross-Cultural Study.* Westport, CT: Greenwood. Examines literature on aging from Europe, Asia, the Middle East and classical Greek and Roman periods.

Binstock, R. and L. K. George, eds. 1996. *Handbook of Aging and the Social Sciences.* San Diego, CA: Academic Press. Every five years this essential resource provides cutting edge articles updating key areas of social gerontology.

Cole, T., D. van Tassel and R. Kastenbaum, eds. 1992. *Handbook of the Humanities and Aging.* New York: Springer. A major compilation from the perspectives of history, the humanities, arts, religion and literature.

Crews, D. and R. Garruto, eds. 1994. *Biological Anthropology and Aging.* New York: Oxford University Press. The book to read for those interested in the biological context of aging around the world.

Kaminsky, M., ed. 1992. *Remembered Lives: The Work of Ritual, Storytelling and Growing Older.* Ann Arbor: University of Michigan Press. An edited volume of the essays of Barbara Myerhoff focusing on the role of ritual and symbolic meaning in the construction of old age.

Rhoads, E. and L. D. Holmes. 1995. *Other Cultures, Elder Years.* 2nd ed. Thousand Oaks, CA: Sage. An excellent update of the only available textbook on the anthropology of aging.

Shuldiner, D. 1997. *Folklore, Culture, and Aging: A Research Guide.* Westport, CT: Greenwood. A resource guide with over 1,500 annotated references. It features works on methods and concepts in field research in folklore, oral history, and community studies.

NOTES

1. For a discussion of the broad biological implications of aging, see Rose 1990; Crews and Garruto 1994.

2. In 1982 the United Nations convened a World Assembly on Ageing in Vienna, Austria and later that year the General Assembly of the United Nations endorsed the International Plan of Action on Ageing. In 1990, the United Nations designated October 1 as the International Day of the Elderly and one year later adopted Principles for Older Persons. During 1992 this organization assembled a strategy for the decade 1992–2001, entitled ''Global Targets on Ageing for the Year 2001.''

3. A recent book by Bass (1995) describes the fuller results of this study and other analyses of productive aging in the United States. For an international look at this issue see Thurz, Nusberg and Prather 1995 and volume 21, number 2 of *Ageing International* (1994).

4. In the April 1996 edition of *Science* it was reported that molecular biologists have discovered the gene associated with the accelerated aging of young adults, symptomatic of a very rare disorder called Werner's disease. This may provide important clues to dealing with many age-related diseases such as diabetes, arteriosclerosis and osteoporosis.

5. Two excellent resources for exploring the image of aging in varied cultural contexts are Shenk and Achenbaum 1994; Featherstone and Wernick 1995.

6. For an interesting analysis of new perspectives on retirement in North America, see Savishinsky 1995.

7. For edited books see Myerhoff and Simic 1978; Fry 1980a, 1981; Amoss and Harrell 1981; Hendricks 1981; Morgan 1985; Silverman 1987; Sokolovsky 1987, 1990; Strange and Teitelbaum 1987. For single author texts see: Keith 1982; Foner 1984a; Cowgill 1986; Albert and Cattell 1994; Rhoads and Holmes 1995. For special journal issues see: Keith 1979; Beall 1982; Sokolovsky 1982a; Sokolovsky and Sokolovsky 1983a; Sokolovsky 1991; Nydegger 1984; Gubrium 1993.

8. For an important series of review articles in the anthropology of aging see Rubinstein 1990.

9. For an excellent discussion of how analysis of symbols and ritual can contribute to the study of aging see Kaminsky 1992, 1993. A broad look at the sociological perspective on qualitative methods is provided in Gubrium and Holstein 1997. For discussion of a humanist perspective, see Phillipson 1996.

10. Some of this research I have labelled ''Cross-National'' (e.g., Arnoff, Leon and Lorge 1964; Seefeldt 1984) is described by the authors as cross-cultural. However, the survey questionnaire approach of these studies places them in the methodological camp of what I call cross-national studies and perhaps explains why they find so little differences in the samples they examine.

11. For some classic examples of such studies, see Arnoff, Leon and Lorge 1964; Heikkinen, Waters and Brzezinski 1983; Seefeldt 1984. A good number of cross-national studies on aging were undertaken during the 1990s. The best source of information about this research is contained in Nusberg and Sokolovsky 1994. There is a growing number

of direct comparative studies of the United States with another nation. Three good examples are Borsch-Supan 1994 (United States-Germany), Buss, Beres, Hofstetter and Pomidor 1994 (United States-Hungary), and Hashimoto 1996 (U.S.-Japan).

12. For comparative analysis of intergenerational relations, see Levine 1965; Rubinstein and Johnsen 1982; Simic 1990; Chapter 8 this volume. For age as a basis of social organization, see Eisenstadt 1956; Stewart 1977; Foner and Kertzer 1978; Bernardi 1985. For widowhood, see Lopata 1972, 1987a, 1987b, 1988; Chapters 4 and 15 this volume. For general aspects of female aging, see Bart 1969; Datan et al. 1970; Dougherty 1978a; Cool and McCabe 1987; Kerns and Brown 1992.

13. Despite this, if one includes the disabled and children in ratios of dependent populations, even at the height of boomer retirement, say 2020, the ratio of workers to nonworking dependents will not be as high as it was during the 1960s.

14. For a broader discussion of dependency and aging in India, see Vatuk 1990; Ram-Prasad 1995.

PART I

Culture, Aging and Context

At present [1995], the number of people who cross the threshold of age 60 is over a million a month, more than 33,000 every day. . . . Of this, three-quarters of a million a month, over 25,000 a day . . . are turning aged 60 in the developing regions.

Sandeep Chawla

THE NEW MILLENNIUM OF AGING

Despite the dramatic statistic cited above, excessive interest by social scientists about aging in the Third World might seem a case of misplaced research priorities. In the poorest developing countries, the average span of life from birth remains abysmally low. For example, in 1975 a majority of nations in sub-Saharan Africa had life expectancies of 55 years or less.

In contrast to the almost universally "aged" industrial countries where the elderly account for at least one-tenth of the citizenry, structural population aging is barely apparent in the Third World as a whole. Although exceptions occur (see Chapter 2 this volume), it is typically found that the "agedness" (percent over age 65) of small-scale societies such as the Amazon-dwelling Yanomamo fall in the 1 to 3 percent range. As of the mid-1990s most Third World nations remain demographically "young," with less than 4 percent of their population over 65—Kenya, 2.3 percent; Guatemala, 3.4 percent—or "youthful," with 4 to 6 percent over 65—Mexico, 4.3 percent; China, 6.1 percent (U.S. Bureau of the Census 1995). Over the past 30 years, the agedness of many such countries was static or even declined, as improved health care typically had the greatest impact on keeping children alive rather than reducing mortality in adults. This was clearly the case in the Mexican peasant community I write about in Chapter

9. Over the coming three decades, however, currently young/youthful nations such as Brazil, Indonesia and Mexico will witness the oldest part of their population (over age 65) at least double—and quadruple in the case of Indonesia. The East Asian region, fueled by dramatic drops in fertility levels and rapid industrialization, will begin the next millennium aging faster than any other area of the world.

This is in contrast to the already "grayer" industrial regions designated as either "mature" (from 7.9 percent to 9.9 percent over age 65) or "aged" (10 percent or more over age 65). In 1995, Japan completed the transition from a relatively young to an aged population structure (7 to 14 percent) in the shortest time for any known society. This occurred almost twice as fast as in other rapid transition countries such as Great Britain (45 years, 1930–1975) and West Germany (45 years, 1930–1975). Even with the help of baby boomers, the United States will not complete this demographic maturing until 2012 and will have taken 68 years to accomplish it.

Yet, this set of statistics does not tell the entire story. During the first three decades of the next century, countries such as Jamaica, Tunisia and Thailand will all break Japan's record with regard to speed of population aging (Kinsella and Gist 1995).[1] By the late 1980s, other Third World countries, such as Costa Rica, already had life expectancies comparable to that of the United States. In fact, Costa Rica now exceeds the United States in both male and female longevity.[2] Much of the difference between low-life-expectancy nations and Western industrial societies can be attributed to the very high levels of infant mortality still persisting in the Third World. For example, although the expected 72 years of life *at birth* for males in the United States exceeds that for Nigerian males by twenty years, males at age 65 in the United States can only expect to survive three years longer than similarly aged men in Nigeria.[3]

The implications of these trends have serious consequences for the functioning of societies around the globe (Shantakumar 1996). The National Institute on Aging and the U.S. Bureau of the Census, in 1985, established an International Data Base and later an Aging Studies Branch to address the issue of global population greying. In this volume's first chapter, Kevin Kinsella, chief of this new Census Bureau unit, discusses some of the key parameters which have caught the attention of those who study the demography of aging. In a global survey, he lays out the critical social, medical and policy consequences of the numbers flowing from demographic reports.

THE IMAGE OF OLD

The conception of being "old" seems to be a near human universal and is culturally constructed by a variety of measures. All known societies have words which roughly translate into the linguistic divisions of infant, child, adult, old person. Cross-culturally, the movement from adulthood to some category of "old" or "elder" appears the least ritualized of any stage of the human life cycle. Exceptions, such as among East-African "age-set" societies, tend to occur when passage of persons into elderhood mandates others to also undergo life-cycle transitions, say from child to adult (see Introduction, Part II). In Chapter 2 the analysis of the Ju/'hoansi people by Rosenberg finds that old age is perceived to begin relatively early and can start in a person's mid-40s. This occurs when and if changes in physical capabilities begin to diminish functional ability. Here there are three levels of "old," a beginning early stage, a frail but functional stage and a physically disabled designation. Importantly, while for the Ju/'hoansi the label "old" has some association with physical decline, it is also associated with greater spiritual and emotional strength often put to use by elders in healing rituals. In the Mexican Indian community of Amatango discussed in Chapter 9, the designation of *coli* (Aztec for "old person") is also socially derived, beginning when a person's grandchildren survive past childhood. There, it is only in the last stages of life that conceptions of oldness are primarily redirected toward physical decline with the use of the phrase *yotla moak*—literally, "all used up."

As a number of historians and linguists have pointed out, existing words marking life-cycle periods can show radical changes in meaning over time. For example, the word "hag" derives from the Greek root *hagia* or "holy one," and prior to the thirteenth century referred to a woman with positive supernatural capabilities. During the Middle Ages the Catholic Church felt competition from literally hundreds of new religious movements. Independent older women, especially those working as midwives, came to be seen as a threat. In this context, the term "hag" became synonymous with evil, ugliness and witchcraft (Rhoads and Holmes 1995:3–4).

A GLOBAL VIEW OF OLD AGE

Only one study to date has used worldwide data to systematically examine the beginning of old age (Glascock and Feinman 1981). As noted below in Table I.1, the authors found that in a random sample of 60, mostly non-Western traditional societies, there were three basic means of identifying a category of "old": change of social/economic role; chronology; and change in physical characteristics.

Particularly striking in this work are the following conclusions:

1. It is typical to begin labeling persons as old between the ages of 45 to 55, when people are less likely to link the general concept of old age with the types of physical decrements most associated with the sixth and seventh decades of human life. As is noted for the Ju/'hoansi people, discussed by Rosenberg in this part, entering elderhood is often linked to positive forms of maturity and spiritual growth.

2. A change in social/economic role is by far the most common beginning marker of becoming old. This can range from one's offspring having their own children, to

Table I.1
Percent Distribution of Old Age Definitional Classifications: From the Human
Relations Area Files (Absolute Numbers in Parentheses)

How the beginning of old age is defined?	Single Definition of Aging	Multiple Definitions of Aging
Change in social role	71% (30)	46% (27)
Chronology	19% (8)	34% (20)
Change in capabilities	10% (4)	20% (12)
Total	100% (42)	100% (59)

Source: Glascock and Feinman 1981:20.

general shifts in the types of productive activities one engages in, to beginning to receive more goods and services than one gives.

3. A change in capabilities is the least common marker. Factors such as invalid status and senility are quite rare as primary indicators of a general designation of old. This seems to be the case because societies frequently create a category of old which begins before many people encounter much radical physical decline.

4. Almost a majority of societies in the sample have multiple definitions of being aged. These varied definitions of aging are commonly applied to distinct categories of "old" itself, which include a phase of aging linked to images associated with a movement toward death and the loss of normal functioning.

This last item seems to add a component of both complexity and ambiguity to how societies fully articulate their images of aging. As we will see later on in Part I, confronting an image of the old tilted toward the dimensions of death and incapacity can initiate drastic changes in the attitudes and behavior toward those so labelled.

Rapid demographic changes occurring around the world are pushing many societies to reevaluate the cultural construct of adulthood and the start of old age. In the United States, when the Social Security Administration was established in 1935, only 15 percent of the populace would ever reach age 65 (Achenbaum 1994). Yet, in the 1990s fully 80 percent reach that age, arbitrarily chosen six decades ago as the time for retirement. For males, in just the 30-year period between 1960 and 1990, the percent of their adult life span spent in retirement has tripled from about four to thirteen years (Kinsella and Gist 1995).

According to sociologist Gail Sheehy, age norms have not only shifted, they are no longer normative:

Consider: Nine-year-old girls are developing breasts and pubic hair; 9-year-old boys carry guns to school; 16-year-olds can "divorce" a parent; 30-year-old men still live at home with Mom; 40-year-old women are just getting around to pregnancy; 50-year-old men are forced into early retirement; 55-year-old women can have egg donor babies; 60-year-old women start first professional degrees; 70-year-old men reverse aging by 20 years with human growth hormone; 80-year-olds run marathons; 85-year-olds remarry and still enjoy sex; and every day, the "Today" show's Willard Scott says "Happy Birthday!" to more 100-year-old women. (Sheehy 1995:3–4)

In *New Passages* (1995), Sheehy asserts that in the United States there has been a shift of stages of adulthood ten years ahead with people taking longer to grow up and mature and much longer to die. One result is that the meaning of being past one's fifth decade of life is altering so dramatically that the nature of this part of the life course bears little resemblance to the experience of prior generations.

"FIRST PEOPLES" AND AGING

Anthropologists have long been interested in examining life in societies which, in their traditional ways of life, resemble the earliest forms of human cultural systems. While many tribal societies such as the Amazonian Yanamamo remain on the brink of extinction, the last decade has witnessed an unexpected resilience among indigenous, "first" peoples. These groups, which constitute about four percent of the earth's population, have sometimes managed to maintain their core cultural values in the face of ferocious onslaughts by industrial nations. Among the best studied examples that fit this description are the Ju/'hoansi, described in Chapter 2 by Harriet Rosenberg. They are also part of the Project AGE sample discussed in Chapter 5. The Ju/'hoansi, known variously as the Bushmen, !Kung or San peoples, are a formerly nomadic gathering and hunting group in Botswana. Despite the erroneous image created in the feature film *The Gods Must Be Crazy*, they are not an unchanged people, lacking contact with the outside world.[4] Instead, over the last 25 years they have become a captive group, restricted to a reservation and forced to significantly alter their quite successful foraging lifestyle. Nonetheless, this harsh context imposed by the South African government has not yet destroyed core cultural features of Ju/'hoansi family, community and ritual life, forums in which the elderly still perform valued roles. These cultural niches for the elderly include: being a knowledge repository about kin ties and natural resource management; transcendental curing and performance; entertainment through clowning and dancing; and being an emotional focus for community integration.

Here we clearly see the benefits of long-term ethnographic research in understanding the cultural mechanisms of caring for the elderly. Without having lived with the group for an extended period or having had access to her husband's twenty years of experience with the Ju/'hoansi, Rosenberg might have mistaken the constant "kvetching" (sharp complaining) of most elderly as proof that this is a society which habitually abandons its older citizens in need of care. Instead, her penetrating analysis linking complaint discourse to the egalitarian and communal roots of Ju/'hoansi society shows that outspoken nagging is part of their package of cultural devices that reinforce values of caring and extreme compassion for even the very frail elderly.[5] Importantly, caregiving is carried out evenly by persons of both sexes, avoiding the overdependence on female caregivers typical for industrialized countries.

GLOBAL PERSPECTIVES ON STATUS AND SUPPORT OF THE AGED

One of the promises of a truly cross-cultural comparative gerontology is to gain an understanding of aging divorced from the narrow boundary of a single case such as the Ju/'hoansi. In fact, it is among such types of society—nomadic, nonagricultural, lacking economic stratification, with bilateral descent—that one is statistically most likely to find the very frail elderly having their lives "hastened." The first serious attempt to deal with such issues on a worldwide basis was the massive study by Leo Simmons, *The Role of the Aged in Primitive Society* (1945). However, one must be cautious about his statistical results. As might be expected from one of the first studies using the Human Relations Area Files (HRAF), the methods were flawed by a poorly drawn sample, inadequate statistical controls and an imprecise definition of some key variables. Nevertheless, the many insights Simmons provided have served as a guidepost to more recent, controlled comparisons and holocultural studies seeking to uncover variables which are associated with high status, deference and support shown toward the elderly.

Working independently with small, cross-cultural samples, Cowgill (1972) and Press and McKool (1972) proposed similar variables which account for high status in traditional peasant societies. These involve four interrelated clusters of cultural phenomena:

1. an available role set emphasizing continuity and important responsibilities in community organization and public life;
2. integration into a residentially viable extended family organization;
3. control of some important material and informational resources;
4. a value system praising a group-oriented ideology while deemphasizing individual ego development.

In applying these variables to the Ju/'hoansi people studied by Rosenberg, we can see that their cultural context does not fulfill all of the criteria listed above. This is especially the case in terms of their lack of a residentially stable, extended family organization, such as I studied in rural Mexico (Chapter 9). Yet, Rosenberg found that there is a powerful cumulative effect of the important roles the elderly play in kinship relations, control of knowledge and mastery of the dangerous spiritual force called *num*. When combined with the Ju/'hoansi people's communal ideological orientation, a cultural context in which the elderly are well supported is created.

A series of holocultural studies have corroborated, in many respects, the association of status and deference with the control of informational and administrative roles (Sheehan 1976; Silverman and Maxwell 1987) as well as valued activities and extended family integration (McArdle and Yeracaris 1981). In terms of resource and information control, Silverman and Maxwell have demonstrated that only certain types of control, particularly administrative and consultative, correlate with beneficent treatment of the elderly. Some forms of supernatural information control, especially transformational powers, were in fact a potential threat to the elderly. This is highly relevant to some historically known situations of massive societal change, such as in thirteenth- to sixteenth-century Europe. The typical person burned at the stake for her "transformational knowledge" (witchcraft) was an older female between the ages of 55 and 65 (Bever 1982; Banner 1992; Haber 1997). Similar demographics of witch accusations were found when John Demos studied those most likely to be condemned in seventeenth-century Puritan Massachusetts. Such female suspects were likely to be old and poor, either single or widowed and known as being unusual or irritating to neighbors (Demos 1982). As will also be noted in Barker's analysis of the Niue (Chapter 21), being spiritually close to the ancestors does not always guarantee a pleasant time for those elders still among the living.

THE ISSUE OF ASSISTED SUICIDE

A special concern within the growing comparative perspective on being old is confronting the darker side of aging—various types of nonsupportive and even "death-hastening" behaviors directed toward the elderly. Australia for a year (1996) was the only country with a real right to death law—giving patients the right to die. However, Australian federal lawmakers struck down this territorial law by a close vote in March 1997, and instead tacked on an amendment calling for more pain treatment to ease suffering of the dying. Voluntary euthanasia and assisted suicide go unchallenged in other nations such as the Netherlands, although both remain illegal there.[6] In the United States, the rise of a politically powerful "right to life" religious movement is counterposed by the growing popularity of the Hemlock Society[7] and the assisted suicides attended by Dr. Jack Kevorkian, popularly known as "Dr. Death." This has created a legal, ethical and medical battleground concerning euthanasia as an option for terminally ill aged (Clark 1997). The judicial dilemmas stemming from this issue are worthy of King Solomon. For example, in January 1996, a man from Petoskey, Michigan won custody of his Alzheimer's disease–stricken father in a court case against his own mother. The son had maintained that the mother and his siblings were conspiring to seek the help of Dr. Kevorkian to end the father's life.[8] In May of that year, in another Michigan court, Dr. Kevorkian was acquitted of murder for the third time. Shortly before this, in separate cases, U.S. courts of appeal in both San Francisco and New York ruled that a terminally ill, mentally competent adult has a constitutional right to a doctor's assistance in suicide. By the time this book is published, the U.S. Supreme Court should have made a ruling on the constitutionality of these legal decisions.

As we have already seen in the discussion of the Tiwi, "high-tech" societies are not the only ones to grapple with this dilemma. Anthony Glascock (Chapter 3) throws the question into historical and global relief and finds some disquieting results. A majority of the societies in his sample exhibited some form of "death-hastening" behavior, with less than one-third providing unconditional support. However, few societies enforce a single treatment of their elderly and it was commonly found that both supportive and death-hastening behavior coexist in the same social setting. Glascock's study demonstrates that when anthropologists have cared to probe the later stages of the life cycle, they have found cultural distinctions drawn between "intact," fully functioning aged and "decrepit" individuals who find it difficult to carry out even the most basic tasks. It is persons placed in this latter category toward whom geronticide or death-hastening is most frequently applied. The important and related issue of elder abuse is beginning to be investigated in diverse settings, such as among Native American tribes (Maxwell and Maxwell 1992; Carson 1995) and within North American (Decalmer and Glendenning 1993) and Japanese families (Tomita 1994). In Part VI, varied cultural responses to the oldest old will be more fully explored.

THE FEMINIZATION OF OLD AGE

Women constitute more than a majority of the aged population in virtually all parts of the world about which data are available.[9] At age 15, women in the United States have a life expectancy eight years greater than men, and when they reach age 65 they can expect to survive four more years than their male counterparts. For Third World nations, there is typically about half this difference in life expectancies. In these countries, for those over age 60, the gender ratio is relatively close, about 90 men for every 100 women, while in the more developed nations there are a full 20 percent fewer males still alive than females. However, it is in the former types of societies that the social worlds of males and females are found to be most socially and culturally divergent.[10] This is especially the case in patrilineal societies with a good deal of stratification, where men try to strongly control the sexuality and reproductive history of women in their families (Dickerson-Putman 1994b). In such societies one can "in fact speak of separate male and female subcultures" (Myerhoff and Simic 1978:23).

The typical dominance of males in public arenas is likely related to the divergent imagery of aging created on the basis of gender (Haber 1997). Predominant in this difference is the common hydra-headed perception of older women in the same society, from the positive, nurturing matriarch/granny to the mystical shamaness, and finally to the feared, evil witch. The ethnographic literature now abounds with this type of dramatic alternation between "Dear Old Thing" and "Scheming Hag" metaphors (Cool and McCabe 1987).

It is unfortunate that until quite recently the analysis of aging in such societies has largely portrayed the male perspective alone, despite the importance of older women to the functioning of society. Many authors have begun to document a common pattern in nonindustrial societies of dramatic positive changes of role, power and status by women as they pass into the middle and latter adult years (Foner 1989; Kerns and Brown 1992; Brown, Subbaiah and Therese 1994).[11] A classic description of this process is provided by Kaberry in an early anthropological study of Australian aboriginal women:

As the women become older they often assume more authority, become more assertive, tender their advice more frequently and interfere where the activities of any of their kindred are likely to run contrary to the tribal law. On the other hand, when anger mounts high and threatens the peace, even safety of others in the camp, they take the initiative in stemming the disputes and temporarily establishing order again. Amidst the shouting, the barking of dogs, the voice of an old woman will make itself heard above the uproar as she harangues men and women impartially (1937:181).

Various writers have noted that for women, the fourth decade of life, in its association with menopause, often provides a key turning point. Cross-cultural work in this area has shown the need for sophisticated research which takes a bio-cultural approach to this issue.[12] As Kaufert and Lock note:

Most women know the script laid out in their particular society for the woman in midlife, including what symptoms she should expect from her body.... Women in California are told that a loss in libido is a medical problem to be treated by hormone therapy, whereas a Bengali woman in India knows very well that sexual activity is inappropriate for the postmenopausal woman.... Both the denial and the affirmation of sexuality are social phenomena, but for the California woman the responses of her body have been transformed into a medical problem to be medically managed.... Just as obstetricians and pediatricians would define how women should feel and behave when becoming mothers, gynecologists and psychiatrists tell women what it is to be menopausal (1992: 203).

How the complex interplay of biology, nutrition and culture shapes women's experience of menopause is nicely analyzed by Yewoubdar Beyene's *From Menarche to Menopause: Reproductive Lives of Peasant Women in Two Cultures* (1989). In a comparison of Mayan and Greek women living in rural villages she shows that, despite similar values and behaviors regarding menstruation and childbearing, their experience of menopause differed. She found that Greek women had a substantial, well-balanced diet, married late, and averaged only two pregnancies. Almost three-quarters of these women reported hot flash or cold sweat symptoms and associated menopause with growing old and the beginning of a "downhill course in life." The Mayan women, in contrast, had an inconsistent, much poorer diet, married early, and had closely spaced, successive pregnancies. In this case *none* of the women interviewed by Beyene reported symptoms of hot flashes or cold sweats and they welcomed menopause for its new freedoms and social passage to higher status in old age.

WIDOWHOOD AND CULTURAL CONTEXT

One of the central issues linking gender and aging has been the loss of a spouse (Bradsher 1997). While not exclusively a late-life experience, widowhood does disproportionally relate to the lives of older women (Stevens 1995; Lopata 1996). In one of two chapters in this volume to address widowed status (see also Chapter 15), Maria Cattell uses her long-term research in rural Kenya to draw readers into the experience of older widows among the Samia people. This work adds to the growing cross-cultural literature on widowhood and, importantly, sets her discussion in the broader context of aging women in Africa (Lopata 1987a, 1987b).[13] Cattell shows how postmenopausal Samia women often see widowhood as a way of consolidating social and economic power and independence which they have accrued slowly over a lifetime. A critical factor which shaped the adulthood of these women, like that of so many others in rural Africa, was their work in agricultural activities and trading businesses. Many of the women Cattell came to know had been betrothed very young to older men whom their families had picked for them. While living in a patrilineal society which uses the ancient rule of the levirate—widow remarriage to the dead husband's sibling—elder Samia widows are increasingly refusing to become married again, thus remaining as heads of their households. Cattell also notes the loss of traditional roles for older women in the areas of healing and the traditional education of adolescent girls. However, as is occurring in the United States (see Part II), roles as supportive grandparents have become especially critical as the pace of change is thrusting the young into a previously unexperienced urban industrial context. In the transition from economically independent tribal societies to more dependent peasant economies, African peoples such as the Samia often send large percentages of their young adults to work for long periods outside their rural home areas. Older adults in the kin network play vital roles in holding together the cultural and social integrity of village life and must not be ignored by those who work for rural development in Third World areas (Apt and Katila 1994; Apt 1996).[14] We will again encounter this issue in Chapter 9.

Maria Cattell's chapter shows that older women are not only crucial to the functioning of households and larger kin groupings, but can also act as initiators of changes which have broad importance to the community. It should be noted, of course, that variations in local culture and class standing can starkly alter a female's late-life experience. For example, throughout South Asia as in Africa, most older women are widows and these widows are among the poorest of the poor. The work by Jean Dreze shows that in India households headed by widows have 70 percent less spending power than the national average (1990). She identifies five factors creating constraints on widows in India: their inability to return to the parental home; restrictions on remarriage; very limited access to self-employment outside of agricultural wage labor; difficulty in inheriting property in a patrilineal system; and lack of access to credit.[15]

Such problems are not unique to India. As illustrated below in Box 2, the 1995 Fourth World Conference for Women, held in China, focused a good deal of attention on the common problems older women face globally.

BOX 2. OLDER WOMEN CREATE A GLOBAL NETWORK

Marianne Maloney from Maine, wearing a muscle shirt and shorts, stood smiling beatifically beneath the Older Women's Tent. She had just won a contest sponsored by the China National Aging Committee, the host for the day. But the Chinese mistress of ceremonies explained that Marianne had to perform—sing a song, dance, recite a poem—in order to claim her prize. So Marianne began to sing. And to everyone's surprise it was a song in Chinese! Many Chinese in the audience of 200 began to stand; she was singing the Chinese National Anthem. Eventually Marianne received her prize, a handpainted handkerchief from Tientsin. "Oh, how wonderful!" she said, "I was born in Tientsin 79 years ago!"

Surprising connections like this . . . kept happening to women during the next ten days at Forum '95, the independent non-governmental event held in conjunction with the Fourth World Conference for Women held in Beijing.

On a hill above the Beijing suburb of Huairou, the Older Women's Tent of sweeping yellow canvas welcomed over 2,000 women from every continent. . . . Each day, women crowded under the Tent to hear speakers and hold debates on a wide range of issues—remarriage in old age, fitness, loving one's older body, affirming valuable traditions, nurturing ties to younger generations and loved ones, and protecting the environment for health and well-being.

While Chinese television cameras whirred away, the experts and elderly themselves held forth. . . . Ms. Xie Heng described the recent emphasis on encouraging older persons to remarry. Long taboo in Chinese society, the new program aims to unite couples to overcome loneliness, reduce the costs to the state, and end adult children's responsibilities for caregiving. Opposition often comes from adult children who have a cultural veto power over the remarriage. Most of the audience at the Older Women's Tent questioned why such marriages would help women. The scholar acknowledged that a survey of 45 marriage brokers in Beijing revealed that 87% seeking a partner in old age were male!

continued

Indigenous older women, Winifred Pele Hanoa, a Hawaiian Kapuna; . . . and Pauline Tangiora, a Maori from Australia explained their difficulty in conceptually separating themselves from their communities, either on the basis of gender or age. While acknowledging the leadership that elders often have in indigenous communities, they were reluctant to think of themselves apart from their communities. Recent French nuclear tests in the Pacific Ocean enraged them, endangering their health and threatening fish supplies, their primary source of food (particularly for the old) and jobs.

On the last day of the Forum at the Tent, women decided to build a global older women's network. Despite differences of culture and economy, many core issues are the same across regions: elder rights, economic security, and a desire to participate fully in the life of society. Network members, such as Global Action on Aging, China National Committee on Aging, HelpAge International, Old Women Networks in Europe and Australia, American Association of Retired Persons and many other NGOs want to mobilize grassroots constituents to speak out on aging issues in their communities and nations as well as at international meetings over the next few years. With solid research and communication capability, the Network can produce a serious strategy document on aging by 1999, the United Nations International Year for Older Women.

Reprinted with permission and exerpted from Susanne Paul, "Report from the Older Women's Tent at the NGO Forum in Beijing," *Aging International* 22(4) (1995):53–56.

PROJECT AGE LOOKS AT A GOOD OLD AGE

The focus of this part's concluding article, Project AGE, represents the most sophisticated cross-cultural approach to questions surrounding aging ever undertaken. Integrating both qualitative and quantitative approaches within a common methodology, complex ethnographies of age and aging were conducted at seven sites around the world between 1982 and 1990. The research shows how both "systemwide" community features (such as social inequality) and "internal mechanisms" (such as values) create distinct contexts for conceptualizing the life cycle, establishing age norms, and influencing the perception of well-being and success in old age (Dorfman and Walsh 1996). In Chapter 5, the authors of Project Age address this last vexing issue. Their focus is on how cultures create a sense of a "good old age" and the factors which shape this perception. It is particularly interesting to note that in one of the sites, Hong Kong, despite continuing ideals of filial concern, and actual intergenerational co-residence, old age receives the lowest status compared to other parts of the life course.

KEY RESOURCES

Centers

NIA Exploratory Centers on the Demography of Aging. These nine newly developed centers across the countries can be accessed through the central web site of http://www.psc.lsa.umich.edu/aging/. Some of the centers already provide online data bases and working papers as well as profiles of the projects that are just getting under way.

Data Sets

The National Archive of Computerized Data on Aging (NACDA): This archive has available various data sets, from a variety of international survey studies. Available on diskettes, CD-ROM or e-mail transfer. Write to ICPSR Member Services, P.O. BOX 1248, Ann Arbor, MI 48106–1248. Phone: (313) 763–5010. Some of the databases are available through a web site: http:/www.icpsr.umich.edu/nacda/index/html.

Averting the Old Age Crisis Database. This software edition of *Averting the Old Age Crisis* (see Other Print Resources below) provides on 3½" double-density diskettes, the complete data sets that are used in the print edition. The World Bank, Box 7247–8619, Philadelphia, PA 19170–8619.

Internet Resources

(1) http:/www.census.gov/ is the World Wide Web site for the U.S. Census Bureau. They also have an International Data Base which includes some data related to aging at http:/www.census.gov:80/ipc/www/idbnew.html.

(2) http://www.aoa.dhhs.gov/aoa/post5ed/demog.html. A site listing connections to demographic centers, databases and statistical information related to aging.

(3) http://www.yahoo.com/Society_and_Culture/Death/Euthanasia/Pro_Euthanasia/ is a site giving links to information on assisted suicide, such as http://www.efn.org/~ergo/ which provides a world information directory on this subject.

(4) http://www.aoa.dhhs.gov/aoa/webres/abuse.htm#center supplies links to the issue of elder abuse such as the National Center on Elder Abuse, http://www.interinc.com/NCEA and an international bibliography at http://www.nisw.org.uk/lins/cd/eld.html.

Print Resources

Journals

Journal of Women and Aging; Journal of Elder Abuse and Neglect; Network News (a newsletter of the Global Link for Midlife and Older Women, AARP).

The *Journal of Cross-Cultural Gerontology* has a special section in many of its issues called "Aging Trends." These articles give demographic profiles on specific developing nations.

Special Issue of a journal, "Gender, Aging and Power in Sub-Sahara Africa," *Journal of Cross-Cultural Gerontology* 7 (1992):4.

Bibliography

Wheeler, H. 1997. *Women and Aging: A Guide to the Literature.* Boulder, CO: Lynne Rienner. Contains over 2,000 references, including doctoral dissertations.

Other Print Resources

Apt, N. 1996. *Coping with Old Age in a Changing Africa*. Aldershot, UK: Avebury. An African gerontologist draws upon extensive research experience in her native Ghana to discuss the changing patterns of care for the elderly throughout Africa.

Cambell, S. and P. Silverman. 1996. *Widower: When Men are Left Alone*. Amityville, NY: Baywood. A biographically focused analysis of how men cope with the loss of a spouse.

Chaney, E., ed. 1990. *Empowering Older Women: Cross-Cultural Views*. Washington, DC: American Association of Retired Persons. Discussions on empowerment by women leaders and organizers from a variety of developing countries and the United States.

Coyle, J. 1997. *Handbook on Women and Aging*. Westport, CT: Greenwood. A very large collection of scholarly works on females in late life.

Jecker, N. 1994. ''Physician Assisted Suicide in the Netherlands and the United States.'' *Journal of the American Geriatrics Society* 42:6:672–678. Compares the status of voluntary active euthanasia and physician-assisted suicide in the Netherlands and the United States.

Keith, J. et al. 1994. *The Aging Experience: Diversity and Commonality Across Cultures*. Thousand Oaks, CA: Sage. The central resource for learning about the general results from Project AGE discussed in part I.

Kosberg, J. and J. Garcia, eds. 1995. *Elder Abuse: International and Cross-Cultural Perspectives*. Binghamton, NY: Haworth Press. An important new collection of articles dealing with a most difficult subject.

U.S. Bureau of the Census. 1996. *World Population Profile*. Washington, DC: Center for International Research, U.S. Bureau of the Census. Biannual report of population. Estimates and projections covering all regions of the world.

World Bank. 1994. *Averting the Old Age Crisis*. New York: Oxford University Press. A global analysis of the issues involved with creating and sustaining economic and social support for the elderly.

NOTES

1. Each of these nations will require less than 22 years to shift from 7 percent over age 65 to 14 percent, with Tunisia the fastest, at just 15 years.

2. It should be pointed out that despite the United States lagging behind in life expectancy from birth, a study in 1995 from Duke University found that those in the United States who make it to age 80 survive on average six months longer than a Japanese, Swedish or French citizen and a year longer than the British.

3. Except where indicated the demographic data in this section was provided by Kevin Kinsella of the U.S. Census Bureau.

4. While quite popular with the general public, the 1982 film *The Gods Must Be Crazy* has evoked a storm of protest from scholars. They have criticized the film for depicting an erroneous, benign view of a South African political structure which protects the childlike Ju/'hoansi living in a pristine state of Stone Age existence. In reality the Ju/'hoansi have been placed on a fenced-in reservation, their traditional lifestyle has been prohibited and the men are often conscripted by the South African military to fight guerrilla forces in rural areas.

5. For a general discussion of discourse analysis in gerontology, see Green 1993.

6. Euthanasia remains technically illegal in both the Netherlands and Switzerland, although in these countries guidelines have been developed which permit doctor-assisted suicide under carefully controlled circumstances. In 1996, the Northern Territory of Australia passed the Rights of the Terminally Ill Act. This allowed a mentally and physically competent person over age 18 to request his own death. This had to be supported by three doctors, including a specialist certifying that the individual was terminally ill and a phychiatrist who established that the patient was not suffering from treatable depression.

7. The Hemlock Society is the best known organization which advocates active euthanasia of mature individuals suffering from a terminal illness. The philosophy and practical advice of this group is provided in Humphry 1991.

8. In April of 1996 newspapers reported that the family had reached an agreement which returned the man to his wife and daughter who agreed not to seek euthanasia for him even if it became legal. As of 1997 Dr. Kevorkian had assisted in at least 46 suicides.

9. While no regions of the world have more older males than older females, a recent study lists four countries for which this is the case for the population over 60 years of age: Bangladesh, Zimbabwe, Morocco and Tunisia (Kinsella 1988).

10. Due to demographic, economic and power differences between older women and men, their living situation in old age is often quite divergent. For a recent international analysis of the living arrangement patterns of older women, see Wolf 1995.

11. While some theorists have stressed the cultural turning points linked to procreative and family cycles, others have suggested that universal intrapsychic personality development best explains the frequent reversals observed among older adults (Gutmann 1987). For other cross-cultural discussion of this issue see especially Bart 1969; Brown 1982; Kerns 1983; Cool and McCabe 1987; Gutmann 1987:133–184; Teitlebaum 1987).

12. For other recent works on mid-life women and menopause in various cultures see: Du Toit 1990; Flint and Samil 1990; Kaufert and Lock 1992; Lock 1993; and Callahan 1995.

13. Some of the important references in this growing literature include Lopata 1972, 1979, 1987a, 1987b; Folta and Deck 1987; Palmore 1987; Sered 1987.

14. For a discussion on older women in African urban settings, see Coles 1990; and Kenyon 1994.

15. Ellickson (1988) provides another example in Bangladesh, where the situation for older women, especially widows, is poorer than the prospects available among the Samia people. For a cross-cultural discussion of older women who had never married see Paradise 1993.

CHAPTER 1

The Demography of an Aging World

Kevin Kinsella

In the Netherlands, doctors and families wrestle with decisions about euthanasia, a practice that is officially illegal but unofficially part of Dutch life. In Argentina, angry crowds demonstrate outside of federal ministries, protesting against ceilings on pension payments that are soon eroded by inflation. In southern Africa, HIV/AIDS deaths among younger adults thrust grandparents back into direct parenting roles. In China, the government continues to publicly espouse a one-child-per-couple policy while privately worrying about the implications of such a policy for future family support of the elderly (see Chapter 24).

It is increasingly apparent that we live in an aging world. From one vantage point, a major success story of the twentieth century has been the extent of population aging that has resulted from reduced fertility, better health and increased longevity. For the first time in history, many societies have the luxury of mass aging. Accompanying this broad demographic process, however, are other changes—macroeconomic strains, emergent technologies, new disease patterns, changing social norms—that are difficult for societies to plan for. As indicated above, the intersection of such changes with an evolving demographic background may generate unforeseen issues that become the socioeconomic problems of current and future generations. While few of us pretend to predict economic and technological developments with certainty, an understanding of the relatively predictable process of population aging helps us to anticipate these developments and better prepare for the future.

PERSPECTIVES ON POPULATION AGING

Although virtually all of the world's populations are becoming older on average, the extent and pace of aging may vary enormously from society to society.

Likewise, the meaning of the term "elderly" varies as a result of wide national differences in average longevity and health status. Any chronological demarcation of age boundaries is arbitrary and open to dispute on grounds that it poorly represents biological, physiological, or even psychological dimensions of the human experience (Myers 1985). Attainment of age 80 may be as extraordinary in one nation as it is commonplace in another. Nevertheless, the establishment of such boundaries is necessary for a descriptive comparison of international aging. In this chapter, the term "elderly" refers to persons aged 65 years and over, and the term "oldest old" refers to those who are at least 80 years old.

Proportions of Elderly. Human population aging refers most commonly to an increase in the percentage of all extant persons who have lived to or beyond a certain age. While the size of the world's elderly population has been increasing for centuries, it is only in recent decades that the proportion has caught the attention of researchers and policymakers. In 1995, the 368 million persons aged 65 and over constituted 6.4 percent of the earth's total population. In absolute terms, this represents an increase of 48 million elderly since 1990.[1]

Sweden was the demographically oldest of the world's major[2] nations in 1995, with 18 percent of its population aged 65 and over. Other notably high levels are seen in Norway, the United Kingdom, Italy and Belgium (16 percent each). The elderly share of total population will increase only modestly in most industrialized nations between 1995 and 2010, and may even dip slightly as a function of the relatively small cohorts born prior to and during the Second World War. After 2010, numbers of and percentages of elderly should increase rapidly in many countries as the large postwar birth cohorts (the baby boom) begin to reach age 65.

Sometimes lost amid the attention given to population aging in Europe and North America is the fact that older populations in developing countries typically are growing faster than their industrialized counterparts.[3] In the mid-1990s, the total of the world's elderly was increasing by more than 800,000 persons each month; 70 percent of this change was occurring in the developing world. Projections to the year 2025 suggest that the growth rate of the elderly in the developing world will remain significantly higher than in today's industrialized countries (Figure 1.1). Between 1990 and 2025, developing countries such as Indonesia, Colombia, Kenya and Malaysia may expect a tripling or quadrupling of their elderly populations.

As a result of past trends in fertility and current trends in mortality, age categories within the elderly aggregate may grow at different rates. An increasingly important feature of societal aging is the progressive aging of the elderly population itself. The fastest growing age segment in many countries is the "oldest old" (persons aged 80 and over). This group constitutes more than 20 percent of the aggregate elderly population in industrialized countries, and approximately 4 percent of the total population in Scandinavia, France and Switzerland. In 1995, nine industrialized nations had oldest old populations in excess

Figure 1.1
Average Annual Percent Growth of Elderly Population in Developed and Developing Countries

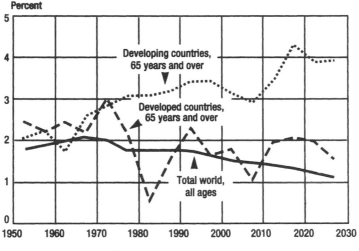

Source: Kinsella and Taeuber 1993.

of one million. While proportions of oldest old are lower in developing countries, absolute numbers may be quite high. China, for example, had approximately 9.4 million oldest old in 1995, more than in any other country of the world.

The demands of the oldest old vis-à-vis policymaking should increase markedly in the twenty-first century due to levels of illness and disability that are much higher than in other population groups. While it may be misleading to simplistically equate growth of the oldest old with spiraling health care costs (Binstock 1993), the fact remains that the oldest old consume social services, benefits and transfers far out of proportion to their numbers (Suzman, Willis and Manton 1992).

Speed of Population Aging. The transition from a youthful to a more aged society has occurred gradually in some nations, but will be compressed in many others. For instance, it took only one-quarter of a century, from 1970 to 1995, for the percentage of population aged 65 and over in Japan to increase from 7 to 14 percent. A similarly short transition period is projected for China, beginning in the year 2000, and for several other East Asian nations such as South Korea and Taiwan beginning slightly later in the twenty-first century. These rapid gains will be driven by drastic drops from prior levels of fertility. In South Korea, for example, the total fertility rate[4] has plummeted from 5 children per woman in the late 1960s to less than 1.8 today. The pace of change in parts of Asia stands in stark contrast to some European countries, where the comparable

Figure 1.2
The Speed of Population Aging (number of years required or expected for percent 65+ to rise from 7% to 14%)

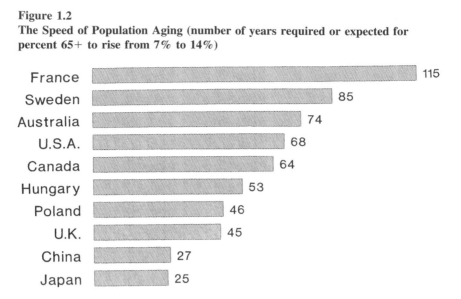

Source: From sources reported in Kinsella and Taeuber 1993.

change occurred over a period of 80 to 115 years (Figure 1.2). Today's rapidly aging societies are likely to face the contentious issues related to health care costs, social security and intergenerational equity that have sparked public debate in Europe and North America. The speed of population aging may even prompt governments to rethink their overall population policies. Singapore, once a prime advocate of fertility reduction, achieved such success in this arena that the declining birth rate became a cause of political and economic concern. Consequently, Singapore's "Stop at 2" [children] policy was modified in 1987 to provide incentives for higher fertility, particularly among better-educated segments of the population (Phillips and Bartlett 1995).

Median Age. Another way to look at population aging is to consider a society's median age, the age that divides a population into numerically equal parts of younger and older persons. While nearly all industrialized countries are above the 31-year level, most developing nations have median ages under 25. In some African and South Asian countries in the mid-1990s, half of the entire population is younger than 15, and high numbers of annual births are likely to keep these countries relatively young in the near future. Yet in developing countries such as Cuba, South Korea and Singapore where fertility rates have fallen precipitously, median ages are rising rapidly and should exceed 40 by the year 2025.

The concept of median age encourages a broader view of population aging which focuses less on the elderly population per se. In many developing countries, the initial effects of population aging will be seen in the relative growth of young and middle-aged adult populations. This trend implies a shift in overall population age structure, with accompanying changes in labor force characteristics, household/family structure and disease patterns. From a business or government-planning perspective, the most pressing aspect of this trend may be the growth in labor force size that produces concern about available jobs. Dramatic percentage increases in labor force size, for example, are likely to occur in Africa and the Near East during the period 1990–2020, and the aggregate number of potential job seekers will more than double. The percentage increase will be less in other developing regions, but the absolute growth will be substantial. In Asia alone, economies will need to generate more than one billion additional jobs during the next three decades simply to maintain current levels of employment.

THE DEMOGRAPHIC TRANSITION

Regardless of how one defines population aging, the process primarily involves change over time in levels of fertility and mortality. Populations with high fertility tend to have low proportions of older persons and vice versa. Current total fertility rates in excess of seven children per woman in Malawi and Niger, for instance, correlate with elderly population shares of less than 3 percent. Demographers use the term ''demographic transition'' to refer to a gradual process wherein a society moves from a situation of high rates of fertility and mortality to one of low rates of fertility and mortality. This transition is characterized first by declines in infant and childhood mortality as infectious and parasitic diseases are controlled. The resulting improvement in life expectancy at birth occurs while fertility tends to remain high, thereby producing large birth cohorts and an expanding proportion of children relative to adults.

Whole populations begin to age when fertility rates decline and mortality improvements occur more at older ages than at younger ages. Successive birth cohorts may eventually become smaller and smaller, although countries may experience a ''baby boom echo'' as women from large birth cohorts reach childbearing age. International migration usually does not play a major role in the demography of aging, but can be important in small nations. Certain Caribbean nations, for example, have experienced a combination of working-age-adult emigration, immigration of elderly retirees from other countries, and return migration of former emigrants who are above the average population age; all three factors contribute to population aging.

Figure 1.3 illustrates the historical and projected transition in population age structure in developed and developing countries. At one time, most if not all countries had a youthful age structure similar to that of developing countries as a whole in 1950. A large percentage of the entire population was under the age of 15. Given the relatively high rates of fertility that prevailed in most developing countries from 1950 through the early 1970s, the overall pyramid shape had changed very little by 1990. However, the effects of fertility and mortality

Figure 1.3
Aggregate Population in Developed and Developing Countries, by Age and Sex:
1950, 1990 and 2025 (in millions)

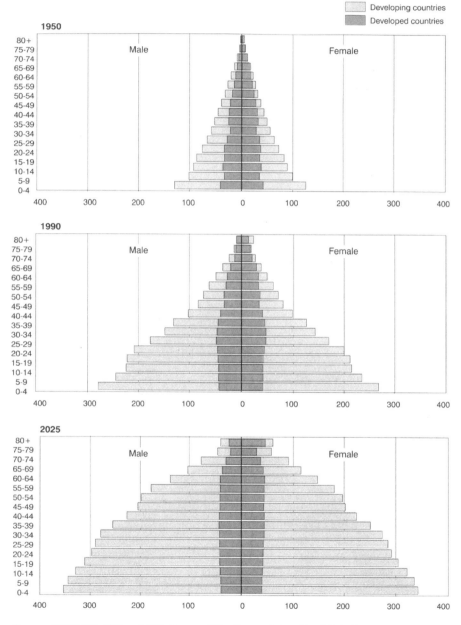

Source: UNDIESA 1991 and U.S. Bureau of the Census, International Data Base.

decline can be seen in the projected pyramid for 2025, which loses its strictly triangular shape as the elderly portion of the total population increases.

The picture in developed countries has been and will be quite different. In 1950, there was relatively little variation in the size of 5-year groups between the ages of 5 and 24. The beginnings of the post–World War II baby boom can be seen in the 0–4 age group. By 1990, the baby boom cohorts were 25 to 44 years old, and the cohorts under age 25 were becoming successively smaller. If fertility rates continue as projected through 2025, the aggregate pyramid will start to invert, with more weight on the top than on the bottom. The prominence of the oldest old (especially women) will increase, and persons aged 80 and over will outnumber any younger 5-year age group.

Longevity. Although the effect of fertility decline is usually the driving force behind changing population age structures, changes in mortality assume greater importance as countries reach lower levels of fertility (Caselli et al. 1987). Since the beginning of this century, industrialized countries have made great progress in extending life expectancy at birth. Japan enjoys the highest life expectancy of all the world's countries in the mid-1990s—the average Japanese born today can expect to live more than 79 years—and the level in various European nations approaches or exceeds 78 years. Three important observations can be made concerning the trends in Table 1.1: (1) the relative difference among countries has narrowed with time; (2) the pace of improvement has not been linear, especially for males. From the early 1950s to the early 1970s, for example, there was little or no change in male life expectancy in Australia, the Netherlands, Norway and the United States, while in Eastern Europe and much of the former Soviet Union, male life expectancy declined in the 1970s and early 1980s; and (3) the difference in female versus male longevity, which universally has been in favor of women in this century, widened with time.

Changes in life expectancy in developing regions of the world have been more uniform. Practically all nations have showed continued improvement, with some exceptions in Latin America. The most dramatic gains have been achieved in East Asia, where regional life expectancy at birth increased from less than 45 years in 1950 to more than 71 years in 1990. Extreme variations exist throughout the developing world, however. While Costa Rica, Hong Kong and numerous Caribbean island nations enjoy levels that match or exceed those in a majority of European nations, the normal lifetime in other countries spans fewer than 50 years (see Table 1.2). Aggregate life expectancy at birth in Latin America (68 years) is 17 years higher than in Sub-Saharan Africa. On average, an individual born in an industrialized country in the mid-1990s will outlive his/her counterpart in the developing world by 13 years according to current mortality schedules.

Where infant mortality rates are still relatively high but declining, as in many developing countries, most of the improvement in life expectancy at birth results from infants surviving the high-risk initial years of life. But when infant and childhood mortality reach low levels, as in developed countries, improvements

Table 1.1

Life Expectancy at Birth for Selected Developed Countries, 1900 to 1995 (in years)

	Circa 1900		Circa 1950		Circa 1995	
Region/Country	Male	Female	Male	Female	Male	Female
WESTERN EUROPE						
Austria	37.8	39.9	62.0	67.0	73.7	80.3
Belgium	45.4	48.9	62.1	67.4	73.9	80.7
Denmark	51.6	54.8	68.9	71.5	73.2	79.2
France	45.3	48.7	63.7	69.4	74.5	82.4
Germany	43.8	46.6	64.6	68.5	73.5	79.9
Norway	52.3	55.8	70.3	73.8	74.3	81.2
Sweden	52.8	55.3	69.9	72.6	75.6	81.4
United Kingdom	46.4	50.1	66.2	71.1	74.2	80.0
SOUTHERN and EASTERN EUROPE						
Czech Republic	38.9	41.7	60.9	65.5	69.9	77.4
Greece	38.1	39.7	63.4	66.7	75.4	80.6
Hungary	36.6	38.2	59.3	63.4	67.9	76.1
Poland	–	–	57.2	62.8	69.2	77.3
Italy	42.9	43.2	63.7	67.2	74.7	81.2
Spain	33.9	35.7	59.8	64.3	74.7	81.4
OTHER						
Australia	53.2	56.8	66.7	71.8	74.7	81.0
Canada	–	–	66.4	70.9	74.9	81.8
Japan	42.8	44.3	59.6	63.1	76.6	82.4
New Zealand	–	–	67.2	71.3	73.1	80.4
United States	48.3	51.1	66.0	71.7	72.8	79.7

Notes: ''—'' Data not available

Figures for Germany and the Czech Republic prior to 1995 refer to the former West Germany and Czechoslovakia, respectively.

Source: UNDIESA 1988; Siampos 1990; and U.S. Bureau of the Census, International Data Base.

Table 1.2

Life Expectancy at Birth for Selected Developing Countries, 1950 and 1995 (in years)

Region/Country	Circa 1950 Male	Circa 1950 Female	1995 Male	1995 Female
AFRICA				
Egypt	41.2	43.6	63.6	66.0
Ghana	40.4	43.6	55.2	58.8
Mali	31.1	34.0	45.4	48.6
South Africa	44.0	46.0	61.2	67.2
Uganda	38.5	41.6	42.9	45.3
Zaire	37.5	40.6	50.4	53.6
ASIA				
China	39.3	42.3	67.4	71.0
India	39.4	38.0	61.4	61.6
Kazakhstan	51.6	61.9	65.8	74.4
Korea, South	46.0	49.0	68.0	75.5
Syria	44.8	47.2	66.0	70.2
Thailand	45.0	49.1	65.7	71.7
LATIN AMERICA				
Argentina	60.4	65.1	69.1	76.2
Brazil	49.3	52.8	64.8	69.4
Costa Rica	56.0	58.6	74.2	78.9
Cuba	57.8	61.3	73.8	77.6
Mexico	49.2	52.4	68.4	74.4
Venezuela	53.8	56.6	69.4	75.2

Note: Data for ''Circa 1950'' refer to the period 1950–1955; data for 1995 represent an average of data for the periods 1990–1995 and 1995–2000.
Source: UNDESIPA 1995.

in average life expectancy are achieved primarily by declines in mortality among older segments of the population. In Japan, life expectancy at age 65 rose nearly 4 years for men and 5 years for women during the period 1970–1991. Under the mortality conditions of 1991, the average Japanese woman aged 65 years could expect to live an additional 20 years, and the average Japanese man more than 16 years.

The greater relative improvement in life expectancy at older versus the youngest ages is not yet widespread in developing regions of the world. However, the proportional increase in life expectancy at older ages is approaching or has surpassed the relative increase in life expectancy at birth in some developing countries, notably in Latin America and the Caribbean (Kinsella 1994).

While global reductions in overall mortality levels have been the norm in recent decades, the HIV/AIDS epidemic now threatens to reverse life expectancy gains, particularly in parts of Africa and Asia. The impact of the epidemic on life expectancy at birth may be considerable, given that AIDS deaths often are concentrated in the childhood and middle adult (30 to 45) ages. Projections to the year 2010 suggest that AIDS may reduce average life expectancy at birth by more than 25 years from otherwise expected levels in countries such as Thailand, Uganda and Zimbabwe. The impact on future population age structure is less striking insofar as the effects of a long-term epidemic become more evenly distributed across age groups (Way and Stanecki 1994).

COROLLARIES OF DEMOGRAPHIC CHANGE

The Epidemiologic Transition. The spectacular increases in human life expectancy that began in the mid-1800s and continued during the following century are often ascribed primarily to improvements in medicine. However, the major impact of improvements both in medicine and sanitation did not occur until the late nineteenth century. Earlier and more important factors in lowering mortality were innovations in industrial and agricultural production and distribution, which enabled nutritional diversity and consistency for large numbers of people (Thomlinson 1976). A growing research consensus attributes the gain in human longevity since the early 1800s to a complex interplay of advancements in medicine and sanitation coupled with new modes of familial, social, economic and political organization (Moore 1993).

One correlate of this interplay of factors has been an epidemiologic transition, which is related to but has lagged behind the demographic transition. The initial mortality declines that characterize the demographic transition result largely from reductions of infectious diseases at young ages. As children survive and age, they increasingly are exposed to risk factors linked with chronic disease and accidents. And as fertility declines lead to population aging, growing numbers of older persons shift national health patterns in the direction of more continuous and degenerative ailments (Frenk et al. 1991).

There is mounting evidence that an epidemiologic transition has occurred or

Table 1.3
Rank Order of the Nine Leading Causes of Death in the Republic of Korea, 1966 to 1991

	1966	1981	1991
1.	Pneumonia	Malignant neoplasm	Malignant neoplasm
2.	Tuberculosis	Hypertension	Cerebrovascular
3.	Cerebrovascular	Cerebrovascular	Accidents
4.	Other infectious[1]	Accidents[2]	Senility
5.	Malignant neoplasm	Senility	Other circulatory
6.	Accidents	Chronic liver	Hypertension
7.	Bronchitis	Traffic accidents	Chronic liver
8.	Meningitis	Tuberculosis	Diabetes mellitus
9.	Hypertension	Suicide	Tuberculosis

[1] Includes parasitic.
[2] Excludes traffic accidents.
Sources: Choe 1989; World Health Organization data files.

is occurring in many developing as well as developed nations. Data from the Republic of Korea in Table 1.3 exemplify the typical shift in causes of death; the infectious and parasitic diseases that dominated South Korean mortality in the mid-1960s have given way to chronic and degenerative diseases. By 1981, cancers had become the number one killer. In 1991, the overall cardiovascular disease category—cerebrovascular (stroke) plus hypertension plus other circulatory—accounted for about 30 percent of all deaths.[5] The role of cardiovascular diseases as the principal cause of death has been well-documented in a large majority of Latin American and Caribbean countries (Pan American Health Organization 1994).

Gender Differences. Women live longer on average than men in virtually all countries.[6] The difference may be slight, as in much of South Asia, or as large as ten years in parts of the former Soviet Union (Figure 1.4). Although human biology produces more male births than female births throughout the world, male mortality rates usually are higher than female rates at all ages. Therefore, the percent female increases and the numerical male advantage disappears as a birth cohort grows older: by age 30 or 35, women start to outnumber men in many countries, and the absolute female advantage typically increases with age. The ratio of women to men among the oldest old may exceed two-to-one, as is the case in Austria and Germany.

The gender difference in absolute numbers at older ages translates into a major difference in marital status. Most elderly men are married. But because women

Figure 1.4
Female Advantage in Life Expectancy at Birth: 1994 (in years)

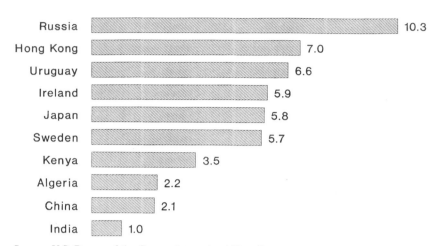

Russia	10.3
Hong Kong	7.0
Uruguay	6.6
Ireland	5.9
Japan	5.8
Sweden	5.7
Kenya	3.5
Algeria	2.2
China	2.1
India	1.0

Source: U.S. Bureau of the Census, International Data Base.

tend to live longer than men, marry males older than themselves, and remarry less frequently after the loss of a spouse, a majority of elderly women in many countries are widowed. In countries that lack a formal social safety net, elderly widows—often illiterate and without significant financial savings—represent an especially vulnerable population that must rely on younger family members for economic support (see Chapter 4).

Altered Family Structures. Several social trends that occur in the context of the demographic transition—for example, urbanization, economic development, increased female education and labor force participation—interact to produce changing household structures. Declines in fertility eventually reduce average household size, as is now gradually occurring in many countries. Concurrently, many nations are in the midst of a shift toward nuclear and away from extended family structures. Also, data indicate that numerous developing nations have increasing proportions of persons living alone (i.e., in single-person households), a trend already common in industrialized nations. This is due partially to changing social norms—delayed marriage, new gender roles—and also to higher rates of marital dissolution and growing numbers of elderly whose spouse has died. The end result is that, in most countries, the number of households is growing faster than the total population. Changes in family and household structure have important implications for social support of, and health-service delivery to, current and future elderly cohorts.[7]

Several decades ago, relatively few people in their 50s and 60s worried about caring for persons aged 80 and over. Now, however, many more people give such care, and for longer periods of time. Today's caregivers provide care that is more physically and psychologically demanding than in the past, especially with regard to the increased number of persons with cognitive diseases such as Alzheimer's (Brody 1985; see Chapter 22 this volume). As medical technology finds more ways to save lives, we can expect the duration of chronic illness, and consequently the need for help, to increase even more.

Demographers often construct population ratios as crude indicators of potential needs within a society. One such gauge of the need for family support of the oldest old is the Parent Support Ratio (PSR), defined here as the number of persons aged 80 and over per 100 persons aged 50 to 64. In a broad sense, this measure relates the oldest old to their offspring who were born when most of the oldest old were aged 20 to 34. In one 50-country study of both developed and developing nations (Kinsella and Taeuber 1993), the PSR was projected to increase from 1990 to 2025 in all but three nations.

In view of a multitude of research results showing that adult women (daughters and daughters-in-law) provide most of the personal care for elderly family members, it may be more instructive to examine a Parent Support Ratio by Females (PSRF), which includes only women aged 50 to 64 in the denominator. In the 50-nation study, country patterns in PSRF were similar to the broader PSR, but the levels were much higher. Most developed countries had PSRFs between 30 and 50 in 1990, while the level in most developing nations was 15 or lower. Projections to 2025 indicate that there could be 91 persons aged 80 and over per 100 women aged 50 to 64 in Japan, the highest level among the 50 countries. The lowest projected level among developed nations would be 48 for both Australia and the United States. Projected levels for developing countries varied from less than 10 in currently-high-fertility nations such as Bangladesh and Malawi to more than 36 in Argentina, Cuba, Israel and Singapore.

DOES LONGER LIFE MEAN BETTER LIFE?

As noted earlier, sustained increases in life expectancy, especially at older ages, have been the norm in most countries worldwide. When individuals live longer, the quality of that longer life becomes a central issue. Are we living healthier as well as longer lives, or are we spending an increasing portion of our older years with disabilities, mental disorders and in ill health? In aging societies, the answer to this question will have a profound impact on national health and long-term care systems, and on the financial well-being of elderly citizens and their offspring. In the future, health expectancy will come to be as important a measure as life expectancy is today.

Since the early 1970s, research has been moving toward the development of health indices that take into account not only mortality but also various gradations of health. While more than 30 nations now have sufficient data with which to estimate healthy life expectancy,[8] strict international comparisons remain problematic. Computational methods are different across countries, and more importantly, the concepts and definitions that define the basic data are different.

Figure 1.5
Disability-Free Portion of Life Expectancy at Age 65 (percent of remaining years lived without disability)

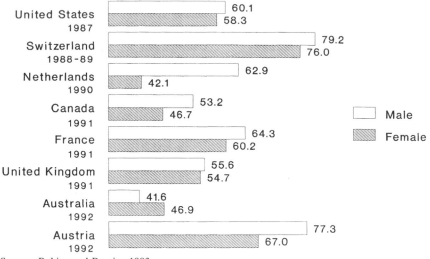

Source: Robine and Romieu 1993.

For example, distinctions among impairments, disabilities, and handicaps lead to different measures of health status (Chamie 1992). In spite of cross-national problems of comparability, two general observations seem warranted on the basis of existing data from developed countries.

For persons reaching age 65, there is a greater range among countries in healthy life expectancy than in remaining life expectancy. Second, women can expect to spend more years in a disabled state than men (Robine and Romieu 1993). Stated another way, men who reach age 65 can expect to spend a greater portion of their remaining years without disability than can women, except in Australia (Figure 1.5). A similar conclusion is supported by preliminary World Health Organization data for twelve developing nations.[9]

In nations where time series estimates of health expectancy are available (for example, Canada, the United States, Australia, England/Wales), two very tentative trends emerge. While overall life expectancy at birth was rising during the 1980s, the proportion of life expectancy with moderate or light disability appears to have declined. On the other hand, the proportion *without* severe disability generally appears to have been stable (World Health Organization 1995).

The uncertainty regarding a global trend in health expectancy may be seen by contrasting Australia with the United States. Data on elderly Australians from two points in the 1980s suggest that the increase in years spent with some degree of handicap was greater than the corresponding increase in life expectancy at age 65. A more optimistic scenario has taken shape in the United States, where longitudinal data from the U.S. Long-Term Care Survey imply that the prevalence of chronic disability among the elderly declined between 1984 and 1989 (Manton, Corder and Stallard 1993).

Researchers have pointed to a number of potential factors—other than actual increases in chronic disease incidence and improved measurement techniques—which might contribute to an apparent increase in disability such as reported in Australia. These factors include increased survival of chronically ill individuals due to improvements in medical care; earlier diagnosis or treatment of chronic diseases; greater social awareness of disease and disability; earlier adjustment to chronic conditions due to improved pension and health care/delivery systems; and rising expectations of what constitutes good health and normal functioning (Mathers 1991; Verbrugge 1989). Clearly, improved data collection and more rigorous analyses are prerequisites for a deeper understanding of trends in health expectancy. Many countries with aging populations now recognize the necessity of longitudinal surveys, not only as a means of mapping adult health patterns, but also as instruments for understanding transitions to and from different late-life economic, social and psychological statuses.

NOTES

1. These and other demographic estimates and projections in this chapter are, unless otherwise noted, taken from Kinsella and Taeuber (1993) and/or the International Data Base maintained by the International Programs Center, U.S. Bureau of the Census and supported by the Office of the Demography of Aging, U.S. National Institute on Aging.

2. Some small nations or areas of special sovereignty, such as Monaco and the Isle of Man, may have higher percents of elderly than Sweden.

3. The country classification used in this chapter corresponds to that of the United Nations, wherein "industrialized" and its synonym "developed" comprise all nations in Europe (including the former Soviet Union) and North America, plus Japan, Australia and New Zealand. The remaining nations of the world are classified as "developing."

4. The average number of children that would be born per woman if all women lived to the end of their childbearing years and bore children according to a given set of age-specific fertility rates.

5. The presence and importance of "senility" as a cause of death underscores the imprecision of cause-of-death data in many countries. Growing numbers of deaths attributed to "old age" imply both an aging population and the need for increased medical training with regard to chronic disease status.

6. The U.S. Bureau of the Census estimates that, as of 1994, male life expectancy at birth exceeds that of females only in Afghanistan, Bangladesh and Bhutan.

7. Heightened concerns about social support of the elderly have sparked a renewed interest in worldwide studies of aging and the family. For additional information on this multifaceted subject, the interested reader is referred to several excellent volumes containing comprehensive analyses: Blieszner and Bedford 1995; Albert and Cattell 1994; and Maddox and Lawton 1993.

8. Healthy life expectancy is not necessarily expectancy free of disease, particularly

long-term chronic diseases such as diabetes and hypertension. Rather, the concept of healthy life expectancy as normally used refers to expectancy without limitations of function that may be the consequence of one or more chronic disease conditions. This concept is sometimes called ''active life expectancy'' or ''disability-free life expectancy'' to avoid the implication that ''healthy'' means ''absence of disease.''

9. The World Health Organization project ''Health and Social Aspects of Aging'' was conducted under the supervision of the Centre for Ageing Studies, Flinders University of South Australia. National data were collected between 1984 and 1989; see Andrews et al. (1986) for selected early-round results.

CHAPTER 2

Complaint Discourse, Aging and Caregiving among the Ju/'hoansi of Botswana

Harriet G. Rosenberg

Old people have long complained: it is an old thing. Even if the child did
everything for them, they would complain.

Koka, age 80

This chapter explores the social basis of caregiving discourses among the Ju/
'hoansi[1] of southern Africa. It looks at how a particular cultural system reproduces the social relations of care for elders, and examines the language through
which care is negotiated. These forms of speech locate caregiving in gender,
family and community relationships. They also reproduce the ideology of caring
for elders in both its public and domestic realm and legitimate this behavior so
that it is experienced as "natural."

Despite the changes in economic and social life that the Ju/'hoansi have experienced in the last 25 years, caring discourse appears to be autonomous in the
Dobe area, in the sense that it is constructed within the culture itself, with very
little influence from state agencies (legal, health, educational, military, social
services) or non-Ju/'hoansi religious philosophies.[2]

THE JU/'HOANSI OF THE DOBE AREA

The Ju/'hoansi (an approximate English pronounciation would be "juntwasi") of Botswana and Namibia are one of the best known and documented
gatherer-hunter peoples in the world. Although their history of contact has been
a complex one, some have lived as relatively isolated foragers[3] well into the
1960s. As gatherer-hunters, the Ju/'hoansi can provide insights into a way of
life that was, until 10,000 years ago, a human universal.

Studies of the Ju/'hoansi have been carried out on a wide variety of topics by over a dozen investigators (including project AGE described by Fry et al., Chapter 5). The Dobe area, where the majority of these studies were undertaken, is a line of eight water holes in the northern Kalahari Desert of Botswana. The area is about 10,000 square kilometers, and has in recent years supported a population of between 800 and 1000 people. In 1986, the 663 Ju/'hoansi shared their eight water holes with about 325 pastoralists, mainly of the Herero ethnic group. Our studies of aging and caregiving covered both the Herero and the Ju/'hoansi but the present chapter focuses on the latter people.

During the 1960s the majority of Ju/'hoansi lived in small camps of about fifteen to thirty people, often centered around a core of siblings, their spouses and children. The groups relied on wild food products for the bulk of their subsistence needs and moved three to six times a year in search of food and water. These camps were characterized by egalitarian social relations and the widespread sharing of foodstuffs—the typical features of a small-scale communal social formation. The language and kinship system were intact and fully functioning.

Missionizing has had little influence in the Dobe area. Indigenous religious practices included belief in two major deities (a high god and a lesser, trickster god) and ghosts of ancestors called *gangwasi*. Trance dancing maintained the health of the community and was used to cure individual sicknesses. At some camps the all-night dances took place two or three times a week. A woman's drum dance was also prominent.[4]

After 1968, conditions began to change rapidly. In 1968, the first store opened, followed by a school in 1973 and a health post and airstrip in 1978. During this period the Ju/'hoansi began to shift over to small-scale livestock and crop production and settle into semi-permanent villages. Cash became a common medium of exchange which coexisted with the traditional regional gift exchange system called *hxaro*.[5] Migrant labor, livestock sales and craft production became sources of cash income. In addition, some young men were drawn across the border into the South African military, where they earned high salaries as trackers in the war against the South West African People's Organization (SWAPO).[6]

By the mid-1980s, in their dress and economy, the Dobe Ju/'hoansi came to resemble the lifestyle of many impoverished southern African peasants. They received drought relief in the 1980s, and bags and containers from overseas countries littered their villages. Their children went to school, but the majority usually dropped out in the early grades. More recently a few have gone on to high school and have become literate in other African languages and in English. People now seek health care at local clinics or from mobile health units, and they often spend their modest incomes on transistor radios, European-style clothing, tea, sugar, tobacco and beer.

Their transition to an agricultural way of life has been far from successful. In the mid-1980s, over half the families lacked livestock, and even the "affluent" herders numbered their stock in the range of ten to twenty head of cattle.

Foraging declined in the mid-1980s with the introduction of drought relief, but bow and arrow hunting has once again increased in Botswana, encouraged by the Game Department (Lee and Rosenberg 1993). The knowledge of Dobe area elders about the environment, seasonal variation and their technical advice about hunting and gathering became highly prized as younger community members intensified foraging activities (Lee and Biesele 1991).[7]

On a deeper level the Dobe Ju/'hoansi are struggling—not without success—to adhere to the values and beliefs of their ancestral culture. It is this cultural context which has continued to generate the motifs, themes, and rationales about aging and caregiving which are explored in this chapter.

AGE AND CHANGE IN JU/'HOANSI SOCIETY

Like most foraging peoples, the Ju/'hoansi were not interested in and did not keep track of chronological age. Birthdays and anniversaries were not social markers and age segregation has been noticeably absent. Major life transition hallmarks existed at the younger end of the age spectrum distinguishing among infants, children, adolescents and adults. No ceremonies marked the onset of old age or menopause, but all elders (including those without children) carry the honorific *na* in their names which means "old," "big" or "great." No ritual occasion marks the moment when one becomes *na*, usually in one's mid- to late forties; certainly, everyone fifty or over is called *na*.[8]

Old age is divided into three broad categories. All elders are *na*, while those who are very old but still functioning are called "old/dead," *da ki*, a term that designates extreme old age and one that is also a joking term. A sick or decrepit elder may be referred to as "old to the point of helplessness," *da kum kum*. *Da ki* and *da kum kum* do not denote a sharp decline in social status. Unlike many societies described in this volume (see Chapters 3 and 21), the frail elderly are not a particular butt of ridicule or a source of fear and anxiety.

It should be noted that growing old and the changes that accompany it are a constant topic of conversation and a source of humor. Linking sexuality and aging seem to make the best jokes and much of campfire discussion features endless stories about decline in sexual prowess, especially among men. Post-menopausal women also delight in engaging in broad sexual joking (R. Lee 1984).

Although the Ju/'hoansi do link old age with degeneration, elders are also associated with generative and life-giving activities, as Biesele and Howell (1981) have pointed out in their analysis of a beautiful folktale of a grandmother/granddaughter relationship. Similarly, elders are felt to have special powers which permit them to eat certain foods (e.g., ostrich eggs) considered too dangerous for younger people to consume. Elders with physical infirmities have taken strong leadership roles, as for example, the case of four blind seniors whose decision-making advice and curing roles were very influential in the political and social life of one water hole in the 1960s (Lee 1968:36). Death is not exclusively connected with old age. Historically, the Ju/'hoansi have had a high infant mortality rate, and now tuberculosis is prevalent in the Dobe area. Thus, death can and does occur at any age.

In the realm of sociopolitical power, Ju/'hoansi elders have had limited prerogatives. Traditionally, they commanded control over defining kinship relationships. A senior person, male or female, has the right to decide who fits where in the kinship system and to determine an avoidance or a joking framework for social interactions. This system of seniority gives elders power within the social universe, but it does not constitute a gerontocracy. Before settling down, the Ju/'hoansi were, for the most part, without property and could not wield the threat of disinheritance to encourage compliance. In 1995 an adult daughter of an elder with cows was asked how cattle ownership affects the quality of care. She responded by saying that "it hasn't changed things. We took care of our elders then and we still take care of them" (Richard Lee fieldnotes May 1995).

However, this mother of six children also indicated that at her passing her eldest child (female) would inherit her cattle and that she alone among her siblings anticipated receiving her mother's property, because she saw herself as the principal caregiver. But she also stated that she might decide to share her inheritance with her siblings (Lee fieldnotes May 1995).

How property and inheritance will, in the long run, influence personal relationships including eldercare is still very much in the process of being worked out. Sedentary life has brought changed patterns in subsistence and marriage customs which may also create significant changes in the lives of Ju/'hoansi elders. In the past, old people, by dint of their personal authority, attempted to construct marriage alliances which seemed sensible to them, but young people often refused such arrangements, thwarting the intentions of their seniors. Nowadays, an emerging pattern of bride wealth[9] in lieu of bride service and an increase in informal interethnic liaisons has made marriage a contentious issue in the Dobe area. As some young women find themselves locked into restrictive arrangements (especially problematic is the new pattern of paternal child custody at divorce within bride wealth systems), many women have chosen to avoid marriage altogether (Lee and Rosenberg 1993; see also Draper 1992). At the same time elders have argued that they see no real change in their own lives as a result of the displacement of bride service by bride wealth, and that receiving a cow at the marriage of a daughter seems to be equivalent to having a son-in-law's hunting skill at their disposal. Lee's 1995 interviews indicate that elders are promoting cattle exchange at marriage in combination with bride service and that they are resisting paternal child custody at divorce.[10] Thus current Ju/'hoansi marriage arrangements are in a state of flux and the implications for elders are unclear.

Another arena of personal authority for elders has been their role as healers. Richard Katz, who has done fieldwork among healers in the Dobe area in the late 1980s, notes that the social status of certain elderly healers is very high (personal communication 1995). These old men are "the healers' healers" and it is their experience and their strength in not being overpowered by the forces with which they work that commands respect. In a culture where boasting of any kind is frowned upon these senior healers are permitted to talk about their skill and achievements. Not all old people develop the power to heal—to sing, dance, go into a trance and "pull sickness" out of others. Those who do can often go on until they are quite old, teaching other healers and participating in healing the community at large. Katz (1982) has described the charismatic energy of some elderly healers and their aura of exceptional strength and spirituality. His recent research (Katz, Biesele and St. Denis 1995) indicates that while some elders say that they are strengthened by their access to *num* (medicine), others have found that healing is very wearing and hastens the aging process.

THE 1986/1987 PROJECT

The discussion which follows is based on field research (participant observation, formal questionnaires and open-ended, unstructured interviews) with the Ju/'hoansi in 1986/1987[11] and updated by Richard Lee in 1995. It also makes use of the accumulated work by anthropologists who have worked with them since 1963. We were, thus, often able to compare our informants' retrospective accounts with field descriptions of observed behavior over a period of three decades. Until recently, however, there has been very little systematic research on aging in Ju/'hoansi culture.

In 1964, 9 percent of the population was over 60.[12] By 1986 the figure was 12.5 percent, with 7.5 percent over age 65. In addition, the birth rate has risen. As of 1986, almost 40 percent of the population was under 15 years of age. Thus, at the time of our field research, 48 percent of the population was between 15 and 49 and supported both young and old.

This project focused on the social experience of aging and caregiving as mediated by (1) narratives of neglect and abandonment, (2) the concept of entitlement, and (3) the social organization of care.

NARRATIVES OF NEGLECT AND ABANDONMENT

To the observer, Ju/'hoansi elders appear to be hale and hearty[13] and well integrated into the social life of their communities. Frail[14] elders are embedded in caregiving networks of several on-site carers, who provide for their needs. Yet the discourse used by elders to describe their situation is often one of unrelenting complaint and blaming. In general, the most common response to the question, "Who looks after old people?" is "Their children." But when we stepped outside the normative system and asked elders, "Who looks after you?" the response was very frequently, "No one. Can't you see that I am starving and dressed in rags?"

Elders frequently complained about the neglected state they were in and told lengthy tales about the deficiencies of those who should be caring for them but were not. While neglect discourse took on a variety of forms, two common styles will be examined here. One is the nagging style and the other is broad melodrama.

The first style is typified by Chuko, age 72, at the time of the interview. In the mid-1980s, Chuko lived with her husband, her daughter and her son-in-law, all of whom shared in the caregiving. Yet Chuko described herself as neglected because she stated that her three half-brothers and their children did not provide for her.

The care that she received from her daughter, son-in-law and husband was scarcely acknowledged. Chuko asserted that caregiving had deteriorated in the present. She maintained that in the past, children were collectively responsible for all elders.

When I say the past was better I mean this: before, the child listened to his/her parents.[15] When children went out to play and an adult who saw an elder ailing came upon them, he scolded them for letting the elder die of thirst and ordered them to attend to [the elder]. Today an adult will merely look and say or think: "Let his/her children take care of him/her." And even the children themselves are not caring by nature.

She then reiterated her complaints against her half-siblings.

Two of her brothers agreed to be interviewed, and they defined themselves as being caregivers to their sister and pointed out that they sent food and water to her via their children and grandchildren. Nevertheless, Chuko maintained a persistent patter of complaint. Far from not wishing to seem a burden or a dependent, she went out of her way to publicly blame her brothers and their families as being delinquent caregivers. Her form of expression was often a quiet oration to no one in particular.

Chuko's complaint discourse can be interpreted in a variety of ways. She may have been detecting changes in the distribution of social obligations that have accompanied settlement, and may indeed have picked up a drift away from sibling care toward a more nuclear pattern. Her family and her brothers had lived together in the past in a traditional sibling core unit, but at the time of the interview, the brothers lived on the other side of Dobe. Two of these brothers have many children, grandchildren and elders to care for and may well have been preoccupied with their immediate situations. The third sibling is often dismissed as a person with no sense who cannot be relied on. Thus, Chuko may be complaining about a new experience of social distance which has fractured horizontal sibling bonds and is delimiting caregiving responsibilities within the nuclear family. But while the Ju/'hoansi may talk constantly about the importance of adult children, they also mobilize other caregiving networks by means of eloquent complaint.[16]

Anthropologists consider the Ju/'hoansi to be "among the most talkative people in the world. Much of this talk verges on argument, often for its own sake, and usually ad hominem" (Lee 1979:372). Thus, Chuko's stream of complaints is not viewed within the culture as unusual or as a particular attribute of old age. Campfire conversation often swirls around accusations of improper meat distribution, improper gift exchange, stinginess and the shortcomings of others.

Complaining is an important leveling discourse and a medium for the expression of a variety of complex feelings (Wiessner 1983). In describing the circumstances leading to and the aftermath of the deaths of three elders, Wiessner (1983) noted vociferous complaints about the adequacy of care in all cases, even in a family where adult children and more distant kin were doing everything they could, including purchasing and slaughtering goats, and holding healing ceremonies. "These accusations," according to Wiessner, are part of "the rhetoric of reciprocity which pervades San life" (1983:1). Complaining is a public exhortation to keep goods and services circulating: It warns against hoarding.

Complaining rhetoric may also have been part of Chuko's individual efforts to keep herself visible. Just as Jewish elders in Barbara Myerhoff's study of a seniors' drop-in center used narration and "competitive complaining" (1978: 146) as a performance strategy to mark their continued presence in the world, so Chuko's constant hum of words may well be her way of saying "I'm still here."

No competing legitimate discourse to the ideology of sharing has thus far emerged among the Dobe Ju/'hoansi. There is no language yet which expresses a world of personal needs which might be at odds with obligations to others, and there is very little leniency shown to those who may have many conflicting obligations. Those who have attempted to limit the circle of reciprocity when they switched from foraging to agro-pastoralism have found it difficult to explain why they were not sharing their crops or killing their goats and cattle to meet the needs of their kinspeople (Lee 1979:412–414).

One woman in her early sixties, a very vociferous complainer, relished denouncing all and sundry for their failure to share. One day, while following one of the research team members while he was packing up camp, she delivered a blistering tirade against his stinginess. Back and forth from tent to truck they trudged, the anthropologist silent, carrying bundles of goods, Nuhka on his heels, yelling at him. Suddenly, she stopped, and like a scene in a Brecht play, she stepped out of character, altered the tone of her voice and calmly announced, "We have to talk this way. It's our custom." Then she stepped back into character and resumed her attack.

The Ju/'hoansi have a name for this type of discourse: It is called *hore hore* or *oba oba* and can be translated as "yakity yak." In the case above, Nuhka stepped out of character to break the tension of the verbal assault she had mounted. In other cases, the tension can be broken by a joke which leaves "the participants rolling on the ground helpless with laughter" (Lee 1979:372). Neglect discourse is, thus, not peculiar to elders but may be invoked by anyone at any time to decry real or potential stinginess. However, elders will frequently avail themselves of the opportunity to complain. In contrast to Chuko's nagging style, others recount their complaints with great theatrical flare.

Kasupe, age 74, a skilled storyteller, responded to the question of who looked after him by denouncing his entire family. First, he attacked his children.

My own children do not look after me. See the clothes I am wearing—these rags I'm wearing—I get them from my own work, my own sweat. None of them have done anything for me. Because they do not look after me. I, their parent say they are "without sense."

He went on to discuss his future prospects:

I do not know who will take care of me when I am old and frail. Right now I can manage; I still have some strength. But as I grow old, I cannot point out a child—a person—about whom I can say, "This one will take care of me." Perhaps I will perish.

Warming up to his tale of woe, Kasupe also denounced his brothers and sisters. In fact, all of his relatives were dismissed as being uncaring. To illustrate the depths of their perfidy, he launched into the following story.

Here is proof of the uncaring nature of my children. I will tell you a story. I'd gone hunting with some Herero [men] and we had split up agreeing to meet later at a certain point. Those Herero warned me that they had set a trap in the direction I was headed. I went on but because it was dark, I could not see and was caught in the trap. It grabbed my ankle. I stayed there and my wife and children were following me. None of them came to see how I was. I was only helped by you Gakegkoshe [the Tswana/Herero translator] and Tontah [Richard Lee, an anthropologist]. You helped me heal and saw to it that I got better. None of [my family] came to see how I was doing. It was only you. Even my brothers and sisters in Southwest [Namibia] did not come to see how I was doing.

At this juncture Gakegkoshe turned to me and said in English, "A big story." And indeed it was.

After the interview concluded, Richard Lee and I returned to camp, fetched a copy of the book *The Dobe !Kung*, and returned to confront Kasupe. There on page 105 of the book was a photo of Kasupe "on the day of the crisis" lying on the ground surrounded by family and Ju/'hoansi healers. The text also included a lengthy account from Lee's fieldnotes describing Kasupe's wife and children sobbing and wailing as community members worked on curing him. Lee administered some penicillin. The next day Kasupe began to improve, and within three months he was hunting again (Lee 1984:104–106).

Feeling some glee in having caught Kasupe in a "lie," we laid the evidence out before him. Here was the story and photograph of his family and community making heroic efforts to save his life. Kasupe's only response was to break out

Kasupe laughing after telling his story, with his friend/Twi seated.

into a loud, long, thigh-slapping laugh which was immediately echoed by the Ju/'hoansi audience and the anthropologists.

Kasupe was completely unabashed and expressed no regret at having "accused" his relatives of neglect, abandonment and death-hastening behavior. Whether there was any "truth" to his narrative was quite irrelevant. His version of events made a good story. It was gripping and dramatic; he was impressive as he told it. The listener was captivated by "the utterance" (Eagleton 1983: 115).

But like Chuko's less melodramatic narrative, Kasupe's performance also had another side to it. Kasupe had expressed what "might" happen if caregivers were not to do their duty. He had described aloud what the world would be like should the caring system not be reproduced. His narrative allowed his audience to imagine the dire scene of family neglect. By negative example, he restated the social contract of caregiving obligations. His laughter, and the audience's laughter, did not mean that the complaint lacked seriousness, only perhaps that he had been topped by a better story this time. But the complaint was important: the Ju/'hoansi system of mutual responsibility and caregiving requires constant lubrication, and complaining greases the wheels.

TALES OF "REAL" ABANDONMENT

In a more serious vein, Xoma, a respected elder, who was not given to extravagant rhetoric, pointed out that there were indeed cases of real abandonment in the past. He explained the circumstances of an abandonment in a previous generation:

They'd leave him/her and go off, because they didn't know what to do with him/her. Naturally, they had no truck, no donkey, nothing. And they were also carrying her/his things on their bodies. Sometimes they'd try to carry him/her where they were going. Someone else would carry his/her things, if there were many people. But if the people were few, or if there was only one man, they didn't know what to do with the old person. They would admit defeat, leave him/her, and go.

It is likely that there have been cases of death-hastening among the Ju/'hoansi in the past. We do not have any sustained ethnographic account of such behavior comparable to Hart's encounter with the Tiwi custom of "covering up" (see Introduction this volume[17]).

The Ju/'hoansi themselves use the equivocal term *na a tsi*, (to leave in the bush), which implies abandonment. As Xoma's dispassionate analysis implies, "burden of care" was often not a metaphor but a concrete description of physically carrying a frail elder on one's back. When this was the only means of transportation, there were likely to have been times when the coping skills of the caregivers were stretched to the breaking point, and the elder was abandoned in the bush.[18]

Settlement has made a difference in eldercare. In the mid-1980s, we found incapacitated elders being scrupulously cared for by kin and community. The conditions of a settled lifestyle, the availability of soft foods and access to vehicles in cases of medical emergencies all make it easier to care for frail elders today in comparison to 30 or more years ago. Furthermore, settlement has meant that Ju/'hoansi practices are now more closely scrutinized by the state than they were in the past. The presence of a legal apparatus and police in the

Dobe district have likely influenced community thinking on abandonment of elders.

The question of what constitutes "real" abandonment was a thorny problem for the researchers and we have found no easy answers. About 90 percent of our informants said that they knew of no cases of elders being abandoned in the past. Many described cases of young people carrying frail elders on their backs from water hole to water hole until they died "in our hands." Many others said that they had never heard of old people being abandoned.

But a few informants recounted explicit stories describing elders being left intentionally to perish. A consistent element in these accounts was that those associated with death-hastening activities were always close relatives—a spouse or children. This finding is consistent with Glascock's discussion (Chapter 3) that the decision to abandon an old person is almost always made within the immediate family, although in the Ju/'hoansi case elders do not appear to be part of the negotiations. What is unknown but nevertheless very important in these discussions of euthanasia is how long the elder was incapacitated before the decision to terminate life was made. It may be that among the Ju/'hoansi, if close family members have been seen to be caring for a decrepit elder for a very long period of time—a culturally acknowledged but unexpressed statute of limitations comes into play and abandonment is permitted, especially if it is *not* presented as a premeditated action.

The discourse of neglect is thus quite complicated.[19] It is used to describe cases in which "real" abandonment may have occurred. It is used as a social regulatory mechanism to reinforce sharing and caregiving. It is used as a vehicle to tell a good story. What is most apparent about this discourse is that it is words and words alone that have up until very recently been the main social regulators of behavior. The Ju/'hoansi themselves have no legal/police system with which to coerce behavior or punish offenders.

ENTITLEMENT

> I would not want to live with my family. They are nice people, very generous but it would not be fair to them.
>
> Eighty-two-year-old Canadian woman

Ju/'hoansi elders do not see themselves as burdens. They are not apologetic if they are no longer able to produce enough to feed themselves. They expect others to care for them when they can no longer do so. Entitlement to care is naturalized within the culture: Elders do not have to negotiate care as if it were a favor; rather, it is perceived of as an unquestioned right.

The needs of elders are not defined as being markedly different from the needs of anyone else. The material aspects of caring for elders was uniformly defined by our informants as providing *da, gu, msi* (firewood, water and food). These are the basics of life which are procured and shared among all members

The elderly Gumi Na clasping the hand of her visiting "European son," Richard Lee, as her daughter Sagai looks on.

of the community. Obtaining these necessities in the past has not been especially onerous, requiring on average twenty hours of work a week in food gathering, from the active population, but today those with herd animals work longer hours. Thus, elders have not been experienced as a particular economic burden or a category of people with "special needs."[20] In fact, in terms of health care, elders are both givers and receivers of care. Even with the arrival of government health workers in the district, healing dances continue to flourish, giving elders a prominent role in community life.

One rarely hears an old person express appreciation for the care which s/he receives and one never hears elders express the desire to live alone in order not to burden the family with caregiving obligations. The desire to live alone is classified as a form of mental illness. "Only a crazy person would live alone," said one young informant.

The following story illustrates how old people make demands. In the middle of a hot afternoon in 1986, Gumi[21] was sleeping in her house next to a small fire. I had never met her before, but she was Richard Lee's (Tontah) social mother and they had had a close relationship for over 23 years. At first sight Gumi, age 83, looked to be very frail, weighing perhaps 60 pounds. Her daughter, Sagai, spoke to her by cupping her hands and shouting about four inches from her ear. Although Gumi had awakened from a sound sleep and had not seen her "European" son for six years, she immediately tuned into the situation, greeted her visitors, and established their place in the kinship system.

Throughout the interview, Gumi gave alert responses to our questions. At the same time she launched her own demanding harangue for gifts: "Give me some medicine . . . Well, I got some clothing . . . Tontah, *hxaro*[22] mi cosisi (give me things). Give me beads. . . . Give me clothing."

At one point during the lengthy interview, her daughter interrupted the steady flow of demands and laughingly said, "Oh, stop going on and on about *hxaro*." Gumi was completely undeterred: "No! No! You tell Tontah that I want to still talk about *hxaro*. Hey, give me things."

When we returned to Dobe, we were asked how Gumi was faring. We described her situation and her persistent requests for gifts. Two elders glanced at each other with knowing looks when we mentioned the demands for *hxaro* and one said, "Even as old as she is, she still knows how to talk nicely. Her thoughts are still sound."

What I had experienced as demanding ingratitude was culturally interpreted as a sign that Gumi was in good mental health. She "talked nicely" in the sense that her words were considered to be appropriate to a gift exchange situation in which she was an active participant. The ability to make demands is a signal of social connectedness, and a symbol of entitlement.

For some, entitlement to care flows directly from the parent/child relationship. Tasa, age 65, described this process of socialization:

When a child is born you teach that child to care for her/his parents throughout the time the child is growing up, so that when the child is older s/he will willingly care for his/her parents. But if that child has a crippled heart, is a person with no sense, that will come from inside her/him and s/he will neglect the parents.

As Tasa pointed out, child rearing practices provide no guarantee of filial caregiving performance. Many of our informants felt that, ultimately, nothing could be done to compel a child with "no sense" to act appropriately.

Others, however, argued that direct sanctions from the spirit world would occur in cases of filial neglect. According to Gai Koma, fear of ancestors underlies elders' entitlement to care. "We feel under an obligation [to care for our parents] because they brought us up. We've drained all their energies. After they die, we would be left with bad luck if we had not cared for them. We could fall ill." Many concur that there is a link between eldercare and the role of *gangwasi* (the ghosts of ancestors) but the relationship between the two worlds is not clear cut. *Gangwasi* have both a punitive side and a charitable side.

The *gangwasi* are not interested solely in eldercare but in all phases of human interaction and their messages to the living are remarkably contradictory. They visit misfortune and sickness on the living to punish but they also "long for" the living and wish to take them with them to the villages of the dead simply

Gumi Na inside her house with her daughter Sagai at her side.

because they are lonely for their loved ones (Lee 1984:107–109; Wiessner 1983). Thus, the reasons for a caregiver's illness or death may be explained either by negligence or devotion; their poor performance may have provoked ancestral anger or their good deeds may have unleashed yearnings among the *gangwasi* to be reunited with their loved one. This ambiguity about motives of the *gangwasi* ultimately lodges the obligation for caregiving in the land of the living.

THE SOCIAL ORGANIZATION OF CAREGIVING

Caregiving is normatively described as being the responsibility of all adult children. All but one informant said that the responsibility should be shared equally among all the children.[23] No elder thought the responsibility was linked to gender or that daughters should be or were doing more than sons. According to Nahka, a woman with many children and grandchildren, feminization of caregiving is not a social norm.

In my household, both my sons and daughters help me. The care they give balances so that I see no difference. I don't think girls are more caring than boys. [Is this the same for others at Dobe?] Yes. I give the example of Nai who has no daughters but the care that her sons give her is of the same quality as that which I get from my children.

Most caregivers subscribed to this version, but a few women felt they were doing more than men. Gumi's daughter, Sagai, was particularly angry with her brother, Toma, and fought with him about his lack of attention to their mother. On the other hand, Toma felt that his sister had not been sufficiently attentive when their father was ill and dying.

For our informants it was not gender which divided the population between active caregivers and delinquents but rather a personal quality or quirk. An elder noted, "If you have a child and that child has a good heart, regardless of whether s/he is male or female, s/he will look after their parent."

Nothing can be done to force a child to be a good caregiver. If a child fails to do his/her duty then others are expected to pitch in, especially if the old person has no children. The situation of Chwa is illustrative.

Chwa was in her late eighties at the time of the interview, had poor eyesight, good hearing and could still walk. She had no children and lived with her co-wife[24] Bau and their husband, both of whom were in their early eighties. Throughout our discussion, neighbors dropped by with food and water. Chwa entered a conversation which compared past caregiving of the elderly to the current situation. One of her neighbors commented that she had never heard of elders being left in the bush in the past. Chwa stated that she had "heard of people carrying those who were sick on their backs from village to village," but "today, people do not look after the old sufficiently." Two of her neighbors immediately disagreed and took turns affirming that the young do *nabe nabe* (care for) the old.

Chwa, however, was adamant. She pointed out that her nephew, Tsau, was derelict in his duty. (Tsau is her brother's son, a man of about 60, married and living at another village.) "He wants to," she went on, "but his wife won't let him. But those who do take care of me are this Nisa here [an elderly neighbor] and that woman there, my co-wife [Bau], while our husband tends the cattle."

She then proceeded to recount this positive description of care, one of the very few that I had ever heard from an elder.

Once, when I was very sick, I was burning with fever, she [Nisa] poured water on me, and then she held me in her arms. These women, Nisa, Tankae [an elderly neighbor], and my co-wife cared for me. I slept in their arms . . . my heart craved bush food and these women collected it for me.

I turned to one of the collectors and asked, "What made you think of doing that?" And Bau, Chwa's co-wife, using her hands for emphasis, responded: "What is there to think about? You see an old person. She is your person. She can't walk. She can't do it for herself, so you do it."

Thus, although Chwa has no children of her own she was firmly anchored in a responsive caregiving network. These ties can be quite distant, in kinship terms, as in the case of Chwa's network. Chwa's neighbor, Nisa, calls Chwa elder sister, although they have a very remote kinship connection. She and other caregivers use the word *ju* to express an affiliation which incorporates a mixture of sentiment based on ethnicity and residential proximity and is expressed in quasi-kinship terms.

The caregiving role for someone who is "your person" is naturalized and it is not feminized.[25] Caregiving is explained as a quality of human, not female, nature. We have observed male and female carers providing food, firewood and water, although the foods may represent a gendered division of labor, with men hunting and women gathering. Government drought relief food will be carried to elders who cannot manage to go to the relief trucks themselves by any of "their people." Both men and women also care in other ways. Massage is an important service rendered by carers. Both men and women will gather the plants and nuts used to prepare the ointments which are used during massage. Women are more likely to provide other, smaller services for female elders, like grooming hair but both men and women spend time visiting, talking and drinking tea with elders. In the delicate area of toileting old people, there did seem to be a gender link. Male caregivers would take responsibility for guiding male elders in and out of the bush and female caregivers would look after the needs of women elders.

Children, regardless of sex, were enlisted in caregiving as well. Sometimes the special relationship of grandparent/grandchild was used to mobilize care. This relationship is quite expandable into an inclusive kinship mode, which draws in distant kin. Elders, for example, may invoke the "name" relationship so that children with the same name as the old person will be regarded as grandchildren and available to perform services like fetching water, if they are willing.[26]

The web of caregiving, thus, moves well beyond the limited confines of the nuclear family[27]: It is located in kinship/community ideology. It is not sentimentalized as a form of self-sacrifice.[28]

Elders are independent and autonomous (as are all members of the community) in the sense that they can do what they wish when they wish. Ablebodied elders forage, fetch water, visit, trade gifts, make crafts, dance, sleep and eat whenever they choose. They live wherever they choose and do not face fears of pauperization with old age or the struggles of living on a "fixed income." Their old age is not filled with anxieties about personal security[29]: They have no fears about interpersonal violence, robbery or abuse. They do not lock themselves in their houses at night. Their conversation is not filled with talk of the "agony of loneliness" (Hillebrant 1980:408), or the difficult decisions about whether to sell their homes and lose a whole way of life in order to seek a diminished but more secure living environment (Draper and Keith 1992).

Frail Ju/'hoansi elders are enmeshed in a network of caregiving. The eight frail elders we interviewed had between four and eight people looking after them for a total of forty-four people undertaking frontline eldercare responsibilities.

Even those who were extremely weak were not segregated from the social landscape. We observed a situation in which Dau, a very sick elder who slept almost all the time, was placed in the center of social life. Around him gathered family and neighbors who chatted, smoked and cooked together. Nearby, his son hacked up the carcass of a kudu, and the old man's wife, Koka, stirred the cooking pot, children played and an infant nursed. As the meat cooked, his wife lifted his head every few minutes and fed him a morsel of food. He chewed silently, his eyes shut. When he was done, he rested his head on the blanket. In the meantime, his wife chatted with those at the fire. Both the old man and his caregivers were rooted in a social matrix which undoubtedly eased the burden of care and perhaps enhanced the quality of this very frail person's last days.

CONCLUSION: THE PARADOX OF SHARING AND COMPLAINING

By North American standards the material situation of the Dobe Ju/'hoansi is poor, but the social circumstances of elders is quite positive (see also Draper and Harpending 1994; Draper and Keith 1992). They have personal autonomy, respect and a great deal of control over the immediate circumstances of their lives. They live in a culture which strongly values caregiving and support. Old people participate in social, political, economic and spiritual life. They may regret growing old and ask someone to pull out the first few grey hairs, but they are also equipped with rich cultural resources for articulating their concerns, fears, and anxieties and for ensuring support.

Yet the Ju/'hoansi complain all the time. They are cranky, funny and loud. They live in a moral universe of high caregiving standards, in which the ideal seems to be that every person is directly obligated to meet the needs of every other person all the time. But since such a perfect world is impossible to obtain, they find ample justification for their complaints of inadequate caregiving. Furthermore, personal preferences, personality conflicts, old unresolved grievances enter into the caregiving equation, making it far from an ideal universe. There is always someone who is not doing enough. And there is always someone ready to denounce that person in terms which are not pleasant or polite.

The cultural forms which reproduce respect and care for elders through complaint discourse reflect deep patterns in Ju/'hoansi culture. Boasting, self-aggrandizement or displays of pride are strongly discouraged as behaviors which impede sharing and may lead to violence. Thus, it is not polite etiquette but "rough humor, back-handed compliments, put-downs and damning with faint praise" (Lee 1979:458)—the rhetoric of complaint—which is in constant use to constrain potentially dangerous behaviors. Complaining is the only social arena in which the Ju/'hoansi are competitive and it is hardly surprising that elders are so good at it; they have been practicing their whole lives.

These discourses have not abruptly unraveled with changes in material culture like the appearance of transistor radios, cassette tape players and bicycles. In other words, cultural formations are resilient and, contrary to the highly romanticized myth presented in the South African film "The Gods Must Be Crazy," the world is not turned upside down by the introduction of a minor artefact of Western society. The Ju/'hoansi of Botswana drink soda pop and still conduct trance dances, still complain about those who do not share and still care for their elders.

Of more far-reaching significance for the Dobe area in general and eldercare in particular are the major infrastructural transformations in subsistence patterns; integration into state educational, legal and medical systems; the role that tuberculosis and alcohol consumption play; and the transformations in southern Africa as a whole with the end of the war in Namibia and the end of apartheid in South Africa. These new elements in the Ju/'hoansi world create challenges that are unpredictable. For the time being, they are meeting these challenges with a powerful cultural pattern of sharing/complaining—one that can still produce the following discourse:

Here are words about caring for an old person. Words like if a person is old, you take care of her. You put your heart into it, and scold others, saying, "Don't you see this person is old? Take care of her today, you take care of her today. Do you say she has strength? She has no strength. Now you put your heart into her." That's what you say to another person. You're telling him/her to put his/her heart into an old person. That's what you say. That's another piece of speech. Now I'm finished.[30]

NOTES

The field research upon which the bulk of this chapter is based was carried on in Botswana between May and July 1986 and January and August 1987. The "we" used here refers to a team of investigators, research assistants and translators. The investigators included Richard B. Lee, who interviewed in the Ju language; Meg Luxton and Harriet Rosenberg, who used translators. We gratefully acknowledge the assistance of Nandi Ngcongco, Dorothy Molokome and Leonard Ramatakwame of the University of Botswana; Makgolo Makgolo, M. A., of Gaborone; and Gakekgoshe Isaaka and Gai Koma of the Dobe region. In addition, Megan Biesele consulted with this project. We thank her for the careful translation/transcriptions she made of interviews she conducted in Ju/'hoansi in Namibia.

The investigators wish to thank the Social Science and Humanities Research Council of Canada for providing funding for this project, "Aging, Caregiving and Social Change in an African Population," file number 410–84–1298.

A version of this chapter was presented to the International Congress of Anthropological and Ethnological Sciences, Zagreb Yugoslavia, July 24–31, 1988. I appreciate the insightful comments made by Christine Gailey and Richard Lee at that time.

In addition, I would like to thank Patricia Draper, Mathias Guenther, Richard Katz, Robin Oakley and Polly Wiessner for their gracious assistance with this version. Finally, thanks go to Richard Lee for gathering additional information for this project while doing research in Namibia in the spring of 1995.

This chapter is dedicated to the memory of Marjorie Shostak (1945–1996), whose work has illuminated the richness and depth of Ju/'hoansi life.

1. The Ju/'hoansi are also known by the terms !Kung San, or the !Kung Bushman in anthropological and popular literature. The word Ju/'hoansi is the people's name for themselves and means "the real people." In the years since this chapter first appeared, the Ju/'hoansi, like many other indigenous peoples of the world, have come to political consciousness and are engaged in a variety of political and economic struggles. The terms "!Kung" "San" and "Bushmen" are moving into positions analagous to "Indian" and "Eskimo" in North America where they are often replaced by "First Nations" and "Innuit" as indicators of pride in cultural identity. The spelling "Ju/'hoansi" was worked out in collaborative efforts between the people themselves and the linguist Patrick Dickens in the late 1980s. The term "Ju" means person or people.

Their language contains clicking sounds which are unique to the Khoisan and neighboring languages of southern and eastern Africa. In addition, the language contains glottal stops and nasalizations. Anthropologists, in committing their words to writing, have developed an orthography, which has recently been revised, to approximate a rendering of these sounds in English.

There are four major clicks: dental, alveolar, alveopalatal and lateral. In this paper, only one click is marked. This is the dental click indicated by a slash. In English it sounds like the mild reproach "tsk, tsk." Nasalization is indicated by an apostrophe. Thus, the word Ju/'hoansi might be approximated in English as "juntwasi" with a soft "j" as in the French "je," a dental click on the "t" and a nasalization of the "a."

2. Influences from Herero practices have been observed among the Ju/'hoansi. The issue of burial practices is discussed in note 17.

3. By foraging I mean a mode of subsistence entirely based on wild food sources, without agriculture or domesticated animals, except for the dog.

4. See Katz 1982; Biesele and Katz 1987.

5. See note 20.

6. See John Marshall's film, "Nai, the Story of a Kung Woman" for a vivid depiction of the effects of militarization on the Ju/'hoansi of Namibia.

7. On the Namibian side of the border, some elders have fared less well with rapid social change. When the war ended in 1990 and Namibia became independent of South African rule, a group of approximately 4,000 Ju/'hoansi, including family members of those who had acted as scouts and soldiers for the South African military, were relocated to Schmidtsdrift, near Kimberley South Africa (Steyn 1994). This newly created community has had significant difficulties and the elderly have been particularly affected: Many were bored, dependent, marginalized and perceived themselves to be largely worthless within the framework of changed values and circumstances (Steyn 1994:37).

8. However, there is a social convention, not understood by the anthropologists, whereby some younger adults in their thirties are called *na*. It may be a combination of the personal magnetism and social stature of a particularly sober and thoughtful member of the community that earns this honorific or some other life experience that is significant to the community.

9. Bride wealth is a common part of marriage arrangements among pastoralist peoples in Africa. The bride's family is given cattle and/or other property to mark the marriage exchange. Customarily, bride wealth is related to the bride's residence with the groom's family (i.e., virilocal residence). Should the betrothal or the marriage fail, the cattle are returned. Furthermore, if the relationship produced children, their custody would normally reside with the father and his family.

By contrast, bride service is associated with the groom's responsibility to move to the bride's family (uxorilocal residence) and to provide subsistence for his in-laws for a specifed period of time, often several years. In marriage systems where the age at marriage for females can be very young, bride service offers a structure whereby the bride's parents can be assured that their daughter is being well treated and that their son-in-law is a good provider. If a divorce should occur, any children would normally remain with the mother and her family.

10. In response to a question about child custody, he was told by one senior woman that "that is very tough. If there is divorce, we would not permit the children to go [to the ex-son-in-law's family] regardless of the cow."

11. Fieldwork was conducted at the three main villages of Dobe, Xai Xai and Kangwa, and to a lesser extent in the smaller villages of Mahopa and Goshe. The 1986 population of Ju/'hoansi in the region was 663, of whom 83 people were 60 or older. The research team interviewed 90 percent of the elders and about 30 caregivers.

12. The Ju/'hoansi themselves do not mark chronological age. The ages used in this essay represent estimates made by the demographer Nancy Howell during fieldwork in 1968 (see Howell 1979) and revisions made according to census updates by Lee during field trips in 1973, 1983 and 1986–1987.

13. In 1967–1968, Trusswell and Hansen (1976) conducted a health survey of the region. They found Ju/'hoansi elders to be remarkably fit and not suffering from high blood pressure or other stress-related illnesses. More recent research indicates that changed diet has produced elevated blood pressures in the population (Kent and Lee 1992; Hansen et al., 1994).

14. We divided the elderly into five categories of functionality: one was the most fit

and five represented those who were completely dependent. "Frail" refers to those in categories four and five, twelve people.

15. The third person singular is not gendered in the Ju/'hoansi language. Thus, the English terms "his/her" or "she/he" are used in the text to translate the speaker's usage. While "he/she" may seem awkward to some English-speakers, it is consistent with the Ju/'hoansi language which does not distinguish between male and female in the third person singular, just as English does not in the third person plural "they" but French does in the forms "ils/elles."

16. This trend may be what Pat Draper detected in 1987–1988, while doing research in the Dobe area for project A.G.E. (see Chapter 5). She reported that the Ju/'hoansi seem to have an "extreme cultural preoccupation with parent-adult child relationships" (Draper and Buchanan 1992:1). Oakley, in a comparison of Draper and Rosenberg's research on eldercare, reviewed Rosenberg and Lee's field diaries and found that 33 of 39 elders interviewed by Lee stated that without adult children "they would be as good as dead" (1992:29). Oakley distinguished between these normative responses and the empirical evidence collected by Rosenberg and Lee which indicated that caregiving networks centered on spouses, co-wives, siblings, namesakes, or more distant kin were significant sources of support. Oakley also noted that support networks play significant roles in eldercare in other cultures, citing Wentowski (1981:600), among others, who has argued that "the presence or absence of informal support . . . [has] been recognized as a crucial predictor of the well-being and autonomy of older people." Nevertheless, these networks are not infallible, as the work of Wiessner (1983) demonstrates.

17. Simmons (1945) accounts of abandonment, based on the work of Ratzel for South African populations (1894 [11]:275) and Bleek for the Naron (1928:35) are unreliable, although often repeated in the literature. Bleek's account of rough treatment and abandonment is repeated almost verbatim by Schapera (1930:162), but is gentler in its moralizing tone. Versions of Bleek's account are also repeated by Hewitt (1986:31). Mathias Guenther, who has done extensive fieldwork with the Nharo or Naron (of the Central Kalahari) has noted that previous German sources (Hahn 1870:122; Passarge 1907:111) offer similar unreliable visions of abandonment; whereas Almeida (1965) describes a very tender scene of eldercare among Angolan Bushmen (Guenther, personal communication, 1994). Ratzel's encyclopedic work is like many nineteenth-century social evolutionary anthropological projects, in casting the "less evolved" Bushmen in crude racist terms at the bottom of a social evolutionary ladder.

18. Wiessner (1983) has given the example of an old woman whose social position in the Xai Xai water hole was weak in that she was from a distant area, had few relatives in the camp, and her son was absent when she became ill. Xai Xai residents let loose a chorus of complaints about the inadequacy of her care, but no one in the community took direct responsibility to provide for her needs or mount a healing dance for her. The circumstances of her death were very painful: Old Bau became delirious, accused people of starving her and ran into the bush to gather for herself, where she died.

The accusations surrounding this death had a very different tone from the everyday discourse of complaining invoked in cases of impeccable care. This was a time when complaint did not generate the bonds of reciprocity as it was supposed to, and the community was shocked. While other deaths in the water hole were followed by a short, cathartic mourning period which included soon-forgotten charges of neglect, the impact of Old Bau's death on the community lingered in an unresolved fashion for months

(Wiessner 1983). This was the kind of outcome that Kasupe may well have had in mind when he wove his tale of callous abandonment.

19. Acculturation to Herero beliefs about death and burial seem to have influenced Ju/'hoansi perceptions about death and abandonment. One traditional way has been to collapse the hut around the person who died in camp or to dig a shallow grave and leave it unmarked if someone dies on the trail. Wiessner (1983) describes a more complicated burial ritual including a deep grave, specific attention to the orientation of the corpse in the grave, ceremonial activities when the body is moved from the house, rituals for the mourners, eulogies and gravemarkers. The postmortem period is not marked by lengthy ritual grieving as it is among the Herero, but by complaint discourse as a way of reframing social relations and restructuring traditional trading relationships.

The Herero, by contrast, have elaborate funerary rituals (Vivelo 1977:127–129) and seem to have been particularly offended by what appeared to them as the casualness of some Ju/'hoansi practices. In discussion with the Ju/'hoansi in the mid-1980s, it seemed as if their own funeral customs were being viewed from the Herero perspective and that statements about the abandonment of elders might be referencing "improper burials."

Suicide among the elderly was treated by informants as an incomprehensible notion.

20. Nor have children been viewed as economic burdens. Until quite recently, children did not participate in subsistence activities until their teens. With settlement and the acquisition of goats and cattle, children now do more work.

21. Old women among the Ju/'hoansi are thus quite different from the passive "Dear Old Grans" described as commonplace among old women in a long-term geriatric ward "who cheerfully surrender [their] autonomy" and "potential to challenge" (Evers 1981: 119–120).

22. *Hxaro* is a gift exchange system for "circulating goods, lubricating social relations, and maintaining ecological balance" (R. Lee 1984:97). Receiving *hxaro* implies that you will also give it. See also Wiessner (1977).

23. She said that it was the duty of the first born, "the one who cracked your bones," to look after an aging parent.

24. Polygyny occurred in about 5 percent of marriages among the Ju/'hoansi in the 1960s and 1970s. In most socially sanctioned forms, men will take two wives, although cases of more than two have been reported historically. Occasionally, irregular polyandrous unions have also been reported.

25. In Western societies, where eldercare is predominantly done by unwaged women workers in the household and women in the waged workforce, expressing the experience of caregiving in ungendered language poses a problem (Finch and Groves 1983). For example, a young man, in trying to articulate his experience in caring for his lover with AIDS, found that

the closest model with which to compare my seven months with Paul is the experience of *mothering*. (My mother brought this home to me. . . .) By this analogy I mean the cluster of activities, characteristics, and emotions associated with the *social role* of motherhood. Whether performed by women or men, mothering—and its analogue within the health care system, nursing—involves intimate physical care of another being, the provision of unconditional care and love, the subordination of self to others, and an investment in separation. (Interrante 1987:57–58. First emphasis [mothering] is mine, second emphasis [social role] is the author's.)

In this context, only the gendered term, "mothering," was found to be able to convey the intensity of commitment Interrante had felt. Interestingly, his insight is substantiated by a footnote referencing three feminist theoreticians—Dinnerstein, Chowdorow and Eherensaft, all of whom have analyzed the social construction of female caregiving.

Mothering carries with it the meanings of long-term, unconditional support. "Mothers" are people who do not abandon no matter how demanding the circumstance becomes. Mothering is thus not only a feminized metaphor for caregiving, it is also highly idealized and sentimentalized.

26. Draper (1976) and Shostak (1981) have pointed out that children were raised in a very nonauthoritarian manner and were normally not expected to work or do anything for adults that they did not wish to do. Even today, with settlement and the beginings of a pastoralist economy which often utilizes child labor, many parents say that they cannot make children perform work if the children refuse. Children are still seen as not owing any special deference to adults.

27. Gubrium (1987:31–35) describes the conflict which follows an elder's creation of a caregiving network which is perceived to be competing with the rightful caregivers—the adult children. Maida, the old person in question, is described as rejecting her "own" children, whom she has accused of not being her "real" children because they have placed her in a nursing home against her wishes. Maida formed close bonds with a small group of co-residents who have constituted themselves as a "family" including the designated the roles of "baby" and "grandma." Both Maida's children and the health professionals identified this alternate caring network as a "problem." The mother's actions were interpreted by the children as a repudiation and described as a sign of mental confusion. The health workers found the group to be cliquish and divisive to equitable caring on the floor. Thus, Maida's stepping outside the discourse of filial caregiving was construed as a contentious and threatening counterdiscourse.

28. Self-sacrifice is not always considered admirable in caregivers in the North American context. Gubrium's 1987 account of a support group for the families of Alzheimer's patients reveals a strong counterdiscourse to expressions of wifely devotion. Caregivers are warned not to burn themselves out and to be "realistic" when assessing the burdens of caregiving. One pointed expression of this counterdiscourse was: "Dear, you're not an old man's lover; you're an old man's slave" (Gubrium 1987:31).

29. The article by Draper and Keith (1992) elaborates on the contrast drawn here between the feelings of personal security among Ju/'hoansi elders and the fears and painful choices of elders within a North American community.

30. From a transcript of Megan Biescle's interview with Nisa in 1987, Gausha, Namibia.

CHAPTER 3

When Is Killing Acceptable: The Moral Dilemma Surrounding Assisted Suicide in America and Other Societies

Anthony P. Glascock

Over the last few years reports of assisted suicide have become front page news in respectable newspapers and lead stories on both national and local TV news programs, as well as fodder for the tabloids and sensational tabloid-style TV programs. At the broader political level, Michigan has taken steps to prevent assisted suicide, while Oregon and Florida have passed laws to allow it. California and Washington state have held referendums on the issue and other state legislatures in New Hampshire and California are considering bills which would allow assisted suicide under limited circumstances. Talk show hosts routinely discuss assisted suicide as an ethical dilemma pitting those who believe in the sanctity of human life against those who place individual freedom as an un-wavering, inalienable right. Leaders of various religious denominations have weighed in with pronouncements ranging from promises of damnation both for individuals who assist and for those who die, to moral dispensation for those who help a person die with personal dignity. Although the result of this discus-sion is very often sensational and often appears to be presented in such a way as to enrage people on different sides of the issue, the fact that this subject is being openly depicted and discussed is a dramatic change within American culture.

Before any further discussion of these complex issues is undertaken, it is necessary to explicitly state what I mean by assisted suicide. Assisted suicide, often termed physician-assisted suicide, is "making a means of suicide (such as prescription for barbiturates) available to a patient who is otherwise physically capable of suicide and who subsequently acts on his or her own" (Quill, Cassel and Meier 1992: 1381). This is different from voluntary euthanasia in which an individual actually administers the means of suicide or the turning off of life support of a terminally ill individual.

As healthy as much of this discussion may be, it is interesting that it is taking place with two implied assumptions: (1) that this is the first time the issue of assisted suicide has been raised within advanced industrial societies such as the United States; and (2) that we are the first society which has ever had to face such a morally vexing dilemma. There are a variety of reasons for these assumptions, but in general there appear to be two main causes for this almost society-wide view. The first explanation derives from the obvious advances in medical technology which allow for the prolongation of life beyond anything that has existed before in our own society or in any other society at any other point in time; a technology which, the argument goes, makes our situation unique. Although the technology may be unique the situation is not, either historically or cross-culturally. As I will show, even though medical technology allows us to prolong life, the same dilemma faced people in our own society prior to the late twentieth century and in other societies; it only happened at an earlier stage in the dying process.

The second explanation is broader and more complex and is not as easily countered. It is hubris—the belief that we cannot learn from other societies and cultures, certainly not cultures which are less technologically advanced than we. If we did turn to these societies for help in answering our own perplexing questions this would be a tacit recognition that we are not morally more advanced and that we could learn from other populations, many of which we would regard as primitive or backward. This is apparently a very difficult viewpoint for us to accept. I will address both of these assumptions in the remainder of this chapter as I first discuss the role of assisted suicide, death-accelerating behavior and euthanasia in American society. I will continue by briefly considering a similar debate over these very same issues in nineteenth-century America, and conclude with a more detailed discussion of the nature of death-hastening behavior directed toward decrepit old people in many nonindustrial societies. It is my hope that this discussion will show that the ethical, moral and legal questions which surround these issues are not unique to twentieth-century American society and that people at other times and in other societies have had to struggle with them just as we have.

AMERICAN SOCIETY

Seven years ago, when I wrote a similar chapter about assisted suicide in American society for the first edition of this book, the subject, although controversial, was relatively simple compared to today (1997). In the last five years, much has happened but in many ways little has really changed. In 1985–1986 the big issue was the Florida case of Roswell Gilbert, a seventy-six-year-old man who shot and killed his seventy-three-year-old wife who was suffering from Alzheimer's and osteoporosis. Gilbert was sentenced to 25 years to life for murder, even though an outcry was raised by a wide range of supporters and sympathizers. While Gilbert was sent to jail, two other men who violently killed close relatives went free. In the same courthouse in which Gilbert was sentenced, a seventy-nine-year-old man who shot and killed his wife, also suffering from Alzheimer's, was not even indicted for a crime. In a second controversial case of the mid-1980s, the New York Supreme Court ruled in 1984 that "a nursing home should not force-feed an 85-year-old patient who was in poor health and had been fasting." The court decided that the man was "entitled to die of his own will [and] that the nursing home was not obliged to force-feed the man" (Hirsh 1985:9). However, just across the Hudson River in New Jersey, an appellate court ruled that a hospital could not remove the nasogastric tube of an eighty-four-year-old man who wanted to die. In California, a hospitalized woman was prevented, through force-feeding, from starving herself to death (Hirsh 1985:10).

The outcry over what many perceived as a cruel injustice in the Roswell Gilbert case and the inconsistency of state laws resulted in much activity over the next decade as political leaders, editorialists, state legislatures, the American Medical Association and the general public were confronted by the moral, ethical, legal and religious issues surrounding euthanasia and assisted suicide. In the late 1980s, ex-Governor Richard Lamm of Colorado and ex-Senator Jacob Javits of New York raised the sensitive issue of the costs associated with the medical care of the terminally ill elderly and even suggested that terminally ill people may have the "duty to die." Although both politicians denied that they supported "mercy killing," both men called for a national debate on these topics and the development of national legislation which would "allow" the elderly to die when they desired (Krieger 1985:13–14). The challenge to debate these issues was met, but not on a national level as Lamm and Javits anticipated. Instead the debate in the 1990s has been held largely at the level of individual states in both state legislatures and voting booths. Although approximately 36 states have laws which explicitly prohibit assisted suicide, this does not necessarily mean that assisted suicide is legal in the other fourteen states (Newman 1991). In fact, the state-level debate has led to confusion rather than clarification, for which Lamm and Javits had hoped.

A couple of brief examples illustrate this confusion quite nicely. In 1992, a referendum which would have legalized assisted suicide and voluntary euthanasia was narrowly defeated in the state of Washington. At almost the same time, the state legislature of Washington passed a law prohibiting assisted suicide which was then declared unconstitutional in 1993 by a federal court because it interferes with individual liberty and privacy (Miller et al. 1994: 120). In 1994, the people of Oregon approved by referendum "The Oregon Death with Dignity Act" which would, in very carefully defined situations, allow for assisted suicide. This law, although approved, has never been enacted because a federal court, in response to a petition from individuals living in Oregon who opposed the Act, ordered a stay until further hearings on its constitutionality could be held. It appears likely that referendums on acts similar to Oregon's will be held in at least two states—California and New Hampshire—within the next two years, even though the federal courts have yet to rule on the constitutionality of the Oregon statute.

As the political and legal process has failed in its attempt to clarify these vexing issues, several individuals have taken a more direct, hands-on approach. The most famous or notorious, depending on your point of view, is Dr. Jack Kevorkian, a retired pathologist who has acted on his beliefs by "assisting" in over 30 suicides. "Assisting" is in quotations because there is much debate as to whether Dr. Kevorkian has undertaken assisted suicide or voluntary euthanasia. It is unclear whether in each and every case he has only provided a means of suicide or whether he has crossed the line to voluntary euthanasia by actually administering the means of suicide, such as turning on a machine attached to intravenous tubes filled with barbiturates. Although the details are somewhat muddled, the state of Michigan passed a specific law to prevent Dr. Kevorkian, who argues that death with dignity is an individual's right, from assisting in anyone's suicide. He continued to assist, was prosecuted, acquitted and has returned to his "practice." Prosecutors, as I write, are considering whether to bring him to trial for a fourth time for once again assisting in a suicide (in this case, of an older woman). However, it is unclear whether a jury will ever find Dr. Kevorkian guilty of murder, even though the Michigan state law was written specifically for him (Margolick 1994:A1).

Are Dr. Kevorkian's beliefs and actions only an aberration, or does the fact that a jury of his peers will not find him guilty of murder reflect a more general acceptance within American society of assisted suicide? "Approximately 6,000 deaths per day in the United States are said to be in some way planned or indirectly assisted" (Quill, Cassel and Meier 1992:1381). This is a surprisingly large number of cases, but one must take into consideration that the 6,000 include people who die because of "the discontinuation or failure to start life-prolonging treatments," in addition to those individuals who die because of the administering of pain relieving medication in dosages sufficient to hasten death (Quill, Cassel and Meier 1992: 1381). In fact, there has been sufficient discussion of the appropriate use of life-prolonging treatments within the medical profession to produce a "how-to" article. Angela Holder, writing in *Medical Economics*, advises physicians how to properly write "Do Not Resuscitate" (DNR) orders so that lawsuits are avoided. She suggests that the orders be explicit and that the family members and the patient be consulted, but the results of DNR orders are that elderly patients are allowed to die when they could technically be kept alive. However, some physicians will not write DNR orders under any conditions, while other members of the medical team often find this cruel (Holder 1984).

Another indication of the complex nature of the debate over assisted suicide in American society is the existence of the Hemlock Society, an international organization which advocates voluntary physician aid-in-dying for the terminally ill. The Hemlock Society has 40,000 members and over 80,000 supporters within the United States, and "believes terminally ill people should have the right to self-determination for all end-of-life decisions. Because Hemlock reveres life, dying people must be able to retain their dignity, integrity and self-respect. They encourage, through a program of education and research, public acceptance of voluntary physician aid-in-dying for the terminally ill" (Hemlock Society of the U.S.A. 1994). The members of the Hemlock Society work to further educate a public approximately 60 percent of whom, according to national polls, supports some form of assisted suicide. In addition, the members of the Hemlock Society actively advocate for the passage of laws which would legalize assisted suicide, as well as to impact the position held by the medical establishment in America which is already undergoing transformation.

The attitudes of physicians toward assisted suicide is extremely variable and even though the American Medical Association's Council on Ethical and Judicial Affairs has issued a report on "Decisions Near the End of Life" (Council of Ethical and Judicial Affairs, American Medical Association 1992: 2229–2233), there is far from a consensus as to the physician's role in suicide of terminally ill patients (CeloCruz 1992; Brody 1992). It is fair to say that the problems surrounding the desire of some terminally ill patients to actively end their lives has been "relatively unacknowledged and unexplored by the medical profession . . . (and that) . . . little is objectively known about the spectrum and prevalence of such requests or about the range of physicians' responses" (Quill, Cassel and Meier 1992:1380). It is clear that whatever position is finally taken by the American Medical Association, no physician will be compelled, as part of a treatment protocol, to assist in the suicide of a patient. However, there does appear to be a discernible move toward a position which would support the right of a terminally ill patient to end his/her life and for physicians, by following very well-established guidelines, to assist in this action (Miller, et al. 1994). Many of these issues are discussed in a comprehensive and stimulating manner in a recent report from the Hastings Center which includes articles on physician-assisted suicide, legal consequences of assisted suicide and the costs to society of assisted suicide (Crigger 1995).

One final topic needs to be briefly considered prior to discussing historical and cross-cultural parallels—elder abuse. It is clear that certain forms of elder abuse accelerate the death of older people in America, but this is a complicated issue and not everyone would agree that it should be included in a discussion of assisted suicide. However, elder abuse in one of its three main forms—physical abuse, financial abuse and psychological abuse—is a growing phenomenon in America (Decalmer and Glendenning 1993).[1] The victims of elder abuse are usually women over the age of 75 who are dependent on others for care. The most common abuser is a son or daughter who is experiencing great stress connected with the care of the older parent and who experienced abuse as a child. There are no easy answers to the question of why elderly individuals are abused, but one can anticipate that the problem will grow as the number of the oldest old, those most dependent upon others for care, increases over the next decades. For a more detailed discussion of elder abuse see Johns, Hydle and Aschjem 1990; and Kumagai 1988.

HISTORICAL AND CROSS-CULTURAL PATTERNS

Historical Evidence

It is interesting to note that the controversy over whether it was moral for terminally ill individuals to take their own lives; what role, if any, should be played by physicians in such suicides; and whether active euthanasia should be allowed goes back to at least Greek and Roman times (Carrick 1985). However, I am most interested in the similarity between the contemporary discussion of these issues in America and a comparable, intense debate in the mid- and late nineteenth century, as a result of the discovery and use of anesthesia. Anesthesia, whether morphine, chloroform or ether, could not only alleviate pain, but could, in sufficient dosages, end life. The debate became especially intense in 1872 when Samuel Williams, a nonphysician, published a book in England which argued that it was the ''duty of the medical attendant, whenever so desired by the patient, to administer chloroform or such other anesthesia as may by-and-by supersede chloroform—so as to destroy consciousness at once, and put the sufferer to a quick and painless death'' (Emanuel 1994:794). Publication of Williams' book generated a considerable discussion on both sides of the Atlantic throughout the 1870s and 1890s. This discussion culminated in various attempts, both within the medical profession and within individual states, to codify various opinions into coherent policy and law. An editorial in the *Journal of the American Medical Association* in 1885 fairly well summarizes the position taken by the majority of physicians and certainly the medical establishment, when it argues that the acceptance of Williams' position on euthanasia was really an attempt to make ''the physician don the robes of an executioner'' (Emanuel 1994: 795). Responding to a growing demand for greater patients' rights, several state legislatures in the 1890s, and for the first few years after the turn of the century, debated legislation which would have legalized some form of what today would be termed assisted suicide. None of these bills became law and after the Ohio legislature rejected in 1906 a bill titled ''An Act Concerning Administration of Drugs etc. to Mortally Injured and Diseased Persons,'' the clamor for patients' rights and euthanasia died down only to reappear in the 1980s and 1990s.

Cross-Cultural Evidence

The above discussion should help refute the assumption that this is the first time the issue of assisted suicide has been raised within American society. I now will turn my attention to refuting the second assumption, that we are the first society which has ever had to face such a morally vexing dilemma. To do this I will turn to ethnographic data which have been collected on a wide variety of nonindustrial societies and employ a methodology—holocultural analysis— which allows for the systematic analysis of data collected from a very carefully selected sample of these societies.[2] Much anecdotal information is available concerning the killing of particular individuals within nonindustrial societies, and almost everyone has heard stories about the old Eskimo woman who is set adrift on an ice floe or the elderly man left behind to die alone because he is no longer able to walk when his relatives move to a new location. Holocultural analysis, on the other hand, allows for the systematic analysis and interpretation of ethnographic material in order to more reliably reach conclusions on human behavior. My research used data drawn from the Human Relations Area Files, which is a compilation of ethnographic information on several hundred societies. However, I did not utilize all societies in the Files, but instead examined a sample of societies which have been selected for very specific reasons to ensure geographical distribution, as well as relative independence from each other. This sample is the Probability Sample Files (PSF) and is comprised of 60 nonindustrial societies (Naroll et al. 1976). The focus of the study was on the treatment directed toward the elderly in these societies.

Definitions

Although the study examined all types of behavior, the most surprising and potentially important finding was that nonsupportive treatment, especially the killing, abandonment and forsaking of the elderly, was widespread. In order to describe these life-threatening behaviors in a coherent manner, I coined the term of ''death-hastening behavior,'' which is a broader concept than gerontocide or gericide and includes killing, abandoning and forsaking of the elderly, and is defined as nonsupportive treatment that leads directly to the death of aged individuals. Four brief examples from the literature analyzed illustrate the type of data found in the Human Relations Area Files and the scope of the death-hastening concept.

Killing

Chukchee—reindeer herding people who speak a Paleo-Siberian language and live in northeastern Siberia, principally on the Chukotsk Peninsula.

Few old Chuchi die a natural death. When an old person takes ill and becomes a burden to his surroundings he or she asks one of the nearest relatives to be killed. The oldest son or daughter or son-in-law stabs the old one in the heart with a knife. (Sverdrup 1938:133)

Abandoning

Lau—a horticultural and fishing people who speak a Malayo-Polynesian language and live in the Lau Islands off southern Fiji in the central Pacific Ocean.

Informants on Fulanga said that when the tui naro (headman) of the Vandra clan became old and feeble he was taken to Taluma Islet in the lagoon and abandoned there in a cave filled with skeletal remains of old people who died there after having left the community. (Thompson 1940:10).

Forsaking—Denial of Food

Bororo—a horticultural people who speak a Ge language and live in the Amazonian forest of Central Brazil.

It is the same for the old people; after a hunt or successful fishing trip, they are brought a piece of meat or a few fish. But also they sometimes are forgotten. The indigent person is then reduced to going without a meal and all night long, alone, utters ritual lamentations (Levi-Strauss 1936:276).

Forsaking—Denial of All Support

Yakut—Yak herders who speak a Turkic language and live in north-central Siberia in the former Soviet Union.

The position of older people who were decrepit and no longer able to work was also difficult. Little care was shown for them, they were given little to eat and were poorly clothed, sometimes even reduced to complete destitution (Tokarev and Gurvich 1964: 277). Aged people are not in favor; they are beaten by their own children and are often forced to leave their dwellings and to beg from house to house. (Jochelson 1933: 134)

Each of these behaviors leads directly to the death of the elderly within the particular society. The example of killing is self-evident—the elderly are not left to die but are rather dispatched directly by members of the social group. The abandoning example is also fairly clear-cut and ranged from the above description, in which the elderly are physically removed from a permanent community, to societal members leaving the elderly behind as the group moves to a different location. The two examples of forsaking behavior given show some of the range of this behavior. Forsaking is the broadest of the three behaviors and includes the denial of sufficient food, medical care, clothing and shelter.

These behaviors contrast with supportive treatment, which is defined as the active support of the elderly including the provision of food, shelter, medical care and transportation. Supportive treatment is more than the expression of deference or respect and must be accompanied by tangible actions that aid in the survival of the elderly individual. Behavior that falls between supportive and death-hastening is, for the present study, defined as nonsupportive, nonthreatening behavior and includes such behavior as insulting the elderly, requiring them to give up certain property and removing them from their normal residence. These behaviors can be unpleasant and may even have long-term detrimental effects on the well-being of the old person, but they do not directly threaten his or her life. Thus, nonthreatening behavior can be viewed as transitional between supportive and death-hastening and may eventually lead to death. A definitional problem was raised by the type of data analyzed—how is elder suicide to be categorized? If an old person asks his sons to kill him, if an old woman wanders away from camp in order to die, or if an elderly individual gives away all of his or her possessions and then wanders from village to village, eventually to die of neglect and exposure, are these examples of suicide and perhaps even assisted suicide rather than death-hastening? To avoid the development of numerous coding categories which would prove too difficult and confusing to employ, the decision was made to include such behavior in the existing categories of killing, abandoning and forsaking. The issue as to who initiates the death-hastening behavior is considered as each of the particular categories is discussed.

Findings

Data concerning the treatment of the elderly were available for 41 of the 60 societies in the Probability Sample Files. In 21 of these societies, a slight majority, at least one type of death-hastening behavior was present (see Table 3.1). While twelve societies directed only support toward the aged, almost an equal number (11) displayed both death-hastening and supportive actions toward their elders. Examining the data more closely, ten societies have a single form of death-hastening behavior, while in eleven societies there is a combination of behaviors. Killing is the most frequent means of hastening the death of old people; it occurs in fourteen of the twenty-one societies. Forsaking is found in nine of the societies, and old people are abandoned in eight societies. The most frequent combination of behaviors is to both kill and abandon the elderly within the same social group—five instances. A combination of forsaking and killing is present in four societies, and forsaking and abandoning are present in only a single society. Interestingly, there is no difference in the treatment directed toward older males and older females.

Importantly, in all but one society in which multiple forms of death-hastening occur, supportive or nonthreatening treatment is also found. The most common pattern is for the killing, forsaking and abandoning to be present with supportive treatment. Intuitively, it would appear to be emotionally, cognitively and behaviorally inconsistent for such extremes of treatment—killing and support—to be present in the same society. This is resolved by answering the questions: Who is to be supported? Who is to be denied food? Who is to be killed? A cultural contradiction is apparently avoided simply by directing different treatments toward different categories of the elderly within a given society. The criteria upon which this differentiation is based are complex and will be discussed in detail in the analysis/discussion section.

The data on death-hastening provided additional details concerning the forsaking and killing of the elderly. In five of the nine societies in which old people are forsaken, there is total nonsupport. The elderly are denied food, shelter and

Table 3.1
Treatments in Nonindustrial societies

Treatment	Number of Societies	Percent
Only Support	12	29
Support and Nonthreatening	4	10
Only Nonthreatening	4	10
Only Death-Hastening	6	14
Death-Hastening and Nonthreatening	4	10
Death-Hastening and Support	11	27
Total	41	100

treatment for illness. Most often, as the previous examples show, the elderly are driven from their homes and forced to either beg or scrounge for food. Interestingly, societies in which the elderly are specifically denied sufficient or "desirable" food tend to be horticultural societies, whereas those that practice total forsaking tend to rely on hunting, fishing or animal husbandry. The existence of relatively frequent "hunger seasons" in horticultural societies appears to result in the elderly being denied food, or only being provided with foods that are low in nutritional value or not easily chewed and digested (Fortes 1978:9; Ogbu 1973:319–323). Even though these "hunger seasons" appear to occur more frequently than is commonly presumed, it is usually only by chance that a researcher is in a community during a period of a severe food shortage. Thus, the forsaking of the elderly through the denial of sufficient food or the substitution of undesirable food is perhaps underrepresented in the available ethnographic literature.

Details concerning the killing of the elderly are generally lacking in the ethnographic material. An outsider is just not going to easily collect specific information on the killing of societal members, regardless of the age of the people being killed. The available data, though, do indicate several interesting patterns. The elderly are killed violently: beaten to death (three societies), buried alive (three societies), stabbed (two societies), or strangled (one society); and no difference based on sex was uncovered. The decision to kill the elderly individual was made, in all but one instance, within the family. The common procedure was for the children and the elderly individual to decide jointly that the time was "right to die." In two societies the elderly individual appears to decide on his or her own when it is the proper time to die. Among the Yanoama, a South American shifting horticultural society, the decision is removed from the family and placed in the hands of the village leaders. The actual killing of the old person is also a family affair. In six of the seven societies on which data were available, a son, usually the eldest, kills his parent. Once again there is no variation based on sex.

Analysis/Discussion

The findings presented above answer three of the main questions posed earlier. The killing of the elderly does occur in other societies and when killing, forsaking and abandoning are combined into the broad category of death-hastening, the elderly are dispatched in 50 percent of the societies with data in the PSF. The sex of the individual does not appear to make a difference since both males and females have their deaths hastened. Children, after consultation with their parents, make the decision, and sons carry out the actual killing. Three questions still remain to be answered: Why are old people killed, forsaken or abandoned? In what type of societies is death-hastening found? How does this behavior compare to the killing of the elderly in our society?

Death-hastening is directed toward individuals who have passed from being active and productive to being inactive and nonproductive members of the social group. This transformation of the elderly from intact to decrepit has long been recognized within the anthropological literature, but the connection between it and death-hastening behavior has only recently been systematically analyzed (Rivers 1926; Simmons 1945, 1960; Maxwell et al. 1982; Glascock 1982). Leo Simmons perhaps best described the results associated with the transformation when he stated:

Among all people a point is reached in aging at which any further usefulness appears to be over, and the incumbent is regarded as a living liability. "Senility" may be a suitable label for this. Other terms among primitive people are the "overaged", the "useless stage", the "sleeping period", the "age grade of the dying" and the "already dead." (1960:87)

Thus, at least two categories of the elderly exist in nonindustrial societies: "normal old age" (the intact) and the "already dead" (the decrepit). In the most simple terms, it is when people are defined as decrepit that they have their deaths hastened.

In fourteen of the sixteen PSF societies in which a distinction is made between the intact and the decrepit elderly, some form of death-hastening behavior is present. In the majority of these cases, as Barker shows in Chapter 21, both supportive and death-hastening treatments occur. The evidence clearly indicates that the intact elderly are supported and the decrepit elderly are killed, abandoned or forsaken. This dichotomization of treatments can be most easily seen in several ethnographic studies. D. Lee Guemple's research among the Eskimo documents well the change in behavior that accompanies the redefinition of an elderly individual as decrepit as his or her health declines. "They [the aged] suffer a marked reduction in both respect and affection when they are no longer able to make a useful contribution. As they grow older and are increasingly immobilized by age, disease, and the like, they are transformed into neglected dependents without influence and without consideration. In short, old age has become a crisis" (1969:69). At this point, "the practical bent of the Eskimo asserts itself forcefully. To alleviate the burden of infirmity, the old people are done away with" (Guemple 1969:69).

Finally, recent research in New Guinea and its neighboring islands shows the transition from intact to decrepit and the resultant change in behavior. "Van Baal reports that the Marind Amin elderly are respected and well treated as long as they are in good health. When they become helpless and senescent they may be buried alive by their children" (Counts and Counts 1985a:13). Research among the Kaliai of New Britain conducted by Dorothy and David Counts provides an example of an elderly man who, because he was suffering from physical disabilities and declining mental acuity, had, in the eyes of his sons, lived too long. The sons, therefore, conducted final mortuary ceremonies, distributed property, and essentially defined their father as socially dead (Counts and Counts 1985b:145).

Although drawn from widely different societies, the above examples show that death-hastening behavior is directed toward a specific type of elderly individual—the decrepit who have experienced actual or perceived changes in their health to the degree that they are no longer able to contribute to the well-being of the social group. This inexorable journey is traveled by males and females alike, but there is some evidence in the ethnographic literature that females begin the journey at a slightly later age than males.

Thus, death-hastening behavior is directed toward the decrepit elderly, but is this behavior found equally in all nonindustrial societies? To answer this question a series of variables selected from the Ethnographic Atlas were correlated with the killing, forsaking and abandoning of the elderly (Murdock 1967). The results indicate that death-hastening tends to be present in societies which: (1) are located in areas with harsh climates, in particular, desert and tundra environments, (2) have no horticultural activity or only shifting horticulture in which grain crops predominate, and (3) lack systems of social stratification. Societies which lack death-hastening and instead have only supportive treatment tend to: (1) be located in areas with temperate climates, (2) have intensive agriculture, (3) have systems of social stratification, and (4) have a belief in active high gods. In other words, death-hastening tends to occur in societies which can be characterized as simple—hunting and gathering, pastoral and shifting horticultural—while societies with exclusively supportive treatment are more economically complex—sedentary agricultural.

Although death-hastening behavior tends to be found in more technologically simple societies, it is common for this treatment to be present in conjunction with support of older people and to be directed toward only the decrepit elderly. Likewise, the supportive behavior found in more technologically advanced societies can vary depending upon internal conditions, such as social stratification, residential location and gender. In many ways it is more desirable to be old in Pygmy society, even if one faces being abandoned and killed, than in some advanced agricultural societies. As long as they are intact, older Pygmies can look forward to respect and supportive treatment, receiving the most desirable foods in an environment which provides abundantly for the general population. In advanced agricultural societies, even though supportive treatment for the elderly is present, it must be put in the context of often harsh environmental and societal conditions; isolated residences, frequent food shortages and exploitive state political systems can put the elderly in jeopardy even if they are generally supported.

CONCLUSION

The discussion of the cross-cultural material on death-hastening should refute the second assumption that we are the first society which has ever had to face such a morally vexing dilemma as assisted suicide. It is hard to conclude that death-hastening is not a relatively common occurrence in nonindustrial societies and that people in these societies did not have to make decisions concerning the decrepit or terminally ill elderly which were morally complicated and emotionally painful. I want to continue with the comparison by now analyzing the way in which the killing, abandoning and forsaking of the elderly in these nonindustrial societies compares to assisted suicide in American culture. I also want to consider how we can learn from the similarities and differences which exist between these behavioral responses in nonindustrial and American society as we struggle to reach some type of societal consensus on what has become a significant moral dilemma. There are some clear similarities between death-hastening and assisted suicide:

1. The behaviors are directed toward people, often old, who have experienced a decline in physical or mental health and who are often terminally ill;

2. These individuals are considered burdens to themselves, their families, and to the community;

3. The decision to hasten death is difficult and involves family members, the stricken individual and often other members of the social group, such as physicians in American society, political and/or religious figures in nonindustrial societies.

There are, however, some significant differences between the behaviors found in American and nonindustrial societies.

First, examples of overt, direct killing of the elderly in America are still relatively rare enough to produce sensational responses in news reports. However, as discussed previously (pages 58 and 59), approximately 6,000 deaths per day in the United States appear likely to be in some way planned or indirectly assisted by the joint decision of family and medical personnel through the discontinuation of or failure to initiate life support, or overmedication. Thus, there is an important difference in American society between dramatic, overt assisted suicide (i.e., Dr. Kevorkian), and more subtle, covert assisted suicide (i.e., discontinuing life support). The behaviors present in many nonindustrial societies— killing, abandoning and forsaking—although emotionally demanding, resemble the less dramatic covert behavior found in American society. There appear to be some definite reasons for this response to death-hastening. Death-hastening is part of the culture of these nonindustrial societies; children have personally experienced the death of close relatives, and as they age they may be called upon to hasten the death of one of their parents, and they in turn may ask their children to do the same. As a result, death-hastening is open and socially approved in nonindustrial societies. In contrast, the covert nature of the vast majority of assisted suicides in American society indicates that there is not a society-wide acceptance of this behavior and consequently it must be kept under cover and not open to discussion.

Second, the people who decide and undertake assisted suicide or death-hastening are quite different in the two types of societies. In nonindustrial societies the decisions are made by the family, often with open discussions with the older person. As Maxwell et al. state, "Gerontocide is usually a family affair" (1982:77). The decision is made by family members and usually carried out by a son. In American society it is often unclear as to who decides— children, spouse, the terminally ill person, medical staff, courts of law or some combination. Most often, the decisions appear to be made on an ad hoc basis, with the family brought in at the last minute and the stricken individual often not consulted at all. As the earlier examples of recent legal cases in America show, when the decision is made and implemented by a single person or undertaken in an overt fashion, the consequences can be severe—people can be charged with premeditated murder. Thus, it is not surprising that people, especially hospital and nursing home administrators and physicians, are reluctant to openly take responsibility for aiding in the termination of life to the point that decisions regarding the discontinuing of life support can end up in courts of law. Social sanctions in the form of prosecution and lawsuits are applied inconsistently, with the result being that most assisted suicide is done covertly and then covered up. In contrast, death-hastening in nonindustrial societies is open and direct and people are willing to take responsibility because the rules are known and accepted by the social group.

Perhaps the most significant difference between assisted suicide and death-hastening is the respective levels of technological sophistication of the two types of societies in which the behaviors are found. As has been shown, death-hastening is most prevalent in societies with simple subsistence/technological systems: hunting and gathering, pastoral and shifting horticultural. Even though the issues surrounding the killing, abandoning and forsaking are similar to those found in our society, the technological ability to maintain life is significantly different. In addition, the need for the social groups in these technologically simple societies to move frequently produces a threat to decrepit individuals as does the inability of most of these societies to store sufficient quantities of food to allow all members to survive severe food shortages. American society is the most technologically sophisticated society that has ever existed. We have the ability not only to maintain life but also to prolong life beyond the point which many people think is reasonable. We are able to provide physically incapacitated individuals with many technological marvels which allow these individuals to live, if not a productive life, one that certainly extends beyond that even imagined by members of nonindustrial societies. Yet we inarguably assist the deaths of large numbers of individuals every day and then struggle over the moral, ethical and legal questions which revolve around these actions. We search for a societal consensus which seems to be further away today than a decade ago. Perhaps it is not possible to reach a similar consensus in a society as large, diverse and complex as ours, but at least we are beginning to openly discuss the issues surrounding assisted suicide.

NOTES

1. Physical abuse includes violent acts against the older person as well as extreme neglect and the denial of medical treatment which leads to bodily harm; financial abuse includes theft or the misappropriation of an older person's valuable property; and psychological abuse is really the dehumanizing of the older person to the point where his or her life is threatened.

2. For a more complete discussion of the methodology employed, please refer to Glascock and Feinman 1980, 1981.

CHAPTER 4

African Widows, Culture and Social Change: Case Studies from Kenya

Maria G. Cattell

Abaluyia widows' words:

"I don't want another husband coming into my house and eating my food."

"God has made it that old women like us can control our own homes. May the Lord be praised!"

In this chapter we look at older women, especially widows, in sub-Saharan Africa to compare their experiences of losing a spouse with the worldwide pattern of widowhood. Some variations within Africa and some widespread African cultural patterns are discussed. Finally, we zero in on Abaluyia widows in western Kenya, using case studies to illuminate the realities of widows' lives and variation in their experience.

WIDOWS WORLDWIDE AND IN SUB-SAHARAN AFRICA

Older Women as Wives and Widows: Worldwide

Throughout the world, cultural beliefs and norms for behavior guide females and males into different roles in family, economy and polity. While there is much variation from society to society, almost everywhere there are broad patterns found which affect girls and women from birth through old age. Females and their work are less highly valued than males and their work. From infancy through old age females have lesser access than men to resources such as food, education, healthcare, land, livestock, employment and pensions. Their participation in the formal or wage economy (labor force participation) is less. Females are more likely to work in the informal sector, and their earnings are lower.

Culminating these and other lifelong inequities, in old age women are likely to be poorer than men. They are more likely to be caregivers, to depend on children for old age support, and to be childless. They are also more likely to live long enough to become frail.[1]

Women are also more likely to be widowed, and to be widowed for many years. This comes about because of women's greater longevity and the fact that wives are usually younger than husbands. In 95 countries with available data, the proportions of widowed older persons vary greatly. But there is no exception to the pattern of substantially higher rates of widowhood among women (Table 4.1). The lowest proportion of widows (26%) occurs in the United States; the highest (60% and over) in Bangladesh, India, Indonesia, South Korea and six African countries.[2]

In most societies a woman's status and access to resources are closely linked to marriage. Since being a wife matters in a woman's life, what difference does being a widow make? A widow's social status may—or may not—change for the worse. Remarriage may be an issue, depending on a widow's childbearing status and local cultural rules, though in general older women are unlikely to remarry. Women's claims to resources and family support may be diminished or lost when husbands die. However, experiences of widowhood vary widely around the world and even in different cultures in the same geographic area. Among the Gusii in rural western Kenya, for example, a widow's rights to land are secured through sons; a woman without sons may lose home and farmland on her husband's death (Håkansson 1994; see also Ncube and Stewart 1995). Not far away in Samia (the focus of this chapter), even widows with no son remain on the husband's land—a crucial difference in terms of a widow's ability to support herself and her children, grandchildren or other dependents.[3]

SOCIOCULTURAL CONTEXTS OF AGING IN AFRICA

There are hundreds of different societies in sub-Saharan Africa, but throughout the continent one finds similar themes in the sociocultural contexts in which women—and men too—age. The themes include the importance of marriage and kinship to widows' rights, obligations and opportunities. For example, widows may have rights to housing and productive resources through marriage and the husband's lineage and/or through their natal kin group. However, a single dyadic relationship is central in African women's lives and crucial for old age support. This is the relationship between a mother and her children, especially mother and son(s). Another African theme is the economic self-sufficiency of African women—as wives and as widows. Throughout Africa the setting is one of rapid change: transformations in Africa resulting from collisions with European economic and political expansion, Africa's incorporation into the world political economy and African responses to the situation.

These are not separate and distinct issues. They are intertwined and inescapable in the lives of all Africans and certainly in the lives of African widows.

Table 4.1
Percentages of Men and Women (Age 60+) in Selected Countries Who Are Widowed

	Percent widowed	
	Men	Women
Sub-Saharan Africa		
Cameroon	10	62
Sudan	6	54
Zaire	9	54
Botswana	9	53
Kenya	7	50
Senegal	6	54
South Africa	11	49
Zimbabwe	6	48
Tanzania	8	48
Uganda	9	48
Mali	5	46
Malawi	6	43
Less Developed Countries		
Indonesia	17	68
Bangladesh	8	66
India	19	64
Korea, South	13	64
Morocco	7	62
Egypt	12	60
China (PRC)	27	58
Brazil	12	47
Mexico	12	38
More Developed Countries		
Germany	15	51
Japan	12	49
Israel	14	47
France	13	45
Australia	12	43
United Kingdom	14	43
Canada	11	40
Sweden	12	37
United States	6	26

Sources: UN (1993); U.S. Bureau of the Census (1991).

THE DEMOGRAPHY OF AFRICAN WIDOWHOOD

Sub-Saharan Africa's population is "young." It is the only major world region where the proportion of elderly (defined as those age 60+) is under 5 percent in most countries. However, there are plenty of old people in Africa and as everywhere, older women outnumber older men. Most elderly Africans reside with children or grandchildren and sometimes other kin; few (3 to 5 percent) live alone.[4]

Relatively few African men are widowed because they tend to be older (sometimes much older) than their wives and/or to have more than one wife, so that a man can remain married even if one wife dies. By contrast many African women are widows. Some are young but relatively few are under age 40. The pace of widowhood picks up for women in their forties and increases rapidly after age 50. In 27 African nations with available data, about 42 percent to 62 percent of women age 60 and older are widows (UN 1993; Table 4.1).

SOME MEANINGS OF WIDOWHOOD IN AFRICA

Being widowed brings changes in a woman's life. At the least, there are emotional issues and loss of whatever support the husband was providing. Widows may have problems similar to those of women who have lost husbands—and claims to resources—through abandonment or divorce. They may have to struggle to support themselves, their children and other dependents with fewer resources than they had as wives, even being chased away from their husband's homes (Folta and Deck 1987; Ncube and Stewart 1995).

But in many cases African widows retain their rights of residence and access to productive resources or have alternatives—most often, rights with natal kin groups (maternal kin). As widows they may head their households, manage their husbands' estates and make decisions formerly made by husbands—more work but also more freedom and autonomy. Further, in many African societies, as in many societies worldwide (see Kerns and Brown 1992), older women and in particular older widows may be free of many of the restrictions placed on wives and younger women. They are likely to have greater freedom of movement and behavior, more time for their own interests and activities, and increased personal and social power. At the least a widow no longer has to serve or get permission from a husband. Older women are likely to have greater power than younger women within women's kinship age hierarchies and in their families and communities.[5]

Will She? Won't She? Marrying Again—Or Not. Remarriage is important in widows' lives because it can be crucial to women's rights of residence and access to resources. Through remarriage widows may gain benefits for themselves and their children—or they may see better opportunities in not remarrying. Widows' degrees of freedom to make choices about remarriage vary from high in some societies to low in others—unless the widows are postmenopausal.

One can safely say that women still of childbearing age are likely to remarry; older, postmenopausal women usually do not. But this is not saying much, since this is the situation worldwide, not just in Africa.

The African twist is that there are numerous forms of marriage and remarriage. Marital possibilities for African widows range from remaining a widow or marrying for ritual purposes only (to cleanse the pollution of death) through the levirate, widow inheritance, and "full" marriage with the usual rights and obligations. The levirate is marriage with a man (often a brother) from the deceased husband's kin group. Its primary purpose is to beget children on behalf of the dead man. Widow inheritance is much like the levirate, but differs in that any children born are children of the inheritor, not of the dead husband.[6]

The levirate has been often opposed by Christian churches because it tends to put widows into polygynous marriages, since inheritors often have at least one wife already (Kirwen 1979). It has also come under attack from colonial and modern marriage laws aimed at promoting the conjugal unit over lineages (e.g., Guyer 1986). Both the levirate and widow inheritance may be less commonly practiced these days, especially as women themselves are resisting these customs and even resisting marriage altogether.[7]

Another pattern of cultural influences on widow remarriage occurs among African Muslims, for whom divorce and remarriage are common throughout the life course. Muslim women usually have a good deal of choice in marriage decision making. Among Muslim Hausa in Nigeria younger widows are likely to remarry, reside with husbands and accept their seclusion. Often their decisions are related to issues of childbearing and residence with their children which promotes close mother-child bonds. Most Hausa women have in-home businesses, and older Hausa widows—secure in relationships with their children—may choose to remain single because it has business advantages, since widows are not secluded. If they choose to remarry, they may arrange marriages which allow them to maintain a separate residence or not be in seclusion (Coles 1990; Schildkrout 1986).

Home and Home Folks: Where Widows Live. Residence is not merely a matter of having a roof over one's head. Residence determines the people with whom a woman has conflicts and emotional bonds, those with whom she shares her daily social and work life. It is related to rights in property and other material resources, rights to the labor of others, and physical and emotional security in old age. In Africa it also involves the sense of the continuity of generations, individuals' relationships with their ancestors, and—as they grow old—their own impending death and ancestorhood.

In patrilineal societies spouses usually live in the husband's home. Here women are "strangers" or "visitors" with few rights and many duties, especially as young wives. In matrilineal and duolineal societies residence tends to be more flexible, even to the husband's living in the wife's home.[8] This is a big plus for a woman as she has a stronger position with her maternal kin than among her husband's people. Among matrilineal Ndembu in Zambia, many villages were constituted through females: clusters of brothers lived where their mother lived—a good setting for the mother's old age support (Turner 1957). In some societies where a woman resides in the husband's home, widows and older wives may have the option to live with a son or return to their natal group. Such "retirement" from marriage is socially acceptable and expected; it occurs in patrilineal as well as in other kinship systems. Women make their choices according to what they perceive will give them a better life in old age, including social and political power, respect and support.

For example, wives among the matrilineal Akan (Ashanti and other groups in Ghana) usually live in their husbands' hometown or on husbands' cocoa farms. But they keep up lifelong ties with their matrikin through gift giving and other forms of assistance. They are likely to return to their hometown, the village of their brothers, in their later years even if their husbands are still living (Stucki 1992; Vellenga 1986). In their hometowns, Akan women have strong rights in houses (or at least a room in a house) and in land for farming. They also have strong positions in their matrilineages, including possible leadership as lineage elders.

Overworked and Underpaid: Women's Work. The most consistent finding about widows in ten African societies was that widows have a high degree of economic self-reliance (Potash 1986a). In this widows do not differ from wives. Being widowed makes little difference in women's responsibilities and usually not in their access to productive resources. This does not mean that life is easy— far from it. The overall context is one of women's economic marginalization, hard work and poverty. Older women may have advantages over younger women. This includes greater command of others' labor, more influence and authority by virtue of leadership positions in the arenas of kinship and ritual, greater self-confidence and stronger personalities. But older women continue to be overworked and underpaid.[9]

WIDOWS IN WESTERN KENYA: AN ANTHROPOLOGICAL CASE STUDY

Doing the Research

We will now take a closer look at widows among the Abaluyia people of western Kenya, among whom I have been doing fieldwork since 1982.[10] I made a five-week preliminary site visit in 1982, then lived in Kenya for two years (1983–1985) and returned for four- to six-week periods in 1987, 1990, 1992, 1993 and 1995. My research has focused on aging, the lives of the elderly and family life in circumstances of rapid socioeconomic and cultural change. It was done in rural western Kenya among two Abaluyia subgroups, the Samia and to a lesser extent their neighbors, the Banyala, and among families of my rural informants in the cities of Kisumu and Nairobi. The research has been carried out by the methods of participant observation, including informal and in-depth

Doing Research in Samia: author Maria Cattell being greeted at the house of her research assistant, J. B. Owiti.

interviews and field-designed questionnaires, one of which was used in a survey of 416 older Samia women and men in 1985, the "Old People of Samia" survey.

In the course of my research I have observed and interacted with numerous people in many homes, on roads and footpaths and in other public places such as markets, churches and schools. I have shared daily activities, serious illness, theft, house fires, the struggle to educate children, marriages, births and deaths. My contacts have included females and males of all ages with a range of social and economic characteristics. Two Samia women (Tekela and Manyuru—Cases 3 and 5) appointed themselves my mothers. I have been incorporated into two Samia families and a third family in Bunyala—an important route to insider information, though I am always to some extent an outsider.

Sociocultural Context: A Century of Change

The Samia and Banyala people live in southern Busia District (county) in the Western Province of Kenya. They reside in Samia and Bunyala Locations (county subdivisions equivalent to American townships)[11] (see map, Figure 4.1). These people are two of sixteen or seventeen culturally and linguistically related

Doing the Old People of Samia Survey: research assistant Rosemary Apeli interviewing
Pamela Silingi.

communities grouped into the Abaluyia, a major Kenyan ethnic group of over
3 million people. The 1989 Kenya census counted 60,000 Samia and 38,000
Banyala. In that same year, Busia District (county) had 20,000 persons aged
60+; this was 5 percent of the total population.[12]

The Banyala and Samia live in the tropics in savanna woodland. Because of
population pressures, land is intensively cultivated though soils have only moderate fertility. Two crops are raised in one year, especially the staple grains,
maize (corn) and sorghum. However, droughts are frequent and periods of food
scarcity are common.

A century ago the Banyala, Samia and other Abaluyia lived in small, kin-
based groups in fortified villages. They were self-sufficient subsistence farmers,
growing their own food, raising cattle and goats, making the tools and other
items they needed. Money and markets were unknown. These people were almost completely untouched by the world economy or outside cultural influences
(except for local migrations) until the arrival of the British explorer-geographer
Joseph Thomson (1885) in the late nineteenth century. From then on things
changed radically under colonialism and then nationhood, which was achieved
in 1963.

The introduction of money changed many things. As older people say, ''When

Figure 4.1
Map of Kenya: Major Cities; Western Province and Its Districts as of 1985
(Bungoma, Busia, Kakamega); Samia and Bunyala Locations (Townships) (inset
shows Kenya's location in Africa)

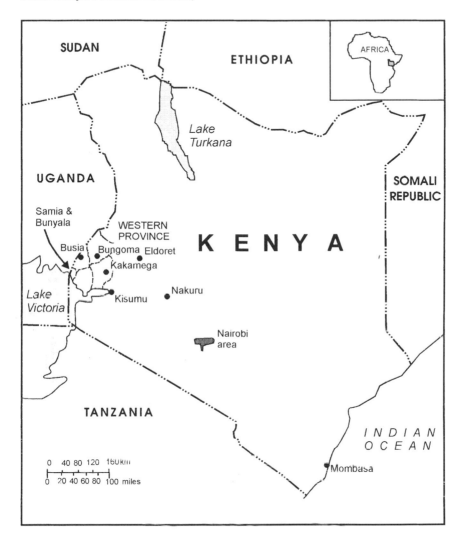

I was young, things were free; but today it is a world of money.'' Money quickly
became a necessity. This led to rapid development of cash cropping and extensive labor migration to the growing cities of Kenya and Uganda. Many now go
to urban areas looking for employment and stay away for years, though often

retiring to their rural homes. In the rural area, most people today are peasant farmers who grow much of what they eat and also raise cash crops (primarily cotton) and earn money through a variety of other activities. In spite of all the effort, however, poverty is widespread.

Added to these economic changes was the hegemony of European languages, ideologies and institutions such as Christianity, Western medicine and formal education.[13] For example, early in the twentieth century people spoke only local languages, Lusamia or Lunyala. This is still true of older persons, especially older women, most of whom never attended school or went to urban areas for employment. However, today most Kenyans (girls as well as boys) get at least some education and about 60 percent complete eighth grade. English, the official language of Kenya, is also the language of classroom instruction; Swahili, widely spoken throughout East Africa, is also taught. Expressing their unease with the changes, older people complain that ''Young people only want to speak English'' or ''They go to books to learn.''

Many other things came during the lifetimes of those now elderly. These include churches, schools, medical facilities,[14] telephone and electric lines, police, government administrators, roads, public transportation. Today's elderly were yesterday's innovators who participated in these changes—especially males. For it was boys and men who went to school, served in the military in World Wars I and II, went outside their home areas seeking wage employment, spent time in newly urbanizing areas, learned to speak Swahili, and in general had much greater exposure to the new influences than did women. Until the last few decades, women, for the most part, stayed in the rural area, managed their households and farms and worked harder than ever to make ends meet in conditions of increasing poverty and scarcity.

In spite of these modernizing influences, people in Bunyala and Samia today remain agrarian or rural in work and lifestyle. This means that for most persons modern amenities are few and work is labor-intensive. Farmwork is handwork; it is done with hoes, machetes and other hand tools. Though there are roads, they are dirt roads. Though there is public transportation, it is unreliable; private ownership of vehicles is rare. Most travel is on foot. In any case, many homes are quite a distance from a road and not accessible by vehicle. Most people live in mud-walled houses with grass-thatched roofs without telephones, electricity, plumbing or appliances such as stoves and refrigerators. Radios (battery-operated), however, are common. Toilets are pit latrines; bathing, laundry and dishwashing are done in plastic basins and pails. This translates into going to streams and wells for water, gathering fuelwood from the hills and cooking over open fires—all being women's work.

One must be strong and able to walk in order to work, get food and water, engage in ordinary social life, attend church and carry out other everyday activities. Getting water and cooked food is little problem for men, who depend on women to do this work. Most men, even the oldest, are married. Their wives or wives' helpers bring water and cook food for them. But women, married or widowed, must supply their own food and water or depend on others if they become weak and have difficulty walking. Frail older people who cannot walk have to reduce or give up attending funerals, church services and other important social events which occur outside their own homes. Getting to a clinic or hospital for medical care also becomes more problematic.

Family positions and roles are important for Abaluyia in both rural and urban areas. Every child is born into the clan (*oluyia*) and patrilineal descent group (*enyumba*) of the father and remains a member for life. Females are valued for their hard work, for bringing bridewealth to their families, and increasingly, as potential sources of support for elderly parents—a duty formerly assigned primarily to sons. Land is inherited by sons from their fathers; women rarely own land but their rights to cultivate a husband's land are generally secure. When women marry they go to live in their husbands' homes and cultivate their husbands' lands to raise food and cash crops. But they continue to have important duties in their *enyumba*, the lineage of their father. From time to time women return to their natal villages to participate in important family matters such as marriage decision making and funerals. This gives women identities and rights not dependent on their husbands nor under a husband's control.

Daughters are valued, but a girl is destined to be subordinate to almost everyone during her early years. Gradually—as she moves up the kinship ladder—a woman acquires prestige and power. By the time she is old (when childbearing and menstruation have clearly ended),[15] a woman is likely to have spent years directing the activities of daughters, daughters-in-law and perhaps co-wives and managing the family farm during her husband's absences for employment. She is likely to be a woman respected by kin and community for her hard work and achievements as well as for her senior position in her family. Age and generational seniority, for women as for men, are the foundation for respect and the right to claim the obedience and services of juniors—ideals often expressed and often put into practice.

Older Samia women are much more likely than men to be widowed. Of those in the Old People of Samia survey, a majority (55.5 percent) of women age 50 and over (n = 200) were widowed compared to only 17 percent of the men (n = 216). By age 70+ nearly all women were widows, whereas no men in their fifties were widowers and relatively few were found even in the older age groups (Table 4.2).

CHANGING ROLES IN A CHANGING SOCIETY

The past century has brought role changes for everyone. In indigenous societies, women had various roles in their families and in craft production, healing and religion. Older women in particular were teachers of the young, midwives and spirit mediums. They carried out rituals connected with birth and childrearing. Today these roles have been transformed by foreign ideas which disrupt indigenous practices but also bring new opportunities.

Table 4.2

Widows and Widowers in Samia (1985) (percentage by gender and age groups)

		Total	Ages			
			50-59	60-69	70-79	80+
Women						
	N	199	62	78	44	15
	%	55.5%	32%	54%	82%	87%
Men	N	216	62	82	53	19
	%	8.0%*	-0-	7%	17%	10%

*Of these 17 men, 14 were widowers, 3 had been divorced by their wives.
Source: Cattell 1989b.

Healers. In the past many Abaluyia women were healers such as herbalists, spirit mediums, midwives and *abalumikhi* (specialists in counteracting illness and other problems caused by the "evil eye"). These healers worked in a system which dealt with illness in its sociocultural context and treated sick persons within their families and communities. Today the indigenous system exists in tension with Western biomedicine, which focuses on the physical body and medical technology. This "cosmopolitan" medicine has usurped, stigmatized or transformed indigenous healing roles (Nyamwaya 1992). Indigenous herbal remedies, long condemned by medical practitioners but still widely used by local people, are now the focus of efforts to bring their use under medical control. The government licenses and regulates doctors, nurses, clinics and hospitals. Midwifery entails taking a government-approved certificate course.

At the same time, cosmopolitan medicine has provided new opportunities in community health work, as in the program developed by Sr. Dr. Leda Liboon, a Medical Mission Sister at Nangina's Holy Family Hospital in Samia. The program recruits local people to work as volunteer community health workers (CHWs); they also become teachers of new CHWs. Often these are older women who are more likely to have the time and freedom to do the work. CHWs learn about health promotion and primary health care. Regina (mentioned below) and Tekela (Case 3) were CHWs; both were proud of their accomplishments in their communities.

Religious Leadership. Religious leadership in sub-Saharan African churches is usually by males. But African women have a long history of important roles, such as spirit possession and prophesy, in indigenous religions. The "saved" movement of born-again Christians gave women, especially older women, new opportunities for leadership after the movement reached the area in the early 1970s. The saved, while continuing their affiliation with recognized churches (e.g., Roman Catholic), also have their own "tea groups" which hold weekly prayer meetings in private homes and act as support groups for members. Women predominate as group members and often as leaders.

Elitist assumptions and separatist behaviors of the saved have brought conflicts to families and communities, and also to the Catholic Church in Samia. For several years the church has been trying to "cool down" the movement by encouraging the saved to participate in the church's lay group, *Legio Mariae*. As will be seen in Case 1, these tensions often emerge at funerals, when decisions about widow inheritance are expected to be announced.

Widow inheritance in these Abaluyia cultures involves remarriage of a widow to her husband's brother, a co-wife's son or another male of her husband's lineage. For younger women this may mean a "real" marriage: a woman may have children with her new husband. For women past childbearing, remarriage has primarily ritual implications for clearing the pollution of death. However, it gives the new husband claims to the widow's goods and services—claims women resist. As one woman said: "Yes, I was inherited, but only to clear the taboos. Then I chased him away. I'm now an old woman and don't want another burden. I have just enough for myself."

In the past most widows were inherited, like the 30 widows of Anyango (see Case 5). Today some—especially older women—are refusing it completely. While their rationale is religious, rejection of the custom is also a rejection of patriarchal power and the possibility of domination by a new husband. Older women prefer the freedom of widowhood which allows them to manage their own resources without having to feed and care for a husband. Having reached the top rung of the kinship ladder, older women have the confidence and assurance of age and experience, and can be leaders in this aspect of the politics of gender relations.[16]

Funerals are held in the home where the dead person will be buried. *Obulori* are a central feature of Samia funerals. The same word, *obulori*, is used for confessions to a priest and the confessions of the saved in their prayer meetings. At funerals *obulori* are the witness or testimony made by family members and others about various matters including the circumstances of the death and what rituals will be done. *Obulori* are also part of an ongoing Samia discourse on contemporary issues. Case 1 is an account of what three widows said about widow inheritance and gender relations at a funeral: no to renewed male domination, yes to the freedom and autonomy of widowhood.

Case 1. Witness to Revolution: The Widows Say No

It is December 1984. Oundo, a very old man, died a few days ago. Oundo was Catholic but not saved. Oundo leaves two widows, Anna, the elder wife, who is Catholic and saved, and Elizabeth, who is Protestant and not saved.

Present at the funeral in Siwongo village are two choirs, one Catholic, one Protestant. The mourners are also divided in their religious persuasions. The deepest divisions are not interdenominational but between those who are saved and those who are not saved.

It is time for *obulori*, during which the widows will announce their decisions with regard to funeral rituals and widow inheritance. Since the death itself is not controversial, these issues are central. What the old women say on this day constitutes a witness for revolution, for radical change in gender relations and gender power.

Anna, the saved senior wife, speaks briefly. She tells the assembled mourners the date she was saved, says she had eleven children with Oundo, and praises him as a good man who always took care of her. She ends with a description of how she came to marry Oundo: "We married when I was still a child . . . as it used to be in the old days that your father could arrange with a man and then you could go. You'd just go. You didn't refuse. So I came and married this man. May the Lord be praised!" Anna has not addressed the questions the mourners are waiting to hear about, though they expect her, as a saved woman, to refuse inheritance.

The younger wife, Elizabeth, who is not saved, follows Anna. Her words suggest that the two women discussed their decision privately prior to the funeral. Elizabeth says she also had eleven children with Oundo. She says that Oundo spoke his last words to her. Oundo told her God was coming to take him on a journey. "The Lord relieved my husband of his problems. So there is no one who can say that any person did anything [e.g., witchcraft] to Oundo." By these words Elizabeth is saying that Oundo's death was not caused by human agency but by God. Hence no *emisiro*, no funeral or purification rituals are necessary.

"The second thing," she continues, "is that there is no one who will bring here advice of inheritance of wives. Oundo refused. I am not saved nor am I Catholic but . . . I cannot break his advice." In this way Elizabeth calls on the authority of the dead husband to support his widows' refusal of funeral rituals and widow inheritance. At her words some of the saved in the audience say "Thank you, thank you" to Elizabeth, and the Catholic choir breaks out into a hymn. But the not-saved people are quiet.

Next the widows' sister-in-law speaks. She is Anjelina, a tough-minded woman in her sixties who refused to be inherited when her husband (half-brother to Oundo) died some years before (Figure 4.2 shows these relationships). Anjelina is Catholic; she is saved. Like Anna, the senior wife, Anjelina begins with a description of how she was forced to marry. "Oundo took me from the house of my mother when I was still a little girl. He came with Wandera to pay brideprice. . . . I refused that I could not marry an old man. My mother said, 'Oundo, carry that child on your shoulder.' Which he did. What God planned with those old men and girls is what happened. God's path is the right path. Let the Lord be praised!''

Figure 4.2
Oundo Family: The Widows Who Said No

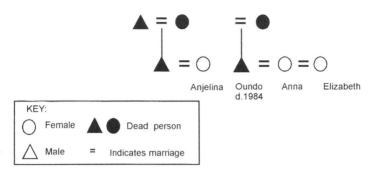

KEY:
○ Female   ▲● Dead person
△ Male   = Indicates marriage

Thus, Anjelina accepts her youthful forced marriage as God's will—the way God arranged things in the old days—but she has seen the light of God's new path and now speaks out strongly against traditional marriage customs. First she condemns widow inheritance as incestuous.[17] The saved in the audience agree with her by clapping and exclaiming "Let Jesus be praised!" The not-saved are very quiet.

Anjelina continues: "I praise the Lord very much. When the inheritor [new husband] comes and finds my son has brought me a kilo of sugar, he comes in and prepares tea for himself. And when I tell him to go out, he refuses." There is more clapping by the saved, and more praise of Jesus, and Anjelina goes on: "We thank God who has given us light. He has really given us peace." The not-saved laugh at this. But Anjelina has a punchline to deliver: "God has made it that old women like us can control our own homes. May the Lord be praised!"

Grandmothers. Another example of role transformation is that of Abaluyia grandmothers. Historically, grandmothers were teachers of granddaughters and younger grandsons. The youngsters slept in the grandmother's house, where they conversed after supper. Grandmothers were socially recognized as the "owners" of important knowledge who had responsibility for "advising" the young. Among other things, grandmothers taught girls about sexual and marital behavior. In effect the old women controlled significant aspects of adolescent sexuality and the intergenerational transmission of knowledge.

Today, older women's cultural expertise and social authority have been eroded by new knowledge—the knowledge of books, the knowledge of Europeans—and by formal education in languages (Swahili and English) most older women do not know. Children spend much time in schools where the teachers are mostly young people. As one grandmother, Regina Makuda, said, "I don't go in the house of my grandchildren. If I go, they are in their studies. Nowadays it isn't easy to advise the young." Regina, who never went to school, meant she did not have the right knowledge to advise her grandchildren.

Nowadays young children often sleep in their grandmothers' houses, but by the time they reach adolescence, girls are likely to sleep in their mothers' kitchens (a separate building because of the fire hazard). Here the girls can talk among themselves about things about which grandmothers know little such as modern contraception. In their grandmothers' day, virginity at marriage was the ideal and the practice. There was even a virginity test on the wedding night. Today's girls do not want to know how to remain a virgin until marriage. They want to know how to prevent conception while having sexual relationships. In this, grandmothers cannot advise them.

This loss of elders' control of adolescent sexuality has led to a boom in premarital pregnancies. However, here grandmothers have come into their own again. Of 252 older women and men (a subsample of my Old People of Samia survey of 416 elders), 29 percent said that they had at least one grandchild for whom they were responsible, most often because these grandchildren had been born outside marriage. Families must deal with the stigma and also care for the child if the mother returns to school, seeks employment or marries a man other than the child's father (few men will accept another man's child into their homes). Usually, maternal grandmothers accept responsibility for these children, even to paying school fees.[18]

While such grandchildren mean extra work, caring for them can also be a source of feelings of usefulness. This was the case with Regina Makuda (mentioned above), whose unmarried daughter gave birth to a girl in 1984. Contrary to the custom of naming children for dead ancestors, the child was named after her living grandmother Regina. Some criticized this and predicted problems, but under her grandmother's care the child thrived. "She has grown up," said Regina. "Had it been she was named for a dead person, she could have died, for I have been caring for her." Clearly, Regina regarded this as a worthy accomplishment despite her inability to advise her older grandchildren.

Many of these themes are seen in the following case study of an unusually successful business woman who used her widowhood to advantage. She is also seen in her role as grandmother.[19]

Case 2: A Widow's Achievements: Paulina Mahaga

When businessman Fabianus Mahaga died in 1970, he left four widows and many children (Figure 4.3). All the widows were inherited by men Fabianus called "cousin." After the purification rituals, the two senior wives, Paulina and Marita, sent away the cousin who had inherited both of them. They did not want him interfering in their lives. As Paulina said: "I didn't want another man because when you get a man you have to take care of him." The man respected their decision but remained a friend of the family. The third and fourth wives were inherited by other "cousins." Each had a daughter with her inheritor, after which the relationships faded. All four widows stayed in the Mahaga family

Figure 4.3
Paulina Mahaga's Family

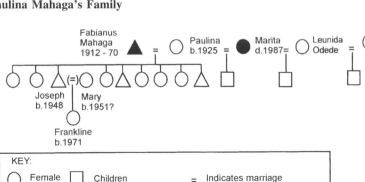

compound or homestead (Figure 4.4) under the management of the first wife, Paulina.

Paulina Stella Ayiemba Mahaga was about 45 years old when Fabianus died. She had already developed her own trading business, traveling long distances by public transport to purchase farm produce for resale in the small lakeside community of Port Victoria in Bunyala. She inherited her husband's businesses, a restaurant and a small shop selling food and household items. A strong determined woman, Paulina managed the family homestead and the many people who lived in it along with the businesses. She saved money, bought land, and made sure her own and her co-wives' children were educated.[20]

Today her oldest son Joseph continues to expand the store. Another son (employed in Nairobi) recently built a modern motel on land his mother gave him. Paulina has "retired" to a small roadside stand where she sells vegetables, fried fish and the doughnuts which she gets up before dawn each day to cook. She is still the family head and is consulted by her middle-aged sons frequently. She lives in a large new house built for her by her son Joseph—the house, as always, at the center of her homestead and herself at the center of her family (Figures 4.3 and 4.4).

In 1971 a daughter, Frankline, was born to her son Joseph and his girlfriend. Joseph, still in school, asked his mother, Paulina, to care for the child. Little Frankline was cared for by her father's younger sisters and by housegirls and other employees. In the evenings she ate supper with her grandmother and they slept in the same room. Here Frankline recited accounts of her day, and Paulina listened and commented, supporting her granddaughter and advising her how to get along in the world. "My grandmother was so strict on education, and she taught me 'a-e-i-o-u' and how to count in English up to 5," said Frankline, "and she made sure my father got me books and pens. She also had me help

Figure 4.4
Mahaga Homestead, 1992

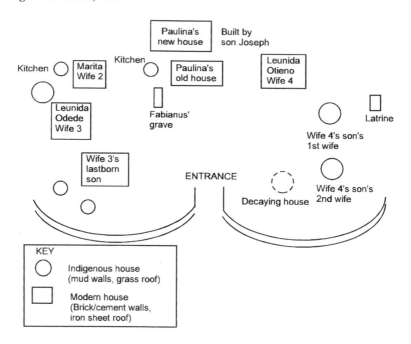

her in her shop so I could begin learning business.'' Paulina also paid the fee
so Frankline could attend nursery school.

In 1978, Frankline was enrolled as a boarder at Nangina Girls Primary School
in Samia. Paulina paid the first year's school fees. Then Frankline's father, by
now a successful business person like his parents, took over. But it was Paulina
who came almost every Saturday to visit her granddaughter during school visiting hours, to see how Frankline was getting along and make sure she did not
lack for anything she needed. When Frankline was leaving for secondary school,
again as a boarder, ''the last person I saw was my grandmother, and she told
me, 'You are going to a different place. You have to respect people.' ''

In June 1993, Frankline received her B.A. in Business from the United States
International University (USIU) in Nairobi. The ''upcountry'' grandmother who
became her surrogate mother and was always Frankline's chief supporter and
adviser was a proud observer at the commencement ceremony. In thus preparing
herself for a business career, Frankline is following in Paulina's footsteps, in a
modern transformation of her grandmother's business career—a transformation
encouraged and approved by Paulina, the widow who parlayed her widowhood
into a position of wealth and power.

Let Her Eat Cake: Update from the Field, 1995. In June 1995, Paulina and
I were present when Frankline received her M.B.A. from USIU. Later, in her

son's Nairobi home, Paulina offered me some packaged cupcakes. As we ate them she told me: "I still like to do a little business so if I want to eat cake, I don't have to ask anyone. I can just buy it for myself." Is it any wonder her son teased this independent woman with, "Mama, you should be going to the women's conference in Beijing"? And Paulina was ready to go!

SOCIAL CHANGE, FRAILTY AND OLD AGE SECURITY

The cultural values of respect and reciprocity in family relationships are important resources for elderly Abaluyia in gaining family support and long-term care.

"Respect" (*esitiwa*) is a word often spoken. It is not an empty word. Respect for parents, elders in general and ancestors—for those more senior in age or kinship status—is a strong value among contemporary Abaluyia. I have witnessed many instances of respectful behavior toward one's seniors. Children are quiet around adults and prompt to do any task an older person sets them. Middle-aged people are courteous and deferential toward their seniors. Clearly, respect and respectful behavior continue to be salient in ordinary, everyday social relations.

Being respectful includes helping one's parents throughout life and caring for them when they become frail.[21] The cultural ideal remains that old people should be able to "sit and eat," as people often say. To be able to rest from working in old age increases one's status. One Samia man in his mid-sixties gave up a night watchman job because he worried that his neighbors and kin would think his children were not taking care of him. This would shame the children and reduce his own status as an elder who should be able to relax, to sit (i.e., not work) and eat. Some years later this man got another job as a watchman. This time his children went to him and implored him to give it up, as they did not want others to think they were not providing for their father. He gave up the job.

Reciprocity is also a strong motivation. This refers to goods and services exchanged over lifetimes. Children owe their parents for life itself and for having fed and educated them (cf. LeVine and LeVine 1985). As one man said: "How can I not help my mother now that she is old? Did she not feed me when I was young?" To sit and be served by younger people, to be cared for in old age—that is respect. It is also returning to parents the care they once gave their children.

This is not to say that behavior always lives up to the ideal! But often it does, or people are at least trying to live up to it. In my Old People of Samia survey and the pretest in a single village, only 23 of 487 old people had no living child. Of the 464 with at least one child, 94 percent said they were receiving help of various kinds from their children. They were not boasting. If anything, they underplayed the help from children in the hope of getting something from me or spurring their children on to better efforts.

Even with the best will, caring for aging parents is not easy. Family members often are not at home. They may be away at school (many schools are boarding) or working or looking for work in a city. They may be able to come home only a few times a year. Geographic dispersion has reduced the ability of families to exert moral persuasion to do the right thing. Such norm enforcement works better in small-scale, local communities like those Abaluyia were living in before British colonization. Poverty is another factor. The shift from self-sufficiency to a market economy was accompanied by poverty. When difficult choices have to be made, paying children's school fees may take precedence over the needs of an aging parent.[22]

In general, older Abaluyia—especially the oldest old—live in multigenerational households, often with daughters-in-law and grandchildren present. Sons often are away for employment. Elderly men, nearly all married, are cared for by their wives. Elderly women, the majority widowed, must depend primarily on sons for financial and material support and on sons' wives for personal care, though daughters also provide assistance. Even married women are likely to be cared for by a co-resident daughter-in-law, as husbands do not provide personal care to wives. The quality of care a woman receives is likely to vary with the quality of her relationship with her primary caregiver, her daughter-in-law, as shown in Case 3 (good care) and Case 4 (neglect). Case 5 shows the difficulties of a frail woman with neither a son nor daughter-in-law.

Case 3. Tekela Musungu "Sits and Eats"

Tekela was born in Uganda in 1908. She was baptized in 1924 in the Catholic Church at Mumias, a day's walk from her home, and married the next year to Musungu. "I was still young when I married," she said. "The priest asked, 'How is it such a young woman is marrying such an old man?' " They were married nearly half a century! Musungu died in 1973 and is buried just outside his widow's house in the village of Bukiri.

Tekela saw the world as few women her age have. She was head singer of a dancing group which performed several times for President Kenyatta in Nairobi in the 1960s and 1970s. She was a woman of curiosity and action, known for being "always on the go." "If I were not so old," she told me, "I would come to America with you." I'm sure she would have! She did the next best thing: she called me daughter and told everyone she had been married to a white man who had gone back to America with me when I was a baby! (Her name, Musungu, helps; it means "white person.")[23]

Although she never went to school, Tekela was active in developing a local primary school; her son later became headmaster there. She was a regular attender at Nangina's Catholic Church, taking one and one-half hours to walk there (a walk which took me two and one-half hours). When Nangina Hospital inaugurated its Community Health Worker program in 1976, Tekela (then 68 years old) was one of the first volunteers. In 1985 she led a two-week seminar

Tekela Musungu and a few of her grandchildren.

for CHWs. She was active in the program until 1987, when dizziness and difficulty walking began to keep her at home. She also had to give up attending church, though she regularly received Communion at home from the priest or his catechist.

Tekela gave birth to many children, perhaps as many as eighteen; quite a few died young. In her old age five sons and three daughters were living (Figure 4.5). The two oldest sons lived in a city and paid little attention to their people in Bukiri; they did not even build houses at home. The other three sons had large brick houses in the Musungu homestead. Of these sons, the eldest had two wives, each with her own house. The next son lived with his wife and children in the city of Kisumu 70 miles away, but was building a large retirement house in Bukiri in the early 1990s. The lastborn son worked in Sio Port (in Samia) but his wife (a schoolteacher) and children stayed in a large modern house very

Figure 4.5
Tekela Musungu and Her Caregivers

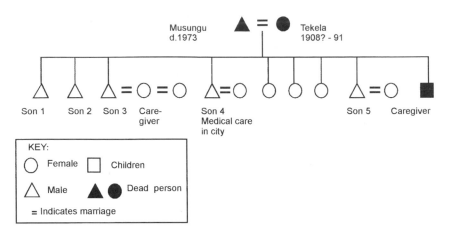

near Tekela's. Many grandchildren lived in these homes and often spent time with their grandmother.

Tekela became increasingly frail in the late 1980s and was blind by 1990. Several times she went to the city of Kisumu for hospitalization, afterwards recuperating in her son's house there. Back home in Bukiri she was well cared for by her daughters-in-law. She had always been especially close to Felesta, elder wife of her son Sirili. Felesta was her main caregiver, though Teresina, the youngest son's wife, also gave much help. Tekela died at home in 1991.

The next case study illustrates conflict between a mother and a daughter-in-law who had never been on good terms. This is not unusual, because mothers-in-law supervise the work of their daughters-in-law and tensions and conflicts are inevitable (Cattell 1996). It is usually daughters-in-law who are caregivers for older women, on behalf of the sons who are responsible for a mother's care. The consequences of such conflict can mean difficulties for the older woman if she becomes frail, requiring personal care and help getting food and water.

Case 4. Lucia Sometimes Waits in Vain

In August 1985, Lucia was around 70 years old. She was a very small woman, short and slender. Lucia's mother, a potter, died before she could teach her daughter how to make pots. When Lucia married, about 1933, she learned potting from her mother-in-law. She herself has taught others, including one daughter-in-law.

Lucia had three children, two sons and a daughter. When she became a widow "many years ago" she earned money for school fees by selling her pots. She educated all three children. In 1985, Lucia was still making pots, though she

Figure 4.6
Lucia and Her Caregivers

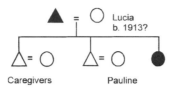

had given up making the huge beer pots—five feet high, taller than their maker and too wide to embrace. It used to take her six days to shape a beer pot and a month to fire it. But she had become too weak to make these giants. Lucia admired my leg muscles, especially my fat calves (*ndumbu*): "I used to have fat *ndumbu* like yours, but look how thin they are now. I cannot walk far any more." For Lucia her problems with walking had serious consequences.

Things had been fine until her older son decided to move his wife and children near his place of work at Nangina, about ten miles from Lucia's home in southern Samia. Lucia had been well cared for by this son's wife. But with her departure Lucia was left with only Pauline, the wife of her second son, a woman with whom she had never gotten along well (Figure 4.6). Pauline's hostility led her to neglect Lucia, who needed help in daily necessities and also in getting clay for potmaking. The food the daughter-in-law provided was often inadequate, though there was enough in the home. Water, carried from a distant stream, and clay, brought from far, were slow in coming. The daughter-in-law even forbade her children to assist their grandmother, thus denying Lucia the help and companionship of grandchildren. Had Lucia's second son been living at home, things would have been different, but he was away most of the year in urban employment. Even the son who worked in Samia could come home only occasionally. So Lucia had to suffer her daughter-in-law's physical neglect and also the social deprivation of being cut off from her grandchildren.

The Caregivers Return: Update from the Field, 1995. I had hoped to see Lucia's older son when I was in Samia for two weeks in June 1995, but I failed because he had been selected to become an administrative chief (a government civil service post) in his home area and had returned there. His former associate in Nangina told me that Lucia is happy to have him back and that she is still making small pots.

In my survey of 200 elderly Samia women, 28 had no living son. Manyuru was one of these 28 women. Although very frail, she lived a marginal existence for many years with help from her extended family. Some frail elderly are even less fortunate than a sonless widow like Manyuru. Some have no family members, or at least, no family member comes to care for them or even, sometimes, to bury them (as happened in one case I heard about from a reliable source).

Figure 4.7
Manyuru and Her Caregivers

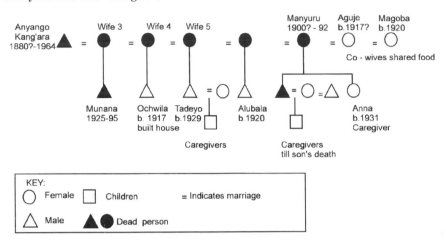

Case 5. Manyuru: A Sonless Widow Struggles to Eat

Elizabeth Manyuru was born about 1900. She was one of the many wives of
Anyango Kang'ara, a colonial chief in Samia. When he died in 1964, Anyango
left 30 widows to be inherited by men of his family. Of her inheritor Manyuru
said scornfully: "Mine was not a real husband. He only did the rituals and left.
All he did was eat my son's inheritance."

Of Manyuru's four children, one son and one daughter lived to adulthood.
After the son's death some years ago, his widow remarried and moved to another
village. She no longer visited or helped Manyuru. That left only daughter Anna
on whom Manyuru could depend, but Anna lived a day's walk away. She came
to see her mother once or twice a year to repair her house and give other help.
Occasionally, she sent a small sum of money. But that was all she could do.

In 1985, Manyuru was living in Bukhulungu village near two younger co-
wives, Aguje and Magoba (Figure 4.7). Each woman had her own house. The
co-wives' big houses were built by their inheritors, Chief Anyango's sons Alu-
bala and Munana. But Manyuru—her only son dead, her "husband" not helping
her—lived in a tiny, tumbled-down house built by Nangina's Community Health
Workers. In the hills surrounding the homes of these three widows lived many
of their husband's sons. Manyuru called these men "my son"—but such sons
did not feel as strong an obligation to care for her as her own son would have.
She also "adopted" me as a daughter and I helped her a little.

Manyuru was a potter in her younger days, and of course a farmer, but in
her later years she was too weak to work. She was thin and bony, partially blind

from cataracts, and could walk only with a walking stick. Her co-wives some-times shared the food they grew and prepared, but on most days Manyuru hob-bled to a stepson's home for a meal. Most often she went to the home of Tadeyo, whose children carried firewood and water to her house. Manyuru was often hungry. "We old people only think about food," she said.

By 1987, blind from cataracts and untreated eye infections, totally unable to walk, she was confined to her house. She continued to receive minimal neces-sities through her extended family, especially from Tadeyo. Another stepson, Ochwila, built Manyuru a new house to replace the decrepit structure in which she had lived for many years. She died in that house one night in 1992, when the thatch roof caught fire. A thatch roof burns and collapses into the house in just a few minutes. Manyuru was unable to crawl out nor could her co-wives (asleep when the fire started) reach the house in time to rescue her. She was buried not far from her house, next to her husband's grave.

Dancing with Her Daughter, Visiting Her Co-Wives: Update from the Field, 1995. While I was in Samia this year, Anyango's son Munana (Figure 4.7) died. The week after the funeral I went to his home to greet "the in-laws" who had come to pay their respects. This was a cheerful occasion, except for the three brothers-in-law, who were terribly stiff and solemn (as in-laws should be). I danced to Zairean music with a woman I did not know. Later she came to see me. She was Manyuru's daughter Anna, whom I had never met. "You really gave me a hot dance!" said she. And we laughed together, we two daughters of Manyuru.

I also visited Aguje and Magoba, Manyuru's co-wives, whom I've inherited as "mothers." Aguje is noticeably frailer than she was two years ago. The two old widows are as close as the fingers of one hand. I couldn't help but wonder how the survivor will get on when one of them dies. Three months after my visit, I got a letter telling me that Aguje has also left us.

FINAL OBSERVATIONS FROM THE FIELD, 1995

In June 1995, I spent two weeks in Samia. New information led to slight revisions of one case study and updates of others. These updates also show how anthropologists do "participant observation."

Every time I go to Samia I make a list of "new things." My previous visit was in 1993. The 1995 list includes many more "modern" houses built of cement blocks or bricks with metal or tile roofs. Some new houses are designed to add future electrical wiring and telephones. As Sokolovsky (Chapter 9) also found in rural Mexico, TV antennas have sprouted like mushrooms. People run them off car batteries, requiring a weekly recharging, so there is also a new local business: battery recharging. What will such innovations mean to social life? Families? Old people? Tekela Musungu, visiting her son in Kisumu, got up from a few minutes of watching TV and told me, "I'll leave this for the young people. They understand such things.'' But will the old people walk away from TV when it's in their own homes?

The Catholic Church's controversy with the saved has become more intense. Before my visit the priest chased all saved people out of the church, an event reported in a Nairobi newspaper. My old friend Maria Ochwila (married to Anyango's son Ochwila, Figure 4.7) told me that she is prepared to go in hand-cuffs if the police arrest her for attending an illegal meeting of the saved people. (Police permits are required for any meeting of more than five people, even in private homes. The saved meet in private homes—without permits.) Civil disobedience! From a woman in her 70s! Really, what's the world coming to? Paulina chased her inheritor away so she could operate her family and businesses her way. The old widows Anjelina, Anna and Elizabeth said ''Praise the Lord!'' and ''No'' to widow inheritance. Paulina was ready to go to the women's conference in Beijing, Maria was ready to go to jail. Old people are old-fashioned? Behind the times?

Younger women are also participating in this revolution, if that is what it is. For example, Florence's husband died in December 1994. She was left with eight children to raise on her own. Can she do it? Florence is a hardworking farmer who raises much of her own food and also owns several cows her brothers gave her. She is employed and thus has a regular but modest source of cash income. She also has moral and spiritual support: she is saved. And she is a daughter-in-law and neighbor of Maria Ochwila, the one ready for the handcuffs. Florence and Maria are very close. Florence and I had a few moments to ourselves as we stood in the cool shadow of a cashew tree. I asked her about widow inheritance. ''I just chase the brothers-in-law away,'' she said. ''Men would just eat me. They know I have a job and that is their aim. They would come and eat and contribute nothing.''

''Is widow inheritance a good thing?'' I asked Pamela Silingi (age 71) in June 1995. ''It is useless, completely useless!'' was her immediate reply. When her husband died three years ago he left three widows. The older wife was inherited symbolically by a grandson, the younger was inherited by a son of the husband's brother. She herself refused to be inherited. ''But I have found that those who were inherited are just the same as me who was not inherited,'' said Silingi. ''We are all working hard and all surviving. So inheritance is useless.''

African widows on the march? Resistance—or revolution? Down with the patriarchy?

NOTES

1. For the significance of gender in old age, see Cattell (1992a, 1995); Rix (1991); Rossi (1985); Rubinstein (1990); Sennott-Miller (1989); World Bank (1994).

2. For more on the demographics of aging, see Albert and Cattell (1994); Kinsella (1988, 1990, 1992b); Myers (1990, 1992); Okojie (1988); U.S. Bureau of the Census (1991).

3. For further examples of variations in experiences of widowhood, see Drèze (1990); Lopata (1987a); Potash (1986b).

4. Data from Kinsella (1990); Okojie (1988); U.S. Bureau of the Census (1991).

5. For further details, see Cattell (1992a); Potash (1986b); Udvardy and Cattell (1992a, 1992b).

6. Gray (1964) suggests that both the levirate and widow inheritance might better be called "husband succession."

7. See Abu 1983; Coplan 1987; Etienne 1983; Goebel and Epprecht 1995; Case 1 this chapter.

8. In duolineal descent systems, people are members of two lineages at once, their mother's and their father's.

9. In this discussion older women are taken as proxies for widows, since most data on women's work do not indicate marital status. This is reasonable given that most older women are, in fact, widows.

10. I am deeply grateful for the invaluable help over the past decade of my Abaluyia field assistants, especially John Barasa "JB" Owiti from Samia, who has been with me throughout, and Frankline Mahaga (see note 19). Thanks also to the Medical Mission Sisters and Holy Family Hospital (Nangina), Nangina Girls Primary School, and Samia officials, among others; to the University of Nairobi's Institute of African Studies, where I was a Research Associate, 1984–1985; and to my late husband Bob Moss, who helped in countless ways. Above all, *mutio muno* to the many people of Samia and Bunyala who have allowed me to share their lives. The research was partially funded by the National Science Foundation (grant BNS8306802), the Wenner-Gren Foundation (grant 4506), and Bryn Mawr College (Frederica de Laguna Fund grant). I am grateful to Margaret A. McDowell of the Department of Geographical and Environmental Sciences, University of Natal-Durban, for redrawing Figures 4.2 through 4.7.

11. *Banyala* and *Basamia* are the people, *Bunyala* and *Busamia* are the places. In English the prefixes *Ba-* (indicating people) and *Bu-* (indicating place) are dropped for *-samia* and retained for *-nyala*. Don't ask why. That's just the way it is.

12. These figures are from the 1989 Kenya population censuses (Kenya 1994).

13. For details see Cattell (1989a, 1989b); Seitz (1978); Soper (1986).

14. Infectious diseases affect everyone. Malaria and related anemia are endemic. AIDS is a rapidly growing problem. Very little research has been done on the impacts of marriage patterns and changes in those patterns on the spread of AIDS and other STDs (Carael 1994). One possible effect of AIDS might be male reluctance to inherit widows. In 1995, a Samia man with a recently inherited wife told me: "At first men just feared [to inherit a woman] especially if the husband died a long slow death and got very thin. But now AIDS is just taken as normal." Whether he is right is open for investigation.

15. The main criterion of old age for men is loss of physical strength, which is more open to interpretation, hence people say, "Women grow old sooner than men."

16. The saved and widow inheritance are both discussed at length in Cattell (1992b).

17. She says: "Is there any child in this world who takes the blanket shared by his father and mother and shares that blanket with his mother?" The referent for her metaphor of incest is the fact that a widow can be inherited by the son of a co-wife, who is also her son in Samia kinship.

18. See Cattell (1989a); Khasiani (1985); Kilbride (1990); Kilbride and Kilbride (1990, 1992).

19. I thank Frankline Teresa Mahaga for her help with this case study, including

interviews with her grandmothers; and her extended family for welcoming me into their homes in Port Victoria and Nairobi.

20. Unlike most women her age, Paulina attended school for a few years. She was—and is—a great believer in education as the key to getting ahead in life.

21. For fuller discussion of the ideal of respect and examples of its behavioral expressions, see Cattell (1989b, 1990, 1993, 1994, 1997). Thomas (1992) has an interesting analysis of the concept of respect among Meru people in central Kenya.

22. Education is not free. School fees are a heavy financial burden for most families. Many children who complete eighth grade cannot attend secondary school because of the expense.

23. In April 1991, my Kenyan mother, Tekela Musungu, died in Kenya and my ''real'' mother, Anna Gleaton, died in America. Even to a skeptic like me it seems a strange coincidence.

CHAPTER 5

Culture and the Meaning of a Good Old Age

Christine L. Fry, Jeanette Dickerson-Putman, Patricia Draper, Charlotte Ikels, Jennie Keith, Anthony P. Glascock and Henry C. Harpending

For centuries humans have quested for a good old age. In fact, that is what everybody would like. Yet when we connect "good" with "old age," conceptually something is a little off. Certainly "good" and "old" fall together quite reasonably when the reference is wine, furniture, automobiles or even cheese. When humans are involved, however, good and old are less comfortably combined. Our experience with old people who are frail and experiencing difficulties suggests that "a good old age" might be an oxymoron.

On the other hand, a good old age is not as flagrantly false as is the fountain of youth. Nowhere on earth do people remain eternally young. No drug has yet been discovered to halt aging or even to slow it down, much less to bring about its reversal. Nevertheless, the fountain of youth is enshrined in the myth of Shangri-La. In this exotic place, a select few who choose the contemplative life and ingest a mild narcotic may live for centuries in the isolation of the high Himalayas (see introduction to Part VI). Explorers have supposedly discovered a few longevous populations, but all have since been found wanting.

Since there really is no Shangri-La, then everyone experiences aging and will encounter old age. In this chapter, we explore culture and the meaning of a good old age in seven different communities around the world. Our intent is to link what constitutes a good and a difficult old age to the context in which they are experienced. First, we describe the project which led us to investigate aging in Africa, Europe, North America and Asia. Second, we look at the meanings of a good old age in specific cultural contexts and draw our conclusions.

PROJECT AGE

Project AGE is a cross-cultural research project which takes a team approach to cross-cultural data collection and analysis (see Keith, Fry, Glascock, Ikels, Dickerson-Putman, Harpending and Draper 1994 for a detailed account). As its major goal, the project sought to investigate, through comparable field studies, how different kinds of communities shape the experience of aging and pathways to well-being for their older members (see Table 5.1). In this team project, the codirectors (Fry and Keith) formulated and coordinated the research design. Principal investigators worked in specific communities around the world, adapting that research design in culturally sensitive ways to the local cultures.[1] In 1982 the project began in North America and Hong Kong. By 1986, a second phase of data collection was initiated in Ireland (also see Chapter 18) and in Botswana. Fieldwork was completed and data analysis began in 1988.

Our units of analysis are communities and neighborhoods. Seven research sites were selected on the basis of cultural and structural diversity across these settings. Table 5.1 outlines the differences across the seven communities. They are not intended to be representative of the respective nations. They are, however, strongly influenced by national-level policies and national social structure. Economies range from an international port of trade (Hong Kong) to cattle herding (Herero) and a combination of foraging and farming in a desert habitat (Ju/'hoansi; also see Chapter 2). They represent different settlement patterns with urban apartments and public housing at one extreme and cattle posts or small scattered villages around permanent water holes at the other. Change is ubiquitous, but different in each community. This varies from near instantaneous response to world markets, to longer-term adjustments to suburbanization, out-migration, deindustrialization, and to European colonization.

METHODOLOGY

Because Project AGE involves a cross-cultural research design, it required multiple methods. In each community, participant observation was a continuous activity throughout the project, informing and framing the more targeted data collection strategies. A structured interview was an important component of our research to systematically obtain information on the life course, individual residential and work histories, kinship networks, health status and well-being. A major part of this interview was designed to investigate perceptions of the course of adulthood and changing concerns associated with aging. People were asked to study cards describing realistic people who were of different ages. In each community, somewhat different, community-specific characteristics were used to describe these "persona." Their task was then to place the realistic people

Table 5.1
Project AGE: Communities and Characteristics

African Sites
Ju/'hoansi & Herero

POPULATION: Low & Scattered
Ju/'hoansi- 780 People
Herero - 5000 + with seasonal
variation

ECONOMY: Subsistence - No wage
Labor - Minimal technology
Ju/'hoansi - Foraging & Gardening with
craft work & herding for Herero
Herero - Pastoralism (Cattle &
Small Animals)

KINSHIP: Familial division of labor
Ju/'hoansi - Bilateral Kindreds &
neolocal residence
Herero - Matrilineal lineages
corporate ownership of cattle

STATE: minimal services and
penetration in the Kalahari
Desert

Irish Sites
Clifden & Blessington

POPULATION: Moderate & Nucleated
Clifden - 805 Town & 852 Townlands
Blessington - 1322 Town & 678 Townlands

ECONOMY: Wage Labor
Technologically Intensive
Clifden - Farming, Fishing
Shopkeeping & Tourism -
19% Unemployment
Blessington - Service, Light
Industry, Commuting to Dublin
7% Unemployment

KINSHIP: Bilateral Kindreds &
neolocal residence
Kin usually geographically
proximate, but Clifden high
emigration.

STATE: Welfare State - dominates
local economies - state services
for older people

U.S. Sites
Momence & Swarthmore

POPULATION: Moderate & Nucleated
Momence - 3400 Town & 4000 Hinterland
Swarthmore - 5950 Town

ECONOMY: Wage Labor - Intensive Technology
Momence - Agribusiness;
Light Industry, Service &
Commuting to Chicago
10% Unemployment
Swarthmore - Service,
Commuting to Philadelphia

KINSHIP: Bilateral Kindreds &
Neolocal Residence
Momence - kin proximate
Swarthmore - kin dispersed

STATE: Welfare State - dominates
local economies - state services
for older people

Asian Site
Hong Kong

POPULATION: High & Nucleated
Hong Kong - 5,000,000
Very Dense

ECONOMY: Wage Labor - Intensive
Technology - Industrial
International Port of
Trade

KINSHIP: Patrilineal Stem
Family; Neolocal Residence;
Extended households for the
old

STATE: - a Colony of the U.K.
Minimal state services for
older people - primarily health
services - state policies dominate
the local economy as well as
international trade

(social personae) into piles representing different age groups or life stages.[2] Once the sorting task was complete, we then proceeded to use the groupings, defined in the respondent's own terms, to ask questions about each life stage—names of life stage, best things, hardest things, transitions between, and chronological age. In total, between 105 and 210 individuals were interviewed in each community (Ju/'hoansi 105, Herero 170, Clifden 130, Blessington 170, Momence 210, Swarthmore 202, Hong Kong 204).

In our interview, when we focused on the last age group or any age group the respondent had indicated was older (if they had more than one "old age" group), we asked very targeted questions relating to the quality of life of older people. First, we asked each person to think of a real individual living in his or her community who would be in that older age group, and who he or she thought was doing very well for their age. We then recorded information about that individual—age, gender, relationship, last time seen, and most importantly, why they were viewed as doing well. Secondly, we repeated the question, except we wanted an example of an individual who was experiencing difficulties in the same age group. In Africa, the United States and Hong Kong, the responses to our questions are based on older people known to our respondents. In Ireland the questions were changed to "What is good in old age?" and "What is difficult in old age?" The rural Irish were found to be particularly sensitive to being questioned about neighbors. This caused us to alter the questioning here to avoid compromising the people being interviewed in the two Irish communities.

WHAT MAKES FOR A GOOD OLD AGE?

Across our seven sites, there is consistency in the factors that can produce either a good or a difficult old age. Four major issues were mentioned by our respondents as they talked about older people who were experiencing a good or difficult old age, or about the positive and negative aspects of old age: (1) Physical Health and Functioning; (2) Material Security; (3) Family; and (4) Sociality. Consistency, however, does not mean uniformity. Although these concerns were mentioned in each site, we find major differences in the importance and implications of each issue for old age as well as in the specific ways it is manifested. These are clearly linked to the social, economic and political context of each community.

In the sections that follow, we will consider each of the issues, by first hearing what respondents from each site told us about that factor as it influenced either a good or difficult old age. Next, we will examine their relative importance by considering the frequency by which these factors were mentioned as a reason for individuals doing well or poorly. Finally, we will discuss the reasons for similarities and differences in terms of the cultural contexts in which our respondents live.[3]

PHYSICAL HEALTH AND FUNCTIONING

Rather obvious components of successful aging are health and the physical ability to function as a normal adult. Despite global variation in genetics and lifestyles, in general, aging bodies have more difficulties than young in responding to physical insults and demands. Indeed, respondents at all sites discussed health and functionality as a factor in promoting both a good and a difficult old age (see Figure 5.1).

Physical Factors as Defining a Good Old Age. On the positive side, health and functionality mean having physical capacity to do things. Successful agers are people who have energy, vitality and interest in activities. For Ju/'hoansi and Herero, good physical health means being able to work, being able to see and to be strong.

> If he/she still has eyesight and can get food, pick berries, that is good.
>
> Ju/'hoansi

> He has strength, cattle, no illness, sour milk, and meat.
>
> Herero

In Ireland, health is seen as declining with age and limiting what activities one can accomplish.

> Health. Young is the good life. Takes a lot out of your health in your old age.
>
> Clifden

> If you were healthy it would good. You could do what you want.
>
> Blessington

Momence and Swarthmore respondents talked about people who were vigorous and physically able to do many things.

> Still does housework, gardens and yard work. Cans, freezes. No health problems.
>
> Momence

> Vigorous, still doing volunteer work. She walks, she looks great, she seems younger than she was when working.
>
> Swarthmore

People in Hong Kong also saw good physical health as allowing older individuals to do the things they had always done.

> Not physically incapacitated, lots of energy, movement and eating is almost the same as the ordinary young people.
>
> Hong Kong

Figure 5.1
Physical Factors in Defining a Good Old Age

PHYSICAL HEALTH
DEFINING A GOOD OLD AGE

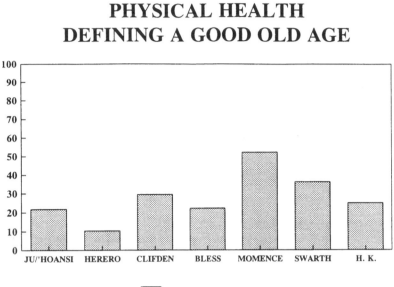

PERCENT OF CASES

PHYSICAL DIFFICULTIES
DEFINING A POOR OLD AGE

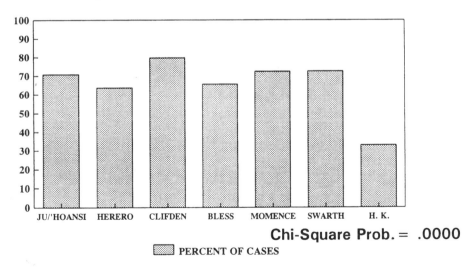

Chi-Square Prob. = .0000

PERCENT OF CASES

Physical Factors as Promoting a Difficult Old Age. Physical decline means loss of mobility, frailty and signals a deteriorating quality of life. Full adult status is threatened since one can no longer do what adults usually do in ordinary living. The Ju/'hoansi and Herero tell us that illness, blindness and not being able to walk seriously compromise life because one can no longer work and must just sit.

> Not having the ability to walk and if he/she can't see.
>
> > Ju/'hoansi

> He does nothing, just sits around.
>
> > Herero

> She can't fetch water, collect wood, go to village meetings, or build a house.
>
> > Herero

In Clifden and Blessington, frailty and not being able to get around and do things signal a social death. When one becomes severely disabled, then the support of others is needed.

> Can be just like being dead if can't get around.
>
> > Clifden

> If not able to walk, or had to go to loo (toilet) and couldn't.
>
> > Clifden

> You can't do things for yourself. Someone has to do things for me.
>
> > Blessington

In the U.S. sites, references are to mental as well as physical decline.

> She's very crippled up and can't get around on her own and her mind is reverting back to childhood.
>
> > Momence

> Mind totally gone—no awareness of present—needs full-time care of nurse.
>
> > Swarthmore

Hong Kong Chinese see age and illness as linked and as very inconvenient.

> Old, sick, her functioning has deteriorated. She is going to die. She is very clumsy.
>
> > Hong Kong

Clearly, good health and functioning are an ingredient for successful aging while illness and physical losses promote difficulties. In Figure 5.1 it is apparent that physical difficulties are a major defining feature of a poor old age. With the exception of Hong Kong, over 60 percent of our cases in each site mentioned health and functionality in giving a reason for a difficult experience of aging.[4] This is *the* primary reason for a negative old age in these six sites. On the other hand, physical issues are much more modestly represented in definitions of a positive old age. Only in the U.S. sites do we find 30 percent or more of our cases discussing the health status of individuals they see as having a good old age.

To better understand how different social and cultural contexts shape this linkage between health and successful aging, we must turn to the settings in which people live their lives. If deteriorating health can be a threat to adult status, then what tasks must most adults be able to do reasonably well in the context in which they are living? How serious are the consequences of not being able to do that task? What supports are available to compensate for physical inability to carry it out?

The most significant contrasts are between the African sites and those in industrial nations. For Ju/'hoansi and Herero men and women, most of the tasks of daily living require significant stamina (Glascock 1994). With the nearest market town a two-day motor vehicle drive away, food (meat and milk) must be obtained from cattle, in gardens or foraged from the bush (hunting and gathering). In the absence of electricity, gas service or plumbing, firewood and water must be hauled for warmth and cooking. In the dry season, Herero men must lift water by buckets just to keep their herd alive. To visit a relative, they must be prepared to walk several kilometers or ride a donkey there. Roads are dirt tracks and traffic is infrequent and unpredictable. Physical incapacity not only erodes adult status, but it threatens survival itself. In this setting, there is little to compensate for disabilities other than direct personal services supplied by family members. As Rosenberg showed in Chapter 2, when a person experiences limitations on strength and mobility, the relatives, especially children and grandchildren, bring food, water and fuel. Most of the Ju/'hoansi and Herero statements about physical health also referenced food.

On the other hand, people in industrialized nations experience their lives in an abundance of technology and labor-saving devices. Food and commodities are purchased in the marketplace. In the United States, central heating, plumbing and energy services (electricity and gas), are standard features of nearly every dwelling. Daily life in these contexts does not require great stamina and strength, particularly in old age. Adults are expected to work (older people usually are retired), do their marketing and maintain their dwellings (cooking, cleaning and, if necessary, yard work). When physical limitations make those tasks difficult, relatives and friends may offer help or a cleaning or lawn service may be hired. Even when sight, hearing, walking or some basic biological function is threatened, there are compensations in the form of medicine and prostheses (glasses, hearing aids, wheelchairs). Adult status may be tarnished, but people can live a long time with one and even more chronic disabilities.

MATERIAL SECURITY

Wealth along with health set a firm foundation for old age. Indeed, our studies of well-being in old age indicate health and material wealth are the most prominent dimensions of a good old age. In cross-cultural research, however, wealth is far too restrictive a concept to use comparatively. Wealth implies ownership of money and access to resources and commodities. Many peoples of the world, including the Ju/'hoansi, have worked out lifeways that are not based on the accumulation of wealth. Yet the Ju/'hoansi are concerned about certain material things and the comforts they can bring. Consequently, we use a broader construct of "material security" in comparing the seven Project AGE sites. More inclusively, material security refers to subsistence and the assurance that food is available. It also means the satisfaction of basic physical requirements such as shelter, warmth and protection against environmental insults (Figure 5.2).

Material Security Promoting a Good Old Age. Because the economies of each of our sites are quite different, what people perceive as constituting material security is variable. In our African sites, security is very directly defined as food. Ju/'hoansi mention bush food, government-provisioned mealie meal and cattle. Cows, smaller livestock and kin are the Herero's safety net.

> If the government helps the old person and there is bush food, the old person has some life.
>
> Ju/'hoansi

> She has one hundred cattle, four daughters, three sons, and eats a lot of food.
>
> Herero

In Ireland the welfare state shores up security in old age through pensions and other benefits (see Chapter 18).

> Getting the pension and other benefits is really the best thing.
>
> Clifden

> Well looked after by government.
>
> Blessington

Our respondents in the United States see pensions, retirement benefits, money and material accumulation as a material basis for a good old age.

> Retired, getting good benefits, worked for all of this, has garden tended, three cars, two buildings, has worked hard.
>
> Momence

> Always going to bank and putting money in—has good business.
>
> Swarthmore

Figure 5.2
Material Factors in Defining a Good Old Age

MATERIAL SECURITY
DEFINING A GOOD OLD AGE

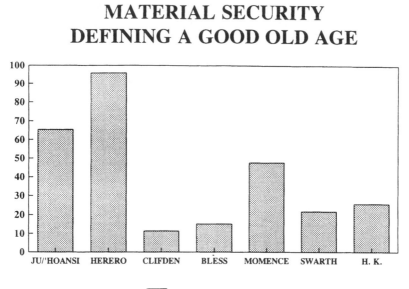

PERCENT OF CASES

MATERIAL DIFFICULTIES
DEFINING A POOR OLD AGE

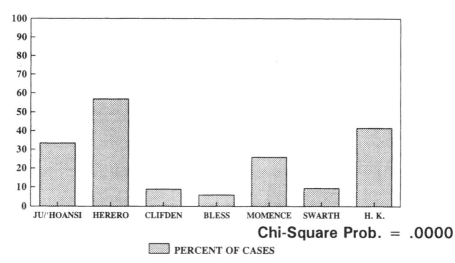

Chi-Square Prob. = .0000

PERCENT OF CASES

Hong Kong respondents are aware of the material effects of social stratification and work.

> All our friends are in the older groups. All are well off. I do not know who is financially not well off, unless my maid.
>
> Hong Kong

Material Issues Promoting a Difficult Old Age. Material difficulties can ultimately result in hunger and starvation. Ju/'hoansi and Herero are very direct in seeing the results of resource depletion.

> Hunger, thirst, cold.
>
> Ju/'hoansi

> All resources used up, hunger.
>
> Herero

In Ireland and the United States the concern is less with food, but is focused on money and maintaining an income once one has retired. In both countries this is through government pensions, Social Security or private pensions and savings.

> If you hadn't money to be warm and fed.
>
> Clifden

> Not having enough money to manage on their own.
>
> Blessington

> Not old enough to draw Social Security and having trouble keeping work, in real trouble.
>
> Momence

Likewise in Hong Kong, material difficulties mean the lack of money. Unlike Ireland and the United States, there is no state-funded old age pension plan. Income is maintained through continuity in work, reliance on children to provide, and if these fail, government welfare.

> Their posterity are grown up, but are unable to make a sufficient living. Therefore, their posterity cannot support them. They have to depend on the assistance given by the home for the aged and the government.
>
> Hong Kong

Material security is a rather obvious basis for a good quality of life. However, as we see in Figure 5.2, it is more variable across our sites than was physical health as a component of a good old age. Clearly, for the Herero and Ju/'hoansi, material security is *the* primary definition of a good old age. In our industrialized sites, we see considerably less emphasis on material issues. Momence is an exception, where almost 50 percent of the older people cited as aging well were doing well for material reasons. In comparison with predominantly middle-class, professional Swarthmore, Momence is far less affluent. Jobs are primarily blue collar and income is more modest. According to the U.S. Census, in 1989 the median income in Momence was around $25,000 with nearly 40 percent of the households reporting less than $20,000. Because poverty is a very real possibility, adequate finances are the basis for a good old age. For older people seen as aging well, incomes are stabilized through Social Security and Medicare and expenditures for mortgages and children are much reduced. Consequently, old age can be more financially secure than earlier life stages which were much more prone to uncertainties in getting and keeping blue collar jobs. Poverty is a very real threat when one is unemployed or underemployed.

In undermining old age, material difficulties are most salient among the Herero, Ju/'hoansi, in Hong Kong and Momence. In these four sites, material reasons are the second most prevalent reason given for a problematic old age. Given the Irish Welfare System and the fact that Irish respondents were discussing a generalized life state and not a real person, we would not expect financial concerns to dominate. Also, in more affluent Swarthmore, older people experiencing difficult old ages because of financial problems are comparatively rare.

FAMILY AND KINSHIP

An important part of everyone's safety net is the people they live with, especially family. As with economies, kinship in the seven sites of Project AGE is also variable. The Herero are our only people to have lineages.[5] Our analysis of Herero herds has revealed that Herero lineages are in all probability matrilineal descent groups in transition to patrilineages. Men are stewards to the herds owned mostly by their sisters and mothers. The Ju/'hoansi kinship system links nuclear families and individuals to a bilateral network of relatives, called a kindred.[6] Under foraging conditions kindreds were very effective in moving people to scarce resources through extended visits among these kin. In Ireland and the United States, bilateral descent and kindreds are also the norm. Here mobility is high, but the economic role of kindreds is reduced. Hong Kong Chinese, as in China, are noted for the ideal of a patrilineal stem family (see Chapter 24). In this type of family parents cultivate one son who upon marriage will continue to reside with his father and mother, manage a common household and eventually be the principal heir. A filial son and his wife (his parent's daughter-in-law) are expected to look after and provide for the senior generation.

Families as Promoting a Good Old Age. Clearly, families contribute to a good old age. What they contribute, however, differs significantly according to the roles they play in people's lives. Among the Ju/'hoansi and Herero, families are essential in physical and material support.

> God helps that person and the children of that person help him/her.
>
> Ju/'hoansi

> She can't milk, fetch water, cook food, fetch firewood. She just waits for her children to do those things.
>
> Herero

In Ireland and the United States, family members play less central roles in providing economic and physical support of their older members. Families in these societies are companions, confidants and people who can be trusted. Home is where intimacy is permitted and kin are enjoyed for their personal growth and individuality.

> More time for family—own grown up and gone can concentrate on individuals.
>
> Clifden

> Having grandchildren around you.
>
> Blessington

> She went through a loss and is holding up fairly well—has lots of grandchildren to keep her busy.
>
> Momence

> Because he really enjoys his grandchildren and gets to see them and enjoys them.
>
> Swarthmore

In Hong Kong filial children live with parents and look after their needs. Under these circumstances, an ideal family is based on harmony and respect.

> Daughter-in-law shows filial piety to her and she helps in performing housework. Everyone puts forth his strength in the family.
>
> Hong Kong

Families as Promoting a Difficult Old Age. If families provide for a good old age, they can also trigger difficulties. Our respondents tell us problematic aging is mostly found in the absence of a family or the fact that family members do not perform their roles. In our African sites, the absence of or abandonment by children has profound implications for survival.

> If no child or no relatives feed her/him.
>
> Ju/'hoansi

> No daughters, no wife, no cattle.
>
> Herero

In the United States and Ireland, family difficulties stem from loss of spouses and difficulties with children. Either social relationships are strained or children are not successfully launched into adulthood and return home.

> If your family doesn't want you.
>
> Blessington

> Kids all moved back home and grandchildren too. He shouldn't have to have children home. No privacy. He should be man of house and not to have kids home.
>
> Momence

> His wife died and he was very close to her, it shattered him.
>
> Swarthmore

For Hong Kong Chinese it is the failure to bear a son that foreshadows a difficult time in old age. With no daughter-in-law, there will be no one to look after an older person. Also, children who are not filial make for a trying old age.

> Her children are not filial to her. Her children cannot get along with her. For example, when it rains, she tells her son to carry an umbrella, but her son rebukes her and says he does not like to carry an umbrella.
>
> Hong Kong

In comparing the prevalence of family issues in promoting either a good or difficult old age, from Figure 5.3, it is apparent that respondents in Hong Kong and the Ju/'hoansi mention it the most. In Hong Kong, family issues are mentioned the most frequently for both good and difficult aging. The Ju/'hoansi mention family nearly as often as material security issues for good aging and physical problems for poor aging. Herero see family problems characterizing about 30 percent of the people seen as enduring a poor old age, while our respondents in Blessington see family as promoting positive aging in 24 percent of the cases.

Why do Ju/'hoansi, Hong Kong and, to a lesser extent, Herero respondents see family issues as central to aging well? Conversely, why are families not as dominant in our answers from Ireland and the United States? Everyone has kin, but lives in highly variable families. Culturally, we define who are kin and what relationships we expect to have with them. The Ju/'hoansi see their kin as a flexible family that has figured out how to live and work together. Family members work jointly and share with each other. In a different way, Herero lineages link generations. Cattle ownership ties fathers, sons, wives, mothers, daughters into economic interdependence. Herero relatives are expected to work for each other and especially the senior generation. Under very different circumstances in Hong Kong, the patrilineal stem families have adapted to an urban industrial

Figure 5.3
Family Factors as Defining a Good Old Age

FAMILY
DEFINING A GOOD OLD AGE

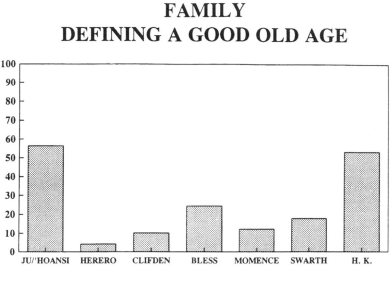

PERCENT OF CASES

FAMILY DIFFICULTIES
DEFINING A POOR OLD AGE

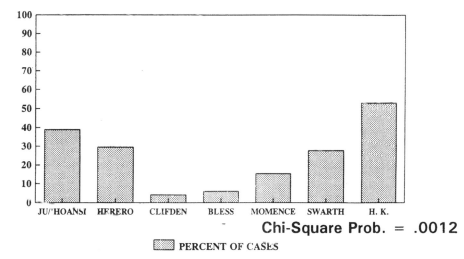

Chi-Square Prob. = .0012

PERCENT OF CASES

economy. Parents invest in their children's futures through education. If children's prospects are improved and they are successful, then the chances of a comfortable old age are increased. A son is expected to be filial and, with the help of his wife, to meet the needs of aging parents.

In the United States and Ireland, family members do not usually work with and for each other. Extended, multiple-generation families do not typically share living quarters, but live in autonomous households. Although family members may support each other economically, they do not and are not expected to do so on a long-term basis. Relatives are not co-workers contributing to and relying on a common "family fund." Instead, relatives are important people for their personalities, sociality and common origins. Kin are valued for their trust and the intimacy possible within the family (Fry 1994). Thus, in Swarthmore, Momence, Blessington and Clifden we find that families play different roles in the lives of older people as compared to Botswana or Hong Kong. Consequently, when a frail elder is in need of caregiving, a family crisis arises. Schedules, jobs, finances and living arrangements must be renegotiated.

SOCIALITY

Physical health, material security and family relationships can be seen as a three-legged stool upon which successful aging is assured. Remove one leg and it all falls down. Our respondents in Ireland, the United States and Hong Kong informed us of another leg to the stool which we identify as "sociality." The sources and content of sociality are very different within each site.[7] Yet in Figure 5.4, it is apparent that sociality is a major reason for aging well in Clifden, Blessington and Swarthmore, and a near second for Momence (after physical health) and for Hong Kong (after family). In our African sites, sociality as a reason for a good old age is almost never mentioned. Sociality refers to qualities which facilitate interaction between an ego and an alter. A very important component of sociality involves affect. Factors such as sentiments, emotion, mood factors and perceptions of qualities that make a social relationship enjoyable or difficult are at the core of sociality. As with the other three factors, sociality is associated with both successful and difficult aging.

Sociality as a Quality of a Good Old Age. What qualities are socially positive? In Ireland responses to our questions about what is good about old age included contentment, peace, relaxation, toleration, reflection and the freedom to do what you want to do as the prevalent themes. Our Irish respondents are talking about old age as a life stage and not referring to real persons, as in the other sites. Consequently, the qualities mentioned are referring to generalized states older people normatively can look forward to that make this time of life attractive.

Able to look back at your successes, no longer anxious about future.

Clifden

Figure 5.4
Sociality Factors in Defining a Good Old Age

SOCIALITY
DEFINING A GOOD OLD AGE

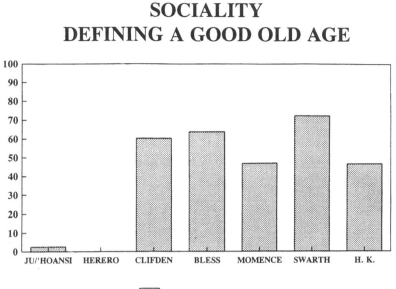

PERCENT OF CASES

SOCIALITY
DEFINING A POOR OLD AGE

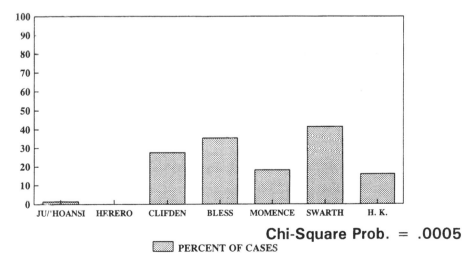

Chi-Square Prob. = .0005

PERCENT OF CASES

Contentment—You're not worried about living and not concerned about dying.

Blessington

Having leisure time and being able to look back on a fruitful life with satisfaction.

Blessington

In the United States and Hong Kong, our respondents told us about real people. Both in Momence and Swarthmore the dominant theme is being "active." Active implies social involvement, visibility and vitality. Along with being active, respondents talked about pleasant personalities, a concern for others and the freedom to do what they want.

Always on the go, never sits around, doesn't let self whither up.

Momence

She's such a wonderful woman, open, vital. She's such fun to be with.

Swarthmore

She finds things to do and is not preoccupied with herself.

Swarthmore

Our Hong Kong respondents told us a different story. Here the themes focused on open-mindedness, toleration of others, not imposing one's opinion on others and not being too nagging. In multiple-generation households toleration is advantageous.

Not too nagging (annoying). Loves her grandchildren. She does not express much opinion of young people. Maybe this is good.

Hong Kong

Sociality as Characteristic of a Difficult Old Age. Sociality has a negative component as well. In Ireland, loneliness and bitterness are potential social downsides of old age.

Become cranky.

Clifden

Loneliness, especially at night.

Blessington

For the real people who are having an affectively difficult old age in the United States, they are inactive, self-centered, disturbed and have bad dispositions and are complainers. They are difficult people who let others know about it.

Not getting out and feeling sorry for self.

Momence

Outspoken and people don't agree with his views.

Momence

She doesn't even go to vote because she's not up to it. She stopped driving. She stays at home and watches TV.

Swarthmore

The opposite of open-minded is to be a nag. In Hong Kong, people also negatively referenced not knowing how to be a human being. This means being unable to overcome narrow personal interests and take responsibility for others (Ikels 1989).

Don't know how to be a human being.

Hong Kong

Nagging.

Hong Kong

The most striking feature in Figure 5.4 is the observation that social qualities are nearly absent from the African sites while quite prominent for Ireland, United States and Hong Kong. Does this mean that Ju/'hoansi and Herero hide their emotions and social issues in evaluating others? Certainly, the biography of Nisa, a Ju/'hoansi woman (Shostak 1981), and Chapter 2 in this volume are strong evidence to the contrary. The reason people in more complex societies use socially affective criteria in explaining how a person is doing in old age is because of societal scale and the relaxed constraints of kinship. In a small-scale society, the social world is very different. Life is lived in a public arena and is dominated by kin. There is comparatively little social and economic life beyond families. In these small-scale and subsistence-based societies, temperamental variations (good and bad) are well-known, but are not highly significant. Given the structural nature of society, people have to make a go of their relations with kin. Kin may be pleasant and cooperative or just downright mean. The realities of kin-based cooperation outweigh temperament. Old Ju/'hoansi and Herero get the same kind of treatment, despite their interpersonal style, unless they are too far away from an accepted norm. Older, even incapacitated Ju/'hoansi effectively use complaining to remind others that they are still here and to mobilize kin to meet their immediate needs (Chapter 2 this volume). Yet not one Ju/'hoansi respondent in our sample complained about the complainer. Instead they were sympathetic and pointed out the cause and consequences of the difficulty.

In comparison, the lives of people in complex societies are less dominated by kin. The social world beyond kinship is characterized by a tremendous variety of organizations, institutions and social roles. In fact, the majority of people in one's social world are not relatives. The economic role a family plays in people's lives is diminished. Kinship, especially beyond the household, is less restrictive.

Families see their relatives as persons with personalities to be enjoyed, tolerated or avoided. Relatives and acquaintances don't have to put up with one's eccentricities, no matter what. Consequently, people in these more complex societies encounter situations in which personal qualities of temperament, style, affect or sentiment figure more prominently in defining interpersonal relationships. Thus, respondents in Ireland and the United States told us about the social qualities that made an older person attractive or trying.

Hong Kong, however, demands special comment. Here certain kin are important economically, especially the stem families. Sons not chosen to live with their parents form their own nuclear families. Daughters join their husbands' families. Within the stem family it can be difficult to maintain harmonious relationships under crowded living conditions and multigenerational households. Sociality is fostered through open-mindedness, and tolerance makes life more pleasant. Pushing one's own interests at the expense of others and nagging make domestic life more difficult.

VARIATIONS ON A GOOD OLD AGE

Have we found an answer? Is a good old age possible? If it is, what is it? Good and old are not by definition an oxymoron. In each Project AGE site, individuals were able to point out people who were having a pretty good time in their senior years. Yes, we have found answers, but not a singular solution.

Africa. For the Ju/'hoansi the most important ingredient is food, material security, especially followed by kin who work together and have the physical strength to provide for each other. Threatening this good old age is declining strength and illness which, when combined with a lack of or an uncooperative family, results in hunger and starvation. Herero also find their answer in material security—cattle. Inability to work compromises continued care of cattle which results in fewer cows, milk, goats and a difficult time in old age.

Ireland. Old age is good, since it is a time of contentment, reduced responsibility and freedom to do what you want with good health and government pensions. The biggest threats are declining health, potential loneliness and needing someone to look after you.

United States. Being vital, active and involved with others are the signs of a good old age. Good health and comfortable pensions do not hurt either. Health problems can erode success in one's elder years, bringing a social withdrawal and a more self-centered old age.

Hong Kong. Family and social qualities which show tolerance and open-mindedness are the most important for a comfortable old age. Families provide for the material necessities of life. Threats come from difficulties within the family which result in material compromises.

Diversity in the meaning of goodness in aging is exactly what we should anticipate from disparate cultural contexts. We now return to the contexts in which old age is experienced to interpret their significance for our understanding of aging. Although Project AGE sites are located in vastly different culture areas with major differences in economics, political integration and kinship, we find systematic variation in the scale of the society in which each community is located. Hong Kong is clearly the greatest in scale followed by Swarthmore, Momence, Blessington, Clifden, Herero and finally Ju/'hoansi at the smallest in scale.

Scale is not to be confused with modernization (see Part III). Increases in scale see community size grow along with an increase in interdependency between people of different kin groups and with other social units. At the core of this process is the evolution of hierarchical political institutions and centralization of power in a state. States function to maintain order, stimulate capital wealth and to reduce risks associated with production for their citizens. States promote a political economy which can be predatory on local economies through taxes and tribute. Bureaucracy becomes the trademark of the state. Markets rationalize and penetrate local economies, becoming the safety net where most of the essentials for life are purchased.

Is an increase in scale and state formation bad for older people? Within the past half century we have seen vast increases in scale marked by envisioned global villages linked to a global economy. Yet, life is lived at a local level. As seen in the Project AGE communities, globalization of change and marked increase in scale are not experienced uniformly. Consequently, for successful aging we find a mix of good and bad features. To further understand this we consider economic, social and political issues.

Economics and Material Culture. Increases in wealth and reduction in subsistence risks would appear to benefit all people. Certainly, the Ju/'hoansi and Herero see material issues as central in determining whether old age will be good or bad. In industrial economies material concerns diminish as factors perceived as shaping the quality of old age. However, the case of Momence reminds us that wealth is not uniformly distributed. For those at the edge of poverty, one mistake and material resources become a major problem, especially in retirement. On the other hand, material culture and labor-saving devices have the potential of improving the quality of life for people who have access to them.

Family and Kin. Families are the safety net for older people in need of caregiving (Draper and Keith 1992; Keith 1992; Troll 1986). Observers have been rather alarmed by the changes in families in the industrialized world. Fertility has declined, resulting in smaller households and fewer relatives to do the work of family. Furthermore, families no longer have the same kind of control over their members as we see in the tribal world. Kindreds whose members work for wages are not as economically interdependent as lineages herding cattle and relying on the family fund. Fewer kin who are bonded in a more volunteeristic way would appear not to favor a supportive old age (Nydegger 1983).

Are the changes in kinship really detrimental to older people? In Africa and Hong Kong, families are dominant institutions in people's lives. Your kinship network is your safety net. By comparison, in Ireland and the United States, respondents talk about the *quality* of family relationships. With smaller kindreds, it is possible to invest in these people as individuals. As people become more individuated, sociality becomes more central in maintaining social relationships. Here smaller, individuated kinship networks bound together by affect are not seen as contributing to a bad old age. The low frequency with which the quality of family relations is mentioned for either a good or bad old age is striking for Ireland and the United States. Kin are not the safety net. Instead most needs (goods and services) are purchased in the market. With increased wealth and state-backed income maintenance programs, the need for a family fund declines. Thus, the changes in kinship do not result in a problematic old age except, potentially, in the last year of life. With declines in physical health and inability to purchase what is required, the smaller and more fragile kindred can be placed in the role of caregivers. Once that happens, the unthinkable has happened and the older person "becomes a burden to her/his family."

Politics of Old Age. To answer how beneficial or detrimental states are for older people, we need to know if any of the political economy is directed toward the welfare of its older citizens (e.g., Chapter 11 this volume). Through our Project AGE communities we can see the effects of four states and their policies in the daily life of people (see Chapter 18 this volume for an expanded analysis). Botswana is a fairly young African nation with a youthful population. In the isolated Kalahari desert the effects of state policies are manifested in free health clinics, veterinary services, food distribution, a primary school and government wells. Older people are not targeted as a special group in need of attention. On the other hand, Ireland and the United States have followed the path of most of the industrial democracies of Europe and North America. Welfare states, such as the United States and Ireland, recognize that if any significant part of the population is denied access to the market, the state and especially the economy do not benefit. Income transfer programs such as state pensions or Social Security guarantee that older people who are no longer working can still purchase their necessities. State-managed insurance programs such as Medicare or a free public health service for older people gives access to another part of the market. In the United States the Older Americans Act has established an "aging enterprise," a network of services such as senior centers, congregate meals and meals on wheels (Estes 1993).

Hong Kong is a colony established to facilitate trade and generate wealth. The Hong Kong government has largely avoided income transfer programs for older people. This is based on assumptions about the Chinese stem family and the support it ideally gives to the parental generation (Ikels 1993). Only health care is state supported and is provided to all citizens regardless of age.

Our evaluation of the effects of increases in societal scale is mixed. In state-level societies, all citizens potentially benefit from increases in wealth and risk reduction. On the other hand, states are associated with marked social stratification and some people are better off than others. An increase in scale can bring about profound changes in a community as development occurs and outsiders move in and new linkages are made (See Chapter 18 this volume for what happened in Blessington). Even in states where a significant part of the political economy is targeted for older people, there are costs. When age becomes the basis for entitlement, "old" becomes a bureaucratic category. Stereotyping the old as poor, disabled and dependent masks the variability and potential of most older adults. Within Project AGE sites, it is in the largest-scale communities (suburban and urban) where older adults are most likely to become socially invisible.

COMMUNITY CONTEXTS AND SUCCESSFUL AGING

Where should I live in old age? Project AGE anthropologists are often asked this question as are other researchers who have investigated aging and diverse cultural contexts. From Sun City to ethnic enclaves to exotic cultures, we have been in search of Shangri-La. Unfortunately, there is no Shangri-La. It would be ill-advised to recommend one or even two of the Project AGE communities as a haven in old age. Likewise a ranking of the anthropologically best retirement spots of the world is not recommended except as a real estate promotion in the Sunday paper.

In our cross-cultural study, we heard from respondents in each community that there are strengths and positive aspects for all residents. For all sites, health and functionality are the singular factor promoting unsuccessful aging. Health problems and disabilities detract from a good old age and can have profound consequences for quality of life. Sociality, making an older person socially attractive, is seen as promoting successful aging in large-scale societies. Here people are viewed as individual personalities and their social fields are much more fluid and filled with choices. In small-scale societies, people are seen as members of collectivities (kin groups) with whom they live, work and give and receive support. Under these circumstances being a nice, socially attractive personality is not seen as a factor in a relationship or successful aging.

On the other hand, all cultural contexts have their weaknesses as well. Where the Ju/'hoansi have little wealth and simple technology, compensation exists in the form of personal support from family and kin. In marked contrast, in Swarthmore, where wealth and technology are quite adequate, kin support is less available and less acceptable because of mobility and values placed on independence. Shangri-La is only a myth. All we have are human communities that are variable in environment, economics, social life, values and the nation-state of which they are a part. Our best advice about selecting a place in which to grow old is to choose the community you now call "home." Live in it for a long time and invest in its social relationships. Your investment will pay off in an old age in which you are perceived and supported in individual terms, not as an "old person."

NOTES

The research upon which this chapter is based was supported by grant #AG 03110 from the National Institute on Aging. The authors acknowledge the work of Joanne Adams, Rebecca Morrow-Nye and Edwina Jones, all graduate students at Loyola University, who were involved in the complex task of managing the textual responses on which this chapter is based, and in reading the text to assure comparability in the themes used to describe successful aging.

1. Project members met on a regular basis to discuss research design and problems of analysis. Also, the project co-directors visited each community while the research was in process.

2. For instance, a respondent might place a persona describing a man as working, married with two preschool grandchildren, and active in the chamber of commerce in a "Late Middle Age" group. In contrast, the same respondent might place another persona describing a man as retired, widowed with great-grandchildren and living in a nursing home in a "Late Old Age" group.

3. In responding to our questions, a respondent could and often did name more than one factor which contributed to a good or poor old age. Analysis of the data subsequently permitted the respondents' answers to be placed in more than one category. In Tables 5.1 and 5.2, the bar graph represents the percent of respondents who mentioned the respective factors.

4. For people in Hong Kong, family factors are far more important in promoting a good old age and can be responsible for a poor old age. Health and functionality are also important in a good old age, but health and mobility problems also mean that family (a daughter-in-law) becomes a caregiver.

5. In the past the Herero have been identified as double unilineal (tracing descent through both male and female linkages).

6. Kindreds are a way of reckoning who your relatives are and to whom one owes support and can expect support from on the basis of kinship. Kindreds are a sibling-centered circle of kin defined by descent and bounded by a degree of collaterality as calculated by the distance of a cousin. Rarely does a kindred extend beyond a fourth or fifth cousin. Within this circle of kin are lineal kin (parents, children and extensions thereof) and collateral kin (siblings, uncles and aunts, nephews and nieces). Kindreds are associated with bilateral descent.

7. Because sociality is a composite dimension consisting of five subthemes, a comment must be made about the meaning of sociality. Such themes as having social qualities that make a person easy to get along with: social connectedness (loneliness in the negative); states of mind; or being an active, outgoing person are clearly dimensions of sociality. Also included are responses which describe a person as having leisure time, the ability to do what they want, and who have accomplished something. The reasoning behind this is that individuals who are perceived as leisured, confident and enjoying life are socially positive and are endowed with socially positive characteristics. In the negative, people who are not leisured are pressured and potentially stressed.

Across the five sites in which sociality appears as a reason in defining a positive or negative old age, we find differences in the frequencies in which the subthemes are mentioned. In Ireland, with more normative answers, sociality defines a good old age primarily as leisure and states of mind (82–83 percent of the response category). In the

United States, being active, leisure and states of mind define between 85 and 92 percent of sociality. In Hong Kong, 82 percent of sociality consists of social qualities and states of mind. In defining a negative old age, in Ireland between 77 and 88 percent of sociality is loneliness. For the United States 80 percent of negative sociality is defined in terms of loneliness and states of mind. Finally, in Hong Kong, social qualities form a core of this category (39 percent), followed by states of mind and loneliness.

PART II

The Cultural Construction of Intergenerational Ties

Subj: AARP IS EVIL
Date: 94–11–20 13:52:43 EST
From: KennyJames
"ATTENTION MEMBERS OF AARP—HOW DOES IT FEEL TO BE
ROBBING YOUR CHILDREN AND GRANDCHILDREN OF THEIR FU-
TURE? YOUR ORGANIZATION IS A CLEAR EXAMPLE OF THE 'ME
FIRST' APPROACH TO LIFE—YOU SHOULD BE ASHAMED."

Subj: Re: AARP IS EVIL
Date: 94–11–28 20:50:09 EST
From: HUTCHCO
"ONLY IN AMERICA COULD A BLITHERING IDIOT BE ALLOWED
TO SPEW HIS DRIBBLE."
    —From *St. Pete Times*, January 16, 1995, p. 1, by John Cutter,
           "Generational Warfare in Cyberspace"

GENERATIONS APPROACH THE MILLENNIUM

At the tail end of a fifteen-year period marked by a dramatic reduction in the
size of the middle class and the greatest shift of material resources to the rich
since just before the Great Depression, intergenerational squabbling has found
a new venting medium, the Internet. While the young still have a decided advantage on the electronic superhighway, numerous "SeniorNet" programs have
cropped up on college campuses and in senior centers around the country.[1] These
are providing older adults with training in the use of computers, enabling them
to access databases and communication forums on issues such as Social Security,
health care reform and generational equity.

 Meredith Minkler (1990) argues that the 1980s marked a transition in the

United States from a prior "compassionate ageism" stereotype of the aged to a more powerful, but dangerous, image of the elderly as an active, assertive and financially secure group whose costly government programs were depleting the federal budget. She notes that during that decade, the developing notion of generational equity or "justice between generations" mistakenly sought to link the increasing poverty of our youngest citizens with the cost of entitlements to older adults.[2]

In the 1990s, associations such as "Americans for Generational Equity" or the "Third Millennium" have begun to proffer an apocalyptic vision of the future, where the productivity of younger adults would soon be eaten up by the costs of keeping the elderly well fed, healthy and entertained (Guillemard 1995; MacManus 1996).[3] They point to what market analysts call WHOOPIES, or "well-off older people." While the Census Bureau estimates that in 1993 twice as many children lived below the poverty threshold than the 12 percent of elderly designated as poor, this difference is primarily an artifact of the relative wealth of white married aged. Single women over age 65, a major category of America's aged, have precisely the same poverty rate as children. Moreover, the increased poverty rate among children is directly related to the fact that from 1973 to 1987 the adjusted income of the poorest 20 percent of families with children declined by 22 percent.

Some scholars see the graying of our society as threatening the American economic dream (Howe 1995; Peterson 1996).[4] Others, and I think, appropriately so, argue that "generational equity" is an ideological smokescreen intended to turn public attention away from the dramatic enrichment of a wealthy elite at the expense of economically crippling the working and middle classes (Adams and Dominik 1995).[5] This second view is supported by data showing entitlement spending as a percent of GNP having been quite stable over the past two decades (Quadagno 1996). It is important to note that a cross-national perspective shows that "generational equity" is not such a major issue in most other Western industrial nations, where the demographic "burden" of older folks is even greater than in the United States.

Despite the very real hostility associated with this generational debate, it has been helpful in situating problems associated with the aged within larger and more general issues our society needs to address. This was seen during the latest White House Conference on Aging, held in May 1995.[6] For the first time there was a conscious attempt to promote the meeting as an intergenerational event concerned about the future of the nation's youngest generation. Resolutions were developed supporting preventive health care for all ages, expansion of nutrition programs and long-term care based on disability, not age. Delegates also focused energy on preserving the limited supports already built into the Social Security system, the Medicare program and the Older Americans Act, the existing cornerstones of the "safety net" for older citizens.

AGE AND SOCIAL BOUNDARIES

While most other primates live in multiaged communities, only human societies have developed systems that require high levels of prolonged material and social interdependence between generations. As noted in Part I, this connection of people in different parts of the life cycle is universally reflected in age-linked language categories. Definitions of when and how persons move through such markers of age-based status are highly variable. The expectations attached to each category strongly shape the culturally differentiated perceptions of time, aging and generation (Fry 1996).[7] In Chapter 13 Jane Peterson shows that chronological age and even the terms "old age" and "aging" have little cultural meaning for African-American women in a Seattle community. Rather, "maturity" and having reached a socially linked "age of wisdom" are the key linguistic markers for older, adult women, who are called "the wise."

Social boundaries associated with age-based statuses show great variation in the degree to which they allot power and esteem to the differently named categories of persons.[8] For example, the Mbuti pygmy hunter-gatherers of Zaire have four loosely defined age grades (categories): children, youths, adults and older persons. There are neither elaborate rituals marking the passage from one grade to another nor barriers to easy interaction between those in different age categories. However, there are well-known norms of behavior and responsibility assumed to be the reserve of a given grade. Despite having great regard for the aged, who as a category of person are called mangese—"the great ones"—the Mbuti have one of the most balanced, egalitarian systems of linking generations that is known in the ethnographic literature. Unlike the Tiwi, Mbuti elders do not practice hoarding or "sanctified keeping" of esoteric knowledge, and they do not attempt to control the lives of the younger generations (E. Maxwell 1986). As Colin Turnbull notes:

The responsibility allocated to childhood was that of ritual purification, most specifically in the daily act of lighting the hunting fire. The youths had full control of the political arena, and the adults were fully occupied with all the major economic responsibilities. The role of the elders was the one, as vital as all the others, of socialization. During the daytime, when youths and adults were off on the hunt, the elders mostly stayed behind in the camp, looking after the young children. By playing with them, acting out great sagas of the hunting and gathering days of yore, or just by lying back under the trees and telling stories, old women and men, the tata of the camp, filled the youngsters with their own love of the forest, their trust in it, and their respect for the forest values that made life so good. (1965:55)

In contrast, one can find societies where age grades are transformed into sharply ascribed age sets, where different spans along the life cycle are sharply set apart by spectacular ritual, distinct dress, specialized tasks, modes of speech, comportment and deferential gestures (Spencer 1996). In societies with age sets, persons move through the life cycle collectively and form tightly bound groups performing specific tasks. While societies where age groupings play such a powerful role in ordering social life have been found in Africa, among certain Native American groups, Australian aborigines and in Papua New Guinea, their global occurrence is relatively rare (see Stewart 1977; Bernardi 1985). The most elaborated forms of such cultural systems are found among East African nomadic herders, such as the Samburu of Kenya (Spencer 1965).[9] Here age sets of males initiated together move through the life cycle collectively. Over time and through elaborate ritual, they progressively enter as a group age-bounded roles of herders, warriors and finally, various levels of elders. In their fifth and sixth decades these elders gain substantial power through maintaining large, polygynous households, holding wealth in their numerous cattle and having a ritual link to the ancestors, whom they can call upon to supernaturally curse younger persons who misbehave. As is the case for most such age-based societies, a Samburu woman's social maturation is accomplished through individual life-cycle rituals and status is much more tied to the her place in family units.

Age set organizations for women in non-Western societies seem much rarer than what is reported for males. Examples include the Afikpo, Ebrie and Mbato peoples of West Africa, the Meru of East Africa and the Shavante of the Brazilian Amazon (see Kertzer and Madison 1981; Bernardi 1985:132–142). Samuel Thomas, who studied women's age sets among the Meru, suggests that one reason for the lack of importance attributed to women's age organization in Africa has been the difficulty of male ethnographers learning about a realm of culture purposely kept secret from men (1995).

All too often, cultures such as the Samburu have been held up as exemplars of places where the elderly are well-off and truly respected. It is important to note that this is frequently accomplished at the expense of intense intergenerational conflict, of exploiting and repressing the young and preventing women from gaining an equitable place in the community. Among the Samburu, older women do not share the very high esteem accorded to old men. Upon becoming widowed they suffer far greater loss of material and social roles than older African women in societies such as the Samia described by Cattell in Chapter 4. The construction of ideas about successful aging has relied too heavily on studies of gerontocratic societies and the lamentation that old age is not worth much since these old ways have fallen into disuse. It is time to shift away from glorifying Old Testament models of social order that center on the power of old men to control younger males and have access to nubile females. Observers in North America and Europe should look further for paragons of aging, seeking examples which reflect equality between genders and generations as well as the untapped potential of older citizens in community life.

FAMILIES AND GENEALOGICAL GENERATIONS

A basic structural difference between kin-based, small-scale societies such as the Tiwi or the Ju/'hoansi and the United States is that elderly in the first type of society have continuous access over the life span to essential resources derived from membership in kinship groupings. In such cultural settings, the wide embrace of family frequently provides what Simic (1978a) calls a "life term arena"—a stable setting for the engagement of an entire life. Even in the age-set societies noted above, the intense ties among age-mates or the ritual bonds across "social" generations do not destroy the links between "genealogical" generations—forged from the developmental cycle of family formation (Baxter and Almagor 1978).

In capitalist, industrial societies, it is more typical that access to resources and status over the life span requires productive participation outside of one's kin group and the transition through numerous "short-term arenas." Careful historical research has shown that this pattern is not new in North America or Western Europe (Kertzer and Lazlett 1994; Hareven 1995a, 1995b). However, over the last two decades many gerontologists have marvelled at the "discovery" that our system of urban industrialism had not totally destroyed extended family contact and intergenerational bonds (Sussman 1965; Gratton 1986; Gratton and Haber 1993). For instance, almost 80 percent of the elderly live within one hour's drive of a child and see that child at least once a month. Various studies have decried any easy assumption that the elderly are socially divorced from their younger kin (Shanas 1979; Climo 1992; Silverstein, Parrott and Bengtson 1995). Although fewer than one in ten of our elderly live in three-generation households, research has shown the persistence of a so-called modified extended family, composed of partially independent, nuclear families engaged in frequent contact and support between the generations (Antonucci and Akiyama 1995). Family networks in the United States have not been destroyed, but transformed. Marjorie Cantor has suggested several such changes: (1) families' support systems are becoming more "vertical," with more relationships that cross generational lines and fewer links to siblings and cousins; (2) a shift toward "top heavy" family caregiving roles, with a middle-generation woman now likely to spend more time dealing with dependent parents over age 65 than with children under 18; and (3) the development of "reconstructed" or stepfamilies, emerging out of increased divorce, single-parent families and changing patterns in the timing of childbearing (1992.67).

Nevertheless, relatively little attention has been paid to understanding the cultural factors shaping such interaction (Rubinstein and Johnsen 1982; Fry 1995). The three chapters in this part seek to remedy this situation.

One attempt to conceptualize the cultural contrast of generational interaction in different societies is found in the work of Andrei Simic. In a good example of cross-cultural analysis, he has examined value systems and socialization processes to draw a strong, qualitative contrast between intergenerational relationships among south Slavic peoples of Yugoslavia and those of the United States (Simic 1990). Here two opposing models are analyzed. A white, middle-class North American pattern of self-realization, independence and generational replication is contrasted to one ideally stressing kinship corporacy, interdependence and generational symbiosis.

Simic notes that the replication of genealogical or family-based generations in the United States tends to permit only certain types of exchanges which would not impinge upon the independence of individuals. This can be relaxed somewhat during the interaction of alternate generations, such as between grandparent and grandchild. However, performance of this role relationship among middle-class families of Euro-American background still must not interfere with the perceived actions of the middle generation as self-reliant parents. It is especially important to cross-culturally examine roles of the elderly, such as grandparenthood, which are universally embedded in family relationships. In such an examination, one can show both the potentials and limitations of this dimension of older adult life. For example, by examining the changing face of grandparenthood in the United States, one can note two important things related to Simic's ideas. First, new patterns of grandparenting are altering modes of generational relations, even for middle-class whites; and second, for certain ethnic groups, American ideals starkly clash with cultural variation (Jackson, Jayakody and Antonucci 1995; Detzner 1996).[10]

IS NECESSITY THE GRANDMOTHER OF INVENTION?

In *The New American Grandparent*, Cherlin and Furstenberg note that in the 1950s psychologists were talking about the appropriate distancing of grandparents from younger generations, and some even elaborated on a negative "grandparent syndrome," implying potential harm from meddlesome behavior to grandkids and adult children (1992:3). The authors also discuss how societal attitudes toward the value of grandparents has changed in a positive direction, prompted by powerful and growing changes in American family structures over the last three decades.

For certain American ethnic groups, a parenting role for grandparents has always been a normative, anticipated option (Johnson 1983a). Joan Weibel-Orlando, focusing in Chapter 6 on Native Americans she studied in urban California and at a reservation in South Dakota, makes a strong contribution to our knowledge about how cultural context affects the grandparenting role.[11] Compared to Euro-American background families, less restricted boundaries between genealogical generations often provided the possibility for grandparents to have crucial roles as "cultural conservators" and even to request that they bring up as their own one or more of their offspring's children. However, in her sensitive portrayal of contemporary Native American life, Weibel-Orlando shows that there are quite diverse grandparenting models among the peoples she studied (Schweitzer 1987; Schweitzer forthcoming). These different ways of being an Indian grandparent reflect not only ancient, indigenous patterns, but needs generated by poverty-imposed stresses placed on the parenting generation (John, Blanchard and Hennessy 1997). In following these grandparents over time, she also explores how frailty alters the experience of this role.[12] The lessons from her study can be profitably added to the chapters on the ethnic aged in Part IV.

Throughout the United States, grandparenthood appears to be increasing in status at the same time more pressure is on older adults to assume a reparenting role (Kornhaber 1996; Robertson 1995). These changes are reflected in the creation of a national Grandparents' Day (first Sunday after Labor Day), and a growing state level movement to enact "grandparents' rights" legislation.[13] As Maria Vesperi points out in Chapter 7, the "Grandparent Information Center," established by the American Association of Retired Persons (AARP) in 1993, was immediately deluged by calls seeking assistance. At the same time, this need has prompted the rapid growth of local support groups such as Second Time Around Parents, GRAM (Grandparents Rights Advocacy Movement) or ROCKING (Raising Our Children's Kids).[14] It should be noted that while chapters in this part and Part IV stress the centrality of older women in grandparenting, other studies have shown contexts in which grandfathers contribute powerfully to family support systems (Kivette 1991).

Maria Vesperi, drawing upon her dual background in anthropology and journalism, shows that current, end-of-century medical and socioeconomic crises which have thrust seniors fully into the child care arena also marked last century's close. Her chapter connects the lives of homeless "newsies" a hundred years ago to today's grandparents, struggling to succeed at full-time parenting of their grandchildren. In doing so she reminds us not to treat these issues as isolated "child" or "old person" problems but to address the reasons families and communities fail to thrive (Bengtson and Greenwell Forthcoming).

While recent studies indicate that children raised solely by grandparents are relatively healthy and well-adjusted, few states allow relatives to be eligible for foster care programs and the associated monetary and legal supports.[15] More significantly, as the AARP Grandparent Information Center points out, ongoing attempts to replace the current welfare system make little attempt to recognize the situation of grandparents raising grandchildren, many of whom cannot meet needs for food, medical care and housing without help from public benefit programs (AARP 1995).[16]

THE FAMILY CONTEXT OF CAREGIVING TO THE ELDERLY

One of the central issues in research on intergenerational relations is the degree to which the elderly can expect to receive various types of support from their younger relatives (Kendig, Hashimoto and Coppard 1992; Kosberg 1992; Blieszner and Bedford 1995).[17] Leo Simmons, in his classic examination of the role of the aged in 71 nonindustrial societies, observes that "throughout human history the family has been the safest haven for the aged. Its ties have been the most intimate and long-lasting, and on them the aged have relied for greatest security'' (1945:176). In Third World nations this is still generally the case, even in urban areas where a majority of older adults reside with younger relatives and must rely exclusively on familial resources for survival (Hashimoto 1991). In the Western Pacific Survey, for example, it was found that in the nations of Fiji, the Republic of Korea, Malaysia and the Philippines, between 75 and 85 percent of the elderly reside in extended family settings. However, as Sokolovsky's (Chapter 9, this volume) study of a peasant village in Mexico shows, the specific nature of kinship systems and how they link up to public domains greatly influence the family's capability for support in rapidly changing Third World contexts.

The consistent survey reports on the living arrangements of the elderly in East Asia must be balanced against the impact of extremely rapid industrialization, which can mimic the dislocations families suffered throughout Europe during its industrial growth in the first half of the last century. For example, in the early 1990s, Australian epidemiologist John McCallum was reviewing a program seeking to create awareness of aging in Indonesia, Philippines, Singapore and Thailand. National experts from these countries consistently told him that despite rapidly increasing geographic family mobility, families were still very effective in providing for the day-to-day needs of the aged. However, contrary data were obtained when he ventured outside the information network of predominantly male public analysts and spokespersons. McCallum gives as an example the situation in a fast-growing urban fringe settlement which provides workers for new industries at one of the research sites. The pressures of work and getting children to school were such that ''a majority of families were placing their elderly early each day, sometimes with little sustenance, in an open field without shade and collecting them in the evening'' (1993:2).

Although many of the world's poorest countries—such as Afghanistan, Chad, Mali, India, Haiti—have legislated some type of public pension system, often less than one-third of the economically active population are eligible for benefits which, when applicable, amount to only 40 to 50 percent of preretirement wages (World Bank 1994). Such entitlement programs seldom reach rural sectors, where 75 percent of the Third World elderly live. Commonly, the rationale for the failure to extend pension programs to peasant populations is that the family can tend to the needs of all its members. However, in just the last decade, rapid urbanization and economic dislocation have radically changed the kin-centered basis for support in many developing countries (see Part III). For example, ''in Malaysia, the Philippines, and South Korea, rural households were found to be smaller and less likely than urban households to include elderly persons living with their offspring'' (Kinsella 1988:29).

Historical research has also found this to be the case during the process of industrialization in nineteenth-century New England (Gratton and Haber 1993). Two major factors linked to this unexpected finding were the greater tendency of younger rather than older adults to migrate to cities and the scarcity of urban housing. Although strong support can be provided by children and other close relatives not living in the household, rapid out-migration can mortally disrupt the fabric of intergenerational caring and reciprocity. This can be an especially hard blow to the life satisfaction of rural elderly, who spent much of their lives caring for their aged parents in the prescribed manner and now find that they are all too often on their own.

Such a situation can be particularly stressful for middle-aged and older women in rural areas, where they often bear the brunt of both agricultural labor and caring for their older spouses and kin (M. J. Gibson 1985; Doty 1986a; Apt 1991). In areas of rural Eastern Europe, the Mediterranean and Africa, this situation is particularly critical. The dynamics of this are aptly noted for Botswana, Africa, by Benedicte Ingstad and her co-authors (1992). They describe the vital role of older women in keeping together the infirm and very young, who remain in the village to survive by the subsistence farming of senior women and the sporadic remittances of younger relatives who work for long periods outside the community.

Even where the structure of the extended family persists in "traditional societies," policymakers should not harbor unqualified optimism about intergenerational kindness or the capacity of family systems to ensure the well-being of aged relatives (Levine 1965; Nydegger 1983). This was illustrated by the results of a study of Hindu households in Kathmandu, Nepal, where 61 percent of all aged individuals lived with at least one son (Goldstein, Schuler, and Ross 1983). It was noted that while the "ideal" form of the patrilineal extended family existed, the material and psychological foundations of filial support were rapidly disintegrating. The authors found it particularly ironic that given the Hindu ideal value of depending on a male child in old age, "the most truly miserable elderly parents were the very ones who objectively were completely dependent upon a son" (p. 722).

In North America the nature of eldercare as well as the assistance provided by elders to their adult children and grandchildren is beginning to alter views about unpaid work and traditional gender-based roles related to intergenerational support (Gallagher 1994). In *Women on the Front Lines* (Allen and Pifer 1993), the authors argue that care for dependents will no longer be solely based on the concept of motherhood.[18] They assert that basing care responsibilities on a child care model has delimited the efficient integration of family eldercare, paid employment and public sector supports. As industrialized nations have commonly experienced rapid increases in surviving dependent parents and in female participation in work outside the household, a crisis in the family basis of eldercare has emerged. Summarizing the results of a six-nation study of this crucial issue sponsored by the International Labour Office, Irene Hoskins states: "the traditional model of family care will become increasingly dysfunctional because the elderly themselves do not necessarily expect or prefer it and, without proper support, female caregivers, most of whom are in the work force, will no longer be able to provide it'' (1994b:62).[19]

The relatively few attempts to conduct cross-cultural studies of family support systems for the aged have been marred by a lack of attention to the qualitative, internal mechanisms that may belie superficial similarities measured by frequency of interaction or ideal statements about the desire to support one's parents. Chapter 8 in this volume seeks to avoid such a limited perspective. Using a variety of qualitative and quantitative approaches, from individual case studies to national surveys, Akiyama, Antonucci and Campbell provide a path-breaking study of intergenerational transactions between women in Japan and the United States. Drawing on exchange theory and Antonucci's concept of a life-long ''Social Support Bank,'' the authors clearly delineate how the cultural construction of reciprocity regulates the flow of goods, services and emotions between adult daughters and their mothers. The comparison of these two societies is particularly important as it allows us to hold relatively constant the factor of urban-industrial development while comparing the effect of dramatically different cultures on the lives of the elderly. Here we see that in Japan the continuing pattern of high elderly co-residence with adult children is embedded within a cultural system with different values and perspectives on the nature of intergenerational reciprocity (Maeda and Shimazu 1992; Hashimoto 1996). In Part III, Chapter 10 will expand on the caregiving role of women in Japan for their elderly parents and in-laws and discuss the dramatic changes which are altering these patterns.

KEY RESOURCES

Centers

American Center on Indian Aging (currently being developed), University of New Mexico of Center on Aging, 1836 Lomas Blvd., N.E., Albuquerque, NM 87131–6086. Phone (505) 277–0911. E-mail: marius@unm.edu.

AARP Grandparent Information Center: Social Outreach and Support, 601 E. St., NW, Washington, DC 20049. Phone (202) 434–2288. E-mail: jrwade@aarp.org. A national clearinghouse for information on grandparenting. They are in the process of developing a minority grandparent component to their work.

The Center for Intergenerational Learning at Temple University, 1601 North Broad Street, Room 206, Philadelphia, PA 19122. Phone: (215) 204–6970. Fax: (215) 204–6733. Fosters the development of innovative cross-age programs, the provision of training and technical assistance. They produce a newsletter which you can read through their small web site at http://www.temple.edu/departments/CIL.

Research Project

''Longitudinal Study of Generations'' is an ongoing project at the University of Southern California, which has followed intergenerational relations in a large sample of families since 1971. Some results from the project can be found in Bengtson 1996, Richlin-Klonsky and Bengtson 1996, and at the web site http://www.usc. edu/dept/gero/4gen/index.htm.

Computer CD-ROM

''1995 White House Conference on Aging CD-ROM.'' All the documents produced by this huge event are found on this new resource. Key word searches can be made within the CD. Available through the government printing office. Cost is $16. It can be purchased by calling (202) 512–1800 and asking for item # 040–000–00674–5.

Internet Resources

(1) http://www.siu.edu/offices/iii/ The site for the Illinois Intergenerational Initiative.
(2) http://www.soulzone.com/soulzone/commzone/agp/indx.html. The site for a Native Elders assistance program called ''Adopt a Grandparent.'' This program developed after three Lakota Sioux elders were found frozen to death in their cabins on the Pine Ridge Reservation in South Dakota during the winter of 1987.

Print Resources

Special Issues of Journals

''Resource Allocation and Societal Responses to Old Age.'' Ageing and Society 15(2) (1995); ''Grandparenting at Century's End.'' Generations (Spring 1996); ''North American Indians and Aging.'' The Journal of Cross-Cultural Gerontology (forthcoming).

Other Print Resources

Bernardi, B. 1985. Age Class Systems. London: Cambridge. An in-depth analysis of societies which use age as a primary basis for organizing society.

Fry, C. 1996. ''Age, Aging and Culture.'' In Handbook on Aging and the Social Sciences, 4th ed. R. Binstock and L. George, eds. New York: Academic Press. A synthesis of cross-cultural studies on age as a social category and of the life course as a cultural unit.

Haraven, T. ed. 1995a. Aging and Generational Relations Over the Life Course: A Historical and Cross Cultural Perspective. Berlin; Walter de Gruyter and Co. An edited volume with good coverage of East and Southeast Asia.

Hashimoto, A. 1996. The Gift of Generations: Japanese and American Perspectives on Aging and the Social Contract. Cambridge, UK: Cambridge University Press. A comparative sociological study of generational relations in two small cities, West Haven, Connecticut, and Odawara, Japan.

Kaiser, M. and S. Chawla. 1994. ''Caregivers and Care Recipients: The Elderly in Developing Countries.'' Ageing International 11:42–49. Summarizes results of a United Nations study of family support of the aged and intergenerational exchange in Chile, Sri Lanka, the Dominican Republic and the United States.

Kendig, H., A. Hashimoto and L. Coppard, eds. 1992. Family Support for the Elderly:

An International Experience. New York: Oxford University Press. A variety of articles based on a major cross-national study funded by the World Health Organization.

Merrill, D. 1997. *Caring for Elderly Parents: Juggling Work, Family, and Caregiving in Middle- and Working-Class Families.* Westport, CT: Greenwood. Documents how working- and middle-class families manage to provide care for their frail, elderly parents.

Narduzzi, J. L. 1994. *Mental Health Among Elderly Native Americans.* New York: Garland.

Schweitzer, M. Forthcoming. *Bridging Generations: American Indian Grandmothers—Traditions and Transitions.* Albuquerque: University of New Mexico Press.

Urban Institute. 1993. *Hunger Among the Elderly: Local and National Comparisons.* Washington, DC: The Urban Institute. An important study which documents the inability of over three million aged to feed themselves adequately.

NOTES

1. The SeniorNet idea was developed in 1986 by Professor Mary Furlong of the University of San Francisco. It is now a nonprofit organization called SeniorNet International. Another interesting change in how culture shapes generational relations in Western industrial societies is the creation of "Universities of the Third Age," where special programs have been established for and by seniors in universities and colleges (Hazan 1996). Most universities in the United States also currently have special registration procedures for older citizens which allows them to attend classes at minimal or no charge.

2. Beginning in the mid-1980s, and regularly since then, articles began to appear in many popular magazines raising an alarm about "greedy geezers" bankrupting the country.

3. The Third Millennium is an association which is said to represent people born after 1960. Groups such as this have been particularly motivated by a report in 1994 by the Social Security trustees that the system would go belly-up in 2029, seven years earlier than predicted in 1993 (Howe 1995).

4. This line of thought is also developed by Lester Thurow in *The Future of Capitalism*, William Morrow and Company, 1996.

5. For a good discussion of perception of the elderly as "well off" see Schulz 1996.

6. This conference has been held once a decade since 1971.

7. For other important references dealing with the life cycle, see Smith 1961a; La Fontaine 1978; Fry and Keith 1982; Kertzer 1982; Fortes 1984; Spencer 1990. For a discussion of the transition into North American retirement, see Savishinsky 1995.

8. Increased conflict between perceived generations in industrial nations is occurring at the same time as the cultural categories and the very structure of age groupings and the life course are in flux. In the 1980s British historian Peter Laslett suggested, in his book *A Fresh Map of Life* (1989), a "new division of the life course":

First comes an era of dependence, socialization, immaturity and education; second an era of independence, maturity and responsibility, of earning and of saving; third an era of personal fulfillment; and fourth an era of final dependence, decrepitude and death.

He later goes on to define the rise of Third Age societies where at least half of a country's male population can expect to survive from age 25 to age 70 and when at least a quarter of adults, those over 25, are beyond the age of 60 years (Laslett 1994a).

Some see the rise of Third Age societies as presenting a real societal dilemma where there is an accumulation of citizens from age 50 to 75 who have completed their main career work and the raising of children, but who in their mental and physical vigor would not be considered old. ''These men and women have much to offer but often are barred by outmoded social attitudes and customs or their own discouragement from making the economic and social contributions they could well make—and should.'' England was so concerned about this issue that from 1990 to 1993 it undertook a massive inquiry into the implications of this situation for issues like employment, leisure, education, health, community life and their role as carers and volunteers (Pifer 1994).

9. For discussion of other East African groups see, Legesse 1973; Baxter and Almagor 1978; Sangree 1986, 1988.

10. For a recent study of rural grandparenting patterns, see King and Elder 1995.

11. It should be noted that a transition is currently going on between the elder generation of respondents studied by Weibel-Orlando who refer to themselves as ''Indians'' and their children and grandchildren who are more apt to use the term ''Native Americans''.

12. For discussion of health among Native American elders, see Shomaker 1990; Kuntz and Levy 1991; and John and Blanchard 1996.

13. Grandparents' Day was established in 1978.

14. As of 1996, the AARP Grandparent Center reported that there were over 400 support groups for grandparents across the nation.

15. There has been great concern throughout the country with the legal problems and barriers for grandparents who assume a parenting role. One source of help is provided in a new book by T. Truly (1995), *Grandparents' Rights* (Clearwater, FL: Sphinx). For further discussion of this latest issue, see Burton and DeVries 1992; Solomon and Marx 1995; Mullen 1996.

16. For additional information on the connection between societal change and the increase in reparenting in the United States, see Burton 1992; Roe, Minkler and Barwell 1994.

17. Classic works on this subject which provide some international perspective can be found in Little 1983; M. J. Gibson 1984; Wenger 1984; Doty 1986b.

18. There is a small but growing literature on men as caregivers; see Kaye and Applegate 1994 for a good discussion of this issue.

19. Countries in the study include: France, Sweden, Canada, Japan, Australia and the United States.

CHAPTER 6

Grandparenting Styles: The Contemporary American Indian Experience

Joan Weibel-Orlando

Much of the grandparenting literature and especially the descriptions of American Indian[1] grandparenting focus on status and role shifts which aging women experience in relation to their parents, children, grandchildren and society in general (Amoss 1981; Nahemow 1987; Shanas and Sussman 1981). Primarily focused on the social, cultural and psychological outcomes of attaining grandparenthood, these studies, with a few noteworthy exceptions, assume grandparenthood to be shaped largely by social and biological factors over which the aging woman has little personal control (Schweitzer 1987; Tefft 1968).

Grandparenthood, however, is neither defined by the narrow constraints of biological and reproductive attainments nor executed solely within the parameters of cultural consensus. Rather, grandparental roles are expressed across a range of activities, purposes and levels of intensity so varied as to be identified as distinct grandparenting styles. Six grandparenting styles—cultural conservator, custodian, ceremonial, distanced, fictive and care-needing—are identified and discussed.

The findings presented here are based on the reflections of the North American Indian grandparents with whom I have worked since 1984, and my observations of their interactions with their grandchildren. The grandparenting styles listed above are defined by seven factors: (1) the quality and intensity of the relationship across the grandparent/grandchild generations; (2) the grandparents' cultural and/or individualistic perceptions of what grandparenting roles should be; (3) accessibility of the grandchildren by the grandparents; (4) social and familial integration of the grandparents; (5) personal lifecourse goals of the grandparents; (6) social, economic and psychological stability of the children's parents; and (7) the age at which grandparenthood is attained.

Freedom of choice in the creation of one's particular grandparenting style is considerable. Some American Indian grandparents petition their children for the privilege of primary care responsibilities for one or more grandchildren. When parents are reluctant to relinquish care of a child to the grandparents, individuals who relish continuing child care responsibilities past their childbearing years develop alternative strategies both traditional and contemporaneous in origin. Establishment of fictive kinship, provision of foster parent care, and involvement in cultural restoration programs in the public schools are among the alternative roles available to older American Indians whose grandchildren, either because of distance or parental reluctance, are not immediately accessible to them.

While custodial, fictive, ceremonial and distanced grandparenting styles are evidenced cross-culturally, I suggest that the cultural conservator grandparenting style, if not particularly American Indian, is essentially a phenomenon of general ethnic minority-group membership. Fearing loss of identity as a people because of the relentless assimilationist influences of contemporary life, many ethnic minority members view their elders as vital cultural resources for their children. Grandparents as cultural conservators constitute a cultural continuity in that responsibility for the enculturation of the youngest generation was traditionally the role of the grandparents across American Indian tribal groups (Amoss 1981; Schweitzer 1987). Cognizant of the powerful influences which attract their urbanized, educated and upwardly mobile children away from tribal pursuits, many contemporary American Indian grandparents understand their roles as conservators and exemplars of a world view and ethos that may well disappear if they do not consistently and emphatically impart it to and enact it for their grandchildren. The ideological, enculturational and behavioral components of this grandparenting style are special concerns of this chapter.

DESCRIPTION OF THE SAMPLE

Between 1984 and 1986, I interviewed 26 North American Indians who had lived for at least 20 years in either the West Coast urban centers of Los Angeles or San Francisco or in rural areas at least 500 miles away from their original homelands. All of the Sioux and Muskogean interviewees had returned to their childhood homelands in South Dakota and Southeastern Oklahoma less than five years before they were interviewed.

Upon retirement, strong family, economic, friendship and aesthetic ties pulled increasing numbers of older, "urban" American Indians back to tribal homelands. Retirees' reduced incomes go further in American Indian communities where the cost of housing, utilities, medical services and some foodstuffs are federally subsidized. Rural family lands and ancestral homes provide the older American Indians much relished sanctuary from the hustle-bustle of urban city life. And lifelong friends and family provide easily accessed affectional supports, in contrast to the increasingly attenuated ones in urban centers.

Aside from being two of the three most heavily represented tribal groups in Los Angeles, the Sioux and the Muskogeans were also among the very first

Native American urban relocatees[2] to come to Los Angeles (Weibel-Orlando 1991). It was reasonable to assume, then, that they would be most heavily represented in the retirement-age American Indians I could identify. Aside from widely separated traditional territories, the Sioux and Muskogeans represent two distinct cultural traditions (Kroeber 1939).

The Lakota Sioux of the Pine Ridge Reservation were, at the time of Western European contact, nomadic, big game hunters of the northern plains. No one has written more persuasively about Sioux personality development than psychoanalyst Erik Erikson (1963). Yet, in over 50 pages of descriptive text about Sioux child-rearing patterns, Erikson provides no clue as to the role of the grandparents in the enculturation of the Sioux child. There are, however, lengthy discussions of the mother's role in shaping the world view of the developing child. From my observations of contemporary Sioux child-rearing practices and the predominance of both mother and grandmother and the shadowlike nature of fathers' and grandfathers' involvement in the enculturation process, I suggest that now, as then, the Sioux family presents a strongly matrifocal profile.

Traditionally, the clear division of labor by sex (men did the hunting, women maintained the hearth and home) resulted in the absence of the Sioux men from the hearth for long stretches of time. When the men were on the hunt, or off on raiding forays, the women were left to their own devices in the rearing of the young. With work of their own to do on behalf of their husbands and families (preparing hides, gathering seeds and tubers, and curing meats), young Sioux mothers often left weaned toddlers in the care of their older siblings or other female members of the three- and, occasionally, four-generation band or residential unit. Often from the same generation as the children's biological grandmothers, these women, as well as the biological grandmothers who shared their daughters' teepees, would be addressed by their charges as *unci*, the Lakota term for grandmother. It is assumed, then, that Sioux grandmothers had as much input into the enculturation of the young child historically as they do today.

The Muskogean-speaking people (Creeks, Chickasaws and Choctaws) of this sample were originally village farmers from the southeastern states of Georgia, Alabama and Louisiana (Driver 1969). In the 1830s, however, their ancestors were summarily removed from their thriving communities and resettled in the territory which now comprises most of Oklahoma's southeastern quadrant (Foreman 1934).

Again, what data we have about child-rearing practices and grandparenthood among these tribal groups are extremely sketchy and provide only hints as to possible enculturation practices during historical times. All three tribal groups were clearly matrilineal. Families were matrifocal as well as matrilocal. The typical family constellation consisted of three generations living in the ancestral village home or in its near vicinity and carrying out a yearly round of agricultural chores on behalf of the most senior female head of household. Use of large agricultural plots was passed through the matrilineage, though husbands and brothers worked the gardens outside the protection of the village palisades.

When the men were not gardening or holding elaborate fertility rites around the agricultural calendar, they engaged in the many and continuing intertribal skirmishes and, by the eighteenth century, numerous wars with offending European interlopers (Driver 1969; Foreman 1934).

As with the Sioux, the Muskogean men were usually otherwise occupied and, therefore, had minimal roles in the care of the young children. We can assume that, as among the Sioux, much of the parenting responsibility of young children was "women's work." The younger Muskogean women, too, had work which carried them away from the hearth. Smaller family gardens within the village compounds were the responsibility of the women (Driver 1969). It seems likely that grandmothers would be expected to tend children while their parents gardened and prepared food.

Although the two culture areas represented in this sample are widely disparate, traditional ecological adaptations, they share several core cultural traits: division of labor by sex, predominance of the three-generation extended family residence pattern, and relative absence of male involvement in the care of offspring during early childhood. I, therefore, suggest that child-rearing patterns and, particularly, the role of the grandparents in that process in these two culture areas were probably as similar historically as they are contemporaneously.

The eleven men and fifteen women in the sample ranged in age from 56 to 83 in 1984. Twelve people (seven women and five men) are Sioux and were living on the Pine Ridge Reservation in South Dakota. Fourteen participants live in the area traditionally known as Indian Territory in southeastern Oklahoma. Five of these (two men and three women) are members of the Creek and Seminole tribes. Six (three women and three men) are Choctaw, and one man and two women are Chickasaw.

The 26 participants represent seventeen households. Five women and one man were single heads of households. Out of fourteen families who had biological grandchildren, only five did not have grandchildren living with them. Of these five families, all had grandchildren who still lived on the West Coast or at least 500 miles away with their parents.

Seven families lived in the three-generational family setting Harold Driver (1969:236) described as the modal North American Indian household configuration. One family had at least one member from each of its four generations living under one roof. Eight grandparents were the primary caretakers for at least one grandchild. In seven cases, the parents of the grandchildren were not living in the primary caretaking households at the time of the interviews. In an eighth case, the mother lived at home but worked full-time. Here, the resident grandmother was the primary caretaker of the three grandchildren in the household during the work week.

The number of grandchildren in the household ranged between one and five. One family cared for a great-grandchild at least half of the day while his mother attended high school classes. All fourteen biological grandparents had other grandchildren who were not living in their homes at the time of the interview.

These demographics illustrate that a substantial percentage of American Indian grandparents still assume primary caretaker responsibility for their grandchildren. Additionally, the multigenerational household still appears to be the modal family composition in the two focal tribal groups.

GRANDPARENTING STYLES

What little literature there is on the role of the North American Indian grandparents in the enculturation of their grandchildren during historic (sixteenth-nineteenth centuries) times tends to be sketchy, ambiguous and highly romanticized. Grandparents are depicted as storytellers (Barnett 1955:144). Grandmothers were mentors to girls about to become socially acknowledged as women (Elmendorf and Kroeber 1960:439). Grandfathers advised and spiritually supported boys old enough to embark upon the first of many vision quests (Amoss 1981). Grandparents became primary caretakers of children left orphaned by disease, war or famine (Schweitzer 1987). In all cases the literature depicts Indian grandparents as protective, permissive, affectionate and tutorial in their interactions with their grandchildren. Only more recently has Pamela Amoss (1986) offered an intriguing analysis of the ambiguous nature of Northwest Coast Native American grandmother myths in which the old women have the power both to protect and to destroy their progeny.

The generally acknowledged model of Indian grandparenting presented above fits most closely the cultural conservator and custodial models to be discussed. In both cases, I suggest that the impetus for such grandparenting styles in contemporary American Indian family life springs from the same conditions and concerns that shaped historical grandparenting modes: practical issues of division of labor and the efficacy of freeing younger women to participate more fully in the economic sector of the tribal community; nurturance of unprotected minors so as to maximize the continuance of the tribe as a social entity; and the belief that old age represents the culmination of cultural experience. Elders are thought to be those best equipped to transmit cultural lore across generations, thus ensuring the cultural integrity of the group.

In the sections to follow, six observed grandparenting styles are defined and illustrated by excerpts from life-history interviews with individuals who exemplify a particular grandparenting style. Grandparenting styles are not mutually exclusive categories. Rather, the grandparents who shared their life histories with me, over time, have manifested attributes of several caretaking styles both with the same children and across their assortment of other grandchildren, both biological and fictive.

Although this chapter deals mainly with women as grandparents, ten men in the study interacted on a continuing basis with their grandchildren. It, therefore, seems more precise to label the relational styles described as grandparenting, rather than grandmothering, styles. The grandfathers, although present in the homes, are less absorbed in the ordering of their grandchildren's lives than are their wives. As described in nineteenth-century ethnographic accounts of American Indian family life, the grandfather, like the father, is more likely to be the soft, affectionate, shadow figure in the family constellation who leaves the discipline and socialization of the grandchildren to his wife or her brothers (Pettitt 1946). Rarely, and in this study only in the case of two men who were religious leaders, did grandfathers take on assertive roles vis-à-vis their grandchildren's socialization. Today, as in the nineteenth-century accounts of Native American Indian life, raising children is essentially women's work.

THE DISTANCED GRANDPARENT

Of the seventeen families in this study, only three are best described by the term "distanced" grandparent. In all three cases the grandchildren are living either on the West Coast with their parents or far enough away to make regular visits difficult. Nor do summer school vacations herald extended visits from the grandchildren in these families. Occasionally, the grandparents will make the trip west to visit their grandchildren. These visits, however, are infrequent and do not have the ritual qualities of the scheduled visits of the ceremonial grandparents. The distance between grandparent and grandchild is geographical, psychological and cultural. For the most part, the distanced grandparents understand the lack of communication with their grandchildren as the effect of children's and grandchildren's changed lifestyles. As one Choctaw grandmother told me: "Oh, they've got their own thing in the city. You know, they have their friends, and their music lessons and school activities. They'd get bored out here if they couldn't get to a mall or the movies."

In one case, the grandfather had had a child from a failed first marriage whom he has not seen since her birth. He was told that she has children of her own whom he also has not seen. Instances of geographical and psychological distance are highly unusual and almost nonexistent among American Indian grandmothers. For example, one Sioux grandmother not only knew all of her grandchildren from her children's formal marriages or publicly acknowledged, long-term liaisons, but also all of her biological grandchildren from her sons' informal sexual encounters. In fact, the issue of grandparental responsibility to a new grandchild was such a strong cultural tenet, she sought out the assistance of a medicine man in determining the truth when a young woman presented herself as the mother of one of her son's children and the young man refused to acknowledge the paternity of the child. Of concern was the child's right to know who his family is and her responsibility to grandparent all of her grandchildren regardless of their legal family status.

The distanced grandparent, then, is a relatively rare phenomenon among North American Indian families. I find no reference to this kind of grandparenting style in the literature on traditional American Indian family life. If it occurred, it was usually viewed as a cultural aberration due to separation of family members through capture by enemies, death or marriage out of the group. Rather, the distanced grandparent appears to be an artifact of an earlier (1950s to the 1970s) migration of American Indians into urban centers. The distancing is gradual, accumulative and only exacerbated by the second and third generations remaining in the cities to work, go to school and become acclimated to urban life when grandparents decide to return to their homelands upon retirement.

THE CEREMONIAL GRANDPARENT

Only two cases of this grandparenting style were identified. In both cases the grandchildren live some distance from the grandparents who, as with the distanced grandparents, have returned to their ancestral homes after living for many years in urban centers. The quality, frequency and purpose of their family visits, however, distinguish their grandparenting style from the distanced grandparent. These families tend to visit with regularity. Every year, summer vacations are planned to include a sojourn with the grandparents. Flowers, gifts of money, clothes or plane and bus tickets are forwarded to the grandparents at most holidays and birthdays.

When grandchildren visit grandparents, or vice versa, the host communities are alerted. The entire family attends a steady round of ethnic ceremonial gatherings and social activities at which announcements of their visits are made and applauded. Frequently, the public announcements make references to the distances traveled and the venerable ages of the visiting or visited grandparents. That these features of intergenerational visits are equally and enthusiastically applauded by the spectators underscores the importance of cultural values, such as family cohesion and reverence for one's elders, which are ritually enacted and legitimized by these public displays of the ceremonial grandparents.

Ceremonial grandparenting is expressed in other public forms as well. Grandparents are often asked to say prayers, lead honoring dances, or stand and allow the community to honor them in ceremonies which dramatize the traditional attitudes of respect and reverence for those who have had the spiritual power to live to old age. Families gain honor and visibility in their communities for fostering the health and well-being of their ancient members. Therefore, the ceremonial prerogatives of old age are sought out and perpetuated both by the elderly person as one way of maintaining a public presence and by the elderly person's family as one way of enhancing group membership and family status within their ethnic group.

Ceremonial grandparents provide ideal models of "traditional" (correct) intergenerational behavior for their children, grandchildren and the community. In time-limited interactions with their grandchildren, the venerated grandparents embody and enact those behaviors appropriate to their age and prestige ranking in the community. By watching the ceremonial displays of age and family cohesiveness, the children learn the appropriateness of veneration of the elderly and how adherence to community mores qualifies older individuals for displays of respect and love in old age. The children are taught appropriate ceremonial

"Grandpa Whitecloud" (Pueblo) and his great-grandsons prepare to fancy dance at a Saturday night Many Trails Club powwow in Long Beach, California.

behavior toward their elders: assisting the unsteady of gait to the dance floor, fetching food and cold drinks for them and formally presenting them with gifts and performance in special ceremonies such as the Siouan powwows and give-aways and the Muskogean church ''sings.''

The ceremonial aspects of contemporary American Indian grandparenting are certainly consistent with historical accounts of public behavior toward tribal elders (Schweitzer 1987). In fact, insistence on public veneration of the elderly may now be exaggerated so as to underscore, once again, what is assumed to be the more positive approach to aging in American Indian culture vis-à-vis Anglo society. Both American Indians and non-Indians are aware of mass-media ruminations about the American preoccupation with youth and the warehousing of its elderly. As a counter to this, there is an insistence on elder spiritual leaders at Sun Dance processions and communal prayers at powwows and sings. In general, both aged men and women are expected to be in attendance at public events so as to be recognized and honored simply for being there at their advanced age. Such events tend to convince community members and non-Indians alike that American Indians know how to treat their elders.

THE FICTIVE GRANDPARENT

Fictive grandparenting is an alternative to the lack or absence of biological grandchildren. All three fictive grandparents in this sample are women. Two of the women had biological grandchildren living on the West Coast whose parents would not relinquish their care to the grandmothers. Solutions to their grand-childless homes included a variety of ingenious strategies. One Sioux woman applied for and received foster home accreditation. During the first two years of her return to reservation life she harbored seven different, nonrelated children in her home for periods of four to eighteen months. At one time she had four foster children living with her at the same time.

Well, I got to missing my grandchildren so much. And none of my kids would let me have one of their kids to take care of so I decided I had to do something. And there's so much need out here . . . so I felt I could provide a good home for these pitiful Sioux kids whose families couldn't take care of them. So I applied for the foster parent license. I was scared that maybe they would say I was too old at sixty five. But, you know, within a week after I got my license I got a call from them. And they had not one, but two kids for me to take. (Sioux woman, age 67, Pine Ridge, South Dakota)

One Choctaw woman, a teacher's assistant in the public school system, became involved in the development of teaching materials designed to introduce American Indian and non-Indian students to traditional Choctaw life. Simple readers and instructional sheets in English that provide study outlines for the acquisition of traditional Choctaw dances, games and foods have now evolved into a full-fledged Choctaw language-learning course. The grandmother's skills

as a Choctaw-speaking storyteller have allowed her access to dozens of kindergarten to third-grade children who fill the widening gap she recognizes between
herself and her West Coast–based grandchildren.

One grandchildless woman had an informally adopted son living with her
who was young enough to be her grandchild. (She was 83 and he was 25 when
interviewed in Los Angeles in 1984.) He subsequently accompanied her to
Oklahoma when she decided to return to her hometown in 1985.

> He needed a home. And he didn't want to live with his mother no more. And we didn't
> know where his Dad was. And all I had was my daughter, who works all day and is
> practically blind, so she isn't much help around the place when she gets home at night.
> I needed someone around here who can look after me, drive me places, help me with
> the shopping, and all that. So I adopted him when he was around seventeen and he's
> been with me ever since. (Creek woman, age 83, Los Angeles, California)

Fictive grandparenting was not initiated by any of the men in this study. That
is not to say, however, that men do not facilitate these types of relationships
upon occasion. In fact, some older men, particularly if they are in command of
medicinal or spiritual lore, will apprentice young men who they later adopt as
kin if there is no blood tie between. Older women tend to initiate fictive kin
ties for the broader personal, emotional, social, cultural and purely pragmatic
reasons stated above.

THE CUSTODIAL GRANDPARENT

As Burton and Bengtson (1985) rightly and importantly point out, grandparenthood is not a status to which all aging women devoutly aspire. The ease and
enthusiasm with which the status is acquired depends, to a great extent, on
timing, personal career path aspirations of both the parents and grandparents,
and the relative stability of the extended family structure. Although Burton and
Bengtson's findings are based on black family studies, the same can be said of
the range of responses to grandparenthood among the American Indians I have
interviewed. Custodial grandparenting occurs across cultures where unantici-
pated family trauma (divorce, death, unemployment, abandonment, illness, neglect or abuse) separates child and parents.

Three families in this study are best described by the term ''custodial'' grandparenthood. In all three cases, the grandchildren were those of daughters who
had either died, had their children taken from them by the court system or had
been abandoned by the children's fathers and could not keep the families intact
with their meager earnings or child welfare stipends. In all cases, the grandparents' roles as primary caretakers were solicited either by the children's parents
or the courts, not by lonely grandparents rattling about in their empty nests.

In one family the grandmother was not only caring for a daughter's three
children but also one son's child, as well as a great-grandchild, when inter-

viewed. The custodial role essentially had been forced upon her by the misconduct or lack of parental interest of two of her children. She, begrudgingly, accepts the role in the best interest of her several troubled and abandoned grandchildren.

When is it ever going to end, that's what I would like to know? All my life I've had these kids off and on. Especially with my daughter's kids . . . Atoka[3] has been with me since she was a year and a half. Her mother would go out and would be partying and someone was left with the child. But that person took off and left Atoka by herself. And the neighbors called me to tell me the child was all by herself, crying. The judge wouldn't let her [the daughter][4] have her [Atoka] back so he gave her to me. Lahoma, she's been with me since she was born, I guess. Pamela went with somebody. I think she was placed in a home, then she would come to stay with me for a while, then her mother would take her back, and then get into trouble again and the whole thing would start all over again. . . . [And] then, there's my sixteen-year-old granddaughter. She's going to have a baby. And guess who's going to take care of that baby when it comes? (Choctaw woman, age 57, Broken Bow, Oklahoma).

For the cultural conservator, having a houseful of grandchildren is an expected privilege of old age. In contrast, the custodial grandmother is often relatively young and unprepared to take on the caretaking responsibilities culturally appropriate to the status of grandmother.

Pressured by cultural norms and familial needs, this fifty-seven-year-old, soon-to-be great-grandmother feels powerless to act in her own personal behalf. Suffused since childhood with fundamental Christian values (charity, self-denial, motherhood, the sanctity of the family) and spurred on by the promise of heavenly rewards to those who endure an earthly martyrdom, she resentfully accepted her custodial great-grandmotherhood as her "cross to bear."

THE CULTURAL CONSERVATOR GRANDPARENT

Being raised by one's grandparents is not an enculturative phenomenon unique to either twentieth-century rural or urban American Indian experience. In fact, grandmothers as primary caretakers of first and second grandchildren is a long-established Native American child care strategy.

The cultural conservator role is a contemporary extension of this traditional relationship. Rather than accept an imposed role, the conservator grandparents actively solicit their children to allow the grandchildren to live with them for extended periods of time for the expressed purpose of exposing them to the American Indian way of life. Not surprisingly, the cultural conservator is the modal grandparenting style among the families in this study.

The grandparental style of six families is best defined by this term. One Sioux woman who had two of her grandchildren living with her at the time of the interview exemplifies the cultural conservator grandparenting style. The enthu-

On the occasion of the great-grandmother's ninety-first birthday, four generations of Seneca women were called forward to be honored at a Saturday night powwow in Long Beach, California.

siasm about having one or more grandchildren in her home for extended periods of time is tempered by the realization that, for her own children who grew up in an urban environment, the spiritual magnetism of reservation life is essentially lost. She regards their disdain for tribal life with consternation and ironic humor and consciously opts for taking a major role in the early socialization of her grandchildren. She views her children as being just "too far gone" (assimilated) for any attempt at repatriation on her part. Her role as the culture conservator grandmother, then, is doubly important. The grandchildren are her only hope for effecting both personal and cultural continuity.

The second- or third-generation Indian children out [in Los Angeles], most of them never get to see anything like . . . a sun dance or a memorial feast or giveaway or just stuff that Indians do back home. I wanted my children to be involved in them and know what it's all about. So that's the reason that I always try to keep my grandchildren whenever I can. (Sioux Woman, age 67, Pine Ridge, South Dakota)

She recognizes the primary caretaking aspects of her grandmotherhood as not only a traditionally American Indian, but also as a particularly Lakota thing to do.

The grandparents always took . . . at least the first grandchild to raise because that's just the way the Lakota did it. They think that they're [the grandparents] more mature and have had more experience and they could teach the children a lot more than the young parents, especially if the parents were young. . . . I'm still trying to carry on that tradition because my grandmother raised me most of the time up until I was nine years old.

She remembers her grandparents' enculturative styles as essentially conservative in the sense that those things they passed on to their grandchildren were taken from traditional Sioux lore. The grandparents rarely commanded or required the grandchild's allegiance to their particular world view. Rather, instruction took the form of suggestions about or presentation of models of exemplary behavior. "Well, my grandfather always told me what a Lakota woman wouldn't do and what they were supposed to do. But he never said I had to do anything." She purposely continues to shape her grandmotherhood on the cultural conservator model of her own grandparents. "I ask [my children] if [their children] could spend the summer with me if there isn't school and go with me to the Indian doings so that they'll know that they're Indian and know the culture and traditions. [I'm] just kind of building memories for them."

Those cultural and traditional aspects of Sioux life to which this grandmother exposes her city-born grandchildren include a wide range of ceremonial and informal activities. An active participant in village life, she and her grandchildren make continual rounds of American Indian church meetings, senior citizens' lunches, tribal chapter hearings, powwows, memorial feasts, sun dances, funerals, giveaways and rodeos. The children attend a tribe-run elementary school in which classes are taught in both English and Lakota. The children actively participate in the ceremonial life of the reservation, dancing in full regalia at powwows and helping their grandmother distribute gifts at giveaways and food at feasts. Most importantly, those grandchildren who live with her for long periods of time are immersed in the daily ordering of reservation life. Through the grandmother's firm, authoritative tutelage, complemented by their gentle and affectionate grandfather, and through the rough-and-tumble play with rural age-group members who, for the most part, can claim some kinship with the urban-born visitors, they learn, through observation, example and experimentation, their society's core values and interactional style.

As stated earlier, the grandparenting styles are not mutually exclusive categories. Rather, this woman's primary caretaking responsibility also includes elements of the custodial model. She sharply contrasts the stability of her home with the turbulence of some of her children's urban social and psychological contexts.

I think I have a stable home and I can take care of them. Especially if the mother and father are having problems. This next June, Sonny [her daughter's son] will be with me two years, and . . . Winoma . . . she's been with me a year and a half. But this is an unusual situation. The parents . . . are going to get a divorce. That's why I didn't want them around there [Los Angeles] while this was going on. I think they're better off with me.

Marjorie Schweitzer (1987) suggests that adults, especially women, welcome becoming a grandparent and are proud to claim that status. For the cultural conservator, primary caretaking is a role eagerly negotiated with children. For the Sioux woman in question, having her youngest grandchildren in her home and under her absolute custody for extended periods of time is just one more example of her acceptance and enactment of behaviors expected of properly traditional, older Sioux women. Her active grandmotherhood fulfills what she sees as an important cultural function not only for herself but also for her future generations. She exercises that function in ways that would have been familiar to her arch-conservative grandparents—a cultural continuity she finds particularly satisfying. "I think it's a privilege to keep my grandchildren. When they're grown up, they'll remember and talk about when I lived with my grandmother. . . . Like I talk about living with my grandmother."

DISCUSSION

The five divergent perceptions and expressions of grandparenthood presented here are clearly consequences of the individuals' sense of personal control and initiative in shaping the style in which they carry out their grandparenthood. Clear parallels to the distanced and custodial grandparenting styles can be found in the descriptions of contemporary American grandparenthood (Stack 1974; Burton and Bengtson 1985; Simic 1990; Minkler and Roe 1993; Vesperi Chapter 7). Those factors which prompt these interactional styles among American Indian families—migration, psychological estrangement between the parental generations and relative instability of the parental household—also produce instances of these grandparenting styles among non-Indian families. Interestingly, neither of these styles is the cultural ideal for either American Indians or non-Indians. Popular American literature deplores the psychological distance between generations, yet also views the child reared by grandparents as culturally and psychologically disadvantaged. While American Indians equally deplore the distanced grandparenting style, the grandchild in the custody of a grandparent, however, is seen as potentially advantaged by that experience.

Incidence of the ceremonial grandparenting style among non-Indians is not clearly indicated in the literature. I suggest, however, that it does exist in some form (the inclusion of grandparents in national and religious holiday celebrations, for instance). Where ceremonialism between grandparents and grandchildren occurs in Anglo-American families, however, it is prompted by different motivations. As the literature suggests, (Holmes 1986; Simic 1990) the noninterfering, affectionate grandparents who live independently in their own homes at some distance from the nuclear parental family but who join the nuclear family on ritually appropriate, if time limited, occasions is the Anglo-American cultural ideal. In contrast, the ceremonial grandparenting style among North American Indians is a compromise—at once pleasing and incomplete. It is symbolic behavior, enactments of one aspect of American Indian family life, in the wake of missing day-to-day intergenerational interactions.

Both the fictive and cultural conservator grandparenting styles are particularly American Indian adaptations. Current motivations for both styles are consistent with historical ones. Pragmatic concerns for providing emotional and economic supports in the absence of biologically mandated ones prompt fictive kinship designations today as in the nineteenth century. And the need to care for children while parents work and to fulfill a sense of continuing participation in family and community life prompted the cultural conservator grandparenting style then as now.

Today, however, presenting one's grandchildren with traditional cultural lore has become a critical issue of cultural survival vis-à-vis a new and insidious enemy. Faced by consuming cultural alternatives and unmotivated or inexperienced children, American Indian grandparents can no longer assume the role of cultural conservator for their grandchildren as practiced historically. Rather, grandparents, concerned with continuity of tribal consciousness, must seize the role and force inculcation of traditional lore upon their grandchildren through a grandparenting style best described as cultural conservation.

The status, grandparent, is imbued with considerable sociostructural weight in that it, across cultures, automatically confers both responsibility and rewards to the individual upon the birth of the grandchild. The roles associated with grandparenthood, however, can be and are negotiated. Satisfaction with both status and role is an artifact of the individual's sense of creating a grandparenthood consistent with both personal and cultural expectations.

CONCLUDING REMARKS

It is now more than a decade since I first talked with older Sioux and Muskogeans about their grandparenting experiences and fully six years since I wrote the first sections of this chapter. During that time I have kept in touch with approximately half of the grandparents of the original study. This longitudinal perspective prompts the cautionary tone of my concluding remarks. Most importantly, the ephemeral, situational, flexible and time-limited nature of the practice of a particular grandparenting style by contemporary American Indians must be underscored.

The grandmother who, in 1984, had actively constructed and was carrying out her chosen role as a cultural conservator, was capable only of ceremonial grandparenting in 1995. This major shift in family role is the result of a number of situational factors. Her daughter moved to Rapid City (a 90-minute car drive away from the grandmother's reservation home), found work and took her four children with her. The grandmother's struggle with diabetes mellitus and heart disease leaves her insufficient strength to care for her now adolescent and teenaged grandchildren. Her grandparenting currently consists largely of occasional trips to and participation in annual powwows with her grandchildren and their sojourns at her prairie home during holidays and their parents' summer vacations.

The relatively short American Indian life expectancy and deplorable morbidity rates vis-à-vis those of the general population are well-known and exhaustively documented (National Indian Council on Aging 1979, 1981; U.S. Senate Special Committee on Aging 1989). The life trajectory of the woman who personified the custodial grandparenting style a decade ago also illustrates the fact that American Indians can expect their grandparents to be with them for shorter periods of time than can non-Indian Americans. In 1985 the, then, fifty-eight-year-old custodial grandmother was diagnosed as having cancer. Already metastasized by the time the growth was discovered, the malignancy took her life within eighteen months of its diagnosis. The younger of the four grandchildren and great-grandchildren living with her when she died were taken in by various aunts and uncles. The teenaged grandchildren returned to Los Angeles to search for their drug-addicted mother. They periodically reappear at the homes of or phone their Oklahoma-based relatives when help is needed. Their preference for the urban pace and their peer group's lifestyle in Los Angeles proved too strongly seductive to be extinguished by their grandmother's attempts to bring them into the Choctaw Christian fold during their short time with her.

A third life trajectory not included in the 1990 version of this chapter underscores the influence of health and the aging process on grandparenting style. In 1984 a Hopi/Cherokee friend and colleague embodied the cultural conservator grandparenting style. Living in Los Angeles, one of her grandchildren had been with her since he was a toddler. Weekly she, with him in tow, attended local powwows and powwow dance classes. By the time he was six years old he was already winning powwow dance contests in his age class.

This woman's grandparenting career also exemplifies the stylistic range with which individual American Indians practice grandparenting. To a number of her grandchildren she was their ceremonial grandmother, going with them to powwows and enrolling them in powwow dance classes even though they lived with their parents some distance from her home. To hundreds of Los Angeles-based American Indian children she functioned as a fictive grandparent in much the same way the Oklahoma-based Choctaw schoolteacher did. The director of the Educational Opportunity for Native Americans (EONA) program in the Long Beach Unified School District for over twenty years, she ensured that Native American school children had the opportunity to learn about their Indian heritages in culturally appropriate ways.

In 1995 she was no longer in Los Angeles. As with so many aging American Indians, her twenty-year struggle to control the onset of diabetes had taken its toll. Approximately a year earlier a complication of diabetes had legally blinded her and a mild stroke had left her partially paralyzed and speech-impaired. She had taken an early retirement and had been moved by her family to her sister's home in Arizona to recuperate. Her now teenaged, live-in grandchild had returned to his mother's home. The woman's state of health had reduced her family role to distanced grandparenthood.

This woman's chronic and progressive illnesses underscore a grandparental condition not immediately apparent to me a decade ago because of the relative youth of the 26 grandparents in the original sample. In fact, the passage of time prompts the conceptualization of a sixth grandparenting style. I think of it as care-needing grandparenting. Although I allude to this condition in the earlier discussion of the ceremonial grandparent, it did not occur to me to consider it a full-blown grandparenting style until now.

Native American children and grandchildren are expected to care for their failing family elders in their homes. Children are expected to read to their live-in, sight-impaired grandparents, to help them to the dance floor and to steady their gait by dancing hand-in-hand with them at powwows. Older grandchildren and their parents are expected to fix meals, run errands and handle the substantial paperwork involved with Medicare, Medicaid, Social Security and Indian Health Service entitlements. Ironically, the frailest elders have among the most important cultural lessons to teach their grandchildren. The culturally expected quality and range of interactions between the needful grandparents and their grandchildren underscore and illustrate core values which have always sustained the integrity of American Indian family life—respect for the elderly and the interdependence of all family members.

"Mitak oyasin"
(Lakota for "all my relations")[5]

NOTES

This research was funded by grant 1RO1 AGO 3794–2, from the National Institute on Aging.

1. The appropriateness of the use of the labels, Native American versus American Indian, has been discussed and disputed in the anthropological and historical literature for at least the last 25 years. I have used both, often in the same article or chapter. Because I am talking about older tribal people who generally use the term American Indian to label themselves, I feel it is appropriate to use the term in this chapter.

2. In 1953 the U.S. government initiated a program to relocate Native Americans in economically depressed rural areas to urban centers. In the following 40 years the U.S. Native American population shifted from a largely rural to an evenly distributed urban/rural mix. This dramatic demographic shift was due, in large part, to the federally-funded urban relocation directive.

3. In all cases fictitious names have been used to protect the privacy of those people who generously shared their life histories and views on grandparenthood with me.

4. All words and phrases in brackets have been added by the author to make the verbatim translation of the narratives intelligible to the reader.

5. This phrase is spoken during and at the end of most Lakota ceremonies. It is meant to remind the participants that they are related to and share responsibilities for all living things. It is meant to underscore interrelationality as a core cultural value.

CHAPTER 7

Without Parents: Multigenerational Strategies for the Survival of Community

Maria D. Vesperi

Life in postindustrial U.S. society is increasingly marked by the number of children who are left without parents due to economic disenfranchisement, residential displacement, drug addiction, homicide, high rates of incarceration and disease. Such children are increasingly likely to reside with their grandparents. According to the U.S. Census Bureau, the number of grandparent-headed households increased by about one-third between 1970 and 1990. At the beginning of this decade, these households included roughly 3.4 million children. By 1994, a U.S. Census Current Population Survey update found more than 3.7 million children living in grandparent-headed households (AARP 1996), a stunning increase of 375,000 since the 1993 sample. Within this group, grandparents were found to be raising an overwhelming 342,000 additional children on their own, with no parent present in the home.

Books and articles on the subject of contemporary grandparental roles draw heavily from census data, and from a wellspring of specialized local studies. In their introduction to *Grandmothers as Caregivers* (1993), for instance, Minkler and Roe point to an Oakland, CA, finding that grandparents were serving as parents for more than 20 percent of children enrolled in a local Head Start preschool program during 1992. At one junior high school in the same district, more than half of the students did not live with their parents. In some urban neighborhoods, these authors tell us, it has been estimated that 30 to 70 percent of all children are receiving primary care from grandparents or other kin. In this book, Minkler and Roe are concerned with the impact of cocaine on grandmother-centered caregiving networks. This is a problem that many policymakers seem to regard as a new phenomenon, unique to our era.

Yet, addiction, economic exclusion, children orphaned by epidemic disease— all of these painfully contemporary dilemmas were present historically as well.

Then as now, public awareness of why families fail to thrive was limited and ideologically focused; efforts to find solutions to complex problems were concomitantly distorted. In his 1990 book, *The American Journalist: Paradox of the Press*, Loren Ghiglione discusses the contrast between the romanticized image of children who hawked newspapers on urban street corners a century ago and the realities of their brutal, often truncated lives. Such children were called "newsies," and they were the subjects of songs, paintings, novels and films until at least the 1940s. In truth, these children were neither the heroic figures of the anonymous 1866 novel, *Luke Darrell, the Chicago Newsboy*, nor the wily, sturdy, Dead End Kid–types romanticized in black-and-white films. Ghiglione puts it graphically: "The early newsies of fact often were homeless waifs, hawking newspapers to survive. They slept huddled together in abandoned stairwells, packing cases, and wooden barrels. Unscrupulous saloonkeepers solicited their business, feeding them liquid lunches of whiskey at three cents a glass" (1990:117).

Two factors brought these children to the streets of northern cities: the punctuated but continuous internal migration of whites and African Americans from rural areas to industrial centers and the influx of new immigrants. The same technological revolution that drew adults with the promise of jobs allowed for the mass production of penny newspapers. In the mid-1800s, according to Ghiglione, a child could earn about 33 cents for every 100 papers sold.

A half century before any form of federal assistance existed in the United States, the only hope available to many parentless children was the occasional "newsboy home" sponsored by a private charity or religious organization. These shelters provided room and board and sometimes even offered night school education.

The public was not spared discussion of the grim realities facing such children. Even the stories about newsies in children's books could be quite graphic; suffering and death were treated with equanimity, as candid cautionary tales. Ghiglione cites *The Roosevelt Bears Go to Washington*, a 1907 children's book by Seymour Eaton, in which a homeless child freezes to death when he fails to earn enough money selling papers for his night's lodging.

Ghiglione traces several thematic elements used to reconcile the discrepancies between the lives of abandoned children and the public's perception of their plight. One is familiar to us as the signature Horatio Alger theme, although it was exploited by other authors as well: "Ned Nevins, the hero of Henry Morgan's 1866 novel, has no father, no education, and no money. But he supports his sick mother by picking coal at a dump and by hustling newspapers. He explains his hard work, 'I want to be free—that is, what mother calls self-reliant.' " At the same time, and equally relevant: "The newsies of fiction demonstrate that—despite poverty and privation—one could live by a code, a clear notion of individual honor and individual justice" (Ghiglione 1990:118).

Much more graphic stories can be found in actual news accounts from the period. Then as now, however, the public bore a very high tolerance—one might even say appetite—for stories about domestic tragedy, brutalized and suffering children, urban chaos. Then as now, discussion was heated. Then as now, there seemed to be a marked discontinuity between awareness and social responsibility or action. What prevents us from moving the debate on such critical issues beyond the level of orthodox rhetoric?

WHY HISTORY REPEATS ITSELF

All too predictably, low-income, inner city families have provided the initial focus of attention in contemporary discussions of parental absence (Minkler and Roe 1993). Although the problems clearly transect demographic, economic and regional divisions within the United States (Minkler 1994; Slorah 1994), they also belong to social theorist Pierre Bourdieu's "universe of the undiscussed" (Bourdieu 1977). The label means precisely what one would suspect—rocks that are never turned over, ideas that are not entertained, questions that those who share a world view are not motivated to ask.

Bourdieu's term can be fruitfully applied to the arena of social welfare policy. The failure to ask relevant questions is always a clue to more complex sets of underlying assumptions. In the nineteenth century, immigrant and minority families were regarded as the source of social problems, imported as so much cultural baggage. Motivation to respond to their needs at a policy level was low because the system itself was not examined as a potential source of trouble. In the case of contemporary grandparents serving as parents, efforts to tailor national social welfare policy have also been obscured by assumptions about race and ethnicity, gender and age. These are the same assumptions that prevent us from asking relevant questions about other aspects of contemporary family formations as well. Put plainly, many people seem to assume that the majority of caregivers who need help are single, African-American women below traditional age, whether they be mothers, grandmothers or both.

A different picture is emerging from a research project conducted by the American Association of Retired Persons. Since 1993, AARP has been collecting telephone data from people who request information from its Grandparent Information Center in Washington, DC. The Center is a busy information clearinghouse established with a grant from the Brookdale Foundation Group. During the first year alone, AARP noted that 83 percent of the grandparents who called were white, with an average age of 55. Most callers over age 65 were actually great-grandparents who were caring for great-grandchildren, and possibly other generations as well. Significantly, 54 percent of the callers worked part-time, 39 percent reported incomes of $20,000 or less, and, contrary to most stereotypes about so-called "dysfunctional" intergenerational families, 68 percent were married couples (Woodworth 1994).

These figures closely resemble data collected by the U.S. Census Bureau as reported by Chalfie (1994). Working with the results of a 1992 Current Population Survey, Chalfie found a median age of 57 for grandparent caregivers, 68 percent of whom are white and approximately 75 percent of whom are married. Similarly, in Patricia Slorah's 1994 study of former grandparent caregivers who later experienced estrangement from their grandchildren, married couples comprised 70 percent of the sample. In another recent study, 76 percent of the grandparents were married.

Substance abuse by the middle generation was cited as a reason for caregiving by 44 percent of the AARP callers. Child abuse was the number two reason. In her study of grandparental rights among mostly white, middle-class grandparents in Florida, Slorah found that child maltreatment by the middle generation figured heavily into intergenerational conflict over grandparental visitation. In families where abuse and/or neglect had occurred, including instances in which children were removed from their homes by the state and temporarily placed with grandparents, these grandparents were frequently denied access to the grandchildren once the parents had restabilized. When these grandparents turned to the same state agencies that had actively sought and gratefully accepted their assistance in times of crisis, they were told that they had no rights.

Grandparents are often the most accessible and sometimes the only alternatives to the foster care system, and in many studies they have been quick to identify themselves in this way. At the same time, as recent research among both white and African-American grandparental caregivers also indicates, they are *not* always eager to become full-time parents again and may openly acknowledge the toll of the parenting role on their health, finances and social networks (AARP 1995; Minkler 1994; Slorah 1994; Smith 1994; Minkler and Roe 1993; Minkler, Roe and Price 1992).

These caregivers—and again, they are currently heading households that include 3.7 *million* children—are suspended somewhere in Bourdieu's universe of the undiscussed. At the level of traditional kinship status they retain the title "grandparent." At the level of role behavior, however, many have experienced a collateral descent, dropping one generation or even two to assume full parental duties for children who are no longer living or who have been incarcerated on a long-term basis. This represents a fundamental transition from their widely recognized roles as active participants in extended families. Indeed, one could argue that the term "extended family" is no longer appropriate in such contexts, and does not provide an adequate framework for the development of medical, social and economic policies to meet their overwhelming, rapidly evolving needs. These grandparents are, in essence, generationally decontextualized.

From a social welfare policy perspective, it is clear that state and federal agencies perpetuate stereotypes about grandparental eagerness and readiness to assume parenting roles because it is in their best financial interest to do so. During the mid-1990s in Florida, for instance, foster parents received about $300 per month for the subsidized care of a child, while a grandparent *with no other source of income* would only have been entitled to $180 for the same care (Miller 1996). If the sweeping provisions of the welfare reforms passed in 1996 are fully enacted, grandparents will no longer be eligible for federal assistance to help them care for dependent grandchildren. At the same time, experts say, the withdrawal of federal support will make it impossible for the poorest parents and children to stay together, forcing even more children into foster care (Miller 1996).

Such bottom-line calculations are masked from public view by persistent, politically convenient assumptions about the roles of older women, particularly older African-American women. While African-American families continue to be the centerpiece of neoconservative rhetoric about the demise of the family, so-called pro-family legislation is, as Slorah notes with regard to grandparental rights, "designed to narrow the focus of the American family to the nuclear model" (Slorah 1994:121).

ADAPTATION AND FAMILY SURVIVAL

Policymakers who would reverse the well-documented, widespread innovations within kin-based networks mistakenly assume that family structures must be static to remain stable. With or without a government stamp of approval, families will continue to adapt to meet changing needs. Margaret Platt Jendrek's study of the relationship between grandparental roles and life transitions among adult children is of interest here (Jendrek 1994). Jendrek conducted in-depth interviews among 114 mostly white, middle-class grandparents residing in or near Butler County, Ohio; she selected this area because it was demographically representative of the state and, in some respects, of the United States in general. Her sample fell into three broad groups: 52 "day care" grandparents, 26 "living with" grandparents and 36 legal grandparents. The day care grandparents identified their children's work schedules as the primary reason for their daily involvement in grandchildren's lives. Among the two groups of custodial grandparents, the "living with" grandparents were often helping an adult child who was struggling as a single parent, and who might also be living with them. Among those with legal custody of their grandchildren, Jendrek found that emotional problems or drug and alcohol use by a child's parent was cited as a predominant reason for grandparents to assume care. In her presentation of this research at the 1994 meetings of the Gerontological Association of America, Jendrek also noted that while the "living with" grandparents often received some financial support from the middle generation, those grandparents who had assumed permanent custody were the least likely to have access to financial support from the middle generation.

The AIDS epidemic provides dramatic examples of generational shifts in the responsibility for child rearing. It is important to consider the parameters of this issue in the 1990s and how it might be configured at the turn of the century. An article published in the December 1992 issue of the *Journal of the American Medical Association* provides some relevant insights. In "Estimates of the Number of Motherless Youth Orphaned by AIDS in the United States," David Michaels and Carol Levine produced a range of sobering figures based on several factors, including data about HIV-related deaths among women ages 13 to 49, the number of children born to this group adjusted for HIV-related declines in fertility, infant mortality and pediatric AIDS deaths, and calculations pertaining to the relative numbers of children who might be orphaned from birth to age 18 and above. "The number of children and adolescents made motherless by the HIV/AIDS crisis in the United States is large and rapidly increasing," the authors found. Projections for 1995 included 45,700 orphaned children and adolescents, with 24,600 under age 13 and 21,000 ages 13 to 17.

Newer statistics indicate that the combined figure can be expected to reach roughly 100,000 by the turn of the century. Again, a comparison to the past is enlightening. An estimated 40,000 homeless children lived on the streets of lower Manhattan alone during the mid-1800s (*Leslie's Illustrated Weekly Newspaper*, August 2, 1856, cited in Ghiglione). They were male and female, some as young as age three (Hughes 1981, cited in Ghiglione).

Michaels and Levine predicted that the number of women under age 50 who died of AIDS and related causes, leaving children under age 13, would reach 3,900 by the end of 1992. Thirty-four hundred of these women would have left adolescent children. As Michaels and Levine pointed out, "The CDC recently commented that the emergence of a disease and its appearance as a leading cause of death in the same decade is without precedent. The emergence of a new group of motherless youth because of that disease may also be without precedent" (1992:3461). Most women who die of AIDS today are in their thirties and forties, but as Michaels and Levine have suggested, increased risk of infection among younger women may well lead to a larger number of orphaned children.

Cross-cultural comparisons, while certainly not directly transferable, offer an alarming preview of what happens when the so-called "sandwich generation" disappears and grandparents are left without support. In his 1989 book, *Ageing in Developing Countries*, Ken Tout identified the cornerstone weight that grandparents are called upon to bear when such epidemics weaken the wage-earning, child-rearing generation. Tout pointed to the larger crisis in AIDS-pandemic regions of Africa, where HIV infection may be all but absent among those over 60 years of age. Here, older woman must care for their dying children without medical support and then rear the surviving grandchildren in AIDS-decimated communities where other once-productive young adults are also terminally ill. A woman might ultimately look up to find that the "entire weight of productivity, commercial activity, transport, and even local government in the community may have devolved upon a random group of grandmothers like herself" (1989:296–297).

In the United States, the mothers of women in their thirties and forties are themselves in their fifties, sixties and seventies. Although it has been noted that the fastest growing HIV-positive population is comprised of people over 60, the oldest remain least at risk for HIV infection. Viewed from this perspective, every study of AIDS, drugs, guns or economic barriers to family formation that ignores the multiple roles of older survivors and caregivers is a missed opportunity. Despite the popular assumption that people in the United States are becoming parents and grandparents at earlier ages today, most assume grandparenting roles for the first time when they are in their forties and fifties, much the same as they did 100 years ago (Cherlin and Furstenberg 1992).

Gerontologist Linda Burton, who has conducted long-term ethnographic research in several communities, stresses that multigenerational support can take many forms. Discussion of ''the'' grandparental role is as misleading as most other efforts to generalize too quickly from particular examples. Families in the United States have always been diverse, but civil law and social welfare policies have yet to reflect their realities and needs. A note of encouragement was sounded when the 1995 White House Conference on Aging adopted a broad resolution that would address many of the legal, financial and social needs of grandparent caregivers. Turning such resolutions into law is another matter, however.

In the meantime, it is not surprising that neoconservative lawmakers could dare to propose placing large numbers of children in orphanages when their mothers, cut off from public assistance under welfare reform, are no longer able to house, feed and clothe them. In the late nineteenth century, homeless children were treated as miniature adults, capable of fending for themselves and forming alternative households. In the late twentieth century, low-income parents have been stereotyped as dysfunctional children, undeserving of entitlement programs and incapable of using them to help maintain stable families. Under such conditions, it is no accident that grandparent caregivers are often singled out and romanticized as aging Horatio Algers, struggling mightily in the private sector to make ends meet and uphold family values. While media feature stories exploit every detail of their individual dilemmas, the larger issues that have normalized and institutionalized the society-wide proliferation of children without parents continue to be ignored.

CHAPTER 8

Exchange and Reciprocity among Two Generations of Japanese and American Women

Hiroko Akiyama, Toni C. Antonucci and Ruth Campbell

The purpose of this chapter is to explore exchange patterns and exchange rules of social support for older persons in two vastly different cultures. We examine them by focusing on the relationships between two generations of women, older women and their adult daughters and daughters-in-law, in the United States and in Japan. Mother/daughter relationships in the United States and mother-in-law/daughter-in-law relationships in Japan have been traditionally considered vital sources of support for older women. Consequently, these relationships have a significant impact on their well-being and adjustment to aging. Furthermore, given the large proportion of the elderly's social interactions which take place within the family and the central role of women in kinship networks in both societies, it is particularly appropriate to focus on these relationships in addressing primary rules of support exchange in old age.

We explore here the exchange of support between two generations of women by focusing on the concept of *reciprocity*. We believe that the norm of reciprocity governs how individuals accept and provide social support and that reciprocal relationships contribute in complex but important ways to successful aging in both the United States and Japan. To examine this, we begin with a consideration of the concept of reciprocity and its manifestations in the two societies. We then present relevant data from three studies conducted in the United States and Japan. The differences in the intergenerational roles of women and the patterns of support exchange offer interesting insights into how the norm of reciprocity operates in the two societies. The data, from very different sources, suggest that the concepts of exchange and reciprocity are vital parts of the lives of these women, but operate in strikingly different ways in the two societies. Finally, the data also offer evidence that gradual changes in exchange rules are taking place in both societies.

THE RECIPROCITY NORM OF SUPPORT EXCHANGE

Our definition of the term *reciprocity* is most consistent with that proposed by Alvin Gouldner (1960) in his early, seminal article on the norm of reciprocity. By the term reciprocity, we refer to equal or comparable exchanges of tangible aid, affection, advice or information between individuals or groups. This limited definition is generally accepted without controversy, referring simply to the notion of exchange, that is, of giving and receiving.

The past two decades have witnessed growing interest in support exchange and reciprocity in gerontology. Earlier, James Dowd (1975, 1984) suggested that the norms of reciprocity, beneficence and other social exchange notions are critical to an understanding of the status of the elderly in the United States. His central argument is that old age includes a necessary reduction in the possession of valued exchange commodities. This decrease in valued resources results in a lessened ability of older people to interact successfully with younger people who do have valued resources and who like to seek valued commodities from others.

Gary Lee (1985) has extended the work of Dowd by considering intergenerational supportive interactions and their consequences for the well-being of older persons within the context of social exchange theory. For example, referring to the study of Brody, Johnson, Fulcomer and Lang (1983) on attitudes of three generations of American women toward the care of older parents, he notes that older people are often unwilling to accept the support offered by their children. Lee argues that studies of informal support networks have ignored the tremendous value placed on independence and autonomy by the American elderly. Older persons, even if they really need help, are often hesitant to accept it if they feel unable to reciprocate. Unbalanced exchange relations which develop dependence could have seriously detrimental psychological or emotional consequences. "Thus while older people may experience many concrete benefits from the services their children and other kin provide, and while these benefits may be instrumental in maintaining their quality of life, ironically the receipt of these benefits may detract from their quality of life in other ways" (G. Lee 1985:31).

In Japan, the norm of reciprocity has also been demonstrated as a useful frame of reference for understanding social behaviors (Befu 1986; Lebra 1986). For example, the concept of *on*, which refers to a favor or benevolence granted by A to B and to a resultant debt B owes to A, is clearly defined in terms of reciprocity. *On* has had its root in the Japanese culture for at least several hundred years. It still permeates almost every area of contemporary Japanese society and has played a pivotal role in explaining various social relations in Japan (Bethel 1992; Lebra 1986; Reischauer 1977). Every individual owes limitless *on* to his or her parents for life, for care received, and, therefore, for what he or she is today. Thus, one is compelled to attempt to repay even a small portion of this debt throughout one's lifetime. For many Japanese, this urge to repay the *on* to their parents is a steady source of drive for lifelong achievements. "Successful" employer-employee relationships in Japan are also bound by the sense of *on*, in which *on*-governed employees show persistent loyalty and devotion to their father-figure employer. Furthermore, the Japanese language is rich in a vocabulary of words which expresses one's indebtedness to another. One example is *sumimasen*, which literally means "I have not cleared off the debt" but is widely used to mean "I am sorry." The frequent use of those words in daily conversation distinctively indicates the cultural emphasis on the reciprocity norm in Japan.

However, it is not clear that the same reciprocity norms which Dowd and Lee have observed among the American elderly can be applied to the support exchange among the Japanese elderly as well. In the following sections we examine this question based on the empirical data from three studies, each of which provides information about the intergenerational support exchange between older women and their daughters or daughters-in-law. In particular, we attempt to identify and compare how the reciprocity norms operate in these intergenerational relationships and how the norms differentially affect the adjustment to aging in the two societies.

RECIPROCITY AND EXCHANGE: RECENT FINDINGS

The first study was originally conceived as a cross-cultural comparative study of the rules for support exchange among family members in the United States and Japan (Akiyama 1984). The study explored how people in the two societies exchange six kinds of basic interpersonal resources (i.e., money, goods, services, information, status and love) with their family members and what the underlying rules of exchange behaviors are. There were two parts to this study. The first part involved a questionnaire about the views of female college students on resource exchanges in various dyadic family relations at different stages of the lifecourse. The second part consisted of in-depth interviews with older women focusing on the rules and rationales which explain their resource exchanges with family members.

In the initial part of the study, approximately 500 college students in each country were asked how likely people are to engage in a certain kind of resource exchange with a family member. The central question here was, what do people give and receive in the family? A respondent was presented with six hypothetical exchange situations, in each of which a family member X (e.g., daughter of age 45) gives one of six resources (e.g., services) to another family member (e.g., mother of age 70). Each situation was followed by fifteen pairs of statements, where each statement described the behavior of Y reciprocating X with a certain resource. Two different resources were paired in those statements. Because there were six classes of resources, fifteen pairs allowed for the combination of each resource with every other one. The respondent was asked to choose from each pair the statement which was more likely to be observed in actual family settings.

Analyses of these data from the two countries identified two distinct exchange patterns. College students in Japan reported that the exchange of different kinds of resources (e.g., money and love) was quite common in the family, whereas American college students reported that they were more likely to exchange similar resources (e.g., money and money) rather than different kinds of resources. Specifically, compared with the United States, expressive resources such as love and status are granted a much broader range of exchangeability in Japan. They can be exchanged not only with other expressive resources but also with material resources such as money and goods. Material resources and expressive resources are unlikely to be exchanged for one another in the United States.

We examined family dyads relevant to this chapter and asked what the appropriate response might be to the receipt of various resources in mother (age 70)/daughter (age 45) and mother/daughter-in-law dyads at similar ages. In both types of dyads, the Japanese were considerably more likely than their American counterparts to feel that love or status was the appropriate resource to reciprocate with, regardless of type of resources originally received. Americans were significantly more likely to feel that the exchange of similar resources was appropriate. Thus, the Japanese might report that when mother-in-law received services from daughter-in-law, she was likely to reciprocate with love and/or status, but Americans were likely to feel that the appropriate response would be reciprocating with the same resource, that is, services.

The in-depth interviews of 32 elderly Japanese and 30 American women replicated the findings from the questionnaire study. In the interviews the respondents were given hypothetical exchange situations involving older women and their daughters or daughters-in-law and asked whether or not the exchange would be typical, appropriate, fair and emotionally satisfying. A content analysis of the interviews with those 62 older women identified two exchange rules distinctive to each of the two family systems, and evidence for more acceptability of elderly dependence in the Japanese system than in the American system.

Analysis of these interviews suggests that the American family system prescribes one exchange rule, symmetrical reciprocity, which mandates repayment by a resource in kind and of equivalent value in a relatively short time period. This American rule suppresses one-way transactions characterized by the failure of equivalent repayment and thereby reduces the development of dependence which not only embarrasses a debtor but may also disrupt the relationship between a debtor and a donor. When one cannot maintain reciprocity, it leads to the disturbance of stable relationships. Even in casual exchanges of services or goods between mother and daughter (also between mother-in-law and daughter-in-law), reciprocity needs to be carefully maintained in order to secure a good relationship.

The following responses in the interviews with older American women demonstrate such characteristics of the American exchange rule. Receiving a small gift from her daughter-in-law, a woman said, "Of course, I would accept it with love and a thank you. But I would also find a way to return a gift. You can't always accept without giving." Given a hypothetical situation in which a married daughter came a couple of times to do some chores around the house when her mother had a bad cold, another woman responded by saying, "If that happened to me, I would offer my daughter some kind of help such as staying with her children when she and her husband go out. I would feel better if I could reciprocate, even though I know my daughter is not expecting anything in return for what she does for me. Just receiving would hurt my spirit . . . or pride, you know. Reciprocity is very important even between mothers and daughters."

The following case of a seventy-two-year-old American respondent, a retired store clerk, exemplifies how the same exchange rule operates in a somewhat more deprived situation. Mrs. B. had been living in a small midwestern city for the past 50 years. She raised thirteen children there. All of them have completed college and are doing quite well. She proudly showed their pictures to the interviewer, pointing out who is a physician, accountant, teacher, rancher's wife, and so on. She is now widowed and living alone in a one-room converted-garage apartment. Due to severe arthritis and heart problems, she is confined to a wheelchair and requires help in daily domestic chores such as cooking and cleaning. During the interview, a volunteer of the local meals-on-wheels program delivered a hot lunch. She repeatedly apologized for the mess of her apartment. After completing the interview, she pointed to one of the shoe boxes piled up in a corner of the room and asked the interviewer to open it. In the box, there was a stack of uncashed checks sent from the woman's children, along with birthday cards and Christmas cards. She was tickled to report that, on her birthday a couple of years before, the children surprised her by presenting a blueprint of a small house designed for a wheelchair-bound person. She was also amazed how creative her daughters and daughters-in-law were in making excuses for bringing "leftover" food and for offering to scrub the floor and to do other household chores because they needed the exercise or wanted to lose weight. She had gratefully declined to accept all these offers. She said she would not feel comfortable accepting a gift or favor when she could not reciprocate. Even if she sometimes experienced inconvenience or scarcity of resources, she preferred living this way.

As shown in such interview cases, the American women appear to apply basically the same exchange rule, that is, symmetric reciprocity, to both daughters and daughters-in-law. This finding is also supported by a national survey study of social support of older persons in the United States (Kahn and Antonucci 1980; Antonucci and Akiyama 1987) in which detailed data were collected on the exchange of six types of support: confiding, reassurance, respect, sick care, talk when upset and talk about health. Respondents over age 50 were asked to provide specific information about who they provided each type of support to and from whom they received each type of support. Focusing on support exchanges between older women and their daughters and daughters-in-law, an analysis revealed a quite similar exchange pattern in the two types of family dyads. The older respondents reported they *exchanged* supports and maintained reciprocal relationships with both their daughters and daughters-in-law. In general, however, they were much more likely to exchange supports with their daughters than daughters-in-law. In other words, the support exchanges in those two family dyads in the United States differ in frequency or quantity but they appear to be quite similar in terms of the exchange rule.

By contrast, the Japanese family system applies two clearly distinct exchange rules for family members and for nonfamily members. The rule for family members is asymmetric reciprocity wherein expressive resources hold high value and broad exchangeability. On the other hand, the rule for nonfamily members is one of symmetry and equal exchange within a prescribed time period. The latter is similar to the American rule. The single exchange rule in the United States and the double rules in Japan may derive from the different family structures in the two countries. A nuclear family, defined as the favored basic unit of organized relationships in the American family system, usually forms strong bonds with its close kin through frequent contacts and mutual aid. Thus, a kin network emerges, which has been conceptualized as the "modified extended family." It assumes equal partnership and autonomy and often results in strong collateral relationships among members (Sussman 1976).

The traditional Japanese family system, however, has the stem-family structure in which descent and inheritance pass from the father to the eldest son. The eldest son remains in the family home with his wife and offspring, while younger sons form branch houses. In such stem-family systems, "family members" consist of the members of a three-generation stem household and its branch households. Others are regarded as "nonfamily members." The fact that in Japan, family and nonfamily are formally defined may be particularly relevant here. For an older woman, her daughter-in-law is a formal family member and the mother and daughter-in-law relationship is completely governed by family-member rules. However, again formally speaking, her married daughter is no longer considered to be a family member. Since the married daughter formally belongs to her husband's family, the mother and daughter relationship is expected to abide by the nonfamily exchange rule.

The exchange rule for family members in Japan prescribes repayment for virtually any type of resource by an expressive resource. Repayment with a material resource in the family is often perceived to imply distance or even insult toward the exchange partner. Resource exchanges governed by such exchange rules are both diffuse and lacking in specificity in terms of equivalence of return within a specific time period. Reciprocity involving expressive resources is difficult to recognize, because love and status are not always quantifiable. Due to this unquantifiable nature of expressive resources, one can never feel the debt is completely discharged. This indeterminateness of debt discharge

A ninety-year old grandmother with her two-year-old and one-month-old granddaughters.

was demonstrated by interviews on mother-in-law and daughter-in-law relationships, in which older women reported that they were uncertain of fairness when they repaid their daughters-in-laws' services with love and/or status, although they considered such exchanges to be quite common, appropriate and satisfying. With a certain amount of ambiguity as to whether the debt has been repaid, one is never free psychologically from the obligation to reciprocate with more expressive resources such as affection and appreciation. Before one debt can be repaid, more material resources are usually received, so that the recipient can easily be placed in a *perpetual debtor* position in which one must be continually vigilant for another repayment opportunity.

Therefore, it is quite common that resource exchanges in the Japanese family are carried out over time. A classic example is the repayment by adult children to their aged parents for what they received as dependent children many decades before. Furthermore, under certain circumstances where direct repayment within a dyad is difficult or inappropriate, a third party, sometimes fourth and fifth ones, could be involved as an intermediary of resource exchanges. More than a few older Japanese women reported in the interviews that, in repaying the devoted services of a daughter-in-law, it was more effective to address affection toward grandchildren than to address it directly to the daughter-in-law. However, it should be noted that these daily family interactions are not usually perceived as a flow of resource exchanges. The prevalence of these long-term indirect exchanges among the Japanese is another factor which contributes diffuseness to the Japanese family exchange rule. Such diffuseness and indeterminateness of the Japanese exchange rule acts as a mechanism that inhibits complete repayment, thus maintaining indebtedness and dependence. It consequently serves to regulate and sustain family solidarity based upon dependence.

The following case exemplifies how the mother-in-law and daughter-in-law relationship works in a typical working-class family residing in an urban area of Japan. Mrs. M. is a relatively healthy seventy-one-year-old widow who is living with her son, a taxi driver, and his family in a small, four-room house in a suburban community outside of Tokyo. She shares a room with her granddaughter. On typical days, she gets up at 5:30, sweeps around the house, and waters the shrubs. Her daughter-in-law calls the family to breakfast when it is ready. After breakfast Mrs. M. usually goes to a local senior citizen center. She told the interviewer that since she started going to the center, the amount of family dissension, particularly between herself and her daughter-in-law, had significantly decreased. ''Our house is too small for two women,'' she said. On her way to the center, she often buys some candies or fruits to share with her friends at the center. ''I receive 100,000 yen [about $1,000] yearly from the government. Although the amount is small, having my own money is something new. My mother never had any money of her own. I can buy snacks to take to the center and can occasionally give my grandchildren extra spending money. It is a really good feeling to have my own money,'' she said with a smile. She spends most of her time at the senior citizen center talking with her regular group of friends and participating in a few of the activity programs such as folk dancing and doll making. Her favorite part of day is soaking herself, along with her friends, in a hot tub which is heated by the city garbage. After dinner, she usually helps her daughter-in-law clean up the table and watches television with her grandchildren.

In her household, as in those of most women interviewed, the daughter-in-law does most of the domestic chores. Mrs. M. helps, as expected, whenever she is needed. A couple of years before the interview, she had surgery to remove

blood clots in her leg. During the entire period of hospitalization and recuperation at home, her daughter-in-law spent countless hours caring for her. She has
reciprocated these hours of service by her daughter-in-law with appreciation and
praise. She always tells her neighbors, friends and relatives how caring and
diligent her *yome* (daughter-in-law) is and how happy she is to have such a
wonderful *yome*. Responding to a question of whether or not she might have
reciprocated her daughter-in-law's services in any other way, she said she had
never thought of giving a gift or doing something special for her. "She [daugh-
ter-in-law] enjoys her reputation of being an ideal *yome*. The good reputation
and respect from others, not a piece of jewelry or clothes, are the most rewarding
things you get from your hard work, I think,'' she added.

While resource exchanges between mother-in-law and daughter-in-law are
prescribed by the family exchange rule, a married daughter is formally defined
as nonfamily and the mother-daughter relationship is expected to be governed
by the nonfamily exchange rule. In fact, women reported in the interviews that
it is not *common* in Japan for a married daughter to provide her mother with
services. The daughter is expected to maintain certain distance from her "parent
family" as a measure of her respect for the wife of the brother with whom her
parents live. It is not appropriate for a mother to visit her married daughter to
provide help, either. This is particularly true for the daughter who lives with
her parents-in-law, although it is becoming more acceptable for a mother to visit
and help married daughters who are not living with their in-laws. The relationship between mothers and daughters in Japan has been undergoing substantial
change during the past few decades. It is now more acceptable to provide each
other with some degree of support beyond that traditionally prescribed.

Interestingly, and perhaps indicative of a new trend, the exchange rules for
such informal transactions between mothers and married daughters have not
been clearly defined. It appears to be common and acceptable for a mother to
reciprocate her married daughter's minor services, if she receives any, only with
affection and/or respect. However, when the daughter provides a considerable
amount of services such as spending several days caring for her sick mother,
the mother is likely to reciprocate with a material gift to both her daughter and
her daughter's family in acknowledgment of her services and the patience of
her family for the inconvenience caused by her absence. On the other hand, a
mother would not reciprocate her daughter-in-law's services with a similar material gift, because the mother and daughter-in-law belong to the same family.
It is considered *mizukusai* (lack of intimacy) to reciprocate any kind of resource
with material resources such as goods and money within the family.

Similar revisions of the traditional exchange rules in the Japanese family
system have been observed in the transaction of goods between mothers and
married daughters. Gift giving among nonfamily members is a minor institution
in Japan, with complex rules defining who should give to whom, what occasions
require a gift, what sort of gift is appropriate on a given occasion and how the
gift should be presented (Befu 1986). It has been the custom for a mother and

her married daughter or, in a more restricted sense, their families to exchange gifts on specified occasions. Such gift exchanges are strictly governed by the rule of symmetric reciprocity. Besides such formal gift giving, more informal transactions of goods between mothers and daughters are now becoming increasingly common. In the interviews, the older Japanese women reported receiving small gifts such as a box of their favorite candies, kitchen scissors or a new hairbrush from their daughters. Those gifts were often given without the knowledge of the daughter's husband and in-laws. Unlike formal gift exchanges, both mothers and daughters seem to apply the exchange rules for family members to such informal gift giving. It is most appropriate for a mother to reciprocate such small gifts only with affection and appreciation.

Clearly, the mother/daughter relationship in Japan is undergoing transition. The trend is that mothers and daughters are choosing to maintain continuously close relationships and frequent support exchanges as family members even after the daughter's marriage. It is obvious that such changes in the mother/daughter relationship are affecting the current mother-in-law and daughter-in-law relationship. This is demonstrated in the findings from a third set of data which compared the family relations of two groups of older Japanese women, those who live in three-generation households and those who live independently from their children. We can see here the direction of future changes in family exchange relationships in Japan. In this study (Campbell and Brody 1985), two groups of women were compared: (1) a joint-living group composed of 128 mothers-in-law and 136 daughters-in-law and (2) a separate-living group of 136 mothers and their daughters. About 80 percent of the older women living with their sons and daughters-in-law also had daughters living separately. The findings reported here pertain to the older women's relationships with their daughters and the younger women's relationships with their mothers.

When asked about visits within the past month, women living apart from their children report both paying more visits to and receiving more visits from their children than did those living in joint households. Consistent with the discussion above, mothers appear reluctant to visit their daughters who are living in joint households. Only 9 percent of daughters living with the husband's parents report receiving visits from their own mothers, as compared to 31 percent of daughters living separately. However, it is important to note that over half the women living in joint households were visited by their own daughters within the past month. The women living in joint households are, on the average, older than those living separately and perhaps would have more difficulty going out to visit their daughters. That many of them receive visits from their daughters demonstrates the diminution of traditional norms of distance between households.

Yuzawa (1994) writes that the weakening of the *ie* system has led to married women feeling more comfortable about visiting their parents as often as they like. He reports that a 1990 survey conducted by the Economic Planning Agency found that 38 percent of women in their twenties thought of their mothers as the person who understood them best, underlining the strong mother/daughter bond which continues through the daughter's marriage. A five-nation comparative survey on the frequency of contact with children living separately, conducted by the Management and Coordination Agency in 1990, showed that contact between elderly parents and their children living separately was less common in Japan than in Britain, Germany or the United States. However, 61.5 percent of older people in Japan reported that they had contact with their children living separately at least once or twice a month. Although the traditional structure of intergenerational relationships still carries considerable force in Japan, the more "natural," affective ties seem to be gaining in strength.

In the area of gift giving, there is somewhat more gift exchange reported by women living separately. The exchanges of food and clothing are high and relatively equal between the two groups, supporting the findings from the previous study that informal exchanges between mothers and daughters in joint-living households are gaining in frequency. A striking difference appears when daughters are asked if they have had dinner with their mothers within the past month. Forty-four percent of those living separately reported having had dinner with their mothers as compared to only 9 percent of those living with their husband's parents.

The question of living arrangements came up frequently in interviews with both generations. Although the majority of older Japanese live with their children, the percentage of those over age 65 living separately has increased from 13 percent in 1960 to 41 percent in 1994 (Statistics and Information Department, Ministry of Health and Welfare, 1994). Furthermore, recent surveys indicate that Japanese of all ages view living separately as a reasonable option when the older couple is healthy. As older persons become ill or widowed, they are more likely to prefer living together with children. Overall, although the Japanese seem to be widening the boundaries of what is possible, the staying power of traditional patterns of support exchange, despite modernization, is remarkable.

EXCHANGE RULES AND AGING

From an exchange theory perspective, the problems of aging are essentially problems of decreasing exchange commodities. Older people as a statistical aggregate suffer from lower income and poorer health than younger people. Consequently, they are physically and financially limited in entering into exchange situations. They might not be able to afford to exchange holiday gifts with children and grandchildren in the way they used to do, or to watch grandchildren in return for the help which they receive from their daughters or daughters-in-law. This is particularly true for the very old. Many of them have very little of any instrumental value to exchange.

How do the exchange rules affect the support relationships of older persons in the two societies? As described in the previous section, the American rule is characterized as symmetric reciprocity, which prescribes repayment by a resource in kind and of equivalent value within a relatively short time period.

Under this rule, faced with diminishing instrumental resources, the American elderly would find it difficult to repay with resources in kind in order to maintain reciprocal relationships. There is a widespread fear that the failure of equivalent repayment develops dependency. On the contrary, the exchange rule in the Japanese family prescribes repayment by an expressive resource regardless of the kind of resource received. Since expressive resources are essentially inexhaustible for any individual, Japanese elderly are expected to be better able to cope with declining material resources by reciprocating with expressive resources.

Thus, due to their exchange rules, American elderly seem to have more difficulty than their Japanese counterparts in adjusting to their decreased material resources. How do American elderly cope with this difficulty? There are several observations and explanations for adjustments in exchange behaviors as well as exchange rules which older Americans make as they age. For example, it is commonly observed that older individuals withdraw from exchange situations. This is clearly considered to be a coping strategy in which older persons still maintain the norm of reciprocity and simply choose not to enter exchange situations to prevent nonreciprocal relationships when they do not have resources to reciprocate.

Other explanations indicate modifications of exchange rules applied to older people. Antonucci's (1990) concept of a Social Support Bank seeks to explain support exchanges across the life span and help clarify the reciprocity issue in old age. The notion of a Social Support Bank emphasizes the enduring aspect of interpersonal relationships and long-term reciprocity in a continuing series of exchanges of support in close relationships. It suggests that individuals utilize a generalized accounting system in the supportive exchanges they experience. That is, they maintain a mental record of how much and to whom they have provided supports as well as how much and from whom they have received supports. This accounting system is thought to be informal and, for the most part, a cognitive activity conducted with little conscious attention on the part of the individual. This cognitive support account can be considered analogous to an individually maintained savings account at a local bank. One can think of the Support Bank account in a similar fashion, as an attempt to "save up for a rainy day." One strives to maintain, at minimum, a balance between what is deposited and what is withdrawn, but the development of a support reserve, which can be drawn on in time of need, is optimal. Thus, one is motivated to provide support to people in close relationships. These essentially constitute deposits. On the other hand, receiving support from others is similar to making withdrawals from one's savings account. In time of need, one can rest assured, at least if deposits have been made in the past and interest accumulated, that support will be available. It is conceivable that, with diminishing exchange commodities, older people (and probably their social network members as well) come to emphasize this long-term reciprocity notion of a Social Support Bank and define their support exchange by this norm. Therefore, they can receive a great deal of support from others who are close and important, potentially for an extended period of time, and yet feel relatively unindebted.

James Dowd argues that a completely different rule governs the exchange of social support involving older people, particularly the very old who are largely limited in resources. Even in this contract-oriented society of reciprocity, non-contractual elements are not completely absent. No longer bound by the norm of reciprocity, older people are entitled to benefit by the norm of beneficence. "The norm of beneficence requires individuals to give others help as they need and without thought of what they have done or can do for them" (1984: 103). It is acceptable, in other words, that the very old receive more than they are owed under the norm of reciprocity. These observations and explanations are obviously not exhaustive or mutually exclusive. Today's old-old population lives in an uncharted territory in terms of behavioral norms.

SOCIAL CHANGES AND EXCHANGE RULES

Both American and Japanese societies have been undergoing substantial changes in many aspects. Demography, social systems, values and norms are changing. Some of the changes are common to the two countries. The others are more country-specific. In this final section of the chapter, we consider how social changes affect the intergenerational exchange rules in the two countries, focusing on changes in societal age structure, family structure, distribution of wealth and women's social roles.

The past several decades have witnessed dramatic increases in life expectancy. People not only live longer but also stay relatively healthy longer. Also, economic statistics indicate that the current elderly population is better off compared with previous cohorts. These historical changes in the health and economic status of the older population mean that the current cohort of older people, particularly the young-old (aged 60–70), have more exchange commodities (i.e., money, goods and services) than their predecessors. In fact, the statistical profile of the intergenerational transfer of wealth in the United States indicates a significant increase in the flow of wealth from older persons to their offspring during the past decade (Soldo and Hill 1993). Such resource increase has allowed contemporary older Americans to maintain reciprocal relationships until more advanced ages than their preceding cohorts.

At the same time, however, the lengthening life span has resulted in a rapid growth of the old-old (aged 80+) population who tend to have fewer exchange commodities. Today a large number of very old people live with few valued commodities for many years. This segment of the population is expected to continue to grow in both countries. As noted earlier, the traditional American exchange rules of symmetric reciprocity often hinder the old-old from maintaining their social relations, because they may not have appropriate resources to reciprocate in exchange. Currently, there appear to be no rules commonly accepted to apply to support exchanges involving an older individual in this familiar situation. The old-old and those who associate with them are applying whatever rules (e.g., immediate reciprocity, long-term reciprocity, benevolence, etc.) which, they think, work best for a particular exchange situation. The two parties involved in the exchange might not necessarily apply the same rule. Such exchange may leave awkwardness, hurt feelings and/or resentment in the relationship. Thus, the lack of rules guiding exchange behavior can be detrimental to older persons' social relations and consequently to their well-being.

The living situations of American families are also changing, influenced by the increased longevity, socioeconomic status and cultural norms. Most older Americans strongly prefer to live alone or with a spouse if economically or physically feasible. With the increased longevity of most Americans, a two-stage process appears to be evolving wherein the young-old live alone in their own homes until such time as they are no longer physically able. At that time they are likely to move closer to or in with an adult child, most often a daughter and her family. A smaller number of older people enter a skilled care facility.

With increased home care services, day care and care management, older Americans will be living longer in the community and entering institutional care at a much more advanced age. Already, adult children spend more years caring for their parents than they did for their children. The issue of reciprocity and support exchange will become even more important in the future, complicated by the large number of women in the work force and the divorce rate and questions of responsibility for parents of former spouses as well as present ones.

Compared with the American exchange rules, the traditional Japanese rules are more accommodating to the reduction of material resources in old age. However, other aspects of social change have been slowly but irreversibly undermining the Japanese exchange rules. First, the transformation of family structure has had indisputable effects on people's exchange behavior. A review of the Japanese census data over the past several decades suggests that older persons' living arrangements have become increasingly diversified. Three trends are particularly pertinent to our topic. First, as noted earlier, the number of older persons who live independently of their children has been steadily rising (see Figure 10.1, this volume). Second, the number of people who live with their married daughters instead of sons is increasing, although the number is still relatively small. Third, it is becoming more common to maintain semi-independent households even if three generations of family live under one roof. Many recently built or remodeled houses for three-generation families have two sections, each of which has a main entrance, kitchen, bathroom and bedrooms. They often have separate utility meters. The two units may be built side-by-side under one roof and connected by a door or hallway; or one unit may be on the first floor and the other on the second. This growing trend of nontraditional living arrangements makes the boundary between family and nonfamily less clear. It also often creates ambiguous exchange settings which make it more difficult to apply customary exchange norms, either the rules for family members or those for nonfamily members. Japanese families are experiencing these situations without clearly defined alternatives.

This flexibility in living arrangements seems designed to minimize the conflict inherent in the traditional situation, particularly between the mother-in-law and daughter-in-law. One young man described how his family built an annex onto their house where his parents and sister lived. He and his grandmother continued to live in the main house, easing the tension between his grandmother and his mother. As one middle-aged woman described it, "I have one daughter. On the same land, I built two houses. We live separately. We do everything separately . . . meals, bath" (Elliott and Campbell 1993). When family relationships are so tied to living arrangements, the road to change for strained exchange rules is to alter the structure of the living situation.

Moreover, as Jenike shows in Chapter 10, a marked increase in women's labor force participation has brought a powerful addition to women's social roles. This additional role has affected women and their families' lives in various ways. It certainly has fostered obligations which compete with duties toward family. It has considerably reduced women's time and energy that used to be available for providing services to family. Yet, probably more significant is a shift in the relative importance among women's social roles. Today, a woman who is successfully juggling her career and motherhood generally gets more respect than a diligent *yome* (daughter-in-law) who stays home and cares for her frail in-laws. Consequently, being an ideal *yome* does not give a woman as much status as it did in the past. In other words, an inexhaustible expressive resource (praise for being a good *yome*) which older women have been using for generations to reciprocate for services from their daughters-in-law is gradually losing its exchange value. At the same time, similar to their American counterparts, the Japanese young-old are healthier and financially better off compared with the preceding cohorts. It means they have more material resources such as money, goods and services, which provide them with alternatives and flexibility when facing uncharted exchange situations.

Parallel to these changes has been the growth of community services such as adult day care, home helpers and private retirement centers for people with means. The Golden Plan, adopted by the Japanese government in 1989, proposed a ten-year strategy to greatly increase the availability of medical and social services both in the community and in institutional care. The acceptance of these services has increased along with their availability. Furthermore, a proposal for a national long-term-care insurance system by the government has gained wide support from political parties and the general public (see Chapter 10). However, monetary compensation for services provided by family members is certainly a novel concept in the tradition of Japanese family relations. These community services and the widespread debate on a national long-term-care insurance system have contributed additional force to the pressure to alter exchange situations and rules.

Today, in the United States and Japan, older persons often encounter exchange situations in which they find it difficult to apply the conventional exchange rules. Both Americans and Japanese appear to keenly recognize the urgency of a transformation in their respective family exchange patterns and are searching for customs more suitable to the "aging society" within its distinctive sociocultural contexts. Such changes will affect the well-being of virtually all members of the societies where over eight out of ten newborns are expected to live to old age.

PART III

Aging, Modernization and Societal Transformation

THE MODERNIZATION MODEL AND ITS CRITIQUE

The dramatic upsurge of older citizens remaining alive in Third World countries is a legacy of the last two decades. This demographic change has been intertwined with alterations in economic production, wealth distribution and the often violent devolution of large states into smaller successor nations. How has this affected the life of the elderly? A simple answer was provided by Leo Simmons's terse dictum, "Change is the crux of the problem of aging" (1960:88). Few could doubt the power of this statement after reading Nancy Scheper-Hughes's poignant study in western Ireland, detailing the demise of a rural "gerontocracy" (1987). In her work within the parish of Ballybran, she detailed how a fourfold population decline stimulated the collapse of community economic cooperation, drastic reductions in support from children, forced retirement and a radical transformation of customs regarding aging and death. Scheper-Hughes found that the once dignified movement of the elderly couple to the sacred "west room" of the house was commonly replaced by unceremonious "warehousing" of the elderly in old age homes and mental institutions. Fortunately, less traumatic changes occurred in eastern Ireland, and rural communities there retained greater cultural integrity. We will see in Part V that the increasing integration of city and country surrounding the urban area of Dublin has brought a mixed blessing to the rural inhabitants there.

Just as dramatic has been the substantial drop in the quality of life for the elderly in Russia and many of its successor states (Velkoff and Kinsella 1993). Studies in the 1990s have shown how the move to market economies in Eastern and Central Europe has resulted in falling living standards and increasing marginalization of the elderly (Laczko and Payne 1994). In Russia, elderly in the last decade have not only increasingly become impoverished and seen a significant drop in life expectancy, but in the mid-1990s reports indicate that a substantial number of aged are murdered each year to obtain their apartments.[1] Tremendous stress is being placed on older women to bolster collapsing family economic and social resources. One report observed, "It sometimes seems as if the whole engine of life in this country is run by millions of little old ladies" (Network News 1992).

On the other hand, studies of Samoa (Holmes and Rhoads 1987), China (Olson 1990; Davis-Friedman 1991; Chapter 24 this volume) and the famous Abkhasians of Soviet Georgia (Benet 1974) demonstrate that significant social change is not always a disaster for the aged. In fact, a careful examination of the history of the Abkhasians reveals that substantial alterations in their societal structure since the end of the nineteenth century have improved what was already a strong situation for the elderly (Inal-Ipa 1982).

Until quite recently, the primary model for considering how massive worldwide change has impacted on the elderly has been "modernization" theory. Most briefly, modernization theory has developed as an extension of a functionalist interpretation of societal evolution. It tries to predict the impact of change from relatively undifferentiated rural/traditional-based societies with limited technology to modern urban-based entities. This shift is marked by the use of complex industrial technology, inanimate energy sources, and differentiated institutions to promote efficiency and progress. Third World countries are said to develop/progress as they adopt, through cultural diffusion, the modernized model of rational/efficient societal organization. While such a transformation is often viewed as an overall advance for such countries, a strong inverse relationship is suggested between the elements of modernization as an independent variable and the status of the aged as a dependent variable. Donald Cowgill, first by suggesting a number of discrete postulates and later in developing a more elaborate model, has been the most dominant writer on this subject (1974, 1986). The hypothesized decline in valued roles, resources and respect available to older persons in modernizing societies is said to stem from four main factors: modern health technology; economies based on scientific technology; urbanization; and mass education and literacy.

Validation of this paradigm has been uneven and has spurred a small industry of gerontological writings, which debate the proposed articulation of modernization and aging (see Rhoads and Holmes 1995:251–285 for an excellent review). Historians have sharply questioned the model, saying it is not only ahistorical but that, by idealizing the past, an inappropriate "world we lost syndrome" has been created (Laslett 1976; Kertzer and Laslett 1994).[2] For example, summing up research on the elderly living in Western Europe several hundred years ago, historian Andrejs Plakans states, "There is something like a consensus that the treatment of the old was harsh and decidedly pragmatic: dislike and suspicion, it is said, characterized the attitudes of both sides" (1989).

Goldstein and Beall (1981) argue that the concept "status of the aged" must be constructed as a multidimensional variable with no necessary assumption of covariance between the different dimensions of status. The ethnographic evidence shows that the impact of change on the elderly is quite varied and depends on such factors as gender, class, social organization of the local community and how the nation-state's political economy transfers modernizing changes into the local region.[3]

A good example of the complexity of this issue is seen in a study of three untouchable communities in India (Vincentnathan and Vincentnathan 1994). The authors show how in the poorest communities, the assumption of respect and high status as a prior condition did not hold. Here the elders had no resources to pass on. Modernization programs which included providing material resources for the elders became a new basis for binding together the young and old. However, increased education of the young led many children and young adults to feel superior to parents, fostering a distinct change in generational relations, closer to the predictions of modernization theory.[4]

Perhaps the most far-reaching challenge to modernization theory stems from "dependency" or "world-systems" models of global development. From this approach, the lack of development in Third World countries is not predicated on a failure to adopt "modern ways," but determined by a historic process of continuing "underdevelopment" (Sanderson 1995). This is based on an international division of labor which allows capital accumulation to take place in wealthy, core nations of a capitalist world system, while these countries control the developmental process in poorer, semiperipheral and peripheral areas. Overall, it is contended that the tie of dependent nations to core industrial powers through multinational corporations and foreign aid has resulted in the enhanced position of favored urban elites at the cost of growing rural impoverishment and internal inequalities. Jon Hendricks (1981), one of the few writers to consider aging from a world-systems perspective, suggests that the situation of the elderly will be determined by their "use-value" relative to the demands of the core sector or the extent to which they "embody old ways inimical to core interests" (p. 341).

There has been a slow recognition of the necessity to figure in the social and economic patterns of aging when planning for the consequences of change in rural sectors of the developing world (Woodsong 1994). A recent UN-sponsored comparative study in Chile, Thailand, Sri Lanka and the Dominican Republic documented the role of the aged in these developing countries as productive citizens. The elders, besides contributing to economically productive activities such as gardening, tending animals and food preparation, carried out other key cultural activities. These included socializing and entertaining children, teaching of vocational skills, leading religious discussions and having a special role in joint family activities such as ritual (Kaiser and Chawla 1994).[5]

SOCIETAL TRANSFORMATION AND AGING

While a significant majority of people in Third and Fourth World nations still live in rural villages, the rapid growth of mega-cities and the sharp rise in overall urbanization is substantially transforming the social worlds of people in such regions. The world's most populous nation, China, is still largely rural, but this will change early in the next century (see Chapter 24). Incredibly, only four of the top fifteen largest cities in the world are in "developed" countries; all the rest are found in nations like Mexico, Brazil and South Korea. Mexico City, estimated to have over 20 million people residing in its metropolitan area, looms as a dramatic example. In the 1940s Mexico was 80 percent rural, but in the mid-1990s about 60 percent of its citizens were urban dwellers, with almost one-quarter of the entire population living in Mexico City alone. Recently, the country has endured very difficult economic times, as in the 1990s when the value of wages dropped by one-half. This is reflected in Bialik's study of 1,000 older women from Mexican urban areas and their high degree of impoverishment: a third had no personal income and 12 percent earned only $5 per month (1992).[6] Despite this, until quite recently there has been little serious research on aging in Mexico or elsewhere in Latin America (Vargas 1992; Checkoway 1994; Sennott-Miller 1994).[7]

The first chapter in this part is set in Mexico and illustrates the integral connection between seemingly isolated rural communities and nearby large urban centers. It focuses on my twenty years of fieldwork in a peasant village whose indigenous culture has helped it creatively adjust to life in the shadow of Mexico City. In the wake of dramatic changes, I found that the elderly have been provided a more satisfactory place in their community than would be predicted by modernization theory. This work illustrates how local control over vital economic resources can become the catalyst for very traditional cultural systems to initiate modernizing change in ways that support the interests of their oldest citizens. It would be instructive for students to consider how the elderly are impacted by the different relationships between rural and urban zones among this area in Mexico, the Samia region in Kenya (Chapter 4) and the rural township of Blessington, Ireland (Chapter 18).

Equally important to consider is the role of older females in agrarian societies. In a recent article, Monica Dos Gupta discusses different patterns in the female life course within rural peasant settings. One pattern typified by preindustrial northern Europe stresses the rights of the conjugal couple over cross-generational ties and the transfer of lands and power with the marriage of the inheriting son. A different pattern in northern India stresses a joint extended family, primacy of intergenerational links and the gradual shift of wealth and authority to the next generation. The first pattern is characterized by greater autonomy and power for women, but increased generational conflict and lack of security in old age. In southern Asia, the motif was reversed with diminished competition across generations, but with women being marginalized through their young and adult age periods, while making gains in autonomy and importance in their elder years. My work in rural Mexico found a pattern that was closer to the Asian model, but possessing some significant differences. Here, not only was there strong support for older women, but the typically harsh impact of peasant life on younger females was moderated. Unlike in India, most mates come from the same village, so that while after marriage, most women live in the domain of their husbands' parents, their own parents and extended kin network are also close at hand.

The varying impact of change on the ties between the old and young in traditional societies is clearly seen in Box 3, which looks at generational relations in the West African nation of Mali.

BOX 3. MODERN WAYS ERODE MALI'S TRIBAL TRADITIONS: WHEN VALUES COLLIDE

Tradition has it that Malians develop a strong sense of themselves and their role in the clan while they are young and reach old age secure in the knowledge that they will be well cared for by their offspring. Tradition, however, is breaking down. The steady pressure of modern life has eroded ancient African customs more deeply in cities such as Bamako, Mali's capital, but the impact of shifting values can be felt throughout the country of 5 million people.

Tension between the demands of modern and traditional life is often expressed as conflict between the generations. Closer examination reveals that the intensity of this conflict varies widely. There are roughly three types of intergenerational relations.

The most supportive situations develop when the older person, either a man or a woman, has managed to integrate into modern life without sacrificing traditional values. Often found among successful merchants or artisans, their offspring maintain close family ties.

Less successful relationships are found among city dwellers whose children are better educated than their parents. Unemployment rates among urban youth are high and attitudes toward low-status jobs quite negative. As a result, most youth of this type cannot contribute to family upkeep, as tradition decrees they must, nor afford to live independently.

In the rural version of semi-alienation, the older person commands respect but not affection. Youth fear the power, both real and magical, of older villagers who, in their turn, fear losing their authority.

In the worst cases, the generations are completely alienated. Older residents of rural areas express this by refusing to cede any authority to younger villagers. In two villages studied, the great majority (from two-thirds to three-fourths) of all decisions regarding agriculture were made by older people. This exclusion from decision making worsens tensions between the generations and speeds up the exodus of young people.

In the urban version of complete alienation, tensions become so extreme that

continued

cohabitation becomes impossible. Both generations lose the community that is critical to maintaining a sense of self in the clan system that characterizes most of African life.

Reprinted and excerpted from *Global Aging Report* 1(2):6.

TRANSFORMING FIRST WORLD SOCIETIES

Third World countries are not the only types of societies undergoing change which affects the elderly. In the industrialized West, radical changes in labor markets, the growth of the welfare state, and seemingly instantaneous alterations in lifestyles have created new contexts in which aging is experienced. Added to this is the growing "agedness" of these countries, where up to 18 percent are over age 65 (in Sweden), and of these persons, typically eight out of ten are no longer employed. Given that the United States is still one of the youngest of the Western industrialized nations and has barely begun to define national policy on the elderly, it has the fortuitous possibility of learning from efforts of other nations addressing this issue.

In just such a way, Bruce Zelkovitz in Chapter 11 analyzes Sweden's attempt to use its "middle way," between U.S.-style capitalism and centralized, planned socialism, to enhance the quality of life of the aged. He uses a political-economy approach to show how this Scandinavian country has created state mechanisms of support which seek to be positively "transformative." This is in strong contrast to the defensive, crisis-management type of welfare system in the United States.

Political economy approaches are useful in resisting the attempt to blame the victims of societal-level changes. Estes (1996) and Walker (1996) have presented powerful arguments that the public policy and the resultant political economy of nations such as the United States and England shape not only the experience of aging but the public response to older citizens. As Jon Hendricks also notes for the United States, "we have designed entitlements and accommodations for nonaffluent elders in terms of their presumed personal worth as reflected in their work history, or in terms of a welfare mentality that requires near-destitution to claim public largesse" (1995:59).

In the 1980s, Sweden's policymakers recognized that in the past a major problem had been *overcare* in institutions and *undercare* within households. They embarked on a national program to promote the independence, integrity and meaningful participation of the aged in community life. In updating his original work done while these reforms were just underway, Zelkovitz discusses how "The Aging Enterprise" in Sweden has coped with serious economic recessions, deficits and high unemployment. While this country has had success in reducing its share of aged in "overcare" (institutional) settings, a downturn in the economy has forced reductions in home-help services with accompanying stress on family carers, primarily women. This is an important warning for the

United States as it contemplates moving toward community-based care. Of the Scandinavian countries, Denmark seems the most successful in this area, replacing in various localities traditional institutional care with sheltered housing in combination with flexible and generous home services (Daatland 1994; Shenk Chapter 16, this volume).

THE EAST ASIAN "MIRACLE"

Another important national level comparison is provided in the context of contemporary Japan. Prior to 1980 it was one of the youngest industrialized nations, but by 1996 its population exceeded the "agedness" of the United States. In the 1990s, Japan posted the world's highest life expectancy and in the past two decades its population has undergone the most rapid aging any nation has ever experienced. Potentially buffering the negative effects of such changes on the aged is the high status and prestige accorded the elderly in traditional Japanese culture (Palmore 1975).[8] This is promoted by cultural patterns which include: the Japanese version of Buddhism linking ancestors and the aged to a family system stressing filial devotion; an age-grading system favoring seniority; and a corporate emphasis which strengthens the place of the elderly in multigenerational households (Keifer 1990; Wada 1995; Tsuji 1997).

There has emerged a lively and controversial debate over the ability of traditional culture in Japan and other East Asian nations to resist erosion of the status of the elderly in light of extensive modernization (Rhoads and Holmes 1995: 277–283; Bass, Morris and Oka 1997).[9] Some Asian scholars are beginning to strongly question the continued reliance on family support systems as the best cultural medium to sustain the aged. For example, Yow-Hwey Hu shows that in East Asian industrial societies such as Japan, Singapore, Taiwan and Hong Kong, the high level of three-generation families, even in urban areas, is found in conjunction with exceedingly high rates of suicide by those over age 65 (1995). The difference between East and West is particularly noteworthy for older women. Prior to their mid-forties, women in countries like Japan and Taiwan kill themselves at about the same rate (11.6 and 10.4 per 100,000) as their counterparts in the United States and France (8.8 and 13.9 per 100,000). Yet past age 65, women in the former two nations end their own lives at a dramatically higher rate (39.3 and 34.6) compared to the latter countries where the level of female suicide actually drops (6.6 and 9.7). Yow-Hwey Hu also finds that there is a subtle bias in the questionnaires such countries use to find continued support for elders preferring three-generation residential life. He argues that more objective questions would change the results dramatically, toward a preference for separate but nearby residences.[10]

In Japan since the 1980s there has begun a radical rethinking of the place of older citizens in society, countering the glowingly positive view presented in Erdman Palmore's *The Honorable Elders: A Cross-Cultural Analysis of Aging in Japan* (1975a). This work and a revised volume (1985), with Japanese gerontologist Daisaku Maeda, is largely based on statistical patterns of household organization and ideal cultural norms. It has been criticized by scholars both in North America (Plath 1987; Rhoads and Holmes 1995) as well as in Japan (Koyano 1989).[11]

By the early 1980s a popular slogan for potential brides seeking the ideal husband was *ie-tsuki, ka-tsui, babanuki* ("with car, with house, without granny"). A decade later women in their sixties dealing with newly retired, stay-at-home spouses began mocking them as "wet fallen leaves," similar to the foliage which clings to a broom, making it sweep less effectively. One recent response to this situation has been the creation of "Silver Human Resource Centers" which rely on both government incentives and market forces to create part-time jobs for older retirees, especially men (Bass and Oka 1995).

The concluding chapter in this part by Brenda Robb Jenike draws many of these concerns together by expanding on the issue of intergenerational support, comparatively discussed in Chapter 8. Her paper gives a powerful voice to Japan's transitional generation of mid-age women. They have had to endure the arduous traditional support of much longer-living parents, knowing full well that such sustenance by their own children is unlikely when they themselves shortly enter old age.

Japan's retention of the highest co-residence rates for any major, urban in-dustrialized society has collided with its unparalleled success in promoting lon-gevity and the growing trend of adult women who desire to remain in the workforce. Corresponding to Robb Jenike's research is a study by Tokyo's Met-ropolitan Institute of Gerontology. This investigation found almost half of the caregivers to the elderly "burning out" from a combination of emotional and physical exhaustion, depersonalization and a decline in overall personal satis-faction with their lives. Almost 90 percent of these caregivers were women, most about 60 years of age, caring for elders averaging 80 years of age, two-thirds of whom were also female (Ageing International 1994:8).

Japan's societal response to such problems has been to undertake an ambitious plan of public sector supports for the social, economic and health needs of their oldest citizens. However, Robb Jenike notes some broad cultural issues which are lowering enthusiasm for national programs versus those which are locally based.[12] How Japan handles this dilemma is of great interest to other family-oriented, Asian Pacific Rim nations, also pushing the limits of rapid demo-graphic aging (Asis et al. 1995).

We can see with academic hindsight that the prevailing models of moderni-zation and aging are too simplistic. They have failed to consider how the eco-nomic underpinning of cultural systems and the linkage between domestic and public domains mediates the impact of change. Perhaps we are in a position to rephrase Leo Simmons's axiom from "change is the crux of the problem for the aged," to "change is the crucible of opportunity for the aged"—it can either greatly enhance their lives or crush any meaning in life during late adulthood.

KEY RESOURCES

Research Project

"Comparative Study of Elderly in Four Asian Countries Project": This important cross-national study in Asia was conducted from 1989 to 1994. Participating countries were the Philippines, Taiwan, Thailand and Singapore. This is being followed up with a new, multiyear study, "The Rapid Demographic Change and the Welfare of the Elderly Project," being directed by Albert Hermalin and John Knodel at the Population Studies Center, the University of Michigan, 1225 South University Ave., Ann Arbor, MI 48014. Discussion of results from the first project can be found in Hermalin, Ofstedal and Chang 1995; Knodel, Chayovan and Siriboon 1995; and Uhlenberg 1995.

Internet Resources

(1) http://www.aoa.dhhs.gov/aoa/webres/int-swed.htm. Provides links to academic gerontology centers in Sweden.
(2) http://www.aoa.dhhs.gov/aoa/webres/int-jpn.htm. Provides links to academic, governmental and public sites in Japan. For example, you can find here a detailed summary of a 1995 government report on the health and welfare of Japan's seniors (at http://www.mki.co.jp/senior/seni24.html).

Print Resources

Special Issues of Journals

Bulletin on Aging (1994), double issue, numbers 2/3. This United Nations publication focuses on older workers and their interaction with economic development around the world.

Other Print Resources

Bass, S., R. Morris and M. Oka, eds. 1997. *Public Policy and the Old Age Revolution in Japan*. Binghamton, NY: Haworth.
Formanek, S. and S. Linhart, eds. 1997. *Aging: Asian Experiences Past and Present*. Vienna: Verlag der Osterreichischen Akademie der Wissenschaften. An edited volume with research from some of the newer scholars doing research on aging in Asia.
Kinoshita, Y. and C. Kiefer. 1992. *Refuge of the Honored: S
Social Organization in a Japanese Retirement Community*. Berkely, CA: University of California Press. An ethnographic study of Japan's first planned retirement community.
Kinsella, K. and Y. Gist. 1995. *Older Workers, Retirement, and Pensions: A Comparative International Chartbook*. Washington, DC: Bureau of the Census. An up-to-date compilation of data relevant to labor force participation of the elderly and societal development.
Sen, K. 1994. *Ageing: Debates on Demographic Transition and Social Policy*. London:

188 Societal Transformation

Zed Books. A good summary of data (especially health issues) on aging in developing countries.

Sennott-Miller, L. 1994. "Research on Latin America: Present Status and Future Directions." *Journal of Cross-Cultural Gerontology* 9:1:87–97. Best available summary of aging in Latin America.

United Nations. 1995. *National Perspectives on Population and Development*. New York: United Nations. The report provides a synthesis of the 168 national reports prepared for the 1994 International Conference on Population and Development.

Walker, A. and T. Maltby. 1997. *Ageing Europe*. Buckingham, England: Open University Press. Presents data from a policy-oriented study, "Observatory on Ageing and Older People," conducted throughout Europe.

NOTES

1. From 1989 to 1994, life expectancy dropped from 65 to 58 years for men and from 74 to 71 years for women.

2. See also Fischer 1978; Achenbaum 1982; Quadagno 1982 for discussion of historical data and the modernization and aging controversy.

3. Some basic literature related to these factors are: class (Harlan 1968; Vincentnathan and Vincentnathan 1994), values (L. D. Holmes 1987), gender (Roebuck 1983; Cool and McCabe 1987; Counts 1991; Yu, Yu, and Mansfield 1990) and age-cohorts (Foner 1984a).

4. A 1995 nationwide survey in India conducted by HelpAge India showed that almost 30 percent of India's aged have no family to live with or cannot live with the family they have. See Dandekar 1996 for a general discussion of aging in India based on sociological surveys.

5. For a broader discussion of general labor issues related to the elderly around the world, see the 1994 combined issues, numbers 2 and 3 of the *Bulletin on Ageing*, published by the United Nations.

6. For other discussion of older women in Mexico, see Robles 1987; Contreras de Lehr 1989, 1992. For a broader view of older women in Latin America, see Pan American Health Organization 1989.

7. For additional comparative discussion of aging in Latin American peasant communities, see Press and McKool 1972. Other early ethnographic information is to be found in: Holmberg 1961; Lewis 1963; Gutmann 1967; Press 1967; Moore 1973; Velez 1978; Kerns 1983.

8. For some classic references on aging in Japan, see Benedict 1946; Smith 1961b; Plath 1964, 1972.

9. This debate has spanned two decades and can be accessed with such references as: Sparks 1975; Plath 1980, 1987; Maeda 1983; Palmore and Maeda 1985. An interesting comparison of the transitions in South Asia with preindustrial Europe can be found in Cain 1991.

10. A broad international perspective on suicide and aging can be found in Pearson and Yeates 1995. For a discussion of Japanese *Pokkuri* cults where elders pray for a quick death, see Young and Ikeuchi 1997. For more general studies of family life and aging in east Asia, see Hermalin, Ofstedal and Chang 1995; Knodel, Chayovan and Siriboon 1995; Uhlenberg 1995.

11. For example, Koyano, writing from the Japanese perspective, argues that *tateme*, or ideal norms toward the aged are very different from *honne*, real feelings: "We Japanese feel ashamed at reading Palmore's indication, because we know that people's behavior and regime, which might be taken as manifestations of respect for the elderly, are mostly courtesy custom without substance, and that Japanese respect for the elderly is merely *tateme*" (1989:343).

12. For discussion of some of the cultural barriers to empowerment of the aged see Sodei 1995.

CHAPTER 9

Aging, Family and Community Development in a Mexican Peasant Village

Jay Sokolovsky

A MCDONALD'S NIGHTMARE

I did not quite know what to expect in June of 1989, when, after an eleven-year hiatus, I drove my rented car toward the village of San Gregorio Amatango, high in the central mountain region of Mexico. From 1972–1973 I had lived there with a family while doing Ph.D. work in anthropology, and had returned for two short visits during the late 1970s to begin studying aging in the community. A week before my return to Amatango I began to have nightmares. Some involved learning that children from the household I had lived in during the 1970s had succumbed to the high child mortality rate then still prevalent. In another dream, the road up to the village was nicely paved and the Aztec-era house mounds lining that road were covered with condominiums and American-style fast-food restaurants. In 1972, this road was a deeply rutted dirt path, strewn with boulders that were sometimes two feet in diameter.

Fortunately, my dreams were only slightly clairvoyant. I was to find that it was no longer likely that three or four of ten children would die before age five, and this was starting to change how young adults and even the elderly felt about reproduction. Doña Concha, the woman of the house where I lived, had lost four of six children prior to my first stay in the village. To my great relief, little José and Lucia, who had been ages 7 and 2 back then, and two of their siblings born in the mid-1970s were all alive and healthy. José, now age 24, had a wife and three children of his own. Following village tradition, he remained in the dwelling of his father, Jeronimo, age 58, while Lucia had just been wed and had gone to live with her in-laws on the other side of the village.

While a McDonald's was not yet within sight of village lands, global cultural influences were becoming very much part of daily life. The access road to the village was in fact newly paved. However, fancy apartments were not atop the archeological ruins and Amatango's farmers were busy trying to reclaim the soils along the road, which overgrazing by the Spanish Conquistador's goats and sheep had ruined 400 years ago. In the village, small stores were opening up almost on a monthly basis, selling a wide variety of household products, previously available only in cities such as Texcoco or Mexico City. Even the room I had slept in during my first field research had been converted into a tiny general merchandise store, selling everything from Coca-Cola to toilet paper. Sixty percent of the houses had TV antennae on their roofs, and cassette tapes of American rock bands were a popular trading item among teenagers.

Yet, amidst newly installed speed bumps, reruns of Bonanza, several fledgling teenage street gangs, six popular music bands, adolescents wearing "Metalica" tee-shirts, microbuses running every ten minutes to the nearest city, one could still hear and see the face of tradition holding a very tenuous sway against the hurricane winds of modern urban culture sweeping rural Mexico. It was seen especially in the eyes of young children as they cautiously approached an older relative, gently bowed to plant a ritual kiss on the uplifted hand and whispered in classic Aztec, *nocultzin* (revered grandparent). It is also observed in the public fiesta dances, where a child of eight shared the same dance platform and ritual significance with a man or woman of age 40 or even 70. Such symbolic acts are still embedded in familial and public domains which give aging adults a place in their society that transcends simple platitudes such as "show respect to your elders."

Since my research trip in 1989, I have made two other short field trips, in the summer of 1993 and in January of 1994, each time focusing on how the life of the elderly was faring in the face of significant and rapid changes in Amatango. It will be the purpose of this chapter to explore how the elderly's place in the domestic and civic arenas of community life has functioned to buffer the potentially deleterious impact of rapid socioeconomic changes in peasant communities such as Amatango.

PEASANT LIFE IN THE GLOBAL VILLAGE

I was initially sent to the central highlands of Mexico by a well-known archeologist to document cultural continuities from the pre-Hispanic historical period for my Ph.D. research. I settled into the community I refer to here as Amatango, nestled in a mountain valley 8,500 feet above sea level and adjacent to the archeological remains of the residents' Aztec forbearers.[1] Amatango is one of 27 *pueblos* (rural villages) in a municipal unit politically led by the city of Texcoco, about 12 miles away.[2] In 1972, Texcoco was a sleepy municipal capital of 25,000, but by the mid-1990s its population had swelled to about 140,000. Its old market had acquired a wide array of electronic gear with accompanying audio and video tapes, allowing families from Amatango to become consumers of North American popular culture. With its banks, appliance stores, movie theaters, medical clinics, Fuji and Kodak film shops and Volkswagen and Nissan car dealerships, Texcoco serves as a juncture for the diffusion of urban national culture as well as international ideas and products. It is here that inhabitants of Amatango also must come to register titles to land, obtain a civil marriage, pay their electric bills or complain about an injustice that cannot be handled by their own authorities.

In the early 1970s the village economy centered around subsistence corn farming combined with occasional wage labor, playing music in traditional *fiesta* bands and the sale of decorative flowers and wooden crates in Texcoco or Mexico City. At that time, the roughly 2,000 villagers of Amatango, who identified themselves as *indios* (Indians), were then thought to be the most ardent followers of indigenous traditions in their region.[3] They were bilingual in Spanish and the classic form of the Aztec language, *nahuatl*. Close relatives were always greeted by a distinctive bowing and hand-kissing respect gesture, women used the Aztec sweatbath (*temazcal*) in many of their healing regimens and the populace kept the Aztec deity, called *nahuake*, in their spiritual pantheon.[4] Moreover, they continued a regular system of communal labor and a very traditional *fiesta* complex in which families took on time-consuming and costly responsibilities for ritually celebrating the lives of various roman Catholic Saints.[5] Along with four other *nahuatl*-speaking villages in the high mountain lands, Amatango remained culturally distinct from the rural communities in the lower ecological zones stretching down toward Texcoco. Inhabitants of such villages spoke only Spanish and disdained the "backward" *indios del monte* (mountain Indians) while touting themselves as *mestizos*, agrarian exemplars of a more cosmopolitan, urban style of life.

What originally drew me to study Amatango was a seeming paradox. How could its strong traditional cultural features coexist with a series of locally initiated, "modernizing" changes which also made the village the most rapidly transforming of the *indio* communities in its region? Some changes, such as village electrification and the building of a new elementary school, had begun a few years before I arrived. Others were transpiring during and within five years of my initial research stay. These changes included construction of a passable, flat dirt road, the creation of a potable water system and building a medical clinic and a high school. What is critical to understand is that Amatango was not a passive receptor of these changes. It has sought through its collective action to initiate these projects and recast itself in terms of local concepts of a "civilized" place. Fortunately for the elderly, Amatango has resolved this paradox of remaining the most traditional while also being the most changing community by relying upon its most customary aspects of belief and village organization to pursue the goal of community transformation. However, we will see that over the last decade a family-planning program and the dramatic expansion of Mexico City into the world's largest metropolis have created new challenges which may test the best of cultural intentions. To understand Amatango's ability to respond in positive ways to the modern world, it is necessary to briefly trace the historical context of this community's metamorphosis.

HISTORICAL CONTEXT OF AGING AND CHANGE

As a peasant community, Amatango has always been incorporated to some degree within larger political spheres. It was founded in the late fifteenth century when the king of Texcoco had an irrigation system developed from the springs located in the mountain forests overlooking the contemporary village (Pomar 1941:7). Access to the large mountain forest zone above its residential area favored the specialty production by Amatango's families of raw materials and finished products derived from the trees and pastures. Some items, especially charcoal and firewood, were sold as far away as the Aztec capital, Tenochtitlan (now Mexico City), with the rest being traded in the large, pre-Hispanic market in Texcoco or bartered for different specialty items in other peasant communities. Such general entrepreneurial patterns have continued to the present day and represent a key economic strategy for the majority of three-generation households.

Very little is known about preconquest village life and the actual functioning of elders in the context of peasant communities.[6] According to historical sources, the elder chief of the highest ranking clan, along with a council composed of other clan elders, regulated the distribution of communally owned lands, settled disputes and saw to the training of warriors and the payment of taxes by the entire community (Soustelle 1961). Aged males and females of any rank had some special roles: Men made ritual speeches and prepared corpses while women arranged marriages and served as midwives. Persons past age 70 also had the privilege of drinking alcohol in public without the severe sanctions imposed on younger individuals who imbibed.[7]

At the household level, Aztec-era elders appeared to command filial respect approaching that of the ancient Chinese. Among a child's first lessons were admonitions about showing esteem toward elders (Simmons 1945:62). Marriage seldom occurred without parental consent and the father had the power to pawn or sell his children into slavery if his economic situation was severe enough.

In the process of Spanish colonization of Mexico, the Texcoco region as a whole gradually moved away from irrigated corn farming. However, peasant communities in the piedmont and higher mountain zones, where Amatango is located, generally continued corn farming and traditional specialty production.[8] Until the 1910 Mexican Revolution, Amatango was subject to a small *hacienda* (private estate) in its mountain lands that set up a glass-making factory and grew wheat on high altitude fields. The village retained ownership of much of its irrigated lands, although partial control over communal forest, water and grazing resources was lost. Other communities closer to the city of Texcoco were not so lucky, and by 1910, many peasants there had given up subsistence agriculture in favor of wage labor in the city or on the haciendas. After the Mexican Revolution, Amatango regained its high mountain territory and water rights through the *ejido* program, which involved the reclaiming of previously expropriated lands.[9]

These lands, although not very agriculturally productive, contain a multitude of resources which have fostered the viability of extended household organization and community solidarity. They have been used to maintain traditional agrarian pursuits and provide the raw materials for some new patterns of economic adaptation. However, by the early 1950s steady population growth had pushed the community size beyond the capacity of the land to feed the villagers. Access to the mountain forests and irrigation waters stimulated the development of two economic activities which helped families resist the wholesale need for full-time laboring in industrial zones, which already had disrupted household integration in villages closer to the city. The first new economic activity involved producing sturdy wood crates which were welcomed by Mexico City fruit merchants who purchased all the community could produce. This work drew upon indigenous woodworking knowledge and allowed for teams of fathers and sons or brothers to gather the wood and make the crates on simple machines in their own courtyards. Crate making had the additional advantage of allowing land-poor villagers a way to resist permanent migration or factory labor. At about the same time, villagers began to convert parts of their irrigated fields to the cultivation of decorative flowers, which would be gathered by family labor and sold in urban neighborhoods of Mexico City.

In 1973, I found that almost two-thirds of extended households which included members over age 60 were producing at least one of these specialty products. These two activities not only provided a fair amount of cash, but the work was best accomplished within a multigenerational domestic work unit. Moreover, the economic utility of the aged, especially males, was enhanced as they were more likely to continue contributing to these cash-producing endeavors long after their effectiveness in other agricultural work had diminished.

Partly as a result of these factors, Amatango reached the 1970s as a highly integrated peasant enclave, depending largely on patterns traceable to Aztec ancestors but shored up by new economic innovations. Yet the benefits from these changes were limited by an inefficient irrigation system, lack of a passable road for motor traffic and the low level of education. Fortuitously, it was in the late 1960s and early 1970s that the state government, with Mexican federal assistance, began to selectively invest in improving rural infrastructure through electrification, road building and eventually the expansion of rural health care services. As a start, the community combined its traditional communal labor system with state government–provided materials and engineers. These initial efforts improved their irrigation system and built a small bridge over a ravine, which had been a serious obstacle to motorized vehicles entering the community. With these successes in the 1960s, Amatango's leaders began to petition for the other "modernizing" changes mentioned previously.

Table 9.1
Aging and Demographic Change in Amatango, 1960, 1970, 1993

Year of Survey	1960*	1970*	1993**
Percent Over Age 65 (agedness)	4.1	3.5	3.4
Old Age Dependency~	7.6	6.7	6.25
Youth Dependency~~	76.5	84.1	78.2

Sources:
*Perez y Lizaur 1970; Mexico, D.F. 1973.
***Source:* Census of community nurse.
Definitions:
~Old age dependency was calculated as the ratio of persons over age 65 to persons age 15–64.
~~Youth dependency was calculated as the ratio of persons less than age 15 to persons age 15–64.

AGING ON THE EDGE OF A MEGACITY

Mexico, like many other Third World nations, has been very slow in seeing the needs of the aged as competing with other issues. In 1995 a little over 4 percent of its populace was age 65 or older, and this rate had barely risen since 1965 when the figure was 3.9 percent. However, like countries such as Indonesia, India and China, in another 30 years the proportion of Mexico's elderly will double.

In Table 9.1 we can see how these national figures are reflected in the rural community of Amatango and view some of the demographic underpinnings for continued support of the elderly in the village. From 1960 to 1993 the agedness of the community and the old age dependency ratio had slowly declined, from 4.1 percent over age 65 and 7.6 elderly per 100 adults, to 3.4 percent over age 65 and only 6.25 elderly per 100 adults. This change was related to significant natural population increases, especially during the 1960s and 1970s when large numbers of children were born in the village. Importantly, by the 1970s, in villages closer to Texcoco the percent of the aged and the old-age dependency rates were nearly triple that found in Amatango. This was primarily due to the permanent migration of adults age 20 to 40 from these areas.

When I began my research in the early 1970s, Mexico was undergoing economic expansion and Amatango, like many other rural regions, witnessed a population explosion. By the end of that decade the population had increased by 62 percent to 2,950 persons. This resulted from a continuing high rate of births, averaging 9.39 per family, while the general and infant mortality rates began to decline (Millard 1980). As usable wood from their forest lands diminished and competition from other flower-growing areas intensified, families began to rapidly abandon box making and flower growing. During this period the population of the Texcoco and Mexico City urban zones dramatically increased and opened up new economic opportunities for Amatango.

By the early 1980s Mexico City was on its way to becoming the second largest urban area in the world with a population of about 12 million inhabitants then (over 20 million today).[10] Here, families from Amatango found new, burgeoning areas in which to sell local goods produced by extended family labor.[11] This type of work was greatly facilitated by the improved village road and more frequent bus service. A majority of families who had previously grown commercial flowers began to buy them cheaply in other communities for resale in urban markets, some even having their own little stores or stalls for this purpose. Throughout the 1980s increasing numbers of younger males and females sought employment in nonagricultural labor outside the village. By the 1990s men in their sixties and seventies were having a hard time finding their sons around to work the fields during critical parts of the agricultural cycle. Some fields were not even planted for lack of labor.[12]

Also significant was a change in the work pattern of young unmarried women. Up to the 1980s the only typical wage work sought by teenage girls was to work as live-in servants for middle-class families in Mexico City or Texcoco. However, in the 1980s, the town of Chiconcuac on the outskirts of Texcoco began to abandon its traditional small-scale production of wool products for large-scale production of inexpensive synthetic fiber clothing.[13] For the last 100 years Amatango's families had provided much of the wool for Chiconcuac's once famous serapes and sweaters. Now they began to provide their teenage daughters to help produce inexpensive dresses, shirts and other clothes for markets throughout Mexico and even the United States.

By the 1990s, Amatango's young women were also adopting new reproductive strategies and the population was increasing at a much lower rate. These women were starting to use modern birth control techniques, despite strong initial resistance from their husbands and mothers-in-law. Introduced slowly in 1983 by a local nurse who worked at the village clinic, by 1993 some form of birth control was used by about a third of the almost 900 women still in their reproductive years. In 1973, when I would ask young men and women what the ideal family size was, the standard response was "only God knows." At that time, couples almost universally sought to have as many children as they could. In the 1990s, attitudes had changed dramatically. Almost like a Greek chorus, adults in their twenties would repeat the maxim, "*dos hijos es mejor, pero cuatro es el maximo!*" (two kids is ideal, but the maximum is four). Of the women who were practicing some form of birth control, the majority would only begin after they had given birth to three or four children. This shift in reproductive behavior was influenced by the fact that with the establishment of a medical clinic in the community, infant mortality had plummeted to levels almost comparable with national figures.[14] For example, infant mortality was 390 per 1,000 in the 1960s, but by 1989 had plummeted to 53.5 (Mindek 1994). Young parents were also acutely aware of the rapidly rising costs of supporting children, especially in the area of education.

PERCEPTIONS OF ADULTHOOD AND AGING

The attainment of adult status for both men and women comes through marriage. For the first few years, the young couple will usually live under the roof and command of the groom's parents. This provides entree into a variety of responsibilities which link the couple to broader community roles. Married men not only must labor in regular public works projects but also be willing to accept the financial burdens entailed in sponsorship of cycles of religious festivals. Young adult women focus their lives on raising children and working with their mothers-in-law to feed the family and manage household resources, especially any livestock.

Individuals will attempt to retain the image of a fully functioning adult (*Tlacatl*-man, *Suwatl*-woman) as long as possible. However, it is recognized that sometime during the sixth decade of life, men and women must gradually give up total executive control of field and hearth to one of their married sons and his wife. People will begin to refer to such persons as old by generically using the term *cultzin*[15] (grandparent) or *culi* (old person) for both males and females. They will begin to be talked about as *culi* when several grandchildren have survived childhood.

However, the *culi* label is not consistently applied to a person until the early to mid-sixties, when changes in strength and vitality reduce work capacity in some way. Once persons are accepted as *culi*, they will be excused from communal work groups and most public ritual sponsorship. There is a noticeable lessening of social constraints on the behavior of older women, and they are allowed greater latitude in social interaction, especially with male age peers. By the time a woman is 60, she may be seen on occasion casually chatting with a group of men or guzzling a beer at a public festival, things forbidden to younger women. This shifting of gender boundaries does not carry over into politics and community leadership roles, as has begun to happen during the 1990s in a number of villages nearer to Texcoco.

However, in midlife, through their forties and fifties, women may cultivate skills in nondomestic arenas. One of these is midwifery and/or some other traditional folk healing specialty such as *tepatike* (general healer), *tlamemelawa* (massage) or *tlapupua* (herbal medicine). Of the four most active midwives, two are in their mid-forties, one is 55 and the other is 75. Each of these women practices at least one of the other healing traditions in addition to assisting with childbirth. To date, the local nurse and the doctors annually sent to the village medical clinic have maintained a good relationship with these midwives. Although more of Amatango's women now give birth in the clinic or even in a hospital in Texcoco, the population growth over the last 25 years has assured these midwives many clients.

A second area of activity for mid-age women is in the entrepreneurial realm. After menopause, women have the opportunity to venture to urban markets by themselves to sell. Most typically this will involve hawking flowers, herbs, food or animals in the crowded satellite urban areas around Mexico City. For example, by 1994 Maria Juarez, age 64, had been a widow for a decade and lived with her married son and his children on a tiny, unproductive plot of land. She began selling sheep and goats about fifteen years earlier. Later, she used this money to trade in flowers and put a deposit down toward the purchase of a small textile-making machine from the factory where her son was working in Chiconcaoc. They started to produce sweaters in their house and eventually used the profits for Maria to set up a paper and notebook store in the late 1980s. This enterprise has done quite well with the completion of Amatango's own high school, soon after the store opened.

As is typical in the life cycle of peasants elsewhere, women in old age show a greater continuity in the roles they play than do men (Cool and McCabe 1987). Most elderly women, almost to the time of their deaths, continue a familiar domestic regimen centering on food preparation, weaving, nurturance of children and the care of small livestock. Continuing this work pattern keeps old women deeply embedded in a network of both age peers and younger women from four to six households, who must cooperate to produce the huge quantities of food consumed on ritual occasions.

Men, even after relinquishing control of their farms, will continue to undertake arduous work alongside sons until their mid- to late sixties. It is after this point, when they can no longer easily plow or plant, that they switch to more sedentary tasks such as preparing cactus beer, repairing tools or collecting wild vegetables from nearby corn fields. For males referred to as *culi*, almost any decrease in vitality will substantially diminish their value in exchange networks which involve demanding tasks such as rapidly planting corn, house building or digging irrigation canals. No longer are they asked to join younger men in the cooperative labor used to perform the agricultural tasks of neighbors or the weekly village-wide work crews. Over the last twenty years, some specialized roles for older men such as *teseuktero* (person who ritually prevents hail storms) or as leaders of certain religious performance traditions have all but disappeared.[16] We will see however, that these men still have other avenues for public acclaim.

WHO ARE YOU CALLING USED UP?

My more recent probings about cultural definitions of aging, in July 1993, revealed a wider range of Nahuatl words about aging than I had encountered before. The experience also bruised my ego. On my second day back in the village I went to visit Santiago Velazquez, who, at age 58 and in exceedingly good health and vigor, was frequently mentioned as someone who was aging well. We had not seen each other since 1989 and now, at age 46, my once deep black beard was showing a good deal of grey. When he saw me he immediately looked quite concerned and said *"pues Don Che, que paso, parece yotla moak."*[17] I had only first encountered this Nahuatl phrase *yotla moak* the day before, and was shocked when I translated in my head this well-meaning greeting by an old friend to mean, "Well, Jay, what has happened? You look all used up!" Although I thought I was in fine shape for my age, having lost weight recently in preparation for playing a tennis tournament in Maryland, to Santiago my thinned face and torso combined with rapidly graying beard portrayed a very ancient personage, who was "all used up" and at death's door. We were almost immediately joined in conversation by Santiago's father Juoquin, age 85. Only in the last few years had he become quite hard of hearing, started to wear thick glasses, and to walk slightly bent over with a cane. When I asked Juoquin about the phrase *yotla moak*, he gave a nervous laugh, patted himself on the chest, implying but not saying that this described himself. Immediately, he excused himself and said he had some wood posts to cut for a new fence around his house.

Over the following week I made it a point to visit Juoquin's house every day and he made it a point to tell me each activity he was about to do such as cutting wood, or walking halfway up the mountain to gather sap from his maguey plant to make fresh *pulque* (cactus beer). When we looked at old pictures I had taken of him working with Santiago in his cornfield in 1972, he thought back to how strong he had been then, in his early sixties, and readily admitted that now he was a "culi," just plain old. He would never admit to being *yotla moak*, although many people were beginning to say this when he was not around. This term was not used often but summed up more precise Nahuatl words which described the loss of real adult functioning.[18]

By the time people would be labelled *yotla moak* they would generally restrict their daily activity to their house compounds and rely on nearby grandchildren and great-grandchildren to assist with their activities of daily living. The only time I observed an instance of public ridicule of an elder was when a thin, small seventy-four-year-old man, Jose D., attempted to join a community work crew of about 40 men repairing a road:

10:30 A.M.: Going to the work site the group of men passed Jose's house and shouted that they needed to borrow a shovel and continued on. A few minutes later at the work site down the road, Jose appeared with a shovel over his shoulder and with a toothless grin, announced that he was ready to begin digging. After mild laughter by the men, several began to taunt him and wrestled away the shovel. One said Jose was lucky to have walked there with such a heavy tool and that digging with it would surely cause his death. An angry Jose directed some weak blows with his fists on the shoulder and head of one of his tormentors, but the man just chuckled and pushed away the older man. Jose, wishing no further humiliation, returned to his house as the other men returned to work with a few muttering under their breaths, "crazy old man" (Field notes, June 10, 1973).

THE FAMILY CONTEXT OF AGING

Such events are rare, as few older citizens will step much beyond accepted age norms. Rather, the elderly in Amatango will consistently draw upon two bases of support and prestige: the extended family and a hierarchy of civil-religious roles. Both of these systems are highly linked, since individuals participate in community affairs as family representatives and not as isolated actors. In Amatango, extended family organization is the normative form of residence older adults hope to generate over the long run.[19] Ideally, as male offspring get married, at least one is expected to raise his children in his parent's house and provide the core basis of support in old age.

In 1973 a clear majority (60 percent) of persons 60 years of age or older (see Table 9.2), lived in such three-generational settings, with 90 percent of such households having no more than one married son in residence. This statistic alone does not give a true picture of family life, then or now. More often than not, at least one other married son resided in a physically independent house, a moment's walk from his elder parent's dwelling—just across a courtyard or down a dirt path. In only four instances did aged individuals live alone. One-third of the aged lived with unmarried children or other single kin, most typically a grandson. In 1993 an informal survey I did of 45 households with at least one person over age 60, showed that almost two-thirds were organized around extended family settings. The other living arrangements did not show significant structural alterations since the 1970s.

Behind this strong statistical consistency lay some important changes related to the position of the elderly in Amatango's families. From the 1920s to the early 1970s, a major shift has involved the significant reduction of very large extended households, where two or more married sons stayed in the house compound to work with and eventually care for their parents. Such "joint" patrilineal (male-linked) households, containing 12–25 persons, were enclosed within 120 by 70-foot-long rectangular compounds protected by 15-foot-high adobe walls and at least two dogs. By the early 1970s, reductions in per capita land holdings and the rise of new money-making activities outside the village had stimulated a shift from "joint" to "stem" patrilineal groupings, where only one married son would remain with the parents.[20] At that time the proportion of joint, patrilineal households with more than one married son living under the parent's domain had been reduced by about half. Of more recent vintage is the formation of extended households by incorporating an adult daughter's family into her parent's residence, either by themselves or along with a married son. My small 1993 sample showed that this new pattern increased the percent of elderly parents connected to joint households—almost one-quarter of extended

Table 9.2

Amatango Household Patterns of Persons over Age 60 (1973, 1993)

	Extended Households		Nuclear Households	Living Alone
	Elderly Parents/Parent		Elderly Parent(s)	
	with		unmarried children/	
			or other kin	
	1 married	2 married		
	son/daughter	sons/daughters		
1973*	44(54.3%)	5(6.2%)	28(34.5%)	4(5%)
n=81				
	[60.5%]			
1993**	25(55.6%)	6(13.3%)	11(24.4%)	3(6.7%)
n=45				
	[68.9%]			

*Source: total household survey by author.
**Source: limited household survey by author.

households sampled were created in this way. In 1973, only two women with their families lived in their parents' home and in each case their married brothers also resided with them. In 1993, I found five of the regular extended households being formed just with married daughters and in another four cases, married daughters or single daughters with children joined their married brothers in living with their elderly parents.

Significant changes in village life have not altered the fact that the lives of the elderly in the 1990s were thoroughly embedded in the social matrix of surrounding households, headed by their adult children, siblings and cousins. As most marriages (about 80 percent) take place within the village, this imparts a particularly intense geographic density to the social networks of the aged, especially for males. While a woman's kin group is more physically dispersed from her abode than a male's, this does not imply that females are more isolated in old age. In fact, due to their greater role continuity, women past age 65 will typically maintain reciprocal support networks with more personnel and have greater frequency of exchange than their male age peers.

Elders are in constant contact with children, if not with a resident grandchild then with a wide range of very young kin and godchildren living within a few hundred yards from them.[21] The child-minding aspect of grandparenting has, in fact, increased over the last decade, as in many households at least one of the parents is working in the city during the day. Relations of the very old with their grandchildren are especially important. As seen in the photos on the following pages, adolescent or teenage children are sometimes sent to live with and help grandparents who might otherwise be living alone. In multigenerational homes, young children were observed sleeping in the same bed as a grandparent. This seldom seemed a matter of space, but rather a case of mutual need. The children help to warm up old bones and the grandparent provides emotional security at night when various spirits and demons are thought to travel through the village.

One of the dramatic and consistently adhered-to aspects of intergenerational kinship behavior is a formal system of deferential gestures. Upon seeing an older relative, a villager will, with respectful comportment, rush to that person's side, solemnly bend to ritually kiss his or her right hand and whisper the proper Nahuatl reverential term (e.g., *Nosicntzin*, my revered grandmother). Kinpersons of roughly equal age also ritually greet each other, but with simultaneous and more perfunctory bows and hand-kissing gestures. This display of ''sacred respect'' (*respeto*) functions to regulate the traditional lines of authority and maintain proper social distance within the kinship system.

The sacred nature of this gesturing behavior increases with genealogical closeness and the age of the relative being greeted.[22] Despite the dominance of patrilineal descent, kinship ties generated through one's mother are also acknowledged by *respeto* behavior and have great practical importance. Maternal relatives comprise a significant portion of a household's total personal network of support. It is through the exchange of labor, tangible goods, and money that families are able to carry out costly and time-consuming public ritual.[23]

During my earliest research in Amatango I found that *respeto* masks an underlying tension and fear which embraces the realm of kinship. A system whereby a man's access to adult roles and community status is largely predicated on inherited lands engenders not only filial conflict but also tension between brothers and certain male cousins (the sons of a father's brother). The total acceptance of *respeto* behavior is thought to help avoid the display of angry emotions among relatives, an act which itself is thought to cause illness or invite sorcery with its subsequent misfortune.[24] While any adult in Amatango can be a potential witch, the quest for a suspect usually begins among one's poorer relatives.[25] Despite this ominous possibility, it is a person's cousins who throughout life form the core of an unremunerated reciprocal work exchange network needed for agriculture, house construction and ritual sponsorship. As the range of economic activities has increased since the 1970s and children are not so tied to replicating their parents' agrarian lifestyle to gain adult status, intragenerational competition seems to have decreased, along with accusations of witchcraft.[26]

In the early 1970s, the emotional structure of family systems was quite authoritarian, dominated by the elder couple, especially the male. Following Aztec legal tradition, parents could take disobedient children to the community judges

Fifteen-year-old boy sent to live with his widowed grandmother, 1993.

for punishment in the form of hard labor for the community or a fine. I witnessed several such cases during 1973.[27] Over the twenty years since my first fieldwork stay, indelible change has clearly occurred in generational dynamics. Most notable has been the reduced control of senior kin over the actions of junior relatives. For example, the last public trial for parental disobedience was held a decade ago. On a more subtle level, in the early 1970s, when I talked to aged parents about divergence from customary behavior by younger people, they

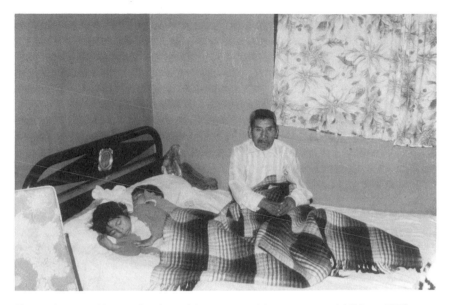

Ninety-six-year-old man sleeping with two co-resident great-grandchildren, 1978.

responded with restrained hostility. They accepted that such things were possible but adamantly insisted that they would see that the *costumbres* (traditions) would be followed. Now, in the 1990s, when confronted with a daughter-in-law who uses birth control or a son who prefers urban factory work to cultivating corn-fields, they are likely to respond with a shrug, saying "*cada quien*" or "to each his own." When I returned to the village in 1989, I had expected to find more generational dissention and a rapid decrease in the importance of extended family life. However, as families had successfully incorporated new village-based, productive strategies in previous decades, in the 1990s households have adapted to the outside wage work of young adults.

Some families have anchored themselves to agrarian pursuits supplemented with both home-grown and industrial-based labor, while others have economically forsaken the land for commercial pursuits centered in urban zones. This is illustrated in the two cases discussed below.

THE AGED IN EXTENDED FAMILIES: 1990s

The first family is that of elderly Juoquin Velazquez and his fifty-eight-year-old son, Santiago, mentioned previously. In 1994 their large household of thirteen persons included four generations living in a large, walled compound. This particular house was known as *tlashcal* (Aztec for tortilla).[28] Santiago's wife Julia, age 59, gave birth to fourteen children, ten of whom survived childhood

Juoquin Velazquez (second from left, holding sword) serving as one of the leaders of a dance troupe for a fiesta in Amatango, 1973.

diseases. Five of her unmarried offspring still lived there, including thirty-year-old Gregoria and her five-year-old daughter. Gregoria had met and married a man from Texcoco, but he had abandoned her four years ago and she returned to her parents' home. She and her mother manage a little produce store built into the side of their house. The oldest two generations have focused their lives on combining peasant agrarian labor with specialty work of the most traditional sort. Juoquin, 86 years old in 1994 and a widower since age 72, passed on executive control of the family fields and animals to Santiago in 1974. He continues to do minor maintenance around the house, and will try to gather cactus sap and wood in the foothills within a half mile of his residence. Santiago is Juoquin's only son who survived childhood. When I first came to Amatango in 1972, Santiago had just been elected *delegado* (mayor), the most important local political role. This was a position his father had held twenty years before. In each case, these men had served the village in several important and costly religious sponsorships as a prerequisite to being deemed worthy of leading Amatango. Into his early seventies Juoquin continued to be an active member of the several religious dance groups which performed at village *fiestas*. He is seen performing in a position of honor during such an event in the photo above, taken in 1973 when he was 65 years old.

Since late adolescence, Santiago not only worked side-by-side with his father in their cornfields but also learned from an uncle to play the trumpet. As an older teenager he began to work in this relative's fiesta band. Santiago still earns extra money by playing in this band, which performs for local ritual events and those in the surrounding region. Santiago has passed on this musical passion to two of his co-resident adult sons. One, Jorge, age 34, is married with two children and commutes daily to earn a regular salary by playing in the military police band in Mexico City. In 1993 the other son, Miguel, age 23 and single, started a new popular musical band, "Realidad," with a group of his village friends. The band plays for family parties and occasionally at concerts in nearby towns. Such musical work has great appeal to traditional extended households, as in most cases this activity would not hinder significant contributions to agricultural tasks.

Just down the road from *Tlashcal*, the house called *Shalali* (sandy soil) contains another extended family which has taken a different path in adapting to the modern world. By 1994, Jeronimo Juarez and his wife, Concha Duran Juarez, both in their early sixties, had made an uneasy truce with life in their rural community. As a young adult, Jeronimo found he did not like farming very much and would on occasion take temporary jobs in Texcoco. Since his mother had given birth to four sons and two daughters, when his father died in the early 1960s the agricultural lands they inherited were not nearly enough for the families of those brothers. The youngest son liked city life even more than Jeronimo and at the first opportunity left the village to live in Texcoco, eventually getting a job in a fertilizer factory and marrying a poor girl from that city. In 1968, Jeronimo was offered a job in a small chicken-processing plant in Texcoco owned by an urban godparent of his youngest brother. Over his wife's strong protest he moved her and his small son to the city. Within six months, Concha fell into a deep depression and threatened to commit suicide. Admitting defeat, Jeronimo moved back to Amatango. When I met Jeronimo in 1972 he was fluent in Nahuatl and enjoyed participating in the traditional *fiesta* system, but he was deeply conflicted by the agrarian way of life. At this time, when I began to live in their house, Jeronimo and Concha headed a nuclear family with just two young children. Their lives, however, were deeply embedded in a kinship web sewn by the nearness of his two brothers remaining in Amatango. The oldest, Miguel, then age 54, lived 50 yards behind him with his married son, daughter-in-law and their child. Another married brother, age 25 lived in a small house adjacent to Jeronimo's.

Over the next two decades two other children, Ana and Angel, were born and survived into their teenage years. Their older brother, Jose, married at age 18, taking a very traditional village bride to live with his parents. During this time Jeronimo seldom planted his fields but let his older brother and his nephew sow it with corn and squash, sharing the harvest between the households. Instead, he sometimes worked in urban factories or making change on buses. Jeronimo also made wooden crates for sale with his oldest son, or bought and sold flowers with his wife in the shanty towns springing up around Mexico City. In 1988, they used their small savings to convert the front room of their house (my former

Jeronimo Juarez and his wife Concha with their three grandchildren, who live in their house. Behind them is the ''micro'' bus which Jeronimo has leased to drive as part of the intercity transport system.

bedroom) into a small convenience store which Concha managed. With population and urban congestion booming in the Texcoco regions by the 1990s, the government encouraged individuals to lease buses or vans to enhance the existing intercity public transport system. By 1994, Jeronimo had leased both a large van and a small bus which he and his two sons would drive in long shifts to support the household. That year he would seldom drive the bus, as he had been elected to the important ''presidency'' of the community group which carried out all work projects on roads, the irrigations system and public buildings. By this time Jeronimo and Concha were on the edge of being considered and referred to as *culi*, as their resident daughter-in-law Maria had provided them with three healthy grandchildren over the prior decade and another was born on the last day of my field trip that year. Also, by their own admission, they were beginning to slow down and could not work as hard as they used to.

THE ISSUE OF NEGLECT

Unlike the situation with the Ju/'hoansi people described in Chapter 2, my initial attempts to elicit cases of neglect of the aged were met with puzzlement and outright denial. In only two instances did I encounter expressions by the elderly of neglect and poor care. In one instance, I met Emilia, an eighty-year-old woman who was visiting the house of her niece and family near the center of the village. She was a widow who had no living children and resided alone in the more isolated mountain section of the village. When I asked about her living situation she became angry, saying that nobody cared about her. She repeated several times that *"mi casa es mi panteon"* (my house is my grave). In later discussions with Emilia's niece and other community members I learned that this elderly woman was considered to have been mentally slow and very peculiar since childhood. Although she had no close relatives nearby, Emilia refused to leave this area and live with her niece's family, despite their willingness to have her. Other villagers thought her kin were making a good effort to support her.

The second case of possible neglect represents a situation where both the elder and the community defined the older person as being abandoned. This case is intriguing in that the elderly man, who proclaims to all who will listen that his sons have abandoned him, actually lives with one son while another lives next door and the other two reside within a few hundred yards. Why, then, is seventy-five-year-old Miguel Juarez considered to be *"yamoucachiwe encaño,"* that is, abandoned while living with his family? A widower for about ten years, Miguel lives with Eduardo, who is 40 years old, mildly retarded and the only one who works with his father in the family cornfields. Eduardo has never married, and is described as "a little crazy" by other people. Miguel has had a serious drinking problem since early adulthood. During his married life, he would get drunk quite often and beat his wife. Frequently in debt, he eventually sold small plots of land for money, land which he should have kept to give to his sons. None of his three married sons ever developed a very strong interest in farming. Two work in small sweater factories in Texcoco and a third makes his living by playing in the local *fiesta* bands. Although in close proximity to their father, the three married sons ignore Miguel, although if he complains to them they let him know how much they resent him for having abused their mother and for selling off part of their birthright.

AGING BEYOND THE FAMILY

Beyond the family, the most important source of prestige, respect and power during middle and old age derives from the carrying out of community ritual and civil responsibilities. Known in Latin American scholarship as either the *cargo* (literally, "burden") system or the *fiesta* system, this involves a hierarchy of ranked positions (*cargos*) occupied for short periods of time by specific households (Cancian 1992).

In Amatango, community roles are loosely ranked, with the higher ones generally requiring more money and/or time but yielding more prestige and authority. The positions are divided between *cargos* of the church and those associated with political office; the former carry out costly folk Catholic rituals (*fiestas*), while the latter form the local government.[29]

In 1994, the religious hierarchy consisted of a twenty-member "church committee" which carried out an annual cycle of four *fiestas* and was responsible for a single year of ritual. These men as a group are led by a senior and junior *fiscal*, who take care of the material possessions of the church and provide elaborate meals for the priests who perform mass at every *fiesta*. The senior *fiscal* position is the most prestigious religious position, with election to this post predicated on prior service in at least two other major religious *cargos* and one significant civil role. There is an expectation that over a lifetime an individual will have undertaken at least one important sacred *cargo* and thereby be worthy of public esteem.[30]

At the center of local political authority and administration is the first *delegado* (commissioner), who serves for three years as the combined mayor and head judge. The second commissioner serves as his chief assistant by recording necessary documents, while the third is in charge of collecting fines and community taxes. The first *delegado*, referred to in Nahuatl as *altepetatli* (community father), is expected to oversee the community paternally, settle most levels of internal disputes and protect local interests from any outside forces. He leads all village meetings and must solicit opinions from all present until a general consensus is reached. Other personnel in the political hierarchy distribute irrigation waters, protect community boundaries and organize the traditional system of unremunerated collective labor which carries out public works projects. It is this civil wing of community service that, since the late 1960s, has initiated and carried out the series of modernizing projects of which Amatango is so proud.

Wealth will condition, to a certain degree, the extent of public prestige and power men and their families will garner as they age (Sokolovsky and Sokolovsky 1983b).[31] Nevertheless, virtually all older men from Catholic families had carried out at least once the sacred burden of ritual sponsorship, which gives them lasting honor in the eyes of the community and the saints.[32] By the time most males reach age 60, even those who are relatively poor will have shouldered at least some local political responsibility.

Besides ritual sponsorship and administrative positions, the *cargo* system affords other opportunities to enhance public esteem in old age. All of the *fiestas* involve dance troupes and elaborate processions. Elderly men, and to a lesser extent women, can volunteer to take roles as dance leaders, instructors, special musicians or simply as participants.[33] Such activities proclaim not only moral uprightness and continuing prestige, but also that one is still actively involved in the life of the community.

Despite the emphasis on age, hierarchy and formal deference between generations in family formations, this pattern is not totally replicated in the public groupings that carry out ritual. Although the *fiesta* system performs an implicit age-grading function, it also provides one of the only community-wide arenas where males and females of all ages can participate as relative equals. This occurs in the large dance groups that perform at most *fiestas* as part of the community's "folk" version of Roman Catholic pageantry. As seen in the

A fiesta dance involving both men up to age 75 and children as young as age 7.

photograph above depicting a ritual dance of the "Christians" versus the "Moors" during a *fiesta* in 1973, participants range in age from about seven to the mid-seventies. Even in the case where teenagers introduced a new dance formation based on an urban model, middle-aged villagers eagerly volunteered to dress up and perform as *caballeros y caballeras* (cowboys and cowgirls).[34]

Although women participate in the masses, processions and dancing associated with each *fiesta*, they assume no overt public leadership position in these activities. In the 1990s, with the establishment of Amatango as a parish center, the resident priest has encouraged middle-aged and older women to become leaders of a children's catechism group. Yet, during major public ceremonies, older women generally operate behind the scenes, directing the production and serving of huge quantities of the special foods required for successful ritual sponsorship. In accomplishing this they rely on, and in turn support, a wide circle of female age-peers and younger women drawn from their bilateral kin network. The reciprocal flow of assistance stimulated by the annual cycle of *fiestas* provides a regular source of extrahousehold engagement for all but the most frail women.

Perhaps the most important change with regard to older people and the *cargo* system has been the reduction in their political roles in favor of younger and better-educated leaders.[35] Prior to 1950 it was unheard of for a man to be considered for first *delegado* or senior *fiscal* before the age of 50 and persons chosen were often at least 60.[36] Even today, the directors of the religious hierarchy (senior *fiscal*) range in age from 50 to 65 and these men exert great influence in public decisions. Yet, for the last 40 years, first *delegados*, holders of the most potent political position, have been 41 years of age or younger with the youngest having been 31.

Despite the steady drop in age of the community mayor, the village has often sought to select men between 55 and 65 as the third *delegado*. In addition, still older men are used as judicial go-betweens in difficult cases where parties initially refuse to abide by legal decisions of the *delegados*.[37] By this pragmatic use of human resources, Amatango has put the prestige and authority accumulated over a lifetime behind political and judicial decisions.

CONCLUSIONS

The information I gathered over the last twenty years in Amatango seems to be at variance with some of modernization theory's predicted dire consequences for the elderly (see introduction, Part III). This is particularly unusual as under similar conditions of ''modernizing'' change, the aged of Amatango have fared better than those in many other Latin American peasant communities, studied in earlier decades. One reads, for example, that in the Colombian highland village of Aritama: ''There is no room and no use for them. Old people are not respected, feared or loved. Their advice is not sought by the younger generation, nor are they thought to possess any special knowledge which might be useful'' (Reichel-Dolmatoff and Reichel-Dolmatoff 1961).

This is an extreme case, but, judging from other ethnographic studies, the situation of the aged in rural communities of the region unfortunately seems closer to the conditions in Aritama than in Amatango (Adams 1972; O'Nell 1972; Kagan 1980). All too commonly, one finds a despairing elderly population rapidly bereft of support. They are caught in a demographic vacuum caused by departing young adults and in a cultural lacunae epitomized by the withering away of *cargo* systems.

This is exemplified by the case of Tepotzlan, made famous by the studies of Redfield (1930) and Lewis (1963). Although overtly similar to Amatango in its Nahuatl Indian cultural patterns, Tepotzlan was forced by population pressure on a diminishing land base into a significant commercialization of agriculture, even before the Revolution of 1910–1920. Eventual return of some communal lands after the revolution did not reverse this trend. The growth of wage labor and commercial production, high levels of internal inequality and the loss of political autonomy to new organs of the federal government severely hampered the viability of both extended family systems and the indigenous community organization. Even by the mid-1940s, Oscar Lewis found that Tepotzlan's elderly had developed a most insecure place in that community. The custom of hand-kissing deference was disappearing and few elderly people retained any roles in a crumbling *cargo* system. Many of the aged preferred to live alone. While there was still an expectation that children support their aged parents "there are cases of extreme neglect and the theme 'I would rather die than depend upon my children' is frequently heard'' (1963:53).

Why has the situation for the aged been more favorable in Amatango since the 1970s? Ironically, its isolated location and the mediocre quality of its agricultural lands protected the community from severe exploitation by a landed gentry in prerevolutionary times. Thus, substantial land and irrigation resources were retained and eventually expanded upon in the early twentieth century, prior to the onset of the pressures which had caused the demise of indigenous institutions and beliefs in similar villages. This economic strength helped sustain cultural features through which the aged have maintained societal value in the light of rapid change.

In fact, it is some of those very patterns of traditional life which have been used to carry out ongoing economic development projects. When, in the 1950s, a rising population provoked the need for new sources of revenue and the development of village capital infrastructure, solutions were largely based on local ecological and social resources.

As a consequence of this, the familial and village niches providing roles for elder individuals were not dramatically altered. Particularly crucial has been the vitality of the *cargo* system, which has not only served as a bulwark of Indian identity but also provided the organizational basis for community transformation. In other Latin American peasant communities, either the total collapse of the *cargo* system or the sharp separation of political and ritual components has severely limited the possibilities of maintaining public esteem in old age (Adams 1972; O'Nell 1972; A. Moore 1973).[28]

For Amatango, community solidarity bolstered by an economic base has enabled the village to transform itself largely on its own terms. This is the answer to the paradox of how the village could be both the most traditional and the most changing community in the region. While many aged are ambivalent about such things as the new schools, which downplay the use of Nahuatl, they are still very much a part of the system that brought these changes about.

NOTES

My research in Mexico could not have been possible without the gracious support of Professors Carmen Viquiera Landa and Patricia Torres Palerm, and their graduate students of the Department of Anthropology at Universidad Iberoamericana. I have profited greatly from the work of Dubravka Mindek who carried out master's dissertation research in Amatango in the late 1980s. Parts of the life history materials on Maria Juarez are taken from Mindek's dissertation. Also, the generous encouragement and support of Professor Luis Vargas is greatly appreciated. The research for this chapter was supported in part by a grant from the University of Maryland System Center for Study in Mexico.

1. The name Amatango is fictitious.

2. A *municipio* is a Mexican political subdivision similar to the American township. A *pueblo* is a politically dependent rural community. However, the *pueblos* in the *mun-*

icipio of Texcoco are comparatively independent, owning their own lands and forming distinct sociopolitical organizations.

3. For an interesting discussion of the use of Nahuatl *indio* identity in other parts of Mexico, see Schryer 1993.

4. The *Nahuake* were not incorporated into any modern cycle of ritual but were conceived as tiny, dwarf-like supernatural beings who dwelled in the mountain springs and controlled the rains and other weather patterns related to agriculture.

5. In many respects, the village in 1973 was culturally what Robert Redfield erroneously thought the Mexican community of Tepotzlan to have been like in the 1920s. Lewis (1963) presents a persuasive argument that even in 1927, when Redfield studied Tepotzlan, many important aspects of social organization, such as communal cooperative labor, had already broken down.

6. Recent historical research has indicated that during the first 200 years of colonial government in central Mexico, significant changes imposed by the Spanish world view and legal system substantially diminished, in Nuhua communities, the role of women beyond the family in ritual and political domains (Kellogg 1995).

7. Today, in Amatango there is a strong social sanction against women drinking in public prior to menopause with no similar restrictions imposed on men of any age. For older males, intoxication from drinking a cactus beer called *pulque* is indeed a significant problem in Amatango; according to the medical clinic records for 1993, alcoholism is the most common chronic health condition in the village.

8. The Spanish more intensively dominated the Piedmont villages with their flatter lands and warmer climate, while impinging much less on the lives of the people of Amatango and the other four communities of the more rugged mountain zone. This fact largely explains the persistence of indigenous Aztec, ethnic cultural traits and identity in these peasant villages and the turning to more *mestizo* cultural patterns in the Piedmont area.

9. Article 27 of the 1917 Mexican Constitution calls for land redistribution in the form of *ejidos*—land parcel grants to communities rather than individuals. Although historical documents show that Amatango began to request return of its lands as early as 1912, it had to wait until 1930 for the granting of its *ejido*, giving it back most of its original lands.

10. At that time it was estimated that about 2,000 persons a day were streaming into Mexico's capital, and many large new communities were formed on the city's eastern edge, closest to Amatango.

11. In certain cases they were able to create new specialty products with extended family labor. I observed an excellent example in 1993, where wedding cake mannequins were made within one of the larger extended family groupings in the village and transported to the market area in Mexico City specializing in matrimonial products. Smaller families would also go into the wholesale markets areas, buy food products, and then travel to these new urban areas to sell these items.

12. My observations in 1993 and 1994 indicated that between 5 and 10 percent of cornfields were not being worked due to lack of interest or sufficient labor.

13. This was in response to a flood of cheap textiles entering Mexico's market from Asia.

14. In the 1960s, general mortality in Amatango was 33 per thousand, but by 1989 had dropped to 6.5. In addition, a study done in the mid-1970s (Millard 1980) showed

that almost three-fourths of women sampled had lost a child to disease, while at the end of the 1980s a similar study showed that only 42 percent of women suffered such a loss.

15. The noun *culcn* is almost never heard in this form as invariably in daily speech the suffix *tzin*, meaning "revered," is used, forming the word *cultzin* (revered grandparent).

16. While some *teseukteros* were still alive, none were practicing their ritual craft for others in the 1990s. As part of the change in the *fiesta* system, especially with the coming of the permanent parish priest, some performances such as the dance of the pastorelas had stopped when the last leader died at age 79, in 1986. Similarly, older men twenty years ago were leaders of two *bandas Aztecs* (Aztec-style bands) playing indigenous music at certain *fiestas*. None of these bands have performed in Amatango for at least a decade.

17. It will be noted that in this sentence the phrase *Yotla moac* is in *Nahuatl*, but all other words are in Spanish.

18. This went beyond saying someone was a *culi* (old man) or *sicn* (old woman). The most common specific terms linked to perceptions of extreme old age and frailty were: *akmukilnamiki* (cannot comprehend); *yomopaltilw* (he) (is incontinent); *akmunnenemi* (cannot walk); or *aqueli itlaayi* (cannot work). A typical conversation about a very old relative considered *yotla moak* might provoke the following statement: "*noachsitntzn y kipia yosio(wk) aqueli itaayi*" (my revered great-grandmother has more than 100 years, she is very weak and cannot work).

19. The household organization of the community centers on an ideal of patrilineal, patrilocal, three- and four-generation households. This kin-based network of relationships forms shallow lineages which are organized on the basis of about three dozen surnames such as Mendez, Duran or Velazquez, which are passed on, along with the mother's surname, to descendants. At any given time, only about a third of all residences contain such family forms. This is not a new pattern, but has been quite consistent from at least the 1920s until the 1990s. In 1927 a community census revealed just slightly lower figures (57 percent) than in 1973 (60 percent) for the percent of nuclear families and virtually identical portions of extended households. A more recent, limited survey done by a Mexican graduate student in 1989 showed that the proportion (64 percent) of extended family households has hardly altered even since the 1920s (Mindek 1994).

20. In 1994 there were still some huge joint households. The two largest in the village had 24 and 22 persons, respectively, living within single-bounded house compounds, where four to six nuclear families lived under the direction of the elder parents. In both cases the households were among the more prosperous and entrepreneurial in the village.

21. As in most Latin American rural communities there is an elaborate system of personal ritual sponsorship, whereby a couple will be asked to be godparent for a specific event such as baptism or marriage. Accepting this responsibility in Amatango forges a very strong bond not only between the godparents and godchild, but also with the godchild's parent who will be called *compadre* (co-parent).

22. Hence, one's grandparents, parents and godparents receive the highest levels of public deference.

23. According to older respondents *respeto* etiquette should extend bilaterally to the fourth degree of relationship, but it is seldom observed beyond second cousins who form the outer edge of a functional, cooperating kindred. This fact serves as a source of minor consternation to people over 50 who sometimes complained of a decline in "proper" respect shown by the younger generation.

24. People who cannot control anger are thought to be susceptible to a folk illness called *muina*, which greatly weakens the individual and may even cause death.

25. Those who know you well are thought the most likely to catch you off guard. Perhaps a cousin may be a secret *tetlachiwe* (witch) who can dislodge your soul with his powerful breath or construct a doll from bits of your clothes, which, when impaled with cactus needles, will cause excruciating pain and even death.

26. In 1993 I was told that there had not been a formal accusation of withcraft brought before the *delegados* in seven years.

27. In the most traditional families, all money earned by the sons would be given to the parents, who would then decide how best to spend the collective resources. This could be the source of simmering conflict, especially in those families where the sons started to work for salaries in factories in Texcoco or Mexico City.

28. Most house sites are known by the Aztec name associated with the plot of land it is built on. These names often depict some aspect of the location, such as the type of land, nearness to the cemetery or a special kind of vegetation. Increasingly, names are being given in Spanish when new houses are constructed. The house names given in the examples do not correspond to the actual households to which they refer.

29. The operation of such a system has traditionally acted as an informal age-grading mechanism for males with ideally: teenagers and young married men (age 17–25) being bell ringers or political errand boys; older married men (26–35) serving as policemen or sponsors of simple ritual; middle-aged men (35–55) shouldering onerous religious duties or significant political positions; and, finally those approaching old age (55–70) being selected for the most crucial positions in the entire hierarchy. With respect to stratifying populations by age, *cargo* systems differ significantly from East African age-set organizations (see introduction to Part II). The former institution does not move men through a series of roles as a group nor is everyone expected to traverse all levels of the system. Consequently, unlike age-sets, the *cargo* system does not typically engender a sense of generational solidarity or shared roles which could give the elderly any power as a group.

30. Since the early 1970s the *fiesta* complex in Amatango has changed in two important ways. First, the number of annual celebrations has been reduced from eight to four and the number of ritual sponsorship positions from 32 to 20, eliminating the low-level positions such as bell ringers. Second, whereas previously each *cargo* for a particular *fiesta* had a variable cost to the individual, now the expenses for a particular saint's celebration are shared equally by its ritual sponsors. This reduction in the number of *fiestas* is happening throughout Mexican peasant villages. In the case of Amatango this is related to several factors. In 1992, Amatango became the center for a new Catholic parish serving the Indian-speaking communities in the mountains and as such has had a parish priest residing there since then. He has worked to concentrate on the *fiestas* which are least "Indian" and more connected to ritual recognized by the Catholic Church. Also, during the period since my first fieldwork, there has been a significant increase in households practicing religions other than Catholicism. In 1994, there were about 100 households practicing either Protestantism or some form of spiritualist religion. Finally, with more adult men working outside the village and becoming dependent on wage labor, it has become more difficult to recruit men to take their ritual responsibilities.

31. Unlike other peasant areas of the world such as rural India or Africa (see Chapter 4), where distinct class formations are completely embedded in the local social order, Amatango's rich and poor share a common ideology and lifestyle. Men from the wealthier families did not form any permanent landlord-tenant relations with poorer village

members. Not only did they all work in the typical round of agrarian tasks but they made an attempt to avoid giving the appearance, through dramatically different clothing or house styles, of being a class apart from poorer neighbors. However, during my research in the 1970s, I showed that men from wealthier families had a significantly higher chance of being selected to the highest political posts.

32. It should be noted that since the 1950s there has been a gradual growth in the number of protestant families in the community. In 1994 at least 100 families were non-Catholic and did not participate in the *fiesta* system.

33. A special honor is bestowed each year to several men over 50 who will guide sacred processions dressed as particular saints.

34. In the last few years the new priest in the village has encouraged the development of separate dance groups for children. For the most part, however, there continues to be a great degree of age integration in the *fiesta* processions and dance groups.

35. Almost from the beginning of the Mexican Revolution there has been considerable national pressure to separate the two parts of the community hierarchy. The intention here was to establish a local power base tied to the dictates and patronage of the national ruling political party. To a certain extent, Amatango has been able to control these processes. While the civil and religious hierarchies are by national law separate, they are unified in the village under a single moral order. It is the political leaders who help the religious stewards collect monies for *fiestas* or who light skyrockets to scare away hail-storms brought by Aztec water demons called *Nawake*. More fundamentally, no person could hope to become first *delegado* without having successfully shouldered one of the major sacred sponsorship positions.

36. Just after the Mexican revolution several very young *delegados*, under the age of 30, were selected to head the community, but the village reverted to leadership by older men by the end of the 1920s.

37. As of the 1980s there were still some Aztec villages where councils of elders still functioned in helping communities make important decisions (Sandstrom 1991).

38. For a discussion of programs to assist the poor and frail elderly in Latin America, see Abraham 1989.

CHAPTER 10

Gender and Duty in Japan's Aged Society: The Experience of Family Caregivers

Brenda Robb Jenike

Author Sawako Ariyoshi brought to light the heavy emotional and physical demands of caring for an elderly parent with her best-selling novel *Kōkutsu no Hito* (1972).[1] Her story concerns the plight of Akiko, a working, married woman in Tokyo with a teenage son, who must face caring for her demented father-in-law as his condition rapidly deteriorates. Realizing with both frustration and anxiety that she has no viable alternatives, she eventually foregoes much of her outside work responsibilities to provide round-the-clock care for her father-in-law at home. Yet, despite the hardships of caregiving, which include tasks ranging from changing the once authoritative man's diapers to preventing him from wandering or choking on his food, Akiko, by the end of the story, has not only resigned herself to taking full responsibility for her now infantile father-in-law, but has also established a caring, understanding relationship with him, to the point where she mourns his absence after his death. She has, in fact, assumed the role of a model daughter-in-law. Two decades after its publication, this tale of caregiving in Japan has only grown in pertinence, as multitudes of Japanese middle-aged women continue to be confronted with the dilemma of caring for frail elderly parents and parents-in-law at home.

Japan's population is aging more rapidly than in any country in the world, yet care of the frail elderly remains primarily a family responsibility, and more specifically, the domain of women. The social prescription of the daughter-in-law bearing the primary responsibility for the care of her parents-in-law persists, as does the gender-based ideological division of labor of women at home and men at work which has kept care for the elderly a woman's task. With increased longevity, however, the time women must devote to care of their elderly family members has reached unbearable levels. In the last few years, public outcry over this unmanageable burden has resulted in sweeping social welfare reforms that will essentially shift care of the elderly from the family to an integration of family, community and state care.

Modernization theory as advanced by Cowgill (1972) predicts such a reduction in extended families and family responsibility with the growth of state-supported infrastructure. Following Cowgill's model, the status of the aged in Japan would decline with these shifts. Yet, rather than readdress the debate on the status of the elderly in Japan, this chapter examines the effects of the ongoing shift in parent care responsibilities from a perspective seldom entered into the modernization and aging debate, that of the women providing the care.[2] Through the voices of those women who have supported the Japanese system of family care with their labor, I explore how Japanese women have framed their prescribed social roles within the context of their own lives, and, further, how these experiences have influenced their own aging processes. In these women's voices we can sense the true ambivalence behind the fulfillment of parent care duties in present-day Japan, and begin to understand the personal impact of current changes in Japan's social welfare policy for the aged. I conclude with a discussion as to whether the role of the family in care of the elderly in Japan is actually being replaced by state institutions, in which case modernization theory would be applicable, or whether state programs are serving to support family responsibilities, thus strengthening them rather than eroding them.

AN AGING SOCIETY, HOME CARE AND WOMEN

Demographic Background

In the late 1980s the crisis of an "aging society" (kōreika shakai), an umbrella term referring to both the demographic phenomenon and the ensuing socioeconomic crisis of caring for the burgeoning elderly population, hit the forefront of national consciousness in Japan. Four demographic aspects in particular signaled that the traditional, family-centered system of care could not continue to absorb the social welfare needs of the elderly: the rapidity of the aging of the population; the increase in single elderly households; the high rates of severely disabled elderly needing long-term care; and the growth in labor force participation among married women. I will briefly explain each of these trends in turn.

With the implementation of health reforms by the American Occupation government and the legalization of birth control after World War II, Japan made the swift transition from a high fertility/high mortality society to one with a low fertility and low mortality. Today, the Japanese continue to have the highest longevity in the world (76.3 years for men at birth and 82.8 years for women), and a birth rate well below the replacement level (1.43) (Yomiuri Nenkan 1997). In 1995, on the eve of Respect for the Aged Day, held annually on September 15, the state's Management and Coordination Agency announced that the percentage of elderly (those 65 and over) in the total population had reached 14.5 percent, or 18.2 million persons, making Japan an "aged" nation (*Yomiuri Shinbun* 1995). While this figure puts Japan on par with or slightly below other industrialized nations, Japan's transition from a young society (7 percent elderly) to an aged society (14 percent elderly) has occurred in only 25 years. This is twice as fast as any other nation. If current demographic trends continue, the percentage of elderly will nearly double to 25 percent by the year 2020, making Japan the "most aged" nation in the world in a span of just over two decades (Ministry of Health and Welfare Population Research Center, *Yomiuri Nenkan* 1995).

What has the Ministry of Health and Welfare most worried in terms of provision of care is the continuing increase in single elderly households (now at 17 percent of all households with elderly). The results of the Ministry of Health and Welfare's national census on household composition can be seen in Figure 10.1. While absolute numbers of joint households with elderly have risen (from 5.6 million in 1975 to over 7.6 million in 1994), the percentage continues to fall by one point per year, from 78 percent of all households with elderly in 1975 to 60 percent in 1994.

When looking at such figures, one must consider that the national census, by counting household heads, does not consistently account for those elderly who live in separate but adjacent residences to their adult children. This living arrangement, which is increasing in popularity, may have contributed to the statistical rise in single and elderly couple households. I will return to the subject of changing household structure in the conclusion.

Japan, as well, continues to have a high rate of *netakiri* (bedridden) elderly, many of whom are cared for at home. The term *netakiri* encompasses all physically impaired elderly unable to perform ADLs (Activities of Daily Living).[3] Over 900,000 or 4.9 percent of the elderly in Japan are bedridden.[4] This is significantly higher than other nations where comparable figures would be 0.4 percent for Denmark, and 0.5 percent for Britain and Sweden (Ministry of Health and Welfare 1992, 1996). Of the current bedridden elderly, over 70 percent have been incapacitated for more than a year, with 40 percent being cared for at home. The high rate of physically disabled is reportedly due to a correspondingly high rate of strokes, and lack of rehabilitative therapy. In Japan, elderly patients stay confined, or even strapped to their beds during their hospital stays, and often return home bedridden, even if they were ambulatory when they entered. Medical anthropologist Christie Kiefer has reasoned that this lack of rehabilitation comes from a combination of limited space in facilities, a shortage of physical therapists, and a reluctance on the part of both family members and hospital staff to force patients to suffer the physical pain inevitable in lengthy rehabilitative therapy (Kiefer 1987). Stemming from growing concern over the high rates of bedridden elderly and the low quality of life for such people, more attention is now, however, being paid to the benefits of rehabilitation programs for physically impaired elderly. Yet, as the majority of hospitals in Japan are

Figure 10.1
Composition of Households with Persons 65 and Over in Japan, 1975–1994

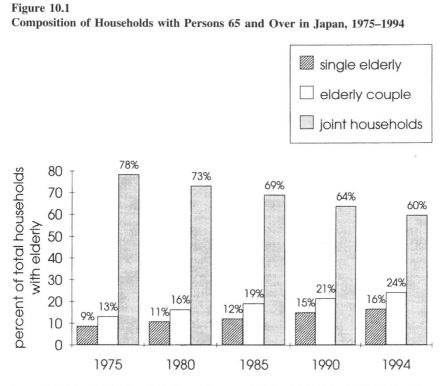

Source: Ministry of Health and Welfare, "Survey of National Life," in *Asahi Shimbun Japan Almanac* 1996:50.

actually small private clinics, space constraints and lack of qualified personnel still hamper the widespread implementation of such programs.

In addition to the rise in elderly living alone and projections for high numbers of bedridden elderly, the increasing number of middle-aged women in the labor force is also viewed as problematic for the social welfare system. The women in this cohort have been the traditional care providers for the aged. Women made up 40.5 percent of the total labor force in 1995, with 57.7 percent aged 40 or above (Management and Coordination Agency 1996). Although the majority of these women are part-timers (which usually means they work 40 hours a week, but with no benefits or security), they often work out of economic necessity. They may, therefore, be unable to leave work in order to care for elderly relatives. In the last few years, there has also developed a concern over younger women in their twenties delaying or rejecting marriage in order to have a career or escape the burden of caring for parents-in-law (Witter 1994). While such trends might suggest the need for strongly expanding formal support systems, the Japanese government has focused largely on programs that serve to reinforce the traditional system of home-centered care for the elderly, called *zaitaku kaigo*, over that of formal care in institutions.

"At Home" Care

As noted in Chapter 8, the elderly in Japan have traditionally been supported and cared for by their grown children. Specifically, the prewar patrilineal *ie* (stem family) system dictated that aged parents would continue to live with their eldest son and his wife, who would care for them until their death. In exchange for this care, the son would succeed as the head of the household, inheriting the family business or property. While the *ie* system has now been replaced by the household (*katei*) or family (*kazoku*), current state social welfare policy encourages the formation of the extended family (as a residential unit) over that of the nuclear family (Kelly 1993b:210). Figure 10.2, a flier from the city of Kawasaki for a public symposium on health and welfare for the elderly, depicts this idealized image of a modern, three-generation family. A healthy and happy grandfather and grandmother are seated at the center of a lovely family picnic, surrounded by their smiling grandchildren, their son and his wife.

The continued promotion of home care by the state coincides with the cultural construct of welfare as shameful among the current generation of elderly in Japan. To this generation, assistance is provided by one's inside group, usually the family or immediate community. To accept public welfare, then, is seen as a mark of shame on oneself and one's family. According to a chief social welfare policymaker in the city of Kawasaki,[5] this reliance on one's family and local community has resulted in a reluctance on the part of many Japanese to support the inevitable raising of taxes for a national, rather than local, system. Paying for such a national system would mean providing help for complete strangers rather than one's own family and neighbors. The national consumption tax, introduced in the late 1980s to help pay for welfare for the elderly, was indeed met with great resistance. In trying to corroborate this official's statements with informal interviews among both young and older acquaintances in Tokyo, one of my middle-aged respondents described welfare as separate from her life and "not a natural part of our system in Japan." She said, "It is just not expected to have things done for you." She saw welfare and volunteerism as a part of a "Christian-based society," not the Japanese belief system.

The subsidized public services now being offered and expanded at the local level are part of the 1994 "New Gold Plan," a strengthened revision of the 1989 ten-year national welfare strategy known as the "Gold Plan" which supports the home care system of public welfare over that of formal long-term care. Although fees and availability differ by locality, most municipalities in Japan now offer the services of city-certified "home helpers" (nurses' aides who make home visits), visiting nurses, short-stays and day care at local nursing homes, and bathing services (Japanese-style hot baths). Training classes for "family caregivers" (*kazoku kaigosha*) are also offered. Need for these services exceeds

Figure 10.2
Public Flier for "Kawasaki City's Public Symposium to Consider Plans for Health and Welfare Services for the Elderly" (March 27, 1993), Depicting an Ideal Image of a Modern Extended Family (Kawasaki-shi, Kawasaki-shi shakai fukushi jigyōdan)

both local resources and available personnel. Priority is thus given first to elderly without family members to care for them, next to elderly cared for only by a spouse, and then to elderly cared for by a single, working child. Those elderly being cared for by a housewife have the lowest priority for such services. As availability expands, however, more families in need are gaining access to these services. In 1994 a national caregiving insurance system was proposed by the Ministry of Health and Welfare that will provide further expansion of home care services through an integration of resources from volunteer organizations, private businesses and public comprehensive care institutions. As the bill now stands, all Japanese aged 40 and over will pay monthly premiums to ensure receipt of long-term care services if they become disabled (as defined by government specifications). Care will primarily be in the form of home services, but will eventually include institutional care. Although the details of this insurance scheme are currently under heated debate, it is likely to be implemented in some form by the year 2000 (three years later than originally proposed).

Nursing homes (rōjin hōmu) have also increased in number since 1989, but are still far below demand, with long waiting lists (three to four years on average) and highly selective criteria for admittance. Unlike in the United States, most nursing homes in Japan are public. Each nursing home serves a set geographic area, which means residents can only enter their one designated facility. If that facility is full, they must wait. Priority for admittance into public facilities is also focused on those elderly with no family members to care for them. As for private homes, high costs exclude all but those wealthy enough to pay. Contrary to our Western concept of a nursing home, however, the various categories of rōjin hōmu in Japan are not medical facilities, but caregiving facilities. They are thus for elderly who, with assistance, are still able to function on a daily basis (i.e., not be "overly physically or mentally impaired").[6] Further, entering a nursing home carries the stigma of being abandoned by one's family. For the majority of the severely disabled, then, the main options are long-term hospitalization, or continued family care. Even when a family chooses hospitalization, the burden of providing care is not necessarily alleviated, for, in Japan, hospitals will often rely on family members of patients to perform basic nursing duties. In addition to the greater availability of respite services over that of formal long-term care options, there are also financial incentives for home care. Families can receive housing subsidies to remodel their homes into joint households, and a tax credit if supporting an elderly parent. This credit increases in accordance to the severity of the parent's condition (Maeda and Shimizu 1992:246).

From a purely institutional perspective, then, there has been and will continue to be considerably more support for home care, and the establishment of joint households, than for formal, long-term care (in nursing homes or hospitals). This lack of viable alternatives to home care may in part explain the continued high rate of joint households with elderly in Japan despite modernization. To understand the whole picture, however, we need to look at what predominant cultural mechanisms, in addition to the historical reluctance to accept or contribute to a national welfare scheme, have been utilized to support the promotion of "at home" care.

Filial Piety as the Ideal; Women's Work as the Reality

Western and Japanese scholars and media alike continue to attribute Japan's high rate of home care to "the persistence of Confucian moral prescriptions about filial obligations to parents" (Ogawa and Retherford 1993:588). Such an emphasis has both produced and been a product of the moral component in the promotion of home-based care in Japan: the reinforcement of the virtues of parent care based on the theme of filial piety, or *oyakōkō*, in the mainstream media. During the early 1990s, documentaries such as *"Uchi de Shinitai"* (I Want to Die at Home) reported that elderly prefer to be cared for at home, as they equate any form of institutionalization with "abandonment." A plethora of moral-oriented television shows dealing with themes such as the camaraderie and follies of a modern, extended family in the city ("Double Kitchen"), the personal satisfaction of caring for one's parent ("Son's Return Home"), or, for children, the severe remorse faced if one does not appreciate grandparents ("Blessed with Grandma"), have been aired in the last five years.

Yet cultural ideals do not necessarily coincide with social reality. From the well-known folk tale *Obasuteyama* ("Throw Out Granny Mountain"), in which elderly parents are carried to a mountaintop and left to die, to contemporary cartoons satirizing the elderly and elder care, to the use of derogatory slang such as *baba* (old bag) and *jijī* (geezer), contradictions to the Confucian-based cultural ideal of revering the elderly abound in Japanese society.[7] The same can be said for the cultural ideal of parent care based on filial piety. For, what continued to be absent in this mainstream discourse of family care in the early 1990s was the acknowledgment of the crucial role of middle-aged women as the main caregivers to the elderly. After all, as social welfare officials would readily admit when pressed, "home care" and "family care" were but euphemisms for care provided almost exclusively by women family members.[8] In the Japanese family care system, the daughter-in-law or adult daughter must shoulder the burden of home care, not their husbands, children or other relatives. Lock cites a 1990 study by the Ministry of Labor which found that 81 percent of 500 people nursing elderly in their homes in Tokyo were women, with an average age of 56 years (Lock 1993a:53). In the Ministry of Health and Welfare's "Survey of National Livelihood" for 1989, 87 percent of the noninstitutionalized, bedridden elderly were being cared for primarily by co-residing family members. Out of those caregivers, 43 percent were daughters-in-law, 32.4 percent were spouses, and 20.6 percent were the adult daughters, with the remaining 4 percent reported as "other" relatives (cited in Higuchi 1992:493).

Furthermore, the vast majority of respite care-workers recruited by local governments in Japan are women, again mostly middle-aged, whereas the policy-

Figure 10.3
Brochure to Recruit Volunteers for Kawasaki City's "Home Helper"
Certification Program: "Free Time: Guide to Joining the Home Helpers"
(Kawasaki-shi shakai fukushi kyōgikai, 1993)

フリータイム

ホームヘルパー募集の

ご　案　内

社会福祉法人

川崎市社会福祉協議会

makers are overwhelmingly men (Jenike n.d.). One policy official in Kawasaki who assisted me greatly in my research had written an article in the welfare trade paper which explains the benefits of recruiting more middle-aged women volunteers for the home helper training program. Middle-aged women are seen as having the greatest time to spare for volunteer activities in their communities as they are (assumed to be) not involved in work, school or child care and are still physically healthy. Further, they are the ones "most skilled" at care tasks such as cooking, cleaning and shopping. As seen in Figure 10.3, the cover of the recruitment brochure for city home helpers in Kawasaki underscores this image with the cartoon of a smiling, rosy-cheeked, middle-aged housewife riding through the clouds on a cane underneath the words "free time."

In the last two years the discourse of home health care has expanded to include the opposition of feminist scholars and politicians. The main agenda of these feminists has been to fight for the expansion of respite services for family caregivers (the proposed national caregiving insurance system). Increased respite will help to alleviate caregiver burden, but does not change the gendered nature of the social welfare system. Home care in Japan, ardently promoted by social welfare policy officials, and sustained by the revitalization of an extended family-oriented society (paraphrase of Lock 1993:46), remains a system of a gender-based division of labor. In 1992 feminist professor and social critic Keiko Higuchi referred to home care as a silent system, one that places stress and burden disproportionately on the lives of women (1992:493). While the system is no longer "silent" to the burdens faced by women, the fact that millions of Japanese women must still fulfill their roles as caregivers out of a perceived social duty remains unchanged.

My aim, however, is not to force a Western feminist framework of perceived exploitation onto the lives of Japanese women, but to carefully examine the framework created by those women who have supported the Japanese system of home care with their labor. By letting these "family caregivers" speak for themselves, I explore how these women have framed their prescribed social roles within the context of their own lives, and, further, how their experiences have influenced their own aging processes. It is through these women's voices that we can sense the true ambivalence behind the fulfillment of parent care duties in present-day Japan.

METHODS

From February until the end of August in 1993, I conducted fieldwork under the auspices of the Kawasaki Public Welfare Bureau to investigate the extent to which home health care for the elderly was a cultural construct of gender, duty and a lack of alternatives, rather than a manifestation of a culturally rooted respect for the aged. I visited the city's pilot project nursing home and caregiver training facility, observed home helper training classes, attended public symposiums on welfare services for seniors and interviewed staff, nurses and city care-workers. During this time, I met with and interviewed in-depth five middle-aged women living in Tokyo and Yokohama who had cared for elderly family members. As I am primarily interested in social roles prescribed to middle-aged women, in which women from the middle generation must care for the elderly generation, I did not interview women caring for their husbands at home.[9] This study should therefore be taken as a look at parent care in particular, rather than at caregivers to the elderly in general.

The guiding questions of my study were: (1) What was the experience of parent care in these women's lives, and what words do they use to describe it? (2) Do these middle-aged women who cared for their frail parents or parents-in-law accept or resist popular discourse on the ideals of home care? (3) How responsible was filial piety in their decisions to give care? and (4) How has their experience affected their own aging process and expectations for the future?

CASE STUDIES

The following are the self-reflections of these former caregivers, whose ages ranged from 48 to 64. Two are single working women, the youngest daughters in their families, who had cared for their own parents. Three are wives of eldest sons who had cared for their parents-in-law. Their caregiving duties had ended with the death of the elderly family member or members two months to ten years prior to the interview. None, however, was through with the prospect of caregiving, as they all had other elderly family members who would be needing care in the near future. Note that at the time these women were full-time caregivers, they did not have access to the range of respite services now available. I contend, however, that while their anxieties and exhaustion may be more pronounced than women who are now using such resources, their personal experiences in caring for elderly family members remain valid.

For the purposes of presentation, I have organized these women's narratives into the following themes: the personal burdens of caregiving and the availability of personal support networks, the decision to caregive at home, the personal benefits of caregiving expressed in the concept of filial piety, and, finally, current expectations for old age.

The Burdens of Caregiving and Support Networks

Daily caregiving duties vary according to the mental and physical impairments of the elderly family member. Mrs. Muraoka (64), a housewife who had worked full-time before quitting to care for her bedridden mother-in-law, describes a typical day of caregiving:

In the morning I would wake her, wash her, feed her breakfast, give her her medicine, do the shopping, and it would be noon. I'd feed her lunch, and at three begin to prepare dinner. During all this I would be taking (mother-in-law) to the toilet, adjusting her in bed and such, and the day would be over. . . . I would have to adjust her again and again, over and over, countless times each day and throughout the night.

Her only time to herself was the ten minutes each day she spent exercising to a television yoga show. She remarked, however, that she did not realize how little time she had to herself when she was caregiving, as she did not think of it in those terms.

Whether assisting the frail parent with meals, toileting, bathing and dressing, housekeeping or providing companionship, the caregivers clearly remembered the physical and mental tolls involved in the strenuous routine. Ms. Yamamori (52), single and the youngest of three children, had her parents move into the apartment next to hers so she could care for them. Together with her mother, she cared for her bedridden father for three years. Working full-time, she qualified for city home helper and nursing services during the weekdays. Still, she recalled:

Each night after work I would be at my parents' until dad was asleep, and everything was done—the housework and such. After that I would return to my own place, about midnight, take care of my things, and go to sleep. In the morning I would go straight to work. Towards the end, when his death was near, I checked on his condition in the mornings, too. . . . I was exhausted. I lost weight. I didn't get enough sleep. More than me, it was mom who was tired. She would say she was going to die before dad.

Ms. Somiya (55) is single and the youngest of ten children. She had lived with her mother since her father's death, but put her mother in a hospital for the elderly when her mother's condition rapidly declined. Ms. Somiya stated, ''I worked during the entire caregiving period. I didn't have time to relax. As my mother deteriorated towards the end, it became mentally difficult for me.''

Whereas all women commented repeatedly on their physical and mental exhaustion involved in caregiving, as well as the impingement on their own time, Mrs. Kawabe (52) focused more on the difficulties involved in the personal interactions between family caregiver and care recipient. She had had the more unusual situation of caring for her mother-in-law as well as her husband's aunt and uncle, as the aunt and uncle had helped to raise her husband upon the untimely death of his father. Both the aunt and uncle had suffered from dementia and physical impairments. The two generations had lived in separate residences on the same lot for 29 years. She said:

Aunt took pride in being able to bathe herself and go to the toilet on her own. She could fall down anywhere, but you couldn't reproach her. She suffered a severe burn in the bath when she let the water boil. The hardest thing was to know when to intervene. . . . Diapers became necessary, but were difficult for both her and me. They were a blow to her pride.

As for time to herself, the separate but adjacent living arrangement provided relief only to a point.

At first I had small intervals of time to myself, but finally it felt like I was caregiving from morning until I slept at night. I was bustling from their house to our house, back and forth. I didn't go out much. Even if I did, I'd have to return soon.

Faced with such mentally and physically daunting work, what coping mechanisms had these women developed? Housewives can be the most vulnerable to suffering from stress and loneliness due to lack of emotional outlets and support systems. Mrs. Muraoka, a housewife who cared for her bedridden mother-in-law ten years prior to our interview, reported the most difficulties in caregiving in terms of mental and emotional costs. She also had the longest period of full-time caregiving, and the least emotional support, with "no time" to communicate with her friends. When I asked Mrs. Muraoka if she had received any help from her female in-laws, she said no. Her husband's older sister would come to visit with her mother, but not to help with the caregiving. The younger brother's wife had once tried to help with caregiving, but returned home after only one day, unwilling to continue. Such behavior of her in-laws was acceptable, as the responsibility of caregiving is that of the eldest son's wife, not of the daughter who, once married, becomes responsible for her own parents-in-law, nor of the younger daughter-in-law. Mrs. Muraoka added, "Even if all the siblings agree to care for the parent, you can't shuttle the parent back and forth from one child's house to another for so many months at a time. The old person becomes anxious and uneasy that way." She then remarked, "It would be a lie to say there was a person who didn't feel resentful at some point for having to do all the caregiving."

Mrs. Kawabe, also a housewife, but whose elderly relatives were not bedridden, had had the chance to talk with friends. She explained, "There were a lot of us with elderly family members. We helped each other, passing on information. To have other people understand what you're going through, that gives you the most strength." She also created her own emotional outlet and coping strategy in the midst of caregiving.

(My husband and mother-in-law) hadn't allowed me to work. But I made a promise to myself that I would be able to do what I wanted after aunt and uncle died. There was a university close by, and I thought, even though I was past 40, I was going to go there and graduate no matter how many years it took. I was really busy. I kept aunt as my priority. School was what I did for my free time, to enjoy. It gave me meaning in life (*jibun no ikigai*).

Note that what I term as these women's support networks consisted of advice and emotional support from other women. One may wonder what emotional support the married women had from their husbands. Mrs. Muraoka stated that her husband did not help out with caregiving whatsoever, and she did not include him as someone who helped her emotionally. Mrs. Kawabe described her husband's role as a reluctant participant.

I couldn't complain directly to my in-laws, so I would complain to my husband. I thought I would die if I couldn't complain about them. They were his own relatives, so he really didn't want to hear it, even though he understood. I knew that, but if I didn't tell him about it, I couldn't keep calm. There wasn't anything he could do (to help), but I wanted his understanding.

The two daughters caring for their own parents, Ms. Yamamori and Ms. Somiya, were able to rely on advice and support of home helpers and nurses who came to care for their parents while they were at work, as well as help from their female siblings. Their main coping strategy was using work as a form of respite. Ms. Yamamori said that while she was away at work, she could actually forget about her father at home, and concentrate on the business of the day. She could also discuss her caregiving frustrations with her colleagues at work.

Even with these varying systems of support and emotional outlets, caregiving at home was a personal hardship for all. Why, then, had they "chosen" to continue to caregive at home?

Why Home Care?

More than the simple response of "it was my duty to caregive," the most important factors in the decision-making process to caregive at home were the existence of reciprocity in the lifelong relationship between caregiver and care recipient (see Chapter 8), and the viability of alternative forms of care. Mrs. Muraoka's comments exemplify the importance of reciprocity in the caregiving relationship between in-laws:

My husband was the one who decided to have his mother come live with us. I was working, so she was to take care of the children for me. I thought it was a great idea. But when she thought about it later, she felt she had made a mistake. Her rural life was gone. She had no friends in Yokohama and was lonely. She poured all her affection into her grandchildren, for twenty years. . . . Her raising the children while I worked was the most important thing. I can't ever thank her enough. I owed it to her to look after her.

Contrast this reciprocal relationship to Mrs. Gonno's (48) relationship with her mother-in-law.

She never helped me with housework nor child care because she lived far from us. She later moved in so that I, the daughter-in-law, could care for her. When she weakened, I would help her with meals as expected of a daughter-in-law, but when she got too sick, we put her in a hospital.

Mrs. Gonno said that she would have liked to have cared for her mother-in-law at home, but her children had been too young. In Japan, fulfilling one's role as mother takes priority over all other obligations. Child-rearing responsibilities are perhaps the only socially acceptable way to excuse oneself from parent care duties.

For Mrs. Kawabe it had been "expected" that she care for her husband's mother, and aunt and uncle. She recalled, "My husband said if they didn't come live with us, it would become a problem when they were older. I didn't think about what conditions would be like when they got older. I was nervous and unsure of myself then.'' The relationship that formed, however, did have elements of reciprocity. "They let me depend on them, too. It was a close relationship.''

For the single women, it had been a "natural" decision as, being the youngest children in their families, they were the most attached to their parents. Also, they were unmarried, and thus seen as still responsible to their natal families. Working full-time, they were eligible for public support services. They did, however, still express their frustrations over the unavailability of quality long-term care alternatives. Indeed, all women told me their hospital horror stories. For example, after months of encountering the three- to four-year waiting lists at nursing homes, or being told her mother was "too sick" for admittance, Ms. Somiya placed her mother in a hospital close to where she lived. "It was an awful hospital!" Somiya moaned. "There weren't enough nurses. We had to come in and care for my mother in the nurses' place.''

Hospitals in Japan, besides relying on the family members of patients to perform basic nursing duties on a daily basis, are seen as places where the condition of the elderly worsens. No one liked the high doses of medications their family members were given in the hospitals. Ms. Yamamori said her father lost the use of his legs after taking a dementia preventative at the urging of his physician. She also noticed that "his head got funny when he entered the hospital, like he had gone senile. But when he returned home, he would be fine.'' Mrs. Kawabe's aunt, hospitalized after her burn in the bath, was strapped down in her hospital bed after she had episodes of wandering. "After that," Mrs. Kawabe said, "she couldn't keep food in her mouth. For the next three months until she died, food would just drop from her mouth. She never regained her senses.''

Compounding these concerns, the elderly family members had adamantly refused to be institutionalized. Even during short stays in the hospital, they had pleaded to come home, saying they were lonely in the unfamiliar surroundings. Mrs. Kawabe said,

Being at home was the most enjoyable thing for the old people. Aunt was nervous about strangers, maybe due to the dementia she became especially agitated. When an elderly person doesn't want to be institutionalized, you can only hospitalize them if you, yourself, cannot look after them adequately.

The women thus felt that home care was truly their only alternative. Ms. Yamamori summed up the sentiment by saying, "At home, we could watch him the whole time. He wasn't neglected like in a hospital. We knew when he was going to die. If he had been in a hospital, we might have been too late.''

In addition, then, to a perceived higher quality of care, what had been the personal benefits the women saw in caring for their elderly relatives, and how did this tie into filial piety?

Personal Satisfaction and the Expression of Filial Piety

Palmore and Maeda (1985:81) describe Ruth Benedict's explanation of *oya-kōkō* (filial piety) as an unconditional *on* (debt) one repays to his or her parents for having raised them. They define it as *gimu*, or an obligation. Yet, to the family caregivers, *oyakōkō* is not an obligation, but a "natural" impulse of a child to help his or her own parents if the relationship is good. Obligation (*gimu*), on the other hand, was used to describe the relationship between a daughter-in-law and her parents-in-law. Ms. Yamamori, thought of by her friends as having demonstrated strong *oyakōkō*, employed that concept as she described her reasons for caring for her father at home until his death.

Dad was the most important thing, caring for him for as long as he lived. I have no regrets. I quit all my clubs and activities outside of work, but I didn't want to do anything else. I knew he would never get better, so I think it was for my own sake so that I wouldn't think back during my life that I should have done more for him. . . . *Oyakōkō* you are happy to do. Willing to do. It's not an obligation. It's a good part of our culture. As my parents aged, I wanted to help them.

Ms. Somiya concurred with this "natural" wish to help her own mother:

From the time I was a little girl, I had always been the one to help my mother. Her eyes were bad from cataracts, and I would have to lead her around by the hand. . . . If the relationship is good, you naturally help them. Before the parent notices, you naturally see what you need to do. That's *oyakōkō*. Something you don't think about.

Mrs. Gonno, who was interviewed with Ms. Somiya, added, "If you do it out of obligation (*gimu*), it's not *oyakōkō*. Not at all." The other two daughters-in-law agreed, speaking of *oyakōkō* only in terms of their own parents.

The daughters-in-law did, however, get a sense of accomplishment from fulfilling their caregiving duties to their in-laws. Mrs. Kawabe remarked, "After caregiving, I could say 'I did it.' If you put them in the hospital, you are only left with a sense of remorse." Mrs. Muraoka referred to this sense of achievement as a "Buddhist outlook":

It was my obligation (*gimu*). Even so, I grew very tired of it. But, looking back, caregiving was not for (mother-in-law's) sake; it was laying the fertilizer for myself, so my life would grow into something splendid. You caregive, then you can spend all your energy on yourself. Caring for the elderly is giving a plus to yourself. It adds to your own good fortune. Of course, when I was caring for her I didn't have these feelings.

Thus, the personal salience of filial piety seems to be a natural, affectionate role of helping one's own parents, and, while the driving force behind Ms. Yamamori and Ms. Somiya's decision to care for their own parents, it was not associated with the duties of the daughters-in-law in caring for their in-laws.

What is associated with caregiving for in-laws is a societal obligation, one that, if filled, is a mark of personal achievement deserving of good fortune in return.

Although filial piety is most often referred to in the context of a caregiving relationship in old age, the concept involves a lifelong relationship between children and their parents. This personal construction and expression of filial piety needs to be understood at the individual level. It should not be over-generalized nor simplified as an inherent societal, or timeless "Confucian" virtue determining individual choice toward parent care in present Japan.

Expectations for Old Age

As these women had intimate knowledge of dependency in old age, I asked them if they, too, wished to be cared for at home by family members in their old age. Takie Lebra has written that older Japanese, when asked this question, tend to reply with unease or embarrassment that they do not want to become a burden (*meiwaku*) (1984:278). Because of the frequency of this answer, Margaret Lock believes that it is probably rhetoric (1993a:73). I, too, received this culturally acceptable answer, but the women's further responses revealed thought-out strategies that cannot be dismissed as rhetoric.

For example, Mrs. Gonno first gave the expected answer. "When I get bad, I of course don't want to be a burden to my children. I'll be at my own home just as long as I'm able to care for myself." She then added, "If I lived with my children, I wouldn't have my freedom. It's bothersome from both points of view." The two single women, knowing they had no children on which to depend, wanted to stay at home as long as possible utilizing public home health services, then enter a nursing home.

Anthropologists Takie Lebra (1984:286), and David Plath (1987:149), among others, have noted that the wish for an abrupt death (*pokkuri*) rather than death from a lengthy chronic illness is strong among older Japanese, pointing to an unwillingness to enter a period of dependency. It also comes out of the experience of watching the slow and painful deterioration of loved ones. Mrs. Muraoka said:

Considering how the elderly feel is important, but it's absurd for people to just expect to be cared for. (They think) she's the daughter-in-law so it's natural that she should take care of her mother-in-law. That's very selfish. My spirit won't let me be dependent. Until the end I want to try to take care of myself to the best of my ability. I am thinking of entering a nursing home, or retirement community rather than home care.

Again, these plans for independence in old age come out of a pragmatic understanding of the changes in norms in Japanese society. Ms. Somiya stated, "The entire Japanese society is suddenly changing. Before, the elderly lived with their eldest son and daughter-in-law. That was expected. Now, people want to be independent." Mrs. Gonno concurred, "No one lives together in the same house like I did.'' Although statistics prove otherwise, her comments show that she senses her former lifestyle as a daughter-in-law, living with and caring for her mother-in-law, is a pattern of the past.

With expectations changing, then, what will be necessary in the future for an elderly parent to receive caregiving from a daughter or daughter-in-law? All women stressed the importance of an established relationship based on inter-generational exchange before caregiving occurs, and the need for more respite services from the government to free up time for the caregiver. The true success of caregiving, however, would depend on the compatibility of the personalities of the caregiver and the elderly parent. In other words, there had to be affection. As for the extended family, the women considered adjacent but separate house-holds to be ideal. Mrs. Kawabe, who lived in such an arrangement for 29 years, said:

"At a distance where the soup won't get cold" (sūpu no samenai kyōri) is about the best. It means you are able to help each other live with food from the same hearth. The space of your lives is different, the way you think, too. Many things differ. If you're in a place where you have close contact, mere trivialities grow out of proportion.

CONCLUSIONS: CHANGE

As previously stated, these five women's experiences occurred primarily be-fore the social welfare programs of the 1989 "Gold Plan" came to fruition. Their ordeals are representative of the system of home care in the past, and their responses are for the most part recognizable and expected by Japanese for women of their particular generation. Foremost on the minds of social welfare policy planners, gerontologists and family caregivers at the time of interview, however, was that the social welfare system, and society as a whole, was in the midst of transformation. The women I interviewed related to me that they felt caught in the middle of this transition. They felt compelled to provide full-time care to their parents and parents-in-law, but knew that they could no longer expect such care from their children. What is this "transition," and how will it impact later life for women in Japan?

A prominent goal of the Ministry of Health and Welfare is to "educate" the public on the need to pay for a national system of support, that is, to educate young Japanese on the concept of state social welfare. But Japan is not likely to become a welfare state. Japanese policymakers have keenly studied Sweden's welfare state model (see Chapter 11). While admiring the high quality of long-term care provided, they know that such total state support is not feasible, as the population is unwilling to pay the high level of taxes required. Further, the cultural emphasis on self-sufficiency of the family is strong in Japan. There is a great desire of many elder and middle-aged Japanese to stay within their communities, where their identities and personal networks are established, rather than move into retirement or nursing homes. Living "at home," however, does not necessarily imply a wish to live with adult children. As Mrs. Gonno pointed out, living with one's grown children is bothersome for both generations involved. Just as many older and middle-aged Japanese are reluctant to move into retirement facilities, they are equally determined not to become burdens to their children or to society, but to live independently in their own residences.

Japan's social welfare model for the future reflects these preferences. The emphasis of the Gold Plan, to provide elderly with access to care services in their own homes, has enabled elderly Japanese to stay independent longer. The proposed national caregiving insurance system, which most likely will begin by the year 2000, will further increase services through a publicly funded insurance scheme. Based on a combination of German and British models, this scheme promises to provide individually tailored care service packages to all elderly Japanese who qualify as disabled. The main obstacles to this optimistic plan at present are the shortage of personnel to perform the services, especially in the case of night care, and the objections of municipal governments who must foot the bill.

Are family responsibilities in Japan thus being replaced by state-orchestrated "community care?" Over the last few decades there has indeed been a steady decline in the percentage of elderly Japanese in extended households, and a subsequent increase in the percentage of single and elderly couple households. This does not necessarily mean, however, that family responsibilities are being replaced. To understand this, we must look beyond the extended family/nuclear family dichotomy, and think instead of the cyclical nature of household structure in Japan. Akiko Hashimoto has criticized the notion that "modernization leads to the disintegration of the extended family" as "a misleading projection, based on a generalization from a Western experience" (1993:26). She contends that the legitimacy of dependency within the Japanese family is still culturally recognized, and that the old model has simply been adapted to changing economic circumstances. Today, young Japanese couples are in fact more likely to form a separate domestic unit at marriage. Their parents also increasingly reside in their own households. However, when the parents reach an advanced age and their health necessitates daily care, the two generations (by now three generations) often form an extended household. This household may be one residence, or, if they can afford it, two separate residences that are adjacent or in close proximity. Since the middle generation is still providing care for the elderly generation, the two residences should be viewed as one household, an extended family. Co-residence is therefore postponed, but support arrangements for advanced old age have not been radically altered (p. 25).

As the elderly stay independent longer, postponing co-residence with adult children, the period and intensity of caregiving will most likely decline, or at least become more sustainable. In Japan, much talk is given to the concept of *ikigai*, translated as "one's meaning in life," or "self-fulfillment." For Japanese women, *ikigai* lies "in conjunction with social structure, . . . interlocked with and programmed by (their) structurally assigned roles" (Lebra 1984:306). A

Japanese woman's primary cultural roles have been first as a mother to her children, and then as a full-time caregiver to aged parents and parents-in-law. *Ikigai* was to come from the "sacrifice, hardship, and endurance" of fulfilling these roles (Lebra 1984:306). But as the social structure has changed, so have acceptable forms of *ikigai*. Today middle-aged women are finding *socially acceptable* self-fulfillment outside the family realm: in their work, organized activities, interpersonal relationships (expanded social roles) or, as in Mrs. Kawabe's case, in the achievement of self-set personal goals such as completing one's education. With this expanded sense of self-fulfillment comes the desire and ability to free themselves from complete devotion to duties of caregiving.

Thus, family structure and women's roles are diversifying, while a strong preference remains for a combination of home-based care and independence among the elderly and their adult children. In this light, Japan's new social welfare policies, which integrate family care with state and private care, do seem the most promising solution. Contrary to modernization theory, family responsibility for care of the elderly in Japan is not being replaced by state institutions, but supplemented and strengthened. From the perspective of quality of life in one's advanced years, this is a positive advancement. From the perspective of women facing caregiving duties, the benefits remain to be seen. Continued increases in availability of services act to postpone caregiving responsibility and help alleviate anxiety of caregivers and elderly alike. Yet, one vital change is still needed: the alleviation of the undue burden of caregiving on women, as a gender, has yet to occur.

Although caregiving is now being recognized as "work," it is seen as "women's work"—work for which women have experience and skills. In Kawasaki, very few men attended the public caregiving symposiums, or had received home helper certification. Those who did participate were looked on as anomalies. Before grown men's attitudes toward "domestic work" can change, expectations of mothers, fathers and siblings in Japanese homes must first change. Men as caregivers, either to their parents or as volunteers, will have to become more culturally acceptable to both women and men. This change in attitude would also have to pervade the corporate setting so men could take leave from work to help with caregiving of the elderly.[10] Only when this ideological, gender-based division of labor breaks down will women gain true respite from their caregiving duties. Until that time, caregiving to the elderly will remain firmly entrenched as the domain of women, and a predominant concern for Japanese women in middle and later life.

NOTES

This chapter is an expanded version of "Home-Based Health Care for the Elderly in Japan: A Silent System of Gender and Duty," in *Aging: Asian Experiences Past and Present*, S. Formanek and S. Linhart, eds. Vienna: Verlag der Osterreichischen Akademie der Wissenschaften, 1997. Both articles are derived from my Master's thesis, "Family

Caregivers to the Elderly in Japan: A System of Gender and Duty,'' University of California, Los Angeles, 1995. I wish to thank the UCLA Center for Japanese Studies, Sasakawa Fund, for funding this research; my respondents for their time and generosity; and Francesca Bray, Mariko Tamanoi, Douglas Hollan, Emily Abel, Sasaki Tsuneo, Tani Sumie, Tamura Shizuko and Jay Sokolovsky for guidance and input.

1. The direct translation is ''a person in ecstasy,'' with ecstasy being a euphemism for senile dementia. The English translation is published under the title *The Twilight Years* (1984).

2. See Palmore and Maeda 1985; Plath 1972, 1987; Kiefer 1990 for discussions of status of the elderly in Japan.

3. The seven ADLs are bathing, dressing, eating, transferring, walking, getting outside and toileting.

4. By the year 2000, the Ministry of Health and Welfare estimates there will be one million *netakiri* elders in Japan.

5. Kawasaki is the ninth largest city in Japan, with a population of 1,153,000. It is essentially part of the same crowded, urban sprawl of Tokyo (to the north and northeast) and Yokohama (to the south). It was through the city of Kawasaki's Public Welfare Bureau, Aged Society Comprehensive Countermeasures Department, that I conducted the majority of my research on current social welfare policy for the elderly.

6. Personal communication with director of Kawasaki's Special Care Home for the Aged (*Tokubetsu Yōgo Rōjin Hōmu*), May 1993.

7. See Plath 1972 regarding *Obasuteyama*; Kelly (1993a:155) for cartoons satirizing the elderly; and Kiefer (1990:187) for derogatory slang for the elderly.

8. Stated in regards to discourse of home health care in the United States as well (Brody 1990:5).

9. Even when a wife cares for her husband, the daughter or daughter-in-law may still be the primary or secondary caregiver.

10. A pilot project of this sort was enacted at a major Japanese corporation in Tokyo five years ago. Men nearing retirement could take a year of paid leave to intern full-time at a local nursing home.

CHAPTER 11

Transforming the "Middle Way": A Political Economy of Aging Policy in Sweden

Bruce M. Zelkovitz

Good government consists of knowing how much future to introduce in the present.

Victor Hugo

INTRODUCTION

The political economy perspective has contributed significantly to the social scientific study of aging. This approach goes beyond conceptualizing aging as an individual phenomenon and as a problem of individuals in society, situating aging in a concrete and dynamic context linking the past, present and future. It is defined as:

the study of the interrelationships between the polity, economy, and society, or more specifically, the reciprocal influences among government . . . the economy, social classes, state, and status groups. The central problem of the political economy perspective is the manner in which the economy and polity interact in a relationship of reciprocal causation affecting the distribution of social goods. (Minkler and Estes 1984:11)

Political economy builds on the anthropological tradition of connecting age-related phenomena such as ageism to industrialization and other macrotrends. Social policy on aging is seen as largely determined by "competing social forces and the visions they carry of the good society" (Myles 1984:4). In this chapter, I apply the political economy perspective to Sweden.[1]

There is a growing body of literature on aging in Sweden, but it remains "scattered" and primarily descriptive, often indicating services provided and comparing them to services in other countries (see Baldock and Evers 1992; Habib, Sundstrom and Windmiller 1993; Johansson 1993; Daatland 1994). I utilize political economy to examine two crucial aspects of the Swedish "aging enterprise"[2]: the official aging ideology[3] promulgated by the national government, and the application of that ideology to residence options for the aged. I explore official aging ideology and its implementation as they reflect broader political and economic currents.

My research suggests, however, that it would be a mistake to view the aging enterprise as only a passive "mirror" of larger trends, for it has sought to reform Swedish life over the past two decades. In this chapter, I examine this unique and most important transformative character of relatively recent Swedish aging policy.[4]

Virtually all studies analyzing aging policy in industrial societies from a political economy perspective assert that it is "reproductive" rather than transformative. From this view, policy reproduces inequities in these societies by segregating the elderly, meeting their survival needs and defusing political resistance. Hence, such industrial societies inevitably generate conservative aging policies. I argue, however, that Swedish aging policy is an exception because: (1) it seeks to transform itself, (2) it attempts to transform the elderly, and (3) it provides an infrastructure to transform Swedish life.

METHODOLOGY

I initially did fieldwork in Sweden during a six-week stay in 1984. Open-ended interviews were conducted with twenty officials in the aging enterprise and with twenty-one elderly Swedes, as well as with the younger family members of five elderly Swedes. Participant observation was carried out in fifteen facilities of different types, including residences and day centers; and for a two-week period in the home of a Swedish family with elderly relatives living in a single apartment, a nursing home and a home with adult children.[5] I visited Stockholm, on the Baltic coast, the cosmopolitan seat of the national government; Boras, near the western port of Gothenburg, known as the "Manchester of Sweden" because of its tradition of textile production; and Linkoping, south of Stockholm, a commercial city dominated by computer production and aviation technology, seen as the center of innovative aging policy in Sweden.

Returning briefly to Sweden in 1989 and 1991, I was able to gather documents and reports on and relevant to aging policy. Recently, I communicated with scholars, consulted colleagues' fieldnotes and reviewed aging literature. Data accrued since 1984 add a time-depth dimension to this study.

SWEDEN: POLITICAL-ECONOMIC BACKGROUND

Sweden is a northern European country about the size of California (173,731 square miles), bordered by Norway, Denmark and Finland. With about 8.7 million citizens, it is the most populous of the five Nordic nations. Among the

Scandinavian countries, it also has the largest percentage (18 percent) of its citizens over age 65, and leads the world in this statistic. The majority of its population is urban and is concentrated in the south. Ethnically, as of 1994, the nation was 91 percent Swedish, with a small Finnish minority (3 percent). The remainder of the population is comprised of Sami (Lapps) and immigrants of diverse ethnicities. Some 94 percent of the population at least nominally belongs to the state Lutheran Church, with a minority participating in evangelical sects and other religions. The government is a constitutional monarchy, with King Carl XVI Gustav its titular head. Political parties spanning the political spectrum compete through direct election for seats in the single-chamber Swedish parliament (Riksdag), with national political leadership vested in the prime minister.

A complete sketch of Sweden's historical development lies beyond the scope of this chapter.[6] What is significant for our purposes is that industrialization developed late in Sweden compared to the rest of Europe. After 1870, social reformers and a rapidly organizing working class joined forces to deal with the problems of the new industrial order. This alliance culminated in the 1889 founding of the Social Democratic Party, which was very radical (left of liberal) by current American political standards and has remained the dominant political party in Sweden. During the worldwide Depression of the 1930s, Social Democratic Leaders helped to enact various economic measures, such as government-subsidized employment for the jobless. This set the tone for the subsequent expansion of the welfare state. In 1938, "The Pact of Saltsjobaden," a historic agreement between workers and industrial owners, sketched the parameters of Sweden's "Middle Way" between an economic and political order dominated by owners and one with significant government and worker control (Childs 1980). Swedish workers promised a minimum of strikes and strike threats in return for expanding taxation to finance a wide range of social welfare programs.

Sweden's economy is 90 percent privately owned. Income has largely been equalized, but wealth has not. It is within this context that the Social Democrats have retreated in recent decades from their earlier focus on worker ownership of technology, concentrating instead on workplace democracy, wage solidarity and codetermination of technological change, leading one sociologist to characterize them as "reformist socialists" (Sandberg et al. 1992; Korpi 1978:55).

Tangible gains for workers under the Social Democrats have been made in medical care, family and child care support, old age pensions and living facilities. Sweden has cushioned the worst effects of global economic fluctuations by developing a "societal corporatist welfare state" demarcated by "social bargaining" among employers, workers and government bureaucracy (Ruggie 1984:16). It has consistently ranked high among industrial societies in terms of quality of life,[7] with virtually no homeless people or slums (Hadenius and Lindgren 1992). Health care is universal, inexpensive and of high quality. As noted in Table 8.1, this is reflected in Sweden's very high levels of life expectancy, second only to Japan, and the low figures for infant mortality.

Table 11.1
Selected "Quality of Life" Indices

	Sweden	United States	Japan
Population	8,778,000	260,714,000	125,107,000
Per Capita – Gross Domestic Product	$16,900	$23,400	$19,800
Life Expectancy at Birth in Years			
Males	75	72 (1992)	76
Females	81	79 (1992)	82
Infant Mortality (per 1,000 live births)	6	10 (1992)	4
Hospital Beds (per person)	1/175	1/211	1/74
Physicians (per person)	1/395	1/406	1/588

All figures are 1994 estimates, except as noted in parentheses.
Source: The World Almanac, 1995.

Yet, Sweden is not without problems. Alcoholism and related crime and domestic violence exist along with ageism and other forms of discrimination, despite extensive efforts by the government to alleviate them (see Hyden 1994; Lenke 1990; Stahl 1991; Westin 1992). A growing resentment among youth toward their obligations to the social welfare system and a corresponding yen to "make a killing" on the stock market, combined with declining production and inflation, threaten the possibility of a "system shift" (Mahon and Meidner 1994:58). Support for such a shift grew in the 1980s, and in 1991 a conservative coalition ascended to governmental power, seeking to erode worker and governmental power and to give fuller rein to the market. This system shift, however, did not materialize as the Social Democrats regained power in 1994.

In the face of these pressures, a rhetoric of lowered expectations crept into government ideology amidst persistent talk of privatizing services provided in the past by government. At the same time, the Social Democrats today have retained a commitment to social transformation embodying democratization and integration. Democratization refers to promoting greater personal and political control in decision making. Integration refers to bringing groups in society together, physically and in terms of status (prestige).[8] Swedish policymakers see these transformative components as reducing social inequities such as ageism and racism, hence contributing to their vision of the good society.[9]

OFFICIAL IDEOLOGY OF THE AGING ENTERPRISE

The official ideology directed toward the elderly is based on five "guiding principles" expressed in the Social Services Act of 1982. While articulated by the state through Parliament and the Ministry of Health and Social Affairs, the guiding principles have been implemented nationally by the National Board of Health and Welfare and on the local level through two bodies: municipalities and county councils. Municipalities handled social welfare needs while county councils ministered to medical care. In 1992, a reform measure integrated these public spheres under the jurisdiction of municipalities to streamline their implementation (Swedish Institute 1994). The guiding principles are:

1. Normalization, which means that to the greatest possible extent each individual should be given the opportunity to live and function in as normal a setting and under as normal conditions as feasible.

2. Viewing a Person as a Whole, which means that the overall psychological, physical, and social welfare needs of a person are assessed and dealt with in a single context.

3. Self-Determination, which means that personal integrity is respected. People should have the right to determine their own lives and make their own decisions.

4. Influence and Participation, meaning that individuals should be able to influence not only their own environment but also society as a whole.

5. Properly Managed Activation, which implies meaningful tasks carried out in close partnership with other people in a normal stimulating environment. (National Commission on Aging 1982:17)

These principles exercise influence today, having become "process goals" (Olsson Hort 1995) officially incorporated into aging social policy. They are explicitly transformative, supporting increased democratization and integration.

In 1984, national and local officials described an aging social policy that, prior to the 1980s, was reproductive rather than transformative. It was dominated by inadequate care for those remaining in their homes and excessive care in intermediate care facilities and nursing homes, making the elderly uninterested, immobile and passive. Even with the addition of new forms of residence options and assistance for those old persons who wished to remain in their houses or apartments, too much was done for them. A decade ago, an official of the National Board of Health and Welfare said that, "We need to train staff of all kinds to see the elderly as human beings and to keep away from doing everything for them." Such sentiments were echoed by a geriatric physician in a Boras hospital who told me, "We want to treat the whole person, to take a more humanistic approach."

Emphasis upon a normal setting helps to account for the reorientation of official ideology away from closed-care and toward open-care, away from closed institutions such as intermediate care facilities, nursing homes and geriatric wards and toward options that encourage and enable the aged to remain in their own homes or in settings as autonomous, and "as homelike," as possible (see Amann 1980; Little 1982). In 1984, a local official in Boras stated, "If we can mix the young and the old, it will be like going back to older generations where people lived together in close communities." He continued, "We want to build all kinds of apartments, for the young, the old, and the disabled, so that they and others can live together," as well as remodelling existing facilities for the same purpose. He emphasized that elderly and disabled persons from all social class backgrounds should have equal access to available residences. With pride he noted that even though "palatial" residence options were available in the private sector for the wealthier elderly, they too were desirous of aging enterprise housing.

In 1984, a Linkoping social worker stressed the importance of spontaneous initiative. In her view, social policy had become synonymous with government coercively "knowing what was best for people." Being sensitive to this, the aging enterprise sought to provide varied enticing contexts. To foster democratization and integration, day centers, libraries which house aging enterprise functions and apartments connected to day centers and nurseries were built to encourage the young and the old to make contact with one another and potentially bond (Jonsson Gardens Document 1983:11).

The guiding principles emerged in social context. The principle of properly managed activation illustrates government taking responsibility for the needs of Swedes. The elderly were not left to fend for themselves, but were given premises, staff and emerging networks to promote activity. Normalization and wholeness of person were shaped by a social bargaining among economic classes, that resulted in an emphasis on dignity and quality of life for all by reducing differences between age and lifestyle groups. Self-determination, influence and participation were an extension of a historical process through which workers have had a powerful impact on democratizing and integrating the workplace.

RESIDENCE OPTIONS: THE OFFICIAL IDEOLOGY OF THE AGING ENTERPRISE IN PRACTICE

As of 1994, most elderly Swedes (92 percent) lived in a rented apartment or a one-family house, compared to 90 percent in 1984 (Swedish Institute 1986, 1994). Other dwelling options, progressively embodying democratization and integration, include: (1) a room in a geriatric ward in a hospital; (2) a room in a nursing home; (3) a room in an intermediate care facility; (4) a room in a group dwelling for those who are disabled; (5) an apartment in a service house; and, (6) an apartment, including service apartments, in a clustered complex.

For the aged now living in their own apartments or houses, in-home technology and structural adaptations are provided by the government, either free or through substantial subsidies. To minimize isolation and reduce autonomy, day centers, home help services, transportation services and home nursing are all available (Swedish Institute 1994).

Day centers, either free-standing or attached to intermediate care facilities, service houses, or nurseries engage the elderly in leisure pursuits. In 1984, I observed dual game rooms at a center linked to a Stockholm service house. One room was used for the fast-paced playing of cards or other games, while in the other, the playing pace was slower. Reading was popular, and, at a day center connected to a service house in Linkoping, readers were available. Weaving, a traditional Swedish handcraft, was another popular activity, with many looms present in all the day centers I visited.

Day centers are also a locus for meals, entertainment, political discussions, meetings and medical services such as pedicures and treatment by district nurses. In a significant recent change, municipalities yielded control of day centers to the elderly (Swedish Institute 1994).

Since 1984, home help services have become crucial in enabling the elderly to remain at home. These formal, or government-provided services have reduced the need for institutional care, engendering increased independence. This has been facilitated by the following services: shopping, cooking, cleaning and personal hygiene and health care. Such services, although expanded in the past decade, have been rechanneled recently to concentrate on the very oldest (Swedish Institute 1994). Home help provision reflects the expectations of Swedish elderly. As is the case in Denmark, they prefer that the government meet their care needs rather than becoming burdens to family members (Boise 1991; Baldock and Evers 1992; Chapter 16 this volume).

As Swedish women have expanded their participation in paid labor, the pool of service sector providers has diminished. The aging enterprise has responded by making workers who also give informal home care to relatives or close friends eligible for paid leaves of up to 60 days per year, per person. Also, those informal caregivers not in the labor force can qualify as paid employees of municipalities while administering such care (Baldock and Evers 1992; Swedish Institute 1994). Baldock and Evers, comparing informal caregiving in Sweden and the United Kingdom, found that such caregivers are paid more in Sweden than their counterparts under a similar reform in the United Kingdom (1992).

By remaining out of institutions, the elderly can interact with different types of people. Such interaction, as I illustrate below with my 1984 fieldwork, can diminish ageism and various types of discrimination. But intergenerational and other intergroup interactive possibilities were not promoted prior to the 1980s in intermediate care facilities, nursing homes and geriatric wards, and are promoted today only to a very limited extent in these contexts.

In 1993, those aged 65 and over residing in institutions in Scandinavia averaged between 5 and 7 percent (Daatland 1994:187). Over the last fifteen years or so, Sweden has experienced a significant reduction in the institutionalization of the elderly. In intermediate care facilities,[10] for example, the number of beds provided was reduced from 56,417 in 1982 to 37,534 in 1990 (Fernow 1992: 2). By 1994, the number had diminished to 34,500, about 2 percent of the elderly population (Swedish Institute 1994:2). As of 1994, nursing homes, which are skilled care facilities,[11] had places for around 31,000 persons, also about 2 percent of the Swedish elderly, as compared to approximately 36,500 places in 1981 (Conference of European Ministers Responsible for Family Affairs 1983: 15). Geriatric hospital wards are an option for the very debilitated elderly. A recent small-scale alternative environment, called group dwellings, offers full support staff while emphasizing integration and democratization. This is collective housing for six to eight disabled persons who, for example, may be afflicted by some form of dementia. Providing for some 7,000 occupancies as of 1993, the elderly have their own rooms here and share communal facilities (Malmberg and Zarit 1993; Swedish Institute 1994).

In 1991, there were about 41,000 elderly in service houses, most of which were erected in the 1970s and 1980s (Swedish Institute 1994). Service houses, or sheltered housing, constitute assisted living promoting independence and self-determination for those who can no longer live at home. Their apartments are equipped with alarms and convenience technology, and they are smaller than nursing and retirement homes.

Service apartments have also been made available in a variety of other contexts. In Linkoping, several apartment buildings combined flats of this kind with ones occupied by people and families of various ages, a common dining hall, and a day nursery. Day nurseries were placed in service houses and apartment buildings with elderly living in them so that they could potentially play a part in child care, an outcome that I witnessed in 1984.

At that time, some aging enterprise officials saw clustered complexes as the "wave of the future," the most developed embodiment of the official ideology's transformative thrust. Here, young and old, disabled and able, and ethnic and social class mixes were encouraged to live independently, yet communally. This was seen as not only constituting a microcosm of a more equal society, but also as providing a structural arrangement that could change negative attitudes faster than any other living option. Daily life, then, supported by a high level of economic growth, was to prefigure an increasingly integrated and democratized society. I shall illustrate this with examples from Vasa Hills near Stockholm and Jonsson Gardens in Linkoping, which continued to exist in 1995.

Built in the mid-1970s, Vasa Hills is a community center with integrated social welfare facilities including apartments for the elderly (Vasa Hills Document 1976). Its three service houses have 172 apartments with one, two or three rooms and a kitchenette. They are connected to a cultural area (with restaurant, music rooms, photo laboratory and a ceramics workshop), a library, a nursery, a primary and a secondary school, a senior high school, a sports center with gymnasium, ice rink, ice hockey rink (in the summer converted to tennis courts), a sauna, a cafeteria, a conference room and a hospital.

Jonsson Gardens, built during the late 1970s and early 1980s, has six conventional five-story apartment houses with 108 apartments and collective housing with 184 apartments in buildings with between three and seven apartments (Jonsson Gardens Document 1983). Collective housing has eleven different kinds of apartments from one room and a pantry to five rooms and a kitchen (Jonsson Gardens Document 1983). Thirty-five of those apartments are service apartments for pensioners, while nine are for the mentally or physically disabled. Common premises are on the ground floor, with a restaurant, study/meeting rooms, a library, coffee room, gymnasium, workshops and entertainment facilities. Day nurseries are included. Collective housing attempts to integrate young families, the elderly and the disabled in a socioeconomic mix.

As I have pointed out, the guiding principles were set out to transform aging policy itself. A major development in the last decade has been the expansion of the support network enabling elderly Swedes to remain at home, bolstering the democratization and integration of open-care. In such contexts, the day centers have continued to be a force against isolation and passivity. The extension of home help services and technological support have increasingly avoided the shunting of the elderly to more institutionalized settings. However, along with such positive developments, the aging enterprise has experienced a major setback: a cutback in the construction of clustered complexes due to economic constraints. This undercuts the more far-reaching and immediate aspects of transformative aging policy.

In 1984, aging enterprise officals also spoke of remodelling, reshaping and restructuring closed-care. At a geriatric ward in a Boras hospital, democratization and integration were at work. Two advanced Alzheimer's patients were bedridden in a large room, spotless, well and naturally lit, traditionally furnished and well supplied with greenery. A geriatric physician apologized for crowding two patients into the room. He emphasized that while these patients were virtually comatose, they still deserved the same normal, private surroundings that others would choose. Recently, small-scale group dwellings have been designed to support transformation in the closed context, part of the recognition that closed-care in its modified and even traditional form still has a place in Sweden. Sweden, like Denmark, while emphasizing informal care, continues to spend on closed-care (see Chapter 16 this volume). But, Sweden spends more (Daatland 1994).

Privatization is a force confronting both open- and closed-care. An integral component of system shift, it emphasizes meeting the needs of the elderly through market solutions. While privatization has been introduced into political debate with such policy suggestions as voucher systems, which would enable group home occupants to select private home help providers, it remains less popular among Swedes than formal care through the aging enterprise (Baldock and Evers 1992; Fernow 1992).

The transformation of the elderly has also had uneven results. In 1984, I observed some elderly individuals participating in what would be considered transformative activity under the official ideology of the aging enterprise. Peter G., a Jonsson Gardens resident, was politically active through the residence administrative council and intergenerational activities that were part of his apartment building. He felt that he was a force in decision making and that he had made younger residents feel more respectful of the elderly. Perhaps activity like this had an impact on increasing the power of the elderly in day centers in the 1990s. And Jock D., a pensioner confined to a wheelchair, received daily support from other residents to work for the rights of the disabled along with his wife Anna. Along with Peter G., he may have contributed to youth maturing over the last decade supporting the Middle Way by aiding the Social Democrats in their return to power. At the same time, however, Britt O., an official at Vasa Hills, indicated to me that even with these encouraging developments, too many of the elderly remained passive. She felt that it would take time and a continued supportive context to get more of them to play a part in their own transformation.

Other residence officials in 1984 also expressed disappointment over a lack of widespread elderly activity. At a service house outside of Boras that I visited then, each hallway and end-of-the-hall alcove was traditionally furnished and decorated to stimulate interaction. Yet, as officials told me and as I observed then, these areas often remained deserted. Many people preferred to stay in their rooms or, if they were weaving or playing cards, they stayed away from inter-group involvement. A staff member and a resident at Vasa Hills and Jonsson Gardens told me that integrated activity was not all that it had been played up to be. Many of the elderly did not like to be in the presence of the young or saw them as a "nuisance," undercutting the democratic and integrative thrusts.

On the other hand, since the mid-1980s, democratization has been furthered by giving the elderly more power in caregiving and in running day centers. Beyond choosing to remain at home, the elderly have been vaulted into poli-cymaking. This outcome could lead them to become involved in community political dialogue beyond the boundaries of day centers. Such a development could give the elderly a vantage point for heightened visibility among other age and status groups. Swedish sociologist Sven Olsson Hort has referred to these day centers as "low budget integration and democratization" (1995).

The impact of official ideology on societal transformation through residence options has also been mixed. On the one hand, an example from my 1984 research illustrates what was foreseen as a positive outcome of clustered com-plexes. Lena S. and her husband Lars, young professionals living with their two children in Jonsson Gardens, described the development of their son Leif. They told me that Leif was aloof from older and disabled residents, who along with younger and healthy residents, lived in their building. But, through collective meals and rotating responsibility for building activities, he had come to view them more positively when encountering them outside of Jonsson Gardens, for example, in parks and on trains. They felt that their living arrangement had heightened the respect for the elderly and the disabled, that Jonsson Gardens had struck a blow against discrimination. Also, they thought that more experi-ences such as theirs would continue develop a microcosm of the good society.

On the other hand, obstacles to the success of this process have emerged. Advocates of clustered complexes pointed out ten years ago that they had to provide much of the impetus for integrative interaction. According to them, many elderly persons did not want intergenerational, intergroup activity, even if it could undergird a more equal society. And, since clustered complexes were envisioned to hasten democratization and integration, a slowdown in their construction has indeed hampered transformative aging policy.

THE POLITICAL ECONOMY OF SWEDISH AGING POLICY: 1995

Swedish aging policy has not existed in a vacuum. It has not only unfolded within Swedish culture, but also, the continuities and changes marking it in the past decade can be seen as responses to national and international events and forces outside of the aging enterprise.

Just as Sweden's political-economic structure has been characterized as a Middle Way, other aspects of Swedish culture steer a "middle" course which may seem contradictory to outsiders. Swedes have been Christianized since the twelfth century and the vast majority belong to the Lutheran Church; yet, in their summer and winter solstice celebrations, they enthusiastically reenact portions of their pre-Christian past. Swedes are descended from legendary Viking warriors, yet have not participated in war since 1814. They have had a central law code since 1350, but their provinces cling proudly to their distinctive folk dress, insignia, music and crafts. They are on the cutting edge of new technologies, while at the same time never waxing more eloquent than when describing a trip to the forest to pick mushrooms or to discover that ultimate delicacy, *smultron* (wild strawberries). Swedes are sometimes characterized by American critics as dependent on government. However, they are not content to be passive observers, being active in the social networks that surround them (some 33 percent of Swedes belong to a sports organization, for example). Their sense of privacy, also highly valued in Denmark (see Chapter 16), and what a Brazilian observer described to me as their "discretion" sometimes strike the American observer as coldness, but, in their unwillingness to tolerate privation in their midst, they have what may well be the most highly developed sense of community responsibility in the industrialized world. Perhaps it is this cultural "balancing act" which leads the Swedes to regard being *lagom* (measured) and *melan-massigt* (middle-of-the-road) as character traits to be prized.

Among the international developments that have influenced recent aging policy have been changes in the nature of international socialism. The political upheavals that began with the Polish Solidarity Movement and culminated in sweeping systemic change in the former Soviet Union and its eastern satellites in the years 1989–1991 inspired worldwide debate about the viability of socialism. To the extent that Swedish social policy since the 1930s has been predicated on the existence of an organized, self-conscious working class taking at least some of its inspiration from the existence of an international socialist movement, these events called forth some comparatively strong responses in Sweden.

At the far left of the political spectrum, the communists abandoned their name and platform and became the Left Party. On the political right, the New Democratic Party endorsed greater play for market forces on the grounds that government intervention in economic affairs had been discredited. Although the implications for the aging enterprise were not always explicitly spelled out in party platforms, they suggested that future changes could include greater reliance on entrepreneurial provision of services, a switch from universal to paid access and the use of charity and volunteerism rather than tax monies to subsidize services.

Swedish social policy, including its aging enterprise, has assumed an expanding economic base permitting comparatively high tax rates and a balance of power between owners and workers. Whether benefits of such can be sustained and/or remain universal entitlements in the face of these recent political-economic trends has become a subject of considerable debate in Sweden, as elsewhere in Europe. That moves toward more "free" market policies did not immediately produce "a tide to lift all boats" may help explain why the 1991 conservative victory was short-lived and only brought about the fine-tuning of aging policy. One result of this was the 1992 reform, decentralizing control over the implementation of the guiding principles, rather than creating sweeping changes of the system. As Turner puts it, "(The Swedish people) have chosen the Social Democratic Party as the 'captain' that is best able to steer the Swedish ship of state through uncharted waters that lie ahead" (S. Turner 1994:3). Thus, such discernible and important changes in aging policy as the slowdown in the construction of clustered complexes can be seen as attributable not to a revision of ideology, but to Sweden, like other First World economies, entering a new era of limits.

Comparing Sweden and the United States today results in the appearance of intriguing similarities and differences. Both nations experienced brief ideological flurries in response to the collapse of state socialism in the Eastern bloc. In the United States, excitement over a "peace dividend" and how it should be allocated evaporated even more quickly than did Swedish enthusiasm for the New Democratic Party; today there are calls for increased military spending from various quarters. Both nations have been buffeted by changes in the world system, leading to unemployment, loss of markets and a decline in workers' leverage. In both nations, tensions generated by such changes and desire to protect hard-won entitlements have, for some, been channelled into crusades against immigrants, perceived as siphoning off resources that rightly belong only to citizens (Westin 1992). And, in both nations, politicians have pinned hopes for future economic growth on "free-trade" agreements with nearby nations (NAFTA in the United States, the European Union in Sweden), though public opinion polls show that the general populations of both nations remain divided as to the wisdom of that course.[12]

Yet, there are striking differences. Universal access to the services of the aging enterprise remains a given in Sweden, as it is in Denmark (see Chapter 16 this volume), while in the United States, means-testing for such previously sacrosanct entitlements as Social Security are being proposed by some politicians, and cuts in programs like Medicare are viewed by others as necessary to meet the requirements of a balanced budget amendment. In the wake of the Republican congressional sweep of November 1994, the rhetoric of the free market economy and an end to government intervention as the solution for unemployment, stagnation, and, indeed, most social ills from illegitimacy to crime, are enjoying a revival in the United States that has no real parallel in Swedish political discourse, except perhaps at the most extreme conservative fringes.

In contrast, the 1994 victory of the Social Democrats reinforces the importance of such political-economic factors as a pact uniting social classes and the role of government as the primary provider of social services. The pact may not be unfolding smoothly (Mahon and Meidner 1994:65). But, as Sweden faces a major demographic-aging burden, one significant continuity seems to be that all social classes, including both owners and workers, desire to retain as much of the Middle Way as possible, including the aging policies that appeared so fresh and promising to this foreign visitor in 1984. It appears that Swedes will continue to make their own aging policy, but not under conditions entirely of their own making (see Marx 1963).

NOTES

I extend my appreciation to those persons whom I interviewed and to those who made my observations at various facilities possible. In keeping with anthropological tradition, I use pseudonyms for informants and facilities.

I am grateful to the Swedish Institute, especially Catharina Mannheimer, for most willingly and efficiently facilitating my research, to the Swedish Information Service for its invaluable assistance, and to family members in Boras who labored hard to make my research productive.

My thanks go out to Dr. Sven E. Olsson Hort of Stockholm University for his gracious and informative contributions, Dr. Ken Wagner and Stephen Turner of the Swedish Program at Stockholm University for their pivotal support, Dr. Jay Sokolovsky for his considerable patience and extremely helpful comments and suggestions and especially to Dr. Karen L. Field, without whose inspiration, knowledge and significant input this chapter could not have been completed.

1. Marshalling evidence linking aging social policy to industrialization, the political economy perspective has been applied to the United States and to Western European nations such as the United Kingdom, France, Germany and Italy (see Estes 1979; Guillemard 1983; Minkler and Estes 1984). Scandinavia, however, has remained a curious lacuna in such analysis. For reasons beyond our scope, policies in Denmark, Norway, and Sweden have rarely been subjected to systematic political-economic scrutiny in the English-speaking world. A notable exception is the work of Sven E. Olsson Hort (1993).

2. The term ''aging enterprise'' refers to ''the congeries of programs, organizations, bureaucracies, interest groups, trade associations, providers, industries, and professionals that serve the aged in one capacity or another'' (Estes 1979:2). As used here, the term should be understood as referring in particular to the governmental programs and bu-

reaucracies (both national and local) which serve the aged, since these play such a pivotal role in the Swedish context.

3. The term "ideology" here refers to J. Bailey's definition: "an organized set of convictions . . . that enforces inevitable value judgments," and (that) "hold major implications for power relations, for in enforcing certain definitions of the situation, they have the power to compel certain types of action while limiting others" (Estes 1979:4).

4. I use the term "transformative" in this context to refer to that which is conducive to liberatory social change, that which tends to empower the individual and to allow the development of each citizen's potential independent of limitations linked to class, physical disability, ethnicity, sex or age. The meaning is thus similar to "emancipatory," as used by many radical social scientists. I prefer the term "transformative" because, while still implying some value judgments about quality of life, it is less closely aligned with a political doctrine and seems to me to connote a more "open" future—one in which there may be no single, static state of "emancipation," but rather a continuous struggle for greater human freedom. Central to my use of the term are two analytically separable aspects of liberatory social change: democratization and integration, which I define more fully in the section "Sweden: Political-Economic Background."

5. The formal interview sample was generated for me by Mrs. Catharina Mannheimer of the Swedish Institute. Members of the informal interview sample included friends and associates of the initial group contacted in "snowball" fashion, as well as contacts made during residence in Sweden. The family chosen for participant observation is related to the researcher's wife.

6. Useful historical materials on Sweden include Heckscher (1954), Andersson and Weibull (1973), Koblik (1975), Childs (1980), and Lofgren (1980).

7. In a study conducted almost a decade ago comparing the quality of life in Sweden, the United States, Japan and West Germany, Sweden ranked first (Topeka Capital-Journal 1986). Recent data, which combine West Germany and the former East Germany, find Sweden remaining in a very favorable position.

8. Kurt Samuelsson concurs that "integration" has long been a philosophical keystone of social welfare ideology in Sweden, and that the Social Democrats have conceptualized it as being gradually accomplished "through 'social transformation'; in the long run, integration would be fully realized in a society different from the one in which the work was begun" (1975:342).

9. For one scholar's attempt to sketch more definitively the minimal characteristics of a "good society," with particular reference to the Swedish experience, see Schnitzer (1970:Ch. 9).

10. Intermediate care facilities, or *alderdomshem*, have been referred to in Sweden as old-age homes. The term "old-age home" has largely fallen out of usage internationally. Such facilities, whose construction began to decline in the 1970s and almost came to a halt in the 1980s in Sweden, house residents whose needs cannot be adequately met by home help services. They occupy single rooms, eat communally, and have access to 24-hour nursing care (Barrow 1992:194; Hooyman and Kiyak 1993:320; Swedish Institute 1994:2).

11. Skilled care facilities are for those elderly who are more severely ill than residents in intermediate care facilities. They require more intensive 24-hour nursing care and have access to regularized medical and social services (Barrow 1992:194; Hooyman and Kayak 1993:320; Swedish Institute 1994:2).

12. A referendum on membership in the European Union took place in Sweden on January 1, 1995. The popular vote was 52 percent for, 47 percent against (Turner 1994).

PART IV

The Ethnic Dimension in Aging: Culture, Context and Creativity

Few topics better reflect this book's prevailing theme of culture and context than the issue of the ethnic aged. Ethnicity is the manifestation of a cultural tradition in a heterogeneous societal framework. The expression of ethnic identity and the performance of ethnically rooted behaviors invariably take place under new conditions and in different locales from where the traditions originated. Ethnicity is therefore typically a creative act, meshing ancestral "native" patterns with restraints imposed by the broader society and the demands of the local environment. Anthropologists working in urban sub-Saharan Africa in the 1950s and 1960s found that some of the "tribal" groups they were studying in industrial cities were actually new cultural phenomena forged in the crucible of places dramatically different from their rural homelands. Similarly, Barbara Myerhoff in her brilliant book, *Number Our Days* (1978a), described how a very old Jewish population, disconnected from their kin and the surrounding ethnic community, established an unusual local variant of *Yiddishkeit* (Jewishness) centered around unique interpretations of Jewish ritual and personal performance. Surrounded by the youth culture of Venice Beach, California, these men and women in their eighties and nineties sought refuge in a senior center and created within its walls their own sense of meaning in late life (see Thomas, Sokolovsky and Feinberg 1996 for comparison).

MCDONALDIZED AMERICANS OR A PLURALISTIC NATION?

Despite a prevailing notion of the United States as a melting pot, effectively homogenizing immigrant cultures into an invariant, "McDonaldized" social soup, cultural plurality remains a powerful element of national life (Markides, Liang and Jackson 1990; Stanford and Torres-Gil 1994). In the field of aging this has been recognized by an explosion of new research, the establishment of national centers to study the issue and the invention of terms such as "ethno-gerontology" and "ethnogeriatrics" to designate those with a specialized focus on ethnicity and age (American Geriatrics Society 1996).[1] This surge in interest stems not only from the recent ethnic revival among groups long settled into America, but by a new immigrant wave sparked by the 1965 immigration act which ended over 40 years of restricted and ethnically skewed migration. For example, during the 1980s alone, "some 800,000 Southeast Asians, 100,000 Soviet Jews, and 125,000 Cubans have been granted safe haven in this country" (Gozdziak 1988:1). This new stream of migration has brought more than 16 million immigrants to our shores in the last 30 years and in 1991 registered the highest single year of legal immigration ever recorded—over 1.8 million.

By 2020 groups classified as ethnic minorities—African Americans, Native Americans, Asian/Pacific Island Americans and Hispanic Americans—are pro-jected to represent one-fifth of all older Americans, a significant shift from the current 5 percent. This is already the demographic situation in California, where "elders of color" are expected to comprise 41 percent of all seniors in less than three decades (U.S. Senate Special Committee on Aging 1988; U.S. Census of Population and Housing 1990).[2]

Such changes, during a period when the United States has developed the biggest gap between rich and poor in the industrialized world, have stirred up old fears about being inundated by people of color. The racist alarm sounded in books such as *Alien Nation* (Brinslow 1995) or the 1994 passage of the anti-immigrant "proposition 187" in California, strengthen the need to engage the issue of cultural diversity as it affects persons throughout the life cycle.[3]

ETHNIC CULTURE AND AGING

It must be noted that only a few groups in our society have maintained so-ciocultural systems that are not only highly variant from the American cultural norms but also stress factors that foster high status for the aged (Johnson 1995). Among the most distinct are the Amish, Hasidic Jews and certain Native Amer-ican groups such as the Navaho and Zuni. The long-term positive maintenance of their ethnic divergence has been possible so far as they have remained eco-nomically independent of outside groups.

One of the clearest indications of sociocultural distinctiveness comes from the studies of old-order Amish who have largely rejected the "worldly" nature of our industrial society (Hostetler and Huntington 1971; Brubaker and Michael 1987). In their tightly-knit agrarian communities, old age is defined functionally, with a retirement process which is voluntary and gradual. Movement into the "grandfather house" adjacent to younger married children provides a transition into a valued, active and responsibility-laden role-set, bolstered by an ideology in which "old-fashioned ways" are revered and a knowledge of these customs is perpetuated by the older people. Moreover, prestige resides with age because elders retain not only adequate economic resources (such as their own buggies to drive) but also purposeful religious roles, which end essentially with death. Tying these factors together is a strong value emphasizing the welfare of others, which overshadows self-absorption and preoccupation with personal needs and comforts. In these respects the distinct culture of the old-order Amish provides a near-idyllic, supportive milieu for the aged that incorporates the key factors associated cross-culturally with beneficial conditions for the elderly (Tripp-Reimer et al. 1988).

The Amish stand as a strong contradiction to the rule. Most other immigrant groups have not been able to maintain such a close integration of ideology, social organization and economic tradition. Accordingly, the expression of ethnicity varies tremendously from encompassing communities which can satisfy most material and spiritual needs, to having a repertoire of subjective identity markers (food, clothes, music) or merely perceiving a vague sense of belonging to an historically felt past. In addition to the articles on America's ethnic aged which are grouped here, this book includes a discussion of Native Americans (Chapter 6) and Hispanics (Chapter 22).

It is important to note, as Gwen Yeo and her colleagues point out, that whatever ethnic group we talk about, significant subcultural variation will be found within the categories typically used (Yeo et al. 1994).[4] For example, within the rapidly growing ethnic designation "Asian/Pacific Islanders" are included Japanese elders, three-fourths of whom were born in this country, as well as primarily foreign-born seniors in the Vietnamese and Cambodian communities. Among the large Chinese elderly populations centered on the East and West coasts of North America, at least three different major "Chinese" dialects are spoken by elders born in either mainland China, Hong Kong or Taiwan. The importance of recognizing such distinctions is illustrated by ongoing work in Boston among Chinese-Americans to develop the kinds of dementia support groups discussed in Chapter 22. Initial attempts to use a Mandarin Chinese speaker to reach the varied ethnic community led some to resist recruitment efforts from those who spoke other variants of the Chinese language (Mabel Lam, personal communication).

CONTEXT AND THE REALITIES OF ETHNIC COMPENSATION

A major theme in researching the cultural diversity of America's aged has been the examination of ethnicity as a positive resource for older people— a form of compensation for the problems associated with aging (Cool 1987). In our own societal context a positive dimension of ethnic attachments can promote a nondenigrating component of identity to balance out the potentially negative impact of retirement or the "empty nest syndrome." In a more general sense it has been suggested that ethnicity carries with it:

special resources or ethnically-inflected strategies that may be mobilized to maximize personal well-being . . . in the development of long-term "careers" for successful elders, and in the management of the inevitable . . . crises that individuals must confront toward the end of the life cycle. (Weibel-Orlando 1987:102)

We have already seen in Weibel-Orlando's study of Sioux Native American elders how the reemergence of their ancestral identity in old age served as a source of a key family role for them as cultural conservators. Especially with the recent focus on informal systems of support in enhancing social services, there has been a general assumption that the traditional ethnic family and community could serve as a model for solving virtually all the problems of the aged (Ikels 1986; Gibson 1991; Morycz 1992).[5] It should be noted that, in the case of single, urban-dwelling Native American elders, 50 percent of whom co-reside with their families, the low incomes of these households contributed to social problems that necessitate the custodial form of grandparenting discussed by Weibel-Orlando (Kramer 1991; Kramer and Barker 1996).

In Chapter 12, Jay Sokolovsky looks at the available data to try to assess the limits of ethnic beliefs and support as a compensator for aging in our urban industrial society. A central point of his argument is to debunk a false policy dichotomy that pits family caring against state support of the aged (Tracy 1993). He shows that even among Asian groups, known for their filial devotion, certain immigration contexts can result in a low perceived quality of life by the elderly. Sokolovsky, in line with Henderson's later discussion (Chapter 22) of the ethnic family's approach to Alzheimer's disease, also finds that when dealing with difficult mental health problems, the traditional ethnic response can sometimes actually exacerbate the situation. Among the more important points made in this chapter are that: (1) the female perspective on family support of the aged can be dramatically different from that of males; (2) elderly with social networks linking them to both kin and the broader community have better mental health profiles than those encapsulated totally in the ethnic family; (3) formal supports can be effectively used to strengthen the ability of the family to care for its elderly members. He argues that these ideas should be used as policy touchstones to counter ongoing efforts to dismantle the system of nonfamilial supports built up over the last half century.[6] Important comparative confirmation of the ideas in this chapter comes from the longitudinal network studies directed by Clare Wenger in rural and urban England. She demonstrated how the structure and degree of integration of social networks was vitally related to both the provision of informal helping directed toward an elder and other indicators of well-being. Wenger found that the network type she classified as "locally integrated"—which fused active family, friend and neighbor ties with church and other voluntary organizations—was the most associated with network support, independent functioning and high morale among the aged. Contrastingly, she also found that morale was lowest among those aged situated in "family centered'' networks, showing almost no social engagement beyond kin ties (Wenger 1992).

MINORITY STATUS AND ETHNICITY, IN CLASS CONTEXT

In the United States the cultural dimension of ethnicity must also be understood within the framework of a class system which has created minority groups (Stoller and Gibson 1996). These are groups of people who are ''singled out for differential and inferior treatment on the basis of such characteristics as their race, sex, nationality, or language'' (Jackson 1980:2). While U.S. minority populations discussed in this book—African Americans, Hispanics, Native Americans and Southeast Asian refugees—have a considerably smaller proportion of elderly than Euro-American groups, their income, education, access to quality housing and health care are far below that of the majority of older Americans (U.S. Senate Special Committee on Aging 1991; J. S. Jackson 1993, J. S. Jackson, Lockery and Juster 1996).[7] After a period in the 1960s and 1970s of gradually improving the ''safety net'' for the minority aged, the past decade and a half has witnessed deep cuts in programs such as food stamps, low-income housing, and energy subsidies—entitlements that were targeted toward helping the poorest elderly (Damron-Rodriguez, Wallace and Kington 1994). In the late 1990s, congressional attempts to dramatically cut Medicare and Medicaid could accelerate the ongoing polarization of the aged on the basis of wealth and access to health care. For example, the National Center for Health Statistics, in 1990, noted that while about 15 percent of elderly whites had no health insurance other than Medicare, the figures are more than double that for older African Americans (38 percent) and Hispanics (36 percent) (Gornick et al. 1996).

Minority aging, historically marked by ''multiple jeopardies'' accumulated over the life cycle, continues to be reflected in the disparity of resources among subsets of the aged population (Salmon 1994; Shea, Miles and Hayward 1996). For example, while the poverty rate for the elderly has decreased significantly over the last 30 years, the gap has widened between whites and African Americans, by far the most numerically significant ethnic aged population. In 1966, there was a two-to-one ratio of black to white elders in poverty (55 percent versus 26 percent); in 1983 the ratio rose to three to one, although absolute rates were cut, and in 1990 the Bureau of the Census found that the ratio exceeded three to one. For the black community, impoverishment is highly focused among single, older women, 43 percent of whom live in poverty. Fully 80 percent of these women are very poor, with incomes 125 percent below the poverty level (Belgrave, Wykle and Choi 1993:382). The impact of inequality among these older women also includes great displacement from the work force by technology and higher rates of illiteracy than other segments of the minority aged (Hardy and Hazelrigg 1995). As will be seen in Part V, such conditions also place these women at higher than average risk of becoming homeless.

One historical response of African-American peoples has been to establish community-based mechanisms of support which could buffer the shock of long-term discrimination on the individual (Coke and Twaite 1995; Ball and Whittington 1995). Employing her dual background as professional nurse and medical anthropologist, Jane Peterson (Chapter 13) explores the participation of older women in two key institutions in an African-American community in Seattle. Despite the ever-present specter of multiple jeopardy—being black, aged and female—a family-based role combined with the more public arena of the Pentecostal Church provide a valued context in which successful aging can take place.

Through the case of Mrs. Lottie Waters we see that mature women in their grandparenting capacity fulfill a classic "kin-keeping role": nurturing and disciplining children; being the repository of family history; serving as a key decision maker and convener of family ritual.

Despite the patriarchal nature of the Pentecostal Church these women belong to, "wise" women can also become church "mothers" who can influence the male "elders" of the religious community. Such women add to the typical characteristics of wise women a devotion to spiritual needs and some in the role of "nurses" apply a holistic system of healing based on herbs and faith. Peterson's ethnographic work corresponds nicely with a recent survey study which shows a powerful statistical relationship between religious participation in African-American churches and positive perceptions of well-being (Levin, Chatters and Taylor 1995).

REFUGEE STATUS AS CULTURAL CONTEXT

Increasingly, over the last two decades, with the ending of old colonial regimes and the collapse of the Soviet Union, numerous tragic civil wars have raged, and still continue in parts of the world. In 1995 the United Nations estimated that worldwide, there were about twenty million refugees being forced from their home areas through wars and other disasters. Refugees from the Southeast Asian states of Vietnam, Laos and Cambodia have a particular connection to the United States, which unsuccessfully, through the Vietnam war, tried to maintain the colonial domain France abandoned in this region. Since the mid-1970s, Southeast Asian refugees and immigrants have come to many different areas of America. In Chapter 14, social psychologist Barbara Yee uses a life-span development approach to broadly examine the dilemmas faced by the elderly in these ethnic communities as they experience a cultural system dramatically different from that found in their homelands.[8] In the cases she presents, we clearly see how cultural variation can combine with personal and situational contexts, leading to dramatic success or tragic disaster (Yee, Huang and Lew, forthcoming).

THE ETHNIC COLORS IN "WHITE"

While in the study of aging it is tempting to focus on ethnic groups which markedly differ in cultural traditions from the predominant Euro-American patterns, a number of researchers have pointed out the need to understand the diversity among "white" elderly (Holzberg 1982; Hayes, Kalish and Guttmann 1986; Barresi 1997). All too often bunched together as a homogeneous body of ethnics, those of European background retain some substantial differences which influence how these populations deal with the aging process. In Chapter 15, the authors address the difficult problem of widowhood and how variations in ethnic identity and values among Irish, Italians and Jews in Philadelphia relate to how men cope with such tragic loss. Despite the far greater likelihood that women rather than men will become widows, it is the male in North American society who seems to fare worse psychologically by this experience. As Turner notes:

because women in our society tend to maintain both normative and interactive integration of kinship systems (and perhaps of wider social networks as well) on behalf of men and themselves, the implications of loss of spouse for men tends to be multiplied. Widows lose only their husband, but widowers also tend to suffer the loss of some portion of their wider support system. (1983)

This issue is explored by an intriguing part of the authors' research strategy. In developing life history materials they asked respondents to think of their lives as books and to describe the different chapters. While similarities were noted in the way ethnic values provided a means of overcoming loss, substantial divergence was found in the way loss was conceptualized, how social connections were remade and how a sense of self was reconstituted. This is one of the few comparative studies of widowhood from the male perspective, although as we saw in Part I, a more extensive literature exists on the response of women to this situation.[9]

KEY RESOURCES

Centers

National Resource Center on Minority Aging Populations, University Center on Aging, College of Health and Human Services San Diego, CA 92182–6765. Phone (619) 594–6765.
National Caucus and Center on Black Aged. 1424 K St., NW, Suite 500, Washington, DC 20005. Phone (202) 637-8400. Web site: http://www.social.com/health/nhic/data/hr1600/hr1614.html.
National Hispanic Council on Aging, 2713 Ontario Rd., NW, Washington, DC 20009. Phone (202) 745–2521.
National Indian Council on Aging, 6400 Uptown Blvd., City Centre, Suite 510W, Albuquerque, New Mexico 87110. Phone (505) 292–2001.
National Pacific/Asian Resource Center on Aging, 1511 3rd Avenue, Suite 914, Seattle, WA 98101. Phone (206) 624–1221.

Internet Resources

http//:www.uchsc.edu/sm/nehcrc/library.htm. The Native Elder Health Care Resource

Center located at the University of Colorado was established in 1994 to promote culturally competent health care for older American Indians, Alaska Natives and Native Hawaiians. They are developing an annotated bibliography on "Native Elder Health Care" through their web site.

Print Resources

Newsletter

Aging is a newsletter produced by the Office of Minority Health at the U.S. Public Health Service and is available online by selecting "aging" at http://omhrc.gov/. Each issue has many short articles on new research, funding opportunities and resources dealing with minority seniors.

New Journal

Journal of Aging and Ethnicity. There is also a new special section of *The Gerontologist* which will focus on minority population perspectives derived from the massive Health and Retirement study.

Special Issues of Journals

"Ethnicity," *Journal of Aging Studies* (1994), 8:3.

Other Print Resources

Blakemore, K. and M. Boneham, eds. 1994. *Age, Race and Ethnicity: A Comparative Approach.* Philadelphia: Open University Press. Edited volume about ethnic, minority aging in England and Australia.

Coke, M. and J. Twaite. 1995. *The Black Elderly: Satisfaction and Quality of Life.* Binghamton, NY: Haworth Press. Explores issues such as the role of the Black Church, the influence of West African culture and models for predicting life satisfaction.

Gibson, R. 1995. "Promoting Successful and Productive Aging in Minority Populations." In *Promoting Successful and Productive Aging.* L. Bond, S. Cutler and A. Grams, eds. Thousand Oaks, CA: Sage. Provides a broad framework for understanding the positive aspects of minority aging.

Litwin, H. 1995. *Uprooted in Old Age: Soviet Jews and Their Social Networks in Israel.* Westport, CT: Greenwood. A study of starting all over in late life. An interesting comparison with the work of Yee in Chapter 14.

Markides, K. 1996. "Race, Ethnicity and Aging: Impact of Inequality. In *Handbook of Aging and Social Sciences*, 4th ed. R. Binstock and L. George, eds. New York: Academic Press. A cutting edge discussion of this crucial issue.

Padgett, D., ed. 1995. *Handbook on Ethnicity, Aging, and Mental Health.* Westport, CT: Greenwood. A large, quite varied volume focusing on the use and effectiveness of mental health services by the ethnic aged.

Rosenblatt, P. 1993. "Cross-Cultural Variation in the Experience, Expression and Understanding of Grief." In *Ethnic Variations in Dying, Death and Grief*, D. Irish, ed. Washington, DC: Taylor and Francis. An exploration of the cultural response to death.

Sotomayor, M., ed. 1994. *In Triple Jeopardy, Aged Hispanic Women: Insights and Experiences*. Washington, DC: National Hispanic Council on Aging. Looks at the problems and strengths of older Hispanic women from many angles.

NOTES

1. Since the 1970s the AOA had funded four national centers to carry out innovative projects to improve the well-being of older Native Americans, Hispanics, African Americans and Pacific Asians.

2. Given these figures for California, it is little wonder that the term "ethnogeriatrics" was created at the Stanford University Geriatric Education Center in California. It is important to note that, also by 2020, Latinos, not Anglos, will be the majority ethnic population.

3. British expatriate Peter Brimlow, author of *Alien Nation*, while noting flaws in our immigration policy, sounds a racist alarm against "racially distinct 'visible minorities' " from "completely different and arguably incompatible, cultural traditions."

4. For a good discussion of this issue in Great Britain with regard to African-Caribbean and South Asian elderly, see Blakemore 1989.

5. For more information about the ethnic variation in informal support systems, see Jackson and Harel 1983; Rempusheski 1988.

6. For a good perspective on the major issues of aging policy which are changing during the 1990s, see "Responding to the Clinton Administration," a special issue of the *Journal of Aging and Social Policy* 6(1/2) (1994).

7. The figures in 1992 for the percent over age 65 in these groups were: 8.4 percent, 5.2 percent, 5.8 percent and 6.2 percent versus 12.5 percent, respectively.

8. For a discussion of the problems facing elder immigrants from South Pacific Island cultures, see Tanjasiri, Wallace and Shibata 1995.

9. For a broad-based view of older men, see Thompson 1994.

CHAPTER 12

Bringing Culture Back Home: Aging, Ethnicity and Family Support

Jay Sokolovsky

My inspiration for this chapter developed from a dramatic reaction to a co-authored paper I presented in 1978 at one of the first national conventions on ethnicity and aging.[1] As the last speaker of the conference, I was supposed to present a survey of cultural variation and growing old in the United States. Toward the end of the presentation, I told the audience that after reviewing the available data, I felt it would be a grave mistake for voluntary agencies to put too much pressure on ethnic families to take care of all of the needs of the elderly. At hearing this, the conference organizer, who also directed one of the types of agencies I was referring to, began to choke and actually stopped my presentation, claiming that time had run out. I knew I was onto something.

ETHNICITY AND AGING

The broadest-based view of the link between ethnicity and aging centers on the premise that varying ethnic lifestyles will alter the way old age is encountered, perceived and acted out. Describing precisely how much ethnic subcultures alter the conditions of aging is, to say the very least, controversial. I will address this point by asking the basic question: Do ethnic distinctions make real differences in the experience of aging? More specifically, I will concentrate on the extent to which an idealized view of ethnic subcultures has led to a policy error which places too much emphasis on the ethnic family and informal supports as the savior of the ethnic elderly. Much is at stake as the U.S. Congress of the late 1990s tries to ''remake America'' by dismantling public sector support systems. This is often justified by the misguided premise that government programs reduce the incentives for families to care for their aged along with their other responsibilities.

CULTURE, ETHNICITY AND AGING

To a cultural anthropologist such as myself, seeking the answer to this question requires examining the general relationship between cultural variation and aging. The consideration of ethnicity as a factor affecting old age brings the question of sociocultural variation back home to our own doorstep. Ethnicity is commonly understood as social differentiation derived from cultural criteria such as a shared history, a common place of origin, language, dress, food preferences and values that engender a sense of exclusiveness and self-awareness of membership in a distinct social group. Viewing the variations of aging in our country within the context of ethnicity seems mandated by the continuing cultural pluralism of our nation. While, by the beginning of the 1990s, only about 5 percent of the ethnic elderly were foreign-born, throughout the twenty-first century there will be large numbers of American-born adults from Indo-China, Asia and Latin America entering old age (Gozdziak 1988; see Chapter 14 this volume).

CULTURE VERSUS CONTEXT

When dealing in general with ethnic segments of the United States, we are almost never confronting "culture in the raw," unburnished from Old World or other indigenous origins. Especially in cities, one can easily encounter such designations as "Moscow on the boardwalk" of Brighton Beach, Brooklyn, "Little Havana" in Miami, or the "little Asias" clinging to numerous downtown districts. However, there are precious few ethnic groups whose traditional lifestyles and values have not been altered by the reality of special immigration histories and the continuing social, economic and political constraints imposed by American class stratification and ideology. In examining a number of transplanted Asiatic ethnic groups, each with a strong "ideal" emphasis on filial devotion, one can see the impact of context on culture. For Chinese-American elderly, migration to the United States in the early twentieth century was largely a movement of young, single males who planned to return to China. Despite living in well-defined ethnic communities, studies of these males in old age have found them to have the smallest family networks of any Asian-American group, and relatively few express high satisfaction with life (Weeks and Cuellar 1981; see also L. Yu 1992).[2] While in the last two decades new immigration patterns have evened out the gender ratio of elder Chinese Americans, continuing insecurity focuses on linguistic isolation.[3] By 1990 only 25 percent of these ethnic aged could speak English well, and almost half lived in households where no one over age 14 had good English-speaking skills (U.S. Bureau of the Census 1993).

In contrast, older Japanese Americans, while they came to this country a few decades after the Chinese, immigrated primarily in family groups and expected to become U.S. citizens. These elders are not only more likely to be more deeply imbedded in kinship networks than the Chinese, but also exhibit higher levels of social and psychological success. While a majority (54 percent) of Japanese-American elders in a San Diego study (Cuellar and Weeks 1980) said they were very satisfied with their lives, only 18 percent of older Chinese claimed this level of contentment. We will see later on, however, that being surrounded by relatives in an ethnic enclave does not ensure passage to a geriatric Nirvana. This can also be seen by carefully reading Barbara Yee's poignant discussion of Southeast Asian refugee elders (Chapter 14).

MULTIPLE JEOPARDY OR ETHNIC COMPENSATION

Understanding the context of ethnic aging also requires an understanding of the minority aged, those who "have been singled out for differential and inferior treatment" (Jackson 1980:2). In this particular clash of culture and context, there have emerged in the ethnicity and aging literature two key themes that on the surface seem contradictory. One theme stresses how minority group membership creates "multiple jeopardies" in the context of structured inequality and thereby intensifies the problems of growing old (Gibson 1995). The other theme underscores the benefits or resources accruing to those elderly who remain attached to an ethnic identity and subculture (Cool 1987; Markides, Liang and Jackson 1990).

From this first perspective Ron Manuel notes that "the distinction of the minority aged is not so much a function of the novel conditions of their aging as it is the dire circumstances of their existence" (1982:XV). Numerous studies have repeatedly demonstrated that in terms of income, housing quality, education and rates of chronic illness, the minority aged encounter harsher conditions than the majority of older Americans. Not only are these problems more severe, but the "aging network" set up to provide services according to uniform bureaucratic standards often creates barriers preventing the minority ethnic aged from obtaining resources to which they are entitled (Barresi and Stull 1993; Mui and Burnette 1994; Gerontological Society of America 1994).

The second theme, which I will refer to as "ethnic compensation," often creeps into the discussion of minority aging in an ambivalent fashion.[4] Manuel, after making the statement quoted above, goes on to state, "while relatively more disadvantaged because of the minority experience, the aged have often adopted distinguishable strategies for successfully coping with their problems" (1982:XV). This sentiment corresponds to the prevailing anthropological writings on aging and ethnicity, which largely echo Linda Cool's statement that, "rather than providing yet one more obstacle to be overcome in the aging process, ethnicity can furnish the elderly with a source of identity and prestige which they can manipulate to make a place for themselves in society (1981: 185).

The two themes do not logically exclude each other, but the policy implications of each could be applied to dramatically opposed viewpoints. Ethnicity as deprivation calls for strengthening federal/state resources to overcome lifelong deficits. Ethnicity as compensation or resource could be construed as a rationale to decrease or at least not radically shift material resources toward the ethnic minority aged. However, a major point I hope to make here is that much of the literature on ethnicity as a resource has been overly optimistic, especially in the area of informal social supports and family networks of exchange (Johnson 1995).

I concentrate on the theme of ethnic compensation not because I think it is more important, but because it has been relatively ignored. By stressing this approach, one can also ask significant questions about the nonminority ethnic elderly. Moreover, it is often in this area of aging research that the ways of testing whether the "differences make a difference" have not been up to the questions asked. All too often, ethnic distinctions are measured by mass survey questionnaires, appropriate perhaps for numerically measuring variations in health complaints, the frequency of contact with friends or the proximity of children to an elderly parent's house. However, such measures tell us little about how ethnic differences influence the way illnesses are dealt with, how they affect the perception of old age, if they lead to premature institutionalization or how the action of social networks actually contributes to or diminishes the successful functioning of the elderly in the family and the community.

This is especially the case in studies of the aged of European background, where statistical documentation can potentially mask subtle ethnic differences (Hayes, Kalish and Guttmann 1986). Quite instructive is the work by Cohler, Lieberman and Welch (1977) studying Irish, Italian and Polish Americans in Chicago. Despite statistical similarity in levels of social contact, the authors showed how subtle differences in value orientations between the Italian and Polish communities related to the nature of support systems affecting the elderly.

In this study, the Polish were found to perceive a greater sense of isolation, and they were more likely to feel no one was available to them for aid in problematic situations. This greater degree of perceived social isolation was related to traditional Polish concerns for privacy, self-containment and formality in social relations. The authors suggest that what appears to be greater social isolation among the Polish-American respondents may be a reflection of their preference for formal rather than informal relationships and a tendency to look to the community rather than to the family for support. They argue that there is a tendency here to undervalue informal relations of the family as a source of support in deference to resources through formal ties to the community.

The Italians, on the other hand, emphasized a traditional value of "family centeredness," used chain migration to link up with fellow townspeople in the same urban neighborhood and put an inordinate stress on family relationships. In contrast to Polish respondents, the Italian aged were more willing to seek out family and close friends in crisis situations. Italian women were noted as gaining higher status with age, as they were much in demand to mediate problems in the family network. As we shall see however, there are costs attached to this "mediating Madonna" role.

While ethnic differences are apparent, the ultimate question remains: Do the differences make a significant difference? In fact, Cohler, Lieberman and Welch (1977) suggest that for the groups just mentioned, ethnic saliency for explaining variant patterns of behavior decreases in old age, with middle-aged cohorts more distinct than aged ones. Nonetheless, this does not mean that general cultural differences among the nonaged ethnics will not have an impact on the elderly. This can be especially important in socially patterned decisions about caring for one's aged parent. An indication of this is provided by a Baltimore study comparing Italians and Poles on attitudes toward institutionalization of the elderly (Fandeti and Gelfand 1976). As one might predict from the previous discussion, the authors note that "Italian respondents expressed a significantly stronger preference for using family arrangements than their Polish counterparts." Here is an ethnic difference which not only directly affects differential treatment of the aged, but also argues for awareness of such differences at some level of policymaking.

The general problem of understanding the implications of statistical survey variables often occurs in the discussion of informal social interaction and exchange in family and neighborhood contexts. Numerous studies now exist purporting to compare subculturally variant "network" behavior. With the predominant use of so-called sociometric techniques for gathering data, one is hard-pressed to know if statistically significant differences (or lack of variation) mean anything. A case in point is the well-known "Social and Cultural Contexts of Aging" study conducted in Los Angeles (Bengtson and Morgan 1987). Here whites were compared with blacks and Mexican Americans in terms of social interaction with children, grandchildren, other relatives and friends. Mexican Americans were considerably more likely than white elderly to see children and grandchildren on a weekly basis, although no difference was found for contact with other relatives. The Mexican Americans were much less likely to see friends and neighbors frequently. Older blacks and whites were shown to have almost identical frequency of contact with grandchildren or other relatives, although smaller percentages of blacks reported seeing children and neighborhood friends frequently.

What use can be made of these facts with regard to the function of the aged in familial and community networks? Just because approximately 40 percent of both whites and blacks in Los Angeles see "grandchildren" and "other relatives" weekly does not mean the aged in each ethnic group fit into kinship networks and use such resources in the same way (Chatters and Taylor 1993; Gibson 1995).[5] Various other studies, such as that by Jane Peterson in Chapter 13, or by Nellie Tate (1983), have given us clues to some of the significant differences. One of these distinctions is a greater flexibility in kinship boundaries among African-American families, which results in the absorption of young grandchildren and "other relatives" into households headed by the elderly. This is particularly pronounced for older black women, who are four times more likely than older white females to live with young dependent relatives under 18 years of age. In her study of Philadelphia's black elderly, Tate has suggested how this difference makes a difference: "It appears that absorbed nonindependent younger blacks are more likely to accept their aged who become functionally impaired as a result of chronic conditions" (1983:99). This is dramatically seen in the case of families caring for elders suffering from dementia. My own ongoing research on this issue in Tampa, Florida,[6] corroborates what other studies have implied, that the structure of African-American families significantly reduces the perceived consequences of Alzheimer's disease on the kin caregiving unit, even though the actual disease stressors or patient functional capacity are likely worse than in Euro-American background families (also see Friedman, Daly and Lazur 1995).[7]

Other studies have documented substantial ethnic-based variation in familial and nonfamilial support systems. One of the most comprehensive is the research of John Weeks and Jose Cuellar in San Diego comparing the elderly in nine ethnic groups to an "Anglo," nonminority sample. Variance from "Anglo-White" norms was most prominent among "filiocentric" Asian and Pacific Island groups: Korean, Chinese, Japanese, Filipino, Samoan and Guamanian. To cite the most dramatic case, 91 percent of elderly Korean parents were found to be living with their children, and over 80 percent said they would first turn to family members to satisfy all eight categories of need. By comparison, only 10 percent of the white aged surveyed were dwelling with their children, and fewer than one in ten expected their family networks to deal with all of their basic needs (Weeks and Cuellar 1981:391; Weeks 1984:101). Furthermore, important and substantial differences were noted in comparing the Asian groups among themselves.

I could proceed with other examples showing the impact of the ethnic family in the life of the elderly, but I have already painted myself into a corner, if my intent was to argue against policymakers putting too much stress on ethnic support systems and the family.

THE LIMITS OF ETHNIC COMPENSATION

From where does my pessimism spring? As I interpret studies now available, the evidence indicates that the capacity of the ethnic family in dealing with the most difficult problems of its elderly members is limited. In the context of rapid demographic and economic changes over the last decade, rural ideals are rapidly giving way to urban realities (Himes, Hogan and Eggebeen 1996). Even by the early 1980s, a majority of black elderly and 84 percent of Hispanic-American elderly resided in urban areas. A case in point is the Hispanic-American elderly (Sotomayor and Curiel 1988). Many writers have described the ideal value structure of this group as involving (1) profound family loyalty, (2) dominance of males, and (3) subordination of younger to older persons. Certain studies confirm some elements of this ideal. Marjorie Cantor's triethnic elderly study (whites, Hispanics and blacks) in New York showed that Hispanic elderly received the highest levels of assistance in terms of tasks of everyday living and the receiving of gifts (1979). Similarly, Vern Bengtson's Los Angeles study showed considerably greater levels of family interactions for Mexican Americans than among whites and blacks (Bengtson and Morgan 1987).

However, other authors such as Cuellar (1980) and Gratton (1987) argue that much of the literature on the Chicano elderly is of limited utility due to a tendency to romanticize, distort and stereotype critical elements of the Hispanic life experience. They question the popular assumption that older Chicanos can find significant emotional and social support in the extended family. Various studies, especially in the southern California area, describe situations where, despite the continuing ideal of intense intergenerational family concern and the actual availability of a large kin network in the respective urban environment, obligations and expectations of kin support were radically declining (Markides, Boldt and Ray 1986; Hurtado, Hayes-Bautista, Valdez and Hernandez 1992).[8]

In San Diego, even though Hispanics who lived alone had four times more extended kin in the local area than whites, they were found to be less likely to turn to family members in times of need (Weeks and Cuellar 1981:392). They preferred to "suffer in silence." The consequences of this appear to be high levels of alienation, low life satisfaction, and other psychological problems. Part of the difficulty stems from unmet expectations of family interaction. More recently, in San Antonio, Texas, results from the largest longitudinal study of Mexican Americans show that "those aged with greatest need for a caregiver are the most likely to report that one is not available. Number of children was not associated with reported caregiver availability among barrio Mexican Americans; many identify family other than spouse or children, or nonfamily, as perceived caregivers." (National Institute on Aging 1994:5).[9] Even in the previously mentioned studies in Los Angeles and New York, which showed high levels of family interaction and support for elderly Hispanic Americans, these aged were more likely to display symptoms of mental stress than either whites or blacks (see also Kemp, Staples and Lopez-Aquires 1987; Tran et al. 1996). In both locales the main sources of concern were children and family. Some have even argued that the intense Hispanic pattern of female adult children giving care through extremes of self-sacrifice increases in a negative way the dependence and disability of elder kin, especially women (Purdy and Arguello 1992; Hopper 1993).[10] This should be particularly disturbing to policymakers, as some studies have shown Hispanic-American families to use community-based services at a very low rate, even compared to other ethnic groups surveyed (Holmes, Holmes and Teresi 1983; Mui and Burnette 1994).

THE GENDER DIMENSION OF ETHNIC KIN SUPPORT

An interesting facet of research on Hispanic elderly is that the negative consequences of needs unmet through the kinship network more likely touch the lives of women than of men. A study in San Antonio by Markides and Vernon

(1984) corroborates this by showing that, of those elder Mexican Americans who maintained a very ethnically traditional sex role identity, only among women were there significant signs of psychological distress. They were found to have higher levels of depression than those older women, who were more flexible in their gender roles and less traditionally ethnic.

This work, and another I will now discuss, suggest the unsettling proposition that "although it has been assumed that social relations are inherently satisfying and reduce the impact of life stress it appears that, at least in some instances, such social ties may enhance rather than reduce feelings of distress" (Cohler and Lieberman 1980:462). Bert Cohler and Morton Lieberman base this statement on their previously mentioned study of Irish, Polish and Italian families in Chicago. These findings parallel those for the Hispanic elderly but are even more dramatic with regard to gender, ethnicity and psychological stress. They state that among women "living in communities characterized by particularly dense social networks and complex patterns of reciprocity and obligations with adult offspring and other close relatives, there is a significant negative relationship between extent of social contact and both self-reported life satisfaction and psychological impairment (Cohler 1983:118). This relationship among a kin-keeping role, ethnic embeddedness and personal maladjustment is strongest for Italian- and Polish-American elderly but did not hold in the Irish-American case. Interestingly enough, for older men of Italian and Polish descent, the effect of ethnic embeddedness is opposite to that found for the women—they seem to benefit greatly in terms of adjustment to old age.

In the case of the Italian-American aged, where this bipolar gender effect is most notable, one sees structural, gender-based differences in the nature of the social networks by which persons are linked to the local environment. Compared to females, older adult males, even after retirement, are active in a more diverse array of community-wide social contexts outside of the family unit. In this case, men's social clubs have been a long-existing traditional arena where older Italian males could gain public status, recognition and support. This opportunity to enter old age with vital connections both to lifelong friends in ethnic neighborhood associations and to relatives is seldom obtained by women. Most of the elderly women in this Chicago study appear very much encapsulated within the sphere of kin. As one might predict, it was found that older women who exhibited the lowest levels of psychological stress were those actively involved with friends as well as family (Cohler and Lieberman 1980:454). That is, they had networks more like men in maintaining important social relations both inside and outside the realm of domestic/kin ties.

At a time when younger married women are entering the labor force, the traditional "kin-keeping" role of older women is often nervously mocked by the refrain, "How is it that one girl can bring up ten kids, but ten grown-up kids cannot care for one little old lady?" Analytically, I think the evidence is quite convincing that in terms of material and emotional exchange, women are most often left holding the short end of the stick—giving considerably more through informal kin support networks than they ever receive. The implications for policymakers are clear. Emphasizing certain ethnic family support networks as a primary service mechanism would be of likely benefit to aged males, but may be a disaster for females, who make up the majority of older ethnic citizens.

This observation is reinforced by studies of the most family-dependent of America's ethnic aged, Asian and Pacific Americans. Recall the previously mentioned Korean aged in San Diego, where nine in ten lived with children and almost that number expected to depend on their families to provide for all of their needs. Yet one is surprised to read in John Weeks's analysis of his qualitative data that "among all the groups interviewed the Korean elders were least satisfied with their lives" (Weeks 1984:190). Being poor, primarily female, lacking strong English-language skills and having been followers of their earlier migrating children, they were isolated and lonely within a small, exclusive, family life arena. Sadly, the vast majority found life hard, and one-quarter reported having contemplated suicide. In the transplanted context, generational relations ideally predicated on *hyo*, a Confucian word that means taking care of one's parents and ancestors, has become more a source of tension than a moral precept for successful aging. Studies in other urban areas have continued to corroborate the difficulty older Korean immigrants are having, especially in terms of depression (Pang 1990; Moon and Pearl 1991).

ETHNICITY IN LIFE-SPAN CONTEXT: JAPANESE AMERICANS

However, San Diego's Korean aged offer an extreme example and tell us little about some very positive Asian cultural features which greatly enhance the experience of aging in the United States. Perhaps the clearest demonstration of this is by anthropologist Chris Kiefer (1974) in his study of how the Japanese-American *issei* (first generation migrants) handled the problem of aging in the context of the rapid Americanization of their children and grandchildren.

Much has been written about the high standards and prestige accorded the elderly in traditional Japanese culture (Palmore and Maeda 1985; Chapter 10 this volume). Many have focused on the Japanese version of Buddhism, with its linking of the aged and even the dead to a family system emphasizing filial devotion, an aged role infused with loving indulgence, and an accepted dependence in this "second privileged period." There is also a traditional emphasis on formal socialization into the retired role (*inkyo*) with its greater freedom but also the expectation of increasing skill and wisdom. While strict maintenance of these ideals has not been possible either in modern Japan or among Japanese Americans, studies of the latter group clearly show the salience of Japanese ethnicity for the elderly (Kiefer 1974; Osako 1979).

Despite the significant generational differences noted by Kiefer (1974) and Masuda et al. (1974), most Japanese elderly still live with or near their families, who encourage the *issei* to be involved in family activities and outings. To a great extent, their lives remain focused on core Japanese values such as *kansha* (gratitude), *gaman* (forbearance), *makoto* (sincerity) and *giri* (duty), which culminate in a style of life Kiefer refers to as structural intimacy. This involves valuing cohesiveness and privileges. Seen from the perspective of the individual, psychological and material security are to be achieved through the cultivation of mutually binding relationships more than through the competitive pursuit of individual goals and abstract ends. Kiefer demonstrates how such ethnic perceptions of the self contribute to successfully dealing with specific concerns of the aged such as increased dependency and impending death.[11]

In sum, the practical meaning of ethnicity for *issei* aged hinges on core values that, although somewhat discontinuous through generations, maintain the elderly in nonstigmatized family roles. Just as important, however, is that much of their socialization into old age is provided by age peers who share these strongly held values and allow their traditional basis of self-esteem to guide them through old age. This later aspect of Japanese ethnicity, linking the *issei* into age-peer-dependent mutuality, may be more important than the rules of filial piety most often alluded to.

A particularly important aspect of Kiefer's work is his discussion of how the high cultural value placed on maintaining harmony in the extended family unit can, in fact, be a substantial problem for the elderly under certain conditions. He found that if elderly persons exhibited symptoms of psychological disturbance, families made a great effort to keep such things hidden and simply did not deal effectively with this issue. Relatively minor problems which might have been alleviated by counseling services available through the local ethnic churches often became exaggerated as time went on. Thus, while the manifestation of Japanese culture in the United States can be broadly viewed as a very positive resource for the aged, particular facets of ethnicity can actually create more problems than they solve.

CONCLUSIONS

In this analysis, I am trying to be realistic about the capacity of ethnic family support systems to deal with problems of the aged (Strawbridge and Wallhagen 1992). My negative attitude may seem unusual given my previously published work in the areas of gerontology and mental health (Sokolovsky et al. 1978; Sokolovsky 1986; Sokolovsky and Cohen 1987). In these writings, I often sought to demonstrate the great benefits derived by inner-city elderly and re-leased mental patients from the social networks in which their lives were enmeshed. Having recently completed the longitudinal and applied extensions of these studies, I am certainly more pessimistic than I was in the late 1970s, when some of my publications helped feed ''informal support systems'' euphoria.

By following, over time, the lives of poor elderly residing in urban hotels and in analyzing an experimental intervention program, my colleagues and I readily noted the limits of informal supports. In the case of black women residents whose social networks were comparatively interconnected and contained complex exchanges, these informal structures were adequate for handling many acute health and resource problems. But longer-term difficulties could not be handled well by these intense networks. Especially in the case of alcoholism, attempts by intertwined social network members to provide support could lead to such levels of conflict that these tightly bound social matrices often disintegrated. An experimental project in one hotel to test the efficacy of interventions using informal support found that only about 20 percent of the attempts to use social networks to solve problems (such as obtaining food, getting to a hospital) were successful (Cohen, Adler and Mintz 1983).

Admittedly, SRO environments are characterized by low levels of material resources, high personal alienation and a lack of a sense of ethnic affiliation. One should expect greater levels of success when applying network intervention techniques in strong ethnic communities (Stephenson and Renard 1993). One example is the servidor (community service broker) system in southern California examined by Valle and Mendoza (1978). In this program Hispanic-American community members informally function as a catalyst for the utilization of services by Mexican-American elders.

Most studies indicate that it is those services that John Colen (1979) calls nonmechanism specific—services that can be provided in diverse settings (such as counseling, information and referral)—that are most appropriately handled through the social organization of the ethnic community (Colen 1982). Informal coping mechanisms, which are proportionally more evident in ethnic communities, can and should be creatively used as structures in which the fulfillment of human needs in late life are realizable. These forms of ethnic compensation can be quite effective when coupled with nonfamilial systems of support such as respite and day care programs and health promotion efforts (Yee and Weaver 1994; see Chapter 22 this volume). Such formal systems of care have been found to greatly enhance the capacity of families who seek to care personally for their elderly (Barresi and Stull 1993).

Perhaps the best example of this is On Lok Health Services, a model of community-based, long-term care developed during the 1970s in San Francisco to serve the poor, frail elderly, especially Chinese Americans. Drawing on the "Day Hospitals" developed in England, On Lok (Chinese for "peaceful, happy abode") created one of the nation's first adult day health centers and later expanded to develop a complete system of medical care, social support and housing for nursing home–eligible elderly (Steenberg, Ansak and Chin-Hansen 1993). The On Lok model, although not initially designed to be focused on ethnic groups, uses multidisciplinary teams to assess how the culture and context of the elderly's circumstances can be used to actively integrate family resources with a broad range of formal services (Kunz and Shannon 1996). This system has been quite successful in assisting ethnic families in their effort to keep even quite frail aged from spending their last years in an institutional setting. As of 1997, fifteen states using private foundation and federal funds are attempting to replicate the On Lok model through a program called PACE (Program of All-inclusive Care for the Elderly).

The success of On Lok in San Francisco's Chinatown indicates that when generally dealing with such needs as long-term care, too much emphasis on the ethnic family would be a grave policy mistake. As was seen in the wake of the deinstitutionalization of mental health services, unrealistic or sentimental views of the strength of informal social resources can have the most unfortunate effects. More than a decade ago, gerontologists Marjorie Cantor and Virginia Little urged the development of a single system of social care incorporating informal and formal mechanisms of support for the elderly (1985). Although national political policy is not presently headed in that direction, it would be well worth the effort to harken to their plea. However, the assumption that public benefits for the needy aged merely supplement or displace family help continues to be used by political interest groups whose primary concern is minimizing social welfare costs and cutting programs that constitute the basis for economic well-being and care for the aged (Crystal 1982; Morris 1994).[12] I urge gerontologists interested in the issue of ethnicity not to become unwitting contributors to this destructive trend.

NOTES

This chapter is adapted from "Ethnicity, Culture and Aging: Do Differences Really Make a Difference?" *Journal of Applied Gerontology* 4(1) (1985):6–17. It is reprinted with the permission of Sage Publications.

1. This paper, co-authored with Jim Trela, "Ethnicity and Diversity of the Aging Experience," was presented at the National Conference on Ethnicity and Aging, May 1978, in College Park, Maryland.

2. Although a recent study (Yu 1992) showed considerable ideal expression of filial support by Chinese-American young adults in a Midwestern university town, actual support lagged well behind good intentions.

3. According to the 1990 census, older Chinese-American women now outnumbered men in the same age category (Bureau of the Census 1990).

4. See Jackson and Ensley (1990–1991) for a discussion of the conflict between what she calls ethnogerontology and the concerns of minority elders.

5. For a good general resource on how African-American elderly fit into family and community structures, see Jackson, Chatters and Taylor 1993.

6. This research project, "Social Support of Caregivers for Dementia Patients," was supported by a National Institute on Aging Senior Research Service Award, IF33G05654–01. For an excellent examination of the complex nature of caregiving in the African-American community, see Burton and Sorensen 1992.

7. A recent comparative study of black-white caregiving subsequent to a heart attack found that when the contexts of caregiving were controlled for, no significant differences were found on well-being of the caregivers (Young and Kahana 1995).

8. For a good discussion of Hispanic multigenerational families, see Garcia 1993.

9. See also Talamantes et al. 1996 for an elaboration of this issue and Brink 1992 for general discussion of mental health and the Hispanic aged.

10. One of the most sophisticated studies of the elderly and psychological stress across several Hispanic-American groups is found in Krause and Goldenhar 1992.

11. For a look at the adaptation of Japanese immigrants to another North American national context see Ujimoto 1987.

12. For a good discussion of the changing political mood and aging policy see the *Journal of Aging and Social Policy* 6(1/2) (1994).

CHAPTER 13

Age of Wisdom: Elderly Black Women in Family and Church

Jane W. Peterson

Among all living organisms, the process of birth, growth and death constitutes a familiar biologic cycle. For human beings this process is often divided into phases based on the development of the individual. Variations in importance of one phase versus another of this universal process occur as a result of the cultural context.

Age as measured in years is a fairly meaningless concept for the black American population with whom I worked. For them, age does not measure years on a fixed continuum but reflects those important life events which mature a person. This latter is believed to occur upon overcoming a struggle. One often hears this phenomenon referred to by the phrase, "You grew today." For this population the culturally significant phases of growth and development are: having a child, which is a sign of procreation; raising a child, a sign of maturity; and becoming a grandparent, a sign of having reached the "age of wisdom." This last stage refers to experience and knowledge gained while raising a child, which can be imparted to the next generation.

"Old age" and "aging" are not part of the language of this community, although members understand these concepts as used by white Americans. However, when speaking among themselves these words are not heard. The words used are "maturity" and having reached the "age of wisdom." The old are commonly referred to as "the wise."

For black Americans, cultural meaning grows out of their African heritage, the experience of slavery and their continued oppression within a largely white Anglo-Saxon, Protestant American culture. Today, elderly women in the black community continue the oral tradition of passing on cultural meanings, such as the value of children and self-reliance, to succeeding generations.

It is therefore common for elderly women in the community to announce that "one more came along today" in reference to a birth. Children are highly valued. Because of their dependence on adults, they create the possibility of potential relationships between adults through kinship, biological or fictive. "Wise" women continually instruct others about the importance of human relationships. They admonish against becoming too attached to possessions, for these can be taken away easily. The reference used is "Remember slavery days." Therefore, one does not aspire to accumulate possessions but relies on one's self, an education which is "in your head," and relationships with others who can be "counted on." One way to build such relationships is through the care of children.

Two very strong beliefs, emphasized by virtually every elderly black woman to members of a younger generation, are the importance of family and the importance of religion. This chapter addresses these two issues.

Data are from fieldwork I conducted among a black urban population in the Pacific Northwest between 1979 and 1980, with continued intensive short periods of fieldwork since then. In this work, family matters were defined culturally as "women's area of concern." As a black woman, I was readily incorporated by "wise" women into discussions on family matters. Religion was quite different. My formal instruction came from a preacher, a "wise" man who sat me down with an indexed Bible and made me read passages that he, and only he, could interpret and analyze. When it became a matter of participating in church activities, I was assigned to the Nurses' Unit, a group of prestigious women who had the wisdom and the authority to monitor my behavior. Although I am a nurse, my nursing license was not the credential that allowed me to participate with this group. Rather, the preacher's perceptions of my interpersonal skills and my dedication to understanding the doctrines of the church were my credentials. These informants, the women who told me about families, the preacher and the nurses, were respected elder members in their community, having reached the "age of wisdom."

OVERVIEW OF THE LITERATURE

A brief overview of selected references on the black family reveals that although the elderly are an integral part of the family they are not a major focus of black family literature. The exception is E. Franklin Frazier's (1939) classic study, *The Negro Family in the United States*. The chapter devoted to "Granny" describes black grandmothers as wise, strong leaders. The 1960s literature focusing on women in the family is largely devoted to young black girls as unwed mothers (Moynihan 1965). Although this interest continues in subsequent literature, the focus shifts to issues of sex, marriage and family (Staples 1973) as young girls reach womanhood (Ladner 1971; Dougherty 1978b).

An early study of older women by Jacquelyne J. Jackson (1972) finds similarities between married and single older black women in their instrumental and affective relationships. The author suggests that relationships with oldest chil-

Grandma and baby. Courtesy of Seattle University Publications Department.

dren and closest friends are most important. Faustine C. Jones (1973), writing about older women in families, describes the role of grandmother as highly respected and "lofty." They are a "source of love, strength, and stability for the black family . . . a steady, supporting influence, as well as a connecting link between branches of the extended family" (Jones 1973:19). Elmer P. Martin and Joanne M. Martin (1978) also explicitly address "the old" as members of extended families who impart "old-fashioned" values to "the young." Linda M. Burton and Vern L. Bengtson (1985) describe the timing of entry into grand-parenthood for black women as critical in defining their role. Those women who enter this "elder" phase of life early (25 to 38 years old) feel the pressure of role conflict and tension in the social support they receive. They perceive grand-parenthood as a "tenuous" role. Those who enter grandparenthood "on time" (42 to 57 years old) have less conflict but can also feel the pressure of integrating family and occupational roles. Meredith Minkler (1994) discusses the problems of grandparents who become parents unexpectedly. This can occur when an adult child is a drug or alcohol abuser, divorced or has AIDS, or when a teenager becomes a parent. Other recent literature on family and the older black popu-lation describes demographic characteristics (Jackson et al. 1988), sources of support (Walls 1992; Watson 1990) and gender differences (Taylor, Keith and Tucker 1993) which show that elderly black women maintain stonger kinship, friendship and religious ties than do elderly black men.

In this literature four salient points come through. First, marital status makes little difference to elderly black women in terms of role relationships. Second, gender does make a difference in maintaining kinship ties. Third, grandmothers are highly respected individuals and, fourth, early entry into grandmotherhood and the unexpected parenting create conflict in these roles within the family.

Selected references from the literature on religion and blacks emphasize re-ligion as an outlet for the oppressed. Religious beliefs, as Emile Durkheim (1915) suggests, are a collective representation that belongs to a whole group despite the fact that no one individual possesses total knowledge. Religion cre-ates a social reality; this holds true for blacks and their religious outlook.

Studies on elderly blacks describe religious participation as a way to help blacks cope with stress by offering material and emotional support (Meyers 1978; Watson 1990; Walls and Zarit 1991; Walls 1992; Bryant and Rakowski 1992). Elderly black women, specifically, believe that the church is important in this respect. Robert J. Taylor (1988) shows that church-based support is of-fered to black elderly in the form of material, emotional, spiritual assistance and as information and advice. Similar to these findings, Gurdeep S. Khullar and Beverly Reynolds's (1985) study supports the thesis that females, blacks and the elderly are the groups most likely to attend church services. However, con-trary to these studies, their findings show blacks who score high on "religious participation" score lower than whites on "life satisfaction" indices. The reason for this finding is unclear. Economic security is the one intervening variable that markedly affects the association between "religious participation" and "life satisfaction.'' One can hypothesize that ''life satisfaction'' measures control over one's life, a feeling which many blacks do not share and the very reason they go to church. The church is perceived by these blacks as the one arena in which they have been able to maintain their cultural traditions in face of social ostracism, economic deprivation and political marginality.

Peter Goldsmith (1985) also finds that religious participation is important among blacks in the Georgia Sea Islands. He suggests that ideological principles in church doctrine account for the differences between black Baptists and black Pentecostals. Baptists hold a belief of the accountability of the individual for life events, a view similar to the dominant white culture. They perceive a clear distinction between the scientific and religious spheres. On the other hand, the Pentecostals embrace a holistic view of a ''divinely directed social order'' (Goldsmith 1985:94) in which it is impossible to separate healing from worship, mind from body, man from spirit and natural being from social being. He then concludes that the use of healing in worship services can be seen as an index of nonacceptance of white culture by church members. This is noteworthy as, in the Pentecostal Church discussed here, worship and religious matters are the concern of the preacher and the (male) elders only, whereas healing is also the concern of the wise women who are nurses.

Cheryl T. Gilkes (1985) explores the role of women in the Sanctified Church (of which the Church of God in Christ is the largest denomination), which emphasizes independence, education, economic status and political autonomy. She finds that black women have been a well-organized force, self-reliant and economically independent since slavery. In the Pentecostal Church of God in Christ, where women are not allowed to preach from the pulpit, they have made a place as equal or interdependent with men. The powerful older women are leaders among church women (Gilkes 1986). The structure of the Pentecostal Church is analyzed from a different perspective by Melvin D. Williams (1974). He describes a hierarchy of elite, core, supportive and marginal members who range from socially close to socially distant to the pastor. The elite group includes powerful older women of the church.

The role of religion for older black women, as seen in this literature, is twofold. On the one hand, these women find within the church material and emotional support, especially in times of illness. On the other hand, the church offers them a place to gain power and exercise their leadership skills.

It is through the two themes of family and religion that the meaning of ''maturing'' and ''age of wisdom'' is elucidated in this chapter. The discussion on family centers around a wise woman, Lottie Waters (all names used are fictitious), who has ''twice reached the age of wisdom.'' She is a great-grandmother and, like the wise women before her, keeps track of family relationships traced both through biological and nonbiological ties. The discussion on religion presents data on a group of respected wise church women known as ''Mothers.'' In both instances, wise women are seen as organizers and leaders within their settings.

FAMILY

Here I want to introduce a woman who has reached the age of wisdom. She occupies a traditional family role, that "lofty" and respected position of grandmother. She is also the nurturer and disciplinarian of children, the family historian, the hub of the family network in which decisions are made, and the convener of family events.

Mrs. Lottie Waters is a fifty-five-year-old great-grandmother who invited me to call her by her first name. She was born in a small rural town in southern Texas. When Lottie was born, her fifteen-year-old mother and her father lived with his older sister, Auntie Elsie, who became a midwife. Auntie Elsie and her mother, known to Lottie as Grandma Lucy, delivered Lottie. Lottie was "raised" by Grandma Lucy, who always retained parental rights and responsibilities over her, an uncle and his family, and Auntie Elsie.

Lottie, like her mother, delivered her first child when she was fifteen years old. Lottie says she did her best to "raise" her five children, giving them to Elsie to "keep" when she was unable to care for them. Elsie was by then a wise woman. When Lottie's second child, her oldest daughter, had her first child, Kermit, Lottie joined the ranks of wise women. She was 32 years old. When Kermit's first child was born, Lottie was 52 years old and her daughter 35. Lottie celebrated being the mother of a wise woman as well as having "twice reached the age of wisdom." Lottie Waters's kinship chart relative to this discussion shows these relationships (Figure 13.1).

As a wise woman, Lottie was expected to care for children, her own and those of others. Often when she took her children to the park she "came upon childrun runnin' wild and unruly." She talked to them, teaching them right from wrong, and scolding them when necessary. It is not uncommon for the wise to admonish any youngster who is misbehaving. The wise do not need permission from biological parents to discipline children. It is their duty to teach any child, should the opportunity present itself. It did not take long for these "unruly childrun" to call Lottie "Grandma," follow her home, eat with her, and a few even slept at her house. Two children stayed with her for over a year. As Lottie became mother to these children, their own relatives would visit, introduce themselves and thank her for what she was doing for the children. Eventually, the adults would come to Lottie for advice in child raising or for themselves. Some would run errands for her; others would bring food or clothing. On one occasion she was given a car to "carry the children around."

Lottie's biological children considered all the children in the house brothers and sisters or sons and daughters, depending on their ages. When it came time to have a Waters family reunion, Lottie set the date and supervised its organization. She alone made up the invitation list. Those invited were all her grandchildren and those related to them. She was the anchor of a large family network held together by interactions involving children. All family members knew their obligation to her and honored the woman through whom they were all related.

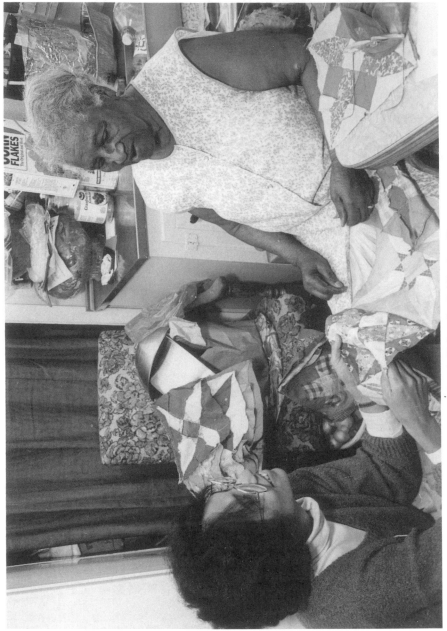

Great-grandma and woman visitor. Courtesy of Seattle University Publications Department.

Figure 13.1
Kinship Chart for Lottie Waters

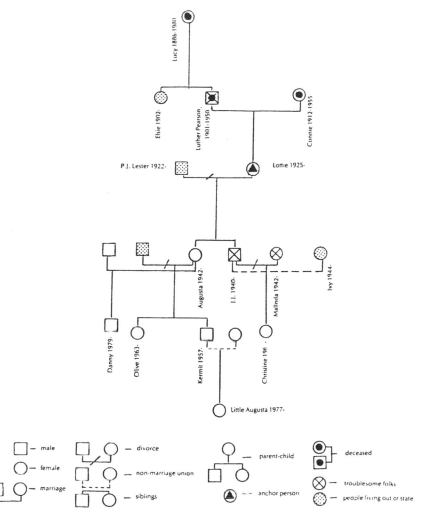

Lottie, the oldest, and her great-granddaughter, the youngest, were the center of attention on that day. Lottie says, "Had Grandma Lucy or Auntie Elsie been there they would have been honored with all manner of fine gifts."

Mrs. Waters is considered a wise woman because she has "raised" two generations and is raising a third. She was fortunate also to have two living generations above her. Those in the younger generations know that only such a wise person can recite a family history. Such a request is honored only when the "wise one" is ready. The task of keeping track of family ties is no easy matter. Wise women, like the griots of West Africa, train and practice this oral skill until they have mastered it. Recounting and reckoning family is still part of an enduring tradition.

The "wisest of wise" were those, like Lottie's ninety-three-year-old grandmother Lucy, who seldom but with great ceremony correct a "wise" one or who are used to legitimize a recitation. No one would dare question Grandma Lucy's description of Lottie's birth. Grandma Lucy saw the caul over Lottie's face at her birth.[1] This unusual circumstance is believed to be a sign of an exceptional child. It is only by Grandma Lucy's account that Lottie's unusual birth is legitimately documented. When Lottie is challenged on incidents in her recitation of the family history, Grandma Lucy with a simple gesture could acknowledge Lottie as a wise woman not to be questioned and scold the questioner for daring to challenge a wise woman.

The position of wise women is also seen in child raising. As one reads even fragments of Lottie's life history one notes that she talks about "havin' children," "raisin' children," and "keepin' children." Her distinctions have to do with giving birth, being a parent with the rights and responsibilities that accompany this and babysitting or temporarily taking care of children, which may be for extended periods of time. The relationship between children and adults or between adults is always clear to those involved. Thus, children can be biological or nonbiological. Because biological parents are not always mature enough to raise their own children, mature or "wise" women can parent or co-parent with biological parents. Thus, a child can be "recruited" into a family (La-Fargue 1981). This means a child might have several mothers and/or fathers. Terms of address and reference for all parents are the same. Lottie had five children; she "kept" many others, feeding and clothing them, and she raised her five plus the two who stayed for an extended period. Her experience with children means that as a grandmother she will be "wise." She will be sought for her wisdom and life experiences.

In analyzing Lottie Waters's account, the role of wise woman as nurturer and disciplinarian is seen. Wise women "keep" and "raise" children. They make a significant contribution to the family in this role both in teaching values to youngsters, as Elmer P. Martin and Joanne M. Martin (1978) suggest, and in freeing adults to concentrate on their occupational pursuits.

The wise are also the family historians, as E. Franklin Frazier (1939) found. Lottie fixes her place in the generations as Grandma Lucy's granddaughter and Kermit's grandmother. Her cultural identity as having reached the age of wisdom is secure. She is also the one to prove through the recitation of the family history that her daughter reached that stage with the birth of her son's child. However, Lottie says her mother never reached the "age of wisdom." Her mother is literally in the same generation as her great-great-grandchild, as neither has raised any children. Lottie can verify that others have reached the age of wisdom or can cast doubt on their life circumstances and retard, if not prevent, entry into that stage of life. She can do this because all important family matters such as parent-child relationships are brought to her. Her decisions are final: only a wise person in a generation above her can reverse her decisions. Older people in this community are vulnerable if they have not raised a child. They have no markers to show they are maturing. They are treated like young persons, who have not yet learned to act responsibly and be accountable for their actions.

Lottie Waters became, at age 32, what Burton and Bengtson (1985) call an "off-time" grandmother. But unlike the off-time grandmothers they discuss, she had a clear position in her family and clear functions to perform. Her fifty-five-year-old aunt and seventy-one-year-old grandmother mentored and prepared her for this role. Lottie's daughter expected her child's grandmother to be someone strong, independent and one whom she could count on for sage advice. The extended family supported Lottie with services, goods, love, status and information when she entered this phase of her life. Her family role was clear: she had achieved the status of wise woman. The only socially meaningful marker of time for Lottie is the passing of generations. She may become wiser with each generation, but it is never spoken of as "older." Grandma Lucy was grandmother to all generations except her children's. It was only when Grandma Lottie called Lucy "Grandma" that one had any inkling of Lottie's chronological age.

Children are highly valued by black families in general (Achenbrenner 1975; LaFargue 1981) and by the Waters kin group in particular. Not only do they demand cooperation from adults for their care and create the potential for increasing adult relationships, they also mark an adult's place in terms of which generation he or she belongs to. The family reunion stresses the relationship between generations with persons such as Lottie linking together the broader kin network. The relationship between child and grandparent forms the basic structure of the family. As Lottie says, "All those related to my grandbabies are my family, and they are welcome." The young parent generation knows that they depend on their children to establish their place in the family and on the wisdom of their parent to legitimize their place in the family. The greater the number of generations between the old and the young the more prestige the wise person is accorded.

RELIGION

The following data come from fieldwork with the Refuge Church of God in Christ. Members of this church refer to themselves as "Pentecostals, Holiness people, or Holy Rollers." The literature also refers to them as members of the Sanctified Church (Hurston 1983; Gilkes 1985). The Refuge Church is part of the larger Church of God in Christ, International. It is Pentecostal in nature because of the belief that the Holy Ghost resides in all believers. The outward sign of a believer is the ability to speak in tongues as occurred on the Day of

Pentecost. The church has a formal structure with traditional, gender-defined roles for its members, yet "it is well understood that men and women complement each other" (Curtis and Cyars n.d.:1).

In the church there are age-grades which cross-cut specific gender roles. For females, these are best exemplified in some of the auxiliaries of the Women's Department. They are: The Cradle Roll for newborns to age four, the Sunshine Band for ages five through twelve, Purity Classes for ages twelve through nineteen, the Young Women's Christian Council (YWCC) for nineteen to "indefinite," and the Church Mother's Board exclusively for wise women, with no specific age stated. The first three age-grades, for ages up to nineteen, are mixed girls and boys. The last two age-grades are sex-specific. The age range is not specified for the YWCC but includes the years of "college, marriage, and motherhood" (Curtis and Cyars n.d.:32). The Mother's Board is composed of women who have raised their children and have also shown a commitment to the church both in their participation in activities and financially. They are able and willing to assume leadership positions within the church organization. They have reached the age of wisdom.

The church uses a reference from Scripture as the basis of its definition of wise woman:

Let not a widow be taken into the number [of elders] under three-score years old, having been the wife of one man, well reported of for good works; if she have brought up children, if she have lodged strangers, if she have washed the saints' feet, if she have relieved the afflicted, if she have diligently followed every good work. (I Timothy 5:9–10)

This passage serves to legitimize women over 60 as "wise." It names the activities a wise woman should have engaged in and reflects values held high by the church.

Within the men's age-grade, "elder" is used to designate those men who have reached the age of wisdom. However, the church precludes the use of the word "elder" for women (Range 1973:159–160). "Mother" is the term of reference and address used for such women. One refers to a Mother by saying, for example, "Mother Gibson will lead the prayer group on Friday." Addressing her as "Mrs. Gibson" is a sign of disrespect or the mark of an outsider. A woman who is a member of the YWCC and a biological mother is referred to as a new or young mother and addressed as "Sister."

Age brings status, respect and prestige to women who have raised a child. Only Mothers teach and instruct and are "seasoned and well informed" (Curtis and Cyars n.d.:18). They understand their obligations to others. Mothers are in leadership positions within the Women's Department of the Church and have the ability to informally cross gender-role lines and influence the elders. Wise women in the Refuge Church of God in Christ are economically autonomous and are the main fund-raisers and contributors of the church. It is a combination of these factors plus Mothers' special knowledge about birth, their experience with illness and death and their strong faith that gives them their power. This is what makes them part of what Melvin D. Williams (1974) calls the elite group, a group in which gender lines are crossed. Among the Mothers, one is chosen to be the Mother of the Church. This Mother has the most experience, shows a deep commitment to the church, is of unquestionable faith, is well versed in the Bible and has alliances with many groups in the church. She is recommended by the Mother's Board to the pastor who appoints her Mother of the Church. This is a lifelong position and the highest one a woman can attain. Because of physical illness or inability to carry out her duties, the Mother of the Church may retire. However, she is still treated with utmost reverence.

The entire denomination stresses education. A Mother who is an educator with ''book learning,'' experience and oratory skills is highly regarded. The Church Mother is the only female sanctioned to teach from the pulpit. She takes the occasion to reinforce passages from the Bible, restate acceptable codes of behavior and remind the congregation of what it means to be a Mother. She usually ends her teaching on an inspirational note. The fourth Sunday of every month is Mother's Day, and the collection taken up at that service goes to her. In turn, she uses the money for her own ''necessities'' and distributes the rest to Mothers in key leadership positions for their work in the Department of Women.

One of the Refuge Church of God in Christ's most important units within the Department of Women is the Nurses' Unit. This unit is composed of women with certain characteristics. They are understanding people, have excellent communication skills, are experienced taking care of the ill, can work compassionately with alcohol- and drug-related problems (two areas the church has targeted) and have a strong religious faith. Most nurses are also Mothers. A license in nursing is needed by only one member to satisfy the legal requirement for giving medications.

Nurses ''serve at meetings, on trips, in the home, funerals or whatever and whenever there is a need for their service'' (Curtis and Cyars n.d.:33). This ability to move in and out of settings is permitted of only a few groups within the church.

For nurses in the Refuge Church of God in Christ, treatment is holistic. The areas of spiritual, mental and physical health spelled out in the *Official Manual with the Doctrines and Discipline of the Church of God in Christ* (Range 1973) overlap in actual practice. However, they are discrete conceptual categories that guide the nurse in her assessment and diagnosis of clients. The spiritual dimension is treated with prayer, scriptural reading and interpretations of biblical passages. The mental health dimension is treated with counseling, teaching and a recommitment to belief in God along with visible proof through practice. Giving up ''evil practices'' (such as smoking and dancing) and being able to have a positive self-regard and high self-esteem are important. The physical aspect is treated with herbs, ointments, teas and referral to professional medical help when necessary.

Among nurses there is a hierarchy. The younger nurses focus primarily on the physical aspects; then with experience and increased understanding of the Bible, they work with the mental and the spiritual problems of others. This latter area is dominated by nurses who are strong in faith and have much experience in successfully healing others. These are nurses who are also Mothers. Only they can care for persons "between," those who are vulnerable to being possessed by spirits or of having their spirits leave their bodies "between worlds." This can occur when a person is unconscious, dying, or during a seizure. At such a time a nurse-mother is needed to protect the ill. This is most clearly seen during the dying process.

During the course of my fieldwork, Mrs. Ella Wilcox, a ninety-eight-year-old retired Mother of the Church, died. Just before her death, the Mother of the Church called the head of the Nurses's Unit, a renowned nurse-mother in her mid-seventies, and asked her to be present when Mother Wilcox died. The nurse-mother was to make sure that the death was peaceful and that Mother's body, soul and spirit were one at the time of death.

In anticipation of her death no artificial orifices were to be made in her body. Mother Wilcox's body should be whole. The spirit is known to be able to leave a body of a sleeping or comatose person and wander around. At the time of death, to be whole means that the body, the soul and the spirit are together. Because Mother Wilcox was comatose and becoming increasingly weaker, several nurse-mothers kept vigil at her bedside. At times they cried and made noise to call the spirit back to the body should it have wandered off. At other times they were quiet and subdued so as not to call the spirit out of the body should it be in the body.

In analyzing perceptions of the elderly in this Pentecostal Church, it is necessary to understand the traditions that underlie the practices observable to the anthropologist. Such tradition is the belief in the wisdom of the ancestors and those who have lived experiences. There is also a belief in the need to keep separate the world of the spirits and the world of the living. Nurse-mothers carefully mediate between these two worlds.

The church reflects the community's values and its social structure. The Church Mother is the center of a redistribution system in which women pool resources and from which they receive material and social support. Such is the case when services were pooled during Mother Wilcox's death. Independent from the men, women have built their own social structure within the church. Elders and Mothers have complementary roles in the church. They are like fathers and mothers in families. They preside over religious celebrations which affirm life. Who better to give meaning to life than those who have reached the age of wisdom? For they know of what they speak when they celebrate life.

Church members respect their Mothers. Mothers are looked to for advice. Their knowledge of history, their lived experience and religious faith give them access to information others do not have. This is the source of their power. Although the Pentecostal Church has a clear and strong patriarchal structure, women have created an alternative structure which provides them with power and authority. Mothers in this religious setting are foremost spiritual role models. They are the powerful, capable women who can provide or mobilize both material and emotional support for persons in need. They are the teachers who endorse power through education. They are the nurses who combine healing with worship. Nurse-mothers simultaneously protect the dying and the living while managing the spirit and everyday worlds. They are among the most powerful and feared women in the church, for they walk between the sacred and the profane.

CONCLUSION

The age of wisdom is a venerated life stage in the black community I studied. I have drawn from both the family and religion to shed light on the meaning of "maturing" and "the wise" for this particular group. The women I have focused on are actively engaged in work which is essential to the continuation of the family and the church. Their wisdom, gained through lived experience, is both sought and respected by others.

Comparing the literature on elderly black women in the family and Lottie Waters, one notes that indeed marital status makes little difference. It is hardly mentioned in the Waters family. However, tracing relationships through children and imparting values to the young are seen as essential roles of a wise woman. Likewise, maintaining strong kinship ties is part of her role. Unlike the literature cited, Lottie's status is conferred by both preceding generations who know of her parenting ability and subsequent generations who establish her position within the family structure. For Lottie, there was minimal conflict in terms of role, despite her "off-time" entry into grandmotherhood. This may be due to the generational pattern of early motherhood followed by early grandmotherhood with the expectation that older women (Aunt Elsie and Grandma Lucy) provided guidance. As a grandmother, regardless of chronological age, Lottie is highly respected.

Comparing the literature on religion and the ethnographic data from the Refuge Church of God in Christ, it is evident that older women can find material and emotional support in the church. However, the data do not emphasize this. What is described are the services wise women contribute to the church and what they receive from the church, namely, material, emotional and spiritual support and information and advice. Specific details of these activities are sparse in the literature. Notwithstanding, the ethnography concurs with the literature when describing wise women who can and do receive prestige and power based on experience, knowledge and service separately from men in the Pentecostal Church.

Both in the family and in the church, experience, not chronological age, is considered the primary criterion for entry into the age of wisdom. For black women in the family this translates into raising a child who can make one's mother a grandmother. This value is also strong in the Refuge Church of God in Christ. However, there is the added dimension that wise women in the church must also possess profound religious faith and behave in the manner described in Scripture. Although this age is acknowledged to be 60, it is not by accident that the Church of God in Christ does not give an age range for members of the Mother's Board. Some women meet the criteria for entry into the Mother's Board before age 60. Therefore, members of this board range in age from mid-forties up. Nurses' ages vary widely. A few nurses are young mothers, members of the YWCC who have the gift of healing, highly developed interpersonal skills, and show a commitment to study church doctrine. These women are permitted to join the Nurses's Unit before they have entered "the age of wisdom." Most nurses, however, are wise women who belong to the Mother's Board and also have the gift to heal.

Aging connotes lived experience. In the family, moving from one generation to the next and raising a child are the experiences women must have in order to reach the age of wisdom. In the church these experiences, as well as being spirit-filled, monitoring life transitions (mainly birth and death) and teaching, are the primary routes to gaining experience and hence becoming a "Mother."

Neither in the family nor in the church do people refer to the elderly as "old." Whether a woman is 32 or 71, she can be described as single, a mother, a grandmother, healthy, disabled or ill but not "old." Old age for black women is a matter of the functions they carry out. For wise women in families this is creating relationships, teaching values and convening the family on certain occasions. In the church, Mothers are religious role models, they establish a system of support for women and children, mediate between the secular and sacred worlds when necessary and maintain independent but collaborative relationships with men in the church. Grandmothers in families and Mothers in churches are the women who have reached the age of wisdom.

This research gives voice to "older" black women born around 1925. They were having children before World War II, became grandparents in the 1950s and were considered "wise" before they turned 65 years old. The historical period in which they grew up was one of overt racial prejudice, idealized traditional European-American family values and segregation, which fostered ethnic communities. Much of the recent research on this population does not address these issues. Instead the research targets current health problems of older black Americans (Gibbs 1988; Edmonds 1990; Wood and Wan 1993; Davis and McGadney 1993; Kart 1993; Spence 1993). Much of this data come from large surveys (Barresi and Stull 1993; Jackson et al. 1988) which do not permit interviewees to choose those areas which concern them. However, more people are able to make their views known on a specific topic, and analysis has generated as many questions as answers. There is however, research on black families which discusses some of the same issues described in this chapter.

McAdoo's (1988) research concludes that support network involvement and kin-help exchange are not class related. The upward mobility of black individuals, she states, is "impossible without the support of the extended family" and is a necessary buffer in "countering the vulnerability of the Black middle class" (McAdoo 1988:166). The initiation of upward mobility and maintenance of black families in the middle class requires intense effort and extensive resources of family members. These resources in turn help to obtain professional training which leads to high-paying jobs and middle-class status. Without this family support, there is a likely decline in class status for families (McAdoo 1988). Billingsley agrees and contends that grandmothers are the backbone of the family support system, for they "provide a great deal of the child care, particularly for the increasing numbers of working mothers" (Billingsley 1990:106). The National Urban League's Black Pulse Survey also documents the "extensive mutual exchanges" among relatives (Hill et al. 1993).

In all three of these works, the sociological notion of class (lower, middle and upper) has a slightly different meaning for African Americans than it does for European Americans. However, as with the Waters family, the cultural construct of exchange, giving and receiving, is important for African Americans.

The black church represents one of the factors, internal to the African-American community, which has a direct impact on the African-American family according to a study by Robert Hill and his associates. Although they do not single out older African-American women, these researchers emphasize the importance of the church, finding that "the overwhelming majority of blacks have a positive attitude toward the black church" with 80 percent feeling that the church has helped the condition of African Americans (Hill et al. 1993:86).

Such research is compatible with the description of older women in the church described in this chapter. While the work by Hill and his associates points to the general themes of positive attitude, self-help in terms of social services for families and especially youth, this chapter describes a particular case to bring life to abstract notions.

Older women have an important role to play in these two institutions: family and church. They move beyond the potential constraints of class, money and blood relationships to reinforce cultural values of the importance of children, the significance of fictive kin, the problem of clinging to possessions and the wisdom derived from lived experience. Although today, some African Americans minimize the struggles they overcame to arrive at their current status, most, upon reflection, will admit that elderly black females in the family and church were key to their success.

Here the ethnographic data of anthropology helps to shed light on specific cases, while survey data used by sociologists situate the data in a larger framework. Both reveal data that are at the same time unique but complementary. When these approaches inform each other the result is better understanding of an issue. In this case, it is a better understanding of the elderly black woman at the level of the lived experience and from a societal viewpoint.

NOTE

1. A child is said to be born with a caul or veil if the amnion or inner membrane of the sac which contains the fetus and amniotic fluid does not rupture and covers the infant's head at birth.

CHAPTER 14

The Social and Cultural Context of Adaptive Aging by Southeast Asian Elders

Barbara W. K. Yee

Southeast Asian elders evacuated during the fall of Saigon in 1975, or who waited years in refugee camps before being reunited with their families in America, experience aging in stark contrast to their lifelong anticipation and positive expectations for the "Golden Years." These elderly Southeast Asians must cope with their rapidly acculturating younger family members, while taking on different roles and expectations in a confusing and often frightening culture that's divergent from and foreign to Southeast Asian cultures.

The social and cultural context of adaptive aging illustrates how universal features of growing older are woven into the rich cultural heritages that are colored by the unique life experiences of the Southeast Asian elderly (i.e., Vietnamese, Cambodian, Laotian, or the Hmong).

These various Southeast Asian groups differ dramatically by social class, Westernization, urbanization, and migration circumstances. Such differences among the ethnic groups that comprise the Southeast Asian population systematically influence adaptive aging. The Vietnamese population in the United States, for example, has been exposed to Westernization by the French and Catholicism (1857–1955) and then by Americans (during the Vietnam War). It appears that this Westernization was more readily adopted by the upper class and highly educated Vietnamese, as evidenced by their fluency with French and later English (Gold 1992). These Western cultural skills and willingness to adopt European and American culture makes the cultural transition to the United States less earth shattering (Portes and Rumbaut, 1990). Vietnamese evacuated prior to and during the fall of Saigon were more highly educated and Westernized than the Vietnamese who came in the late 1970s.

In mid-1975, the Pol Pot Khmer Rouge seized control of Cambodia. Out of a total population of 7 million people living in Cambodia, roughly 1 to 3 million died under the Khmer Rouge regime. They were executed, starved or died of diseases (Algin and Hood 1987). The major issue for many Cambodian people living in America is the cultural shock between traditional Cambodian and American cultures, coupled with extreme family losses and guilt experienced by survivors of the Khmer Rouge holocaust (Mollica et al. 1992). Cambodians and lowland Laotians are diverse in their urbanization, yet are less Westernized than the Vietnamese, with one-third being illiterate in their native languages (Le 1993). The Cambodian or Khmer people have strong cultural ties to Buddhism and this influences their aging.

The Hmong are an horticultural and fishing people who live as migratory tribal clans in the highlands of Southeast Asia. Those who settled in the United States are largely from Laos and the majority practice animism or ancestor worship. Large groups adopted Christianity after being resettled in the United States by church-sponsored resettlement agencies (Le 1993). These Hmong came to America to escape the wrath of communist governments because they helped the CIA during the Vietnam War and feared retaliation. The Hmong are the least Westernized of Southeast Asian populations discussed here and appear to have the most difficult adjustment to urban America (i.e., highest unemployment rates, poverty rates, illiteracy, poorer school performance). The Hmong had the lowest level of formal education in the homeland followed by Cambodian and Lao peoples (Portes and Rumbaut 1990). These rates of literacy in the homeland are inversely related to level of English-speaking ability and Westernization.

A LIFE SPAN DEVELOPMENTAL APPROACH

A life span development approach helps us understand the complex tapestry of factors that contribute to coping and adaptation by Southeast Asian elders living in Western societies (Yee forthcoming a). From this perspective, knowledge of a culture's *age-related* or *normative expectations* provides information about the cultural context in which Southeast Asian elders must adapt.

Personal characteristics could be adaptive tools such as English abilities, or hindrances to positive adaptation in old age such as cultural values, beliefs and behaviors that oppose those that are considered normative in the United States. Lifecourse issues such as life stage, age at immigration and acculturation opportunities all contribute to adjustment and aging of these migrants. For instance, migrating to America in your thirties and growing older here for twenty years prior to being designated ''old'' by society will have significantly different outcomes compared to migrating when you're already considered old. The former circumstance allows the individual to slowly adapt to American age norms and culture, while the latter case instantaneously puts the elderly Southeast Asian in a foreign environment and sets him or her up for culture shock (Yee 1989; 1992).

Personal history, or life experiences, systematically impacts survival skills and adaptation to American life in predictable ways. For instance, the high prevalence of Post-Traumatic Stress Disorder (PTSD) among these refugees is related to the horrors of war experienced during the Cambodian holocaust, or the rapes of Vietnamese women during pirates' attacks as their families attempted to escape persecution in small, leaky vessels (Abe, Zane and Chun 1994; Chester and Holtan 1992). The effects of PTSD can occur immediately or years after the traumatic event. Depression, anger, psychological and family conflict have been identified as major after-effects of PTSD among many Cambodians and other Southeast Asians exposed to extreme trauma (Mollica 1992; Westermeyer 1986). The current environmental context such as cultural and social supports, economic and social opportunities, as well as various stressors will have implications for adaptation and coping by Southeast Asian elders. All these factors contribute to a variety of adaptational and coping strategies adopted by them.

For Southeast Asian elderly, whose spheres of influence have shrunk after migrating to America, maintenance and reconstruction of the extended family is central to adaptive aging (Yee 1989). Cultural gaps between expectations and behaviors to carry out age, gender, work and family roles are the cause of much distress among Southeast Asian elders in this society.

A large majority of older Southeast Asian refugees migrated with their families or have joined their relatives through the family reunification program.[1] As a result, very few Southeast Asian elders have no relatives in the United States. However, the large extended family system that is normative in countries such as Vietnam has large holes in America as perceived by elderly in this country (Yee 1989, 1992). Family reunification is the major goal and focus of many Southeast Asian families, especially for family elders (Yee 1989; Gelfand and Yee 1992).

The purpose of this chapter is to examine the cultural transformation of the Southeast Asian family as seen from the perspective of the elderly generation. This story is only beginning to be told, but the elderly identify family changes in age and gender roles and intergenerational relationships after migration to be most important. Four case studies will be used to illustrate a variety of coping and adaptational strategies. These four cases were collected as examples for mental health crisis intervention workshops conducted by the author over the last twenty years.

AGE ROLES

A consideration of age-related or normative life expectations, and their social roles, is critical to our understanding of coping and adaptation by Southeast Asian elders. Attaining cross-cultural competence may require that people reorient timing of the stages in the life cycle. Many middle-aged Southeast Asians are surprised to find that they are not considered elderly by American society. For example, among traditional Hmong, a young grandparent at the age of 35, whose children were capable of taking over economic responsibility for the family, could retire. In the United States, age 35 would generally not be an acceptable time of life to retire (Yee 1992).

A factor shaping such age-role dilemmas in this country, especially for the more traditional members of these Southeast Asian groups, is the strong influence of Confucianism (Liem and Kehmeier 1979). According to Confucius, the Cult of Ancestors is demonstrated by filial piety and respect for family elders. Age roles within society and the family were hierarchical with strict rules for social interaction. The child was to have total obedience to the father and to venerate him, as was a woman to her father and then her husband. However, a major psychological discrepancy for Southeast Asian families is between the traditional roles of elders in their homeland versus those available to them in the United States (Weinstein-Shr and Henkin 1991).

Weinstein-Shr and Henkin (1991) also found that elderly Southeast Asians lack English-language skills and adequate knowledge of American culture. This decreases their credibility when advising younger family members about important decisions because they find it difficult to deal with the outside, English-speaking world. As younger family members take on primary roles as family interpreters and gatekeepers to and from American institutions, such as the school or legal system, elders lose some of their leadership roles in the eyes of the family and larger American society (Yee forthcoming a). The Southeast Asian elder becomes increasingly dependent upon younger family members for dealing with society and accessing basic survival needs.

Weinstein-Shr and Henkin (1991) further recognize that while Southeast Asian elders try to maintain their role as transmitters of traditional values and customs, grandchildren often reject their cultural heritage in order to lessen their conflicts during acculturation to American ways. The majority of Southeast Asian families are still struggling to survive in work and educational arenas in order to support dependent family members (Le 1993). This translates into very little time left over to show respect toward family elders in the traditional or expected manner (Detzner 1992). The negative consequences of such factors are seen in the tragic case of Mrs. Song and her family.

Mrs. Song: A Case of Negative Adaptation and Elder Abuse

Mrs. Song came to this country at the age of 63, from a Cambodian refugee camp, to be with her only living adult son and his family. Her son, his wife and her grandchildren had been in this country almost fifteen years. One grandson had been born in Cambodia and the other grandchildren were born in this country. Mrs. Song survived the Killing Fields and refugee camps for about ten years and came to this country expecting the streets to be lined with gold. She clearly had unrealistic expectations about life in America. Upon arrival, Mrs. Song discovered that she would not be living with her son and grandchildren. Her son had not been able to find work, and the family was surviving on welfare and living in a two-bedroom apartment. Mrs. Song was sent to live in another apartment by herself. Heated family discussions occurred over expectations that she provide child care and household tasks for her son's family, but was not welcome to live with them. Apparently, Mrs. Song's daughter-in-law did not accept Mrs. Song into her home because she had become accustomed to an independent lifestyle, free from the traditional Cambodian expectations of providing care to a live-in mother-in-law. Mrs. Song expected that her son would provide support until she died and was disturbed with her situation. Her depression and isolation deepened when she got into a fight with her 15-year-old, American-born granddaughter. The argument was over this girl's refusal to use respectful Cambodian terms with her elders and for not being obedient to her grandmother. Mrs. Song was upset with her son and his wife for not educating her grandchildren about filial piety and respect for their elders, and also not expressing their own filial piety by making arrangements so that she could live in their home. Mrs. Song contemplated suicide as the only solution to her situation. She was isolated in her apartment because there were no other persons who spoke Cambodian within walking distance and she feared leaving her residence due to the high crime in her area. Mrs. Song had a massive stroke, was hospitalized, but never recovered use of her entire right side and left leg. Her daughter-in-law, who was forced to care for Mrs. Song around the clock, deeply resented this caregiving responsibility. Mrs. Song was found dead with trauma to her head, and authorities charged her daughter-in-law with elder abuse. Although the case of Mrs. Song ended tragically, the Southeast Asian elderly can draw upon strengths from the culture of origin and provide cultural continuity from the past to the future in the new country.

Elderly Southeast Asians may provide child care assistance and perform household duties for their families (Detzner 1992), although they no longer can offer financial support, land or other material goods as they would have in their homelands. The refugee process strips away these elders' resources that are a source of high status and inheritance in the family. More importantly, the sage role of family elders is seldom available. Southeast Asian elders can no longer provide advice and lend their wisdom because it is derived from traditional culture, tied to the homeland, and not perceived by younger family members to be relevant to life in America. Older refugees find that they are increasingly dependent upon their children and grandchildren for help rather than the reverse (Lew 1991; see review in Yee 1995). This role reversal between the elder and young generation in family authority and access to cultural knowledge or to mainstream institutions has created numerous family conflicts in the Southeast Asian family and communities (Yee forthcoming b).

Research, however, shows an increased interest and appreciation of cultural roots during the late adolescent or young adult period by later generations of Asian Americans (see review in Kitano and Daniels 1988; and Sue and Sue 1990). A quest for one's cultural roots typically occurs during critical periods of the life span when a search for and consolidation of one's identity takes place. During this phase, the family elders may be called upon to help younger family members explore, discover and appreciate their cultural heritage and family history (Lynch, Detzner and Eicher 1995).

Mr. Anh: A Case of Positive Adaptation and Community Treasure

Mr. Anh, a former businessman turned General during the Vietnam War came to the United States during the fall of Saigon at 61 years of age. He was relocated to Fort Chaffee and was resettled by Catholic charities in a southern city in 1975. After working in grocery stores owned by those who helped resettle him in America, he pooled his money with other Vietnamese refugees to start his own Vietnamese grocery store. He was quite successful in his grocery store business and worked to help resettle other Vietnamese refugees who came after him. He enlisted the help of the mental health agencies in the city, and started a Vietnamese mutual aid society[2] to provide crisis intervention, vocational training and English as a second language with cultural orientation courses. This mutual aid society provided such innovative services for Southeast Asian refugees that agencies in other states invited him to provide training in their areas.

Mr. Anh retired from directing the Vietnamese mutual aid society at age 73, and moved to another city so that he and his wife could live with his son's family. Mr. Anh currently lives with his wife, son, daughter-in-law and grandchildren. In his retirement, Mr. Anh started a senior citizens' center with nutrition services; is editor of a Vietnamese-language newspaper; helps care for his grandchildren; and takes an active interest in the political activities in Vietnam. A major contributor to Mr. Anh's successful adaptation is his dedication to helping others cope with life in America. He believes this is best accomplished by maintaining some important aspects of Vietnamese culture, while encouraging youth to cultivate the tools that they need to survive and be successful in America.

INTERGENERATIONAL ROLES

T. V. Tran (1991) found that elderly refugees who lived within the nuclear or extended family had a better sense of social adjustment than those living outside the family context. However, when these elderly were living with their families in overcrowded conditions or with children under the age of sixteen, there was a negative impact on their quality of life. Heightened intergenerational conflicts arose because, living under the same roof, the least-acculturated grandparents and very Americanized grandchildren found daily opportunities to express their vast cultural differences. The cultural schism grows as grandchildren approach early adolescence, a time in the life cycle when aspects of the self, such as individualism and identity, begin to be systematically explored and expressed. This growing acculturation gap leads to greater conflicts between the generations and reduces elderly satisfaction with their new life, since general life satisfaction for Southeast Asian refugee elders is closely tied to satisfaction with family relationships (Yee forthcoming b). Older Southeast Asians have been shown to have poorer adjustment than their younger counterparts because elders experience greater losses and fewer gains after migrating to America than younger family members (Yee and Thu 1987).

In a recent study, Rick and Forward (1992) examined the relationship between the level of acculturation and perceived intergenerational differences among high school students from Hmong refugee families. Not surprisingly, these authors found that students perceived themselves to be more acculturated than their parents. Higher acculturation was associated with higher perceived intergenerational differences. Rick and Forward examined three specific values and behaviors concerning the elderly: consulting the elderly on life issues, taking care of the elderly, and respecting the elderly. They found that basic values concerning relationships with family elders may be quite resistant to change, but how these younger Southeast Asians express those values may shift. For instance, how one takes care of and respects the elderly may mean providing financial support, but not total obedience. Changes in values concerning decisions about the timing of marriage, ideal family size, place of residence or appropriate dress appear to be more readily adopted. Values supporting filial piety are maintained over generations, but what may shift is how cultural values are expressed and translated into actual behaviors.

Mr. Vang: A Case of Negative Adaptation and Shame

Mr. Vang was a sixty-year-old Hmong father who reacted with extraordinary violence to cultural clashes often experienced by many Southeast Asian families transplanted in Western countries. He felt disgraced over his seventeen-year-old daughter's failed marriage plans when her fiancé rejected her because she was too Americanized. It was her parents' duty to socialize her to be a proper Hmong wife and this rejection publicly shamed the family. Mr. Vang was very depressed by his life in America. He was particularly upset by the lack of Hmong cultural training displayed by his own children, still economically dependent on him, and by the financial difficulties his unemployment created for the household. As the elder male in the family, he was not able to fulfill his primary and most important role as breadwinner. He blamed his wife for not properly raising their children, who, like other young people in America, wanted to date and marry whomever they pleased rather than defer to their family's wishes. Mr. Vang hacked his fifty-four-year-old wife to death, sliced off another unmarried daughter's hand and then ended his misery. He committed suicide by plunging a knife into his own heart. In this case, cumulative stressors related to economic difficulties, cultural clashes over Hmong traditions regarding proper socialization of family members and the creation of public humiliation led to this tragic incident.

GENDER ROLES

Southeast Asian elders must cope with gender-role differences as practiced in the homeland versus the United States. Even before migration, traditional gender roles were changing in Southeast Asia as a result of the Vietnam War. Military-aged men were away fighting the war and their spouses were solely responsible for tasks normally divided along gender lines. Once they came to this country, changes in traditional gender roles sped up and became more dramatic. This was especially true for young adult and middle-aged Southeast Asian women, for whom there were more work opportunities. This was the case for these women because their employment expectations fit with the lower-status jobs that were among the few opportunities open to persons with little English skills or scant transferable educational credentials. Age bias against older men and women coupled with poor English skills created the situation in which few elders found gainful employment outside the home. Many middle-aged women and younger Southeast Asians of both genders became family breadwinners. This was a radical change from the traditional role of male elders as breadwinners of the family.

Mrs. Nguyen: A Positive Adaptation and Family Breadwinner

Mrs. Nguyen is a fifty-six-year-old Vietnamese female who came to the United States in 1976 at the age of 36. She was a former schoolteacher in Vietnam and was working as a legal secretary in America. Her husband worked as a volunteer and then obtained a job in a mutual aid society providing orientation classes. For about four years, Mrs. Nguyen was the sole breadwinner of her family, supporting her husband and two sons. She worked for about ten years in the office of a lawyer providing immigration and refugee legal services. While working as a legal secretary she became interested in going to law school and becoming a specialist in immigration law. Mrs. Nguyen and her husband supported both sons through undergraduate school and then law school. Once both sons were out of graduate school and established in their careers, Mrs. Nguyen went to law school at night. Eighteen years after coming from Vietnam, Mrs. Nguyen received her legal degree at the age of 54. She is currently practicing immigration law and assisting other refugees and immigrants. She looks back at her life and says that her success is attributable to her supportive family and especially her husband, who found ways to accommodate to her dreams. It appears that Mrs. Nguyen's successful adaptation to the second half of life was due to her determination to help others, an ability to successfully adapt to America by learning excellent English skills, and the support of her husband. He did not rigidly adhere to traditional Vietnamese spousal roles, but encouraged his wife to fulfill her career goals and acquire skills to help insure survival and the success of their family. Mr. Nguyen gave total support to his wife when he realized that he was not going to recapture his former status as a university professor in Vietnam, and that his wife would be able to more successfully support the family.

The literature on adaptation by refugee populations suggests that there may be a gender (by age or generation) difference in short-versus long-term adaptation (see review in Yee 1989). As compared to males, short-term adaptation to this country—which may be as long as fifteen years after migration—can be more positive for middle-aged and elderly Southeast Asian women. Several investigators have attributed this gender difference to a continuity of females' roles from the homeland to America (Yee 1989; Detzner 1992; Berresi 1991). Female refugee elders perform important but not necessarily honorific roles in the family, such as household tasks and child care. However, male Southeast Asian elders, especially older men, have less clear functional or high-status roles in the family in the new country. This latter pattern is especially evident for Cambodian men (Detzner 1992).

The ability of elder Southeast Asians to perform work roles outside the family also shows a gender-by-generation pattern (see review in Yee forthcoming a). There is an expansion of work roles for both young adults and young middle aged women, and this generalization is especially true for the Vietnamese group. The challenge is that these refugees must also take on roles and responsibilities they had not anticipated for this time of the life cycle.

By contrast, there is a constriction of work and family roles for older Southeast Asian men, especially those who had high-status educational and occupational roles in their home countries. Many also experience significant downward mobility. Migration has frequently created the permanent loss of high-status work, family and community roles. Their job skills may not easily be transferred to the United States, employers may be unwilling to employ an older worker, or their lack of English skills can form an insurmountable barrier to passing American credentialing tests (Yee forthcoming b). After struggling for many years, these elderly refugees may resign themselves to putting all their hope in the younger generation, and give the responsibility to achieve their lifelong goals to their children.

An extreme example of failed expectations is the situation of elderly Vietnamese males previously incarcerated in Vietnam. These prison detainees may be predicted to be at high risk for problematic adaptation to aging in the United States. Such elderly males have lived as long as twenty years apart from their families in Vietnam, and were reunited as part of negotiations with the United States in 1989. While they have spent these many years in Vietnamese jails, their wives and children have rapidly acculturated to American ways, and they may have idealized their former and future lives with their families. The nightmare of these Vietnamese detainees' family reunification process is reported anecdotally by organizations helping former prison detainees.[3]

The pattern for long-term adaptation of Southeast Asian elders is yet to be determined empirically, but there are indications that the long-term adaptation of females may not be as rosy. Middle-aged and elderly Southeast Asian women are integrated within the family in the short term. These women provide house-hold and child care services in order to free younger family members from these responsibilities so they can work one or two jobs and perhaps go to school to insure economic survival of the family. While these elderly refugee women are assisting younger members of the family to succeed in America, they themselves are isolated at home and not learning new language skills or crucial knowledge about American society (Tran 1988). After the family has passed through the stage of meeting basic survival needs, these elderly women may find that they are strangers in their own families and their new country. In other words, elders frequently lack the opportunities to experience exposure to American life that their adult children and grandchildren acquired in school and work settings (J. Anderson et al. 1993; Dinh, Sarason and Sarason 1994). Nevertheless, a recent study has shown that given the opportunity, even quite traditional Southeast Asian elders would adopt more Western help-seeking behaviors and acquire the skills necessary to successfully cope with aging in this country (Chung, Lin and Lin 1994).

SUMMARY AND CONCLUSIONS

Elders have a place and role in the Southeast Asian family. Yet the exact nature of these roles is evolving, and determined in a unique manner by which the elderly person adapts to his or her social and cultural context. Life offers both danger and opportunity. The cases of Mr. Anh and Mrs. Nguyen demon-strate that refugee experiences in middle age and old age can be turned into opportunities for growth and development during the later years. As illustrated by these two examples and supported by many other elderly who have suc-cessfully adapted to America, acculturation during old age does not mean totally giving up one's traditional culture, values and behaviors. Rather, being adaptive in the later years requires the ability to learn new things, compromise and adopt features of a new culture to enable elderly persons and their families to succeed.

The cases of Mrs. Song and Mr. Vang highlight instances of poor adjustment and even tragic response to the refugee experience in the United States. Common features of nonadaptive aging among Southeast Asian elders are fewer personal and social resources, rigid adherence to an idealized ancestral culture and the lack of flexibility when faced with changing cultural demands.

There are indications that elderly Southeast Asian females may experience increasing difficulty as their families become highly acculturated, yet they, while performing family obligations, remain extremely isolated from mainstream America (Yee forthcoming b; Lynch, Detzner and Eicher 1995). The high sui-cide rate among elderly Asian women, especially those who came here from China, is particularly noteworthy and provides a glimpse of what may lay ahead for older Southeast Asian women (Yu 1992).

The interaction of ethnicity, culture and aging is a dynamic process (Baressi 1992). It is *not* unidirectional and unidimensional, but is bidirectional and multidimensional. The migrant from another culture is touched and transformed by American culture although its extent varies across individuals and life contexts. Something not as well recognized, but necessarily true, is that the American culture is forever changed by its association with these new Americans. Our great nation has derived its strength, creativity and vision from contributions made by new Americans; let us not forget and appreciate this diversity.

NOTES

1. The refugee family reunification section of the immigration law allowed parents, siblings and children to join their family members in the United States. The numbers of immigrants coming from Southeast Asian countries were excluded from the caps mandated by Congress from this area of the globe. This in effect pulled about 800,000 Southeast Asians to the United States as refugees and later as immigrants (Le 1993). Immigration law and migration flows significantly influence the fabric of aging in America (Gelfand and Yee 1992).

2. A voluntary organization of refugees or immigrant individuals who help their compatriots through goods, services or loans (Khoa and Bui 1985).

3. These issues were discussed during the Hogg Foundation Refugee Mental Health conference in Dallas, Texas, 1991. Discussion highlighted the extremely unrealistic expectations held by Vietnamese prison detainees regarding their rosy futures in America. These prison detainees had idealized memories of their family members from the time of their incarceration. Unfortunately, twenty years may have passed and their families had acculturated to American ways. Wives were no longer young, obedient and dependent upon their husbands. Children were very distant because they didn't know their fathers. Children had developed American ways and suddenly, their fathers appeared, wanting to go back in time twenty years, to a different place. Family conflicts abounded.

CHAPTER 15

The Dynamics of Ethnic Identity and Bereavement among Older Widowers

Mark R. Luborsky and Robert L. Rubinstein

Ethnic identity exists within complex societies and at the boundaries between all societies. An ethnic identity, with its values, beliefs and behaviors, is often considered to be a subculture within a larger culture. A part of culture, it is a phenomenon that anthropologists have examined with increasing interest. But people and circumstances change over time. Elsewhere we suggest that ethnic identity be thought of as something with both "solid" and "fluid" properties (Luborsky and Rubinstein 1987). By this we mean that there is something ideally unchanging or irreducible about ethnic identity which gives it an enduring flavor of tradition; yet the experience of ethnic identity may change from situation to situation. So we see that ethnic identity is something that people can have to differing degrees. It is not fixed at birth but is sensitive to historic, social, personal and life span developmental events. We need to understand more about how individual and group conceptions of ethnic identity may change over time and how people use ethnicity to achieve a sense of continuity despite change (Gelfand 1994).

There is often confusion about the relationship between ethnic identity, religion and family life. In one view, the family is the focal point of ethnic identity, because it is within the family that ethnic values and behaviors are transmitted. We found, in addition, ethnicity may serve as a language or metaphor for family relations and processes. Ethnic background and religion are not always the same. In some cases, such as Judaism, religious and ethnic identities usually correspond, while for others, such as Catholicism, it may not. Ethnic meaning is complex and most appropriately explored using qualitative methods (Rubinstein 1992; Luborsky 1994b; Luborsky and Rubinstein 1995). Our view is that family life and religion are separate, important aspects of ethnic identity. Catholicism may be equally important to Poles, Italians and Irish, but each group has its own ways of observing the religious traditions and, for members of each, participation in religious activities may be an important expression of their distinct ethnic identities as well as religious beliefs. A notable misconception is that Euro-Americans are now ethnically undifferentiated or homogenized. As born out by the examples below (and many other studies) this is not so.

Social gerontologists and others who study old age find that ethnic identity is a key aspect of how we age (Gelfand and Barresi 1987; Hayes, Kalish and Guttman 1986; Stanford and Torres-Gil 1992). One difficulty in studying this issue, however, is that ethnic identity is built up from interwoven conscious and unconscious behaviors and beliefs. For example, a person may willfully behave in an ethnic way (by attending an ethnic festival), or may unconsciously behave ethnically, as when craving certain foods. Or an individual may consciously reject his or her ethnic group but unconsciously retain traditional attitudes. Despite these complexities, ethnicity clearly does account for a wide range of significant differences including: how people face pain (Zborowski 1969); ideas about illness and death (Suchman 1964; Kalish and Reynolds 1976); types of family relationships (Cohler and Grunebaum 1981); the context of life crises and ritual (Myerhoff 1978a, 1978b); alcohol consumption (Greeley et al. 1980); institutionalization (Markson 1979); and mental illness (Al-Issa 1982).

THE RESEARCH

The study described here concerns such questions about ethnic identity. We report on a project involving Irish, Jewish and Italian men (N = 45), age 65 and older, widowed two to eight years after a long term marriage. We questioned them about how they reorganized their lives after the early bereavement period, the first two years. The focus was on how they reformulated their sense of identity, on changes in health and activity patterns, ethnic identity and lingering attachment to the deceased spouse. One goal was to discover how ethnic identity shapes or is shaped by the bereavement experience. The focus on men permitted us to avoid confounding gender differences.

Loss—especially the death of a loved one—is one of the most significant and difficult experiences. Bereaved persons may pass through several experiential stages leading to some kind of acceptance and reorganization (Bowlby 1980). Often key to the recovery is a period in which some attachments to the deceased remain and are only gradually relinquished. Although a person may "recover" and return to an active life, ties to a deceased loved one are never fully let go. Further, American folk culture ranks the severity of losses relative to age and role. Deaths of youths are considered more serious than elderly; deaths of young spouses more serious than old ones. Yet this does not accord with the subjective reality of bereaved in which all losses are serious. For example, elder parents' death, considered a timely and normative loss, is often personally significant and deeply affects the survivors (Klapper et al. 1994; Rubinstein 1995a).

As we get older, loss becomes a part of the experience of life. The death of a spouse in late life is especially difficult, not merely for the emotional distress of the loss itself, but also for the social and psychological challenges it brings to the survivor to shape a new, whole life. Much research has been done on this topic. The areas most studied include the experience of widowhood for women (Lopata 1979), the first year or two of adjustment after the death of a spouse (Glick, Weiss and Parkes 1974; Parkes and Weiss 1983) and the question of whether men and women differ in how they react to their grief (Arens 1982; Berardo 1970; Gallagher et al. 1983). The focus on these topics is not surprising, since women tend to outlive men, the first two years may be most difficult, and because of deeply embedded gender differences in American culture. The topics of our study, the experiences of men and ethnic differences in long-term readjustment have received little study.

We selected the Irish, Italians, and Jews because of the lack of qualitative material on so-called white ethnics in later life and because of the large populations of these groups in urban areas in the United States, including Philadelphia. Today, many elders from these backgrounds are first- or second-generation immigrants. The countries from which these immigrants' ancestors hailed maintained distinctive cultural and religious traditions. Influenced by a new society and the rapid changes of American life, many customs and beliefs have disappeared. Others have disappeared for a time, only to resurface in new ways, while still others, both conscious and unconscious, were preserved or modified to fit with life as it is today.

Each of the three ethnic groups studied is distinctive. Some important features of Irish-American culture are the central role accorded to the church, the importance of verbal skills, a focus on propriety, a sense of suffering, emotional repression, the use of alcohol and a focus on death as a central life passage (McGoldrick, Pearce and Giordano 1982). Important features of Italian-American culture include a concern with keeping a tight-knit family life; an emphasis on sharing and eating food, and, the family as the unit which provides security, identity and affection; a focus on the expression of emotions and feelings; strong parental roles; and an emphasis on marriage as a central life passage (Rotunno and McGoldrick 1982; Johnson 1985). Important features of Jewish-American culture include the centrality of the family; an ethos of enduring hardships; a high value on intellectual achievement and learning; highlighting of verbal expressions of feelings; and a focus on life cycle events such as bris (circumcision) and Bar Mitzvah (ritual passage to manhood) (Herz and Rosen 1982). While on the surface some features, such as the central value of the family, may be equally important for all groups, there are deep differences in their cultural styles of conducting family relationships.

SOME CASE STUDIES

Here we discuss the role ethnic identity plays in overcoming a profound challenge to one's personal identity in later life, such as that occurring through loss. Our goal is to reveal the nature of ethnic identity and differences in later life and to show how they operate after a loss. Again, we need to note that adjustment to loss is complex, involving influences such as health, personality, opportunities, social support, the historical situation, in addition to ethnic style. We suggest, however, that ethnic identity, while often overlooked by researchers, can represent an individual's most central values and symbols and, as such, is especially worthy of examination in order to understand how people come to grips with change and maintain continuity of self despite change.

In order to encourage readers to build their own views of how ethnicity intertwines with other factors, we prepared three studies of how widowers from each ethnic group reacted to widowerhood. We describe a widower's background, the events of his wife's death and his reactions to it, and an account of ethnic identity as part of this. We show the diverse patterns of: experiencing the loss, reactions to widowerhood and the course of reorganizing a new life. Note, these cases were chosen to illustrate our findings about the contrasting cultural universe of shared meanings, heritages and experiences of each group (Luborsky and Rubinstein 1995), rather than to represent what is "typical" within each group.

Morris Stern: Case One

Morris Stern is a quiet, youthful seventy-nine-year-old man who lives alone. Married forty-three years, he has been a widower for five years. He worked in his family's wholesale business after college until retiring eight years ago. His children, grandchildren and siblings live near him.

Mr. Stern repeatedly described his life as "not over-exciting, but enjoyable." To learn what he saw as stages in his life, we asked, "If you wrote your autobiography, what would be the chapters?" (a task asked of each subject); he listed four chapters. First was "early days," consisting of close friends and school life. Second was college and a new circle of friends. Married life was the largest chapter he reported. The last chapter was the period of his wife's death and his retirement. They shared three years together after he retired. Of his current life, he noted, "I enjoy myself without a hectic existence."

His wife developed heart trouble four years before dying. Because her health declined slowly, few restrictions were imposed on their lives until her final year, when he took over all daily tasks. For some time he was able to care for her, and he felt that the time allowed him to prepare ahead for her death.

Mr. Stern, a Jew, said his parents emigrated from Poland to escape poverty and discrimination. Today, he belongs to a conservative temple and works as a volunteer delivering Kosher meals to homebound elderly. Most of his friends are Jewish and being Jewish is important to him. Key to his life now, his wife is credited with making him more aware of being Jewish. Together they regularly attended religious services and kept Sabbath observances at home. Her family was, in his eyes, "part of the Great Jewish Tradition."

Traditional mourning customs, which he followed scrupulously, included daily prayers and breakfast at a synagogue. This provided a daily structure to his life and helped him recover during the period of grief after her death. "It did me good to go daily to the synagogue to say prayers and to honor her memory," at a time during which he reported feeling despondent. One month is the traditional observance, but he attended both morning and evening services for eleven months. He also observed the tradition of shiva—a gathering of family and friends for seven days after a death—in the home of his son and said prayers with them daily for a month. "It was a big help because I was retired and there was nothing else to stop me from just sitting and moping." These practices let him meet others who were overcoming losses. It was also important to him to feel part of a community of observers. Thus, just as each chapter of his life featured a new circle of friends, so, too, did the bereavement period.

His difficulties in adjusting to her death included learning the daily tasks such as cooking, washing clothes. These were "low on my totem pole when she was here." He felt these difficulties despite her teaching him some skills the year before she died. Many friends told him he would remarry within one year, but he was not interested in dating. Another dimension of this period was a "great sense of uncertainty about what to expect next."

One year later, he said, he no longer lamented his fate and began to live again. "I surprised myself by taking it in the right light, taking things for what they are." He spoke of a transformation of his feelings about the loss. Formerly, he was preoccupied with "lamenting what might have been," but later came to accept and enjoy those people and activities still present. Part of this new perspective hinged on accepting that his wife was dead and would not return.

Mr. Stern's Jewish identity provided him with sources of continuity despite the loss, and a structure for daily life through customary mourning observances at the outset of widowerhood. His family was an important resource, "I had their cooperation, but never told them the big things, they were good to me." That is, he felt he never burdened them with his feelings of loneliness and depression but relied on their visits and sympathy for uplifts. Perhaps, more subtly, the religious observances his wife instilled led him to rekindle sentiments and her daily presence in a positive fashion. That is, by attending the funeral services and mourning practices in the months after she died, he not only honored her memory but also performed roles that relived experiences they shared when she was alive.

Horace McGraw: Case Two

Horace McGraw is a sixty-six-year-old Irish man, stout, and with a sharp brand of humor. He lives in a one-room apartment. Married for thirty years, but childless, he was bereaved six years ago.

Mr. McGraw left high school before graduating to begin a career of unskilled labor, mostly loading trucks. A heavy smoker and an alcoholic (not drinking now), he suffers health problems including emphysema, high blood pressure and diabetes. Today his social network consists of only three "others"; a sister, a niece and "TV, one of my best friends."

His parents came from Ireland. He grew up in a mostly Irish neighborhood. His family shopped only in stores run by Irish, and he got into "good fights" with Irish kids in the next parish after baseball games. He said his family "keeps up the old-fashioned stuff, speaking in heavy brogues," and traditions such as wakes. The family is mostly Catholic; Protestant converts are outcast members. That may represent tension between upwardly mobile Irish assuming positions once held by WASP elites and the mostly urban, middle-class and working-class Irish who retain positions traditionally held by immigrants.

In discussing his life as an autobiography, he labeled the final chapter of his wife's death and health and lifestyle changes as "my craziness." His wife died suddenly of a heart attack just after they returned home from shopping; she had been in good health. After her death he went unshaven and unwashed for many months, "lacking a purpose in life." To him, it was like "living in a dream," as it all seemed unreal. "It seemed like everything was closing in on me." He moved in with his sister, but he left as tensions with her husband grew. After the funeral he developed an alcohol dependence so severe that he lost his job, sold his home at a loss for drinking money, and alienated his friends. For a time, he feared having a nervous breakdown.

A typical day for him during this period included visiting his sister for two hours every morning. Then he went to a bar and stayed until closing time. Once home he was unable to sleep well and watched TV. He sold everything in order to have money for beer. He lost weight and had "an appetite only for beer." The drinking was self-destructive behavior, but it also was a mechanism for coping with pain and feelings of loss and, further, was perhaps a way to rekindle a sense of earlier family life and Irish traditions of "the old days" and the milieu in which he met his wife. In a sense, he also returned to some basic identities by drinking in the manner he believed people did in the past.

This bleak period ended with the help of a friend who helped him get treatment for alcoholism, and helped him get reinstated at work and in his union. Mr. McGraw stayed sober, and after two years of intense grief, began to put his life in order. The friend helped give him "a reason to live again," taking him fishing and doing things with him. Now, however, he was living in poverty, with only a small veteran's disability pension and without the house he and his wife shared for twenty years.

He not only stopped drinking, he "got religion" again. One day he met the local priest and asked to be allowed back in the church, because, he said, he was "afraid of dying," and also "needed to do something socially." Attending church, he believed, led him to "face the fact of her death and that nothing would bring her back." He came to believe that grieving "must be cut off, or like gangrene it will kill you."

"Getting religion" marked a period which he describes as one in which the grief is still with him but is not overwhelming. He is no longer self-destructive. He is still lonely and longs for his wife at times. He does not go often to the gravesite as he gets upset just thinking about her.

Vito Crazza: Case Three

Vito Crazza is a sixty-five-year-old Italian widower whose wife died six years ago. He lives in a very Italian, tight-knit, poor neighborhood, in the same row house in which he was born. His father died when the oldest of nine children was fifteen; some of his siblings were put up for adoption. As a child he worked with his family harvesting crops to earn money to heat the house. He worked a variety of jobs until, suffering an incapacitating injury, he opened and ran a small corner grocery store until a heart attack forced retirement.

He suffers from multiple health problems yet can perform all the daily tasks for himself. Having suffered many losses of friends and family, he is often depressed. While his remaining friends and family are very close at hand, he views himself today as isolated. He misses many lifelong ties and the Italian life of the past, recalled when he walks the neighborhood streets and sees many strangers and new stores. Being Italian is very important to him; most of his friends are Italian. He speaks what he calls ''an Americanized Italian.'' However, when his favorite sister, with whom he went to religious events, died, he ''gave up regular church and the Italian community stuff.''

He pools his monthly cash with a sister and her husband. He eats with them at their house, seldom cooking or eating in the house he shared with his wife. Yet despite, or perhaps because of ambivalence toward his wife, which he felt throughout their marriage, he now experiences a deep sense of longing for her.

The chapters of his life story concern ''day and night'' contrasts between the poor but happy and healthy childhood and today's sadder life with TV, telephones and adequate heat in winter. He often feels that the world is against him today, and all his friends and family are dead. Three years before his wife died they experienced marital strife, and he left to live with a sister two houses away. A severe heart problem led the family doctor to advise him to either move out or settle things with his wife. He reported that they always argued, but it grew very bitter in late life.

His wife underwent a double mastectomy and apparently recovered fully. Thereafter, while still living with his sister, he had ''started coming back to her.'' He intended this to mean that they were getting closer. Six months before her death his wife fell down the stairs and had surgery to repair a damaged vertebra, during which widespread cancer was discovered. She remained hospitalized and he was not told of the cancer, although other family members, he believes, knew of her dire condition. Two months before her death, their son finally told him. Still, the son would not let his father visit her. Mr. Crazza had to stay away because it was felt that if he visited her, she would know her death was near. It was deemed more important to keep a front of ''business as usual,'' although this was produced by unresolved conflict, rather than resolving existing conflicts. He did talk daily with her by phone, however.

When his wife died, new health problems emerged which he related to "nerves" caused by the stress of her death. Not unexpectedly, arranging the funeral and burial plot caused bitter family fights. She was buried in a Catholic cemetery with her family. He will not be buried with her, but rather with his oldest sister elsewhere. He reported being grief-stricken, depressed and remorseful at her death. It took six months to "get over the worst part," including his worries about a nervous breakdown. He emphasized how he tried to "make amends" before she died but never made things up to her.

Two months after her death, while passing by their house (vacant, because he felt he could not live there), he noted, "Finally I decided, it is my house," and his son and sister helped him move back. A typical day for him during this period consisted of visiting his diabetic sister, eating meals there, taking long walks and passing the evenings at home. He confided that Italian mourning customs prohibit "amusements" such as radio and television, but to escape his grief he watched TV with closed curtains so that no one could see the light.

Today, Mr. Crazza reports his feelings of grief and remorse continue unabated. The enduring sense of abandonment is sharpened by his bad health and loss of many friends and family with whom, as with his wife, he had conflictual relationships. He still has dreams of his wife in which they are fighting, and, he reported, in the mornings he fears going downstairs just as he did when living with her. At other times he awakens, believing that she is talking downstairs, and calls to her. He concludes that he feels worse now than when she was alive. Romanticizing about the past of a close Italian neighborhood, friendships, sharing meals and the presence of his wife, he states, "When she was alive I was making a decent living with the store and buying her stuff. It was good then. As kids, we told my mother, 'Do we gotta eat this crap macaroni again?' Now, we miss it and go to restaurants for it. Same with missing my wife. Living at home, I couldn't stand it. She nagged about all the little things, and with my heart condition, as well. But now I think back and miss it."

ETHNIC DIMENSIONS OF WIDOWERS' LIFE REORGANIZATIONS

Morris Stern, Horace McGraw, and Vito Crazza each faced the same objective event, the loss of a spouse after many years of marriage. While there were similarities among their reactions, there also were contrasts in their experiences and behaviors when constructing new lives as widowers. The three cases summarize the experiences of men of their ethnic groups and some of the areas in which ethnic identity enters into reorganization after a traumatic event such as a loss. These cases suggest that ethnicity is significant to bereavement life reorganizations in several ways.

Commonalities emerged among the men's widowerhoods, despite the specif-

ics of ethnic backgrounds. Most significant was that the wife's death left them
with a sense of social isolation and loss of a singularly important intimate con-
fidant. There was only some diminution in the sense of attachment to their wives
over time. That was coupled with a need to come to understand who one now
was in the world, the need to face later life alone, and a heightened concern for
a meaningful family life.

These findings are interesting in light of theories about recovery from grief.
Freud posited that recovery was marked by the replacement of the lost one with
another. Myerhoff (1978b), however, argued that for the elderly, recovery from
grief involves integrating memories and values of the deceased into current life,
not replacement. Our study supports Myerhoff's view.

The cases also showed an increased involvement with activities of earlier
family and locale which themselves may be infused with traditional ethnic sentiments and practices. Each man's distinctive heritage was a potential basis for
involvement in a community of spirit—both religious and cultural—and in social ties. The men may re-form parts of their identities around ethnic values and
themes; some are discussed below. Yet while such involvement fosters a new
life, there is also a sense of the possibility of reengagement with earlier life
patterns when each man was single and times were quite different. In one sense,
it is the fact of being single again that helps to rekindle memories of how things
used to be and forges unexpected continuities where a break existed while their
wives were alive.

What elements of reorganization does ethnicity provide for in a concrete way?
First, ethnic identity, itself, regardless of specific differences among the ethnic
groups discussed here, provides dimensions of continuity for facing a major
late-life disjunction such as widowerhood. The raw material for continuity is
provided by both conscious and unconscious ethnic behaviors and feelings that
may emerge in times of stress. From the array of raw material, each individual
selects those behaviors or feelings that suit his psychological and social needs
and creates new meanings, patterns of involvement and activities. Ethnic identity
thus provides a sense of continuity through both identification with and participation in (1) what are idealized as enduring traditional values, sentiments and
practices, and (2) guides as to what to do in times of stress. Ethnic identity may
be infused with early family values and activities. Refocusing on these can
provide a desired sense of rootedness in a time of turmoil. Such continuity was
clear for all three men described here. Thus, we see in the context of late life
and bereavement that the widowers draw on different elements of their ethnicity
to revitalize their lives, including religion, the parish and synagogue and family
traditions.

Those findings accord with Obeyesekere's (1982) view that commitment to
one's ethnic identity is reasserted when commitment to other identities has
weakened through social, local and individual lifetime changes. But note that
we also saw how revitalizing ethnic and family traditions also may awaken past
difficulties or old feelings of loss or anxiety about one's family or cultural

heritage. This was especially so for Mr. Crazza, for whom neighborhood change was utilized as a means of expressing his continuing sadness.

Contrasts emerged among the three ethnic groups in our study. Each, in a sense, conceived of different meanings for the loss, differences in the social contexts in which they remade significant relationships and experiences of the self, and notions of guidelines for bringing one's self back into some balance. We discuss this last point first.

Our study suggests that differences in ethnicity are associated with distinct styles of locating the disruption and differing notions of a proper state of "self." Widowers in each group described experiences of an "inner" and "outer" self in bereavement. They related that their inner, experiential, individual self was set off balance, but they appear to differ significantly in their notions of what dimensions went askew. Thus, the men share a concept of the desired emotional condition as one of "smoothness," or calm, and the less desired condition as one of "roughness," or turmoil. Yet the nuances of this self-appraisal appear to differ ethnically.

For example, Mr. McGraw reported bereavement created "craziness" inside him. He described acting out angry, wild inner emotions in a self-destructive way. He experienced a breakdown of his emotional balance and of his social life by becoming insensibly alcoholic and "irrationally" selling his home, losing his job, alienating friends and family and ending up in a slum. He lived out these "wild" inner states for several months until his behavior led to intercession by a friend and a priest whom he needed to help calm his turmoil. Today, he feels, as do the other Irish informants, his inner and outer life are again the desired "okay." Mr. Crazza, too, described how his wife's death gave him "nerves," how he feared "losing my mind." But, unlike his Irish counterpart, he struggled to keep a calm, smooth exterior and to adhere properly to daily life. Today he still expects to feel disruption and some craziness inside and continues to work to maintain a smooth exterior as is reported by the Italian widowers. In contrast, Mr. Stern did not describe or seem to manifest "craziness" in his inner or outer sense of self. At his wife's death, he grieved over her loss and felt desolate at being alone, but did not label the feelings of suffering as a kind of "crazy" inner feelings. He describes endeavoring to accept his pain and to present a calm inner and outer self, neither "lamenting" inside nor being irresponsible to his family or community.

Our findings are consistent with Lola Romanucci-Ross's (1982) portrait of traditional Italian perceptions of the individual as beset by a hostile world and urged to display proper behavior, a "business-as-usual attitude" by means of coercive public social pressure and shame. That contrasts with the coercion by guilt typical of the Jewish tradition. Further, we found many of the Italian men fought to keep the dying wife from learning of her exact condition; this also fits the beliefs Romanucci-Ross describes. One wonders if these prescriptions might hinder the resolution of grief, especially if there are ambivalences remaining, as in Mr. Crazza's case.

At this point, the power and limits of in-depth case approaches are apparent. We have discovered some key dimensions and processes of widowerhood experiences and life reorganizations. Our findings are general to the fifteen men from each ethnic group studied. But we are limited in generalizing from this data because of the scarcity of other data on widowers, as opposed to widows, and by our case study approach. Yet we have collected the kind of data, the subjective "emic" aspects of ethnicity, "dramatically needed" (DeVos 1982), since ethnicity cannot be defined by behavioral criteria alone.

It will be useful to speculate about other cultural differences emerging from our study. It appears that the Jewish men tend to express their loss in terms of separation from a valued companion, while Italian men mourn the loss of a dutiful wife, housemaker and moral center of the family. Further, it appears that Irish and Italian men, more than the Jewish men, may assume the wife's role in food and caregiving exchange networks. We speculate that this is a differential mechanism by which Irish and Italian, as opposed to Jewish men, work to rebuild for themselves the ties to community and family which their wives provided for them. These findings concur with Cohler and Lieberman (1980) who found high levels of life satisfaction and psychological functioning among elderly Italian and Irish men who were enmeshed in ethnic relations. Thus, the Italian men's ethnic heritage may predispose them to be more vulnerable than the Jewish men to the disruptions caused by the loss of a wife, since the spouse was a key link to that ethnic community.

We speculate further that ethnic identity shapes the overt behaviors of these three men and the other widowers, in terms of expressions of grief, mourning practices and, more unconsciously, regarding the patterns they follow—for example, in family relationships and food. These men also exemplify the situational and lifecourse fluidity of ethnicity in the recasting of female roles in the family to meet their needs. We found, as did Cool (1981) in her study of elderly Corsicans in Paris, that ethnicity may be a key source of continuity. We suggest again that revitalizing ethnic dimensions may lead to a reemergence of family tensions associated with that identity which Luborsky and Rubinstein (1987) and Ikels (1983) found among Chinese in Boston.

Our observations here pertain to Euro-American groups. Yet populations of many ethnic elders are increasing. Culturally sensitive psychosocial studies on the lives of minority elders are greatly needed. Little is known or published on the bereavement needs of ethnic elders. Data from the present study indicate direct mental health implications for health professionals. The findings suggest the need for culturally sensitive guidelines to use for making ethnically relevant professional evaluations of personal adjustment and recovery behaviors. Examples of these include the need for professional education about ethnic variation in the paths and the long-term traits of life reorganizations, or about the kind of loss perceived to one's whole way of life. The data also may aid informal supports by clarifying helpful and unhelpful support behaviors tailored to the ethnically expected outcomes of bereavement (Lehman et al. 1986).

We have discussed some of the ways that ethnic identity may be viewed as a fixed identity and set of traditions and also a fluid set of vital new meanings which, according to each person's background, shape the experience of bereavement and the rebuilding of life afterwards.

NOTE

The data described in this chapter were collected in a research project entitled "Ethnicity and Life Reorganization by Elderly Widowers," supported by the National Institute on Aging. We wish here to express our gratitude to NIA for its continued support of our research.

PART V

Networks and Community: Environments for Aging

After they married, thirty-five-year-old Slobodan and his wife moved into the small house of his parents near the center of Belgrade, the capital city of Yugoslavia. When the younger couple started having children they began taking over more of the limited space in the dwelling. By the time Slobodan's wife had their third child, his mother was dead and his seventy-four-year-old father, Zvonko, was becoming frail. Slobodan requested that his father give up his larger bedroom to him and his wife. As his children grew, Slobodan haphazardly built a tiny room onto the house and "encouraged" the father to move into this new space, which he did. Eventually, although he was still able to take care of himself, Zvonko was asked by the son to move into a large, new residential complex for pensioners on the outskirts of the city. Two years later, the father died. A month later, Slobodan received a call from the director of the residence for the elderly, asking when he and his family were moving out of the house. Puzzled, Slobodan inquired why the director should ask such a crazy question. He was then informed that Zvonko had been *so* appreciative of how he was treated at the residence that he had deeded his house to the facility for its use.

Story told to Jay Sokolovsky while studying
residential homes for the elderly in Yugoslavia

It was intriguing to hear this story in a country whose constitution mandates care of the elderly by their children. Interestingly enough, similar tales can be found in such divergent places as Japan and among the pygmy hunter/gatherers of the Ituri forest in Zaire. As was also seen for the Ju/'hoansi in Chapter 2, such stories act as powerful narratives of caution. They forecast what can happen if the traditional system does not perform as it should. Part of the aversion to special old-age residential settings in Eastern Europe is a historical comparison of public homes for the elderly to harsh dumping grounds of last resort for the economically dispossessed, the mentally ill and the frail aged.

Still, today, in many countries it is difficult for the populace to cognitively distinguish between age-homogeneous communities of the independent elderly and the variety of long-term care facilities for the very dependent aged. One could briefly cite the example of the nation of Croatia (formerly part of Yugoslavia), which has perhaps the oldest such residence in Europe, built in the seaside city of Dubrovnik in the mid-fourteenth century. In 1981, when I first developed an interest in the issue of nonfamilial environments for the elderly in Croatia's capital, Zagreb, scholars in the United States advised me not to bother. I was told that there was so little interest in homes for the aged that most of the rooms had to be rented out to students or tourists. This was no longer the case in 1983, however, when I found that each of the nine *Dom Umirovljeni* (home for retired persons) in the city was filled to capacity with *local elders*, and some had waiting lists of over one year (Sokolovsky, Sosic and Pavlekovic 1991). I found that, in general, the public was horrified at the thought of such places. Ironically, however, the residents themselves, like the man in the story above, thought such residences were wonderful places and they often felt fortunate to be there. My research showed that the elders in these facilities typically had very few living, close kin. They saw the *Dom* as a vital resource for their survival in late life.

Countries such as Croatia find themselves, along with older Western nations, confronting a true age of aging. Typically, 80 percent of populations born in industrial countries now survive to age 65, and huge masses of people are beginning to experience upwards of two decades of postparental and postemployment life. Throughout such nations, a multitude of attempts are underway to provide some shape and culturally valid meaning to this last phase of active adulthood. These efforts range from numerous social and political movements such as the Gray Panthers in the United States, to a myriad of new residential schemes, care settings and activity centers. As noted here and in Part III, this endeavor also includes the creation of constitutionally imbedded principles for maximizing the potential of the aged in countries such as Sweden and Denmark.

SOCIAL NETWORKS AND SOCIAL SUPPORT SYSTEMS

Despite the proliferation of formal caregiving organizations and specialized personnel oriented toward senior citizens, growing attention has focused on the existence of "natural" support systems, *generated by the elderly themselves* (Chappell 1995). In seeking to understand the importance of informal social ties in meeting the needs of the elderly, one level of analysis has concentrated on the study of "social networks"—ego-centered sets of personal links and their interconnections generated among friends, kin and neighbors (Sokolovsky 1986; Antonucci and Akiyama 1995). Network analysis has been particularly useful

for studying urban settings where social action is not readily understood within
the context of formal institutional structures such as the totemic clans of the
Tiwi or East African age-sets. An excellent example is Sally Merry's study of
the elderly living in a multiethnic housing complex, set in a high crime, urban
area of Massachusetts. This work shows how the lines of informal ethnic networks shape and create perceived spacial zones of "danger"—sometimes erroneously—in a dense city environment (Merry 1996).

The use of social networks to study the life of the elderly and to examine
their place in varying social systems has flourished over the last two decades
(Wenger 1996). This research has provided a natural connection to the theoretical models of "disengagement," "activity" and "exchange," which sought to
account for the patterns by which older adults construct a social world and
transform it in relation to the demands of aging (Lee 1985). Each model has
been used to try to predict how patterns of personal social engagement would
relate to operationalized measures of well-being, life satisfaction or morale.

As noted in the discussion of family interaction (see Part II), network studies
have shown that as people age in industrial societies they are not as isolated as
previously suspected, at least in terms of frequency of contact and the exchange
of some practical resources (Knipscheer et al. 1995). As we saw in Part IV, this
is particularly the case within strong ethnic areas in such nations (Barker, Morrow and Mitteness forthcoming).[1] One of the few cross-cultural studies, in rural
Kentucky and India, of the extent of elders' networks showed very consistent
network sizes from early adulthood through age 75, with only a moderate decrease past that age (van Willigen, Chadha and Kedia 1995). A very interesting
component of this study was that among Hindu elders studied in India, precious
few followed the culturally prescribed disengagement from worldly attachments
during *samnyasa*, the last life stage.[2]

Ironically, while measures of informal social interaction have been viewed as
crucial in gerontological theory and research, too many studies have failed to
examine the qualitative characteristics and cultural meaning that social networks
hold for the elderly. For example, survey studies of aged living in single-room
occupancy (SRO) hotels in the central core of older U.S. cities often depicted
these individuals as totally isolated and incapable of replenishing an impoverished repertoire of social ties (Stephens 1976). However, my own research with
community psychiatrist Carl Cohen in New York City SROs showed that elderly
living there were far from true isolates—only about 5 percent fit this description.
Rather, we showed that the cultural construction of their networks was different
from middle-class elderly patterns and was generated through three network
features: structural dispersion, highly selective intimacy and variable activation
of social ties. We found that many of these elderly described themselves as
"loners." However, this was typically a self-identification which enhanced local
perception of their independence. It combined with their small but active social
networks to connect them to their urban environment in a culturally meaningful
way (Sokolovsky and Cohen 1987).[3]

A central issue related to social support systems among the elderly is the degree to which the development and expansion of formal supports would impede the caring behavior of kin, friends and others—that is, informal caring (Krause and Borawski-Clark 1994). The evidence from the United States to date strongly shows that the infusion of formal services for older citizens does not substitute for informal ones, except on the periphery of an elder person's social network.[4]

As we will see in Part VI, this is particularly critical in understanding how families cope with long-term care of their senior members. A recent analysis of this issue by Myers and Agree shows the importance of informal support for the disabled elderly (Myers and Agree 1994). Using Figure V.1 they show that for those with minor impairment in activities of daily living (1 ADL), 80 percent of the support network was exclusively informal. At maximum impairment levels (5–6 ADLs), such as those with advanced dementia, the figure for exclusive informal support dropped but remained high at 60 percent of the sample.[5] This analysis, based on the 1982 U.S. National Long-Term Care Survey, also found that a mix of helpers [referring to informal and formal networks] appear to provide better, or at least more extensive, long-term care. Their conclusions back up my analysis of ethnic, family support systems in Part IV. Myers and Agree note: "Disabled elderly with both informal and formal helpers received more help more frequently than others at all levels of disability. . . . If mixed networks can provide greater amounts of care, then family care alone may not necessarily be the 'best' form of long-term care for an older individual with multiple functional deficits" (1994:17).

SUPPORT SYSTEMS AND THE RURAL ELDERLY

While network studies of the elderly have most often focused on urban areas, there is a growing recognition that the rural aged may have as many problems in generating adequate support systems as their city-dwelling peers (McCulloch 1995; Wenger 1995).[6] In the United States an increased concern has centered around the collapse of many local rural economies in the 1980s and the out-migration of the younger members of family networks (Coward, Lee, Dwer and Seccombe 1993). More recently, certain areas have also suffered the disintegration of rural health systems (McCulloch and Rowles 1993). This has placed a greater burden on providing formal services in a cultural context where personal, informal networks are often preferred as a way of getting by (van Willigan 1989). Chapter 16 puts this issue in comparative perspective by examining the support systems of older women in rural Minnesota and Denmark. While the women studied by Dena Shenk and Kitter Christiansen shared a strong attachment to the physical and social aspects of their locales, they also had a clear desire for personal autonomy. However, how this independence was constructed in each society was quite different. Older Danish women saw their autonomy as tied to professional service providers who could reduce their dependence on

Figure V.1
Source of Long-Term Care by Disability Level: United States, 1982

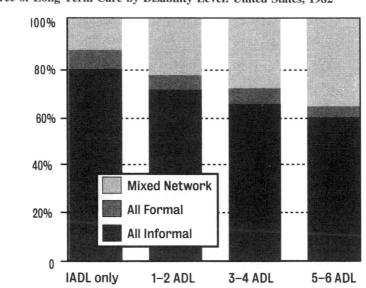

Source: Myers and Agree 1994.

kin and close friends. The women in Minnesota, in strong contrast, saw their independence as linked to an avoidance of formal services. This article also demonstrates the importance of examining how different parts of support systems fit together in varied cultural circumstances.[7]

THE AGED AS SOCIAL PIONEERS

One of the potentials of a network perspective on social life is to show its connection to community organization. This has increasingly loomed as a controversial topic because, following World War II, most industrial societies began developing new types of noncustodial residential environments for the elderly (Stroud 1995). Otto von Mering and Lauric Neff link the rise of a substantial number of "fourth age" persons, past age 75, as the stimulus for the creation not only of a multitude of new domestic arrangements involving unrelated persons, but also utopian communities focused on the needs of people in their seventh or eighth decades of life. They suggest, for example, that "Life Care Communities" will become a major option for middle-class elders seeking alternatives to "frailing" into a nursing home (1993).[8]

By the early 1960s sociologists such as Arnold Rose (1962) were already predicting the emergence of a distinct elderly subculture with a new status system predicated on health and activity levels. This was to be based on a growing age consciousness and a segregation of the elderly from younger people. At the time, it was generally perceived that living in environments such as retirement homes, which enforced a separation of the generations on a daily basis, would result in a decreased quality of life compared to life in "natural" communities. For example, anthropologists George Foster and Barbara Anderson, while admitting that such environments can provide the basis for a healthy self-image and insulate against disquieting societal change, argue that such communities also represent an "escape the system" model of adaptation that operates by ignoring old age and emphasizing a cult of pseudoactivity (1978:294). This is contrasted with what they feel is a more positive, "confront the system" model, one that emphasizes accomplishing a variety of adaptive tasks in response to life in "real" age-heterogeneous communities.[9] Yet, accommodating to growing old is not merely a matter of personal adjustment; it is strongly influenced by the organization of the broader society in which people are embedded.

Gerontological research has usually shown that extreme age density as a community feature did not automatically mandate alienation and social oblivion. This was initially demonstrated by Irve Rosow's (1967) study of Cleveland city housing projects where the aged lived in buildings with a wide range of age distributions. His findings showed that the elderly living in buildings with the highest levels of age-peers possessed the best morale, largest number of friends and the highest level of social integration. Particularly in terms of social interaction, anthropological studies in a wide variety of age-segregated environments in Great Britain, France and the United States have generally corroborated Rosow's findings (Keith 1982, 1994; Lawton, Moss and Moles 1984). It is in such public housing, mobile home parks, RV encampments and private retirement communities that an ethnographic approach to aging has been most frequently used (see Silverman 1987; Rhoads and Holmes 1995: 125–144 for a good summary of this research).[10] These new environments in which aging takes place can also include clubs, day centers, senior centers and even "Universities of the Third Age" (Cuellar 1978; Hazan 1980, 1996; Okley 1990; Jerrome 1988, 1992). Their importance in helping people construct a meaningful old age is just being recognized (see Pratt 1995 for an international perspective).

Dorothy Jerrome, based on her studies of clubs for working-class elderly in England, contends that such organizations provide advantages to their members versus their nonjoiner aged peers (1992). She argues that such groups help the aged positively deal with late-life losses by stimulating social integration, generational consciousness and appropriate contexts for friendship.[11]

Like Great Britain, America since its inception has been known for the tendency of its citizens to join a wide variety of voluntary associations. In the United States, senior centers first developed in the 1940s but were an outgrowth of senior clubs dating to the late nineteenth century. By the 1990s an estimated 10,000 senior centers were in operation, providing a wide range of health, social, recreational and educational services for older citizens (Krout 1994, 1995). The

Older Americans Act of 1965 targeted senior centers to serve as community focal points for comprehensive service coordination and delivery at the local level. However, the qualitative studies done in such environments find that it is the stimulation of informal, personal networks which is of special interest to the participants. Such is the case in Chapter 17 on the Lake District Senior Center, by Japanese anthropologist Yohko Tsuji. Her work provides a noteworthy contrast to the ethnically homogeneous center studied by Myerhoff in California (1978). Through the actions of its diverse participants, we learn how they have used key tenets of American culture to shape the social order of the center into a vibrant organization which adds special meaning to their lives.

As seen in Box 4, culturally distinct senior centers are slowly being created in the non-Western world. In the case of Thailand, such places help compensate for the gaps in family and societal support created by the very rapid aging of that country's population.

BOX 4. THAILAND'S SENIOR CENTERS RELY ON TRADITION AND TRENDS: NUT PASTE AND NUTRITION ADVICE

Thailand's burgeoning aging population, which now makes up 11 percent of the nation's total, has an enormous need for basic and preventive health and social services, and few senior centers to provide them. The centers that do exist fulfill their mission with a holistic approach to health care relying heavily on traditional Asian health practices.

The 50 or 60 clients at Din Daeng Center for the Elderly in Bangkok start their morning as early as 7 A.M. with an hour of Tai Chi, an ancient Chinese exercise made up of flowing movement that Western researchers have begun to hail for its contribution to improved balance and circulation. Physical therapists are available at Din Daeng to work with those whose mobility is impaired by arthritis, a broken hip, or a stroke.

Trained nurses visit the center two days a week to discuss disease prevention, family problems, and nutrition. They serve clients herbal tea and traditional Thai nut paste while assessing needs for additional services such as counseling or home help.

Now in its tenth year of operation, Din Daeng is one of only nine such centers in Thailand and one of only three in Bangkok, population six million. The center offers temporary emergency housing along with food and clothing for up to 15 days. Clients who cannot return home are referred to one of Bangkok's two residences for older persons.

Thailand's older population is increasingly visible and needy in the nation's rural areas, where grandparents often represent the sole caretakers of young grandchildren whose parents have migrated to urban areas in search of better incomes offered by Thailand's rapidly growing economy. The resentment that grows from assuming such late-life responsibility has generally been offset by financial aid,

continued

which may be disappearing as the country's AIDS epidemic spreads among working age adults.

Reprinted with permission and excerpted from *Global Aging Report* 1(3) (1996): 3.

COMMUNITY AND SUCCESSFUL AGING

One of the salient issues emerging from the study of such new modes of organization is how the variable nature of community organization relates to well-being in old age. A good example is provided in Maria Vesperi's book *City of Green Benches* (1985) about St. Petersburg, Florida. Local leaders, in an attempt to change their city's image as "God's waiting room," undertook a revitalization plan which included the removal of the numerous green benches on commercial streets and the tearing down of old residential hotels and small stores along downtown side streets. These were the key sites where elderly residents had generated their own very active and supportive social life. However, some partial compensations did develop. As housing and amenities declined and the remaining population continued to age in place, congregate dining sites, adult day care and a variety of other community-based opportunities for social integration began to increase.[12]

Clearly, community change and urbanization can have a complex impact on how the elderly perceive their local environment as a resource. This is the subject of Chapter 18, on the transformation of an Irish town in the shadow of urban Dublin. Blessington, the site of Jeanette Dickerson-Putman's research, was one of the communities in Project AGE discussed in Part I. This area has undergone changes which are becoming familiar to many North American towns—a rapid influx of young adult urbanites with cultural interests and social connections not rooted in their new residential setting. At the same time, increased support from the Irish state in the form of pensions, medical care and grants for a local Senior Citizens' Committee have provided a level of physical security that is higher than in "the good old days." Yet the influx of "blowins" from the city transformed the makeup of local organization enough that many elderly have removed themselves to the margins of community life.

AGING AND HOMELESSNESS

The last short readings in Part V are both drawn from ethnographic research I conducted among older homeless and marginally housed older adults in New York City. Chapters 19 and 20 are intended to provide readers with a feeling for how elders experience aging under very difficult conditions. Despite the growing number of residential options that are becoming available for the middle-class elderly, it is difficult to stroll along the streets of urban America without seeing the devastating effects on the elderly poor of a radical shift in federal government housing policy and funding begun during the 1980s. As the Coalition for the Homeless has demonstrated in its book *Crowded Out: Homeless-*

ness and the Elderly Poor in New York City (1984), the catastrophe of homelessness has a special meaning for the urban aged (see also Ladner 1992). The combined effects of a virtual abandonment of subsidized housing by the federal government and the actual destruction of a large percentage of low-cost housing stock deprived hundreds of thousands of older adults across the nation of a regular domicile (Christopher and Inui 1993; Rich, Rich and Mullins 1995; C. Cohen 1996a). While many other industrial nations have also seen homelessness increase among their elderly, the United States stands out for the continuing increase in its undomiciled, despite the substantial levels of economic growth and stock market increases over the past decade (for a comparative perspective, see Crane 1994; Lipmann 1995; Cohen and Crane 1996).

The authors of the selection on older homeless men, myself and psychiatrist Carl Cohen, have been studying the inner-city, poor elderly for two decades. In 1975, when we began this research in the single-room occupancy (SRO) hotels of Manhattan, there were over 50,000 rooms available in all five boroughs. About 15 percent were used by older adults, who typically had lived there at least a decade. While some of the SRO hotels we studied in the mid-1970s were dangerous, inadequate places to live, our research demonstrated that these environments, for the most part, provided affordable living quarters where most elderly were able to develop supportive, although small, social networks (Sokolovsky and Cohen 1981, 1987). Only six years later, almost two-thirds of the rooms had been gutted in a gentrification frenzy which was nearly matched nationwide, where about one-half of such housing was lost (Hopper and Hamburg 1984). In essence, the poor, including numerous aged, had been deprived of adequate shelter for the sake of subsidizing condominiums for the rich.

It is little wonder that in the mid-1980s a U.S. government report indicated that 38 percent of people seeking public shelter had been evicted from their prior dwellings (1984 U.S. Department of Housing and Urban Development). The past decade saw a dramatic reduction of new public housing construction and an inadequate supply of apartments eligible for federally supported Section 8 rent subsidies.[13] For example, Keigher and Pratt noted that in the beginning of the 1990s there was an average of six Section 8 housing units available for every 1,000 elderly persons, and in large cities, there were more than eleven applicants for every vacant unit in federally backed Section 202 senior housing (Keigher and Pratt 1991). This substantial lack of affordable housing options has occurred at a time when the woefully inadequate shelters are already overflowing with younger, poor, alienated and sometimes mentally ill homeless who cause the elderly to flee for their very lives. This has put a special stress on older, homeless women, who represent an extreme example of powerlessness and destitution (Roth 1982; Makiesky-Barrow and Lovell 1987; Golden 1992; Cohen et al. 1997).

Chapters 19 and 20 are based on separate, multiyear research projects with older homeless men and women, funded by the National Institute of Mental Health.[14] Conducted during the mid-1980s and early 1990s, these studies gathered intensive interviews with 281 males and 237 females over age 50 who were homeless or near homeless. This was combined with my ethnographic examination of the lifestyles of a smaller number of these individuals. Data from this research were instrumental in helping create a successful intervention program for older homeless men called "Project Rescue" (Cohen, Onserud and Monaco 1992). In Chapter 19, on homeless men, the authors draw upon these qualitative data to let the lives of three older men speak for themselves in showing the reality of being old, poor and homeless in America. This is followed by an edited portion of an interview I conducted early in my fieldwork on the "Older Homeless Women" project.

KEY RESOURCES

Centers

National Resource Center on Rural Elderly, University of Missouri-Kansas City. 5245 Rockhill Rd., Kansas City, MO 64110–2499. Phone (816) 239–1024.

The Center on Aging and Health in Rural America. The Pennsylvania State University, 601 Oswald Tower, University Park, PA 16802–6211. Phone (814) 863–2938. E-mail: hayward@pop.psu.edu. Web site: http://www.pop.psu.edu/about-us/cahra. html.

The National Eldercare Institute on Housing and Supportive Services. Established as a public-private consortium of the Andrus Gerontology Center of the University of Southern California, the National Association of Area Agencies on Aging and the Federal National Mortgage Association (Fannie Mae) to increase the availability and utilization of housing and supportive service programs. A list of their reports, seldom found in other places, can be found at the following web site: http://www.fedworld.gov/ntis/health/3he61512.htm.

Internet Resources

(1) http://www2.ageinfo.org/naicweb/data.html. This site allows you to view and print out selected statistical tables on population and housing patterns of older Americans based on the 1990 census.

(2) http://www.ksu.edu/cfa/policy_center.html. National Resource and Policy Center on Rural Long-Term Care.

(3) http://www.rurdev.usda.gov/ideas/idea_menu.html. Under the "Aging" section of this site there are descriptions of workable project ideas to reach the rural elderly.

(4) http://www.aahsa.org/. The American Association of Homes and Services for the Aging. Its home page has links to information on continuing care retirement communities and many types of not-for-profit organizations which provide housing, health care and services to the nation's elderly.

(5) The Rural Resource. This is a dial-up bulletin board developed for the rural aging network and funded by the Administration on Aging and the National Association of Area Agencies on Aging. It is operated by the National Resource and Policy Center on Rural Long-Term Care at the Kansas State University Center on Aging.

To connect, dial (via your modem) either: 1800903LINK or 1800903NEWS (8 bits, no parity, 1 stop bit).

Print Resources

Special Issues of Journals

(1994) *Journal of Housing for Elderly.* "University Linked Retirement Communities: Student Visions of Eldercare." 11:1; "Relationships Among Women in Later Life." *Journal of Women and Aging* (forthcoming).

Other Print Resources

Counts, D. A. and D. R. Counts. 1996. *Over the Next Hill: An Ethnography of RVing Seniors in North America.* Petersborough, ON: Broadview. A lively account of community formation within RV encampments, by an anthropological couple known for their work on aging in Papua New Guinea.

Estes, C. 1996. "The Political Economy of Aging." In *Handbook of Aging and Social Sciences,* 4th ed. R. Binstock and L. George, eds. New York: Academic Press.

Francis, D. 1984. *Will You Still Need Me, Will You Still Feed Me, When I'm 64?* Bloomington: Indiana University Press. An award-winning comparative study of social networks and community formation among Jewish elderly in Cleveland, Ohio and Leeds, England.

Free, M. 1995. *The Private World of the Hermitage: Lifestyles of the Rich and Old in an Elite Retirement Home.* Westport, CT: Bergin and Garvey. An ethnography of the retention of power by aging members of the Texas elite.

Hazan, H. 1996. *From First Principles: An Experiment in Ageing.* Westport, CT: Greenwood. A "postmodern" ethnographic analysis of a group of seniors in Cambridge, England who come together to develop their own curriculum for a "University of the Third Age."

Heuman, L. and D. Boldy, eds. 1993. *Aging in Place with Dignity: International Solutions Relating to the Low Income and Frail Elderly.* Westport, CT: Praeger. Analyzes emerging innovations in a wide range of countries including Asia, the Middle East, Europe and North America.

Hoskins, I. 1994b. *Combining Work and Eldercare: A Challenge for the 1990's and Beyond.* Geneva: International Labour Office. Report from a cross-national study in France, Sweden, Canada, Japan, Australia and the United States.

Jerrome, D. 1992. *Good Company: An Anthropological Study of Old People in Groups.* Edinburgh: University of Edinburgh Press. A comparative analysis of the meaning and function of social groups for the elderly. Focuses on Europe and the United States.

Kivett, V. 1997. "Rural Older Women." In *Handbook on Women and Aging.* J. Coyle, ed. Westport, CT: Greenwood. A good background article for Chapter 16.

Krout, J. 1993. *Community Based Services for the Rural Elderly.* Newbury Park, CA: Sage.

Litwin, H. 1996. *The Social Networks of Older People: A Cross-National Analysis.* Westport, CT: Praeger. Critical look at the function of social networks in providing care for the elderly in the U.S., Canada, Israel and six European nations.

Mitchner, J. 1994. *Recessional.* New York: Fawcett Crest. A novel set in Tampa, Florida, which vividly depicts life in a fictional, upscale assisted-living facility.

Morgan, L., K. Eckert and S. M. Lyon. 1995. *Small Board-and-Care Homes: Residential Care in Transition.* Baltimore: Johns Hopkins University Press. Describes the results of a multidisciplinary, longitudinal study of unlicensed board and care homes for the elderly in Maryland. An excellent example of the integration of qualitative and quantitative methodologies.

National Council on the Aging. 1995. *Profile of Rural Older Americans.* Washington, DC: National Council on the Aging.

Regnier, V., J. Hamilton and S. Yatabe. 1995. *Assisted Living Housing for the Aged and Frail: Innovations in Design, Management, and Financing.* New York: Columbia University Press. A cross-national look at housing innovations that can make a real difference in the quality of life for the aged.

Schreck, H. 1996. *The Elderly in America: Volunteerism and Neighborhood in Seattle.* Lanham, MD: University Press of America. An ethnographic study of community work with the elderly based on the Volunteer Chore Ministry in King County, Washington.

Stroud, H. 1995. *The Promise of Paradise: Recreational and Retirement Communities in the United States Since 1950.* Baltimore: Johns Hopkins University Press.

NOTES

1. See Singh, Kinsey and Morton 1991 for a study of ethnic networks of elders in the United States and Canada. See Litwin 1995 for research on the social networks of Soviet Jews transplanted to Israel.

2. For a discussion of elders' social networks in another Asian country, Japan, see Koyano et al. 1994.

3. For an ethnographic perspective on older SRO dwellers in San Diego, see Eckert 1980.

4. Critical studies here are the San Diego Long Term Care Program and the National Financial Model Channeling Demonstration, both conducted during the 1980s. In an interesting international comparison between Israel and Sweden, Habib, Sundstrom and Windmiller (1993) show that in these countries, especially Sweden, there has been some substitution of family support by social services. However, this effect is largely found among those aged who live alone, the percent of which in Sweden is quite high at 40 percent.

5. ADLs or Activities of Daily Living are used in gerontology to assess the level of dependence one has on others to accomplish such tasks as: transferring from a bed to an upright position; being continent; feeding oneself; the ability to use the toilet and dress oneself.

6. For a classic article on retirement in rural America, see Lozier and Althouse 1975.

7. For a discussion of older men in rural areas, see Elder, Robertson and Conger 1995.

8. For a discussion of the social networks in such environments, see Stacey-Konnert and Pynoos 1992; Perkinson and Rockermann forthcoming. For an international discussion of housing for the frail elderly, see Pynoos and Liebig 1995.

9. These ideas are based on a very important community study conducted in San

Francisco and focusing on mental health of the aged (Clark and Anderson 1967). For a recent discussion of the connection between housing and health among the elderly, see MacDonald, Remus and Laing 1994).

10. For studies in public housing, see Hochschild 1973; Ross 1977; Kandel and Heider 1979; Francis 1984; Smithers 1985. For hotels, see Teski 1981. For mobile home parks and RV encampments, see Johnson 1971; Angrosino 1976; Counts and Counts 1992, 1996. For private retirement communities, see Byrne 1974; Jacobs 1974; Fry 1977; Perkinson 1980; Stokes 1990; Free 1995.

11. This study drew upon her earlier work on the meaning of friendship among older middle-class women in Brighton, England (Jerrome 1981).

12. For an analysis of a more disastrous impact of urban change, see Teski et al. 1983. This is a study of how the building of casinos in Atlantic City, New Jersey affected the community life of the elderly there. A more positive perspective on planned urban change can be seen in Hornum's (1987) study of the elderly in planned cities in England.

13. Section 8 housing subsidies pay the difference between a unit's actual rent and 30 percent of a tenant's income.

14. This research was funded by two grants from the National Institute of Mental Health Center for the Study of the Mental Disorders of the Aging: (1) "Old Men on the Bowery in the 1980s," grant number RO1-MH37562; and (2) "Older Homeless Women in New York City," grant number RO1-MH45780.

CHAPTER 16

Social Support Systems of Rural Older Women: A Comparison of the United States and Denmark

Dena Shenk and Kitter Christiansen

The roles of formal services and informal social supports for older adults are viewed very differently in various societies. In this chapter, we explore these differing orientations in relation to social support systems for the elderly in the United States and Denmark. In Denmark, formal services are viewed as a *right* to be used by any member of that society who is in need of assistance, premised upon a societal model of mutual self-help. In the United States, formal services are generally viewed as an approach to be used when one's informal network is unable to meet one's needs. The impact of this major distinction on the expectations of a sample of rural older women in each society, and on their uses of formal and informal support systems, will be examined.

A secondary focus of this chapter is the social support systems of rural elders. About 26 percent of the American elderly live in rural areas (Peterson and Maiden 1993).[1] The recent interest in the experience of aging in rural environments has not reversed the still overwhelming bias of the gerontological literature toward aging in urban settings (Coward 1979), nor has it erased the major gaps that exist in our knowledge base concerning the rural elderly (Lee and Lassey 1982). It has signaled the apparent end, however, to a period where the special needs and distinctive features of aging in rural society were virtually ignored by social gerontologists (Coward and Lee 1985). In particular, little research has focused on the specific situation of rural older women.

This chapter is based on a comparative study of the United States and Denmark, but the research in Minnesota was more extensive and was carried out over a longer period of time. The comparison is constrained by the more limited data from the Danish context which include questionnaire data and minimal participant observation, but not life histories or social network data.

Key values of these rural older women, both in the United States and Denmark, include a strong sense of independence, a closeness to the land and a clear sense of the importance of relationships with others. The meaning of ''independence'' is different in the two societies. The American rural elders believe that independence is achieved by avoiding the use of formal services and thus maintaining control over one's life, choices and decisions (see Shenk 1987, forthcoming). The Danish rural elders believe that by having people's needs met by professionals, one can maintain a sense of independence, turning to friends and family primarily for social interactions. The Danish women tend to be comfortable with the knowledge that formal services are available when they have increasing needs for support, allowing them to feel independent. They are not comfortable asking for or accepting help from friends or family.

A major focus of the early literature on rural aging in the United States was the dearth of formal services available in rural areas and the unique features of service delivery in rural communities (Ginsberg 1976; Nelson 1980; Taietz and Milton 1979).[2] Another related concern was the assessment of the needs of the rural elderly (Hynson 1975; Krout and Larson 1980). These needs have continued and even expanded as some communities have experienced the collapse of rural health systems. In much of this analysis, the rural elderly have been viewed primarily as receivers of care. It has not generally been recognized that rural older adults are not passive recipients of services and care but, rather, active manipulators of social support systems through which they meet their needs and the needs of others in their network.

There are both similarities and differences in the rural aging experience in Denmark and Minnesota. Fifteen and one-half percent of the Danish population were 65 or older as of 1989 (Cooney 1990:1), compared to 12.6 percent of the U.S. population. There is of course, also, a difference of scale in the two contexts because Denmark is such a small country, with 5.1 million people living in an area about the size of Massachusetts and New Hampshire combined. So, for example, the cultural institutions are more evenly distributed in rural areas of Denmark, although major differences exist in available services in various counties. There also is not the same strong sense of being an outsider in Denmark if you have moved into a rural community from another part of Denmark. In particular, this is not the case in Lokken (site of this research), which as a resort area has seen lots of ''outsiders'' settling as permanent residents. In the United States, those who move to the area or ''marry-in'' may always be considered newcomers by those who were born there.

Rural elders are often long-term residents of their communities and commonly derive the benefits of involvement in ongoing networks of exchange and informal support. There is generally an expectation by elders growing older in a rural environment in the United States that they will continue to turn to family, friends and neighbors (these categories may of course overlap and in fact, include formal service providers) for support in meeting their increasing and changing needs. For example, 90 percent of the U.S. study participants reported having good friends in the area, which is a high percentage reporting close friendships. While comparable friendship data are not available for the Danish sample, our sense is that the proportion reporting good friends in the area would be much lower. The Danes would be more likely to have acquaintances, rather than close friends.

The distinction between the basic orientation to the role of informal and formal supports is critical to an understanding of the aging experience in a particular cultural context (see Twigg 1989). Danish service delivery has been built on a strong philosophical belief in meeting the basic rights of every individual.[3] There is also a related Danish belief that survival through hard times depends upon cooperation—not competition (Thomas 1990:45). These principles are similar to those discussed for Sweden by Zelkovitz in Chapter 11.

The Danish elderly, along with other members of Danish society, expect to have their basic needs met through formal services which are seen as the appropriate way to meet individual needs. The effect of recent trends is that while Danish older women are comfortable accepting formal services, these services are now less readily available to the extent they have come to expect. At the same time, they are hesitant to ask friends and family for assistance and support. In contrast, elders in the United States are hesitant to use formal services, especially those which they fear will draw them into a network of formal services over which they will have little control (Shenk 1987, forthcoming). American rural elders are typically more likely to turn to family and friends to meet increasing needs for assistance, while the Danes are more likely to draw on available formal services to meet their needs for care.

The system of formal services and programs to meet the basic needs of older adults is one component of the larger Danish system of providing for the basic needs of all citizens, which is characteristic of the Scandinavian countries. The system of health and welfare services is financed essentially by the income taxes paid by all workers, which begin at 51 percent of earned income. Services are free of charge for all residents, except for certain services provided by nursing homes and social welfare. For these services there are sliding fee scales for those earning more than a basic pension.

The social welfare system in Denmark is based on the concepts of normalization and equalization. Normalization is one of the five guiding principles discussed by Zelkovitz in relation to the transformation of aging policy in Sweden (see Chapter 11). The concept of normalization has been described in regard to the mentally retarded as providing the same opportunities and conditions of life to the handicapped as are available to the rest of society and the right to experience and use the environment in a normal way (Bednar 1974:13). Equalization is a related principle. "For many years, the primary goal of Danish social policies has been social equalization, where few have too much but fewer have too little" (McRae 1975). High priority is placed on providing services that preserve and strengthen the capabilities of the dependent elderly, particularly on services that will enable them to remain in their homes as long as possible

(Raffel and Raffel 1987). This is again similar to the principles outlined by
Zelkovitz regarding aging policy in Sweden (see Chapter 11). The basic orientation of the system of service delivery is toward maintaining the elderly's
control over choices, enabling them to lead their lives as independently as possible.

While Denmark developed a comprehensive system of high-quality, govern-
ment-financed services during the economically strong period prior to 1980, the
government is struggling in this new economic climate. Officials are trying to
maintain the level of services in spite of budget reductions, increased numbers
of older adults and increased demand for expensive medical technology (Raffel
and Raffel 1987).[4]

Recent developments in formal services for the aged in Denmark have centered around the theme of "self-help" and have been advanced through the
development of experimental projects. Two of the model programs which have
received publicity are in urban settings, but these efforts are reflective of those
occurring throughout Denmark. The Fynsgade Center in the city of Aalborg, for
example, has become a model of a multiservice center which also includes
sheltered housing. The community center called Koltgarden, in the city of Arhus,
is another example of a center that "contains activities aimed at promoting good
health, preventing disease and stimulating cultural endeavors" (Wolleson 1989:
19). The Koltgarden Centre offers home nursing and home help for residents in
sheltered flats and for the whole community—a form of cooperative care work
that saves resources (Wolleson 1989:20). Clients from the neighborhood come
to the Centre for entertainment but also for offerings which include gymnastics,
talks with a case worker and a home nurse. The Koltgarden Centre is similar
to Havgarden in the research site in Lokken (see Shenk and Christiansen 1993).
Havgarden operates as a neighborhood community center which serves as the
hub for delivery of services to older adults in the community and also includes
24 apartments.

Changing attitudes are reported in Denmark due to the economic necessity of
cutting back on formal services. The elderly still receive formal services because
it is more acceptable and they can receive them without losing face. The current
effort is to get people to "care" more, that is, to develop the informal system
of care through which people help and support their families and friends.

In the United States there is a similar emphasis on encouraging more extensive
family care of the elderly. There is a large body of data from a decade ago,
which suggests that family already provide the bulk of ongoing informal care
and are in need of greater support from the formal sector (see, for example,
Cicirelli 1981; Johnson 1983; Litwak 1985). Several factors have been discussed
in the literature as affecting the assistance provided by the informal support
system. One set of factors related to changes in informal social support networks
is the mobility of the younger generation in the United States since World War
II. It has been suggested that the loss of networks (or decline in their ability to
provide daily assistance) as a function of the mobility of younger generations

may be most detrimental to those elders who reside in small towns and rural communities (Lee and Cassidy 1981). Other literature suggests that older rural residents are more highly integrated into social networks providing informal social support than their urban counterparts (see Lee and Whitbeck 1987; Kivett 1985). Most of these studies focus on the quantity or frequency of interaction with no concept of the nature of the relationship or the meanings attached to those relationships by the participants. The research discussed in this chapter focused on the nature of the individual relationships and the kinds of support being exchanged.

Another factor in the changing nature of informal support networks relates to the changing roles of women. Since women have traditionally been a critical force through which relationships and helping networks across generations have been initiated and maintained, their entrance into the labor force in large numbers has serious consequences for the provision of social support to the elderly (Pilisak and Minkler 1980). Notably, among European countries, Denmark has the highest employment rate for women—81 percent (Leeson and Tufte 1994). The impact of this trend on the rural elderly has not been examined.

In addition, the formal service delivery system in both countries is often not oriented toward working effectively in cooperation with the informal support system, but rather is seen as a substitute. In regard to our present discussion, a primary question is the culturally defined relationship between the formal and informal support systems, which frames how the two work together. In Denmark, the formal system is seen as primary whereas in the United States the informal support system is expected to be the primary source of support. The formal system is viewed as a replacement to be used when the informal system fails to meet an elder's needs.

BACKGROUND AND DISCUSSION

This discussion is based on the findings of a multiphase qualitative study of 30 rural older women in central Minnesota and participant observation and questionnaire data collected from a comparative sample of 30 older women in rural Denmark. The Minnesota research was completed by the first author from March 1986 to July 1987 (see Shenk 1987, 1991, forthcoming). The Danish interviews were completed by the second author during the summer and fall of 1990.[5]

The Minnesota Older Women's Project was completed in several phases which included the collection of: (1) life histories, (2) social network and questionnaire data and (3) photographs of the study participants. The data collection in Denmark was based primarily on a translated, culturally adapted questionnaire.

The Danish research was completed in Lokken-Vra on the northwest coast of North Jutland, Denmark. The area of research includes the towns of Lokken, Vrensted and Vittrup. Lokken, a seaside resort town in this century, was initially a seaport and later one of Denmark's larger fishing towns. There are 1,300 permanent residents in Lokken. Vrensted was a larger center and Vittrup a smaller center for the surrounding farming areas. They are both now merely clusters of houses and farms surrounded by open country. A few stores including a grocery are all that remain of the prior commercial development in each community.

The inhabitants of the area are known as tough and independent people, and were predominantly small-scale farmers and fishermen.[6] The Borglum Monastery (Kloster) was active in the community from about 1130 until the sixteenth century and employed many local people. Then, as a lay manor house, it continued to have a great impact on life in the area until the present. Due to technological advances, it is now run by a few people. A railway line went through the area, but it was closed in 1963. The former station houses in Vrensted and Vittrup are now private residences.

The American research was conducted in a four-county area of central Minnesota including Stearns, Sherburne, Benton and Wright counties.[7] The American study sample was selected to be similar to the larger regional population in terms of key demographic characteristics, including education and income (see Shenk 1987, forthcoming). The Minnesota sample was selected based on both demographic guidelines and self-definition as a rural person. Most of the women live in towns of under 2,500. Several farm wives who had moved into a larger town were included in this sample. Self-definition by the participants was used in determining the extent of "ruralness" of each of the respondents.

The women defined "rural" in terms of both geographic location and the nature of life. Our respondents characterized themselves as rural because "they live out in the country," where it is quiet, peaceful and spacious. They talked about having freedom, not being confined and enjoying the outdoors. They thought of life on the farm as the essence of rurality. Aspects of their lifestyle which they considered to be rural included depending on their neighbors, having more friends and not having much formal education. The rural lifestyle was described as being more "simple" than life in the city. There weren't as many choices, life was less hectic and expectations were thought to be clearer. In summary, rural life was described as more simple and based on close social ties.

The Danish sample was selected by both authors during the summer of 1990, based on earlier research with the older residents of the area by the second author. The respondents were chosen to include a broad range of patterns in terms of key demographic characteristics including marital status, living arrangement and education. A comparison of selected demographic characteristics of the two samples is provided in Table 16.1.

There are striking differences in the attitudes toward the use of formal services by the respondents in Denmark and the United States. A Danish informant explained that the Danish system of services can be understood in light of the cultural value of privacy. When money was available, formal services were used more because of this pattern of maintaining privacy. Those in need wanted to

Table 16.1
Selected Demographic Characteristics

	Minnesota		Denmark	
	(%)	(N=30)	(%)	(N=30)
Age at Interview				
60-64	6.6	2	23.2	7
65-74	33.3	10	40.0	12
75-84	40.0	12	26.6	8
85+	20.0	6	9.9	3
Marital Status				
Married	30.0	9	43.3	13
Never Married	13.3	4	13.3	4
Widow	43.3	13	43.3	13
Divorced	13.3	4	0.0	0
Housing Location				
Farm	20.0	6	13.3	4
Open Country	16.7	5	3.3	1
Farm into town	20.0	6	3.3	1
Small town (<2500)	23.3	7	36.7	11
Town (>2500)	20.0	6	43.3	13
Health (self-rated)				
Excellent/very good	26.6	8	36.7	11
Good	40.0	12	30.1	9
Fair/poor	33.3	10	33.3	10
Religion				
Catholic	56.6	17	0.0	0
Lutheran	16.7	5	96.7	29
Methodist	13.3	4	0.0	0
Other	13.3	4	3.3	1
Income per Month				
< U.S. poverty level	26.6	8	10.0	3
125% poverty level	10.0	3	13.3	4
125-150% poverty	30.0	9	16.7	5
> 150% poverty level	26.6	8	60.0	18
Unknown/refused	6.6	2	0.0	0

stay protected and private and would turn to formal services rather than ask friends or even family for help.

The American system, in comparison, is based on the concept of replacing an unavailable or insufficient informal system of support with formal services. In the United States the need for formal services is sometimes linked to the concept of ''welfare'' and those in need are implicitly seen as lesser beings not deserving of privacy or autonomy. The importance of respecting the elders' needs for privacy and autonomy are not part of the American system of formal service delivery. For example, when the first author visited an American informant in her home late one morning, she found her dressed in a sleeveless shift. She apologized for not being dressed and explained that the new home health aide who assisted with her bath comes at 1:30. ''It's not her; it's what they assigned her. But it's so inconvenient. It's hard for me to get dressed and undressed and dressed again.'' So she stays in her night clothes until the aide comes. She went on to explain that the agency regularly changes the day and time of her bath, as well as the particular aide, and she has no say in it. ''I asked her about coming in the morning and she said that she had to do what the main office told her.'' In Denmark there is generally more importance placed on developing a comfortable relationship between the aide and recipient of support and more of a feeling of choice and control on the part of the elderly.

Clearly, each society must develop a framework for effective interaction of the formal and informal systems of care in meeting the basic physical and social needs of the elderly which is based on cultural expectations (see Shenk 1991). The difference between Danish and American opinion on this point is perhaps one of degree, rather than one of kind. The American women generally were wary of using formal services which would draw them into a network of formal services over which they would have little control. Formal services are seen by these rural American women as options to be used sparingly.

The Danish system of formal services ideally provides alternatives from which the individual can choose. The goal of the Danish system is clearly to enable the individual to remain in control of the decision-making process and to choose the services which best meet his/her current needs.

CASE STUDIES

This comparison will become clearer with consideration of two case studies from each sample which emphasize the use of formal and informal supports in each cultural context. Each case study is presented based on the respondent's life situation at the time of the individual interviews.

Minnesota Case 1

The first American respondent, Harriet Tucker, age 83, showed me the pictures from her fiftieth anniversary party which had been held a year ago, and talked at great length about that occasion when we spent our first day together. She was married two days before her seventeenth birthday to a farmhand on her father's farm. She gave birth to their first child six months later and she confirmed these dates, showing me the family bible.

She raised eight children, two boys and six girls. "I don't think I did too bad. Because he was working all the time. It was mostly up to me." "I was four months pregnant with (her youngest child) when he had his first surgery (after an accident). He was paralyzed on his right side. Then he got worse and used crutches. . . . About four-five years ago he got into the wheelchair."

Harriet was very proud and loved to talk about the celebration of their fiftieth wedding anniversary. I realized that this event was a symbol for her of her success in following the cultural norms and "doing the right thing." After getting pregnant, she married, raised a family and stayed married through difficult times.

Harriet and her husband live in their own home and receive a lot of support from their children. "Our kids come home and help us a lot. And we intend to stay here as long as we possibly can get along without going to a nursing home. It really doesn't make any sense to move away from here and move into town. We'll still have to have somebody come and help, so we might as well stay here." Their youngest daughter lives nearby and helps them several times a week. She takes Harriet shopping and in fact, drives them everywhere they need to go. Without the help of their children they feel they could not get by living at home. They collect "compensation" for her husband's disability but have used only minimal formal services.

Harriet still provides a great deal of personal care for her husband and is dependent on her daughter to provide the assistance which she needs. She has avoided using any formal services, preferring to turn to her informal support network in meeting her extensive needs.

Minnesota Case 2

The second American case is Maurine Strutter, an eighty-one-year-old retired physical education teacher who never married. Maurine's quiet, smiling demeanor and her love of physical tasks (snow-shoveling, chopping wood, woodworking) are what I remember most clearly.

Maurine lives with a close friend in a home overlooking Clear Lake. "You know I don't live alone. (Hilda) and I have lived here for 15 years together. We taught together in Willmar. She moved on to Rochester, but we decided to retire here."

Maurine talks about her life in terms of her family heritage, beginning with her childhood through high school and graduation from college. The themes in her life story are travel, work, hobbies and community involvement. Maurine served on three local committees including the county community-based services committee and was very knowledgeable about the services available to seniors.

She explained about home-delivered meals, for example. "There's a problem with them in the rural area because of the road situation. I've heard that they want to start a program where a van will go and pick up all these people who get home-delivered meals and take them to the nutrition site instead of them staying home. The problem with the home-delivered meals is people don't get out and don't mingle with other people." She had not used any of the available services, however, and could not imagine herself seeking formal assistance. She and her housemate support each other and there is also a neighbor to whom she would turn in an emergency. She talks about the need to stay active and "do my best."

In 1991, Maurine was diagnosed with an inoperable heart condition and told to curtail her activities. This was a difficult time for her, but she never complained. When she had to have a tooth extracted, the dentist was unable to curtail the bleeding and she was brought to the hospital for the last time. In her weakened condition, she was moved to a nursing home where she was visited by her friends until she died. Her housemate Hilda was forced to sell the house and moved to live with her widowed sister.

Maurine had also preferred to turn to her informal system of support in meeting her needs during her final illness. She lived in her lake home for as long as she could. When it became necessary for her to use formal services, she went to the hospital and then the nursing home. These were both in the community where she had taught and had moved away from fifteen years before. Her housemate drove the 120 miles back and forth every other day to be with her, spending the alternate days packing and arranging the sale of the house. She also had visits from her close friends in that community. But the formal system of support, in this case a nursing home, was not used to reinforce her informal support network; rather it replaced the informal system at the end.

Denmark Case 1

The first Danish case study is Mrs. Ingrid Larsen, an eighty-one-year-old respondent who lives with her husband in a one-bedroom apartment with a small kitchen and bathroom in a protected housing unit in Lokken.[8] The apartment is located within Havgarden, the local old age home.[9] They have been together for 66 years and are clearly very devoted to each other, their family and friends.

Her husband was a farmer and she was a farm wife, raising two children on their farm in a nearby community. Mrs. Larsen has been blind since she was 28, due to a hereditary eye disease. She is in good spirits and has coped well with her handicap. The only problem she mentioned was that the children didn't want her to cook the gravy because she couldn't see the lumps, so her husband always did that and was good at it.

In 1964, because of her husband's bad leg, they moved from the farm to a home in town. They had a home helper for four hours every day and home-delivered meals until they moved to protected housing in 1986. She has received a disability pension for many years because of her blindness; now she and her husband collect retirement pensions.[10]

Typically, after waking up, dressing and eating the breakfast brought to them from the central kitchen, Ingrid cleans up around the apartment. She tries to do as much of the housework herself as she can manage. They go to the activity room to have coffee, talk to people and play cards. Ingrid typically works on the hooked-wool pictures which can been seen hanging in their apartment. They have their warm meal at noon in their apartment and their evening meal (bread) is delivered at the same time. Sometimes they return to the activity room again in the afternoon, but more often she works on her hooked pictures and they relax in the apartment.

Her children visit once or twice a week. One set of grandchildren visit once or twice a month, bringing her great-grandchild, while the other two grandchildren visit once or twice a year. One of her major daily concerns is the health of her children, especially whether they will inherit her eye disease. She regularly spends time with neighbors and friends who visit at the center.

Ingrid Larsen died in 1992. Her husband lives alone in the protected housing apartment at Havgarden and spends most of his time in the activity room. He has kept the apartment just as it was when she was alive. It is decorated with numerous pictures of the two of them and their family, as well as the hooked pictures which she made. The formal system of services has been effective in providing for the changing needs of both Ingrid and her husband. The formal service providers work effectively with his family and he is often visited by friends in the larger community and staff who are his friends. There is much more of a blending in this case, with both the formal and informal systems of support being integral parts of their lives.

Denmark Case 2

The second Danish case study is Helga Christiansen, age 67, a respondent who never married. Helga's smile and quiet strength instantly reminded me of Maurine Strutter (Minnesota case 2). Her love of life was demonstrated clearly as we shared lunch at another respondent's home. She later admitted that she went home and napped after too much good food, good company and a little aquavit (Danish alcoholic beverage).

Helga worked as a home nurse for more than 30 years. When she was transferred to this district, she bought the house in Lokken where she has lived alone with her dog ever since. Her father and brother were both architects and her brother had designed her home for someone else. Helga cared for three or four generations in the community, before she retired in 1987 so she would have time to do what she really wanted, while she still could.

Helga is fully independent and she gets around by walking or driving her own car. In 1984, when she was diagnosed with cancer, she had an operation and spent ten days in the hospital and three weeks recuperating at home. She had no treatment afterwards and apart from this has never been ill. She explains that she didn't need any help while she was recuperating because as she put it: "I let the dust stay where it was until I could remove it again." She emphasized her belief, however, that if she needs help she will go to the public services, not her family.

Ms. Christiansen is very active in the community as a local leader of the Red Cross Visiting Friends, a member of the Red Cross Board, a knitting club, an active member of the Senior Club and a member of the Board of the Lokken Museum Association. She also is involved in planning and activities at the local center for elders (including a nursing home, protected housing and day center) and has been active in "Soeroptomist" (the international Optimists organization) for twenty years. This has involved her in traveling abroad to meetings and international contacts. Her biggest daily concern is finding enough time to manage all the things she is involved in and wants to do.

Helga sees her two brothers and one sister-in-law, who live in the area, once or twice a month and gets together with her family from all over Denmark several times a year. She has a very strong network of friends whom she sees once or twice a week, and neighbors she sees daily. She is an independent woman with a strong network of family and friends.

The expectation is that Helga will again turn to the formal system of services when she has future needs. While she maintains close relationships with her friends and family, these are based on the premise that her basic needs will be met through the formal system of services available in the community. For her there is clearly a blending, with the informal system providing emotional support and the formal service delivery system providing for basic needs.

QUESTIONNAIRE FINDINGS

The pattern exemplified in the American cases is to turn first to family and friends, while the Danish women generally turn to formal services to meet increasing needs. These patterns are seen in the case studies, as well as through the questionnaire and social network findings. Relatively few service providers were discussed as part of the social networks of the American respondents. These formal providers of care who were part of the informants' personal networks were very important however, in the lives of those study participants. These rural older women use formal service providers to fill gaps in their informal support system. The Danish women, in contrast, are generally more likely to use formal service providers to meet their needs for assistance. The nature of their relationships with service providers was not fully explored. While they formed comfortable relationships with their service providers, they did not tend to form close social relationships with them.

The differences between the two samples, in their attitudes toward the use of formal and informal supports, can be seen in several areas. There are major differences, for example, in the primary mode of transportation between the two

Table 16.2
Past and Future Use of Formal Services (N = 30)

	Minnesota		Denmark
Have used home-delivered meals	4		3
Would use home-delivered meals	12		28
Have used home helper	9		13
Would use home helper	15		28
	van/bus	volunteer driver	
Have used transportation	8	4	14
Would use transportation	12	14	28

groups, which reflect cultural differences. The Danes are more likely to use public transportation, walk or use a bicycle, while the Minnesotans more often drive their own cars or get rides from family or friends.

Both groups were asked a series of questions about both past and future use of formal services. While a similar number had used each of these services, their attitudes toward the possible future use of formal services were clearly different. A sample of these data are provided in Table 16.2. In general, about half as many respondents in Minnesota indicated that they would use formal services, as compared to the Danish sample. In fact, one of the Danish respondents got annoyed with these questions, indicating that the services are a "right" and demanding to know: "Why are you even asking about this?" Even though many more of the U.S. respondents were already over the age of 85 and more likely to already be in need of transportation services, the Minnesota respondents who reported that they would use transportation in the future represented 46.6 percent compared to 93 percent of the Danes. Most of those indicated that they would use a van or bus or volunteer driver in the future. It should also be noted that public transportation is much more readily available throughout Denmark.

A similar pattern is evident in the respondents' responses to questions about seeking assistance with a range of needs. They were asked, for example, to whom they would turn if they needed help when they became sick. More of the Danish women reported that they would seek the assistance of their spouses and slightly fewer would turn to their children or friends and neighbors than in the Minnesota sample. A similar number in each of the two samples reportedly would turn to other relatives for support. Notably, while 13 percent of the Minnesotan women would seek the assistance of a professional, 33 percent of the Danish women reported that they would ask for such help.

The women were asked to whom they would turn for assistance if they needed to get somewhere quickly, if they needed money, for help around the house, if

Table 16.3
Help with Housework (N = 30)

	Minnesota	Denmark
Self	1	4
Professional	3	6
Child/Grandchild	10	6
Spouse	2	6
Other Relative	3	2
Non-relative (neighbors, friends)	3	4
No response	3	2

they were feeling lonely, needed help with paperwork or help with shopping. Similar patterns were found in response to each of these questions. For example, the Danish women were most likely to seek professional help with paperwork or if they needed money, and less likely to turn to children, neighbors and friends.

Table 16.3 reports on their responses to the question of whom they turn to when they need help with housework. The Minnesota sample turns most heavily to children and grandchildren, neighbors and friends for assistance with housework. More of the Danish women reported receiving no assistance with housework, but those who did turned to the full range of informal and formal supports in equal numbers.

In general, the Danish women were less likely to seek assistance from neighbors or friends than were the American women. Danish women turned to their children for assistance with short-term needs, but were also more likely to seek support from professionals than were the American women.

Family relationships were described as the most important aspect of the American respondents' lives, with spouses, children and in-laws often being depended on for extensive assistance. Relationships with children and grandchildren were a key component of most of these women's social worlds. In talking about children and grandchildren, several women spoke about how these relationships change through time. For example, one American respondent in discussing her grandson explained: "that's Sylvia's oldest. We always were very close. I don't see him much any more. He's married and has a family. It seems when they get big, you don't see them as much. They get their family and all. He used to be around all the time, now I just see him on occasions. They don't visit." These special relationships with particular children and grandchildren often provide an ongoing source of emotional support for these older rural American women, although not necessarily direct care. While the nature of the relationships and the extent of support and assistance that is actually exchanged have changed and may be minimal, the importance of the emotional support should not be understated.

A common image of life in rural areas, which was also reported by these women, includes an expectation of social relationships with friends and neighbors. In reality there is a great deal of variation in the roles that friends and neighbors play in the lives of various rural older women, in conjunction with the pattern of strong attachment to family. Some of the American women and most of the Danish women deal with the rural phenomenon of everyone knowing everyone else by maintaining an emotional distance in most of their relationships with neighbors and friends. As one American informant explained: ''I'm not the kind to put my worries on someone else. I don't usually talk to anyone. I read or knit to get over it. If I have a heavy worry, I go to church. I don't talk to anyone.'' Or as another American informant explained: ''We're not that kind, to watch too close.'' There was generally a perceived need to maintain emotional distance from neighbors because of the geographical closeness. A few of the American women seemed to thrive on openness and intimacy. An informant who has many close friends and people she talks with intimately explained her view that: ''We always need other people. . . . I talk (intimately) with all my friends . . . I'm sorry for people that can't come out of their shell.'' It is also worth noting that fewer of the Danish women reported that they never feel lonely and more of them reported not seeking help from anyone other than themselves. This supports the Danish core value to be independent and to take care of yourself, so that even if they needed help they would not be likely to admit it.

In regard to assistance in each of these areas of need, the Danish women were more likely to turn first to spouses. This is indicative perhaps of the presence of more husbands in the Danish sample who are in better health than spouses in the Minnesota sample. There is also evidence of a different kind of relationship between spouses in the two countries. For example, the Danish women were more likely to turn to their spouses for help around the house than were the Minnesotans. This seems indicative of a different division of labor between the spouses in Denmark, which is less rigidly gender-based than that in the American sample.

When ongoing assistance is needed with intimate personal care, the American women clearly prefer to turn to the formal system, rather than seek help from individuals in their informal support network. They are more comfortable if this personal assistance is received from someone with whom they can maintain a nonpersonal relationship. Eight of the thirty women, for example, reported needing assistance with bathing. All of them are assisted in bathing by home health aides and hired service providers rather than friends or relatives. Even those still living with a spouse did not receive assistance with bathing from their husbands. Personal assistance can be accepted from a formal service provider without feeling a loss of independence or becoming a burden as would be the case in depending on a relative or friend. At the same time, three of the women assist others with bathing. One assists her husband, while two others are paid for providing personal care.

Service providers who came to the American women's own homes were generally essential to their being able to remain in their home. Housekeepers, homemakers and home health aides in particular were very important to these rural American women and were most often listed as being close to the informant. Some of the women reported close friendships with these service providers, occasionally including them within the first tier of their social network. For example, one informant explained about her home health aide through county social services: "Marion is good therapy for me. We talk while she works. She tells me her problems and I talk to her. We talk about everything and it never goes any further." The feeling was similar in Denmark, although we did not collect the specific social network data to support this point.

RELATIONSHIPS BETWEEN THE FORMAL AND INFORMAL SYSTEMS

In the Danish view, while the necessary *social* support is found among family, friends and neighbors, basic needs are expected to be met somewhere else, that is, through formal services. Danish older women are comfortable accepting formal services, but not necessarily asking friends or even family for assistance. The current effort at the national level is to get people in the informal sector to "care" more for each other, as the economic situation worsens. These efforts are being greeted with considerable complaints, because the Danes maintain a clear expectation that basic needs should be met through formal services. It will be difficult to get the present generations to reorient their expectations toward the use of formal services and to get them to expect more from their informal support systems.

In the United States we have the opposite problem of persuading individuals to use formal services effectively in order to reduce the strain on their informal systems of support. The system is not always designed so that rural elderly can use the services as an aid toward maintaining their independence and autonomy. A powerful example is provided by the American informant who discussed the increasing frailty of her ninety-year-old husband and herself. They still managed alone in their farmhouse. They no longer farmed but had gardened until the previous year. She explained that all she needed was assistance with housecleaning. The dilemma she expressed was based on her perceived inability to pay to hire someone to clean and her unwillingness to turn to social services for assistance. "I'm not going to tell them how much we make. That's nobody's business." In fact, having told the first author in intimate detail about her life, friends and family, she was unwilling to indicate the range of her income. Her husband has since died and she has moved into a nursing home. The move was difficult for her and she later wrote: "I am fairly well and I wouldn't be here, but they say I can't be alone. . . . The nurses and aids are so good to me, but I can't seem to adjust to life here. It is such a lonely and depressing place. My many friends are so good about coming to see me which helps me keep my sanity." She was not willing to use the formal system to meet her needs and help her remain in her own home, as she wished. Instead she was institutionalized after the loss of her primary social support, her husband.

The Danish system of services can be understood in terms of the cultural value of privacy. When money was available, the system of formal services was expanded and a range of home and community-based services were available for the asking. It is interesting to note that in the United States also, the most private kinds of care are sought from formal service providers when they are available. The American service delivery system, however, is not oriented toward maintaining the privacy of those whose needs are met through the formal sector. The "welfare system" mentality associated with public sector assistance in American society continues to label those who need to seek assistance from formal service providers as having failed in some way, as demonstrated by their not being able to meet their needs through informal supports.

CONCLUSIONS

Formal services are viewed as a *right* to be used by any member of Danish society who is in need of assistance, premised upon mutual self-help. Having one's basic needs met by formal services allows one to interact with friends and family on a more equal basis. In contrast, in the United States, formal services are more likely to be viewed as an approach to be used when one's informal network is unable to meet one's needs. Rather than functioning to strengthen the informal system of support, formal services in the United States often strain the informal social support network. Formal services are generally seen as a replacement for rather than a supplement to the informal support system. The realization of the full meaning of this distinction is critical to an understanding of the system of informal and formal services for the elderly in both Denmark and the United States.

Services created to meet the needs of aging rural Americans must combine a clear understanding of their specific needs with a recognition of their attitudes and expectations. It is difficult for these women to accept care from a formal system of care, because they are not comfortable with the idea of accepting help from outsiders and do not know enough about such a system to feel they can retain control. Like the rest of the present generations of older adults in the United States, they fear being a burden to others and sometimes feel they have lived too long. They are ashamed of their inability to cope with the changes of aging, and embarrassed because they cannot receive all of the support they need from their family and friends. Their pattern of service preference is also related to the rural concept of a simple life, which does not include a formally structured, bureaucratic system governed by official rules and guidelines. All of these feelings must be recognized and accepted. They can then be used to formulate a system of services which can work with the informal support systems of rural older women to enable them to remain in the community for as long as they possibly can. The formal system of care must be able to fill the gaps in the informal system and service providers must be sensitive to the expectations of these rural elders, rather than expecting the informal network to conform to the structure of the formal service delivery system. Services that are the least structured and the least formal should be built upon to assure the availability of necessary assistance for rural older Americans.

Rural older American women are more likely to participate in programs and services which meet specific needs without drawing them into an all-encompassing system of social services. Living in small communities where everyone knows everyone else, they are very concerned about public opinion and the impressions of their neighbors and friends. Services which are provided on a piecemeal basis are more likely to be acceptable. This is especially true if the individual feels she is in control of which services she receives and even more true if she can choose who will provide the service. Ideally, rural American elders would like to be able to pay for these services, which they cannot always afford. Paying for services allows them to feel independent and in control and not to feel they are overly dependent on others.

The Danish system of services appears to be a response to the societal preference for using formal services to meet basic needs, allowing one to depend on informal supports to meet social needs. The system now clearly perpetuates that preference and their goal is to ensure that the elderly get at least the same services in rural areas as would be available in urban settings.[11] In Denmark, formal services are available to assist the rural elderly to remain in their own homes, including meals, house cleaning, home health aides and home nurses. While it is often difficult for the Danes to ask for and to accept help from family and friends, they are comfortable having their basic needs met through formal services. The interaction between the formal and informal systems of care are clearly quite different in the two countries, based on the different perceptions of the role of each kind of support.

NOTES

Financial support for the Minnesota research was provided by the Central Minnesota Council on Aging through funds provided by the Older Americans Act, the St. Cloud State University Foundation, St. Cloud State University through a research grant, Extramural Support Grant and Summer Research Stipend and the Central Minnesota Initiative Fund to the first author. The Danish research completed in 1990 was funded by a St. Cloud State University Research Grant and research completed in 1992 was funded by a UNC Charlotte Summer Research Grant to the first author.

1. The U.S. Census includes in its definition of rural any place under 2,500 people. Researchers often use various measures of size and density of population to define "rural."

2. It is also to be noted that, in general, rural communities are not able to provide the range of services that are more common in higher density areas.

3. This philosophical tradition is exemplified by the work of Soren Kierkegaard, the Danish philosopher who stated:

If real success is to attend the effort to bring a man to a definite position, one must first of all take pains to find HIM where he is and begin there. This is the secret of the art of helping others. Anyone who has not mastered this himself is deluded when he proposes to help others. In order to help another effectively I must understand more than he—yet first of all surely I must understand what he understands. If I do not know that, my greater understanding will be of no help to him. (Bretall 1951, translation of S. Kierkegaard, *The Point of View for my Work as an Author*, Part 2, chapter 1, section 2:333)

4. For discussion of the historical development of the system of formal services in Denmark, see Shenk and Christiansen 1993.

5. Preliminary research by the first author was completed in Denmark in 1981 and a follow-up visit was completed in 1992 (see Shenk and Christiansen 1993).

6. An ethnographic culture change study by Anderson and Anderson (1964; see also Anderson 1990) provides a picture of life in a similar fishing community outside of Copenhagen at the turn of the nineteenth and early twentieth centuries.

7. The project was completed with the cooperation and support of the Central Minnesota Council on Aging, the regional area agency on aging.

8. Protected housing in Denmark is similar to assisted living as it is being developed in the United States. There are twelve protected housing units at the center, along with a nursing home and other services (see Shenk and Christiansen 1993). Services are provided to residents by staff based on the resident's individual needs.

9. For further discussion about the services for the elderly in Lokken, Denmark, see Shenk and Christiansen 1993 and Shenk n.d. The old age home is integrated into the larger community and a range of services are provided within the facility.

10. Government pensions in Denmark are generally approximately 50 percent of pre-retirement income. Many retirees also have private pensions available to them, although that was not true in this case.

11. For a discussion of the evolution of the aging services system in this rural area, see Shenk and Christiansen 1993.

CHAPTER 17

An Organization for the Elderly, by the Elderly: A Senior Center in the United States

Yohko Tsuji

INTRODUCTION

When I came to the United States in 1976, I encountered a totally unexpected culture shock: the disappearance of old people from my daily life and Americans' strongly negative attitude toward old age. For instance, when my American octogenarian friend from Indiana visited me in San Diego, my roommates treated him nicely but shocked me by their comments after his departure: "I would rather die before I become like him"; "He has outlived his usefulness. He would be happier dead." In my native Japan, elderly people occupied a significant part of my life. I grew up with my grandmother in a traditional, three-generation family and my neighborhood was full of old people who were grandparents of my playmates. I was taught to be respectful and kind to the elderly. The elderly in return nurtured young children when our mothers were not available.

Negative stereotypes of old age and the absence of older people in my American life intrigued me, not only because they were very different from my experiences in Japan, but also because they made me wonder how elderly Americans lived their lives. Years later, in 1987–1988, my interest culminated in an eighteen-month-long fieldwork at Lake District Senior Center in a small town in upstate New York.

Prior to my fieldwork, I reviewed relevant literature and learned that, in addition to the universal problems of coping with physical decline, old age in America presents "unique" problems. Not only does American culture offer no well-established models for aging, but old age is regarded as antithetical to dominant American values, such as independence, productivity and strength. The major aim of my research, therefore, was to find out how elderly participants at Lake District Senior Center dealt with this apparent cultural dilemma and made their lives meaningful. I set out to explore these questions as an outsider in terms of both my age and my cultural background.

Because of the wide gap existing between the realities of old age and American cultural ideals, some previous studies suggest that adaptation to old age is better made outside dominant values through "disengagement" (Cumming and Henry 1961), "deculturation" (Anderson 1972) or segregation of the aged. My research showed, however, older Americans handle problems of aging within the realm of American culture. Being constrained and guided by their culture simultaneously, they negotiate reality to conform to cultural ideals.

This chapter examines elderly Americans' activities at Lake District Senior Center as well as the nature of its organization. The chapter has two major objectives: (1) to explore various functions of the Senior Center, in particular the Center as a stage where the elderly can play a social drama in conformity to dominant cultural values, and (2) to illustrate how culture shapes not only patterns of the elderly's activities, but also the organization of the Center itself.

LAKE DISTRICT SENIOR CENTER

Taietz (1976) postulates two conceptual models of the senior center: the voluntary organization model in contrast to the social agency model. The former is seen as attracting the higher-income elderly who are active participants in community affairs. The latter, on the other hand, regards the senior center as a place to offer programs which meet the needs of the poor and disengaged.

Lake District Senior Center fits neither of these models. Although it is run by a private, nonprofit organization, the heterogeneity of its participants is inconsistent with the voluntary organization model. The Center draws participants from a wide socioeconomic spectrum, ranging from a wealthy widow who owns successful businesses to welfare recipients. The participants' ethnic background also varies. While white Protestants constitute the majority, there are Catholics, Jews, blacks and Asians as well as those who immigrated from Western European countries in their youth. The participants' places of residence are widespread. Some live near enough to visit the Center on foot and others drive a fair distance from neighboring counties. The heterogeneity of Lake District Senior Center makes a striking contrast with the homogeneity of the Jewish Day Care Center studied by Barbara Myerhoff in their participants' ethnic, socioeconomic and residential backgrounds (1978).

Taietz's second model, the social agency model, corresponds to the prevailing stereotypes of the senior center as a service provider for the poor or as a recreational facility for those who have nothing meaningful to do.[1] Lake District Senior Center belies such stereotypes. It departs from such type casting, most notably in the elderly's roles vis-à-vis their Center. It was established in 1952 by a score of private citizens who foresaw the need for an independent organization of older people in their community. In its early days, the Center's operation relied totally on elderly volunteers. Since the idea of the senior center was novel at the time,[2] the charter members faced pioneering work of promoting the significance of the senior center as well as of finding necessary resources to carry out their mission.

Their work had multiple purposes. In addition to offering a place for activities and companionship to the elderly, their mission involved educational programs for better understanding of old age, community services by the elderly and implementation of social services for the elderly. In short, Lake District Senior Center was never an isolated retreat for the elderly. As the only organization in the local area exclusively dealing with issues of aging,[3] the Center played a crucial role in identifying unmet social needs and, together with other public and private sectors of the community, in implementing social services to solve the elderly's problems. Housing and transportation, two crucial services to prolong the elderly's autonomy, would not have been possible or would have taken much longer to realize without incessant efforts by the members of Lake District Senior Center.[4]

One important principle guided their work: self-help. At a promotional gathering, one of the charter members emphasized, "if Senior Citizens were to have happier, healthier lives, they must solve their problems in their own way" (Gabriel 1972:18). A paramount symbol of their determination for self-help is their "Home" where the Center is located now. Lake District Senior Center purchased its permanent home in 1970 when federal money for construction or renovation for senior centers did not exist. Their dream came true after almost two decades of searching, saving and repeated involuntary moves.[5]

As the membership grew and the programs expanded, acquisition of public funds and hiring of nonsenior staff became inevitable. Nonetheless, Lake District Senior Center has managed to remain as a private, independent organization,[6] and self-help has continued to be their most important motto. Today, with the 1,700-plus membership, the Center's day-to-day operation is carried out by nonsenior paid workers. But, for its smooth operation, older volunteers' help is indispensable.[7] Furthermore, it is mostly the elderly who make decisions on the current and future operations of the Center by serving on the board of directors and various other committees. Older people also play a significant role in financing their own Center. One-third of their annual budget, over $300,000 in 1993, is still self-provided.[8]

In summary, the elderly at Lake District Senior Center are not passive recipients of services. Rather, they actively participate in creating, providing and using such services.

ELDERLY PARTICIPANTS AND THEIR ACTIVITIES

Lake District Senior Center is open daily from 9:00 A.M. to 4:00 P.M., Mondays through Fridays, and from 10:00 A.M. to 1:00 P.M. on Saturdays. It offers a wide range of programs: class instructions, group meetings, workshops, seminars and other special events.[9] Some of them are mainly recreational and others more focused on educational and informative aspects. Regardless of their aims, all the activities at the Center contain strong social components. Chatting with their peers is very common and for many people is one of the most enjoyable aspects of going to the Center. Some groups and classes meet earlier than scheduled to have lunch together. Others extend their activities outside the Center and go out together for shopping and dining. One immediate outcome of the elderly's participation in the Center activities is to bring them into social interactions with others and ease their loneliness. Hazel, a widow in her eighties, lives next door to her also widowed daughter, Florence. She recalls their isolated lives before attending the Center: "Day after day, my daughter and I sat in my living room like two rocks."

Social marginality or worthlessness is also regarded as a problem of old age in America. Lake District Senior Center provides some solutions for this predicament because it offers abundant opportunities to help others and do volunteer work and thereby makes its participants feel useful again. Some older people make a new "career" out of their volunteer work. Eleanor, age 84, maintains a busy schedule as Manager of the Center's Gift Shop and leader of the toy-making group. Hazel and Florence, the mother-daughter pair mentioned above, and May, their neighbor, are also active in their volunteer work and known as "the dynamic trio." Their help is highly appreciated not only at the Center, but also at various other community organizations. For example, the elderly volunteers make a significant contribution to the local hospitals, schools, libraries, transportation services and so on. In 1987, the year I was doing research, 435 volunteers contributed a sum of 54,150 hours or $181,402.50 worth of community services.[10]

Important as volunteer work may be for many elderly, there are some who are unable to participate due to physical, temporal or other personal reasons. At the Center, however, the latter also have opportunities for contribution and recognition. For instance, any gathering, whether it be a class or a group meeting, involves some preparations, such as setting up chairs or taking out necessary materials. For the weekly meetings of the Thursday group, Frieda always heats water and prepares the beverage cart. The group awarded her the title of "Kitchen Queen."

Fred's appearance in the art class provides another example of recognition the elderly receive at the Center. Fred, 83, lives in a senior citizens' apartment adjacent to the Center. He likes art, but his poor eyesight and back pain forced him to give up painting. One cold winter day, Fred showed up in the art class. Spotting him entering the room, Doris, a class member, waved to him and announced his arrival to the class, "Fred came to see us in this miserable weather! He deserves a round of applause!" The whole class applauded to welcome Fred. "Anyone who tries deserves recognition," eighty-year-old Frances told me once. The Center people seem to be in agreement with her and acknowledge their peers' achievement no matter how small it may be.

Although I emphasized earlier that Lake District Senior Center is not an isolated retreat for the elderly, the Center is an age-homogeneous community and this fact has various positive impacts on its participants. For instance, people can discuss experiences of growing old as well as of their past without meeting scorn or boredom. At the Center, the elderly can easily find sympathetic listeners when they tell what a chore it is to button a shirt, tie shoelaces or walk to the kitchen to fetch a cup of coffee.

The past is also a frequent topic of their conversations. For the Center participants, a Model T Ford and the Great Depression belong not in a museum or a history book, but in their own actual experiences. When Mabel brought up her father's Model T Ford, everyone within earshot joined in and the room was filled with lively conversation and laughter. Reminiscence is often played as a collective game. One common game is to show pictures of their youth and guess who they are. Another game consists of a series of questions which goes, "How many of you remember . . . ?" People are asked to remember such things in the past as victory gardens, box socials and the first pair of nylon stockings they ever owned. After each question, participants volunteer their stories. Diane, for instance, talked about her late mother, who was an excellent cook. She recalled that her mother's boxed dinner was always in high demand at the box socials. Marge described the moment of happiness and anger in her youth when her husband brought home six pairs of nylon stockings. To give her this surprise present, he had spent the money set aside to buy coal for the following week. The reminiscence game allows people to relive their pasts together and share a good time at present.

Older people are often depicted as living in the past to escape the grim reality of the present. The truth is quite contrary, however. The elderly's reminiscence is more oriented to the present than is generally assumed; it helps reaffirm their personal identity apart from society's characterization of them as marginal and anomalous beings. On the significance of reminiscence, Myerhoff argues, "[Reminiscence] is often the reach for personal integration, the experience of continuity, and the recognition of personal unity beneath the flow and flux of ordinary life" (1978:199–200). Sharing the past with their contemporaries is particularly effective in satisfying these needs, for it enables them to set an individual's private experiences within a common time frame and "[bridges] the gap between private and public experiences" (Vesperi 1985:74–75). Consequently, collective reminiscence contributes to enhancing elderly's sense of belonging.[11]

The age-homogeneity among the Center people also generates different meanings to advanced age. At the Center, advanced age loses its saliency, and this fact has a significant impact on overall feelings of the individual elderly in his or her life. Ward argues:

A stigma attached to the general status of "old person" will have little effect if older people are not attending to age as a relevant personal characteristic; that is, a general stigma associated with old age is not brought to bear on personal assessments of identity and well-being. Old age may be demoralizing when it is made salient to the individual, as with the changes which cause an ''old'' identity. (1984:228)

My research supports Ward's argument. At the Center, not only does advanced age lose its negative connotation, but also becomes a source of pride. Young visitors to the Center remark on the elderly's readiness to disclose their age to virtual strangers. My own experiences confirm their comments. Most of the elderly volunteered their ages upon telling me their names.

It seems that the more advanced their age, the prouder they are of their age. Correspondingly, the Center people treat their peers who enjoy an extraordinarily long life with special attention and respect. The Thursday group confers lifetime membership to its members who have reached age 85. Birthdays of those in their late eighties and nineties receive special attention. On Elaine's ninetieth birthday, a large cake was ordered from a bakery and some longtime friends brought her a gift. Many elderly and the Center staff gathered to celebrate her long life.

Mary, the oldest at age 97, personifies such a positive meaning of advanced age at the Center. Her appearance always commands the special attention of everybody present. People are happy to see her and go to greet her. They also start talking to each other about her age and her admirable qualities: ''She is 97 years old!'' ''She lives alone in a senior citizens' apartment.'' ''She occasionally takes senior citizen bus trips.''[12] ''She still makes beautiful cards using pressed flowers she herself prepares.'' In short, Mary is a ''celebrity'' at Lake District Senior Center. Remarkable as Mary may be, it is her age that makes her extraordinary. Her advanced age is not a curse. Instead, it is treated as an asset, not only for her, but also for other Center participants.

I have examined various positive impacts that participation in the Senior Center has on older Americans. The most significant, though perhaps covert, function of Lake District Senior Center is that it allows the elderly to play a social drama in conformity to dominant cultural values, despite their limited resources. The next section explores this function of the Senior Center further. I will examine various social networks formed at Lake District Senior Center and illustrate how the elderly try to bridge the wide gap existing between cultural ideals and the realities of old age.

SOCIAL NETWORKS AT LAKE DISTRICT SENIOR CENTER

Lake District Senior Center provides an arena where its participants can establish various social networks for information, mutual support and exchange. These networks enhance the elderly's social integration and well-being. They also reveal that three dominant cultural values—independence, egalitarianism and individual choice—play an important role in guiding the elderly in coping with old age.

Support Networks

Support networks are crucial for older Americans to maintain an independent life in the face of declining physical, mental and financial abilities. In many societies, the formation of support networks follows social conventions and is based on such factors as geographical proximity and membership in the communal or occupational organization. The indispensability of mutual support often requires that participation be mandatory. By contrast, among the elderly at Lake District Senior Center, no matter how important support networks may be, participation in them is always voluntary and their formation is based on individual choice. As a result, there are many different ways or reasons to form support networks. Some support partners see each other almost every day while others primarily use the telephone for communication and seldom see each other. The criteria for choosing partners also vary, including former colleagues, neighbors, shared interests (e.g., hobbies), shared experiences (e.g., former occupation) and so on.

Despite these variations and the ad hoc nature of network formation, support networks among the Center people exhibit certain patterns. One such characteristic is their multiple participation in more than one network and, as a result, compartmentalizing their involvement in any one of them. The case of Diane and Helen illustrates the point.

Diane, age 85, and Helen, a decade younger, are both retired teachers and live on the same block. They belong to the same church and some of the same groups at Lake District Senior Center. They also share a ride because Diane drives but Helen does not. Since Diane and Helen spend a lot of time together, the Center people regard them as a pair. If one is present and the other is not, they either inquire what happened to the latter or assume she is simply out of sight. Each of them lives in a big, old house by herself. Neither has been married, nor has close relatives living nearby. Thus, for both Diane and Helen, this partnership is an essential source of support, security and safety. They call every day at designated times to check on each other. Each has a key to the other's house. When Diane fell in the bathtub and was unable to move, she said she was not panicked because she knew Helen would eventually come and call for help. Help did come as Diane had anticipated.

Diane and Helen depend on each other and maintain close relationships. Yet, their seemingly extensive ties do not include economic commitment. They are limited to an exchange of favors and moral and emotional support. In addition, their involvement with each other is not exclusive. Despite their closeness, both have other networks of supporters. Diane claims that there are three friends she could not do without. One is Helen, obviously. The second is Louise. Since Louise and Diane are both avid readers, they exchange books. They also spend holidays together. The third, Marsha, is an old family friend. She is one of the few people with whom Diane, the last survivor of her generation of relatives, can share memories of her family. Helen has friends of similar importance including those she spends holidays with. She also has networks of friends with whom she exchanges hospitality. When Helen hosts a dinner party at her home, Diane drives Helen to the grocery store. But, Diane is invited only on those occasions when she and other guests belong to the same social circle.

This piecemeal participation in support networks, as Diane and Helen's case exemplifies, is a distinctive pattern observed among other participants at Lake District Senior Center. Why do not older Americans form extensive and exclusive ties with others for mutual support? What accounts for such piecemeal participation in support networks?

The answer lies in the elderly's quest for independence. By distributing their sources of support among different people, they avoid total dependency on any one individual.[13] The elderly's quest for independence is also manifested in their efforts to maintain equal partnership in support networks. Although forming support networks is imperative for their survival, it means to depend on others. Dependency, however, is a cultural taboo. Egalitarian relationships with support partners resolve this dilemma. One way to have an equal partnership, and thereby a sense of independence, is to complement each other's missing resources.[14] Diane and Helen's case provides a good example.

As mentioned earlier, Helen no longer drives and depends on Diane for a ride. By return, Helen offers resources Diane finds valuable. For instance, Helen serves as ears and legs for Diane, who is almost deaf and lame. When they drive together, Helen sits next to Diane and draws her attention to significant sounds Diane should know as a driver, such as the turn signal which did not stop automatically. Helen also navigates for Diane when they go to an unfamiliar place. To complement Diane's driving, Helen walks for Diane. Frequently, Helen does errands for Diane at banks and stores while Diane waits in the parked car.

The support relationships between Diane and Helen are mutually beneficial and based on equal partnership. Although both find this partnership indispensable, they also try to minimize their dependency on each other. Thus, Helen sometimes walks to the Senior Center. She also takes a bus. When Helen had an appointment with her hairdresser soon after recovering from a severe case of influenza, she accepted Diane's offer of a ride only after Diane's persistent persuasion. Diane makes similar efforts to minimize her dependency on Helen. She occasionally walks to banks and stores on her own, slowly and using her cane.

Diane and Helen's case shows that forming informal support networks is essential for the very survival of older Americans. It also illustrates that older Americans circumvent the cultural taboo of dependency by establishing multiple support networks and maintaining equal partnership in them.

Social Exchange

As in the case of support networks, social exchange at Lake District Senior Center is characterized by three dominant cultural values: independence, egalitarianism and individual choice. For instance, the principle of participation in exchange relationships is an individual choice. Consequently, there is no standard pattern of participation. At one end of the spectrum are those who go to the Center every day and structure their lives according to the schedules of their Center participation. These people maintain regular and personal exchange with their peers. The Center is a "home away from home" for them. At the other end are nonparticipating members, those who pay membership fees, buy the Senior Discount Card, and send a donation check during the annual "Seniors are Giving" fund-raising campaign. Their exchange at the Center is limited to an impersonal transaction between the organization and the individual.

Individual choice governs withdrawal from exchange networks as well. One outcome of this truly voluntary nature of the Center participation is the fuzziness of the group boundary. It is not always clear who belongs to the group. If regulars are absent from the Center activities, people inquire what happened to them. If they find that absent members are sick or have lost a loved one, they send a get-well card or a sympathy card. When Dorothy, a loyal member of the knitting group, did not show up, her unexplained absence caused some concern. A number of people volunteered what they knew about her. One said that her friend visited Dorothy just the day before and found her well. Someone else told the group that Dorothy was at church Sunday morning. Still another claimed that she saw Dorothy at a bank that very morning.

The Center people's concern and exchange of information about absentees confirms their membership in the group. However, if their absence continues without apparent reasons, people stop contacting them. They assume that their friends stopped coming for some reasons they do not want to share and respect their intentions. During the course of my field work, Dorothy's participation in the knitting group followed this pattern. Dorothy, a regular, became a marginal member. Ambiguous membership, such as Dorothy's, sometimes creates information gaps. At a monthly birthday celebration of the Thursday group, the secretary called the name of a deceased member who had not been seen at the Center for an extended period of time before her death. Apparently, the secretary missed her obituary which appeared in the local newspaper several months earlier. Some members mumbled about her death and an awkward silence followed.

Dowd (1975) and Matthews (1979) argue that, contrary to the common assumption, older Americans' social marginality is not necessarily imposed by society, but is often the outcome of their own volition. Behind such self-imposed isolation is their quest for independence. The elderly's diminishing resources prevent them from reciprocating and thereby create dependency on others. Since dependency is culturally abhorred, they choose to withdraw from exchange relationships.

The manner of social interaction at Lake District Senior Center minimizes the cost for exchange and enables those with meager resources to maintain balanced transactions. That is, the elderly need not withdraw to avoid dependency. How do they minimize the cost for exchange? For one thing, acceptable "currencies" for exchange at the Center are different from those in the outside world.

The most frequently exchanged and highly appreciated resources are small tokens that make others feel good. The Center people make gestures of affection—hugging and patting on the shoulder—and give phone calls to keep in touch. They are also generous in offering kind words. Frequently, what people wear triggers positive words from their peers: "I like the color of your sweater. It brightens a dreary day like today." "What a beautiful brooch you wear!" Class activities are always met by praises and encouragements: "I like the way you draw this blue flower." "You knit very well. You started just last week, and you have finished this much!" There is no monetary cost for engaging in this kind of exchange. Besides, reciprocating brings an emotional gain because it makes both the giver and the receiver feel good.

Another common and inexpensive "currency" for exchange is information: cholesterol-free eggs and bacon, a new type of hearing aid, healthy and easy-to-cook recipes for the elderly living alone and so on. These pieces of information may not be useful for younger Americans. But, for the elderly, they are not only valuable, but in some cases make major changes in their lives. Kathleen's cataract operation provides a good example.

When I met her, her eyesight was so poor that she could not read nor knit. Her right eye was blind due to the failure of a past cataract operation, and the cataract was thickened in her left eye. Although Kathleen needed another eye operation, her past experience made her very reluctant. The casual conversation at the Center changed her life. From her peers, she learned about a new type of operation, went ahead with it, and regained her vision.

Besides the use of inexpensive "currency," group-based exchange also reduces the cost. When someone becomes ill or has lost a loved one, the Center people circulate a get-well card or a sympathy card for signatures and send it to their peer. When the occasion arises, they are reciprocated by a card from a group of participants, rather than a multitude of cards, one from each of them.

A dish-to-pass meal also illustrates the advantage of the group-based exchange. It is a less costly alternative to hosting a dinner party or going to a restaurant. It frees people from the "obligation to return" (Mauss 1967) because giving and receiving take place simultaneously. In addition, by accommodating those who no longer cook or those who have dietary restrictions,[15] a dish-to-pass meal displays another important pattern that characterizes the elderly's interactions at the Center: their avoidance of making distinctions among themselves.

This avoidance has various implications. For one thing, it encourages the participation of those with physical and financial limitations. The Center people show great tolerance toward the handicapped and treat them as their peers. They communicate with the hearing impaired by raising their voices, and move with the lame by slowing their own pace. In addition, at the Center, any project which incurs an expense is carefully handled no matter how small the cost may be. For instance, the Thursday group's plan of having a special lunch or dessert went forward only after members unanimously agreed to pay for it. The amount involved was small: a dollar for strawberry shortcake to welcome spring or two dollars for a hot dog lunch with beverage and dessert to celebrate Independence Day.

The Center people avoid making distinctions not only in their socioeconomic and physical conditions, but also in their ethnic backgrounds. No clear class or ethnic boundary is drawn at the Center, despite the heterogeneity of its partic- ipants. Rather than forming separate groups of their own, people of different ethnicity and socioeconomic backgrounds are distributed among various groups.[16] They sit side-by-side in the same group and are engaged in activities, such as knitting, painting and singing.

It is remarkable that such attitudes go in tandem with their heterogeneity. Why do the Center people avoid distinguishing differences among them? Why do they not "flock together" with those of "the same feather"? One possible explanation may be that the Center is an age-segregated community. In the face of the inhospitable world outside, they are all "insiders" and being old, a com- mon denominator among them, supersedes all the other differences.

Probable as this explanation may be in some cases, it is not sufficient here because: (1) Lake District Senior Center is not an isolated retreat for the elderly, and (2) the Center people do not express the "we versus they" feeling toward the outside world, which may be observed at some other age-segregated com- munities (e.g., Jerrome 1988; Keith 1977).[17]

Class and ethnic backgrounds are important in identifying who one is. How- ever, since human beings are complex aggregates of various facets and accu- mulated experiences, class and ethnicity are merely two of many building blocks of individual identity. Furthermore, in the light of the compartmentalized, rather than total and exclusive, relationships the Center people maintain with their peers, their class and ethnic backgrounds do not necessarily play a significant role in shaping their relationships with others. It is not unusual that the Center people do not have some vital information about their friends: for example, what kind of jobs their friends had before retirement or whether they have any chil- dren or not. Individual choice and the context of social interactions determine what kind of information one shares with others.[18]

Although compartmentalized social ties may undermine the significance of class and ethnic backgrounds, I argue that egalitarianism is the vital force behind the elderly's avoidance of making distinctions among themselves. Maintaining egalitarian relationships is essential for the Center people, not only because egalitarianism is a dominant American value, but because it is a key to resolving their dilemma of depending on others to achieve a cultural ideal, independence.

The examination of social networks and exchanges at Lake District Senior Center illustrates that (1) three dominant values—independence, egalitarianism and individual choice—guide the elderly in coping with old age, and (2) the elderly's participation in the Center helps them bridge the wide gap between cultural ideals and the realities of old age.

CONCLUSION

My encounter with old age in the United States came as an unexpected culture shock. The negative view of aging and the marginality of the elderly in American society are strikingly different from the one I had known in Japan. I was both puzzled and intrigued by such differences. The existing literature explains Americans' negative attitudes toward aging by regarding old age as the antithesis of cultural ideals. That is, culture is the "culprit" in the "problem" of old age. The relevant literature, however, sheds little light on how older Americans cope with this apparent cultural dilemma.

My research shows that, contrary to the suggestions made by some previous studies, older Americans deal with problems of aging within the realm of American culture and that conformity to cultural ideals—independence, egalitarianism, individual choice, in particular—not only provides them with crucial coping strategies, but also enhances their sense of well-being. In other words, paradoxical as it may seem, culture creates problems but at the same time offers resources for responding to them.

The actual experiences of aging I observed at Lake District Senior Center present quite a different picture from the prevailing stereotypes. Hardships of old age in America have been compared to a "shipwreck" (Sontag 1972:29). But, most people at the Center do not succumb to such difficulties and passively wait to "founder on the rocks." Instead, they try to make the best of their lives by exploring new roles and new meanings in life and ingeniously tapping whatever resources are available. In short, elderly Americans are "pioneers." While the absence of well-established cultural models for aging creates many different and seemingly ad hoc ways of dealing with old age, it is their culture that guides older Americans in treading into the unfamiliar territory of old age. In other words, elderly "pioneers" are equipped with a "map" to venture into the unknown world, though their "map" may not provide detailed descriptions of the new territory.

Culture also shapes the organization of Lake District Senior Center. It was established by a score of private citizens in the early 1950s when an organization exclusively for the elderly, such as theirs, was virtually unknown. The Center, therefore, carried out a pioneering task of identifying unmet social needs for the elderly and finding ways to deal with them. It is a voluntary association which Tocqueville (1945) found typically American where a group of private citizens assume public tasks by helping others to help themselves. Lake District Senior Center is an organization for the elderly, by the elderly, in the true sense of the term.

The elderly's participation in the Center activities makes various positive impacts on them. It keeps them busy, rescues them from desolation and enhances their social worthiness. Some Center activities resurrect their pasts from oblivion and make them meaningful. In addition, the age-homogeneity of the Center community transforms the negative connotation of advanced age into a positive

one. Among various roles the Center plays in the elderly's lives, the most essential is to enhance their ability to enact a social drama in accordance with
cultural rules. The Center serves as a stage where the elderly can negotiate the
discrepancies between the "is" and the "ought" of their lives in the face of
their declining abilities.

As a native Japanese, initially I found old age in America was a mystery. My
research, however, has enabled me to observe and participate in the lives of
older Americans and has clarified many unknowns about aging in America. I
was most impressed by older Americans' quest for independence and their in-
genuity in achieving this cultural ideal, because their attitudes show a virtual
opposition to the way Japanese elderly try to find their security, worthiness and
identity in mutual dependency and social embeddedness (see Chapter 10). Aging
is a pan-human experience, but it is also socially and culturally constructed.

NOTES

1. The nation's very first senior center, the William Hodson Community Center in
New York City, is the "precursor" to this model (Krout 1989:16). It was founded in
1943 by the City's Welfare Department to serve low-income elderly (Krout 1989:15–
16).

2. A number of senior centers were established following the birth of the nation's
first one. However, the idea of having such an organization exclusively for the aged was
not as widespread as today. Krout estimates that there were no more than 200 senior
centers throughout the country by the end of the 1950s (1989:16).

3. Other organizations for the elderly appeared much later in the local community:
AARP (American Association for Retired Persons) in 1964, the County Office for the
Aging in 1975, and RSVP (Retired Senior Volunteer Program) in 1977.

4. It is also Lake District Senior Center that initiated the Senior Citizens' Discount
Program in the local community in 1970.

5. A flood and a fire forced them to move from their first and third homes, respectively. The second was demolished. They lost their fourth home when it became a target
of an urban renewal project.

6. A senior center in a neighboring county, which started as a private voluntary
organization in the 1950s, became a public institution under the sponsorship of the local
County Office for the Aging.

7. For instance, updating the Center's long mailing list and mailing a large volume
of newsletters (8,700 in 1995) would be impossible or too costly without their contributions. The elderly volunteers also run the Center's Gift Shop.

8. Fund-raising is one of the most important activities at Lake District Senior Center.
The annual "Seniors are Giving" campaign solicits donations from elderly residents in
the county. The total of the 1993 campaign reached almost $70,000, though the amount
received from each donor was small. A variety of sales—the annual Grandma's Attic
Sales, yard sales, bake sales and so on—also bring in revenue. Other major sources of
self-generated income include membership fees, discount card sales, donations and the
Gift Shop sales.

9. Major weekly programs during the period of my fieldwork included therapeutic

exercise, clay workshop, needlecraft, photo assistance, art class, bowling, swimming, toy-making, quilting, social security consulting, several dancing groups, music history, foreign language classes, the Thursday group meeting, Men's group meeting and so on. Among the special events was the Centennial Tea to commemorate the city's 100th birthday in 1988. A number of dignitaries including the mayor were present.

10. The figure is based on the minimum wage of $3.35/hour at the time of my field-work.

11. Kastenbaum argues that the private nature of the past tends to isolate the elderly from younger members of society. By sharing the past with their contemporaries, "the past is brought alive into the present, and no longer has that solitary, private quality that we Americans tend to suspect and resent" (1966:20).

12. When I went on a day-excursion sponsored by the Center in 1993, Florence was among the group. Although she was 103 years old, she got on and off the bus without any obvious problems and enjoyed lunch, as well as the beautiful fall colors, with the others.

13. The same avoidance is applicable to their own children as well. For this reason, even for those who enjoy frequent and loving intergenerational contacts, it is very important to form informal support networks with their peers. The elderly's reliance on various services and facilities for the elderly, such as using the transportation services and living in the senior citizens' apartments, also reflects their efforts to minimize dependency on others.

14. American efforts to maintain egalitarianism and independence in support networks makes a striking contrast with hierarchical social order and mutual dependency underlying support relationships in Japan. See Tsuji 1994.

15. The former bring something they buy at the store, such as cookies and fruit, while the latter bring their own bag lunches to eat with the rest of the group.

16. The formation of some Center groups is based on their members' occupation before retirement; for example, teachers or machinists. Although these groups are homogeneous in one criterion, their members belong to other groups as well. Also, one of the Center groups consists of residents in the city's black neighborhood and their monthly meetings are held at their community hall. However, the group is not exclusively for black elderly. Eleanor, an eighty-four-year-old white woman, and I attended their meeting once and were met with a warm welcome. Furthermore, members of this group are active in various other groups which meet at the Senior Center.

17. The absence of the "we versus they" feeling at the Center may be attributed to the heterogeneity of its participants.

18. When the local newspaper featured Alice's heroic involvement in the resistance movement during World War II, some of her old friends were surprised to learn about her unknown past. They asked Alice, "Why didn't you tell us?" Alice's answer was, "You never asked."

CHAPTER 18

History, Community Context and the Perception of Old Age in a Rural Irish Town

Jeanette Dickerson-Putman

I was worse off financially in the past. Everyone was in the same situation. Before we had to weigh up every penny. It has gotten much easier especially since we got the pension. Now you can go and buy whatever you want. It came in when the State was formed. We don't have any financial worries now at all. Certainly finances were a major worry in the past. I'm so used to making do with this, that and the other that I still try to stretch things.

Mary from Blessington, age 67

Blessington is not the same to me any more. The population . . . has changed an awful lot as far as I am concerned. Too many blow-ins have moved in from Dublin. They think that they know everything. The blow-ins moving in has been bad for the area. I see people mentioned in the newspaper that live in Blessington and I have never even heard of them.

Michael from Blessington, age 71

People years ago were very great with one another. Neighbors would call into see each other and they helped one another. Everyone got on well together. The young people don't care about visiting now. A lot of them have no time for hearing about years gone by. They are more concerned with the future and looking ahead.

Margaret from Blessington, age 81

Margaret, Michael and Mary have different ideas about the the nature of life for the elderly in the rural Irish town of Blessington. All these people have experienced a great deal of change since their childhoods. Margaret was born in 1920 with a degenerative muscle disease and experienced the destruction of her childhood home in Ballianahown when the Blessington Lakes were created in the late 1930s. She and her husband continue to do some part-time farming and await visits from their six children, who all live within a three-hour radius. Michael is retired and lives in the town of Blessington with his disabled wife, who benefits from visits by the District Nurse. He and his wife, who never had children, ran a shop in the town from 1930 to 1972. They left the business and sold their moderate-size farm to developers from Dublin in 1972. These "foreigners" built the condominiums that attract commuters from Dublin. Today, Michael spends much of his time caring for his wife. Mary is a widow who lives in a low-income tract home in Blessington town. She has twelve children and is considered very blessed because six of her children have married and settled locally.

Between June 1987 and August 1988 I resided in the community of Blessington, located eighteen miles south of Dublin. The purpose of my stay was to conduct a community study for a cross-cultural aging project entitled Project AGE (discussed in Part I). Ethnographically rich data about Blessington and its elderly were collected through participant-observation, structured and unstructured interviews and the collection of life histories. The elderly in Blessington were very interested in my work and were particularly anxious to talk about their lives and the history of the area. When I first arrived I was surprised to find that older people were not highly visible in the town. Only occasionally did you see an older person going to the shops, to the weekly Bingo game or walking to and from one of the two churches. It was also interesting that older people did not seem to congregate in local pubs like they did in Clifden (another Irish community in Project AGE). As my rapport with and knowledge of older community members increased, I began to understand some of the ways in which the particular character of Blessington affected their perception of old age and their past and present participation in the community.

This rural town and the context it provides for aging is the result of various forces including Irish cultural traditions, the continuing development of the Republic, creation of state-level resources for the elderly and the changing quality of relations between the rural town of Blessington and the urban center of Dublin.

IRISH RURAL LIFE

In order to understand how Blessington and other rural communities have changed through time and how these changes have affected the elderly, we first need to consider what rural Irish life was like in the past. Most of the detailed ethnographic descriptions of Ireland reflect rural life in the central and western parts of the country (Arensberg 1968; Arensberg and Kimball 1968).

Irish rural communities usually consisted of small market villages that served the needs of their surrounding farming population. Various factors affected the character and social organization of these communities. First, there was an integration and interdependence between both town and farm and among farmers that was expressed in bonds of reciprocity and neighborliness (Arensberg 1968: 143). Occupational differentiation also affected community life. Major occupations, in their order of ranking, included teachers, clergy, farmers, shopkeepers, traders/craftsmen and laborers (Cawley 1979). Farming supported most of the population. Family history and reputation also affected social life. Descent from core families (families with a long period of continuous residence in the area) gave some individuals greater status than others.

Irish culture is well-known for both its emphasis on familialism and for the honor, power and privilege that it afforded to its elderly. In fact, age and age status structured relations both within families and within and between communities (Arensberg 1968:110). In rural communities fathers and older men had adult status in their families and communities because they headed a farm and made decisions about the allocation of their sons' labor. Sons were subordinate to fathers until the family farm was turned over to a single son. This son could then inherit the farm and marry a bride of his father's choice. Although parents achieved the status of old age at this time, they would continue to be supported by the designated heir. O'Connor and Daly state that "in the eyes of the community, marriage made the 'boy' into a man and the father into an old man" (1983:18).

Great respect was displayed for the elderly within both the family and the community. Older men represented the interests of the community to the outside world. Groups of old men met regularly at specified houses to discuss community interests, to solve family and community problems and to orchestrate community integration (Arensberg 1968:129). In short, the old wielded considerable economic control within the family and also exerted extensive power in both community decision making and community organizations.

Although the above description gives a general outline of rural life in Ireland, it must also be remembered that the quality and specifics of rural life in eastern Irish communities situated near Dublin (like Blessington) probably differed significantly from this model (Hannan 1979; O'Connor and Daly 1983). People in communities like Blessington had greater opportunities and access to urban services. Many of the elderly that I came to know had worked in dairies, as housekeepers and in the quarries that supplied the construction companies in Dublin. These opportunities were especially crucial to noninheriting sons who were expected to support themselves. The availability of employment in Dublin also meant that fewer people were forced to emigrate and thus kin networks were less dispersed.

STATE DEVELOPMENT, RURAL-URBAN INTEGRATION AND THE ELDERLY

Prior to 1900 most older Irish supported themselves or relied on family and community support. Since 1922 state machinery in the Republic of Ireland has had an increasing impact on the resources and lifestyle of the elderly. Some of the government services and benefits now available to the elderly include pensions, fuel allowances, free medical services and a variety of other cash and noncash benefits (National Council of the Aged [NCA] 1984). The work of various voluntary organizations and church-related groups also plays a critical role in the provision of community care for Irish elderly (NCA 1983:24).

The gradual absorption of rural communities into larger urban structures also affects the resources of the elderly in Ireland (Cawley 1979). Cities impact rural areas because they offer employment for rural residents and attract commuters who wish to live in the less crowded and more scenic countryside. Polarization based on occupation, residential segregation and cultural norms can emerge in rural communities with the immigration of commuters (Cawley 1979; Pahl 1965).

An "us versus them" dichotomy often develops in urban fringe communities because "foreigners" have no preexisting links with the rural communities in which they live. They do not fit into the local occupational and prestige hierarchies and local people fear that the "foreigners" will change and take over their communities. This polarization and segregation could undermine both the community integration that contributed to the respect for older people and the leadership positions and power of the elderly in their communities.

BLESSINGTON

Blessington's location in the more developed eastern half of the country and its proximity to Dublin means that its residents and especially its elderly have been affected by the complex nature of state development.

The Manor of Blessington was created in 1669. The devastation and subsequent emigration that many western Irish communities (like Clifden) experienced during and after the potato famine of 1845–1846 was not felt by Blessington tenants. According to local lore, the generosity of landlords to both their own and other tenants actually led to an increase in Manor population during the famine years. Blessington remained a small market village, integrated by kinship and intermarriage and serving the needs of its surrounding rural farming population, up through the early 1930s (Daly 1981).

Respect for the elderly and age stratification affected Blessington life in both the towns and on the farms. Contemporary elderly in Blessington told me that in the past, older farmers, shopkeepers and publicans wielded considerable economic control within the family and undoubtedly exerted extensive power in both community decision making and community organizations.

Blessington, 1935–1965

The effects of state development and urbanism on Blessington dramatically increased during the period 1935–1943, when the Electricity and Supply Board

(ESB) and the Dublin Corporation created the Poulaphouca Reservoir (referred to locally as the Blessington Lakes) and Power Station near Blessington town.

Unfortunately, the Ballianahown Valley chosen for the scheme was also home to about 100 families. As part of the scheme, these families were offered financial compensation for their losses and most used this money to purchase farms outside the Blessington area. Many older people in the Blessington area feel that Ballianahown residents were not treated fairly by the State because they were given only three months to leave and because the compensation was not enough to buy a comparable farm. Increased State development also changed the character of the town and the interdependence between farmers and shopkeepers. A final impact of the creation of the Lakes was the inauguration of tourism, as the area became a popular spot for summer recreation.

Blessington, 1965–1987

The boom period of development came to Blessington in the late 1960s and 1970s when a local development organization effectively marketed the economic and scenic potential of the area. Between 1970 and 1980 the creation of both an industrial park and large tracts of low-income housing attracted many families to the area. In-migration reached a peak between 1971 and 1979 when Dubliners decided to build their dream homes near the Lakes or purchase private tract condominiums in town.

The development of the Blessington area and the immigration of commuters reached a plateau in the early 1980s. In the late 1980s there began a decline in population in the area as young people began to emigrate to find jobs.

Contemporary Blessington

My ethnographic research in Blessington focused on a sample of 170 community residents over the age of eighteen that was drawn from a study zone of about 2,000 persons, hereafter referred to as the Blessington area. This area includes the rural town of Blessington (with a total population of 1,322) as well as some of the surrounding farms and residential areas.

Contemporary Blessington is neither a bedroom community or a suburb of Dublin (Hamilton 1971; Social Studies Course [SSC] 1982). This is in large part because Blessington continues to offer a healthy economic environment for its residents. Over 30 businesses and 49 organizations serve the needs of the local community. In fact, only 7 percent (compared to the national average of 19%) of the residents (age 15–65) are unemployed. About half of the sampled population work locally and another 36 percent of the population commute to work in Dublin. Only about 15 percent are involved in farming.

THE ELDERLY OF BLESSINGTON

Older persons in Blessington comprise 10 percent of the population of the Blessington study area. Over half of older residents are widowed and the most common living arrangement is living alone. As noted earlier, people in town are most commonly seen in church and at the shops. Although there are many community organizations in Blessington, the elderly are most often involved in church-based activities.

A day in the life of Mary provides a good example of the daily activities of the elderly who live in Blessington town. Mary is up and doing the washing from the night before by 7:30 A.M. After making her twenty-year-old son's lunch and putting the wash in to soak, she's off to Mass. After Mass she does her daily shopping and is back home in time for lunch. Various grandchildren stop by to see Mary after school. When their parents come by to pick them up, they stop for a moment and have a cup of tea with their "mum." In the evening Mary cooks a meal for herself and her son. Once a week Mary gets her hair done in town and twice a week she plays Bingo.

As in the other Project AGE sites, a structured interview, a card sort game and the Cantril Self-Anchoring Ladder were used to understand how people conceptualized the lifecourse and the aging process. Most people in Blessington divided the lifecourse into four stages (18–29, 30–49, 50–65, 65+) based on the characteristics of family stage and social responsibility. Although residents strongly resisted naming these stages, further analysis revealed underlying similarities within the above four chronological groups and these were used to create the following named groups: (1) Single Adults/Getting Established, (2) Married/ Older Children, (3) Grandparents and (4) Older Grandparents. The last stage of life is viewed by the elderly as a return to the freedom and lack of responsibility experienced as youths. Older people were also often described as being grandparents and being retired.

The elderly in Blessington gave a high average score (4.9) for their current life satisfaction. When compared to the elderly included in Project AGE, the elderly of Blessington gave themselves the second highest score across all sites. Despite their high well-being score, they were ambivalent about how they perceived their own age category. About 40 percent said they did not like being in the last stage of life. In Blessington and five of the other Project AGE sites, physical problems were most commonly linked to a negative view of old age. A little over a third of elderly residents in Blessington also said they did not like being old because of loneliness. Another 41 percent preferred being in the old age category. When I asked Mary why she liked being old she told me that "my children are raised and I now have the freedom to enjoy my grandchildren."

CONTEMPORARY BLESSINGTON AS A RESOURCE FOR OLDER PEOPLE

Most older people in Blessington feel that the town is a good community for older people. For example, Margaret told me that she and many older people describe Blessington as a "quiet, caring community." There are three aspects of community life that are especially pleasing to older people. First, the town is a good place for older people because of the amenities it provides. Although the total contribution of state benefits to the lifestyles of the elderly is unknown, most (55 percent) Blessington elderly said that state pensions and other benefits contributed to a good old age. State-supported health and community care are also recognized as important resources for the elderly in Blessington. Many older residents said that they greatly benefited from the help provided by the doctor and District Nurse who operate out of the Eastern Health Board Clinic in town. An added bonus is the fact that both these health practitioners make house calls to the elderly. The District Nurse is especially concerned with older people living alone. She visits these elderly once a week in winter and once a month in the summer.

There are no local nursing homes or hospitals in Blessington, and the closest acute care hospital is in the larger town of Naas, a twenty-minute drive by automobile. Older persons can also receive specialized care at Baltinglass District Hospital, 45 minutes from Blessington by automobile. About ten elderly from Blessington are transported by bus once a week to an adult day care center that is part of Baltinglass Hospital. The local doctor "hospitalizes" frail elderly who are unable to live alone during the winter months. Many people don't own vehicles and the lack of well-developed public transportation means that elderly become isolated from family when they are hospitalized or institutionalized.

The availability of family care and support is a second reason why Blessington is a positive place to grow old in. In fact, over half the elderly in the area have daily contact with local relatives. This support usually comes from children who help their parents when they are sick and with activities such as grocery shopping and transportation to church and doctors. Mary feels that family support helped her to deal with her widowhood. She said:

After my husband died (four years ago) I let everything go. My children worried about me. Then my youngest decided to give up his flat in Dublin and move home about a year ago. Having him live with me has made all the difference. I have a commitment to do things now. I make his meals and wash his clothes. Now I have gotten over my husband's death. I can say that in the last year I have settled in to a life.

The presence and activities of the Blessington Area Senior's Citizen Committee is the third reason why older people feel that Blessington is a great community to live in. The Committee was formed in the mid-1960s by two members of the Irish Country Women's Association who volunteered to produce a Christmas dinner for local elderly in the Catholic Community Center. State grants to the Blessington Senior Citizens' Committee further extend community care to the elderly in Blessington. Michael, with a homebound spouse, especially appreciates the help of the Committee because their visits "allow me to get out and about and give my wife and I some time away from each other."

Today each of the twelve committee members, who range in age from 30 to 70, monitors the old in their area. A little over half of the Committee members were born and raised in the area. Most Committee members told me that such things as pensions, free fuel and transportation have given the elderly in the area much more security than they had in the past. Now the members see their main function as creating ties between local elders and providing services that older persons desire, such as the Christmas party and a summer outing every year. Committee members also visit the elderly at Baltinglass hospital and arrange for transportation to day care.

Even though almost nine out of ten elderly in Blessington think that it is a good community to grow old in, over half of these same people also told me that they could not relate to the people that lived in the town as a social group.

In the past, kinship, neighborliness, a homogeneity of experience and values and respect for the elderly contributed to community integration. Today many forms of social differentiation define life in contemporary Blessington. Local people recognize a difference between nonlocals and locals. Locals (35 percent of the population) were born, raised and settled in Blessington. Nonlocals (68 percent of the population) were born outside Blessington. A person remains a nonlocal regardless of how long he or she has lived in the area. Local people (especially the elderly) further differentiate nonlocal people into Council Housing (low-income housing) people and "blow-ins" or bungalow people. Although one could refer to these differences as class differences, local residents refer to these differences in terms of residence and interaction. It is the distinction between blow-ins and local people that is most salient for the elderly of Blessington.

According to the local stereotype, blow-ins build expensive homes near the Lakes and on the road to Dublin. They are college-educated and commute to professional and managerial jobs in Dublin. Blow-ins also belong to many local organizations, most of which they have introduced. They also shop outside of town and send their children to school outside Blessington.

Michael's description of a blow-in is representative of how many elderly people view the newest immigrants:

The Lakes attracted people from Dublin. You'll find a bungalow everywhere there is a view of the Lake. I almost consider myself a stranger in town. They don't have anything in common with me. They aren't really a part of the area because they never spend any time or money in town. Yet they always try to change things. They want to build this or develop that. Local people resent this. I never get involved. They don't know our ways so they shouldn't try to change things. Local people also don't want to fix up their shops or develop the area around the Lake to attract day trippers from the city because we've had enough of Dublin already.

For many locals the presence of the blow-ins is further evidence that Dublin planners wish to develop Blessington as a bedroom community for Dublin. While most natives acknowledge that some growth and development is inevitable, they are opposed to the pattern and style of growth established by Dublin in the 1930s.

Resentment about these past events affects the participation of many locals (especially the elderly) in contemporary community affairs. Many locals will not support even the best new ideas and activities if they are proposed by blow-ins. This is especially true if the goal is to develop the tourist potential of the Lake area.

Some local people also feel that development will slow down if they do not participate in it, thereby preserving what is left of rural life. Although in the minority, local or native people control most of the shops and own much of the land in the area. In this way their lack of participation does affect the growth of the community.

CONCLUSION

Images of the past affect the elderly's perception of the contemporary community of Blessington as both a resource and source of support. So too, images of the past affect the elderly's perception of available resources, what constitutes a good old age and the role that the state plays in this stage of life.

The vast majority of elderly in Blessington feel that the town provides a good environment to grow old in. When community residents like Mary, Margaret and Michael talk about the positive aspects of their town they emphasize the amenities it provides. The elderly in Blessington feel that the state resources available today have brought them greater economic security than what was available in the past.

When focusing on the negative aspects of community life, many residents like Michael and Margaret say that they do not view most community residents as a resource or source of support. In the past, the elderly claim to have been active in community affairs and leadership and saw residents and community groups as a source of support and prestige. The elderly base their current idea of community on their image of the way Blessington was in the past. Rich descriptions of Blessington as it existed prior to the 1940s continue to flavor the conversations and stories of the elderly.

Many elderly like Michael feel that state interference and urban expansion have negatively affected the character of the town and area. A wide variety of new people have moved into the community over a short period of time and as yet no integrative mechanisms have developed to bind them together. Many elderly have withdrawn from community activities but refuse to support efforts to develop the area for tourism and recreation.

A similar set of processes related to urban expansion has affected Momence, Illinois, one of the U.S. sites in Project AGE. These processes, however, did not affect community integration and the participation of the elderly, because the immigration of newcomers was gradual. The gradualness of this process meant that local community dynamics were not disrupted. Contemporary Momence, with its strong residential stability and sense of community, provides a context in which the elderly are both highly visible and active in town affairs. In fact, elderly in Momence continue to gain status, positions of dominance and authority because of their age and length of residence in Momence.

Despite their withdrawal from community interaction and activities, many elderly still view Blessington as a positive context for aging because of the availability of care and support from family, friends and community-based organizations such as the Senior Citizen's Committee. This care reflects the fact that respect and support for the elderly are still very important aspects of contemporary Irish culture. In the future, however, changing economic circumstances leading to the continued emigration of young people may affect the availability of these important resources for the elderly in Blessington and other urban fringe communities. This would place even greater pressure on community-based organizations to fill the gap left by the state and the family. The activities of these groups in rural towns like Blessington may hold the key for the future quality of life for the elderly because these activities themselves could help create the cohesion and integration that is absent from these contemporary urban fringe communities. The creation of new forms of community integration and interaction would pave the way for the reemergence of the elderly into community life.

CHAPTER 19

Uncle Ed, Super Runner and the Fry Cook: Old Men on the Street

Jay Sokolovsky and Carl Cohen

The Bow'ry, the Bow'ry.
They say such things
And they do strange things
On the Bow'ry, the Bow'ry!
I'll never go there any more!

These popular lyrics from the 1891 hit show "A Trip to Chinatown" once helped introduce New York's Bowery to the American public. They also epitomize the contemporary situation of this urban zone, which remains our nation's most infamous skid row. In the mid-1980s, a trip into the world of older men who make this area their home illuminated America's emerging human tragedy of this decade—the dramatic growth in poverty and homelessness. Ironically, as President Reagan was proclaiming, "America is back—standing tall, looking to the eighties with courage, confidence, and hope" (State of the Union Address, January 25, 1984), economic policies of his "opportunity society" were forcing thousands of older adults to find their abodes on the mean streets of cities like New York. This chapter will provide an interior view of the daily existence of three such men who are battling homelessness in old age.

In examining the lives of Uncle Ed, Miles (the fry cook) and Roland (the super runner), it will become apparent that for men who are old, poor and live in or rely on the Bowery for survival, each day is likely to present a major crisis. The three men do not represent by any means the total variety of social types on the Bowery. However, the dilemmas they face daily, the paths that led them to the area and their future prospects constitute key patterns that were repeated in the lives of the several hundred men we studied.

The widespread destruction of single-room occupancy housing has dramatically increased the number of older homeless adults. This photograph shows one such hotel in the process of conversion into expensive condominium apartments.

PROFILE: UNCLE ED, THE CLASSIC BOWERY MAN

It was one of those rare times that Ed showed real anger when he was not drunk. In a rage he shouted, ''How could such a freakin' stupid thing happen to someone who is so needy. I need my food stamps back, you stupid bitch.'' He almost lunged across the table at the thin black woman working the computer in Room 301 of the Human Resources Administration. Instead, he slumped back in his chair, embarrassed at the loss of his usually pleasant demeanor and feeling the wall of bureaucracy pressing on his head. Without another word he left the office and headed back toward the Bowery. Although only 56 years old, Ed worked to fight off a dependent, idle old age, but such frustrating experiences produced feelings of hopelessness and cravings for a bottle.

Before returning to his tiny cubicle, he rested on a park bench and contemplated the oppressive reality of most Bowery lives—profound poverty. From a monthly check of $277.85, Uncle Ed pays $132.18 for a five-by-nine space with thin wooden walls and a chicken wire ceiling. Despite free mission clothing and 25-cent breakfasts and lunches from the Bowery Residents' Committee, between five and six dollars are spent daily to pay for coffee, cigarettes, his dinner and other incidentals. It is indeed a rare month when he does not need to borrow money at the typical usurious rates—borrow ten dollars and pay back fourteen.

Ed is a jovial caricature of the classic skid-row alcoholic. Nicknamed by a nurse after he provided help to others while himself a patient at a sobering-up station, he tries to show a nonoffensive helpful face to all he meets. A clean-shaven, comely person when sober, he is usually dressed in second-hand mission clothes, which as often as not are ill-fitted to his bulky frame and pot belly. As he walks the streets of the Bowery hardly five minutes will go by without someone shouting "Hiya, Uncle Ed." Every other block will find Ed passing some deli or second-hand clothes shop where he used to find casual work running errands. He has been on his own since the age of 16, working menial jobs in restaurants, hotels and construction sites.

Seldom without a cigarette, he chain smokes Camels—lighting up for a few minutes, putting it out delicately with his fingers, clamping the butt securely behind his ear, only to resume smoking a short time later. To emphasize a point while he speaks, Ed will crinkle his pug nose, roll his eyes up into the side of his head and discuss in raspy, measured words his life on the streets. "I have had in the past a bout with alcoholism where I was one time four months sober and then at one time six months sober, but then I went off the deep end, starting to drink again, but this time I'm sober five months." His last major drinking spree began about eight months before, following a bitter argument with a woman he was living with in Queens for a short time. As he put it:

During the night, I guess John Barleycorn [alcohol] talked to me, I just got up. . . . Well, fuck it, I'm going back to the bottle. I've already got it in my mind that the only place I can go is back to the bottle so I drank a bottle. Three-quarters of a fifth of gin, and then I went out to the bus stop and I got on a bus to Penn Station, bought some more gin and came back to the Bowery and this is where I am now. I come right to the Pacific Hotel around three in the morning. I saw the clerk which I know personally, Pete's his name. He said, "What do you want Uncle Ed?" I said, "I want a room. I gotta sleep this shit off."

As Ed was white, old and could pay the $3.50 for the night, he was given a cubicle and began one of his cyclical trips into oblivion.

I'd wake up in the morning and I'd be so discouraged, depressed, knowing that I just had another goddamned day with a bottle where I never made no plans, everything just came as they came, you know. I'm an early riser, up by six, even when I'm drinking, I sleep two hours and I think I got a good night's sleep. I'd usually see if I've got the dollar and a quarter for the first pint of T-Bird [Thunderbird wine] and if I didn't, I'd go out panhandle at Lafayette and Houston streets. There's a good light there where I'd bum a card [panhandle]) and I'd usually walk down Grand Street going up to drivers and they'd give me a quarter, or wipe his windshield and hope he gives ya a quarter. Usually I go up and tell 'em, I don't want a dime for a cup of coffee, bullshit. I just go right up to them and I'd say, "Excuse me, sir, could you pardon me, I'm thirty-five cents short on a drink, could you probably help me out?" And usually I found out that they think more of you if you were man enough to ask them towards a drink instead of the old bullshit you need a quarter for a cup of coffee. That went out. By eight o'clock [A.M.] I've made a bottle, made the price. I would never guzzle it. I'd take a couple of good shots to kind of settle my nerves, put it in my back pocket, and go out and make another one. Usually I make my second before I finish the first. This way, I had reinforcements for the next day. I usually like to drink by myself but sometimes I get despondent and I want someone to talk to so I go to this park on Spring Street, if I've got a bottle or if I haven't, I go there to see who's got a bottle. Without a doubt I would find myself an associate or two. Usually, one would say, "Well, we need a bottle Uncle Ed," and I'd say "let's go make it."

Ed had left Queens with $300, but inside of a week, maybe ten days, it was gone. Even when he still had the money he was often too drunk to get back to the hotel and he would spend the night in a park or a darkened doorway, and for four nights he slept in Penn Station, crawling behind a partition or sitting in a phone booth until the police finally kicked him out. "I was relatively 'holding the banner' [living on the streets] with money in my pocket because I was drinking around the clock until I went broke and my legs went bad." For over two months he slept at night on the subway and sometimes went to the Holy Name Mission to clean himself up. Finally, in a state of exhaustion and with his feet so bloated he could not get his shoes on, he was talked into entering a detoxification unit near the Bowery.

While in the detoxification unit a case worker recertified Ed for Social Security Insurance (SSI) and when he was released nine days later, the Pacific Hotel became his abode once again. In early August 1985 he celebrated at an AA meeting his last five months of sobriety. Each day he struggles to avoid drinking. His daily circuit takes him from his hotel to a local center for older men, for long walks to Greenwich Village to have coffee and read the newspaper in a quiet park, and finally a visit to one of the several AA groups to which he belongs. He is careful to avoid the Spring Street park where his old "bottle gang" usually gathers. Ed talks proudly of the young alcoholic in his hotel whom he recently "twelve-stepped," that is, convinced through personal testimony and persuasion to join his AA group.

Constantly poised between hope and despair, Ed occasionally looks for a quiet job, a night watchman or doorman would be ideal he says, but he has given up looking for the time being. On occasion, to get some money, he will "make a run" for the older men in his flop house who are too frail or too drunk to leave their drab quarters. Having had mild heart attacks in the last several years, he can no longer play the quick errand boy for local merchants. Ed realizes old age is upon him, and each day ends with him wondering if the next morning will find him splayed in the gutter on Spring Street reeking of cheap wine.

PROFILE: MILES, THE FRY COOK

"It's my own damn fault," Miles said repeatedly to himself as he searched in vain for a comfortable sleeping position on the hard wooden bench. As if it had happened minutes ago, he could still feel the ragged edge of a broken mirror held tautly at his throat as a man he knew only as Paco relieved him of his savings. He had met this forty-year-old man from Puerto Rico while spending the prior month upstate at Camp LaGuardia, along with 250 other homeless men. Paco was a friendly type with an easy way about him, and the two quickly became "associates." He had confided to Miles that he could help him get a cheap apartment in the Bronx. Paco claimed to know the super in the building, and Miles would have to put a deposit down right away. At the beginning of July, Miles returned to the City, cashed his social security check, paid off some loans, and went to meet this supposed "close associate." He was promptly mugged by this con artist and relieved of the $380 he had brought along. This was virtually all the money he had in the world.

It was now July 25, 1985, and Miles arose before daybreak from his park bench at East 23rd Street. Despite his tall, lean frame and healthy looks, old age hung on this black man's shoulders like a leaden cloak. At first light he would begin what for him was a humiliating task, collecting returnable soda and beer cans. He had slept even less than usual during the night, as at 12:30 A.M. an old acquaintance, Jack McDonald, wandered into the small park. Jack spotted Miles and offered to share his pint of Wild Irish Rose. Miles politely turned this down, since the cheap liquor sometimes made him sick.

When Jack learned of Miles's plan for the coming day, he was almost indignant when he asked, "What are you doing picking up cans for a living?" Trying to hide the growing depression he felt, Miles replied, "Tomorrow's my birthday, I'll be 63, and I want to buy myself something real good to drink, get some cigarettes, and maybe go take in a movie, uptown." Jack finally dozed off on a nearby bench, but Miles just sat and stared at all the other homeless. By 4:00 A.M. the prostitutes and the cadre of gay men looking for a quick tryst had left the park to the almost 90 people who made this urban glade their home on a warm summer night. Most slept on the benches, but a few were in small tents on the grass.

Over the next two hours Miles smoked a handful of the tobacco stubs garnered earlier during his daily trek across Manhattan. Every once in a while he muttered to himself, "I can take this 'carryin a stick' [living on the streets] every once in a while, but I can't take much more 'pickin shit wit the pigeons' [scavenging in the street]."

Miles's life had not always been this way. Just after World War II he started working as a cook's helper at a famous seafood restaurant in Brooklyn. Miles developed great skill at cooking fish, and within five years he became one of the main fry cooks at one of the City's better places to eat. He would work at this same place from 1946 until 1972, when the restaurant was closed. By the early 1950s he had a good apartment in the Bronx and was living with a woman who worked for the electric company.

It was two decades later that his life began to come apart. In 1972, at the age of 50, he had the first of several minor heart attacks, and shortly after he was released from the hospital, Lundy's restaurant closed down. Without his old job, in poor health, he began a pattern of periodic drinking; eventually he had to give up his apartment. Miles lived in a series of run-down SROs (single-room occupancy hotels) on the upper west side and later, midtown Manhattan. Every couple of years he was forced to look for a new place to live, as gentrification began to decimate the available housing stock for low-income inner-city dwellers.

Although this proud black man has only twice slept on the Bowery for very short periods, by the early 1980s he had begun an economic and residential lifestyle common to many of the older skid-row men. For most of the spring and summer he would live in cheap hotel rooms and take short-term manual labor jobs around the City or in one of the many Catskill Mountain resorts. If his money ran low or if his hotel was converted into expensive condominiums, he would spend a week or two "carrying the stick" [living in the streets] until he could afford another "livable" room. During the winter, when jobs were scarcer and he tended to drink more, he would live for several months in upstate New York, staying at various retreats for homeless men. Miles would remain at one such state-run place called Camp LaGuardia for up to three months.

When speaking about the Bowery, Miles literally spits out angry words expressing his feeling of humiliation in just walking through the area. "I told this social worker, I'm not trying to be funny or smart. I refuse to sleep on the Bowery. I don't consider myself Bowery material 'cause I can remember years ago when I used to come down to the Bowery just to have a ball, because they had nice bars and shows down here." He is also quite aware of the continuing de facto segregation which offers blacks rooms in only the very worst flophouses. This is in an area where even the best accommodations are barely fit for human habitation.

More than anything, Miles is a victim of one of the worst housing crises New York City has ever faced. His last residence for any length of time (26 months) was a run-down SRO, with the rent ($260) eating up over one-half his monthly social security check. When he complained about the horrendous conditions in the hotel he was harassed by the management; he was forced to leave after being robbed by thugs hired by the management. Fearing for his life, Miles left shortly after this, retreating to the "holy mountains."

Now, three years later, he was back in the "carrying the stick" segment of his annual cycle. With almost no money to his name, he spent July sleeping in a park in good weather or taking to the subway when it rained.

Following the recent robbery, he was able to get just $21.50 from the Welfare Department and promptly went to see Tony, the "buy and sell" man, where he pawned his watch and ring for another $15. Although Miles had not had any contact with his relatives in Alabama since 1960, he still retained two close friends whom he has known for the last 40 years. Both these black men were in their mid- to late sixties, had their own tiny apartments, but subsisted on very low incomes. One man, Charles, kept Miles's suitcase in his apartment when he lived on the streets. The other person, named Jim, worked as a cook's helper at the Bowery Residence Committee and had talked Miles into going there for the almost-free lunches. From these friends he was able to borrow about $30 dollars following the robbery.

Miles could have gotten a ticket for a free room through the Municipal Shelter or even paid for a couple of weeks at one of the lesser flophouses. The first option was ruled out; during his last visit to the "Muni" he had been violently attacked by a young man strung out on drugs. Paying for a room was not considered, as Miles refused to panhandle and he wanted to husband his resources in hopes of finding a better place to live next month.

All the other times Miles had been homeless he stayed by himself, but this time it was different. He had recently witnessed many attacks on older men and had himself been robbed. Each night he slept with a group of three other black men whom he had come to know only in the last month. Two of them, Walt and John, were about his age, while the other was in his mid-thirties. He had met John one evening while waiting on a line for sandwiches at the St. Francis of Assisi Church. Miles had offered the other man a cigarette, and, as they struck up a conversation, they not only came to like each other but also discovered that they had been sleeping at opposite ends of the same park. Back at the park Miles was introduced to the two other men who had been staying together for the last month, and it was decided they would all sleep together, two men to each long bench.

For now he would sleep in the small park that stretched two blocks long and one block wide in a neighborhood that was safer for old men than the Bowery. To homeless men who lived in this area, skid row had come to be called "Little Vietnam." In fact, Miles was constantly scared living anywhere out on the streets, and attributed his drinking a pint of wine a day to this situation. Besides witnessing various brutal attacks on older men by young thugs, twice in the last year he had been robbed and beaten. Miles usually arose first in the morning and would gently shake his sleeping partner and inform him that he would be leaving soon. The four men spent most of their waking hours apart. When they congregated in the early evening they would swap the day's news and information about the menus at various soup kitchens, trade surplus food, and perhaps split a pint of wine. Walt and John had steady jobs while James did household repairs and sold old soda cans. James had introduced Miles to this latter trade.

The day before Miles's birthday started off badly. Although he had enlisted Jack to help with the collection of cans, they had only made only about $15. Some merchants simply refused to take dirty cans even though the mayor had declared this unnecessary due to the severe water shortage in the city. He began to have the same suicidal thoughts which almost ended his life in 1972. However, over the course of the day he would meet up with all three of his oldest friends who each remembered his birthday and had given him gifts of money totaling $14. Better still, one of these buddies related to Miles a rumor that "his" old restaurant might be soon opening again.[1]

That night at the park benches he celebrated by sharing several bottles of vodka with Jack and his newly formed sleeping group. The liquor and the thought of his social security check coming next week made him almost ebullient as he discussed two plans he had for the coming week. First he would buy a copy of the *Amsterdam News* and begin scouting for a cheap apartment. Next, he would take the D train to Brooklyn and see if anyone could use a real fine fry cook.

PROFILE: ROLAND, THE SUPER RUNNER

"Not even the cops will bother me here," Roland thought confidently as he closed the top of his room for the night, a cardboard carton which last housed a new refrigerator. As a final ritual to evoke momentary security he pulled his woolen cap over his gaunt, well-scrubbed cheeks and curled up into a ball. Satisfied for the moment with his comfort, he was less certain of how he would fare in the icy rain predicted for this night. His flimsy shelter had some big rips that were difficult to repair with the newspaper he had collected during the day. For the past week he had been scouting out this secret flop in a tiny alley off Bleecker Street where a short landing of steps led down to a basement door which was nailed shut. By 1:00 A.M., having prepared the steps with cans to warn of intruders, Roland drifted off into a light sleep. His last conscious thoughts that night were "just six more months until my sixty-fifth birthday, then I dig up my money, start collecting my social security checks and get away from here."

It was the week before Thanksgiving, a time of the year which forced the street-dwelling homeless of New York to make life-and-death decisions. Roland had recently taken to wearing several layers of clothing and using extra caution in choosing his flop for the night. Not only was he now leery of marauding young black skid-row men, but the mayor had declared that all homeless persons would be removed from the streets when the temperature dipped below 32 degrees. Just last month he had been sleeping in a cardboard box set behind a big shrub on a tiny street at the edge of Greenwich Village. The police had stumbled upon his abode and asked him to come along with them, but Roland told himself, "They're not taking me to the hospital and givin' me no electric shock treatment." Despite a strange new pain in his left leg he ran like a frightened rabbit. The two patrolmen just stood there and laughed, glad to have chased another bum out of their patch.

Yet Roland is no ordinary bum. He has the money and, more importantly, the connections to get a room in a cheap hotel. Many years ago when he was still drinking he slept with 400 other men in a dormitory-style flophouse, resting on cloth-covered planks of wood. Periodically, he would lose most of his accumulated money by either going on month-long drunken binges or being robbed in his hotel. Now a decade later he will relate with a slight shudder how he left the flop, began living in an abandoned building uptown, and simply

Roland delivering food to the homebound in a flophouse.

decided that life on the street as a drunk was too dangerous. He ceremoniously broke his remaining bottles of wine and just sat in his room for a week of hell until the tremors of withdrawal had gone away. Since this time the streets have been his home.

Although for the last ten years he has slept somewhere on the streets of New York, he remains meticulously clean, has, through his own willpower, completely stopped drinking, and works a steady 40-hour week at various jobs on the Bowery. He is in fact a super runner. A "runner" does errands for cash. Roland is a super runner in that he has graduated from the "get a bottle and keep the change from the ten" level to working only for social workers, priests and nuns. He is now an amazingly fit and energetic sixty-four-year-old.

Roland is a do-gooder who labors for the charity establishment rather than the tavern owners or hotel managers, because he has acquired the social work ethic. Each weekday at noon he becomes the delivery unit of the Bowery's main "Meals on Wheels" program. Up and down the steps of flophouses he can be seen effortlessly hefting a cart laden with prepared lunches from a local soup kitchen. Moving in a fluid half-run through each building, he deposits a meal, shouts "How ya doin," and accepts the quarter tip he receives in each of the 40-odd rooms he will visit. He is constantly ferreting out hotel-bound and homeless old men who need food and clothing and bringing them together with the

Bowery's social service resources. He will not buy a bottle for you, but he will get your prescription filled.

Although Roland rapidly moves through the streets with a gait seemingly born of confidence, his active participation in life dangles on a thin thread. In the course of being a super runner he is sometimes asked to operate a machine or deal with keys, often with disastrous results; not because he is careless. He attacks any job with metronomic precision, but he will always try to avoid work that involves any technology whatsoever. New employers, however, will take advantage of his great energy and willingness to help and press him into locking up or running a dryer or a dishwasher. Roland is no worse at these things than anyone else, yet when the inevitable happens, when a fan belt breaks or a key is lost or a fuse goes, Roland becomes frantic. He knows he has broken whatever he was working on. It must be his fault. Inevitably he flees and avoids the embarrassment of dealing with his screw-up. His life is cast in cycles of such stories, which are used to explain how he came to the Bowery and why he has not had any contact in years with his sister or other relatives in nearby Connecticut.

Roland's affect, motor and speech patterns are quite unusual. Constantly in motion or asleep, his appetite is prodigious. Weighing not more than 140 pounds, with a wiry body that looks no more than 40 years old, he eats perhaps five times what other older men do. Many of his jobs involve food as well as cash payments. He talks in bursts, as if to mimic verbally his mode of motion and work. A voracious newspaper reader, he readily offers opinions on both front page and obscure items. Obsessed with stories of gore and violence, especially those perpetrated on Bowery men, he is a walking local history of murders and bizarre accidental deaths. If you walk the streets with him, every few minutes another sordid story will unfold. Passing a boarded-up paper processing factory, he will tell of a drunk old bum who slipped in late one winter night to sleep warmly between layers of cardboard. Unfortunately, the man slept too long and was tragically crushed to death when the bailing machines were started up in the morning.

Despite his varied jobs in Bowery institutions he always sleeps alone in one of several places off the Bowery. One is under the Manhattan Bridge, and several others are dispersed on the edges of the Greenwich Village area. Where he flops on a given night depends on the weather and his judgment of its safety, based on a scouting of the area. After spending his day on the Bowery he will walk a winding two-mile route to the West Village where he meets a close associate who attends an Alcoholics Anonymous meeting there. En route he constantly scans the streets for two things, money and muggers. As he passes a garbage can he will quickly examine the top layer of refuse hoping to repeat a recent windfall when he found five twenty-dollar bills neatly folded in an empty pack of cigarettes. After a meal at McDonald's with his associate and an hour or so of casual conversation, the two men will separate and Roland makes his way to one of his "homes," always arriving around midnight.

Roland had not slept indoors more than a handful of times over the last ten years, giving in only when the winter weather reached Arctic dimensions. Now, on this night in late November, while Roland dozed in his leaking cardboard shelter, the temperature hovered just over freezing, and a mixture of rain, sleet and hail pelted the City. Virtually paranoid over the possibility that the police would again try to drag him off the street he would use his secret sleeping place. The bottom of the landing where he lay in dreamless slumber was impossible to see even from a few feet away.

Roland was startled awake at 5:00 A.M. by a stinging pain that ran up and down his left leg and almost made him cry out. Most of his body was soaked, and he felt colder than he had been all last winter. What frightened him the most was that his lithe frame could not be supported by his usually dependable legs. Although almost 65, his physique and energy level would be the envy of most men half his age. Now it was a great effort to move let alone walk. A terrifying thought ran through his mind—"My god, have I got AIDS or somethin'?"

Fueled by his mounting fear, Roland willed himself to half crawl, half hop to the Holy Name Mission, one of the several places he worked on the Bowery. After two agonizing hours he had negotiated the mile to his hoped-for sanctuary and lay on his side across the street from the Mission doors. However, he could not move another inch. Fortunately, he did not have to wait long before he could hail a young homeless man seeking an early morning shower. Roland gave him a dollar and asked him to call Father Charles in the Holy Name. The priest came out with another man and carried Roland into the Mission and a temporary warm bed.

Later that day a doctor examined Roland and decided that he suffered from a severe sciatic nerve inflammation and prescribed some medicine and several weeks of rest. For the next month, he slept at the Holy Name, and then, to the shock of everyone who knew him, Roland checked into the best flophouse on the Bowery. This was the first time in over ten years that he had slept for any length of time with something more substantial than cardboard covering his head.

THREE LIVES IN PERSPECTIVE

These three profiles illustrate the world of recurrent crises which confront older Bowery men. These men face acute crises that include falling through holes in the welfare "safety net," rapid deterioration in health, physical assault, alcohol craving and loss of shelter. These short-term episodes are embedded within the patterns of chronic crises of impoverishment, alcohol abuse, physical and psychological disability, sporadic work opportunities, a public policy of reducing entitlement programs and destroying the housing stock available for low-income people, and the stigma attached to life on the skids.

It is easy to react to the plight of such individuals through popular stereotypes of the poor skid-row derelict. The men of these images are homeless by choice, unwilling to work, constantly inebriated, possibly psychotic, reluctant to conform to norms of personal hygiene and dress, beyond redemption. In order to address the problem of homelessness it is necessary to avoid such standard characterizations and to examine the interweaving of the numerous elements that generate and sustain these individuals.

To many, Uncle Ed must seem like their typical image of a "Bowery bum." In his worst moments, he can be seen as a hopeless drunk, living for days in the same wine-soaked garments and panhandling quarters for his next bottle. Yet, like so many of the older Bowery men, he desperately seeks employment beyond the occasional "gofer" job, in a quest for dignity and enhanced economic stability. Ed is convivial, articulate, of great support to others, and maintains a wide range of social relationships including women friends and kin. Despite frequent bouts of severe depression, he still nourishes the hope of staying sober long enough to escape the vicious consequences of his addiction and poverty.

Superficially, Miles would appear to be a shiftless old street alcoholic. His street living, however, originates in the housing policy which has greatly depleted the stock of affordable apartments and hotels rooms. In fact, a 1985 survey indicated that 55 percent of the elderly in New York City shelters had lived independently in their own apartments or in SRO hotels before entering the shelter system; a majority of them had been evicted because of inadequate funds (Human Resources Administration 1987). Miles's drinking problem is nurtured and exacerbated by fear and anxiety brought on by street living. Due to his strong desire to secure an apartment, he prefers to sleep on a park bench rather than pay even small amounts for the inhuman housing available for blacks on the Bowery. His intelligence is reflected in his ability to maximize the meager resources available to men on the street.

Roland is a man who, due to his bad experiences in flophouses, has opted for a homeless existence that many would consider insane. His unusual speech and affective patterns amplify this image of a "crazy" person. If Roland were captured by the mental health system, and he has been there at times, he might be labeled a chronic schizophrenic. But, in his element, on the streets, Roland is a successful entrepreneur who provides useful services to more needy Bowery men. He does not drink, use drugs or panhandle. Roland represents a rare type, but he is hardly unique. He may be homeless but he is not a bum.

NOTES

This chapter is adapted from chapter 1 of *Old Men of the Bowery: Strategies for Survival Among the Homeless*, Carl Cohen and Jay Sokolovsky, Guilford Press, 1989. It is reprinted with the permission of Guilford Press. Research for this chapter was supported by grant number RO1 MH37562 from the National Institute of Mental Health.

1. Unfortunately, the rumor about the restaurant was just that. It did eventually open, but not until late 1995.

CHAPTER 20

One Thousand Points of Blight: Old, Female and Homeless in New York City

Jay Sokolovsky

Unfortunately, one thousand points of blight is too generous a title for this chapter, considering the growing dilemma of the poor elderly.[1] Throughout the nooks and crannies of our cities and suburbs, the older men discussed in the prior chapter have been joined by female age peers, as well as younger men, women and children. They are sleeping in parks, train stations, temporary shelters, alleyways, under bridges, in their cars and over heating grates (Golden 1992). This includes evicted families living in armories or doubled up with relatives, battered wives concealed in shelters trying to retain their lives, sanity and most of all, their children. Among these suffering ranks, women are the fastest-growing single category and 20 percent of this particular new homeless group are over age 50.

Homeless women are not new to the American scene. While they were found among female camp followers of revolutionary times or the numerous depression era "box-car Berthas," even the 1930s did not produce the numbers of homeless older women now undomiciled. The increase of homelessness among older women is obscured by the movement of young men and young single women with children into the undomiciled ranks. Older women have been much harder to count as they tend to shun the large public shelters and choose either tiny charity shelters, drop-in centers or the streets.[2] While the percent of older women counted as homeless has dropped in the last decade, their absolute numbers are actually increasing (Cohen 1996a; Cohen et al. 1997).

When older homeless women have been conceptualized, it has either been as totally stigmatized adjuncts to alcoholic skid-row men (depicted in the novel *Ironweed*) or as the feisty, psychotic bag ladies dangerously alone in their own minds and lugging mysterious packages through the streets (as portrayed by Lucille Ball in the television drama "Stone Pillow"). Media coverage in the

1980s tended to romanticize these bag ladies and mythologize about their former lives as highly placed professionals—one report even claimed to have found a former anthropology Ph.D. on the streets. During the depression, "sisters of the road" as they were sometimes called, were never accorded the symbolic, care-free panache of the male hobo, glamorized in song, movie and novel. They were regarded as adventurous, *unredeemable* deviants who should not exist. In our culture the only way such women can exist is as individuals of "spoiled iden-tity"—a category of person almost impossible to recast as "normal." Older women, typically, are socialized more than men to be linked to the private, domestic sphere of home and intimate social relations which involve some flavor of "kin-like" feelings.

Yet, the experience of homelessness forces older women into a physical and social world which is the antithesis of "home" and enduring kin relations. As will be seen in the following case illustration, such women can quickly exhaust the resources of kin and then are thrust into an inversion of the basic spheres by which our culture normally judges the realms of public/private/domestic. The culture of homelessness is dominated by large communal areas for accomplish-ing eating, sleeping and hygiene. These environments have been designed to accommodate the poor single male, who is more likely to have at least experi-enced such environments in the military, in boarding houses or in jail. Many of these women are presented with a terrible cultural and psychological paradox: by choosing to accept being housed in typical public shelters, they are moving even farther away from the cultural links to "home" than might even be created while living on the streets.

In a follow-up study to the "Old Men of the Bowery" project mentioned in the previous chapter, in 1989 the National Institute of Mental Health funded a five-year study of older homeless women scattered throughout New York City. The larger project included a sample of 237 women age 50 or over. The fol-lowing short piece is from my ethnographic fieldnotes recorded in the early stages of this project.[3]

SETTING

July 12, 1991, 10:30 A.M., Women's Shelter (located in a U.S. Army Ar-mory). I was told today by the head of social work that the Army does not want the shelter here and has fought efforts to improve ventilation and provide air-conditioning. It is very hot today, in the mid-90s; there is still no air-conditioning up here and the big fans just blow the hot stale air into my face. As I enter the room where the case workers are sitting, I notice a woman, likely in her early sixties who is hounding one of the case workers as he enters the room. They are having a loud argument (it seems to be over needed bus fare). The case worker seems totally exasperated and quickly enters a nearby office and shuts the door. The woman storms around the room for a minute and gradually calms herself down and lingers outside the big office. I go over and introduce myself and tell her about our study of older homeless women. She seemed eager to tell her story and I suggested we go to a nearby coffee shop to talk.

INTERVIEW

Question: Tell me a little about yourself and how you came to this shelter?

Just call me Val. I'll be 60 soon and my sister is pushing 70. We grew up in the Bushwick section of Brooklyn. I was working in a factory in Queens, before they moved to New Jersey and I lost my job. I didn't know what to do, I was living with my sister and her grown daughter in the Brownsville section of Brooklyn. Before we got burned out of the apartment building, we were living in a two-family house nearby, but it was eventually sold. Our last place was four nice little rooms in a City-owned six-family building. We had lived there four years. But a fire destroyed the place. What the fire didn't take, people stole. Now we got nothin', except for a few pieces of clothing the shelters have given us. Together, we get about $500 a month, what can you do with that, today?

First we went across the street to my friend's place—it was just her and her husband, but my sister's daughter could not take it and went her own way. We stayed there about a month and a half. Then we went to my niece's place in downtown Brooklyn, but she has eight kids so it is rather crowded there. It was tough, her husband and my sister were always getting into fights. We were tossed out at 2:30 in the morning. My niece had to choose between her man and us and she chose him. We went to the Red Cross and the welfare sent us to a drop-in center on Bond St., downtown and they sent us to some woman's shelter for the day. They fed us and transported us to the assessment shelter that night and we stayed there the required 21 days before coming to this shelter for older ladies. I felt totally disorientated: I kept on saying to myself, over and over again, "I'm actually homeless!" Well, you see, people read about homelessness and even sometimes sit down and converse about it with other people. And then when it's you, reality doesn't hit you until then. It's a frightful thing, it can blow your mind. This assessment shelter was for tough young people, a lot were lesbian, gay kids and it was hard to cope; and you really had to block a lot of situations out to cope, just to get to the next day.

Did you ever see this picture with Olivia de Havilland called *Snake Pit*? Well, this is the way the assessment shelter is. People talking to themselves and screaming at night; it's nothing you can describe, it's like a picture, quiet before a storm.

Lots of people around here need to be in a mental hospital. You line up for everything; that isn't so bad; but, you got to show your meal ticket, and they throw food at you. If you want another piece of bread you have an hour's wait, but then, you see the staff eating anytime. They curse you and talk to you like you're not human. It's bad enough just to be homeless, but it's worse when you are degraded and more or less, spit on. . . . That is hard to take.

Question: What were the first few days like?

It was like walking into living hell. I was glad in one sense 'cause I had a place to put my head. The place was very full when we were there; they let a pregnant woman sleep on the floor in the basement. . . . They give you a bed, but they put you through a degrading process, so that some people crack. If you were 5 or 10 minutes late they would snatch you out of bed and take it away and give it to a newcomer. Fortunately, we were in a small room like now—12–14 in a room. We were in one of the quieter rooms with ladies in our age group. But we had to sit in the TV room most of the time with the TV and stereo blaring, there was fighting and carrying on; I tried to stay mostly by myself. We had to be out of our rooms most of the day (from 8:30 A.M. to 6:30 P.M.). Much of the time I took a book and went out and read until meal time. My sister would generally do what I did.

The food wasn't too good either. For Mother's Day, we had frozen cheese and string beans. They give you meals like dogs in there. . . .

Well, we finally get transferred here, to this better shelter for older women and the second night, when my sister is going to bed, a mouse runs up her arm and she has a heart attack, right there, and has been in the hospital for awhile.

My whole life now is getting my sister to kin in Georgia, and finding me a place, where I can close the door and have a key!

NOTES

1. The beginning part of the title of this chapter is a purposeful alteration of a phrase—"A Thousand Points of Light"—used in former President George Bush's Inaugural Address on January 20, 1989.

2. Drop-in centers in New York City provide limited respite from the streets and usually for relatively small numbers of homeless. They typically provide a place to get a meal and wash up. They are often linked with religious institutions which provide sleeping places overnight. Studies funded by the Bureau of the Census, in 1989, to evaluate their methods for counting the homeless, showed that those homeless in non shelter environments were the hardest to count. Census takers may be missing 50 percent or more of this population.

3. This research was funded by the National Institute of Mental Health Center for the Study of the Mental Disorders of the Aging: grant number RO1–MH45780, "Older Homeless Women in New York City,"

PART VI

Health, Aging and Culture

A recent visitor to an Abkhasian family was being entertained at a feast, and following local custom, raised a glass of wine to toast a man who looked no more than seventy. "May you live as long as Moses [one hundred twenty years]," the visitor said. The man was not pleased. He was one hundred nineteen.

Sula Benet

THE QUEST FOR GERIATRIC UTOPIAS

During the 1960s and 1970s exciting reports filtered into the gerontological literature and popular press about a small number of mountain peoples who possessed extraordinary longevity. Not only were their ages said to exceed that of the man being toasted in the quote above, but their health was said to be like that of spry sixty-year-olds. In the Caucasus region of the Soviet Union, gerontologists by the 1950s claimed to be studying, among the Abkhasian people, a well-documented group of 500 *dolgozhiteli* (very long-living people) ranging in age from 120 to almost 150. Similar assertions were made for a peasant village in Vilacabamba, Ecuador, the Hunzakut of the Karakoram Mountains in Pakistan, and the inhabitants of Paros Island, Greece.[1]

It is usually very disquieting for my students to learn that *none* of these claims for a modern fountain of youth appear to be true (Leaf 1982; Palmore 1984; Beall 1987). In the case of the Abkhasian super-centenarians, we are dealing with one of the great scientific frauds of the twentieth century (Medvedev 1974). For this population, the oldest documented age is actually only 114, and in Vilacabamba none of the reputed centenarians were found to be older than 96 (Mazess and Foreman 1979).

Despite false claims for breaching the normal limits of the human life span, we seem to be dealing, at least in Abkhasia, with an exceptionally healthy group of ninety- and one-hundred-year-olds. Interestingly, the details of their lifestyles, when compared with those of healthy centenarians in the United States and other countries, point to a number of common factors in promoting long life. Such persons tend to have low-fat, low-calorie diets, refrain from much caffeine, tobacco and alcohol and have been physically active throughout their lives (Hadjihristev 1988). In fact, a 1996 report by the MacArthur Foundation Consortium on Successful Aging noted that only about 30 percent of the features of aging are genetically based and that by age 80 there is little genetic influence on determining what happens after that point. This project identified several non-genetic factors influencing successful aging: regular physical activity and social connectedness; the ability to bounce back after suffering a loss; and having a feeling of control over one's life.

One may wonder about the benefits of living more than two decades past the century mark. A person who has done this, Jeanne Calment, of Arles, France, has received considerable international media attention. Now age 122 (reached in 1997), she is recognized by the *Guinness Book of Records* as the longest-living human whose date of birth can be authenticated.[2] This French woman, who watched the Eiffel Tower being built and claims to have sold paint brushes to Vincent Van Gogh, celebrated her 121st birthday on February 21, 1996, by releasing a compact disc about her life called *Mistress of Time*. People revel in her status as an extreme post-centenarian and her nursing home has become a pilgrimage site for those seeking the secret to long life. Yet, it is important to note that she has lost her sight, is partially deaf, and has outlived not only her children, but *all* her descendants. A widow of 50 years, Calment offers laughter as a recipe for long life and when asked on her 120th birthday to describe her vision of the future, she replied, "very brief."

While it is exciting to note that the number of centenarians in the United States has doubled every decade since 1970, it is important to realize that all populations must cope in some way with the biomedical imperative of aging (Crews and Garruto 1994). In human populations, typically fewer than .005 percent are 100 years or older, and starting before age 40 many human functional capacities begin a steady process of decline. Of course, the level of physical functioning at any age is influenced by many factors such as diet and activity patterns, as well as the cultural construction of personhood and disability over the life cycle. As I can attest from my research experience in Mexico (see Chapter 9), many a twenty-five-year-old North American anthropologist has been worked or walked into the ground by trying to keep up with a healthy seventy-year-old peasant.

AGE, AGING AND THE "AT RISK" ELDERLY

Not only does culture influence the degree of physiological change associated with aging but it also defines when old age is thought to begin and how it relates to the rest of the life cycle. In the United States, with a bureaucratic, public designation of 65 as the beginning of old age, there is a common linkage of the aged with illness and severe decline in most areas of life. When those both under and over 65 are questioned, a majority believe that persons past age 65 are in poor health. This stereotyping view of linking illness and old age has a long history in Western thought, going back to Hippocrates, and is still embedded in the diagnostic schema of Western medicine (Sankar 1984).

However, as Glascock also shows in Chapter 3, a large number of these same societies recognize more than one phase of old age. It is these later stages which are usually defined by the appearance of bodily and mental deterioration and minimal levels of functional capacity. Older persons bearing labels of "decrepit," "near dead," or "childlike" are the ones most likely to be mistreated by society. It is important to realize that the actual level of frailty is not the only factor involved. Maxwell and Maxwell found, in a worldwide comparative study, that while physical decline was a key predictor for negative treatment of the aged, lack of family support loomed as the most important variable (1980). This notion is consonant with studies in the United States showing that, controlling for other factors, elderly with weak kinship networks are the most likely to enter institutional forms of long-term care. Once again, culture meets context (Freedman et al. 1994).

The complex dimensions of this issue are often lost in statistical analyses employing the coded data from hundreds of societies in the Human Relations Area Files. It is necessary then to turn to holistic ethnographies such as that found in Chapter 21. Having worked as a medical anthropologist on the Polynesian island of Niue, Judith Barker explores the paradox of how a society known for its beneficent treatment of the healthy aged and disabled young could show seemingly heartless disregard of the unfit elderly. She shows that understanding the neglect directed at "decrepit" older folks does not yield to simple mechanical explanations. Such disregard is neither part of a uniform way of treating all disabled persons nor an ecological expedient dictated by low surplus production. Rather, it is crucial to view how the label of "decrepit" itself is negotiated (again linked to the level of kin support) and constructed within Niuean conceptions of the life cycle, death and ancestral states. In Chapter 24 we will encounter, in the case of urban China, a different package of cultural reactions to late-life impairment.

Of the demographic changes occurring in the world, the one that will be most related to the health needs of the aged is the rapid growth of the "oldest old,"— persons over 85 years of age (Suzman, Willis and Manton 1992; World Health Organization 1995). By 1994 in the United States, the "oldest old" accounted for about one percent of the total population. Over the last 35 years their numbers have increased by 274 percent while the entire country grew by only 45 percent (U.S. Bureau of the Census 1995). These are the aged who are most "at risk" of having their abilities to function hampered by chronic diseases (Albert 1995; Johnson and Barer 1997).[3]

There is a general perception that it is the health needs of the "oldest old" which is the universal, "real" crushing problem causing health care costs to become unmanageable. However, a recent comparative analysis by Robert Binstock (1993) shows this assumption to be inaccurate. In fact, during the 1980s the United States was one of the only industrialized nations where the rate of change in the number of persons over age 80 meant an equal or greater percent increase in the Gross National Product (GNP) devoted to health care. In the five countries with the most rapid growth of the oldest old, health care's share of national GNP rose only a small fraction of the population rise of the very oldest persons. In the case of Sweden, the GNP spent on health care actually *dropped* by over 10 percent while the percentage of change of those over age 80 jumped threefold. Binstock draws two crucial conclusions from this analysis: (1) there is little evidence showing that a very elderly population mandates "out of control" expenditures on health; and (2) the structural features of and response to systems of health care delivery are considerably more predictive of the cost of care than are demographic trends. These facts give great salience to the examination of the response to population aging in countries such as Sweden, Denmark and Japan, where the rapid growth of many grey heads has not put as crushing a burden on the overall cost of medical care as might be predicted by numbers alone.[4]

Nevertheless, as we saw in Part I, in most countries, especially in the developing world, this older, high-risk group is the fastest-growing component of the elderly. In nations like China, Ghana and Croatia, health service providers have come to realize that with regard to the aged a major shift is needed, involving less intervention for acute care and more continuous care for chronic states (Heisel 1985; Manton, Dowd and Woodbury 1986). For example, during the early 1980s in what is now the European nation of Croatia, the rising number of older citizens with hypertension began to create a crisis for medical services.[5] Physicians found themselves hard-pressed just to perform basic tasks of blood pressure regulation, let alone to cope with the increased risk of disability related to unregulated high blood pressure. One response has been to promote locally based self-help groups, trained collectively by medical personnel to take their own pressures and maintain required diet and drug regimens. In a study of such groups of hypertension patients during the mid-1980s, it was found that while most of these groups were initially successful in stabilizing the pressures of a majority of their members, unless health institutions made a long-term commitment to the groups, many would eventually collapse (Sokolovsky, Sosic and Pavlekovic 1991).[6]

An expanding international literature has attested to the explosive growth of such self-help/mutual aid groups, especially in industrial societies (Silverman 1986; Kurz 1997).[7] These groups can emerge as a critical resource facilitating a "health-promoting" approach to illness or psychosocial crisis as distinct from a traditional "sickness approach" (Borman 1983; Kaye 1995).[8] The essence of all these associations is a collection of people who share a common problem and band together for mutual support and constructive action toward shared goals. The types of social entities that touch on the lives of the elderly tend to take three forms: life-cycle/crisis transition groups (such as widow-to-widow); affliction groups (hypertension, alcohol); and support for carer groups (carers for Alzheimer's patients).

This last type of group is the subject of Chapter 22. While in the United States less than 10 percent of all those over 65 suffer from some form of dementia, up to 30 percent over age 85 may be afflicted with this cognitive disfunction (Graves et al. 1994).[9] Medical specialists now recognize over 70 different causes of dementia, but in most populations, Alzheimer's disease is the most common type and evokes great fears among old and young alike. Ethnic elders may wax rhapsodic about the strength of their family support system, but, few things can test the veracity of such claims as caring for victims of dementia (Valle 1989; Wood and Parham 1990; Young and Kahana 1995). As a chronic disease with severe and progressive cognitive and physical impairments, Alzheimer's imposes a great challenge to the provision of noncustodial long-term care (Kitwood and Bredin 1992; LaNavanec and Vonhof 1996).[10] For instance, studies indicate that home care for patients with a severe level of impairment requires an average of eight hours of care per day, and that, in general, Alzheimer's demands 50 percent more time than caring for physically disabled aged (Hu and Cartwright 1986). Despite this, relatively few family members caring for cognitively impaired kin use formal services other than a physician, and then only sporadically or in late stages of the disease (U.S. Congress OTA 1990). One consequence of this is a heavy psychological toll on family carers, with caregivers for memory-impaired adults typically suffering several times the number of stress-related symptoms than their age peers who are not caregivers (D. Cohen et al. 1990; Jones and Miesen 1992).

Over the past decade a rapidly enlarging international and cross-cultural literature has emerged, which explores both the prevalence of dementia and the cultural response to this condition (Osuntokun et al. 1992; Graves et al. 1994; L. Cohen 1995; Yeo and Gallagher-Thompson 1996).[11] There has also developed a national awareness of the need to adapt diverse strategies to reach ethnic families, typically the most reluctant to seek professional help in dealing with the consequences of dementia (DHHS 1992; Hart 1996).[12] With rare exception, memory disorder clinics in major medical centers have had a very difficult time recruiting ethnic minority families to use their services (Picot et al. 1997).[13] The work of Neil Henderson in Chapter 22 addresses this issue by combining a focus on the ethnic context of aging and the promotion of a new social formation to deal with this problem. His work provides a unique study of a support group for Hispanic Americans established in Tampa, Florida. It illustrates the impact of formal institutions, such as gerontology centers, in providing an organizational and educational role in strengthening the "natural" support systems which provide community-based care for the elderly.

An important lesson of this article is that informal and formal supports seem to function best when they act together to strengthen each other rather than functioning as totally separate components of a care system. Yet, the effective interaction of formal institutions and ethnic families is no simple matter of providing information and help. Henderson clearly demonstrates how an understanding of the cultural context can overcome ethnic-based problems stemming from overreliance on females as caregivers, generational differences and low "service user" patterns in the Hispanic community (Wallace and Lew-Ting 1992). Unfortunately, within less than three years of its formation the group ceased to function.[14] As was noted previously in the Croatian case, left on their own, support groups have a high likelihood of collapse unless they are assisted by broader community coalitions or health institutions.

Since 1990, one response to this problem by the National Institute on Aging has been to establish 27 Alzheimer's Disease Center Satellite Clinics, nationwide. Their goal is to enhance knowledge and treatment of cognitive impairment among ethnic communities.[15] One of these centers in Atlanta reported in 1995 that contrary to popular opinion, Alzheimer's disease is the most common cause of dementia among African Americans.[16] Importantly, a third of the patients have dementia caused by multiple factors including combinations of stroke, depression, alcoholism and vitamin deficiency.[17]

DISABILITY, LONG-TERM CARE AND THE INSTITUTIONAL ENVIRONMENT

Clearly, chronic illness and disability tend to increase during the last decades of human life.[18] Among noninstitutionalized elderly the percentage who need help doing everyday activities doubles with each successive decade up to age 84, and triples between ages 85–94 (American College of Physicians 1988; German 1995). As we learned in Chapter 1, there is a big difference between gross measures such as longevity versus healthy longevity. For example, in the United States, a male of age 76 has an expectation of living 6.3 independent years and two dependent years. A female of the same age can expect about one more year of independent functioning, but double the dependent years of men (Kinsella 1992a; Guralnik et al. 1995).[19]

Disability, Aging and Culture

The cross-cultural study of health and disability has been a focus of the World Health Organization since the early 1980s. It has developed a useful framework for distinguishing among impairment, disability and handicap. Here "impairment" means diminishment/loss of physical function, "disability" refers to a diminishment/loss of activity, and "handicap" constitutes a diminishment/loss of role performance (World Health Organization 1991).[20] As Albert and Cattell note, "while impairment involves clear physical properties, its expression as disability and handicap depends on cultural factors" (1994:208).[21] An excellent example is found in Albert's own work among the Lak people of Melanesia.

He found that perceptions of certain impairments, such as cataracts, did not translate into the Western view of disability or handicap (1987). Despite a high incidence of cataracts among the Lak elderly, this condition did not become a disabling feature of late life. Their impaired vision seldom interfered with participation in gardening, household assistance or ritual activities. Contrastingly, North American elders with similar levels of impairment typically experience cataracts as a disabling condition, which limits valued activities because of the cultural emphasis on reading, driving or other tasks requiring acute vision.

The impact of disability in late life has received increasing attention by qualitative researchers such as Gay Becker, who looked at deaf elders (1980) or Sharon Kaufman's study of how stroke victims reconstruct a sense of identity (1988). Chapter 23 by Monika Deppen-Wood and her colleagues, and Chapter 24 by Charlotte Ikels follow in this tradition. First, in the work of Deppen-Wood, Luborsky and Scheer we encounter the story of Henrietta Evers, a single, sixty-six-year-old African-American woman, who lives in the city of Philadelphia. Since early childhood she has had polio and has suffered from this impairment throughout her life. Yet, in this poignant case study we see how the notions of impairment, disability and handicap are mediated by patterns of African-American culture and the nature of the local urban community. These factors allow Mrs. Evers not only to garner a wide array of social supports, but to make important contributions herself, within a broad kin network.

Next, Ikels draws from her larger study of urban life in Guangzhou to analyze the Chinese cultural reaction to disability in old age and China's evolving system of long-term care (Ikels 1996). Her findings are clearly distinct from the situation on Niue Island (Chapter 21). In China even elders who are quite impaired (by Western standards) are perceived as having limited difficulty and being worthy individuals. Particularly striking is the cultural response to dementia. In contrast to the Hispanic families studied by Henderson (Chapter 22), the Chinese view the symptoms of this kind of disease less as a type of mental illness, and more as a normal part of aging (Ikels forthcoming).

In urban China, although most impaired aged live with children or other relatives, the success of family caregiving involves tapping the resources of neighborhoods, work units and paid carers. China now shares with the rest of industrializing East Asia the demographic dilemma of economic success (Olson 1990; Chen 1996; Davis 1997). This country has the world's largest group of adults over age 60, constituting more than 20 percent of our planet's seniors. Over the coming decade China will be second in the world to Japan in the rate of population aging. A new National Committee on Aging fears what it calls the 4:2:1 ratio: four grandparents and two parents cared for by one adult child.

Nursing Homes as Social Environments

Although about 80 percent of the aged in the United States report that they can get around by themselves, it is the rapidly growing number of the "oldest old" which is creating the greatest challenge for our system of long-term care

(Binstock, Cluff and von Mering 1996). Currently, only about one percent of the "young old" reside in long-term care institutions, as compared to 6.1 percent of the seventy-five to eighty-five-year-olds and 24 percent of those over eighty-five. However, one study predicted that of the persons who reached age 65 in 1990, about 40 percent would spend some time in a nursing home prior to their deaths (Kemper and Murtaugh 1991). With an average admittance age of 83, such places have become the abodes of our most frail elders. A majority have some form of dementia and a similar percent are incontinent.

For at least the last fifty years most industrial nations have recognized the necessity to construct settings outside of the home to attend to the needs of the very frail and dependent elderly (van Nostrand, Clark and Romøren 1993). Even Japan has embarked on a policy of rapidly increasing the number of such places (Brown 1988; Robb Chapter 10). Western European countries facing demographic pressures earlier than the United States have developed a broader range of options and stronger geriatric medicine programs to deal with the medical needs of the elderly (Baldock and Evers 1992; Doty 1993).[22] Despite movements in many countries to institute an "open care" system stressing both multiple-care options and the goal of maximizing the time elderly remain in their own homes, there persists the need for some forms of nursing care in specialized medical settings (Amann 1980; Little 1982; Scharf and Wenger 1995).[23]

Nursing homes have had an infamous place in the spectrum of care settings built predominantly for the elderly. Ethnographic studies of such environments go back almost 40 years and provide a sometimes unwelcomed window into our own culture. For instance, in the mid-1950s Otto von Mering turned an anthropological gaze toward the geriatric wards of mental hospitals and showed how our cultural devaluing of old age led to a withdrawal of psychosocial care for the geriatric patient (1957; see also Henry 1963; Gubrium 1975). More recently, Maria Vesperi, in reflecting on the qualitative study of long-term care environments, evoked the jarring disjuncture between life inside institutional settings and the outside world:

It is possible to pass through a nursing home without observing how differently life is actually lived there. Some visitors remember the experience primarily as a sensory assault, with few social details; some focus on a single person or task and develop tunnel vision with regard to the rest. For an ethnographer, however, the experience of stepping outdoors after visiting a nursing home can be as disconcerting as a certain image from one of Alfred Hitchcock's last films, *Frenzy*. Here the viewer is first utterly absorbed as the murderous protagonist attracts his victim; the outside world fades to insignificance as the pair mount the stairs to a drab apartment. Then, just as he overwhelms her, the camera backs slowly from the room, down the stairs, out to the sidewalk and across the street to a busy curbside market. As each threshold is crossed, the cries from the room recede and the lively bustle of a London neighborhood becomes more audible. The moment of true discomfiture occurs as the camera lingers on the mute facade of the apartment building, leaving viewers to ponder the proximity of chaos to the comforting, familiar routines of daily life (1995).

For good reason, much of the early literature on such institutions focused on the high level of abuse, especially in those proprietary care units where profit can attain a higher value than caring for residents (Henry 1963; Vesperi 1987; Johnson 1987).[24] It took over a decade of federal hearings and a scathing report by the Institute of Medicine on the poor medical care in nursing homes before Congress passed the 1987 Nursing Home Reform Act. This comprehensive legislation, also known as the OBRA regulations, set national standards for such things as patient care, staff training and residents' rights.[25] Such federal guidelines have provided much-needed protection for the over three million residents in long-term care facilities.

However, as Renée Shield demonstrates in Chapter 25, even in a well-run, nonprofit nursing home, factors other than physical elements of care can be crucial to the resident's quality of life (Powers 1988b; Henderson and Vesperi 1995).[26] Shield uses anthropological models of life cycle–focused ritual to show how placement in a nursing home begins the change of status from adulthood to death.[27] Seldom, however, is the ritual cycle completed, leaving the initiate in an incomplete liminal stage, having to endure an endless transition to oblivion. Students can profitably compare such a cultural transformation of personhood with that found among the Kaliai of Papua New Guinea, where very frail elderhood can be associated with a predeath ritual signifying that the person is in the process of dying and is already socially dead (Counts and Counts 1985b). Here, as in the nursing home context, some elderly resist this process and seek to declare, "I am not dead yet!"

The eclipse of personhood in exchange for a barely sustained physical form is the Faustian bargain many nursing home residents must accept. Like the older homeless men and women discussed earlier, residents are stripped of personhood by being unable to sustain a semblance of individuality rooted in a domestic setting. In Chapter 26, anthropologist Joel Savishinsky tells how his field research in the Canadian arctic with a people who spent six months a year traveling and hunting by dog sled, led to his involvement in one of the early programs of pet therapy in U.S. nursing homes (Zisselman et al. 1996). Asked to evaluate the bringing of dogs to institutions in upstate New York, he and his students became involved in a study which lasted seven years and resulted in an award-winning book, *The Ends of Time: Life and Work in a Nursing Home* (1991). He found that as symbolic markers of a lost domestic life, the animals in many cases broke a wall of silence, evoking memories of youth, work and children. Residents could express emotions and stories with the pets which when said aloud to themselves led to their being regarded as crazy. Savishinsky's chapter provides a counterpoint to the absence of discussions of death in the nursing facility studied by Renée Shield. He found that thinking about the death of loved pets made it easier for residents to more openly discuss mortality and sometimes even joke about it.[28]

KEY RESOURCES

Data Sets

"International Longevity Project." International Leadership Center on Longevity and
Society, Mt. Sinai School of Medicine, Box 1070, New York, NY 10029–6574.
Phone (212) 241–0102. This project is compiling a numeric data base with key
indicators from 46 countries, available in print and on diskette.

"The Health and Retirement Study." This is a longitudinal survey project conducted by
the National Institute on Aging under the auspices of the University of Michigan's
Institute for Social Research. Research begun in 1990 and continuing through
2005 will examine comparative health, wealth and retirement among 13,000 individuals who were between the ages of 51 and 61 when the project began.
Students can find out about this project and access data sets from the web site at
http://www.umich.edu/~hrswww. Discussions of initial findings are found in
"The Health and Retirement Study: Data Quality and Early Results," Special
Issue of the *Journal of Human Resources* (1995):30.

Research Project

"Determinants of Healthy Aging." This World Health Organization project began in
1992 and will last until 1997. It involves research in Costa Rica, Israel, Italy,
Jamaica, Thailand and Zimbabwe. For more information contact: Alexander Ka-
lache, Chief of the Aging and Health Program, WHO Geneva, 20 Avenue Appia,
1211 Geneva, 27, Switzerland. E-mail: kalachea@who.ch.

"Project Reach." Resources for Enhancing Alzheimer's Caregiver Health is a new five-
year initiative launched in 1996 by the National Institute on Aging and the National Institute on Nursing. It seeks to develop and test new ways for families
and friends to manage the daily activities and stresses of caring for people with
Alzheimer's disease. There will be a special focus on African-American and Hispanic families. Students will be able follow the progress of this research through
the following web site: http://www.nih.gov/ninr/pubs/reachrel.html.

Research Center

Stanford University Geriatric Education Center, 703 Welch Road, Suite H1, Stanford,
CA 94304. Phone (415) 723–7063; FAX (415) 723-9692. They have an Ethno-
geriatric Resource Center which reviews materials related to the health care of
elders from different ethnic groups. Their most important resource for students is
a series of literature reviews on aging and health for each of the federally designated minority populations. A list of these publications is available at their web
site: www.stanford.edu.dept/medfm/gec/other.html.

Internet Resources

(1) http://www.hookup.net:80/mall/aging/agesit59.html. The Aging Research Center provides information related to the biomedical study of aging.

(2) http://www.biostat.wustl.edu/alzheimer/. Compiled by the Alzheimer's Disease Research Center at the Washington University (St. Louis) School of Medicine. It has links to many Alzheimer's-related sites.

(3) http://www.aoa.dhhs.gov/aoa/hcbltc/profiles/ is a site developed from a report on "State Long-term Care Profiles" and uses a map of the United States to allow viewers to click on a state and get a summary of 25 data tables for that state.

(4) http://www.aoa.dhhs.gov/aoa/stats/agetrend/ageguide.html provides a 1994 report on "Vital and Health Statistics: Trends in the Health of Older Americans." This includes numerous tables on disability, health status, health expenditures, and other topics which can be viewed, printed, and downloaded.

(5) http://aspe.os.dhhs.gov/daltcp/home.htm is the home page of the Office of Disability, Aging and Long-Term Care Policy at the federal Department of Health and Human Services. At this site you can get access to a report based on a nationwide study of assisted living environments being completed in 1997 and the "National Study of Assisted Living for the Frail Elderly: Literature Review Update."

Longevity Game. On the home page of the Northwestern Mutual Insurance Company— http://www.northwesternmutual.com/games/longevity/. Students can find there a game which shows how lifestyle alters the predicted life expectancy in the United States of 73 years. For example, if you smoke two or more packs of cigarettes a day, anticipate losing eight years. But, if both your parents made it to age 70 without cardiovascular disease, you can add back two years toward expected years of life.

Print Resources

Journals

Journal of Aging and Health; Journal of Mental Health and Aging; Health Care in Later Life; International Psychogeriatrics.

Special Issues of Journals

"Hispanic Aged Mental Health." *Clinical Gerontologist* (1992) 11; "Aging and Disabilities: Seeking Common Ground." *Generations* (1992) (Winter); "Home Health Care and Elders: International Perspectives." *Journal of Cross-Cultural Gerontology* (1993) 8:4; "Cultural Contexts of Aging and Health." *Medical Anthropology Quarterly* (1995) 9:2; "The Nursing Home Revisited." *Generations* (1995–1996) (Winter); "Ethnogeriatrics: Impact of Cultural and Minority Experiences on Geriatric Rehabilitation." *Topics in Geriatric Rehabilitation* (1997) 12:4.

Bibliography

Koff, T. H. et al. 1995. *Long Term Care: An Annotated Bibliography.* Westport CT: Greenwood.

Other Print Resources

Barresi, C. and D. Stull, eds. 1993. *Ethnic Elderly and Long Term Care.* New York: Springer.

Bethel, D. 1992. "Life in Obasuteyama, or, Inside a Japanese Institution for the Elderly." In *Japanese Social Organization*. T. Lebra, ed. Honolulu: University of Hawaii Press. Provides a good comparison with the description of North American nursing home life in chapter 25.

Bonita, R. 1996. *Women, Aging and Health: Achieving Health Across the Life Span.* Geneva: World Health Organization. A short but useful report prepared for the Third Meeting of the Global Commission on Women's Health which was held in 1995 in Australia.

Chen, S. 1996. *Social Policy of the Economic State and Community Care in Chinese Culture.* Aldershot, UK: Avebury. A new study of the evolving system of community care in China by a Chinese scholar.

Ferrucci, L. et al., eds. 1995. *Pendulum: Health and Quality of Life in Older Europeans.* Florence, IT: Instituto Nazionale Ricovero e Cura Anzianni. Draws on data collected for the European Longitudinal Study on Aging to discuss "health related" quality of life in Belgium, Finland, Germany, Greece, Poland, and Ukraine.

Haven, B., ed. 1996. "Long-Term Care in Five Countries." Special Issue, *Canadian Journal on Aging* 16(1). Studies from Australia, Canada, the Netherlands, Norway, and the United States draw on the work of the International Collaborative Effort (ICE) on Measuring the Health and Health Care of the Aging to analyze variable challenges facing long-term care.

Henderson, J. N. 1990. "Anthropology, Health and Aging." In *Anthropology and Aging: Comprehensive Reviews*. R. Rubinstein, ed. Norwell, MA: Kluwer. A comprehensive discussion of the contribution of ethnographic and qualitative studies to understanding health and aging.

Henderson, J. N. and M. Vesperi, eds. 1995. *The Culture of Long Term Care: Nursing Home Ethnography*. Westport, CT: Greenwood. An edited collection of ethnographic analyses in a variety of long-term care environments.

Hopper, S. 1993. "The Influence of Ethnicity on the Health of Older Women." *Clinics in Geriatric Medicine: Care of the Older Woman* 9:231–257. Comprehensive discussion of ethnic variation, older women and health. Provides access to clinical research often overlooked by social scientists.

Lamb, V. 1996. "A Cross-National Study of Quality of Life Factors Associated with Patterns of Elderly Disablement." *Social Science and Medicine* 42(3):363–377. A study of different patterns of disablement among non-institutionalized elderly from Bahrain, Burma, DPR Korea, Egypt, Indonesia, Jordan, Sri Lanka, Thailand and Tunisia.

Olson, L. 1993. *The Graying of the World: Who Will Care for the Frail Elderly?* Binghamton, NY: Haworth.

Poon, L., ed. 1992. *The Georgia Centenarian Study*. Amityville, NY: Baywood. This volume details results from the largest study of centenarians in the United States. Updates on this project can also be found at http://omega.geronuga.edu/gcs/html.

Scharf, T. and C. Wenger. 1995. *International Perspectives on Community Care for Older People*. Aldershot: Avebury.

Stafford, P., ed. Forthcoming. *Gray Areas: Anthropology and the Nursing Home*. Sante Fe, NM: School of American Research. A new compendium of provocative articles about the "inside" culture of nursing home life in the United States.

Woolfson, P. 1997. *Old Age in Transition: The Geriatric Ward*. Westport, CT: Greenwood Press. An ethnography of how frail elderly are evaluated by the medical and social service staff of a geriatric ward.

NOTES

1. The references for each of these localities are: Vilacabamba, Davies 1975; Halsell 1976; the Hunzakut, Leaf 1975; and Paros Island, Beaubier 1976.

2. Prior to this, the world's longevity record of nine days short of 121 years was held by a Japanese man, Chigyen Izumi, who died in 1986. As of January 1996, the oldest authenticated living male is a 113-year-old American, Chris Mortensen, who lives in a retirement home in San Rafael, California. There have been numerous unauthenticated claims of longer life, such as by Charlie Smith, an African-American, who claimed to have been 130 years old when he died and by a Brazilian woman, Maria Jeronimo, who asserts that she has lived 125 years as of 1996.

3. For a good discussion of the cultural construction of very old age see Sankar 1987.

4. Various studies have shown that the aging of people in industrial countries over the last 40 years typically has accounted for less than one percent annually of the rise in medical costs.

5. At the time of the study mentioned here, the contemporary country called Croatia was a republic in the Yugoslav state.

6. For a comparative discussion dealing with hypertension in different countries, see Sheppard, Robinson and Cuervo 1988.

7. Other classic articles on self-help groups dealing with medical problems include: Caplan and Killilea 1976; Guzlow and Tracy 1976.

8. These kinds of groups are especially critical in facilitating access to health services by ethnic populations which avoid using formal health care institutions (Lew 1990).

9. A recent study by David Snowden mentioned in *Public Health Reports* (110:4, 1995) reports that Alzheimer's disease might not actually be a disorder of aging, but a distinct disease affecting only a minority of elderly. This was indicated by the finding that although the disease increases significantly from age 75 to 89, after that point its incidence declines. Due to the complexity of diagnosing this disease there is a wide range in prevalence rates, both within societies and between them. See Graves et al. 1994 for a good discussion of the international data.

10. For up-to-date discussion of diagnosis, treatment and family care of Alzheimer's patients, see Cairl 1995; Eisdorfer and Kumar (forthcoming).

11. For discussion of the cultural variation in other psychological problems, such as depression among the elderly, see Krause and Liang 1992. A general discussion of mental health among the Third World aged is provided in Levkoff, Macarthur and Bucknall 1995.

12. For information about how Vietnamese immigrants cope with dementia see Braun, Takamura and Mougeot 1996.

13. It also should be noted that the diagnostic tests for dementia were developed for Euro-American populations, and that when used among ethnic populations, especially those with relatively little education, results can be unreliable (Wilder et al. 1995; Kaufert, J. and E. Shapiro 1996; Whitfield 1997).

14. For discussion of the problems with a parallel project in the African-American

community of Tampa, see Henderson, Gutierrez-Mayka, Garcia and Boyd 1993. For a study which looks at the use of churches in the African-American community in St. Louis to disseminate knowledge about Alzheimer's disease, see Chadiha, Morrow-Howell, Darkwa and McGillick 1994.

15. For a look at the impact of culture on the clinical approach to dementia in the Chinese-American community, see Elliot 1995 and Elliot et al. 1996.

16. For an excellent discussion of African-American cultural elements which influence the perception of dementia as a health issue, see Gaines 1988–89. A more recent study among this ethnic group which looks at the reaction to chronic illness is Groger 1994.

17. There has developed a controversial debate over studies in both Western and non-Western societies which link more education to a lower incidence of Alzheimer's disease (Li et al. 1991; Mortimer and Graves 1993). However, Cohen (1996b) has suggested that there is equally compelling evidence suggesting that greater poverty and lower education might diminish cerebral reserves and cause a higher incidence of Alzheimer's disease among poor, uneducated individuals.

18. For a recent analysis of trends in disability among the U.S. elderly, see Manton, Stallard and Corder 1995.

19. It was initially speculated that as longevity enlarged, most of these years would simply be added to a dependent old age. Yet, it seems that the whole life span has stretched, with physical old age being increasingly delayed—people are more physically youthful at an increasingly greater age. Recent analysis of the National Long-Term Care Survey shows that the proportion of those over age 65 able to perform activities of daily life independently has steadily grown by 1–2 percent since the early 1980s. Between 1982 and 1995 these lower disability rates have saved Medicare about $200 billion (Global Aging Report 1996).

20. For an excellent general discussion of aging, culture and disability, see Albert and Cattell 1994:191–220. For a recent comparative analysis, see K. Avlund, M. Luck and R. Tinsley 1996.

21. They also suggest that the role of culture in the disablement process is likely to increase as people age, as the definition of disability becomes less tied to one's ability to remain fully economically active.

22. Important sources of information about international innovations dealing with the aged include: Teicher, Thursz and Vigilante 1979; Little 1982; Nusberg, Gibson and Peace 1984; Thursz, Nusberg and Prather 1995. Students should also see the newsletter *Global Aging* published by AARP.

23. For a discussion of the early stages of a move to open care in Europe see Amann 1980; Little 1982.

24. For a recent discussion of abuse in nursing homes see Payne and Cikovic 1995.

25. The acronym OBRA derives from the fact that the reforms were included in a large budget compromise bill called the Omnibus Budget Reconciliation Act.

26. There is a growing literature on how culture influences the experience of long-term care and living in nursing homes (von Meering 1996). See Watson and Maxwell 1977; Chee and Kane 1983; Longhofer 1994 for discussion of ethnicity in these settings, and Miller et al. 1996 for a general discussion of the use of community long-term care services by minority groups. See Conn and Mace 1996 for a general analysis of quality of life, and Kayser-Jones (1981) and Holmes and Holmes (1987) for works dealing with cultures outside the United States. See Foner 1994 for an ethnography dealing with the

work experience in nursing homes and Farmer 1996 for an ethnography of the way nursing homes are organized.

27. For a general discussion of the varied cultural response to death, see Kagawa-Singer 1995.

28. For further discussion of the impact of pet therapy on the elderly, see Kongable, Buckwalter and Stolley 1989; Savishinsky 1991.

CHAPTER 21

Between Humans and Ghosts: The Decrepit Elderly in a Polynesian Society

Judith C. Barker

The distinction between decrepit and intact elders is now recognized as being an important one in all societies (Foner 1985; Glascock 1982; (Chapter 3 this volume). Frequently, frail elders are seen as burdens on society and even are subject to "death-hastening" behaviors, such as neglect or abandonment by the rest of the community. Certain aspects of Polynesian life, however, lead to an expectation that the senescent old will not be abandoned or neglected but rather will always remain a focus of attention and concern. Is this in fact the case?

Until recently (Counts and Counts 1985a; Holmes 1972, 1974; R. Maxwell 1970; Nason 1981; Rhoads 1984), relatively few works dealt explicitly with the status of the aged in Pacific nations. By and large, the picture we have of old age in Polynesian societies, showing that elders are not forgotten or devalued but powerful and active family and community members, comes from ethnographic studies, such as those of Firth (1936), Hanson (1970), Mead (1928) and Shore (1982). Generally, these works fail to distinguish between the treatment accorded the intact, mature elder and that given the frail, senescent old. Where this distinction is mentioned, the impression is given that frail elders are treated much like their intact peers: "The infirm aged are cared for with matter-of-fact kindness within the family, mostly by women and older children" (R. Maxwell 1970:140). Any variation in treatment accorded the frail elderly Polynesian is assumed to be idiosyncratic, a mere aberration having no societal or cultural basis.

Fieldwork on a little-known western Polynesian island, Niue, reveals the existence of considerable differences in the treatment of very frail and of intact elders.[1] Very frail, decrepit elders, whom I came across when doing other sociomedical research, were by Western standards neglected. My encounters with these old people were so vivid, so at odds with my expectations derived from the literature and from observation of the lives of intact elders, that they remain indelible. The impression I formed about the lives of decrepit elders is confirmed through investigation of medical records and archival documents and by accounts from others.

This chapter shows that variation in the treatment of the elderly on Niue is not only well-established and systematic but also makes cultural sense. Discussion shows not just how decrepit old people are treated and who constitutes this group of elders but also considers several different reasons why they appear to be neglected by family and community alike. The individual threads of discussion eventually intertwine to produce a complex understanding of how those aspects of Polynesian culture that lead to respect for the aged give way, in the face of severe physical or mental infirmity, to other values.

Certain striking similarities are evident in all Polynesian societies; similarities, for example, of language, ecology, social organization, and myth and history (Keesing 1953; Oliver 1961; Ritchie and Ritchie 1979; Topping 1977). Nonetheless, each Polynesian society is unique, different from all others. The description given here of Niuean responses to the elderly is a case study: It is merely suggestive but not proof of the existence of similar social processes in other Polynesian societies.

THE ELDERLY IN POLYNESIAN SOCIETY

Said to be well past the giddiness and frenzy of youth and comfortably settled into the responsibilities of marriage and family, elders are stable and influential figures. These people are in the prime of life, full of vigor, with complex political and social (including family) roles and responsibilities. An elder in Polynesian society is not necessarily an old person but simply an adult of mature years with some social standing. While traditional roles allotted to the elderly sometimes chafe modern youth, the elderly themselves are still highly regarded. In the face of sometimes sweeping socioeconomic changes, Polynesian elders sustain their high status (Holmes 1974; R. Maxwell 1970; Rhoads 1984).

Having acquired political and social influence by middle age, a competent person maintains that power into advanced old age. Because the role of elder is well established before a person reaches chronological old age and begins to experience significant decline in physical or mental abilities, elders suffer little disruption of roles as a result of mere chronological aging. Throughout this chapter the term ''elder'' is used to refer to those who both currently or formerly held important sociopolitical positions and have reached chronological ''old age,'' that is, are 65 or older. Continue to bear in mind that the role of elder is well established by the time these people reach numerical old age.

Elders are respected not just because of family background or accomplishments but also because they are chronologically older. Not only is attention to relative age linguistically symbolized but it is bolstered by the entire social, religious, economic and political organization of Polynesian life. A focus of socialization throughout Polynesian life, especially during childhood, is the inculcation of respect for those who are older (Ritchie and Ritchie 1979, 1981; Shore 1982). Older people are to be obeyed, respected, served and emulated. In return, elders will nurture, teach, love and protect. This form of relationship continues throughout life, younger persons always being socially obligated to care for older ones.

From these values comes an expectation that even in advanced old age or physical infirmity the aged will be well-looked-after by children and grandchildren, because they are still important family members and because it would be shameful to neglect an elder. Most ethnographers of Polynesian societies argue that this expectation is fulfilled (e.g., Holmes 1972, 1974; Holmes and Rhoads 1987). My research, however, casts some doubts about this.

NIUE ENCAPSULATED

Relatively little is known about Niue. Observers of Niuean life have been few in number and somewhat reticent about writing (Ryan 1984:xi). Two dated ethnographies exist (Smith 1983 [1902/1903]; Loeb 1926), both based on very short periods of fieldwork over 50 years ago. More recent works are frequently difficult to access (e.g, Barker 1985; Bedford, Mitchell and Mitchell 1980; Chapman 1976; Frankovich 1974; Mitchell 1977; Niue Government 1982; Ryan 1977).

Captain Cook made a fleeting first contact with Niuean society in 1774 (McLachlan 1982; Ryan 1984). Except for shipwrecked sailors, traveling missionaries and itinerant traders, the island was seldom visited until after the 1850s when mission stations were first established and some trade contacts set up (Niue Government 1982). Because it was outside the regular trade routes, had little commercial potential and was not strategically or militarily important, unlike many other Pacific islands, Niue was not colonized until very late. Britain annexed the island in 1900 but promptly handed over control to New Zealand (Niue Government 1982).

Administered by New Zealand from 1900 to 1974, Niue is now an independent nation, although New Zealand continues to provide Niueans with citizenship, with protection against foreign powers and with considerable economic aid (Chapman 1976, 1982; Connell 1983; Fisk 1978; New Zealand Coalition 1982; Pollard 1979). The island inherited, upon independence, an infrastructure of communications, roads, and health and social welfare services of a standard far in excess of its nearest neighbors.

An isolated single island of raised coral, Niue does not fit the popular image of a tropical isle. It has no fringing reef, no sandy beaches, no lagoon. Access is difficult via steep cliffs 25 meters high, which rise directly out of deep ocean. Located about 600 km southeast of Samoa, at 19°S and 169°55'W, this large (16 km × 10 km) island is covered by relatively sparse vegetation growing in shallow pockets of fertile soil between pinnacles of sharp coral rock. There are no streams or ponds, no surface water on this drought-prone island.

Slash-and-burn (shifting) agriculture, arduous and labor-intensive, supplies the populace with its basic subsistence needs and is supplemented by fishing, hunting and gathering. In contrast to most other Pacific nations, the economic base of the island has changed recently from being primarily agricultural to service provision (Connell 1983), so that now nearly 80 percent of employed adults on the island work for wages for the Niuean government. This gives Niue a high standard of living compared to other Pacific nations. Money, from wages or supplemented by cash cropping of passion fruit, limes or coconuts, is used to buy durable consumer goods such as motorbikes, outboard motors and refrigerators (Pollock 1979).

Demographics

Niue is thought to have been originally settled from 120 A.D. by successive waves of Tongan and Samoan voyagers. Although large in area for a Pacific island, Niue has never supported a population greater than about 5,000, probably because of the arduous nature of agriculture on this difficult terrain (Bedford, Mitchell and Mitchell 1980). Depopulation, not overpopulation, is Niue's greatest worry (Bedford, Mitchell and Mitchell 1980; Niue Government 1985, 1988; Walsh and Trlin 1973). Out-migration started in the late nineteenth century when young men left temporarily to work on plantations on neighboring islands; recently, emigration has taken a new and more serious turn. Now out-migration is permanent and consists mainly of unmarried youth and of mature adult couples and their school-age children, going mainly to New Zealand to settle. In each of three five-year intercensal periods between 1971 and 1986, Niue lost 23 percent of its population. Such migration has had a considerable effect on the island's population structure.

The total population of around 2,500 now left on the island contains an increasing proportion of elderly adults (Barker 1994). A 1988 census revealed a total of 178 natives on the island who were aged 65 or older (Niue Government 1988). Elders thus comprise 8 percent of the total population on Niue. This is low compared to the United States, where in 1980 older people made up 11 percent of the population, but high compared to other less-developed regions of the world such as Africa, Latin America or Asia, where the proportion of over-sixty-five-year-olds is estimated to be under 4 percent (Hoover and Siegel 1986; Soldo 1980).

Aged dependency (those 65 or older per 100 people aged 15 to 64 years) on Niue is high for an underdeveloped nation. At 15.3, Niue's current aged dependency is nearly three times that generally encountered in less-developed nations (Hoover and Siegel 1986:15), but it is still less than aged dependency in highly developed countries such as the United States, which in 1980 had an age dependency of 18.4 (Soldo 1980:39).

Hence, elders form a visibly large demographic group on Niue. Moreover, with a life expectancy at birth approaching 67 years and a decreasing mortality rate (Taylor, Nemaia and Connell 1987), elders will continue to form a large part of Niue's population in the future.

Central Niuean Values

Contemporary Niue has both a language and a social organization similar to but different from other western Polynesian societies (Loeb 1926; Pollock 1979; Ryan 1977; Smith 1983 [1902/1903]). Daily life and interaction on Niue is much like that on any other Polynesian island (see Hanson 1970; Holmes 1974; Levy 1973; Shore 1982).

Although typically Polynesian in many respects, such as in child rearing and family organization, major political forms and central religious values, Niue is also atypical. The most distinctive features are a rudimentary and very flexible social hierarchy, egalitarian ideals, an emphasis on individual achievement and a strong work ethic (Frankovich 1974; Pollock 1979; Ryan 1977). The influence of these features of Niuean life on the status of elders is clearly exemplified during political processes.

Political power on Niue is reserved for those, both male and female, who demonstrate competence and knowledge, from the wider world or accumulated in the course of a long life. Any person in a position of political or social power on Niue has arrived there through a combination of personal and social attributes, and their position is maintained because they continue to demonstrate competence and an ability to control younger, ambitious persons and to measure up to the demands of that position. Each of the thirteen villages on the island is represented in the *Fale Fono* (Niuean Assembly) by one person elected by the residents of that village. These representatives are generally older men with prestigious backgrounds, as pastors, government officials or successful planters. The *Fono* is completed by the addition of six island-wide representatives elected by all eligible voters. These Common Roll Members, as they are known, tend to be younger, to have been educated outside Niue and have worked as teachers or doctors before becoming politicians.

Thus, modern Niuean politics conforms to tradition by having elders represent individual villages at the same time as it deviates from convention by rewarding individual achievement. A flexible social hierarchy, egalitarian ideals and an emphasis on individual achievement work against elders' maintaining their privileged position once their competence is in any way compromised.

THE ELDERLY ON NIUE

The ethnographic picture of the aged in Polynesian societies, presented briefly above, portrays well the intact elder on Niue. Those in good health, those with important social functions, are respected community figures, political leaders and vital family members. Their life is well discussed in the general literature on Polynesian societies (such as Holmes and Rhoads 1987). The frail, infirm Niuean elder, however, presents a very different picture. Decrepit elders are frequently ignored, even neglected, by kin and community, left to fend for themselves without any longer having the physical or psychological means to succeed. Exactly how are impaired elders treated on Niue? What kind of treatment do they receive from their kin and community? How is this possible?

The Treatment of Impaired Elders

I met elders with urinary or fecal incontinence, with wheezing chests and running eyes, with infected sores, with bleeding gums, or with painful joints, none of whom had been seen recently by a doctor or nurse. One elder I saw lay semicomatose on the floor, evoking rueful smiles from visitors and kin and comments about "going out the hard way."

Too frail to summon a physician themselves, these elders relied on their caretakers, who seemed not to bother asking for medical help. It is not difficult to get a physician to visit. A doctor visits each village on the island four times a week. A red flag hanging by the roadside brings the doctor in his van right to the door. Public health nurses, too, can be fetched in the same way on their monthly rounds to assist in the care of patients. All medical services, including hospitalization, are free.

When cases such as these do come to the attention of the medical profession, they are quickly attended to. Elders comprised a yearly average of 8 percent (N = 276) of all admissions to hospital on Niue between the years 1977 and 1982. Fourteen elderly patients (5 percent), most of whom remained in the hospital for over a year, were admitted solely for nursing care (Barker 1988).

Several types of old people were generally left unattended or received minimal care. They were: those old folk who yelled constantly, swearing at neighbors and kin; those who fought all the time, hitting out at all and sundry; those who forgot people's names or forgot what they were doing; those who wandered away at all times of day and night; those who talked only of events in the remote past, who conversed with absent friends and long-dead relatives; those who stared vacantly about them, constantly drooled or were incontinent. Little effort seemed to have been made to bathe these elders, who were generally clad in filthy rags, to clean their homes, or to provide them with any material comforts. Many of these elders complained of being constantly hungry.

Just as a pregnant woman is warned not to steal from others lest her unborn child be punished for the act by being born with a withered arm, so were explanations found for the causes of some degenerative processes which afflict the old. Facial tics, involuntary vocalizations, and limb palsies in old age are regarded as belated punishments for evil-doing. Elders with these problems were held up as examples for children: "Old Togia makes noises like a chicken all the time now. That's because when he was young he must have stolen chickens and never confessed to doing so. If you don't want to be like that when you get old, don't steal.''

Those old folk who were bent over or walked oddly or tried ineffectually to fend for themselves were figures of ridicule. It amused everyone that an elderly man was concussed by a dry coconut falling on his head. The danger of a dry nut falling from a tree is constantly pointed out to young children, who quickly learn this lesson. An old person who fails to avoid a falling nut demonstrates the loss of critical skills inculcated early in life.

Similarly, people were amazed that extreme thirst late one afternoon would cause an eighty-five-year-old partially blind woman to go searching for water only to end up falling into a disused water tank, breaking her arm and dislocating her shoulder. Her feeble cries for help were finally heard by school children on their way home from classes. The children did call for help—amid much hilarity about the old lady's plight and some teasing and swearing at her for creating such a situation.

Anyone who gets injured on Niue is likely to be greeted with gales of laughter and ribald comment. Mocking, teasing and ridicule are common strategies of social control, of making abnormal situations appear normal. These strategies are used especially to get children to acquiesce to adult wishes or to accept painful medical treatments (Levy 1973:308–314). Giggling and laughing also hide nervousness, fear or embarrassment at some unusual event. Hilarity not only covers an underlying concern for the injured but also reinforces the fatalistic, stoic acceptance of misfortune that is expected of victims.

The children's laughter over the old lady's fate was at a pitch and intensity that revealed that they were especially disturbed. Teasing her, ridiculing her and making rude jokes about her and her fate were attempts to establish control over the phenomenon, to make it conform to Niuean expectations, to normalize the unusual. Events of the sort in which the elderly sustain injury are not unusual. Between 1977 and 1982, for example, accident or injury was a leading cause of death for Niueans over 70 years of age, accounting for 14 percent of all deaths of elders (Barker 1988; Taylor, Nemaia and Connell 1987). Old men were especially likely to die as a result of accident or injury.

Late in 1982, a visitor from New Zealand, a nurse with many years of experience in caring for geriatric patients, made an informal inspection of elderly people on Niue. Her findings paralleled mine. From this evidence, I concluded that some frail elders on Niue were not receiving the kind of care and attention I had expected they would. By Western standards, some elders were clearly being neglected.

The Concept of ''Neglect''

Each society has its own standards for conduct toward other persons, for conduct that is honorable, respectful, acceptable, proper, indifferent, demeaning, brutal, abusive or neglectful. The age, sex and relative social ranking of the persons involved in the relationship, as well as individual characteristics of the protagonists and the history of their interactions, have a lot to do with the conduct of one to the other and how it is defined. What is deemed "neglect" by Western societies may be acceptable, expected, normal behavior elsewhere.

When I say decrepit elders on Niue were ignored or neglected by their kin or community I do not mean they never received any attention or care. They were not completely abandoned but rather received inadequate care or minimal attention. Old people would be visited by kin but not necessarily every day, and then often only by youngsters sent to check on their well-being. They would be given food but in scant amounts, really only enough for one meal and not an entire day, and they would no longer receive the choice morsels they formerly enjoyed. They would be clothed, but in rags that were rarely laundered. It is this type of treatment that I refer to as neglect.

When Glascock (Chapter 3 this volume) describes a group's behavior toward the frail elderly as "death-hastening" or "neglectful," he means the outcome of the acts of behavior do not enhance the well-being of the aged individual from *our* understanding of the physical and mental processes involved. From the perspective of the people concerned, however, the outcome might be seen as helpful, if not to the individual at least to the group. In this chapter, behavior toward the elderly is first described using Western notions of "neglect," and then it is related to other aspects of Niuean society to show why this apparently "neglectful" behavior is in fact understandable, even correct. Such behaviors cannot be understood outside their proper cultural context.

Frail and Decrepit Elders

Most elders either retain their abilities and relatively good health well into advanced age or die from acute disorders or accidents before they reach a stage of decrepitude. A recent survey found that less than 20 percent of the Niuean population aged 65 or over was extremely frail or had many impairments (Barker 1989). Only about half of these frail elders are decrepit, however. Of the approximately 200 elders on the island during the fieldwork in 1982–1983, for example, I met eleven old people (about 5 percent) whom I considered decrepit while another four or five were rapidly losing their ability to maintain an independent existence and appeared to be on the road from frailty to decrepitude.

So, I have been concerned with understanding the behavior of Niueans toward a small but nonetheless interesting segment of their society. I explore the cultural conditions that make it possible for behavior radically at odds with the expected norms to become comprehensible.

As a group, the characteristics of decrepit elders contrast sharply with those of the general elderly population on the island. A survey of the latter was performed in 1985 using a 50 percent random sample of elders whose names appeared on the Niuean government pension list. In general, being over 75 years of age, being male, having never married, and having few children left on the island to care for one, are all associated with impairment (Barker 1989). All these factors are even more strongly associated with decrepitude. Table 21.1 documents the major differences between decrepit elders, those who experienced some degree of neglect, and other elders on Niue.

Contributing little to their families, decrepit elders fail to maintain even minimal social roles in the general village community; in particular, the important social role of churchgoer ceases. Furthermore, decrepit elders experience more limitations in work activities, more confusion or mental deterioration, and more sensory problems (blindness, especially) than do other elders on Niue.

Niuean Explanations for Neglect

Niueans themselves expressed ideas about the care of "oldies," as they commonly call all elderly people. In general, Niueans espoused respect and admiration for old folk, vehemently contrasting what they perceived as Western indifference to elders (signaled by the placement of elders in nursing homes) with their own respectful concern and loving care for the aged. Niueans did recognize, however, that their treatment of decrepit elders was not the same as their caring for intact elders, and they gave several explanations for their treatment of decrepit elders.

Niueans said some degree of decrepitude was to be expected in advanced old age and should be accepted, not complained about. Combined with a degree of fatalism (McEwen 1974), Niueans have the general Polynesian tendency to display little empathy for others (Levy 1973:312). As we have seen with respect to the old woman who fell into the disused water tank, even those experiencing severe pain or in very adverse circumstances receive little overt sympathy.

Another explanation was that in old age people receive their "just deserts." Those who had been excessively individualistic, materialistic, ill-tempered or nasty at a younger age are simply reaping the harvest of unpleasant seeds they previously sowed. Further, people who cared for kin and displayed their love throughout life are not neglected. People who took no time to raise a family, to help siblings and other family members through life, to establish a bond of love between themselves and younger kin have no one to call on in old age, have no one who is obligated to assist.

Men more than women are likely to have failed to demonstrate love for kin. Generally, these are men who failed to marry and so have no children whom they raised and were obligated to provide care for, or who left the island for work and returned only in old age. Biological ties that are never properly and continuously "socialized" will not suffice to ensure that an elder is adequately looked after in old age. Claims for help on the basis of biological connections alone usually induce a polite but minimal and or temporary response.

There is a striking parallel between this native explanation for neglect in old age and the demographic characteristics of the decrepit elderly. Males predominate in the decrepit sample, with a relatively large proportion of them never-

Table 21.1
Characteristics of Elders on Niue*

	Elders in Survey (N = 63)	Decrepit Elders (N = 11)
Average age#	under 75 years	over 80 years
Sex	30% males	64% males
Married	40%	19%
Living on own	14%	54%
Regularly attend church	71%	0%
Limited in doing work/family activities	48%	100%
Severe mobility impairments	14%	100%
Partly or completely blind	29%	45%
Some memory problems or confusion	16%	45%

*See Barker (1989) for an extended discussion of the health and functional status of the elderly on Niue.

#Interpreting attributed age for Niuean elderly is extremely difficult. There is a tendency for chronological age attributed to the very old or the very frail, especially men, to be inflated (see Barker 1989).

married, childless, or recently returned from overseas. Almost half the decrepit old men (43%) I encountered had never married. One of these was an aggressive, confused seventy-year-old living on his own next door to a niece. He had only recently been sent back to Niue from Pago Pago, where he had lived for most of his adult life. Another decrepit old man without children of his own had just moved to live with a nephew, having rotated from village to village, kin to kin, over the previous five years. No one was certain how long he would remain, as his previous relationship with this kinsman had been very distant and tinged with hostility.

Some Niueans said old people now have a tough time because out-migration has so severely depleted the resources available to any one extended family that there are no longer several adult women available in any one household to care for both children and old people. There is undoubtedly some merit to this explanation, as the domestic workloads of individual adults, especially of women, has increased recently. What this explanation reveals, of course, is that care of old people comes low on the list of domestic priorities, well after the care of other adults and children. Indeed, doubts can be cast about whether decrepit old folk ever received adequate care even before permanent out-migration and demographic changes disrupted family organization.

Glascock and Feinman (1981:27) note that supportive treatment of the intact aged and nonsupportive, even death-hastening treatment of the decrepit elderly can coexist in one society without strain, as these behaviors are aimed at different populations. Niueans even signal the difference between the intact and the decrepit elderly populations linguistically. The term *ulu motua*, meaning "gray-haired one," refers to socially active, powerful, respected, intact elders. In contrast, the terms *penupenu-fonua* or *mutumutu-fonua*, "grey fish of the land," are graphic if rather morbid metaphors used to describe very elderly, incompetent, decrepit old men. Obviously, senescent old men are not in the same category as other old men.

Negotiation of the Label "Decrepit"

Elders do not become decrepit overnight. Decrepitude is a gradual, degenerative process during which negotiation over the applicability of the label "decrepit" constantly occurs between the elder and the rest of the community. Becoming decrepit is a process of "fading out" (Maxwell 1986:77). It is a process in which elders begin to deploy their resources differently, often in a more self-centered fashion, while displays of deference by others toward them are correspondingly recast. When an old person is unable or unwilling to use his or her resources to maintain even a minimal social role, the community successfully applies the decrepit label, then the elder accepts it.

Decreases in competence are fought against, minimized in several ways. One strategy is for elders to cease doing strenuous "bush work" but to continue engaging in household chores. The very strong Niuean work ethic insists that every person—man, woman and child—assist in supporting the household. From an early age (three to five years), children are assigned and expected to perform regularly important household tasks, including weeding gardens, feeding livestock, washing clothes and dishes, or child-minding. An elder who can no longer perform any of these tasks places a greater burden on the family than does any other member except an infant. Unlike caring for a frail elder, however, caring for an infant carries the promise of future rewards: in a few years a child will be an able worker, in a few years the elder be no more able than at present.

A second way elders can minimize their impending decrepitude is to adopt new but valued social roles inappropriate in younger persons, roles such as "storyteller" or "clown" (Holmes 1974; Holmes and Rhoads 1987; Huntsman and Hooper 1975). In contrast to the behavior expected of younger folk, old

people, especially women, can tell lewd tales, can mock high-status public figures, and can act generally as court jesters at important social events or ceremonies such as weddings. This joking and ribald behavior is tolerated, even
valued, as a commentary by which elders delineate social norms and indirectly
control younger persons.

An elder too frail to do any household tasks or to engage in public jesting
has little to offer his or her family or community, except perhaps being a teller
of tales, a repository of lore and ceremonial knowledge. Unlike other Polynesian
peoples, however, Niueans have long been noted for their negligence in recording traditions and their relative lack of oral histories (Ryan 1977:33). Thus, even
a role demanding little physical skill and involving memory tasks most often
maintained by frail elders, that of tale-teller, of oral historian, is generally unavailable to the elderly on Niue.

One exception concerns the role of traditional healer, *taulaatua*, which is still
important on Niue and essentially is reserved for elders (Barker 1985:148–153).
Some healers are specialists who treat cases of major disorder from all over the
island; others deal only with more minor problems within their own village. An
elder in each extended family usually knows and uses healing recipes. Because
of the secret nature of the herbal ingredients, of the proper preparation and use
of the recipes and of the incantations, curers who become so frail that they can
no longer gather the required herbs themselves begin to lose even this role.
Some elderly healers maintain power through the gradual revelation of their
secret knowledge to a grandchild or other younger relative who shows aptitude.

A third major way to demonstrate competence is to continue to raise children
(Kirkpatrick 1985a). As Counts and Counts put it, people "recruit a new dependent whose presence testifies to the continuing ability of an aging person to
care for himself and others" (1985a:5). Adoption of a child by an old person
is both a demonstration of competence and an insurance against neglect in advanced old age or frailty, for adopted children are under great obligation to
repay their parents by caring for them in later life. Most adoptions on Niue,
especially of girls, take place through the child's mother's kin (Barker 1985),
and the driving force behind most adoptions is closely related women, not men.
Elders without daughters or granddaughters will not only make fewer adoptions
than others but will be more likely to adopt children who are male and who are
related only through distant or putative biological ties. This is especially true
for elderly men who never married or are widowed at the time of adoption.
Adoptive boys who have no close biological bond to the adoptive parent frequently feel little obligation to carry out their filial duties when the parent becomes aged. So, once more, men are more likely than women to reach advanced
old age without anyone, even an adopted child, to care for them; decrepit old
men are more likely to be neglected.

IS "NEGLECT" OF RECENT ORIGIN?

Thus a picture of Niue emerges. Socioeconomic change on the island has been rampant, recent and rapid. Demographic change, too, has been of monumental proportions. Niue has a high aged dependency ratio and an increasing proportion of elderly in the community, partly as a result of out-migration (Niue Government 1985), and partly through reductions in mortality and increases in life expectancy over the past 30 years (Taylor Nemaia, and Connell 1987).

It is tempting to see these factors—modernization—as causes for the differences in treatment between the decrepit and intact elderly, a difference that would be recent in origin. But is the distinction between decrepit and intact elders a modern phenomenon on Niue? Documents located in several archives soon dispelled the notion that variation in the treatment of the elderly on Niue is of recent origin. Neglect of the elderly, even in the past to the extent of abandoning them in huts in the "bush" where they literally had to fend for themselves, is not new.

Historical Evidence

In a letter written in November 1885, the European missionary on the island, Frank Lawes, quoted a Niuean *toa* or warrior thus: "It was better to have the skull broken to pieces in war, than to die in old age from neglect" (quoted in Ryan 1977:100). The first ethnographer on Niue, S. Percy Smith, had only this to say about the elderly: "In very old age, it was not infrequent that old people requested their younger relatives to strangle them to cause death" (1983 [1902–1903]:60). The accuracy of this statement is unknown. In 1922, a short article about life on Niue by a visiting scholar noted that Niueans "were not thoughtful of their old folk" (Juniper 1922:612). Edwin Loeb (1926:86), the next ethnographer, writes that the elderly were abandoned in the bush.

Reports by the New Zealand Administration's staff support the views of these scholars. In 1923 the medical officer noted a "tendency for the natives to neglect their old."[2] A few years later he more bluntly reported: "At times one encounters marked cases of neglect, especially of the aged. 'Only an old person' is an expression one commonly hears. In several instances one feels that this callous indifference has been a potent factor in the cause of death."[3]

Reporting an outbreak of influenza on the island in 1932, the Resident Commissioner said: "The old people when sick have rather a poor chance as the younger ones are most indifferent, and do not worry about feeding them or attending to their comforts."[4] Again, in 1945, another Resident Commissioner reports: "Old folk are left in hovels and begrudgingly fed. . . . I am quite convinced that neither the Church nor the people even recognize that it is a problem. It is quite taken for granted and *faka Niue* [the Niuean way]."[5]

Throughout the 1950s and into the 1960s, medical officers continued to report neglect affecting about 10 percent of the elderly population then on the island.[6]

To help stem this widespread custom, a tax was levied from 1958 on to provide old people with a small pension. Abandonment of old folk into "bush huts" had ceased by the mid-1960s, but other improvements were slow in coming about. One 1964 medical report noted that "the elderly [living alone] fare worse than those living with relatives . . . several appeared poorly clad and neglected. Nearly all had inadequate bed clothing and some none at all."[7]

Accounts by Niuean Migrants

The general tenor of these reports is corroborated by Niueans who migrated from the island decades ago and have become acculturated in new communities. These informants recounted the incomprehension they experienced when making return visits to Niue. Their tales of seeing how formerly influential, vital community members were neglected in old age reverberate with now familiar themes: "hunger," "filth," "smells" and "neglect."

When decrepit elders died, families were genuinely distraught with grief and loudly mourned the loss of their cherished family members. My informants asked: How could this be? Why did the community allow these families to neglect the elderly and not punish them for so doing? How could a family neglect an old person in life yet so sincerely grieve his or her death?

CULTURAL VALUES AND "NEGLECTFUL" BEHAVIOR

By now enough evidence has been presented for it to be clear that Niuean neglect of decrepit elders is a well-established, systematic pattern of behavior and not mere idiosyncracy or aberration. Moreover, it clearly is not a new phenomenon, not a response to massive, recent socioeconomic and demographic change. The question remains, however—given strongly espoused values about the aged and a social system organized around elders—how is this variant of behavior possible?

Egalitarianism in a Fragile Ecology

Recall that Niue's agricultural system is fraught with difficulties. Periodic drought, a fragile ecosystem, a harsh terrain—all make food production uncertain, arduous and time-consuming. Subsistence requires constant work from every able body, even young children, and there is little surplus available for nonproducers. A decrepit elder, too sick or frail to garden, to work around the house or even to mind infants and toddlers, creates obligations that he or she is unable to repay. Decrepit elders can easily be begrudged whatever small surplus is produced, especially in times when food is scarce.

Combine this with cultural values that stress hard work and individual achievement—looking out for oneself—and a system that neglects decrepit elders, leaves them to their fate, makes them cope on their own as best they can, starts to become comprehensible. This "ecological" explanation appears rather callous, though, and very different from the sentiments accorded the healthy old. Such an explanation is also at odds with the treatment given other handicapped people.

Others with Disability

As in many Polynesian societies, babies born with physical and mental disabilities are not rejected but rather receive special attention, are lavished with affection. When older, these children are expected, to the best of their abilities, however minimal those might be, to aid the family in meeting its subsistence and communal obligations. A handicapped child might occasionally be mildly teased by his or her peers, but no more so than any other youngster. No child would be excluded from social gatherings or village activities just because of physical or mental "difference" (Kirkpatrick 1985b:230).

Similarly, those who sustain injuries that result in permanent disabilities are not excluded from family or social activities and responsibilities. Adults with handicaps are expected to work to the extent of their abilities and to occupy whatever positions in village life are appropriate to their skills and social standing. One thirty-year-old paraplegic, for example, though confined to a wheelchair, tends his passion fruit and lime gardens by day and regularly attends village dances and other social gatherings by night. People banded together to build him a specially designed house and to pound down into level paths the coral rocks around his garden plots so that he could tend his crops unaided.

So, physically or mentally impaired children or adults are not excluded from society, are not subject to treatment any different from that given others of their age and status. Why then do Niueans neglect their decrepit elders? It cannot just be because of their handicaps or because of their minimal contributions to household welfare. Other cultural values must be at work.

One clue is that despite this acceptance of disability, being of imposing stature, being well built and sturdy is culturally valued in Polynesian societies. High rank and social importance are frequently associated with being tall or fat. Excessively thin individuals or those losing weight or physical robustness are suspected of illness, curse or serious misdemeanor (Finau, Prior and Evans 1982: 1542). Both literally and figuratively, decrepit elders on Niue are shadows of their former selves. Those who when younger were muscular, strong and sturdy are now shrunken, stooped and scrawny. Those who formerly were vital, influential figures are now ineffectual, pathetic beings with little interest in social life.

Such dramatic and obvious changes clearly raise suspicions about their origin. Degenerative changes are fundamentally different from any birth defect or disability resulting from accident and are unlike acute illnesses of rapid onset and resolution. Decrepitude is insidious, slow and cumulative, a gradual and irreversible destruction of vitality. Very traditional ideas about the origin of such misfortunes, about the nature of death and about the proper treatment of the afflicted give us an understanding of why these degenerative processes are suspect. They explain the treatment of the decrepit elderly on Niue.

The Origin of Misfortune and the Nature of Death

In the Polynesian view there are two parallel worlds, this world of humans and the world of the supernatural. Inhabitants of the latter keep a close watch on this world and punish those who offend. A person courts punishment by acting indecorously, by blaspheming, by transgressing the rules of proper conduct or by breaking *tapu*, rules specifying how to behave in certain localities or on special occasions. Punishment usually takes the form of sickness, especially intractable or life-threatening sickness, and is often brought about by possession by *aitu*, ghosts, the spirits of the dead.

In taking possession of a person, an *aitu*, usually a close ancestral spirit, aims to kill eventually, to take the person to the supernatural world, perhaps to avenge its own death. Once an *aitu* takes over, it speaks through the living in trance, delirium or confusion, revealing secrets to the family and community at large, making salacious suggestions and commenting generally upon the morality and correctness of the conduct of all and sundry (Barker 1985:143–152; Goodman 1971; Shore 1978).

As is common in Polynesian languages, Niuean uses the same word, *mate*, to encompass several states that we distinguish as delirium, unconsciousness and death. Thus, there are no clear distinctions, linguistic or conceptual, between being incoherent, being comatose, being dying or being dead. A *mate* person is somewhere out of this world, on the way to the next.

Death in Niuean perspective is not an instantaneous, unequivocal event (Counts and Counts 1985a:17). Rather, death is a process of transition, a gradual shucking of the competencies and responsibilities of this world and a simultaneous acquisition of characteristics of the new world. So death occurs over a period of time, months or even years, perhaps. Death is not unexpected, as all natural living things die. Death is not absolute as there is no irrevocable boundary between parallel worlds, worlds occupied by humans and by supernatural beings, by ghosts.

Burial is merely a disposal of a body, a former container for the soul and animating forces. To encourage the new ghostly being to stay in the hereafter with its supernatural kin and to not return to this world, Niueans bury their dead quickly, usually within twelve to twenty-four hours. Large stones or concrete slabs are placed atop the grave to discourage the new *aitu* from wanting to return to this world, from wanting to remain in the world of humans.

Relations between the Living and the Dying

Decrepit elders, then, especially those who no longer look or behave like competent adults, who rave incoherently, who speak of long-past events or converse with long-dead kin, are being actively courted by *aitu*, are *mate*, in transition. They are "the nearly dead." In touch with the spirit world, they are alarmingly near to becoming *aitu* themselves. Decrepit elders are in transition, inhabiting a twilight world of not-quite-human-but-not-quite-ancestor. As human beings, the decrepit elderly are obsolete, but, as inhabitants of another realm, they are incomplete.

Such near-*aitu* threaten to break the barriers between the worlds. In possession of alarming characteristics from both worlds but not fully competent in either, this human-in-transition, this ghost-in-the-making, threatens to contaminate this world with things from beyond. This threat ceases only when the dying are dead, fully dead; when they have completed the transition to the other world and are buried.

In traditional times, the intractably sick, those possessed by ghosts (by *aitu*) "were removed into the bush and placed in a temporary hut where they were left until they might recover or die. Their relatives took food to them, but no one remained with them" (Murray 1863:367).

Such isolation of the sick conformed to the custom for dealing with ritually unclean objects. Imposition of a long period of *tapu* prevented *aitu* from spreading possession to others (Luomala 1978:147). Hence, we can see that abandoning or neglecting decrepit elders is not simply a rather brutal means of relieving younger people of an economic burden (though that probably plays some role) but is a ritual activity undertaken for sensible reasons. It prevents contamination by ghostly influences from beyond.

Moreover, neglect is appropriate precisely because in reducing the customary ties and emotions between humans it allows decrepit elders to complete an expected transition as smoothly as possible. As Levy (1973) notes (see pp. 225–228, 291–302, 493–497):

too much concern causes difficult processes (usually social or supernatural ones) to become even more difficult and unpleasant. In regard to dying, if you are too concerned . . . the transformed spirit of the dead person may gain power over you. . . . Being casual, then, frees the dying person from you, and you from him or her. (Levy 1973:229)

Men not only have greater power in life but also in death. *Aitu* of socially powerful men, particularly of traditional healers who mediate between the parallel worlds, can be especially malevolent and hard to control. This is yet another reason why it is predominantly males who experience neglect in old age. To abandon decrepit elders or at least to limit contact even to the point of neglect makes sense. They are not elders but some other category of being engaged in a normal, expected and important but nonetheless difficult social process, that of dying. Casualness, "neglect," with respect to decrepit elders is a way of distancing oneself from such powerful and potentially dangerous transformations.

Once the transition between the realms is complete, the cessation of life here can be noted and be grieved over. Thus can a family who apparently neglected an elder at the end of life grieve sincerely for the person who was. They had "neglected" no one whom they knew, no one who belonged in this world. Rather, they had maintained a prudent distance from a near *aitu* during its difficult process of transition between worlds. And if their actions hastened that process along, surely that cannot be thought harmful or harsh or uncaring.

For Niueans to abandon or neglect their decrepit elderly, to engage in what Glascock (Glascock and Feinman 1981; Glascock 1982) calls nonsupportive or death-hastening behaviors, thus makes sense. To laugh at decrepit elders, to deride their feeble endeavors at being competent humans, to ridicule them, to neglect them, to be wary of and distant during interactions with them is not to disrespect an elder but to guard against foreign intrusion. These behaviors are not behaviors involving elders but an entirely different category of being. These behaviors are attempts to deal with "matter out of place" as Mary Douglas (1966) would put it, to persuade a near *aitu* to go to the proper realm, to cease to be human, to leave the land of the living and become an ancestor, a ghost, who can, once again, be revered.

NOTES

1. Fieldwork on which this chapter is based was supported by a project grant from the South Pacific Medical Research Committee of the Medical Research Council of New Zealand. The author gratefully acknowledges this support and the unstinting assistance of the Niuean people. The following notes come from files held in the National Archives, Department of Internal Affairs, Wellington, New Zealand, and from files held in the Archives, *Fale Fono*, Alofi, Niue.

2. Ministerial report in Section A-3 of the *Appendix to the Journal of the House of Representatives*, New Zealand, 1923.

3. Ministerial quotation from the Medical Officer, Dr. Boyd, in the Report in Section A-3 of the *Appendix to the Journal of the House of Representatives*, New Zealand, 1926.

4. Report by Resident Commissioner Captain Bell on outbreak of influenza, 29 April 1932, in reply to a telegraph inquiry by Department of Island Territories, New Zealand.

5. Copy of report from Resident Commissioner Larsen, 6 August 1945, sent to Director General of Health, New Zealand, by Department of Island Territories, New Zealand. Memorandum by Resident Commissioner Larsen, 3 September 1945, on visit by the New Zealand Prime Minister and his reaction to the plight of old people on Niue, sent to Secretary, Department of Island Affairs, New Zealand.

6. Minutes of the Island Council Meeting, 2 October 1958 and 30 October 1958. Memorandum from Resident Commissioner, 9 August 1946, to Secretary, Department of Island Affairs, New Zealand. Minutes of the Island Council Meeting, 31 July 1958. Monthly reports by Chief Medical Officer to Resident Commissioner, March and May 1967.

7. Monthly Report by Chief Medical Officer to Resident Commissioner, May 1964.

CHAPTER 22

Dementia in Cultural Context: Development and Decline of a Caregiver Support Group in a Latin Population

J. Neil Henderson

The Estradas of West Tampa, Florida, lived in a lower-middle-income neighborhood with several houses that had garages obviously converted into additional interior spaces. Numerous mailboxes lined the streets with Spanish surnames on them, and an occasional car was seen with a Puerto Rican license tag or a bumper sticker such as one which advertised a National Hispanic Chamber of Commerce meeting. This area has many people, like the Estradas, who moved here from Cuba in the early 1960s. The Estrada family was distinguished from others in their neighborhood by the fact that Mr. Estrada, although trained as a chemist, was severely impaired with Alzheimer's disease.[1]

Other members of the Estrada family included his wife's eighty-five-year-old mother (who lived in the house with them in order to help her daughter care for Mr. Estrada), his brother who lived next door and his sister who resided four miles away. While Mrs. Estrada implied that she provided nearly all the care, her mother and her husband's sister in fact participated in direct care on a regular basis. In addition, Mr. Estrada's brother provided limited assistance in the form of regular social visits.

The Estradas also have two sons, one of whom lived on the same block and another some six miles away. Mrs. Estrada reported that the two sons were of little help. One was unable to tolerate taking care of his father for even a few hours because it made him "nervous," a nonspecific condition mentioned by many of the Latino families as a very real and acceptable emotional category. The other son had offered to pay to bring in an extra caregiver. Mrs. Estrada rejected this for three reasons. One was that it would only create more difficulties with her husband because he was so irritable and argumentative. Second, Mrs. Estrada described herself as a meticulous housekeeper who was very concerned with odors in the house. She felt compelled to clean her home thoroughly each time before a respite caregiver came to visit. Finally, she felt she would not get any respite anyway because she would have felt obligated to keep the person properly entertained as a guest in the home.

Mrs. Estrada said that at times she had trouble accepting "the disease" because it seemed as though her husband's crazy demands were merely extensions of his very domineering personality from his intact and lucid days. For example, he demanded "real food," meaning complete meals, which typically included a large portion of meat and seasoned vegetables.

When Mrs. Estrada first attended the support group meetings she was often in tears when trying to tell of her caregiving activities. In fact, for a time she was clinically depressed and was medicated by a psychiatrist on an outpatient basis. Therapy was unsuccessful, since she adjusted the medicine because the initial dosage made her "groggy," and she did not know that the sedative effect would wear off with continued use.

During the time that Mrs. Estrada was being treated for depression, she continued to attend the support group meetings, and interviews in the home continued to take place. During one such interview, Mrs. Estrada simply sat by and watched as her husband tried to sit down in a chair in the living room in sort of a half-crouched position, but he was too far away from the edge of the chair. He then slowly and precariously inched his way backwards in the crouched position toward the chair. She gave him no help or instructions. This was clearly a departure from her earlier attentiveness. She also reported an instance when her husband refused medications, and she could not get him to take them by any strategy. He began calling her "dirty names" (which she would never specify), after which she began screaming and pounding the walls with her fists and forearms until they were sore.

Mrs. Estrada said she had never been depressed before. Much of her stress came from her belief that she was a failure because she was unable to maintain the household and caregiving activities unaided. She talked explicitly about holding a self-controlled "face" in front of her family and her children. She said her children had not seen her cry, although she had hidden in the bathroom to cry privately so she could maintain an outwardly powerful image in front of her family. She also reported that since joining the Alzheimer's Latin Support Group she had become aware that other caregivers experience some of the same frustrations. She felt that gave her a better understanding of the disease and that she was better able to cope with the caregiving requirements.

As a Latina with a strong Catholic background, Mrs. Estrada said that her religion told her that she got married "for better or for worse." She felt that she had already had the "for better" and now was getting the "for worse." She referred to Alzheimer's disease in a fatalistic sense, indicating that it was out of her control and that she had to simply endure her lot in life, which seemed in some way to have been supernaturally ordained.

Mrs. Estrada vacillated between the need for nursing home placement and the feeling that it indicated failure as a caregiver. During one interview Mrs. Estrada said, "Latin people, we are very stupid," in regard to an unwillingness to put people in a nursing home as she saw Anglos do. She said, that this would "bury him before he dies," in response to the question of what would happen if she went ahead with the nursing home placement. She reported that her husband was being put on a tranquilizing agent which calmed his behavior so that she could cope with him. Shortly before, she had had a "fit" in which she broke all of the dishes in the house because she was angry with Mr. Estrada. After this episode, she called the support group leader to ask for the phone number of one of the other members with whom she felt she could talk.

Inevitably, Mr. Estrada's dementia continued to worsen. For example, at the end of a very elaborate meal prepared by Mrs. Estrada and her stepdaughter, Mr. Estrada very matter-of-factly said, "We eat only air and water in this house." In addition, he became incontinent and had to be bathed and dressed by Mrs. Estrada.

EPIDEMIOLOGY OF DEMENTIA

The fourth leading cause of death in this nation is dementia, a group of diseases which destroys brain cells (Brody 1982). But, before death, the victim, family and friends can expect two to twenty years of slow, progressive decline in the victim's ability to think, remember and control bodily functions. In fact, these losses are feared more than death by most older people. Family members who care for such patients refer to Alzheimer's disease (AD) and related dementias as "the long goodbye."

At any one time, almost two million older American adults are victims of Alzheimer's disease.[2] In the United States, AD is the most common form of dementia, constituting about 50–65 percent of all cases (Mortimer 1995).[3] Alzheimer's disease is a very complex disease but, in general, the brain cells die because a protein toxic to brain cells is deposited from the bloodstream into the brain tissues.[4] Those cells nearby are killed and cannot regrow. There are new genetic findings that show the rate of deposition of the toxic protein varies among people and is governed by a few genes. Some people who have genes that cause a fast rate of deposition will develop symptoms of AD in their sixties or seventies while others will not show symptoms until much later and possibly not at all (Corder, et al. 1993; Hardy 1994).[5]

The second most common form of dementia in the United States is a group of diseases called vascular dementia which constitute about 20 percent of all cases. An additional 20 percent of persons have a mixed case of AD and vascular dementia. The vascular dementias cause brain cell death due to blood flow interruption in the brain. Blood flow interruption is caused by a stroke in which blood is blocked in its flow by a clot or is lost into tissues due to a blood vessel which literally breaks. Either way, brain cells die (O'Brien 1994). The cognitive result is confusion that is similar to, but not exactly like, AD.

There is not known to be a genetic effect associated with causing vascular dementia, as there is with AD. However, there are diseases which are risk factors for vascular problems. These include diabetes, obesity, hypertension and alcoholism (Main 1994). Such conditions are problems in most populations, but among American Indians they are extremely common and serious. As Weibel-Orlando notes in Chapter 6, within Native American communities there are numerous cases of diabetes of such severity that it is very common to see those who have had amputations of fingers and lower legs (Young 1994). Also, hypertension is extremely common. In an effort to control these problems, intensive educational campaigns are maintained through the tribes and the Indian Health Service Community Health Representative program. One result may be that American Indians are more likely to suffer from vascular dementia even though they are genetically "protected" from AD (Hendrie et al. 1993; Rosenberg 1996).

The increased risk of dementing diseases with concomitant intellectual loss is associated with advancing age. The older a person is, the greater the risk of dementia. This is one of two epidemiologic facts known about the most common type of dementia: Alzheimer's disease. The second known epidemiologic fact is that dementia has a worldwide distribution. No social, racial or ethnic group appears to have total immunity from dementing disease.[6] However, some societies or ethnic groups may have a significant variation in the amount of certain types of dementia. Studies of elders' thinking and memory abilities have shown variance in the prevalence rates of dementia (Jorm 1990). For example, Alzheimer's disease may be more common in Western Europe and North America, with the exception of American Indians (Jorm 1990:72–3). However, Russia, Japan and China may have less Alzheimer's disease and more vascular dementia compared to Western Europe and North America. These studies suffer from comparison problems in research design as well as diagnostic variability.[7]

SOCIOCULTURAL ASPECTS OF DEMENTIA

Sickness episodes have been examined from a sociocultural perspective in two categories: (1) disease as a biologically objectifiable condition; and (2) illness, which is subject to sociocultural influence. For example, Alzheimer's disease can be described in terms of pathological changes in the brain and symptomatic changes over time. However, this does not address the sociocultural context such as that in the Estrada case. The "folk" definition of the disease, interpretation of the symptoms, beliefs about etiology, beliefs about appropriate therapies and social values placed on given disease conditions are all parts of the illness experience. Such aspects of disease are subject to organization and structuring in accordance with prevailing sociocultural systems (Herskovits 1995; Stafford 1991; Gubrium 1986). For complete analysis, the examination of human sickness demands a biocultural perspective incorporating the disease/illness dimensions.

Given the worldwide increase in length of life and the geographic distribution of dementia, many intriguing questions arise regarding the sociocultural response to dementia as it occurs in cross-cultural perspective. To date, little is known about dementia. There is no known etiology, no cure, little accurate mapping of epidemiologic patterns, no ability to predict the length of the disease and little information about differential sociocultural responses to the symptoms of dementia. It is this last issue which will be examined here, using examples from an ethnic population in Florida who are derived from Cuban, Puerto Rican and Spanish ancestors.

Widespread American values such as independence, domination over the environment and high status of youth all operate against the caregiver when dealing with an elderly dementia victim. More specifically, the Alzheimer's-type patient is not only old, therefore losing the status of youth, but also suffers multiple losses of function resulting in the inability to negotiate even the simplest aspects of life unaided. The loss of youth, intelligence and independence produces a social stigma akin to those with severe psychiatric afflictions such as schizophrenia.

Other sociocultural correlates impinging on Alzheimer's disease and care of the patient and caregiver include the American kinship structure, migration patterns and division of labor based on gender. Typical nuclear family organization, dispersed postmarital residence patterns and geographic mobility in the pursuit of occupation and finances all act in concert to create a home caregiving environment in which burdens are placed on only one or two individuals (Henderson 1987). Enormous emotional and physical burdens devolve on an individual caregiver. A popular guide for the home caregiver is titled *The 16-Hour Day* (Mace and Rabins 1981), reflecting the caregiver's perception of his or her job.

SELF-HELP GROUPS AND SOCIAL NETWORKS

The special difficulties imposed by the sociocultural environment on those families coping with Alzheimer's disease have given rise to the spontaneous emergence of mutual aid societies specifically designed for Alzheimer's disease patients and family members. Such mutual aid societies typically go under the rubric of a "support group" and are a specialized part of one's wider social network. Alzheimer's disease support groups can be seen as cultural products that emerged in response to the deficits of an acute care medical system unable to meet the needs of a population experiencing a chronic debilitating brain disease. In fact, the informally organized Alzheimer's support groups developed by Bobbie Glaze in the early 1970s have led to a nationally incorporated network: The Alzheimer's Association, formerly the Alzheimer's Disease and Related Disorders Association.

Alzheimer's disease support groups function socially as fictive kinship groups. They arise in a culture in which fragmented kinship networks are typical; thus, they supplement the immediate, face-to-face interactions and assistance that become more difficult when family members become geographically dispersed. Support groups also fill gaps created by the acute-care medical system in the long-term management of the disease. One of the discrete internal functions of support groups is to provide knowledge as well as the sharing of techniques for in-home management of the demented patient (Yale 1995). The in-home caregiver can also look to guidebooks to better develop the role of the caregiver (Andresen 1995; Feil 1993), while professionals evaluate the impact of caregiving on the caregiver (Young and Kahana 1995). Ultimately, Alzheimer's disease support groups are types of social networks which create a facsimile of a healing community. Social networks develop through contacts with relatives, friends and neighbors, through which individuals maintain a social identity and receive emotional support, material aid, services and information, and develop new social contacts (Berkman 1985; Penrod et al. 1995). Here the population is brought together by a common experience related to brain failure, in an effort to better cope with this drastic and unpredicted change in the latter years of their lives (Henderson 1987; Henderson et al. 1993).

ETHNIC-SPECIFIC ALZHEIMER'S SUPPORT GROUPS

In the mid-1980s, I observed that the Tampa, Florida, Alzheimer's support group showed a virtually all-''white'' user profile. Since Tampa is largely a tri-ethnic community (Euro-American, African-American, and Latin) the support group did not match its predominant population base. Nationally, Hispanic elderly people are 3.7 percent of all elderly (Older Americans Almanac 1994). In Florida, the 65+ age group of Hispanics is 12.2 percent of all elderly (*The Tampa Tribune* 1992). Under the auspices of the University of South Florida Suncoast Gerontology Center I developed a plan for the implementation of an Alzheimer's disease support group intervention in ethnic communities that generally do not use existing support group services (Henderson et al. 1993; Gutierrez-Mayka and Henderson 1993). In 1986, an Alzheimer's disease support group in the Latino community of Tampa, Florida, was initiated by taking into consideration ethnic-specific local history and patterns of illness experiences. However, after two years the support group floundered after the stimulus of the funded project stopped. The complex operational needs of volunteer groups overcame the intent and desire to keep the group viable.

The century-old local Latin history is multifaceted and resulted in participants from various Latin cultures. Most were of Cuban origins arising from needed labor pools for Tampa's hand-rolled cigar industry begun in the late 1800s. Also, political migrations starting around the early 1960s produced additional waves of Cuban immigrants, from which some participants were derived. Second in numbers were Puerto Ricans. Next in participant frequency were the Spanish descendants who came to Tampa in the early part of the twentieth century. Last in numbers were the Afro-Cubans. These people were immigrants from Cuba with genetic and cultural origins from West Africa and Cuba. Their native language is Spanish. There were no Mexican Americans, South Americans, or other Latin Americans in the support group.

The development of Alzheimer's disease support groups in ethnic populations is designed to strengthen the coping capacities of the elderly minority caregiver by extending state-of-the-art information and fostering peer support. As Jay Sokolovsky shows in Chapter 12, ethnicity-based informal supports may be attenuated to the point of dysfunction, due to changing urban conditions and overburden linked to the inherent difficulty of caring for an Alzheimer's disease patient. Therefore, extrafamilial help is commonly needed.

The proliferation of Alzheimer's disease support groups nationwide is direct evidence of the vigor of the informal health care sector in coping with dementing disorders. However, the AD support group system on a national basis is used primarily by a specific and limited population: white, middle-class caregivers. This user pattern constitutes an undesirable and unnecessary bottleneck to ethnic caregivers in need of help. This is particularly true in view of epidemiologic research which indicates that dementing disorders are present in all racial and ethnic populations.

In the last decade, there has been a modest increase in efforts to develop ethnic-specific AD support groups. In the early 1980s, no major city in the United States could boast such a group except fledgling ones for Spanish speakers in San Diego and Tampa (the group described here).[8] Today, there are ethnic-specific support groups for Chinese Americans in Boston (Levkoff, personal communication) and San Francisco (Elliott 1995; Elliott et al. 1996), as well as one for Mexican Americans in San Antonio (Gallagher-Thompson, Talamantes, Ramirez, and Valverde 1996) and very likely others.

A need for cultural specificity in Hispanic health interventions is well documented. For example, the importance of family image in health and disease (as with Case #1 and #2 below), intrafamilial expectations of caregiving (as with Case #1 below), changes in extended family networks (as with Case #3 below), language differences and intraethnic diversity must be understood for effective intervention (Valle 1981, 1989; Henderson and Gutierrez-Mayka 1992).

IMPLEMENTING THE LATIN SUPPORT GROUP

The efforts of this project constituted a model for the implementation of support groups in ethnic minority populations (Henderson 1996; Henderson et al. 1993; Gutierrez-Mayka and Henderson 1993). The basic steps of this model for ethnic AD support group development are: (1) reliance on members of the target communities to coach project staff in the development of community-compatible support groups; (2) understanding of the network of personal, familial and community resources already used in coping with AD relative to the formal and informal health care systems; (3) training of support group leaders from the community; and (4) locating AD support groups in the

Hispanic community. In initiating these plans, the Latin Alzheimer's disease support group received a boost from the Department of Aging Services in Hillsborough County (Tampa is the county seat). Staff in this agency directed project implementers to a senior day care center located in the historic Latin district of Tampa called Ybor City. A bilingual Latin day care center aide who had family experience with dementia was interested in serving as a support group leader. Her supervisor would allow her to have compensatory time for the hours that she would use in conducting a support group, estimated at four to five per month.

The decision was made to train the leader at conferences on dementing disorders conducted by the University of South Florida's Suncoast Gerontology Center and to conduct a series of three small group discussions with her. In addition, it was decided that support group meetings would be jointly led by the project staff so that the local support group leader could observe how to conduct meetings. On a gradual basis, she could exert more influence on group dynamics.

The meetings were scheduled monthly and led by two professionals from the Suncoast Gerontology Center as well as the local support group leader. The location suggested by the local group leader was a Hispanic hospital in Tampa, Centro Español Hospital. Announcements were made via Spanish-language newspapers and radio stations in the community. The leader's work at the day care center provided her several potential support group participants. These activities led to the initiation of a support group meeting that was considered attractive to Latinos, due to the participation of a Hispanic support group leader and the use of Centro Español Hospital, a culturally potent symbol in their health care domain.

As David Jacobson states, "The meaning of 'social support' is intelligible within its cultural context" (1987:58). Therefore, one of the assumptions tested by this project was the appropriateness and utility of support group intervention as a proper means of intervention in "Hispanic culture." Some investigators suggest that group psychotherapy, which is akin to family support group intervention, is prone to failure among Hispanics due to members' concerns about privacy (del Valle and Usher 1982). Reflecting on this issue, one of our support group members referred to the reluctance to discuss Alzheimer's disease in public:

You know what I think happens in a lot of Latin people who have family members with this disease, they feel like they don't want other people to know about it. It is not that they are ashamed of it but I think they like to keep it to themselves. . . . A lot of them feel that way. A lot of Latin people keep their things to themselves. They don't let everybody know their problems, their medical problems. I don't know why but I have noticed that . . . maybe they don't want people to know they are suffering.

Del Valle and Usher do note that with proper empathy from group leaders such concerns can be overcome (1982). Other specialists agree that there are positive benefits of Hispanic group meetings. Acosta reports that although group psychotherapy among Hispanic people is not currently common, it "can be a powerful modality in treating the Spanish speaking Hispanic patients" (1982).

The experience of this model project is consistent with the predictions that the support group will represent a fictive kinship network unit in itself. According to Escobar and Randolph, the extended kinship network is a primary social resource among Hispanics, and the strong reliance on the *concepto de la familia* is a key element in Hispanic culture (1982). Within six months after the start of the support group, members had developed car pooling schedules, phone calling to check on members during nonmeeting weeks and a repeated pattern of conversation in Spanish at the beginning and end of meetings while members arrive and depart. One of the earliest examples of mutual ethnic identity came from members detailing historical events surrounding life in Ybor City, where most of them used to live. Also, they talked about acquaintances they have in common. The number of these acquaintances and the fact that many turned out to be distant relatives came as no surprise to the group. As the support group meeting was started in earnest, conversations spontaneously developed which tapped members for information on the current status of their patients.

The prominence of the Latin dynamics of family structure is very clear in issues related to burden-bearing and responsibility. The foremost of these is the sex-biased pattern of familial transmission of responsibility for care of the demented patient. Members commonly report that women are expected to provide care to the demented person, whether it be the woman's spouse, a parent or a parent-in-law. When the family has both males and females "available" for bearing the major responsibility, it is still the female who is expected to provide that type of care. One respondent reported that during the life of the patient (her father), her mother and she would be expected to provide the bed and body care for the patient; when death occurred, her brothers would take charge of the father because it then entered a business dimension, namely, the cost of the funeral and a matter of public display.

If the family does not have a close "blood-relative" female to provide bed and body care for the patient, these duties will typically be assigned to a nearby daughter-in-law. This provides a source for a variety of intrafamilial irritations. For example, many Hispanic parents are concerned that their adult children may disengage from family responsibilities with the parents. In fact, a daughter-in-law is often the target of great hostility. By marrying the son, she becomes the recipient of his attention and help, thereby reducing the amount of assistance available to the other family members (del Valle and Usher 1982). Nonetheless, the daughter-in-law may be pressed into service to her in-laws. Although a new household has been established, the expectation of direct caregiving support is placed on women. Therefore, selection of a helper from the new couple is strongly biased toward the bride.

Case 1: Vascular Dementia in a Tampa Latin Family

The following case incorporates dimensions of cultural influence in terms of gender roles in a case of vascular dementia in a Latino family.

Sixty-eight-year-old Mr. Perez was hospitalized at Centro Español Hospital with a diagnosis of vascular dementia. The prognosis was not favorable and included complete bed care for the remainder of his life. Consideration of nursing home placement was unthinkable to Mrs. Perez, who elected to care for him at their home.

The Perez local family consisted of Mrs. Perez's able-bodied eighty-eight-year-old mother, who lived with Mrs. and Mr. Perez. The Perez adult children consisted of a married son with two small children and a divorced daughter with three older children and one grandchild for whom she was the babysitter.

Having learned of her husband's diagnosis and prognosis at his bedside, Mrs. Perez led her daughter into the hallway of the hospital and told her that it was up to them (meaning her daughter and her) to provide the ultimate in care for the husband and father at home. The adult daughter recoiled and began to list the nearby family members who could have likewise given direct support and assistance but on whom her mother was not calling. Mrs. Perez was unable to understand her daughter's reaction, in that she was the expected helper of the primary caregiver.

When a support group for the caregivers of dementia patients was formed at Centro Español Hospital, the daughter was actively involved. However, Mrs. Perez attended only one meeting because of her sense of public humiliation due to the nature of her husband's disease. Nonetheless, the adult daughter, who gave occasional ''hands-on'' care, attended the meetings regularly and served as a broker of information and support from the meeting to her mother. The mother responded by initiating use of community services and reevaluating her role as caregiver.

The patient remained at home (with brief episodes of hospitalization) for three and a half years before dying there.

Case Comment. The expectation for female caregivers was brought out very clearly in the case of Mrs. Perez and her adult daughter. This type of expectation of caregiving by women has been observed in this project and reflected in the fact that out of the 36 actual caregivers, 29, or 81 percent, are women. Based on data of caregiving frequencies and types, the ranked preference of Latino caregivers by sex and kinship relation in this study was as follows: (1) wife, (2) sister, daughter or other adult blood-kin, (3) female nonkin, (4) male blood relatives, and (5) male in-laws. Note that even before switching to kin-related male caregivers, nonkin females were relied upon.

Case 2: The Garcia Family

Many Latino caregivers are worried that the community will interpret the sometimes bizarre behavior of the dementia victim as evidence of "craziness in the family." The following case is such an example.

Mr. Garcia suffered from dementia for several years. He was cared for at home with a minimum of fanfare or help from kinsmen and neighborhood friends. Mrs. Garcia discussed the early stages of her husband's dementia. As she began to tell of specific circumstances, she began to explain a Latin ethic. "I tell you one thing about the Spanish, they will get very upset about someone who is crazy or does crazy things." She hastened to add that this is due to lack of education and not that they happen to be of Spanish descent.

Even during a time when her husband was so confused that he was urinating on the living room floor, Mrs. Garcia tried to put up a front that everything was okay, to her neighbors certainly, but also even to her children. Mrs. Garcia said, "How could I tell my family not to bring a girlfriend or boyfriend in here because the house smells of urine?" Mrs. Garcia said that former friends avoided her because they "fear the disease" or just felt uncomfortable about being there. This bothered Mrs. Garcia to the point of wondering if she was being penalized for some past sin.

An event that prompted Mrs. Garcia to put deadbolts without keys on doors of the house involved her husband wandering away from the house at night. She awoke at 5:00 A.M. to find that Mr. Garcia was not in bed. She immediately checked the house but could not find him. Her first response was to get in the car alone and scout the neighborhood for him. Only after this proved futile did she return to the house to call neighbors for assistance. They first checked their backyard pool and then decided to drive in separate cars around the neighborhood while Mrs. Garcia waited at home. A neighbor found Mr. Garcia about two miles from home, "just in his briefs," with blisters on his bare feet. His safety as well as the public nature of his "crazy behavior" mortified Mrs. Garcia.

Case Comment. Alzheimer's disease presents symptoms that the general public interprets as characteristic of someone who is "crazy." The stigma attached to mental disorders is well-known within this culture and many others. Escobar and Randolph (1982) report that, for many Hispanics, mental illness is still seen as a dreaded affliction akin to *mal de sangre* or "bad blood." The issue of a family member being "crazy" was a common one in the Latin Alzheimer's support group meetings. There was often a personal crusade launched to be sure that friends and family understood that Alzheimer's disease is an organic disease and, therefore, not under the control of the individual, thus relieving the patient and family of social liability.

The Latin support group members extended their concern about social stigma and mental disorders into financial arenas like insurance coverage. They complained, as do other families of Alzheimer's patients, that insurance categories place all psychiatric afflictions in mental health domains. Because mental health problems often are not covered by policies, families found themselves negotiating with physicians to enter the diagnosis as an organic brain disease.

Case 3: The Lopez Family

The families in this sample strongly valued the image of being strong, tightly knit and reliant on family resources to succeed in life. However, over time, a "generation gap" has developed. Older Latins are less likely to use social services and community resources than their adult offspring. Attendance at a support group meeting communicates publicly that help is needed; self-reliance has failed. The following case shows the adaptation made to bridge the gap.

Maria Lopez attended her first support group meeting in the company of her oldest son. Her stepdaughter had been summoned to go with her, but her work schedule prevented her attendance. During the two-and-one-half-hour meeting, Mrs. Lopez's son, Roberto, introduced her and provided some details of his father's condition. Mrs. Lopez sat quietly during this discourse, which included commentary and questions from others in the support group which her son answered. During the support group meeting, Mrs. Lopez herself commented only about her love for Cuban coffee and, due to its strength, the "lift" that it produces from the caffeine.

One month later Mrs. Lopez was again accompanied by her son to the support group meeting because the stepdaughter was unable to arrange her job in order to bring the stepmother. This time, Roberto Lopez talked mainly about their former upbringing in the Latino quarters of Tampa known as Ybor City. As discussion turned more toward caregiver issues, his mother began to comment in response to her son's status report of the father's condition. Roberto reported that the father had been very hostile and aggressive for the past few days, to which Mrs. Lopez had said to the group by quoting her own statement to her husband, "I'm tired of this. If you don't straighten up, I'm going out this door." Roberto followed this comment by saying that when his mother responds sharply to his father this "brings him back to reality."

Eight weeks later, Mrs. Lopez is accompanied by her stepdaughter Marcela. Marcela began by saying her stepmother's problem is "lack of sleep." Mrs. Lopez said, "I'm very nervous," and then demonstrated with her hands by shaking them and saying, "Just like this." Maria Lopez now became outspoken and discussed a history of being physically abused by her husband and occasions of running into the street to solicit help from other Latin neighbors. In reference to her husband's condition, Mrs. Lopez became so bold as to demonstrate his stooped gait and short steps while shuffling his feet. Her stepdaughter interjected that, "It's the Haldol" (a tranquilizing medication). It was clear that Mrs. Lopez was willing at last to express her anger through her raised voice, rapid speech and physical mimicry of her husband's condition.

Mrs. Lopez referred to her state of "nerves," which is affirmed by Marcela. Mrs. Lopez said that she didn't take any *medicatinos* (medicines) for herself because she couldn't afford them. But, she did take honey to ward off heart problems. Mrs. Lopez also said that she kept her husband fully medicated with prescription medications in order to "keep him cool."

One month later Mrs. Lopez attended the meeting by herself, having been "car pooled" by other members of the group. As a result of encouragement from the group, an aide came to the home to give Mr. Lopez a bath twice a week. It became clear that Mrs. Lopez spoke openly and freely over time within the group setting, having phased herself into the support group family.

Case Comment. David Maldonado (1985) suggests that Hispanic populations variably respond by age cohorts to available helping services such as Alzheimer's family support groups. This age cohort effect was very clearly observed in the Latin Alzheimer's support group. The most active members were adult daughters and sons of parents who were coping with Alzheimer's disease. The older-generation Hispanics seldom attended the group except when specifically brought by their daughters or sons. Furthermore, when knowledge of additional community resources was made known to the parent generation, arrangements for such resources were negotiated through the adult daughters or sons in the group.

It was common to see the older generation Latin person attending the group with an adult daughter or son. The older person sat quietly and occasionally added an affirmation in response to a monologue delivered by the adult offspring. Usually, however, within a few meetings the older person spoke up, and the role of the adult offspring became less important.

THE FATE OF THE SUPPORT GROUP

The Latin support group no longer exists. After 24 months of testing a model process for implementation of ethnic-specific support groups, the group could not sustain itself after project funding ended. Seven months after funding ended, the group stopped meeting. In spite of its effectiveness and efforts to continue its operation after funding, the support group slowly declined in attendance. The dynamics of this decline are related to lack of finances, the volunteer nature of the group, overburdened caregivers, lack of sustenance by other organizations whether private or governmental, and failure to sustain the infrastructure of organizational vitality.

From its inception, the project had considered its longevity to be a critical factor. Because there are costs associated with group operation, the project staff had tried to get the county aging service unit to incorporate the group into the senior adult day care programs. Local politics prevented such an alliance. Consequently, there was no permanent place to conduct the meetings and no money to pay for utilities of a meeting place.

The efforts to keep the group going included the training of laypeople to operate the group after the funded professionals left. These people were caregivers who expressed an interest in continuing the group as leaders. A six-hour training session was developed for them and presented in a casual, non-"school" fashion. The intent was to make them comfortable with the training and defuse images of school and tests. Five caregivers from the group participated. This training was done five months prior to the end of funding so that trainees could practice their skills under the supervision of professional project staff.

The volunteer caregivers/group leaders were motivated to continue the group because of their reaction to a relative's devastation by dementia. They adopted a "warrior" stance against this terrible disease and "fought the disease" by being leaders of the support group. However, the enormous energy required to provide care for a dementia patient left them exhausted. They could not add the role of support group leader to their overburdened life. To conduct the weekly phone calls to group members, write a short newsletter and otherwise get the meeting organized was simply too much.

Most of all, the support group's organizational infrastructure was starved for attention. The roles played by participants were clear when the professionals and the lay caregivers were in the group. However, when the combined "lay caregiver and group leader" role emerged, the division of authority and labor was blurred. Also, other needs were present. There was the need to bear the costs of the newsletter. Someone would need to be given the authority to levy dues or assign a rotational cost-sharing system to maintain the newsletter. The newsletter obviously required a typewriter or word processing capability. Someone needed to buy snacks for the meeting. During the funded years, these problems were not problems. Yet, a multitude of small but significant elements of organizational operation became barriers to survival of a volunteer group of Latin people trying their best to cope with dementia.

The professional project staff had offered to be available as consultants for any and all questions to assist the new leaders with operating the group. The new group leaders made some use of this offer. For awhile, the newsletter was copied and mailed from the project offices. However, even the task of getting the copy to the office was a barrier to caregivers and this assistance fell into disuse.

It may seem that a solution would be to get noncaregiver volunteers to be the group leaders. However, recruitment is a labor-intensive project. As always, there is a need to meet direct and indirect costs of operation, even if there were noncaregiver leaders. However, the strongest barrier to lay noncaregiver leaders is the caregiver perspective that no one can really understand their trauma except those who have experienced it. A layperson with some training in the disease symptoms and what it must be like to be a caregiver will have very low credibility. For "real" caregivers, intellectualized experience only is no experience at all.

Another option for institutionalizing the Latin Alzheimer's disease support group could have been the local Latin social and health clubs. Unfortunately, these were in financial decline at the time of this project and the health care components no longer exist today. Moreover, the Latin clubs were home to specific segments of the Spanish-speaking population and not universally compatible with all Latins.

While this project showed that there is a need and a way to provide support-group help to Latin caregivers of Alzheimer's disease patients, its longevity was severely compromised. The reason for the support group's demise is multifactorial. It may seem that the obvious explanation is financial. However, this singular explanation neglects the local politics, caregiver attitudes, the wish to be a leader in the absence of sufficient energy to do so, and, certainly, flaws in the project design and staff actions.

SUMMARY

The effectiveness of the Latin Alzheimer's disease support group was high, as judged by sustained participation of members, development of interpersonal linkages between members, recruitment of new members by long-standing members, and direct reports of the comfort received from participants in support group meetings. However, no instruments were used to measure effectiveness in terms of improved mental health or caregiver functioning. Nonetheless, this support group of Latins shows that certain cultural patterns such as extreme reliance on female caregivers, generational effects and "low service user" patterns can be overcome when culturally compatible approaches are used.

Certain unique characteristics of these support group members contributed to the configuration of this ethnographic profile. For example, most participants were middle class and high school educated. All were bilingual and were at least second-generation residents of Tampa. Still, elements of ethnic culture remained very strong in the minds and behaviors of people considered to be highly acculturated. This definitely applied to the members of the Latin support group.

There were vast numbers of poor, monolingual Latinos in Tampa who apparently were not attracted to this type of intervention. Other local factors were revealed by examining another Latin-specific Alzheimer's disease support group operating in the country. Dr. Ramon Valle worked with such a group primarily composed of Mexican Americans in San Diego. Those meetings were characterized by multiple generations of participants, including young children (Valle, personal communication). In Tampa, however, the young children of the adult caregivers in the sample were seldom present. Valle attributes the difference to intraethnic variation. The San Diego group participants were Mexican Americans who came to California 30 to 40 years ago. They exhibited the "Mexican heritage interactional pattern." The interdependence of family members produced a "group" approach to resolving family problems (Ho 1987).

Most older people do not get dementia. For those who do, the devastation and impact on a patient and family members is enormous. The overwhelming impact of this disease on families is being perceived by the American government in terms of programs specifically for dementia victims in adult day care, respite care and nursing home care. However, policies made for the majority population can neglect specific needs of ethnic and minority groups. This appears to be the case on a national basis with lay-developed Alzheimer's disease support groups. Yet, this project shows that, with proper community involvement and sensitivity to sociocultural issues, a helpful intervention can be put in place.

At the time this project was conceptualized and implemented, there was great doubt that support groups, as developed in mainstream society, would work in ethnic minority communities. That notion was proven wrong. As noted earlier, ethnic-specific Alzheimer's disease support groups are now being developed elsewhere in the United States. In fact, the concept of disease-related support groups among elders has proven useful in societies outside the United States, as shown by the development of hypertension support groups in Croatia (Sokolovsky, Sosic and Pavlekovic 1991). However, the fact that the Latin support group in Florida lasted only a few months after funding ended shows that too little attention was given to what ethnic minority caregivers would need to keep the group operating effectively by themselves.

Today, developing a similar intervention could include a relentless effort to integrate the group into the general or ethnic community social service system. Fund-raisers could be undertaken by volunteers from other social service organizations. Whatever the specific mechanism needed to keep the ethnic support groups operating, more creative thought can now be given to the issue of longevity, since there is evidence that the prerequisite questions of developmental feasibility have been answered.

NOTES

This project was supported, in part, by a grant, 90AM0724, from the Administration on Aging, Office of Human Development Services, Department of Health and Human Services, Washington, D.C. 20201, and the State of Florida, Department of Health and Rehabilitative Services; Aging and Adult Services; and the University of South Florida Suncoast Gerontology Center. Grantees undertaking projects under government sponsorship are encouraged to express freely their findings and conclusions. Points of view or opinions do not, therefore, necessarily represent official Administration on Aging policy.

1. Alzheimer's disease results from progressive brain cell death. The early symptoms include short-term memory loss of slow onset. Later, more general and severe cognitive deficits ensue. Ultimately, the person dies from a severely damaged brain (Friedland 1994).

2. The actual number of cases of Alzheimer's disease is difficult to determine. The difficulty relates to the very gradual worsening of symptoms, which makes it impossible to state when a case "begins" and, consequently, can be counted. Also, there are different ways to count cases, such as AD specifically and only, all dementias of any kind, possible cases, probable cases and cases of confusion of unknown etiology. The vagueness in determining the number of cases allows for variation in listed prevalence rates. There may be some exaggeration in rates when, for example, an organization perceives the need to gain attention for its cause. By using various definitions of a case, literature may report rates for AD as high as four million cases while other reports specify only two million cases (Blume, Persily and Mintzer 1992).

3. In a living person, the only absolute diagnosis requires a brain biopsy, but because this is such an invasive procedure, a clinical diagnosis is made by ruling out every other possible medical cause of symptoms relating to memory loss and confusion. If the patient's history shows a slow and progressive onset of dysfunction and no other medical cause can be found, a diagnosis of dementia of the Alzheimer's type is made. At autopsy, confirmation can be obtained by examining brain tissue microscopically.

4. The protein is beta-amyloid.

5. These genetic findings imply that populations will show variance in the amount of AD present in older age cohorts. The gene responsible for the variance of the toxic protein is known to be variable across populations. The gene is known to play a role in fat metabolism. However, it is theorized that its complex chemistry also has a "side-effect" of chemically assisting or inhibiting the deposition of the toxic protein in the brain depending on which genetic combination is present (Hardy 1994). In terms of population prevalence variability, it is hypothesized that the indigenous people of the Western Hemisphere have a low frequency of the genetic combination causing fast deposition of the toxic protein (Henderson 1994a). This implies that American Indians would have low rates of AD. Conversely, Euro-Americans would have higher rates than American Indians because this group has more people with the gene causing fast rates of deposition.

6. Due to variations in diagnostic criteria and methodological designs, comparison of cross-national epidemiological studies is limited to meta-analysis of data (Mortimer 1995).

7. Recent genetic studies which identify specific genes related to the causation of Alzheimer's disease seem to support the variation between Western European/American rates and Asian rates. The genetic profile of Western Europeans and North Americans (not including American Indians) suggests more genes related to Alzheimer's disease whereas the genetic profile of Asians suggests less Alzheimer's disease and more vascular dementia (Corder et al. 1995; White et al. 1996). Extrapolating from these data, American Indians may have an "Asian dementia profile." The characterization of American Indians as having an "Asian dementia profile" is consistent with the prevailing archeologic view of an East Asian source for the peopling of the New World.

8. This project also involved the development of an African-American support group.

This chapter on Latin caregivers was stimulated by and expanded from an invited article in a special issue on Hispanic aging in *The Clinical Gerontologist* (Henderson and Gutierrez-Mayka 1992). For other publications on the African-American support group see Henderson et al. 1993; Henderson 1992; Henderson 1994b; Henderson 1994c).

CHAPTER 23

Aging, Disability and Ethnicity: An African-American Woman's Story

Monika Deppen-Wood, Mark R. Luborsky and Jessica Scheer

As you read about the life experiences of Ms. Evers, a sixty-six-year-old African-American woman living with a physical disability in an American inner city, you might be tempted to consider her race, gender, poverty and age as additive or cumulative burdens. This view, called the multiple jeopardy hypothesis (Salmon 1994; Dowd and Bengtson 1978), has a tenacious but contested place in popular thought and social science research. It assumes that each of these statuses has an incremental negative effect on an individual's life and well-being. Ms. Evers, however, expresses much satisfaction with her life as she draws on her ethnic heritage, her gender identity and even her neighborhood to achieve a sense of meaning and purpose. Thus, it appears that the multiple jeopardy hypothesis is inadequate for describing her actual experience. That perspective lacks two important factors. First, it does not include insights into the *cultural components* of life events and personal circumstances (Murphy et al. 1988). Second, it does not illustrate the complex intertwining of individual character, personal and cultural values and meanings. These factors pattern how individuals *interpret* events and conditions of life.

Let us turn to Ms. Evers's account of her life for the light it will shed on the disparity between how she sees her life and what others might conclude based on the conditions she faces. She told her story during interviews conducted as part of a study on how culture shapes people's experiences of living with a range of impairments from paralytic polio.[1]

POLIO IN EARLY CHILDHOOD AND MULTIPLE LOSSES

Henrietta Evers was born in Georgia in 1929 to a poor farm worker and his wife. She was the youngest of their eight children. Henrietta's memories of early childhood are filled with painful events. She was 3 years old when her mother died and the following summer Henrietta contracted polio.

Ms. Evers maintained that she will never forget the excruciating pain she had to endure due to a country doctor's ill-treatment. She vividly remembers those days:

I had a fever. I was very small and my leg began to draw back and at that time no one knew what polio was. In the county where I was born there was a little Caucasian girl that I heard she had contracted it but she had hospital care. At the time we were poor and I didn't have hospital care. My leg had drawn up, it was bending at the knee and I couldn't bend it out. So, what he [the doctor] did, he just takes it, and pulls the leg out, and breaks all the tendons and all the ligaments. It did hurt! Oh, my did it hurt. You could hear me holler all over Georgia. I remember—I will never forget.

Henrietta's older sisters did their best to care for her; but as it became clear that Henrietta's health was not improving, she was sent, at age 4, to her god-mother in Philadelphia in the hope of receiving better medical care. Despite the doctors' efforts, including physical rehabilitation treatment and an operation at age 11, the damage done by the country doctor was permanent. She was left with a lifelong mobility impairment due to a severely weakened leg.

GROWING UP WITH POLIO: SOCIALIZATION, STIGMA AND INTERDEPENDENCE

Growing up, Henrietta lived with her godmother. When Henrietta was 14 years old her godmother died. She then moved in with her oldest sister, who lived just a few blocks away. Henrietta wore a full leg brace, special shoes, and used crutches. She attended a city school for disabled children.

Ms. Evers describes herself as a quiet and shy person. "I never had much confidence in myself. I was always afraid I couldn't do the right thing, that always worried me. I couldn't do math too well. I would cry because I knew I wouldn't get it." She quickly came to avoid academic subjects and concentrated on home economics. Other students went on to public high school, but Henrietta wanted to stay in the specialized school for disabled girls.

Following graduation from high school, Henrietta's brother in Georgia asked her to come and live with his family to help out for awhile. His wife was expecting their seventh child and she was ill. During her stay, Henrietta became close to one of her nieces and subsequently brought the niece with her when she returned to Philadelphia. This niece's oldest sister joined them in the city some months later. At this time in her life Henrietta lived with her own childless

Henrietta Evers (center) at age 10 with her two older sisters, Wanda (left) and Mona (right). Years later, after the death of her brother-in-law, Henrietta took care of her oldest sister, Wanda, who suffered from Alzheimer's disease until her death in 1994.

sister and husband, within a few blocks from where she grew up with her god-mother. She now took care of the two nieces from Georgia, ran her sister's household, including doing washing, cooking, shopping and cleaning, and fur-thermore, baby-sat some neighbors' children. She describes feeling good about her life of helping others, and her love of children, yet also regrets never having had a husband or children of her own. She attributes these facts to her low self-esteem which, despite her having been attractive, kept her from dating or push-ing to get a "real, good-paying" job.

Ms. Evers does not speak of feeling "burdened" or "used" by these others. Helping out provided valued opportunities to be useful to others, to contribute and take part in a normative social life rather than being dependent upon others for kindness and charity. Discussing gender differences, Murphy (1987) notes that the availability and desirability of such opportunities are fewer for men. Stack (1974) documented how the interdependence of the extended kinship net-work in the black community serves both as a strategy for survival for the group and as a way to provide socially valued roles for individuals. Ms. Evers gained a deep fulfillment from her helping and caregiving role in the family and the community. Although she never had children of her own, Henrietta's life was consistent with traditional gender norms. She performed family service to her extended family composed of blood relatives and fictive kin. In her youth, she cared for her family's and neighbors' children; later, after her oldest sister was widowed, she became a caregiver for older relatives. For example, she nursed, until their deaths at home, her sister Wanda, who suffered from Alzheimer's disease and her niece, whom she called a sister and who had terminal cancer.

Today, as Henrietta's own physical abilities and health are waning, she is the last survivor among all her siblings and immediate family. In the absence of any blood relatives to aid her, she creatively draws on a close-knit community of neighbors and longtime fictive kin. She is neither entirely dependent nor independent. She has always found ways to contribute to the larger good of the "family" or community, and thus her life has been interdependent with the lives of others.

AGING WITH DISABILITIES IN AN URBAN NEIGHBORHOOD

Dynamics of Extended Kinship in Household and Community

Interdependence within a web of fictive kin and neighbors remains a salient factor in Ms. Evers's disability experience. As her health declines and her mea-ger assets make her more dependent on others, she still reciprocates and finds meaning and pleasure in caring for others.

Ms. Evers today is 66 years old. She wears a full body brace and uses a cane or walker due to a worsening of the residual impairments from her childhood polio (Kaufert, Kaufert and Locker 1987). She has a degenerative joint disease in her left knee, a rotator-cuff tear in the right shoulder, and carpal tunnel syndrome in both wrists. Her functional losses and pain are worsened by her home environment. Accessing the two bathrooms in her home provides a daily additional challenge for Ms. Evers due to the fact that one is located in the basement, the other on the second floor. To climb the stairs she pulls herself up the railing, relying heavily on her arms since her legs are weak. This method is getting more difficult due to increased weakness in her legs and pain in her shoulder and arms. Ms. Evers must limit her diet due to other health problems.

Ms. Evers's physical health is poorer than most sixty-five-year-old Americans and her experiences of health and functioning are tied to financial constraints. As government statistics demonstrate, she is not alone in this predicament. Disparities in health status of African Americans and white Americans loom large. African-American women have more chronic diseases and disabilities than any other group. These are related to limited access to health care, lower amounts and quality of treatment, and general socioeconomic factors (AMA 1990; U.S. DHSS 1990; NCHS 1987).

The two-story row house Ms. Evers has lived in since she was 14 years old lacks modifications that would help her perform physical activities of daily life without exacerbating her functional deterioration. It thus directly increases her level of disability, in excess of that due to her own physical limitations (Verbrugge and Jette 1994; Brody et al. 1971; Brody and Ruff 1986). Although she is eligible to have home modifications provided by a city social services agency, she does not own her home and the owner will not allow contractors to remodel the home.

When Henrietta's sister died, she willed the house to a "niece," Margie. Margie is not a blood relative but her deceased sister's best friend's goddaughter. Margie feels that the renovation program requires too much paperwork to qualify, and fears that such remodeling will reduce the resale value of the house after Henrietta's death. The house is a major asset for Margie. She also justifies her point of view by explaining that her "Aunt" really can manage just as she had always done in the past.

Six months prior to our interviews, Margie's daughter, Stacy, and her child asked to move in after she left her boyfriend. Margie's apartment is too small for them. So once again Ms. Evers is caring for a young child. She feeds Stacy's son when he gets home from kindergarten and watches him until his mother returns from her post office job. This unexpected yet familiar and welcome role gives Henrietta much pleasure and enhances her sense of security. But the extra work also increases her physical fatigue and pain.

Thus, her strong, extended "family" network is both supportive and draining. She has assured housing but is unable to alter it to accommodate her needs. She describes herself as very lucky to have Margie around to check on her, and to be useful and needed. But the reciprocal demands increase her physical distress. There is reason to be concerned about her future as her health and function, already compromised since childhood polio, are deteriorating. Will she still get

Ms. Evers and her next-door neighbor's daughter, Dana.

the support she needs once she is no longer able to provide for others? Research in the African-American community confirms that help from the extended family is available as long as there is reciprocity. Assistance becomes less frequent as a person becomes more frail. Older, unmarried and childless persons are at greatest risk of isolation, or even neglect (Hatchett and Jackson 1993; Barker 1990).

Currently, Ms. Evers recruits neighbors to help her with daily tasks. She feels comfortable, not ashamed, to ask them to shop for her or to drive her to the doctor. For example, prior to one interview, she got her neighbor's daughter (whom she baby-sat years ago), to come over and do her hair. She later revealed cheerily: "I was just a mess, my hair, I can't roll my hair anymore, because of my arms, but you know what a nice hairdo means to us women, so I called Dana to fix it."

Ms. Evers draws creatively on many other long-term neighbors and fictive kin. Since she can no longer answer the doorbell in time if she is upstairs or not yet completely dressed, she phones a neighbor across the street to look out and tell her who is at the door. "I don't want to go down there for nothing," she explained. If it is a delivery truck, she may ask her friend to receive the package for her. Ms. Evers's limited range of arm motion makes dressing a slow and difficult process. It requires an hour to put on her body brace, dress, and groom herself. She enlists neighbors into her daily routine without feeling embarrassed that she is imposing or helpless. In her view, she helped them in times of need, and now it is her turn. Now that she is becoming more frail and dependent on others, her sense of life-time reciprocity offsets the negative impact of the wider culture's norm that personal identity should be based on independence and self-reliance (see Clark 1972; Stein 1979).

When she does go out, her choice of assistive equipment reveals attention to both safety and social image. She prefers to use a cane outdoors despite the fact that she tires faster and can't go as far. She limits her use of a four-legged walker to inside her house. Her preference reveals two sources of stigma, one culture-wide and one very local (Scheer and Luborsky 1991; Luborsky 1993, 1995). The derogatory social stereotypic images of frailty and helplessness evoked by using a walker in public leads her to avoid it in favor of the cane to preserve her sense of self-esteem and identity. But there is a more immediate consequence: In her neighborhood, someone using a cane appears more agile than someone using a walker and thus a less likely target for criminals.

Ms. Evers's lifetime illuminates two noteworthy aspects of the role of the wider family and friends. First, there is a broad range of kin involved in the daily life and business of meeting needs. Second, the structural definition of the African-American family includes a wider range of extended kin, such as distant relatives and long-term friends, relative to the emphasis on direct lineal biological blood ties in the European American family. The web of collateral and fictive family ties lends her an array of valued opportunities for social interdependence, a sense of fulfillment and worth to the family as well as for support.

RELIGIOUS FAITH AND SPIRITUALITY

As was shown in Chapter 13, religion and spirituality have a vital role in the African-American community (Raboteau 1995; Peterson 1990; Taylor 1986; Genovese 1974). Medical researchers now identify religiosity and spirituality with better outcomes, survival and positive adaptation during health problems and rehabilitation (Koenig 1988). Ms. Evers believes her deep faith in God helped her overcome the many losses and hardships she has experienced. It also provided her with a specialized perspective on the meaning of her disabilities.

God works in mysterious ways, he knows what's gonna happen down that highway long, even before you get, even before you breathe . . . I seriously believe that all of this was mapped out for me because I had to take care of my sister when she got sick because when her husband died he wasn't here to take care of her.

Ms. Evers reconciles her suffering in light of a powerful belief in God's grace. She believes that the reasons he bestows such hardships are not always apparent to us, but truly believes the Lord knows best. Despite her own lifelong suffering for dignity and survival and being surrounded by hardships, God is her anchor and her salvation. Through religious faith she makes peace with the disabilities and suffering in life; thus she neither seeks self-blame, victimhood nor retribution for her problems. Her faith, combined with her web of relationships in the neighborhood, sustains her sense of well-being and purposeful life meaning.

SUMMARY

Henrietta Evers's story, first and foremost, documents the lifelong social and personal repercussions of living with a physical impairment. The culturally defined normative lifecourse framed the social consequences of Ms. Evers's physical impairment and limited the areas in which she could participate, but it also provided new opportunities to develop a socially meaningful career in her family and community. Ms. Evers developed a strong identification and sense of fulfillment through providing care and assisting others. The value of this is heightened as she reaches the later life stage of development of generativity, which emphasizes investment in others and assisting the success of the next generation and the avoidance of narcissism (Alexander et al. 1991). We do draw attention to many sources of good morale, fulfillment and well-being. Yet it is wise not to underestimate the daily toll of physical pain, functional limitations and extra time caused by her physical impairment and lack of needed home modifications or proper medical care. Simple tasks of walking, baby-sitting or getting to the bathroom or doorbell exact a high cost.

One clear message from her case is that health and biology dictate neither destiny nor experience. Knowledge of her physical impairment alone cannot predict the richness of life, her capabilities (Langness and LeVine 1986) nor her sense of positive or negative well-being. Ms. Evers is neither dependent nor independent, but richly interdependent as family and neighbors depended on her over her entire lifetime and as she draws upon others. Her life illustrates the lifelong complex intertwining of individual character, values and meanings and conditions of life (Luborsky and Rubinstein 1987). If one were simply to add up the long lists of potentially negative adverse conditions due to severe physical disability, race, gender, age, low income, poor neighborhood, one might mistakenly conclude that she would be despondent and helpless. The multiple jeopardy model does not allow us to sufficiently assess how individuals interpret and respond differently to events. Decades of study on disability and disease have shown that standardized factors such as age, disease or income do not relate to individual adjustment or lifestyle in a predictable fashion.

In brief, Ms. Evers's case may sensitize us to be skeptical about several generalizations common in both popular thought and the scholarly literature on ethnicity, aging and disability. First, the centrality of physical limitations in the lives of people with disabilities often gets overstated, sometimes to the neglect of many other abilities (Luborsky 1994a; Wright 1983; Verbrugge 1992). Second, people with disabilities are too often depicted as helpless and dependent, rather than active and productive. Third, urban neighborhoods are often ethnocentrically perceived as desolate environments, devoid of meaningful life involvement. Such a view misses the complex and vital community life that sustains African Americans like Ms. Evers.

While the social consequences of functional impairments affect the lives of all people with disabilities, Ms. Evers's story highlights the significant cultural, social and symbolic outcomes associated with an African-American cultural heritage and thus reveals rich and complex dimensions of the experience of living and growing older with a disability.

NOTE

1. Support for this research project was provided by a grant to Luborsky (P.I.) and Scheer (Co-P.I.) from the National Institute of Child Health and Human Development (#RO1HD31526). We thank our project team members Kathy McGowan, Delia Easton, Carmit Kurn and Hilde Mausner-Dorsch for valuable comments on earlier drafts.

CHAPTER 24

Long-Term Care and the Disabled Elderly in Urban China

Charlotte Ikels

The provision of long-term care to the elderly in China is essentially the responsibility of the family. While this responsibility has its roots in traditional values that emphasize filial obligations to one's parents, it is equally grounded in the contemporary political economy of China. Since at least the early 1980s, the Chinese government has placed greatest priority on developing a market economy, and one of the costs of this priority has been the erosion of the generous subsidies that only a decade ago supported its urban population. These subsidies at one time included a host of wage supplements, guaranteed employment, workplace-provided housing, health benefits, pensions and a welfare net for those unable to work and lacking family support (almost all of whom were either elderly or orphaned youngsters).[1] The withdrawal or reduction of these subsidies has been possible politically only because the standard of living has been steadily, though unevenly, rising and because the brunt of the changes is being borne by those newly entering the urban labor force, that is, by urban school-leavers and migrants from the countryside, and those seeking employment in the evolving private sector.

Most of those who have for years enjoyed employment in the state sector remain relatively protected, continuing to hold their jobs until retirement and to receive health as well as pension benefits upon retirement. They are protected because their work units are able to draw on surplus funds from national, provincial or municipal budgets to compensate for their own economic losses. Although one of the objects of the economic reforms has been to weaken this kind of fiscal relationship, in practice it has not proven easy for government officials to close or penalize unprofitable enterprises under their jurisdiction. Consequently, the most vulnerable urban elderly are those who spent their lives working in the collective sector, in factories and services operated by the lowest administrative level of government (the street committee), because these enterprises are almost entirely dependent upon their own or the street committee's meager profits to support their obligations to their retirees.[2]

The restructuring of China's urban economy has produced many changes, some planned and desired but others unplanned and undesired. Because these changes are occurring at precisely the same time that China's population is rapidly aging, it is perhaps inevitable that policymakers are now struggling to determine how to develop a market economy and simultaneously to meet the needs of a growing army of retirees. While the Chinese government has already taken steps to protect pensions, the provision of long-term care to the disabled elderly has become an increasingly problematic area. In order to clarify the forces that have contributed to the emergence of this problem and the array of alternatives that the elderly, their family members and their workplaces have considered as possible solutions, this chapter presents a case study of the provision of long-term care to the disabled elderly in Guangzhou (also known as Canton), China's sixth largest city.

METHODOLOGY

The data on which this chapter is based were gathered in two waves, in 1987 and in 1991. A random sample of 100 households each containing at least one person 70 years of age or older was selected from each of two of Guangzhou's four core urban districts.[3] In the initial 1987 visit, information on health, functionality, care arrangements and a variety of other topics was obtained from 200 focal elders or a proxy. In 1991, similar information was gathered from 156 of the original focal elders or a proxy (38 elders had died and 6 had moved out of the Guangzhou area since the first interview). All of the interviews were conducted by the author in the homes of the informants, and all elders, whether able to participate in the interview or not, were observed and assessed by the author.

Since the focus of the research was on predicting patterns of care of the elderly, each elder was rated in terms of the extent to which he or she experienced difficulties in hearing, vision, mobility and cognitive function, and whether any of these difficulties (or other health problems) resulted in the need for care. The ratings of none, minor, moderate or major difficulty were derived from estimates of the informant and the observer (the author) and not from any standardized tests. To assess hearing, for example, elders were asked whether they could follow conversations around the meal table with no difficulty while the observer noted the extent to which she had to raise her voice to communicate with the elder in the course of the interview. To assess cognitive function, elders were asked directly whether they experienced any difficulties with memory, when they had last had contact with their various children, and to recall in detail how they had spent the previous day (frequently family members were available to verify the elders' responses).[4]

Although lacking in precision, the ratings appear to have been quite accurate. The Time 2 scores were assigned without reference to the Time 1 scores, and when the two scores were subsequently compared, they were generally consistent with the passage of time, that is, stable or deteriorated. In the case of cognitive function, for example, 74 percent received the same rating both times while 19.5 percent had worsened, and 6.5 percent had improved. The least easily explained Time 2 ratings are those for vision: 62 percent fell in the same category as Time 1 while 22 percent worsened and 16 percent improved. Since vision was the one variable that the observer could not easily rate independently of the elder, it is likely that much of the variation, particularly much of the apparent improvement, reflects instability in informant assessment criteria or, in a very few cases, medical intervention such as cataract removal. Because the rating categories are broad and, in the case of the last (major difficulties), open-ended, the true extent of deterioration is likely understated by these figures; for example, those receiving a rating of '4' (major difficulties) in cognitive function at Time 1 were clearly in worse shape at Time 2 yet necessarily received the same rating.

It is also important to note that the ratings assigned by these methods probably understate the degree of impairment that would have been found by standardized tests. The primary reason for this likely skewing is that both the informants and the observer based their evaluations of capability or performance on the *local standard of everyday normality*, that is, the level of performance required of a person of their age and sex for successful negotiation of daily life. In the case of Guangzhou, where performance demands on the elderly are relatively modest (they are not, for example, expected to live independently in order to retain full adult status), even substantially impaired individuals are likely to perceive themselves as having no or only minor difficulties in managing their daily lives. Standardized tests, by contrast, base their evaluations on *standards of perfection*, that is, the level of capability or performance that a healthy individual could attain under optimal circumstances, such as lifting 50 pounds, or on the *research community's standard of everyday normality*; for example, the ability to drive a car or balance a checkbook (neither of which skills are required of Chinese elderly).[5]

Given that reliance on different standards will result in different findings, how is the investigator to decide which standard is most appropriate? Clearly, any such decision must be based on the objectives of the research. If the primary goal is to compare the frequency and distribution of impairments among societies, some kind of standardized measures that are as culture-free as possible must be used. Alternatively, if the primary goal is to determine the impact of perceived impairments on functioning in the real local world, then culturally sensitive measures must be used and culturally specific performance demands taken into consideration. This research necessarily chose the second of these alternatives.

Table 24.1
Types of Assistance Needed, by Age at Time 2*

Age Range	None		Household Tasks		Going Out		Personal Care		Total	
	N	%	N	%	N	%	N	%	N	%
70–74	15	75	2	10	3	15	0	0	20	100
75–79	53	72	10	14	7	9	4	6	74	101*
80–84	18	46	10	26	6	15	5	13	39	100
85+	6	26	6	26	5	22	6	26	23	100
Total**	92	59	28	18	21	13	15	10	156	100

*Elders are counted only by their greatest need; for example, those in need of personal care also
   need assistance in household tasks and in going out but are not counted in those columns.
**Total exceeds 100 percent due to rounding.

THE LONG-TERM CARE NEEDS OF THE DISABLED ELDERLY

The presence of impairments does not automatically translate into disability and the need for assistance. For example, at Time 1, 49 percent of the elderly acknowledged difficulties in getting around or using their limbs (mobility), yet only 26 percent of all elderly in the study required assistance in any of the following areas: household tasks, going out or personal care. The same phenomenon is observed at Time 2, with 59 percent of the elderly reporting difficulties in mobility, yet only 41 percent requiring any assistance.[6] As the above statistics indicate, the passage of time (i.e., the aging of the sample) is, not surprisingly, associated with higher needs for assistance. This relationship between age and needs is further demonstrated in Table 24.1.

The needs depicted by the columns are generally sequential and inclusive. Barring dramatic events, such as a hip fracture or a stroke that can propel the victim directly into the last column, persons with typical chronic conditions, such as circulatory or respiratory disorders, move from one needs state to the next—from needing assistance with household tasks, to needing assistance to go out, to needing personal care. Because most Chinese elderly (91 percent in this study), including even those in good health, live in multiperson households (see Table 24.2) meeting these needs seldom requires relocation. Thus, the gradually increasing reliance on others that so frequently accompanies aging is much less threatening to Chinese elderly than to American elderly, who are more likely to live alone and who, therefore, often must relocate in order to receive the appropriate care.

Living with or at least in close proximity to one's children, especially to one's

Table 24.2
Household Composition at Time 2

	N	%
Alone	15	10
Couple Only	18	12
Couple and Adult Child(ren)	34	22
Couple and Other Junior Relative	4	3
Elder and Adult Child(ren)	67	43
Elder and Other Junior Relative	13	8
Other	5	3
Total	156	101*

*Total exceeds 100 percent due to rounding.

son, is a cultural ideal. Until recently, this ideal has been facilitated in China by the scarcity of urban housing. With the implementation of the economic reforms, however, urban households (and neighborhoods) now find their enforced unity and stability increasingly a phenomenon of the past. Greater freedom to control their own budgets in the early 1980s led work units to divert funds into building housing for their workers. As a result, young couples can now expect to be assigned housing relatively soon after their marriage and no longer have to spend many years doubled up with the husband's parents. Although young people frequently invite their elders to move with them, the elders themselves are ambivalent about leaving their familiar and convenient neighborhoods to settle in the suburbs, where most new housing is being built.

The most commonly occurring medical conditions mentioned by the elderly in this study are cardiovascular diseases, arthritis/rheumatism and respiratory problems, such as chronic bronchitis and emphysema. These, along with cataracts and glaucoma, are essentially the same major conditions found among the elderly in a much larger study that was carried out in Shanghai in 1987.[7] Perhaps because of their very commonness these diseases are generally accepted as nearly unavoidable concomitants of old age. While they may be sources of annoyance, discomfort and inconvenience and occasionally result in hospitalization (and, in the case of cardiovascular and respiratory problems, often in death), most old people do not waste time fretting about them primarily because the inconvenience they cause can be dealt with fairly easily by the typical family. Generally, the only intervention required is that someone take over whatever household tasks had previously been the responsibility of the elder. Allowing younger people, who are already sharing the household, to take over such tasks is perceived not so much as becoming dependent as simply taking a well-deserved rest.

Nor does the prospect of dementia cause much alarm to either the elderly or their family members. The reasons for this comparative complacency are several, and they support the contention of Lyman (1989), Henderson (Chapter 22 this volume) and Kitwood (1993) that in the West, biomedicalizing dementia has led to the downplaying of cultural and social factors that mediate the impact of the disease. Authors describing the phenomenon of dementia in non-Western societies, such as Polynesia (Chapter 21 this volume), India (Cohen 1992) and Japan (Ariyoshi 1972), have argued that the loss of normal cognitive function among the elderly is viewed, at least by some people in these societies, as signifying that the affected individual is severing ties with the ordinary world and is in transit to the supernatural realm. This common perception does not, however, generate a common response. On the island of Niue, Barker finds that people, wanting to put as much distance between themselves and the near-dead as possible, neglect and ridicule the demented. In India, Cohen notes that social status plays an important role in how demented behavior, such as repetitive or nonsensical babbling, is interpreted. If the speaker is an ascetic or self-styled renunciate, inappropriate speech might be viewed as meaningful if not exactly accessible or proper, but if the speaker is an old widow with no social affiliations, she is likely to be viewed as simply crazy. The caregiver in Ariyoshi's fictional work comes to view her charge as a god-in-the-making and her caregiving as a privilege rather than a burden.

What are some of the cultural and social factors that mediate and moderate the individual and family experience of dementia in China? The first is that the cognitive correlates of dementia do not carry the same weight in China that they do in the West. In China the essence of personhood (or humanness) involves more than the demonstration of a rational thinking self; it requires a moral self. To become a full human being requires an understanding of the proper way of conducting oneself (Ikels 1989). A person who suffers from cognitive deficits yet is still able to behave more or less appropriately is unlikely to be regarded as a pitiable or problematic individual. Mild or even moderate dementia is not seen as necessitating much intervention by the family. The second factor that reduces the significance of cognitive decline in the elderly is that currently there are enormous cohort differences in educational attainment and concomitant cohort differences in standards of mental performance. The vast majority of elderly Chinese, women in particular, have had little exposure to formal learning. In this sample, 71 percent of the women (and 31 percent of the men) had three or fewer years of schooling of any sort. Such elderly are not usually expected to be well-informed about current events, and not being prepared to discuss them or offer an opinion about them is not interpreted as a failing. A third factor reducing the psychological impact of dementia is that to some extent becoming "childish" in old age is a culturally recognized phenomenon.[8] As a symptom of dementia, however, childishness draws the observer's attention to behavioral rather than cognitive changes. Impulsive acts, such as snatching food out of another's bowl, stubbornness and unreasonable demands are much more readily noticed and remarked upon by Chinese than memory loss, which is seen as something much more benign. The chief reason for this different emphasis is, I think, quite straightforward and directly related to living arrangements. So long as the elder lives in a multiperson household, cognitive declines have relatively less impact on both the elder and the family than if he or she were living alone and had to function independently. Yet this same fact, living in a multiperson household, means that the consequences of changes in personality and behavior cannot be easily avoided and so may result in friction in interpersonal relations.

Other factors affecting the impact of dementia include stability of residence, approval of passivity, perceptions of psychological needs and cultural norms concerning the capacity to endure. Dementia sufferers do best when their environment and the challenges they face in everyday life are familiar. Because neighborhoods in Guangzhou have been stable, most elders find themselves living in a very familiar environment. They face few novel challenges, can easily walk to the market and know their neighbors who, equally important, know them and can steer them home if they seem confused or lost. Furthermore, Chinese elders and family members view an unstimulating environment rather differently from Americans. Elders who sit and do nothing are not likely to be regarded as in urgent need of interaction or entertainment. Indeed, the single most favored leisure pastime of the elderly in this study is, by their own admission, "sitting," that is, resting, relaxing, passively observing the activities of others. Finally, with regard to the difficulties family members might face when providing care to any disabled elder, Chinese values have long emphasized the capacity to endure hardship without complaint. As one informant put it, "What is the point of burdening someone else with your hardships [by talking about them] when they are not in a position to do anything about them? All you accomplish is making the other person feel bad."

The most feared condition Chinese associate with old age is paralysis from a stroke. This condition is not only the most personally disabling, it is also the most demanding of family members, and the most difficult for which to find alternatives to family care. Once a stroke patient has been stabilized, hospitals (assuming they have agreed to admit the victim in the first place) are likely to insist on discharge. Once home the elder has little prospect of rehabilitation. At best he or she will be looked after by an unskilled family member, supplemented in some cases by a hired attendant (*baomu*) and monitored weekly by a nurse or doctor as part of the Family Sickbed (home care) program of a nearby hospital or public health clinic.[9] Since the services of neither a *baomu* nor a Family Sickbed worker are normally covered by health insurance, many families simply go without.

When I interviewed the Family Sickbed doctor who was responsible for one of the neighborhoods in which I was interviewing, she indicated that 80 percent of her case load consisted of elderly, paralyzed patients and that the record for a paralyzed patient maintained at home in this neighborhood was 18 years! Of the eight elderly who were bedridden at the time of my second set of visits, three had suffered hip fractures and were hospitalized, while three who had suffered paralytic strokes and two who were in the apparent final stage of dementia were being cared for at home. I asked the Sickbed doctor whether it was better for stroke patients to remain at home or to go to a facility of some sort. She and her superior, the clinic director, both responded immediately that it was better for them to go to a facility. Better for the patient because a health care facility offers more specialized equipment and a better trained staff, and better for the family because they can obtain some relief. The size of dwelling units is so small that patients and families have a hard time. The reality of the situation is, however, that there are not enough facilities and that families do accept this kind of responsibility.

To provide the reader with a better sense of the context in which Chinese families provide care to the disabled elderly, three cases, one involving generalized decline, one dementia, and one a paralytic stroke, are presented below. Following the presentation of these cases we will consider the recommendations of the elderly themselves as to how families can best be helped to meet the long-term care needs of the elderly.

FAMILY CARE OF THE ELDERLY

Case 1

At the time of the second interview, old Mrs. Lau was feeling the weight of her 90 years. She opened her remarks to us by saying: "I've lived too long. If I weren't so old, I wouldn't be deaf. I'm so clumsy [I can't get around]. I would like to buy things myself, but everyone always tells me not to go out. The things others buy at the market aren't what I want to eat." Mrs. Lau's "clumsiness" stems from poor vision (a cataract in one eye) and the fact that she needs a cane to walk any kind of distance. She is also very hard of hearing and, according to her co-resident granddaughter, has in the last few years "become strange." Only two of Mrs. Lau's five children, a son and a daughter, survived to adulthood. Her son, however, died while still young, leaving behind a widow and two young children. When his widow remarried, she left the two children for Mrs. Lau to raise. This action is in accordance with traditional patrilineal kinship rules: Children belong to the father's line and not the mother's. Similarly, men who marry widows usually do not welcome the prospect of raising someone else's children. Mrs. Lau's daughter is herself now a widow and lives with her four children in another part of Guangzhou. Although she visits her mother, it is not possible for Mrs. Lau to live with her.

All of Mrs. Lau's daily care is provided by her twenty-eight-year-old granddaughter, though her grandson, married and living elsewhere in Guangzhou, has occasionally offered his sister a rest by taking Mrs. Lau in for a week or two. Fortunately, Mrs. Lau's needs are still modest; although she requires assistance with nearly all household tasks, she can look after her personal needs. More problematic is Mrs. Lau's wish to leave her ground-floor residence and wander about the neighborhood, in particular to go to the market. Since her granddaughter works full-time, it is not possible for her to supervise her grandmother during the day. The solution to this problem rests on good ties with the neighbors. The Laus have lived in their neighborhood since before the granddaughter was born. Their dwelling is located on a wide lane with an open sitting area, accessible from the main street only by pedestrians and bicycles, and their doorway is close to the local residents committee office. Miss Lau, widely admired for her filial attitude, has successfully enlisted the neighbors to keep an eye on her grandmother—thus Mrs. Lau's opening lament ("everyone always tells me not to go out"). This supervision is not constant, however, and twice Mrs. Lau has been taken advantage of by an unknown young man who entered her premises on the pretext of looking for the granddaughter. The first time he successfully flimflammed Mrs. Lau out of her money; the second time he actually attempted to frisk her.

At the moment Mrs. Lau's support network seems to be holding, but at considerable cost to her granddaughter, who essentially is working full-time both outside and inside the home. Miss Lau, a gentle and attractive young woman, is fast approaching 30, the age at which traditionally a woman was considered well past her prime on the marriage market. With no free time to meet and socialize with people of her own age and no boyfriend in evidence, one wonders about her matrimonial prospects. It is also unlikely that Mrs. Lau will remain ambulatory for much longer. When she cannot get around, will the neighbors be prepared to offer more intensive kinds of care?

Case 2

When I first visited the Lam Household, Mrs. Lam's eighty-four-year-old mother, Mrs. Kwong, seemed to be well on her way to recovering from a stroke she had experienced about a year earlier. At that time she had been hospitalized for over a month, incontinent and unable to talk because of a nasal tube. Finding it too expensive to keep her in the hospital, her family members had carried her home on a stretcher and tended her themselves. During the interview, Mrs. Kwong was an enthusiastic participant, eagerly demonstrating how she could now walk about the living room, but she still needed assistance in getting washed and dressed and could not use the traditional Chinese toilet.[10] She was totally exempt from any kind of housework and spent most of her time passively sitting. Although she could carry on a conversation, more complex cognitive skills had eroded.

Over the next three and a half years Mrs. Kwong deteriorated physically and mentally to the point of being essentially bedfast. She had not left her room in the past three years; in fact, she can no longer walk and can rise from her bed only with support. More difficult from Mrs. Lam's point of view is the fact that Mrs. Kwong has become incontinent again—not seeming aware of the need to urinate, falling off the spittoon when she does attempt to use it, and leaving waste all over the floor. Mrs. Kwong has neither strength nor energy—she cannot so much as wring out a washcloth. When she eats, she drops food all over the place and afterwards does not even realize that she has eaten. Sometimes she doesn't even seem to know that she should eat the items presented to her—she simply holds a bowl of rice porridge when it is given to her. Mrs. Lam notes that her mother has virtually no memory, asks totally irrelevant questions, scolds and can be very stubborn. Most of the time, however, Mrs. Kwong just sleeps.

Mrs. Lam, who is in her mid-fifties and has been retired for several years, feels the burden of looking after her mother. She emphasizes that she provides all the care, although her own two adult sons assist with moving Mrs. Kwong, who is rather heavy. Up until about seven years ago Mrs. Kwong had lived with her younger son and daughter-in-law and helped them to raise their three children, but she had taken her meals with Mrs. Lam, whose family, along with that of her older daughter, lived nearby. When Mrs. Lam's husband's workplace assigned them to this new building seven years ago, Mrs. Kwong joined the Lam household because it had the most space. Mrs. Kwong's older son is in his sixties and lives in Hong Kong. He sends Mrs. Lam the equivalent of U.S.$13 a month to look after their mother; his brother in Guangzhou with whom Mrs. Kwong used to live only sends about U.S.$2! If she had the money, Mrs. Lam would prefer to hire a *baomu* to look after her mother. She raised this issue with her three siblings, but they are all retired and cannot put enough money together to hire someone, since besides paying wages, they would have to provide room and board. Mrs. Lam ended the interview by observing: "Even if you have money, it is still difficult to get people to look after an old person, to do all the dirty things. . . . Old people live much longer now."

Case 3

Even at the time of the first interview Mrs. Siu, then in her mid seventies, was heavily dependent on her family's care. Her body was wracked with the pain of rheumatism (a broadly used term that frequently encompasses the symptoms Westerners associate with arthritis). Mrs. Siu walked only with the assistance of a cane, and her arms were so weak that she needed help washing her hair and placing food in her bowl, though she could feed herself with chopsticks. At that time she lived in private housing owned by Chinese living overseas with her only child (a daughter), son-in-law and three grandsons (the oldest grandson lived upstairs while another had gone abroad).[11] With all of them pitching in, they were easily able to meet Mrs. Siu's needs.

Between the two interviews, both the household circumstances and Mrs. Siu's health condition changed substantially. The oldest grandson moved out of his upstairs apartment to housing assigned by his work unit. The second grandson, his wife (to whom he was married at the time of the first visit but not yet able to live with because of space problems) and baby moved upstairs into the living quarters vacated by his brother's family. One of the other grandsons accepted work in a county outside of Guangzhou and returned to Mrs. Siu's residence only once or twice a month. In late 1988, Mrs. Siu's daughter retired as did her son-in-law a few months later. As it turned out, both of these retirees were almost immediately enlisted in family care, the daughter to look after Mrs. Siu, who had a stroke, and the son-in-law to look after their second son's new baby.

In the spring of 1989, Mrs. Siu suffered a major stroke that left her paralyzed on one side and unable to talk. She was sent by ambulance to one of the hospitals attached to Zhongshan Medical College, where most of the costs of her treatment were covered by her (former) work unit. After lingering for a month in the emergency room, Mrs. Siu was finally admitted to a specialty ward.[12] Five months later, when she had reached the point that she no longer needed a feeding tube through the nose and could talk (though not clearly), the hospital told the family that they could do no more for her and that she was being discharged. While there is a rehabilitation hospital in Guangzhou, as far as this family knew it is only for self-pay patients. Mrs. Siu's unit certainly was not going to pay to send her there, though it did pay a small part of the costs of the weekly visits by the Family Sickbed doctor.

When Mrs. Siu first came home, she was treated by an acupuncturist, but it soon became apparent that she was not recovering any function. Because, in addition to the paralysis, she still suffered from severe rheumatism, Mrs. Siu did not like to move or be moved, and gradually her nerves and muscles began to atrophy. Despite the family's best efforts, after being home for over a year, Mrs. Siu developed bedsores. About a month after my second visit, the Family Sickbed doctor discovered her feverish and, realizing that the bedsores were infected, sent her to the district hospital, where she died only two or three days later.

FACILITATING FAMILY CARE

As the above examples illustrate, Chinese families are generally prepared to provide long-term care to their disabled elderly members, but it would be a mistake to assume that they do so at no personal cost. Everyone recognizes that providing care can mean putting one's own plans on hold. Certainly, Mrs. Lau's granddaughter cannot easily contemplate getting married, and we have witnessed cases of children in other families postponing moves or taking early retirement for the sake of their parents. Perhaps those who suffer the greatest exhaustion are spouse caregivers who either live too far away from their children or have no children available to offer support. When we asked the study participants how families can best be helped to meet their obligations to their disabled elders, they had a great deal to say. Their suggestions ranged from ideas about an elder's responsibility to stay healthy to the state's obligation to increase the availability of alternatives to family care. Let's examine these suggestions below.

Personal Responsibility

A number of informants commented that older people themselves should make life easier for their children.

> If people are happy, they will get sick less. The most important thing is not to scold people or complain about one's daughter-in-law.

> You should do what you can to lighten their burden. Old people should not be so nosey, so nagging . . .

> Take my own case—the kids work far away. They can't just take off. They are needed at work. Old people have to look after themselves; they can't make the young people laborious. Maybe if I know a person in this circumstance, we could help each other. The elderly shouldn't think only of themselves.

> We should have an old people's club—one in which retired people would look after each other. The street committee should set this up. I would participate if there were such an organization.

It is a widely held belief that a complaining or quarrelsome person not only contributes to a strained family environment but also is likely to make him or herself sick. Excessive emotions, including worry, dissipate or derange one's *qi* (internally circulating vital essence); one must learn to cope with adversity with quiet acceptance. Elders also recognize the value of moderate exercise as a preventive health measure. Most of the people in this study who were able went to a park every morning for a stroll, to perform traditional Chinese exercises, or even on occasion to participate in aerobic dancing. Similarly, people are careful about what and how much they eat by trying to avoid fatty cuts of pork and not stuffing themselves. Where tobacco and high blood pressure medications are concerned, however, elders fail to heed their own advice about the importance of prevention. Respiratory diseases and strokes, both associated with tobacco use and the latter with high blood pressure, are leading causes of death in Guangzhou. Nevertheless, tobacco-using elders are nearly impervious to government efforts to reduce smoking (these efforts are seriously undercut by the fact that the government heavily taxes tobacco products and makes substantial profits from it). Similarly, despite their great fear of strokes and their awareness of whether or not they suffer from hypertension, elders take a short-sighted approach to medication. Although many people in the study had prescriptions to manage their high blood pressure, most are slow to refill them and carefully ration their pills, taking them only when they are symptomatic (a practice also common in the West). This reluctance to take medicine stems not from financial considerations (the medications are covered by health insurance and are very inexpensive) but from traditional notions about the wisdom of taking any medicine over a long period.

The willingness of older people to look after each other expressed by the last two informants is a reflection of reality and not merely idealism. As we saw in Mrs. Lau's case, stable neighborhoods in which people are familiar with the individual's background and current circumstances facilitate the involvement of familiar others. We heard many cases of neighbors and even more specifically, co-tenants voluntarily looking in on each other. One elderly man, for example, commented that he personally makes a point every morning of watching for a light in the window of a frail widow living nearby that signals that she is up and about lighting incense. If he doesn't see a light, he goes up and knocks on her door to see whether she is alright. His wife buys vegetables for her (with money left behind by the Hong Kong daughter of her deceased husband's first wife), and others fetch coal for her. While these arrangements seem to have been the spontaneous result of longtime interaction, more formalized arrangements are sometimes worked out by residents committee personnel, who either take on the provision of such care themselves or, for a very small sum, hire a neighbor. The residents committee is likely to become involved, however, only if the needy elder has no family and no work unit.[13]

Hired Helpers

Many elderly acknowledged that the demands of looking after someone who needs extensive personal care or is bedridden is likely to be too much for most families and that the logical solution to the problem is to hire a *baomu*. Certainly, this was an option that Mrs. Lam wanted to explore, but others who had tried this solution found it wanting.

> Get an old lady to look after them if the young people have to work.

> You have to rely on your own family, but they work. It's hard to find a *baomu*, and looking after a paralyzed person is too much responsibility for a *baomu*.

> *Baomu* are not necessarily reliable. It's better to be looked after by retired people in the neighborhood.

> It is impossible to hire a *baomu*. It's better for the elderly to have a place to eat and have some activities—social services. . . . I myself would like such a place—to not have to cook but to be able to go to a central place to fetch cooked food. With these kinds of services you would not have to hire a *baomu*.

Dissatisfaction with the *baomu* option is clearly widespread. They are very difficult to recruit locally as there are many higher paying and more attractive jobs available to urban residents. Families seeking *baomu* must go through their personal networks or labor companies to locate someone from remote areas of the province or even from outside the province. Many families who could otherwise put together the funds to pay a salary cannot provide any extra living space for such a nonfamily caregiver. Moreover, young *baomu* are likely to switch jobs once they come to know more about urban life, while old *baomu* are often not strong enough to manage the care of a bedridden patient.

Workplace Responsibility

As indicated in the introduction to this chapter, the urban workplace has long been regarded as a source of welfare as much as a source of employment. With regard to the typical elder the workplace is especially important as the source of one's pension and health coverage. For the elder with no family the workplace is even more significant as it, rather than the local residents committee, is responsible for the care of its childless retirees. We will return to this point shortly, but first let us consider how the workplace can facilitate the care of the elderly who do have children.

> My daughter-in-law's unit let her take home leave to look after me in the hospital.

> Work units should give compensation time to young people so they don't have to be so exhausted [that they can't help out]. They shouldn't dock their pay because they take a different day off after the factory required them to work on their regular day off.

> These people should be sent to a nursing home. Our unit (the City Bus Company) has four rooms for people who are waiting to die. A lot of times you can't get these people into a hospital or an observation room. If a family member works for this unit, you might be able to get one of these beds.

When people talk about good and bad work units, they employ a number of criteria—nature of the work, quality of the benefits, political atmosphere and so forth. Probably, the criterion that they see the unit as having the greatest discretion over is accommodating the personal needs of the workers. A unit that is willing to bend the rules for its workers is a good unit; one that is inflexible or whose personnel officers require favors before they will consider a worker's special circumstances is a bad one. The first speaker in this section mentions a unit flexibly allowing a worker to be absent from work to look after her mother-in-law in the hospital by officially explaining her absence as home leave. This type of paid leave is available primarily to people whose separation from their families is directly due to their work assignment. Her daughter-in-law's parents live in Weizhou, a city three or more hours from Guangzhou, but in reality the daughter-in-law, instead of going to visit them, remained in Guangzhou (with her unit turning a blind eye) to look after the informant. The second speaker's child, however, seems to belong to a more selfish work unit that puts profits first and squeezes everything it can out of its workers.

The last speaker refers to the practice of some of the larger work units or a number of related work units of operating their own health care facilities. Such work units have long run their own clinics and sometimes even their own hospitals and sanatoria for their employees and their dependents. However, the changing economy and health care needs of the population have contributed to a need for innovation. Specifically sanatoria, originally established in the 1950s to provide a place for TB patients to recover and for high cadres and model workers to undergo rest and recuperation, have seen their occupancy rates sink as TB can be treated on an out-patient basis with antibiotics, and as work units no longer wish to subsidize what are increasingly viewed as nothing more than paid vacations. In this context of declining income, two local sanatoria that I visited in 1991, having noted the growing need for long-term care, had already transformed part of their facilities into nursing homes or geriatric hospitals and made their services available to the wider community.[14]

Most work units do not have the finances to sponsor their own long-term care facilities. Instead they have had to rely on the availability of openings in homes for the aged operated by the City Civil Affairs Bureau and its branches at the district and street committee levels. Until very recently, these urban facilities (as welfare institutions) were open only to those without children and no means of support, but increasingly, in order to generate some of their own funds, they have been opened to the childless elderly with work units who pay for their admission and maintenance and even, in the case of the City Home for the Aged, to private-pay residents. It should be noted that work units rarely, if ever, subsidize the entry into homes for the aged of people with family members to look after them. In addition, while originally these homes required that the would-be occupants be capable of self-care, this restriction has been relaxed at least for the City Home, which now operates several levels of care and charges accordingly.

Street committees without a home for the aged within their jurisdiction may send their and their work units' eligible elderly to their district or the city-level home. Since in 1991 half of the street committees did not yet have their own homes and only one of the eight districts had one, the waiting list for the City Home for the Aged was several years long. Furthermore, the most impoverished work units frequently have the greatest welfare burden and cannot afford to send their eligible elderly to any of these homes. For example, a review of the 1991 figures for one of the neighborhoods I worked in revealed that of a total of 1,045 persons dependent on local collectives for their income, 573 (or 55 percent) were already retired. With a worker-retiree ratio of less than one, there was no way the street committee could sponsor the entry of its retirees into the

City Home.[15] It is facts like these that make family care or no care the normal range of alternatives available to the elderly.

CONCLUSIONS

Let us review here the government and workplace policies that currently influence the provision of long-term care to the disabled elderly. The first is that, in China, family care is the rule by law and by custom, and its availability is heavily influenced by employment policies. As a socialist economy (now in transition), China has emphasized the empowerment of women by employment. Consequently, the overwhelming majority of women are in the labor force full-time. This fact would seemingly augur ill for the availability of family caregiving, but such has not generally been the case for two reasons. The first is that women may retire from the work force at either 50 (if factory workers) or at 55 (if technicians, professionals or cadres) with full benefits. Thus, the exit from employment at mid-life to provide caregiving is not penalized as it is in many capitalist countries. The second is that grandchildren (on lunch break from school or home for the day) are frequently enlisted to look after the elderly.

Two developments, postretirement employment opportunities and the one-child family policy, and a third possibility, raising the age of retirement for women, threaten to alter this relatively secure arrangement. Ironically, it is logical in China for certain work units to reemploy their own retirees rather than to hire younger workers (and for those who have difficulty attracting new workers it is the only alternative now that ordinary workers are free to seek employment on their own). When a retired worker is rehired by his or her own unit, all the unit has to pay is the differential between the retiree's pension and the normal wage (usually on the order of 30 percent of the basic wage). The retiree is already receiving most subsidies as well as health coverage, so the unit is freed from having to add those to its costs as it must if it hires a new worker. We found many middle-aged and even older retirees who had gone back to work at their old units. The attraction to the older worker is that in addition to recovering the extra 30 percent of the basic wage, he or she is also eligible for a share of the bonus money that is distributed monthly to active workers but not retirees. Reemployment not only reduces the availability of family caregivers; it also reduces the availability of neighbors to provide supplementary care (Chan 1993).

Since 1979, China has been vigorously enforcing a one-child-per-family policy in the urban areas, and the vast majority (99 percent) of the households in this study were clearly in compliance. If one thinks of the impact of this policy only on the current *parent* generation, one can safely postpone worrying about its implications for family caregiving for another three decades, because the parents of one-child families are still young. But this inaction would be very unwise because, as we have seen above, grandchildren are substantially involved in the provision of care to the current *grandparent* generation. If the retirement age for women is raised (professional women are already being allowed to work until age 60), the role of grandchildren will become even more important.

The second set of economic policies affecting the provision of long-term care to the elderly is the requirement that work units become increasingly responsible for meeting their own budgetary needs. Financial constraints are having both negative and positive consequences for Guangzhou's elderly. On the negative side, work units are trying every conceivable way to avoid unnecessary welfare expenditures by reducing and haggling over health benefits. On the positive side, work units in the health care field have suddenly had to think about ways of generating new sources of income. Having entered the market economy of supply and demand, these units, former sanitoria, former homes for the (well) aged and even district hospitals, have come to realize the need for institutional provision of long-term care places. For those families able to pay, these new services are welcome.

The third policy with major implications for caregiving is housing reform (here referring primarily to the government's promise to raise average per capita living space). The tremendous increase in the number of apartments has made it possible for young married couples to spend a briefer and briefer period living together with the senior generation. Although this growth in the availability of housing does not yet seem to be a major threat to the security of elders, it has the potential to be very problematic. The reasons for this are threefold: First, new housing is increasingly located far from the urban center and, therefore, far from the health care facilities that the elderly need to use. The elderly resist these moves. Second, new housing is increasingly likely to be built apart from the workplace and to be inhabited by people originating from diverse work units. The close linkages that exist among many families because they share both work and residential ties are being severed. Third, the older neighborhoods risk being turned into geriatric ghettoes with fewer young people around who are familiar with their older neighbors and who, therefore, are unprepared to come to their assistance.

Finally, it is quite obvious that major service gaps remain. With the exception of the Family Sickbed Program, there is no formal home care program to speak of.[16] Respite programs have been talked about as a way of generating income and filling empty rooms in local homes for the aged, but few homes have actually offered this service. Most significant for stroke patients is the scarcity of rehabilitation services. Perhaps these shortcomings will be partially remedied as more market-oriented thinking comes to predominate. For example, homes for the aged whose family members live abroad and can pay in foreign currency have been springing up in the counties between Guangzhou and Hong Kong or Macao. They will doubtless soon appear also in Guangzhou.

NOTES

The research on which this chapter is based was partially supported by a grant from the Committe for Scholarly Communication with the People's Republic of China.

1. The rural population did not receive these same sorts of subsidies, though the vast majority of local communities did operate a cooperative medical insurance system and a minimal safety net for those experiencing extreme financial hardship. The nature of the differences in programs and services for the elderly in rural and urban China is described in Ikels 1990. The impact of the economic reforms on the rural elderly will not be examined in this chapter.

2. Below the district level, Guangzhou city proper is divided into subdistricts known as street (*jiedao*) committees (sometimes translated as "wards") that are further subdivided into residence committees. Each street committee in Guangzhou is usually responsible for an area in excess of 20,000 people. The two street committees that I worked in had, in 1987, populations of 24,900 and 38,000.

A work unit is simply one's workplace, such as a factory, hospital, government bureau or department store. Their size can range from the very small (under 50) to the enormous (thousands of people). The changing nature of employment-based welfare benefits is discussed at length in Ikels 1996.

3. A fuller description of the sample and of the interview can be found in Ikels 1991.

4. These data were supplemented by the observer's evaluation of the informant's ability to participate in the interview; for example, to focus on the topic at hand, to be consistent, to minimize repetitions of incidents or events of long ago and so forth.

5. For a recent review of the literature on the concept of disability and how to measure it, see Kopec 1995.

6. It should be noted that the impact of impairments on needs is somewhat minimized by the way the data were analyzed. That is, if the informant could and did perform the usual tasks of daily living without assistance, he or she was deemed not to need assistance. This way of categorizing obscures the fact that some people met their own needs only with great effort and were generally forced to do so because no one was available to assist them. These very few cases were found among those living alone or as couples only. Those living with other healthy people in their households (the vast majority of the elderly) were automatically assisted or relieved of difficult tasks.

7. Chen et al. 1995. The Shanghai study found that eye diseases (cataract/glaucoma) were even more frequent than arthritis/rheumatism. Eye diseases were also common in Guangzhou but were asked about in a different context in the interview such that people were likely to mention them only if they interfered with daily activities.

8. For a discussion of this same concept of childishness in the West, see Covey 1993.

9. For a fuller discussion of the Family Sickbed program in another Chinese city, see Wang and Schneider 1993.

10. The traditional Chinese toilet usually found in urban households and public restrooms is a formidable structure. The user must squat down carefully over the trench-like fixture and then stand erect without any assistive devices. For many older people with arthritis or weak legs using such a toilet is simply out of the question. The standard alternative is to use a metal spittoon that can be placed anywhere (i.e., against a bed so that one can brace oneself while getting up and down), and whose wide brim provides some support for the body. Spittoons are also used at night as chamber pots by people of all ages in buildings without toilets. A few residences in Guangzhou, some old and some new, have Western-style sitting toilets.

11. In fact, the kinship relationship is a bit more complex. One of these grandsons

(the second of five) had been designated Mrs. Siu's son (i.e., her daughter had turned one of her sons over to her parent[s]). Mrs. Siu's husband had died three years after their marriage with no male descendants. By grafting a grandson through a daughter onto his line as a son, the Sius effectively continue his line. This young man was quite aware of his dual status and seemed comfortable with it.

12. In Guangzhou, hospitals are frequently reluctant to admit patients who appear unlikely to survive or to benefit from treatment. We heard many families express their dismay and anger that their elder was refused admission or left to die in the observation room off the emergency room. Hospitals are familiar with these charges and counter them by explaining that hospitals attached to the city, province or medical college are the most specialized hospitals and as such are expected to treat the most difficult and acute cases. They are usually very full and prefer that older people, particularly those suffering from a chronic condition, go to the lower-level district hospitals for care. Indeed, the district hospitals have both lower occupancy rates and longer lengths of stay than those higher up in the hierarchy. The problem for the families is that they seem unaware of this semi-official division of labor, believe that the higher-level hospitals offer better care and often may not go to district-level hospitals because their work units have made exclusive contracts with one of the higher-level hospitals to provide care to their insurees.

13. For a more lengthy discussion of this topic see Chan 1993. In late 1988, Chan surveyed 24 of the 90 street committee offices (the administrative unit immediately above the residents committees) in Guangzhou to learn what services were available, who provided them and who received them. Of greatest interest for our purposes is the fact that half of the street offices had organized Home-Help Teams. These teams consisted primarily of younger volunteers from schools, the Communist Youth League and the Communist Party, and the nature of help provided to the elderly included assistance with household chores, buying goods and visiting. But these services (with the possible exception of the purchasing of goods) tended to be sporadic (annual cleanings or monthly or less frequent visits), and the number of people receiving them was minuscule. The average street committee had a population of about 50,000; the average number of people served by a Home-Help Team (in those street committees having them) was 17.9 while the median was 9. These services were limited to those with no families and no work units, and Chan suspected that they were targeted primarily at the dependents of martyrs (those killed fighting for the Communists prior to 1949) and ex-servicemen.

14. One of these sanatoria was run by the Transport Department (and originally for the use of commercial seamen) and the other was operated by the Bank of China for its cadres and workers. See also Wong, Ho and Yu 1994.

15. There were several quite desperate cases encountered in the course of the study who wanted, to no avail, to be sent to the City Home. These were usually couples who were totally dependent on one another and could just barely manage. They wanted admission either as a couple or at least for the survivor who would likely be unable to manage alone. That the statistics given for this neighborhood are not out of the ordinary is supported by an article appearing in *Nanfang Ribao*, October 4, 1991, which reported that in the adjacent district, the collective labor force of nearly 30,000 included 15,064 retirees (or 51 percent of the labor force).

16. An experimental nongovernment facility, the Linghai Old People's Center (see

Ikels 1990), which is primarily a residential facility for retired cadres, began a home visiting program in 1990 and also provides skilled workers to attend hospitalized family members. They declined to mention the costs of their services, saying they varied by distance from the facility, the nature of the care provided and so forth.

CHAPTER 25

Liminality in an American Nursing Home: The Endless Transition

Renée Rose Shield

INTRODUCTION

The nursing home environment provides an excellent setting in which to examine processes of community formation and the impact of institutionalization upon the residents living there. Several recent ethnographies have illuminated our understanding of nursing homes (Savishinsky 1991; Diamond 1992; Foner 1994; and Shield 1995). Numerous factors impinge upon the frail old person living in institutions: inevitable functional decline, increased occurrences of disease and the cultural effects of nursing home life. The experience of residing in a nursing home varies according to the particular nursing home and numerous individual factors of the residents. Many nursing homes are for temporary stays in which the individual recovers from a specific procedure or ailment and is then discharged. Nursing homes vary according to size, according to how they are funded, administrative ''culture'' (Shield 1997), current Medicare and Medicaid reimbursement criteria, the presence of special care units and so forth. Many nursing homes allow considerable resident autonomy, though others still do not. In addition, the reorganization of nursing home care due to funding and managed care changes is having a profound impact (see Shield 1996). All of these factors influence whether or not a sense of community is developed within the nursing home and the shape the particular community takes if it does develop.

This chapter seeks to explain the lack of community formation in one American long-term care facility, which was studied for a period of fourteen months between 1981 and 1983. The Franklin Nursing Home, located in the northeastern United States, is a nonprofit, long-term care facility for 250, primarily Jewish elderly who are unable to live on their own in the community.[1] This nursing home, considered to be a good one at the time of the study, enjoys higher staffing ratios, more recreational activities and better facilities than most. One-half to two-thirds of the nursing home residents, whose average age is 85, suffer from Alzheimer's disease or other dementing illnesses. They typically live in the nursing home for approximately four years. Most of the residents die there. Evidence of community was expected, because many of these old people knew each other before admission and are of similar ethnic background. Instead, they were found to be isolated and only superficially involved with each other.

Two factors in particular illuminate the study of communities of the aged. First, entering and living in a nursing home can be understood as a rite of passage: the individual leaves his or her old status behind (separation), enters a new world with like individuals (liminality) and eventually dies (reincorporation). Because there are no rites to accompany this particular passage, the individual undergoing the passage is solitary and unaided. The second issue is how individuals in the nursing home help each other or somehow contribute to the institution. This ability of people to give and take with each other, reciprocate with one another, is an important hallmark of community formation and needs to be considered here.

Here I argue that the residents are undergoing a rite of passage from adulthood in the community to death—their residence in the nursing home is part of an unresolved liminal phase; and their inability to contribute to each other and to the institution exacerbates their dependency and leads to their being considered children by staff members (see also Hockey and James 1993). This liminality is the result of, and in turn causes, a lack of coherence among staff members. Although most of the residents are Jewish, their differences from each other and their frailties are pronounced. The separation between the nursing home and the Harrison community in which it is located reflects an ambivalence by the community toward its institutionalized elderly. This situation exists despite the fact that many of the residents have relatives in the vicinity. In the following, I describe the factors which comprise this unresolved rite of passage and show how reciprocity is constrained. These processes prevent the formation of community.

RITES OF PASSAGE AND RECIPROCITY

Rites of passage and reciprocity are universal cultural forms that take on unique expression in the nursing home. In 1908, Arnold van Gennep's seminal *Les Rites de Passages* showed how rites of passage throughout the world have three parts: separation from the old status, transition (usually called "liminality") between the old role and the new role and reincorporation into the new role. The stages are made less stressful by the rituals that surround them. The liminal part of rites of passage is considered the most dangerous of the three segments because it is "neither one state nor the next" (Douglas 1966:116).[2]

The new initiate is also receptive to learning about his or her new role. As if stripped of all past knowledge, the initiate learns the basics of the new position which awaits him or her. Because rites of passage occur at moments of great anxiety, they are dramatic occasions, naturally or socially provided crises, when the person is most teachable. Tension is heightened by rites, and resolution is eagerly sought (Myerhoff 1982:113).

The anthropologist Victor Turner (1969) expanded the idea of liminality to refer to varied people and situations defined in neither one category of social identity nor another. He stressed the positive aspects of liminality and used the term ''communitas'' to describe the togetherness that initiates in a rite of passage often share with each other.

The aged individuals of the Franklin Nursing Home are also liminal. They have been separated from their statuses as productive adults in the community, and, not having died, they remain in the transition. However, their liminality is not marked by communitas. Instead of the nursing home helping the resident to prepare for the next stage, death, as in other rites of passage, the entire subject of death is avoided. Social and emotional withdrawal from the other residents is coupled with vigorous physical interventions that maintain life. Like other liminal states in other rites of passage, there is dependency and separation, but unlike other kinds of liminality, the dependency is not accompanied by teaching. Preparation for the next stage is actively discouraged; religion and ritual are minimal; involvement by the community is meager; and isolation is prevalent. There is little camaraderie or ceremonial notice to accompany this transition. These conditions are further described in ''Aspects of Liminality.'' Separation and loneliness, not community, result.

RECIPROCITY

To give and to receive are basic in human life. Reciprocal relations are crucial to power, choice and control. Because receiving and giving are cyclical and mutually indebting, humans are bound together. This inherent mutuality is aborted when one side always receives and the other always gives, and there is little or no opportunity for the receiver to repay the giver. Theorists have shown how reciprocity is important among the elderly.[3] Cross-cultural evidence has shown that elderly persons are able to maintain a fairly high status when they have something considered valuable by others in their society to exchange, whether it be customs, skills, historical knowledge, economic resources or in-heritances.

Because the residents of the nursing home are in the liminal part of the passage from adulthood to death, they are already dependent and vulnerable. Another layer of dependency is added because the residents receive care and the staff members dispense care. The lack of resources with which the residents can repay staff members reduces their control and increases their dependency.[4] Given this unequal power balance, staff-resident interactions take on particular forms.

DIVERGENT STAFF BELIEFS

In most rites of passage, there is general consensus regarding the purposes and processes of the rite in question. However, staff groups at this nursing home (administrators, nurses, social workers, aides and orderlies) have different perceptions about the nursing home, including: who the nursing home residents are, how the staff members should behave toward them and what their goals for the residents are (Shield 1988; Foner 1994). The lack of cohesion concerning these cultural constructions of nursing home life prevents the formation of community, encourages competition in staff and promotes isolation among the residents.

These three issues translate into contested bipolar assessments of "home versus hospital," "employees versus friends," "life versus quality of life" and "rehabilitation versus maintenance."

HOME OR HOSPITAL?

Some staff members insist that the nursing home is a "home." The maintenance man sharply retorted when I happened to refer to the place as an institution: "This is not an institution," he said, "This is a home."[5] Opposed to the notion of the nursing home as home is the idea that the nursing home is a hospital; thus medical dictates take over. Esther Marks was obese and had hypertension. On a shopping trip downtown she bought smoked meats, pickled herring and other foods of which her doctors disapproved. When she returned to the nursing home, she bragged about her purchases and announced her intention of eating them. The administrator of the home confiscated the foods. Staff members try to determine whether to allow behavior that is "bad" for the resident or insist on distasteful preventive measures which the residents hate. Did the resident have the right to behave as if she were in her own home, or must she conform to medically determined treatment as if she were in a hospital? Frequently, there is inconsistency and little consensus.

EMPLOYEES OR FRIENDS

The home-hospital dichotomy also influences the nature of staff-resident relationships. At times residents as well as staff members refer to themselves as a family or as friends.[6] However, the inequality of the relationships is paramount. Max Sager wanted to celebrate a milestone with the social worker, Fran Rubin, by sharing a glass of wine with her. She refused and he was disappointed with what he called her rigidity. Since Mr. Sager lives in the nursing home, he may have his glass of wine, but since the social worker works there, she may not. This distinction put Mr. Sager abruptly in "his place." While many staff members act "friendlike" to the residents, residents are more frequently reminded that staff members are employees first. Fingernail cleaning and chart completion take priority over talking or visiting with residents.

LIFE VERSUS QUALITY OF LIFE

The most important division occurs in the use of two slogans, which I call "life" and "quality of life." These two models of care embody the home-hospital dichotomy and stem from the medical model of preserving life and the social work model of advocacy. Nurses and doctors prescribe routines to preserve life at all costs, and social workers argue for more family and resident choice in life-preserving measures.

The resident-care conference is about to break up, but the doctor wants to talk about his decision to resuscitate Mrs. Kerman. Long before, she had specifically told him not to do anything extraordinary for her, "should anything happen." A social worker, Lisa, asks pointedly now, "And did you?" "Yes!" answers the doctor adamantly. Lisa scoffs, "I don't want you to be my doctor!" The doctor says that if someone told him explicitly right before a procedure that he or she didn't want extraordinary measures taken, then okay. He can live with that, with not doing anything. But in this case, there was a long time lag from when Mrs. Kerman first expressed her wish for no intervention until the crisis that called for intervention. What should he do when the patient cannot express her wishes then? The doctor says, deliberately using the double negative, that he didn't want to do nothing. Lisa says, "But you are deciding on her quality of life for her and that's not right." When Mrs. Kerman had told the doctor that she wanted nothing extraordinary done, she had also explained that she'd had a long and full life and that when the time came, she wanted to die. She is angry at the doctor now for what he has done, but the doctor is saying, "I don't think I did the wrong thing." The nurse, Bernice, says with disgust, "No one ever used to talk like this. In all my thirty years of nursing, there was never a question. Our job is to save lives!" She shakes her head at the social workers across the table and walks out. The meeting is over.

Social workers refer to the residents as residents; physicians and nurses, on the other hand, more often refer to residents as patients. While physicians and nurses are trained to preserve life whenever possible, social workers have a priority to improve the "quality of life" of the residents. The medical personnel regard life-saving decisions as automatic, but the social workers question them. For example:

The suitability of an operation to be conducted on a terminal cancer patient who is 87 years old was not questioned by some of the nurses, but was considered unsuitable by social workers. The nurses and the social workers could not understand the others' points-of-view in the matter, and they criticized each other accordingly.

Nurses and social workers also disagree about the appropriateness of cardiopulmonary resuscitation (CPR) in this setting. At times the discrepant points of view are irreconcilable.[7]

REHABILITATION VERSUS MAINTENANCE

The philosophy to rehabilitate residents competes with the ideology of maintaining people at their current function. This belief operates against the physical therapy program, whose explicit purposes are to improve the resident's ability to ambulate and to regain weakened or lost motor control. A stroke patient attended physical therapy three times a week and made steady progress. However, back on his floor, the nursing staff did not follow up with "range of motion" and other exercises.[8]

The effort to rehabilitate residents competes with the opposing notion that maintenance of residents at their current level of functioning is adequate. The divisions among the staff goals that have been described in this section prevent the smooth fulfillment of a team plan for nursing home residents. Two additional factors, described next, further complicate the picture. Residents are very different from each other (but are treated as a group), and much of the Jewish population of the city in which the nursing home is located avoids the nursing home residents in important ways.

HETEROGENEITY OF RESIDENTS

The Franklin Nursing Home cares for residents with varying degrees of neediness.[9] One group is comprised of those individuals who are extremely ill or debilitated. Many of these people are unable to fulfill any of their physical needs, but they may be capable of understanding and communicating. The second and largest group in the nursing home is comprised of those residents who are considered demented and may or may not be physically capable of certain activities. The final group consists of those residents who are considered the most physically and mentally capable. Each group has significant variety within it.

While these groups are fairly distinct and have quite separate needs, they are contained within the same institution and are often treated alike. Problems abound when the competing staff goals, described above, are added to the three different resident groups in the nursing home.

Ambivalence by Harrison Toward the Nursing Home

The fact that the Franklin Nursing Home is linked to and cut off from the Harrison community at the same time helps create liminality. Tension and cooperation alternate in the relationship between the neighboring hospital (where the Franklin Nursing Home residents are almost invariably hospitalized) and the Franklin Nursing Home. While the nursing and social worker staffs of the two institutions are separate, there is little communication between them. The hospital nurses misunderstand the nursing done at the nursing home to be inferior, custodial care, for example.[10]

The Jewish community behaves ambivalently toward the nursing home, too: Although supporting it financially, members of the community tend to avoid personal contact with residents.[11] There is no consensus on numerous decisions facing the future of the nursing home, and it has been difficult to secure a rabbi to come to the nursing home. The services and clinics provided in the nursing home decrease the need for the residents to secure those same services in the community so that dependency on the institution is ensured, and separation from the community is increased.

ASPECTS OF LIMINALITY

Thus far, I have presented certain background conflicts and pressures which exist in the nursing home and in Harrison that create the particular environment into which nursing home residents come to live their last years. They begin their last rite of passage, made more difficult than it might be because it is not aided by already socialized nursing home residents, by staff members of the nursing home, or by individuals from Harrison. Thus, this rite of passage accentuates the lonely aspects of liminality, and resolution is secured only by the physical fact of death.

Entering the nursing home is accomplished by a series of leave-takings: a home is relinquished; a driver's license is given up; various memberships lapse. Separation from a past status and from the mainstream of a community is a hallmark of rite of passage ceremonies. A sense of timelessness coupled with various rigid staff routines creates a unique institutional time. Other characteristics of nursing home liminality are dependency, the belief that old people are like children, the denial and avoidance of death and the lack of religious support and ritual within the nursing home.

TIME

Time is often described as endless or strange in liminal states, and in the nursing home time looms large. It seems unfillable and fraught with future perils. It needs to be broken up because days and weeks seem the same. Certain strategies allow residents to get through the days and the weeks, much like Jaber Gubrium (1975) describes ''passing time'' in his ethnography of Murray Manor.

Time is tracked by the secular calendar, by the Jewish calendar, by clock and by nursing shifts. Knowledge of what day it is is necessary to predict visits, telephone calls, outside doctor visits and events relevant to family members. Residents know staff time because it affects their lives directly. Many become anxious as they anticipate the change in shift.

The charge nurse on the third floor is describing how the atmosphere of the floor changes at about 2:30 in the afternoon. Many of the aides, orderlies and nurses are lolling around the nurses' station, some are already in their coats, and they're chatting with each other animatedly, appearing restless to go home. At the same time, the new shift is coming on, and there are greetings and personal catchings-up that go on between members of the two shifts. Various residents act more disturbed at this time; they appear restless; they repeat their questions with urgent frequency; they are less soothed by reassurances.

Much time is spent sleeping and watching television. Meals, activities, visits, telephone calls and other events further structure the day. Sicker residents are, to varying degrees, the passive recipients of routines performed on them by different staff members. Their attempts to alter staff schedules in their care meet with little success:

Mr. Allen came down the hall again, still in his bathrobe. "May I speak to a nurse, please?" he asked. No answer from the four personnel at the nurses' station. Two of them are charting; two others are in conversation with each other. After a few more tries, one of the nurses looks up and asks Mr. Allen what he wants. "May I please have my shower now?" he asks. The nurse explains that Ned, his orderly, is on his break now, and he will be having his shower later on in the afternoon. "You are not the only person Ned has to take care of, you know," she reminds the resident testily.

The management of time for these residents is more contingent on staff schedule, union-management negotiations and on staff whim than it is on the needs of the residents. "Will you take me to the bathroom, please?" asks Mrs. Behrenbaum. After she repeats this request quite loudly, an aide calls over to her, "I'm not your aide. Wait 'til Bertha comes back."

Contacts with family structure time, as well, particularly on weekends, when the time seems unbroken and long. Receiving or placing daily telephone calls is another way of marking time and filling it: "Is it time to call my daughter now?" Mrs. Deutsch, a somewhat confused resident, anxiously asks Sarah Zeldin, her competent neighbor. "No, dear," answers Mrs. Zeldin patiently. "You always call her after lunch. We haven't had lunch yet. I'll remind you. Don't worry."

Awareness of death and finality provides a prominent counterpoint to the other times at the Franklin Nursing Home, including the cyclical staff time of nursing shifts, the static time of every day being the same as every other, and secular and Jewish calendar time which helps create some anticipation of the future. Cognitively intact residents bluntly acknowledge their closeness to increasing disability and death. They say things such as: Well, we're all here to die. Or: Obviously, this is the last stop. Or: I hope I'll have a chance to pick some of your grapes, if I'm around in the fall, that is. Demented residents appear stuck in the present as their ability to both recall recent events and anticipate the future is impaired. Many of the Franklin Nursing Home residents see their fate clearly in the other residents around them. Residents witness their neighbors become sick, go to the hospital, and either die there, come back well enough to retake possession of their old rooms, or come back at a lower level of functioning. It is a reality that most of the residents acknowledge readily. One resident said: "At least I can still walk and talk. But if I have another heart attack, I might end up like him." Such observations create a time perception of "future peril"—that with each passing day, the risk of experiencing more deficits and of requiring increased care is greater and is witnessed continually in others. This time of future peril is fought by staff denial and cyclical nursing home routines. This contradiction intensifies rather than resolves the ambiguity of the liminality.

DEPENDENCY

Dependency is another marker of liminality. The subjects of rites of passage events are often acted upon by other members of the society. Enduring the transition promotes dependency. In the nursing home, residents guard the independence and evidence of autonomy that they still have, knowing that it is a time-limited, precious commodity. Measures of independence constitute a ranking system among individuals (Shield 1988).

Initiates in rites of passage ceremonies are made dependent by the event, but this dependency seems to have the purpose of preparing the initiates for the next stage. There are tasks and teachings which may be facilitated by the dependency. In the Franklin Nursing Home, however, the dependency is enforced by rules, enhanced by expectations and leads to more dependency.[12] Aides and orderlies do "people-work" duties (Goffman 1961) efficiently; rather than take time to help residents walk, eat or dress, aides and orderlies do these jobs for them. The rehabilitation that is attempted in physical therapy sessions loses ground to maintenance regimes on the residents' floors. Dependency that occurs in the nursing home is not inevitable, but by being expected, it is in part fostered by staff attitudes.

OLD PEOPLE AS CHILDREN

People undergoing rites of passage are often likened to children because they are ignorant about the new role into which they will be socialized. In the nursing home the old person is considered "like a child," "regressed" or "entering a second childhood." But if they are child-like, they are not taught here.

Residents at the Franklin Nursing Home are called by the diminutive versions of their names or by generic terms, such as "honey," "dearie," "sweetie" and so forth. "Good morning, honey," croons Aymara to the still-sleeping form in bed. "It's time to get up now, darling. Okay, sweetie? It's Tuesday, honey; time to get up." She turns to me and says, "Sometimes you have to baby them, you know." Most employees resist the social workers' preference that residents be called by their surnames.

The activities and events that the aged in this nursing home are supposed to enjoy are ones that children love: birthday parties are held monthly, and special outings include excursions to the zoo and the amusement park. One resident commented succinctly: "Whenever they go to the zoo, I don't bother to go. We used to live near the zoo when my children were little. I took them to the zoo every single week. I've had enough of the zoo."

Simple behaviors become evidence of dependencies, inabilities and childishness when framed by the nursing home environment. A person's verbal expressions and actions are ignored, trivialized, or become emblematic of other meanings not intended by the person. A request for something is likely to be interpreted as a complaint. Requests for individualized treatment may be understood as expressions of self-centered childishness:

"Tomato juice is the best part of my meal," Mrs. Zeldin says with satisfaction. When she tells the dietician that the kitchen has mistakenly sent the unsalted kind to her, the dietician denies the charge, implying that Mrs. Zeldin has made the mistake. They assume that she cannot tell the difference, and her complaint is not valid. She finds this occurrence frustrating.

Nonperson status is often reserved for use with children, and some of these behaviors are evident in the Franklin Nursing Home. For example, adults frequently talk to each other about their children as if they were not present. So, too, in the nursing home:

In the resident-care conference the staff members are talking about the resident who is present. The resident is unable to hear what is being said because she has some deafness. The resident interrupts the conversation and asks what is going on. Several staff members look surprised. In an exaggerated way, a staff member turns to face her, and speaks very slowly and loudly. After this statement, staff conversation returns to its previous quick-paced, low-decibel quality.

Sometimes the social worker refers to the resident as "mother" or "dad," when talking to the adult offspring, rather than as "your mother" or "your father." Like children, institutionalized elderly people are expected to enjoy being in each other's company automatically. Residents who do not get along with each other are regarded by many staff as childish.

Along with the perception that old people are like children is the denial of their sexuality. Sexual behavior such as masturbation or residents' appreciative comments about the opposite sex are often treated by staff as inappropriate, disgusting or amusing.

Mr. Bernstein is somewhat senile, and several of the orderlies on his floor have discovered that he has a vivid interest in talking about the females whom he sees. They egg him on, asking him what he thinks about this one, and that one. He is specific in his appraisal of those attributes on the women he admires and those he does not, and the orderlies listen, and giggle, and ask, "What about this one? How about her?"

Attempts to establish sexual relationships take on an adolescent quality as the couples scramble for privacy (in unlocked rooms) and as staff members and other residents view the relationships as illicit or ridiculous. Sadly, residents, too, seem to think that sexual behavior in people their age is inappropriate.

In mundane and myriad ways the residents are supervised. Decision making by residents is hindered by the perception that the residents are like children. While there is a residents' council with elected officials, it minimally influences the way the nursing home operates. Residents witness changes in administration, in policy and in staff, and their roles as passive recipients in the institution remain basically the same. The care that is provided the residents comes at the expense of considerable independence.

DEATH DENIAL

Although death looms at the residents constantly and is a subject they themselves discuss, staff members avoid the subject and cover it up whenever possible. While residents talk and joke freely about it, staff members seem repulsed: Mr. Wolf walked over to an aide in the dining room and said, "When I die, I'd like to be buried in Israel." The aide responded immediately, "Now, Mr. Wolf. We don't talk about dying here. We talk about living."

In other liminal situations one would expect active preparation for the next stage, including talk, but such preparation does not go on here.

Max Abel has been quite confused and isolated for some time. The physician asks if anything has precipitated his state. One nurse thinks he is depressed because of the death of his son-in-law with whom he was quite close. Another nurse does not think so; she thinks he does not know about the death. No one can agree whether he knows or does not know. The nurse says to the social worker that they had been told that they weren't supposed to say anything to the resident about the death. The social worker replies that they wanted the resident to learn the news from another relative. The nurse says that she thinks no one ever told him, and her understanding was that it should be kept from him. The issue is unresolved, and no one knows, first of all, whether he has been told, and second, whether he has the capacity to know, understand or remember being told.

Different beliefs about what the residents should know collide with discrepant information about the resident that the staff have. Another resident has been admitted to the nursing home from the hospital with cancer. He has been told about the diagnosis and the staff thinks he is depressed about the news. The social worker wants the resident and the staff to "deal with" the issue of his cancer explicitly. The nurses are not sure.

When a resident is about to die, most staff members seem to withdraw. As social and emotional supports from staff dwindle, medical props and life-prolonging interventions are fortified.[13] People's work goes on uninterrupted in its repetitive cycle. Nurses, aides and orderlies sometimes discuss the impending death in hushed tones that residents are not intended to hear. When the death finally occurs, the room is closed, the physician is called so the body may be "pronounced," the next of kin is notified, the personal effects are picked up and the body is taken away to the funeral home. Not all staff members agree with this procedure.[14] A social worker told me: "I was uncomfortable each time I saw how death was managed. All the residents are taken into the dining area, and the doors are closed. Mysteriously, two men in black suits appear on the floor with a stretcher between them. They take away the body, and five minutes after the residents have been taken into the dining area, they are let out again. No one ever says what just happened." Residents sometimes attempt to fight the predominant staff attitudes about death. On one occasion a resident organized a memorial service for a friend who had just died. He put notices up around the nursing home and was satisfied that he had expended the effort on his friend. Scoffing about the typical handling of death, he said: "When someone dies, it is as if the person never even existed. They pretend nothing has happened."

The pet therapy program Joel Savishinsky describes in Chapter 26 presents a contrasting approach. Volunteers and their pets provide a bridge to the residents to talk about memories, death and home. The pets seem to help residents and volunteers see common areas of interest between them.

The silence regarding death in the Jewish nursing home may be due to an Orthodox prohibition restricting talk about death, to death anxiety, or to Amoss's (1981) idea that the elderly are degraded as more associated with "nature" than with "culture,"[15] since they are close to death. The overall behavior contrasts sharply with how the hospice movement explicitly deals with death. Preparation for and acknowledgment of death might foster the development of transition-easing rituals that might spur the development of group solidarity and communitas. In rejecting talk of death, however, preparation and rituals are prevented.

The nursing home symbolically embodies the dangerous transition from adulthood to death. It is cut off, clearly bounded, and separated from "normal" life on the "outside." The nursing home residents, tainted as they are by their nearness to death, cannot spread it to those in the community because of the separation. The separation provides artificial safety to the Harrison community. People in the Harrison community and staff members in the Franklin Nursing Home make the nursing home resident into a category distinguishable from them as "other" (see also Fabian 1983). The separation is maintained, continuity is denied and the apparent danger of contamination made remote.

RELIGION IN THE NURSING HOME

More separation occurs within the realm of religion in the nursing home. While Jewishness is obvious among the residents—consisting of Yiddish expressions, jokes and folk wisdom; common historical experiences; a religious identity; values in education and skills of survival; a widely shared though often argued about commitment to Israel; and foods and other sensory customs that have provided continuity throughout their lives—there is little attempt to make Jewishness a vital part of daily life in the nursing home. Few of the very religious people in the nursing home attend the Orthodox services.[16] In order to achieve the proper quorum at the Orthodox early morning service held at the Franklin Nursing Home, several Orthodox men from the community join the half dozen nursing home residents for the service each day.

Few of the nursing home's staff are Jewish, and ignorance of Jewish customs and beliefs is widespread. Virtually no one on the staff understands or can speak Yiddish except for an expression or two. When staff members know a few words of Yiddish, however, they often use the words for instant rapport. For example, one of the residents offers the nurse a piece of chocolate he has received from his granddaughter. "Do I look like I need that?" laughs the nurse, trying to say no. "Just look at that tuchas [rear-end]."

Another problem concerns rivalries among the residents. Certain individuals are said to monopolize ritually important tasks. When honors are more fairly divided, however, there are complaints that the rituals are not performed properly.

When Ida Kanter was admitted, she noticed that there were no Friday evening candle-lighting ceremonies. When she talked to the social worker about it, the social worker suggested that the resident organize it, and she did. Mrs. Kanter remembers to procure the candlesticks, to put on a white tablecloth, and have wine glasses and wine available for the occasions. However, the fact that she is "de facto" in charge of the Shabbos candle ritual has made her the target of other residents who resent her position of assumed authority.

In all, an active Jewishness is not promoted or encouraged. Occasionally, a flicker of information about Jewish history or culture is exploited as the explanation of some heretofore baffling resident behavior. The fact that Jews were in concentration camps during World War II "explains" any reluctance by residents to wear identification bracelets now. These shortcuts to cultural and personal understanding rarely penetrate beyond or dissuade staff members from their original preconceptions. Since residents are not asked "how things were" or what meaning something has, staff members' beliefs about the residents need not be challenged or revised. The fervent debate that Barbara Myerhoff (1979) described among the Jews in their senior center does not go on here. Thus, there is no soil from which newly meaningful forms of formerly meaningful ritual can spring. Instead, the "chicken soup" Judaism of the nursing home acts as a thinly reminiscent shell of the real thing and fails to provide viable answers or to heal.

THE UNANSWERABLE QUESTIONS

Many of the residents have endured difficult lives and have been unable to devise satisfactory answers to the plaguing question, "Why me?" The setting of the nursing home offers no solace, even though some of the residents are bound together by similar experiences. For example, some of the children of the residents have married non-Jewish people or have divorced. Their parents have no good explanation for these events. More disturbing is the fact that numerous residents have outlived their children. The death of a child is considered a particularly harsh tragedy. Many of the residents believe themselves too old to still be living; it seems a cruel joke that a son or daughter of theirs should die from cancer, a car accident or a sudden heart attack. As Sally Falk Moore has written about the Chagga of Kilimanjaro, people expect an orderly timing about the succession of deaths:

Over the course of life, men see themselves moving place by place up the seniority ladder of the lineage. It is clear who is due to die next and who is to succeed him. When people die out of turn, that is something to be explained. It means that something has gone wrong in the order of things, and there may be witchcraft or curses to reckon with. (1978:33)

At the nursing home, people struggle for explanations to satisfy, but rarely succeed. Mr. Sager looks baffled as he describes how his perfectly healthy son "just died" one day at age 50. It does not make sense to continue a strange, day-to-day life in a nursing home for month after month and year after year, when it seems to be far past an appropriate time to die. One resident said, "Every day, I am surprised to wake up. 'Why didn't you take me last night, God?' I always ask Him." Residents do not have a ritualized or formal opportunity to discuss these inexplicable tragedies with each other. They may not know that they are not the only ones who have experienced these losses. Ritual, religion and the companionship of caring others would help.

THE LIMITS OF EXCHANGE: RESIDENTS AS RECIPIENTS

The final major factor which confronts the nursing home residents and inhibits the development of community in this setting is the constraint on reciprocity. Even though initiates in rites of passage ceremonies are the passive recipients of activities, behaviors and expectations by other members of the society, they are active because they overcome the obstacles of the passage and proceed to the next stage. Residents at the Franklin Nursing Home, on the other hand, have their basic needs provided and have no tasks to fulfill. Payment to their caregivers is indirect, whether it is paid by the resident or by Medicaid/Medicare, because it happens in two stages: the nursing home is paid, and the nursing home pays its employees. Residents have few, if any, resources to repay or otherwise affect those who provide the care. Their behaviors toward staff members have few consequences; they receive care, food, shelter and medical attention regardless of their actions. Residents who complain about the conditions trespass the moral rule of reciprocity: They should not complain since they have

no alternatives. Passivity is encouraged, and community formation has no incentive to survive.

The anthropological literature on aging documents the extensive network and
support systems that poor and disabled aged individuals construct for themselves
to fulfill their needs and help each other to survive (e.g., Hochschild 1973;
Becker 1980; Sokolovsky and Cohen 1978). When aged individuals have no
institutional provision for care, horizontal networks between the individuals
stretch among them and maintain themselves through reciprocity. But when care
proceeds vertically from staff to residents in the nursing home, there is no incentive for horizontal networks to evolve. On the contrary: There is reason for
the individual recipients of care to vie among each other for more services. Wax
(1962) has written:

One who observes the residents of such a home may be surprised at the relative absence
of friendships among people of similar status and years, isolated from family and friends.
Yet, friendships, as other human relationships, are built upon reciprocity and those who
lack possessions, strength and health have relatively little to exchange with each other.
What little they have might still be negotiable, except that in a home where the administration is in control of such great benefits in the form of food, shelter, social and medical
services . . . what can be given or gained from one's neighbor is minuscule.

RECIPROCITY AND CONTROL

Jeanie Schmit Kayser-Jones (1981) compared a Scottish nursing home with
an American nursing home and found that the residents in the Scottish nursing
home had more valuable things to exchange than did their American counterparts, and thereby had more control over their lives. Residents of the Franklin
Nursing Home are penalized twice. On the one hand, their inability to exchange
commodities deemed valuable by others leads to dependency on others for aid.
Acceptance of their dependent position and their demand for better services
make them seem like greedy children who deserve the fate of living their lives
in a nursing home. Conversely, attempts at independence and the refusal of staff
supports result in the resident being labeled "difficult." Staff members infantilize and resent the residents as a result.[17]

The actions of residents have few basic consequences. Their actions minimally affect the future and help create the timeless atmosphere of the nursing
home. For example, in the nursing home, recreational therapy fills time. While
some items made during these sessions decorate the institution and are admired,
and some of the other items are sold in the gift shop at the home, there is no
direct connection between the needlework that the residents do and the funds
that these items may procure. The contribution made by the residents seems
symbolic at most.

Many resent being the object of charity, understanding the gratitude and in-
feriority that are due in return. For this reason, some of the residents attempt to

limit the favors that others do for them. ''A resident would like to go downtown and window shop. But she has put it out of her mind because she would have to ask one of her relatives or one of the staff members to drive her. How could she pay back her debt to the person in that case? If she hears of someone going downtown, maybe then she'll ask to go along.''

The responsibility that staff members exhibit toward the residents is also reduced by the constraints on reciprocity. Because residents have little power and always receive, they must be grateful. The staff member's obligation is to his or her bureaucratic duties. Staff members can perform their duties superficially and impersonally; they can decide what behaviors are in the resident's best interests or not; they may allow a resident to wet himself or herself; they may not bother to peel the orange so that the resident can eat it; they may forget to take the resident for a walk outside. If the resident complains, those complaints underscore his or her childish inability to wait. Resentment caused by the caregiving exacerbates victimization of residents, entitlement by residents and increases the wedge between givers and receivers.

CONCLUSION: NO COMMUNITAS—A DIFFERENT LIMINALITY

As Victor Turner theorized in his work, communitas is an important and positive feature of liminal states. But, though existence in the Franklin Nursing Home is liminal, there is more isolation than communitas there. New admissions to the Franklin Nursing Home are effectively separated from their past lives in the Harrison community. But instead of the explicitly harrowing transition found in most rites of passage, the transition in the nursing home rite of passage is seen by staff members to be protected and tame. This perception belies the experience of the nursing home residents, whose passage is harrowing but unshared. As if separated from the ongoing rigors of life and from the deteriorating course of the body, the residents wait. The staff members believe the residents to be protected, but the residents have doubts and fears which they cannot express. There is no cultural, ritual resolution to the passage; it is resolved only by the physical fact of death.

Instead of communitas, residents stay by themselves and try to be good patients. Instead of the exuberance found in communitas, residents often distrust each other, compete with each other, and denigrate each other. There are no difficult tasks to undergo, and there seems little reason for the residents to bond together. Acknowledging that they share a similar fate, knowing that they all suffer from not having alternatives available outside the nursing home, referring to common Jewish customs, histories and holidays—the sharing is minimal, if present at all. The individuals' past lives are not considered relevant to the present by the residents. In the nursing home, references to the past are often interpreted as symptoms of incipient dementia and therefore frequently self-squelched.

The timelessness in the nursing home is very different from that described by Haim Hazan (1980; 1984). Hazan characterized the experience of the elderly in a Jewish day care center as "limbo" because of the paradoxical juxtaposition of two conflicting conceptions of time: a static time derived from the welfare system which gave benefits without repayment and a deteriorating time caused by the ailments experienced by the aged. Hazan shows how these elderly construct an "alternate reality" of time in which they care for each other and are shielded from the outside. Time in the Franklin Nursing Home, in contrast, betrays the certainty of how limited the time actually is for the residents. The time of future peril that intact residents perceive as their fate threatens the quality of resident relationships rather than enhances them. The residents interact superficially and guardedly. Communitas is unlikely to flourish where the present is benignly misrepresented as safe and timeless, the future is known to be uncertain and perilous, and residents serve as reminders of each person's present fragile security and future certain danger.

If, as in other rites of passage, there are rituals that explain and cushion the actors' situation to themselves, there will likely be more communitas and sharing among the residents. In the nursing home, however, staff members disagree about goals for the residents and avoid preparation for the next stage. Staff members splinter among themselves, and residents do likewise. Instead of adapting bits and pieces of old ritual to novel crises and conflicts as in the senior center Myerhoff described (1979), the lack of ritual and of communitas in the nursing home gives way to loneliness. Instead of the Jewish community joining together to forge a new integration of past values, present experiences and common anticipations about the future with the residents, it gives custodial care. If nurses and social workers discussed their differences, they might be able to create innovative approaches to caregiving. If staff members talked with residents about death when the subject came up, the residents might be aided in their preparations for death and might, in turn, help staff members alleviate their own fears about death.

Nursing homes are not all like this one, and nursing homes are changing. Depending upon the leadership of the nursing home, the training levels of the staff members, the values of the community members and the particular needs of the residents who are being served, nursing homes respond to their clientele in varied ways. Federal and state regulations have increased in recent years, nursing home reform has outlawed certain abuses, but public funding has been tightened. Regulations have improved nursing home care in many ways, focusing primarily on better medical care, training for nursing assistants, and resident rights. But no one can mandate better "caring" or attention to many of the issues raised here. These concerns remain critical ones.

The Franklin Nursing Home liminality contains no tasks that residents must fulfill. While learning and trials are the initiate's ticket to admission to the next phase in most rites of passage, nothing is expected of the nursing home residents in their passage here.

This nonreciprocity makes them ineligible for serious treatment as adult persons. Symbolic and concrete ways for the residents to contribute could be found for the nursing home population. However, nursing home residence at the Franklin Nursing Home in the early 1980s displayed a liminal state without communitas: a timeless state which ends when it ends. Unlike other transitions in which individuals can look forward to a new status where certain behaviors, activities and prestige will be expected of them, the residents in the nursing home receive forever. No requirement for reciprocity and little incentive for exchange join the death denial and conflict of staff members to comprise the lonely liminality experienced here. By equating the aged with children, the staff members transform the threat of death into the familiarity of nurturance. In this way, the nursing home residents are made both unthreateningly familiar, as children, and distantly "other," and staff members are relieved of identification with them. The danger inherent in the liminality is thus contained, and the transition for the residents is endless.

POSTSCRIPT

Many changes have befallen the Franklin Nursing Home since I first studied it in the early 1980s. The nursing home expanded ways to take care of the residents, adding adjunct medical services, such as optometry and dental services, for example. It provided educational programs for residents, staff and family members. It also devised a treatment and testing document that recorded residents' choices about how extensively they wanted to be treated in medical emergencies. To accompany this major advance in the respect of residents' rights, the nursing home also formed an ethics committee to discuss ethical issues on a regular basis (some of these cases are discussed in Shield 1995).

However, the nursing home was also beset with continuing problems which ultimately resulted in its closing in the early 1990s. Residents were moved to other nursing homes in the area and managed the transition very well overall. The closing had a major impact on the Jewish community, which responded by setting up various programs to provide Jewish outreach to Jews in all the nursing homes. A small staff—including a director, two part-time rabbis, a volunteer coordinator and others who develop programs, oversee a large group of Jewish community volunteers of all ages who together provide "yiddishkeit" (elements of Jewish culture and tradition), pastoral counseling and friendly visiting to the Jews who live in the area nursing homes. In some ways this program has revitalized the Jewish community's commitment to its elderly. The evolution of this program and the community's response to the nursing home's closing continues, but that would be another chapter.

NOTES

I wish to thank Stanley Aronson, M.D.; William O. Beeman, Ph.D.; George L. Hicks, Ph.D.; Lucile Newman, Ph.D.; and Jay Sokolovsky, Ph.D., for their helpful comments in the preparation of this paper.

1. All names in this paper are pseudonyms.

2. The notion of "double burial" (Hertz 1960) is relevant here.

3. As just one example, Dowd (1975) postulates that elderly persons in the United States are constrained to exchange compliance (in retirement, for example) for benefits related to pensions, old age assistance and social security. Because their control over social and economic resources decreases, compliance becomes the only thing left to exchange for continued security in the social system.

4. Notwithstanding these hindrances, the institutionalized elderly of the Franklin Nursing Home have innovative strategies which are more fully described elsewhere (Shield 1988).

5. Anecdotes throughout the paper, such as this one, come from the author's field-notes.

6. This observation has been noted in "helping" agencies such as mental health clinics (see, for example, Gubrium 1982). In such constructions, the real versus fictive family often depends on who "really" cares for the patient.

7. These and other similar questions were later discussed in the Ethics Committee in the early 1990s (Shield 1995).

8. These are simple exercises to stimulate muscles in arms and legs in order to improve strength and mobility of the limbs.

9. At the time of study, there were three Medicaid-mandated "levels of care," including residents in need of minimal nursing supervision, residents who required 24-hour nursing supervision and those who required skilled nursing care. These designations indicated the specific nursing procedures, such as intravenous feedings, the use of catheters and the like.

10. This belief is different than the reality. Geriatric nursing requires extensive, specialized knowledge and experience. Syndromes manifest themselves differently in aged patients than in middle-aged ones; psychosocial issues are different; many procedures, such as finding veins on aged patients to do bloodwork, require an exactness not necessary for younger patients.

11. In 1985, when there was a strike at the Franklin Nursing Home, community volunteers were numerous and devoted, however. The crisis brought the nursing home and the Jewish community closer to each other.

12. For example, residents are not allowed to bathe themselves. Ambulatory residents are not allowed to push their neighbors' wheelchairs because of insurance and governmental regulations.

13. The social and emotional withdrawal exemplified by these behaviors could be subsumed under Glascock's "death-hastening behaviors," discussed in Chapter 3 this volume.

14. To a considerable degree, the social workers struggle against the conspiratorial silence that surrounds the residents regarding death. The nursing home has recently made some changes in the handling of death, such as notifying residents and holding memorial ceremonies.

15. Where elderly persons do possess skills considered valuable by others, they are perceived as closer to culture rather than to nature; they thereby avoid the association to death and retain prestige. See also: Greene (1980); Fleming and Brown (1983).

16. Residents in need of assistance may be prohibited from coming to services because of insufficient staff on the floors.

17. Whereas Kayser-Jones (1981) has stated that staff resentment of their lowly status in American nursing homes encourages them to dehumanize and infantilize the residents, it seems to me that processes of infantilization and victimization in the nursing home have more to do with residents' liminality, compounded by their inability to reciprocate.

CHAPTER 26

Understanding Life Backwards

Joel Savishinsky

The image of old age in the modern age is a fairly dismal one. A nurse at an institution where I once volunteered complained that the process of getting old is reduced in the popular mind "to the 3-Ds of decline, depression, and death." For years now, her words, and the image she decried, have haunted me. With my students, I have been trying to make sense out of how our society defines the nature of late life.

As an anthropologist, I am supposed to study myths, not live by them. But an anthropologist without myths would be a person without a culture and, as an American, I have been raised on the myths that shape my own society. To many of my compatriots, old age is joyless and terrible, and nursing homes only make a bad situation worse. They are seen as the last resort of those who can no longer help themselves. In the apparent uselessness of one's later years, such institutions symbolize rejection, and they sometimes rub the salt of neglect into the moral wounds of marginality. This sad, spoiled picture of late life contrasts with the equally extreme myth of the Golden Age of old age, a once-hallowed but now suspect image. The imagination of our culture has transformed the old dream into a new nightmare.

Both literature and the social sciences have provided some of the substance on which this new image feeds. Novels, poems, and dramas portray the desperation of the aged, the indifference of some who could help them, the frustrations of others who try. With less vividness but more detail, researchers have tried to record the realities of older people living in their own communities, as well as those who lack the grace of independence and must make their home in an institution.

The imaginative and scholarly results often have a tragic ring. Disembodied and dessicated images pervade our poetry. Eliot's Gerontion is "an old man in a dry month," living like a "dull head among windy spaces." For Yeats, "An aged man is but a paltry thing,/A tattered coat upon a stick." Shakespeare, parading the seven ages of man across the world's stage, declares the "Last scene of all,/That ends this strange eventful history,/Is second childishness and mere oblivion;/Sans teeth, sans eyes, sans taste, sans everything."

Social scientists who look at the aged have tried to see them as flesh and blood and spirit rather than as mere metaphor. One of the earliest accounts of nursing homes was given in Jules Henry's *Culture Against Man* (1963), a book which describes a process of "pathogenic metamorphosis" through which elderly patients were transformed into animals, objects, and other sub-human forms by repeated degradation. A much more benign picture of institutional life was Jaber Gubrium's *Living and Dying at Murray Manor* (1975), a study which nevertheless detailed how isolated administrative "top staff" could be from the "floor staff" who actually gave care to the elderly.

One of the most personal accounts ever written of institutional existence was Carobeth Laird's *Limbo* (1979). Written by an 81-year-old anthropologist who was placed—involuntarily—in a private Arizona facility, the book bears the pointed subtitle, "A Memoir of Life in a Nursing Home by a Survivor." Laird watched with dismay as her independence, assertiveness, and identity dissolved under the regime of patronizing treatment to which she and her peers were subjected. Though she was eventually rescued by friends who took her into their own home, this was only after Laird had nearly lost all sense of hope and self. At one point, she later wrote, she even refused to join a day-trip to a nearby zoo because "I felt too much like a caged animal to enjoy looking at other caged animals."

Unlike Laird, my own connections to both nursing homes and animals have been mercifully more positive. I got involved studying geriatric facilities, in fact, because I had once driven dogteams in the Canadian Arctic, where I travelled extensively among native people leading a hunting, fishing, and trapping way of life. The mutual dependence I observed there between Indian families and their dogteams got me interested in not just the technical, but also the emotional role of domestic animals in other cultures. Several years after I left the North, Cornell's Veterinary College began a series of pet therapy programs in upstate nursing homes, and I agreed to examine and evaluate the impact of these efforts. It was a chance to study a new form of domesticity.

Three of my students and I began this project by visiting the geriatric institutions each week with our own or borrowed animals. We found that the pets not only had many unintended effects on the elderly, but that the nursing homes themselves were a complex and subtle world of their own. At Elmwood Grove, the facility I became most deeply involved in for the next seven years, I came to appreciate how patients, caregivers, and families were caught up in contradictory attitudes toward mortality and morality, silence and touch, altruism and intimacy, and caring and curing. In my book *The Ends of Time: Life and Work in a Nursing Home* (1991), I describe what I learned at Elmwood from the residents, staff, visitors, and volunteers whose lives converged there.

One lesson was the power of animals to break the grip in which silence held the elderly. As symbols of a lost domesticity, pets triggered stories and memories of childhood, families, farm work, and children. Residents who would have been stigmatized for talking to themselves about these topics could talk with impunity to the animals. Many patients soon moved past the pets, however, and attached themselves to the volunteers who had brought them: residents proved to be as hungry for human companionship as for that of animals. This surprised many of the volunteers, who had originally thought of themselves simply as "transporters of pets," as secondary actors in a supportive role; but the elderly placed many visitors at center stage, casting them as members of their "new" or their "real family." The patients' domestic message was impossible to miss. Some volunteers welcomed it as a sign of an unexpected intimacy, an acknowledgement of value they had not anticipated. But others backed away from the demands that the very word "family" implied, finding the expectations for regular support and personal attention to be more than they had bargained for.

Conversations with residents covered a broad spectrum of topics, two of the most compelling being mortality and morality. The pets in the room, for example, were commonly associated by patients with long-lived animals they had once owned; their proud remarks about canine and feline longevity were an indirect means of expressing both the benefits of good care and their long-term hopes for themselves. Anxieties about death could be voiced through the same medium. An elderly couple who lived at Elmwood liked to share bittersweet memories of a brother-and-sister pair of cats they had kept for eighteen years. They told how the brother had passed away within a week of his sibling's death, a sequence that reflected the intensity of this couple's own relationship and their fears about its indissoluble bonds.

The moral tenor of residents' remarks often blended praise and condemnation with humor. One woman lauded her sister and brother-in-law for taking her collie when she had to enter Elmwood. But on another occasion, reflecting on the same events, she decided that they had "kept the dog but got rid of me." A different resident, who had suffered the death of several roommates within just one year, speculated that a solitary goldfish she had been keeping in her room might have died from the same loneliness she was enduring. But on a later occasion, settled in with a friendly new roommate, she joked: "You know, I used to talk to that fish all the time. Not that she answered, but, I think I talked her to death."

Finally, there were things that could not be said and acts that were hard to perform—the words lost in the silence of dementia or withdrawal, the moments of touch which failed to occur because of cultural taboo. It was difficult for staff and visitors to simply *be* with residents without benefit of conversation and where words failed, to reach out physically to those who could not be reached in other ways. I realized that what the chronically ill elderly sometimes needed was the simple laying on of hands and a silent being together—means of communion and communication that Americans find uncomfortable, but which need to be learned if we are to enter the place that is now the world of the old. The pets were not a panacea, but the quiet, tactile presence helped to bridge the chasm between the frail aged and those who could care for, but not cure them.

Understanding the elderly does not take exceptional skill—it does require the will to share part of the common and everyday quality of their lives. For readers who want to enter that realm in print before facing it in the flesh, there are some wonderful books: May Sarton's moving novel of nursing home life, *As We Are Now* (1982); M. F. K. Fisher's memoir *Sister Age* (1983), which tells the tales of the old people she has known; *Number Our Days* (1978) by Barbara Myerhoff, in which aging Jewish immigrants speak of their passions and disappointments; Florida Scott-Maxwell's candid diary of her own life, *The Measure of My Days* (1991); and Ronald Blythe's eloquent *The View in Winter* (1979) are literate and rich experiences. They each give older people a voice and vision of their own, gifts our culture rarely bestows on them. Collectively, they bear out Kierkegaard's insight that while life is lived forward, it is often understood backward.

NOTE

This chapter is reprinted with permission from *The Bookpress* 2(1) (1992): 11, 15.

Bibliography

Aalen, F. H. A. 1967. "Rural Surveys and the Role of Local Development Associations. A Case Study in West Wicklow." *Administration*: 109–127.

Aalen, F. H. A., D. A. Gilmore and D. Williams. 1966. *West Wicklow: Background for Development*. Department of Geography, Trinity College.

AARP. 1995. "The Effect of Welfare Reform on Grandparents Raising Grandchildren." *Parenting Grandchildren* 1(4):4–5.

———, 1996. "The Trend Continues . . .". *Parenting Grandchildren* 2(2):1–2.

Abe, I., N. Zane and K. Chun. 1994. "Differential Responses to Trauma: Migration-Related Discriminants of Post-Traumatic Stress Disorder among Southeast Asian Refugees." *Journal of Community Psychology* 22:121–135.

Abel, E. 1990. "Family Care of the Frail Elderly." In *Circles of Care:Work and Identity in Women's Lives*. E. Abel and M. Nelson, eds. Albany: State University of New York Press.

Abel, E. and A. Sankar, eds. 1995. "Qualitative Methodology." Special Issue of *Research on Aging* 17(1).

Abraham, D. 1989. "Reaching Elderly Abandoned Citizens Housebound." In *Aging, Demography and Well-being in Latin America*. M. D. Alvarez, O. von Mering and K. Tout, eds. Gainesville, FL: Center for Gerontological Studies.

Abu, K. 1983. "The Separateness of Spouses: Conjugal Resources in an Ashanti Town." In *Female and Male in West Africa*. C. Oppong, ed. London: Allen & Unwin.

Achenbaum, W. A. 1982. "Further Perspectives on Modernization and Aging." *Social Science History* 6(3):347–368.

———. 1994. "U.S. Retirement in Historical Context." In *The Columbia Retirement Handbook*. A. Monk, ed. New York: Columbia University Press.

Acosta, F. X. 1982. "Group Psychotherapy with Spanish-Speaking Patients." In *Mental Health and Hispanic Americans*. R. Becerra, M. Karno and J. Escobar, eds. New York: Grune & Stratton.

Adams, F. 1972. "The Role of Old People in Santo Thomas Mazaltepec." In *Aging and*

Modernization. D. O. Cowgill and L. D. Holmes, eds. New York: Appleton-Century-Crofts.

Adams, P. and G. Dominick. 1995. "The Old, the Young, and the Welfare State." *Generations* 19:38–42.

Ageing International. 1994. "Caregiver Burnout." *Ageing International* 21:2:7–8.

Akiyama, H. 1984. "Resource Exchanges in Dyadic Family Relations in the U.S. and Japan: Towards a Theory of Dependence and Independence of the Elderly." Ph.D. dissertation. University of Illinois at Urbana–Champaign.

Al-Issa, I. 1982. *Culture and Psychopathology*. Baltimore: University Park Press.

Albert, S. M. 1987. "The Work of Marriage and of Death: Ritual and Political Process among the Lak." Unpublished dissertation, The University of Chicago.

———. 1995. "New Perspectives on the Elderly: Epidemiology and Public Health." *Current Issues in Public Health* 1:77–81.

Albert, S. M. and M. G. Cattell. 1994. *Old Age in Global Perspective: Cross-Cultural and Cross-National Views*. New York: G. K. Hall.

Alexander, B., R. Rubinstein, M. Goodman and M. Luborsky. 1991. "Generativity in Cultural Context: The Self, Death and Immortality as Experienced by Older American Women." *Aging and Society* 11:417–442.

Algin, D. A. and M. Hood, eds. 1987. *The Cambodian Agony*. Armonk, NY: M. E. Sharpe.

Allen, J. and A. Pifer, eds. 1993. *Women on the Front Lines: Meeting the Challenge of an Aging America*. Washington, DC: Urban Institute Press.

Almeida, A. D. 1965. *Bushmen and Other Non-Bantu Peoples of Angola: Three Lectures*. Johannesburg: Witwatersrand University Press.

Altergott, K. 1988. *Daily Life in Later Life: Personal Conditions in a Comparative Perspective*. Newbury Park, CA: Sage.

Amann, A., ed. 1980. *Open Care for the Elderly in Seven European Countries*. Oxford: Pergamon Press.

American College of Physicians, Health and Public Policy Committee. 1988. "Comprehensive Functional Assessment for Elderly Patients." *Annals of Internal Medicine* 109:70–72.

American Geriatrics Society, Ethnogeriatrics Advisory Committee. 1996. "A Position Paper From the American Geriatrics Society." *Journal of the American Geriatrics Society* 44(3):326–328.

American Medical Association. 1990. Council on Ethical and Judicial Affairs: Council Report. "Black-White Disparities in Health Care." *Journal of the American Medical Association* 263(17):2344–2346.

Amin, S. 1976. *Unequal Development*. New York: Monthly Review Press.

Amoss, P. 1981. "Cultural Centrality and Prestige for the Elderly: The Coast Salish Case." In *Dimensions: Aging, Culture, and Health*. C. Fry, ed. Brooklyn: J. F. Bergin.

———. 1986. "Northwest Coast Grandmother Myths." Unpublished paper presented in the session, American Indian Grandmothers II, of the 84th Annual Meeting of the American Anthropological Association, Philadelphia.

Amoss, P. and S. Harrell, eds. 1981. *Other Ways of Growing Old: Anthropological Perspectives*. Stanford: Stanford University Press.

Anderson, B. 1972. "The Process of Deculturation—Its Dynamics Among United States Aged." *Anthropological Quarterly* 45(4):209–216.

————. 1990. *First Fieldwork—the Misadventures of an Anthropologist*. Prospect Heights, IL: Waveland Press.

Anderson, I. and J. Weibull. 1973. *Swedish History in Brief.* Stockholm: The Swedish Institute.

Anderson, J. et al. 1993. "An Acculturation Scale for Southeast Asians." *Social Psychiatry and Psychiatric Epidemiology* 28:134–141.

Anderson, R. T. and B. Anderson. 1964. *The Vanishing Village—A Danish Maritime Community.* Seattle: University of Washington Press.

Andresen, G. 1995. *Caring for People with Alzheimer's Disease.* Baltimore, MD: Health Professions Press.

Andrews, G., A. Esterman, A. Braunack-Mayer and C. Rungie. 1986. *Aging in the Western Pacific. A Four-Country Study.* Geneva: World Health Organization.

Angrosino, M. 1976. "Anthropology and the Aged." *Gerontologist* 162:174–180.

Anmie, T. 1993. "Managing the Transition from a Family to a Community Oriented Support System in Japan." In *Aging in Place with Dignity.* L. Heumann and D. Boldy, eds. Westport, CT: Praeger.

Anonymous. 1866. *Luke Darnell, The Chicago Newsboy.* Chicago: Tomlinson Brothers.

Ansell, E. and N. Eustis. 1992. *Aging and Disabilities: Seeking Common Ground.* Amityville, NY: Baywood.

Antonucci, T. C. 1985. "Personal Characteristics, Social Networks and Social Behavior." In *Handbook of Aging and the Social Sciences.* R. H. Binstock and E. Shanas, eds. New York: Van Nostrand Reinhold Co.

————. 1990. "Social Support and Social Relationships." In *Handbook of Aging and the Social Sciences.* R. H. Binstock and L. George, eds. San Diego: Academic Press, Inc.

Antonucci, T. C. and H Akiyama. 1987. "Social Networks in Adult Life and a Preliminary Examination of the Convoy Model." *Journal of Gerontology* 42(5):519–527.

————. 1995. "Convoys of Social Relations: Family and Friendships Within a Life Span Context." In *Handbook of Aging and the Family.* R. Blieszner and V. Bedford, eds. Westport, CT: Greenwood Press.

Antonucci, T. C. and J. S. Jackson. 1987. "Social Support, Interpersonal Efficacy, and Health: A Life Course Perspective." In *Handbook of Clinical Gerontology.* L. L. Carstensen and B. A. Edelstein, eds. New York: Pergamon Press.

Apt, N. 1991. "Elderly Women's Economic Participation: Problems and Prospects in Africa." *Bold* 2(1):31.

Apt, N. and S. Katila. 1994. "Gender and Intergenerational Support: The Case of Ghanaian Women." *South African Journal of Gerontology* 3(2):23–29.

Arens, D. 1982. "Widowhood and Well-being: An Examination of Sex Differences Within a Causal Model." *Aging and Human Development* 15:27–40.

Arensberg, C. 1968. *The Irish Countryman.* New York: Macmillan.

Arensberg, C. and C. T. Kimball. 1968. *Family and Community in Ireland.* Cambridge, MA: Harvard University Press.

Ariyoshi, S. 1972. *Kōkutsu no Hito.* Tokyo: Shinchōsha. *The Twilight Years.* English trans. 1984. M. Tahara, trans. New York: Kōdansha International.

Arnoff, F., H. Leon and I. Lorge. 1985. "Cross-Cultural Stereotypes Toward Aging." *The Journal of Social Psychology* 5:41–58.

Aronson, M., ed. 1994. *Reshaping Dementia Care: Practice and Policy in Long-Term Care.* Thousand Oaks, CA: Sage.

Asahi TV. 1993. "Uchi de shinitai" [I Want to Die at Home]. TV documentary.

Aschenbrenner, J. 1975. *Lifelines: Black Families in Chicago.* New York: Holt, Rinehart & Winston.

Asis, M. M. B. et al. 1995. "Living Arrangements in Four Asian Countries: A Comparative Perspective." *Journal of Cross-Cultural Gerontology* 10:145–162.

Avlund, A., M. Luck and R. Tinsley, 1996 "Cultural Differences in Functional Ability Among Elderly People in Birmingham, England and Glostrup, Denmark." *Journal of Cross-Cultural Gerontology* 11(1):1–16.

Baldock, J. and A. Evers. 1992. "Innovations and Care of the Elderly: The Cutting-edge of Change for Social Welfare Systems. Examples from Sweden, the Netherlands, and the United Kingdom." *Ageing and Society* 12:289–312.

Ball, M. and F. Whittington. 1995. *Surviving Dependence: Voices of Elderly African American Elders.* Amityville, NY: Baywood.

Banner, L. 1992. *In Full Flower: Aging Women, Power and Sexuality.* New York: Knopf.

Barker, J. C. 1984. *Niue's Health Services: A Personal View.* Technical Report for Dr. H. T. Nemaia, QSO, Director of Health, Niue. Medical Anthropology Program, University of California, San Francisco.

———. 1985. "Social Organization And Health Services For Preschool Children On Niue Island, Western Polynesia." Ann Arbor, MI: University Microfilms.

———. 1988. "Admission of Geriatric Patients to Hospital on Niue Island, 1977–1982." *New Zealand Medical Journal* 101:638–640.

———. 1989. "Health and Functional Status of the Elderly in a Polynesian Population." *Journal of Cross-Cultural Gerontology* 4:163–194. (Erratum: Journal of Cross-Cultural Gerontology 9 [1994]:419.)

———. 1990. "Between Humans and Ghosts: The Decrepit Elderly in a Polynesian Society." In *The Cultural Context on Aging: Worldwide Perspectives.* J. Sokolovsky, ed. New York: Bergin & Garvey.

———. 1994. "Home Alone: The Effects of Out-migration on Niuean Elders' Living Arrangements and Social Support." *Pacific Studies* (September):17(3):41–81.

Barker, J. C. and L. S. Mitteness. 1990. "Invisible Caregivers in the Spotlight: Non-kin Caregivers of Frail Older Adults." In *The Home Care Experience: Ethnography and Policy.* J. Gubrium and A. Sankar, eds. Newbury Park, CA: Sage.

Barker, J. C., J. Morrow, and L. Mitteness. Forthcoming. "Gender, Informal Social Support Networks, and Elderly Urban African-Americans." *Journal of Aging Studies.*

Barnett, H. 1955. *The Coast Salish of British Columbia.* Eugene: University of Oregon.

Barresi, C. M. 1992. "The Impact of Ethnicity on Aging: A Review of Theory, Research, and Issues." Presentation at the American Society on Aging Conference on March 15, 1992, San Diego, CA.

———. 1997. "Ethnogerontology: Social Aging in National, Racial, and Cultural Groups." In *Gerontology: Perspectives and Issues*, 2nd ed. K. Ferraro, ed. New York: Springer.

Barresi, C. M. and D. Stull, eds. 1993. *Ethnic Elderly and Long-Term Care.* New York: Springer.

Barrow, G. 1992. *Aging, the Individual, and Society.* St. Paul, MN: West Publishing Company.

Bart, P. 1969. "Why Women's Status Changes in Middle Age: The Turn of the Social Ferris Wheel." *Sociological Symposium* 3:1–18.

Bass, D. M. and L. S. Noelker. 1987. "The Influence of Family Caregivers on Elders' Use of In-Home Services: An Expanded Conceptual Framework." *Journal of Health and Social Behavior* 28:184–196.

Bass, S. 1995. *Older and Active: How Americans Over 55 Are Contributing to Society.* New Haven, CT: Yale University Press.

Bass, S. and F. Caro. Forthcoming. "The Economic Value of Grandparent Assistance." *Generations.*

Bass, S. and M. Oka. 1995. "An Older-Worker Employment Model: Japan's Silver Human Resource Centers." *Gerontologist* 35(5):679–682.

Bateson, G. 1950. "Cultural Ideas About Aging." In *Research on Aging.* E. P. Jones, ed. Berkeley: University of California Press.

Baxter, P. T. and U. Almagor, eds. 1978. *Age, Generation and Time.* London: Hurst.

Beall, C., ed. 1982. "Biological Perspectives on Aging." Special Issue of *Social Science and Medicine* 16(2).

————. 1987. "Studies of Longevity." In *The Elderly as Modern Pioneers.* P. Silverman, ed. Bloomington: Indiana University Press.

Beall, C. and M. Goldstein. 1981. "Modernization and Aging: Views from the Rural, Pre-Industrial Hinterland in Nepal." *Journal of Cross-Cultural Gerontology* 40(1):48–55.

————. 1986. "Family Change, Caste and the Elderly in a Rural Locale in Nepal." *Journal of Cross-Cultural Gerontology* 1(3):305–316.

Beaubier, J. 1976. *High Life Expectancy on the Island of Paros, Greece.* New York: Philosophical Library.

Becker, G. 1980. *Growing Old in Silence* Berkeley: University of California Press.

Bedford, R. D., G. Mitchell and M. Mitchell. 1980. "Population History." *1976 Census Of Population And Housing, Niue. Volume 2: Analysis Of Demographic Data.* Alofi, Niue: Department of Justice.

Bednar, M. 1974. *Architecture for the Handicapped: Denmark, Sweden and Holland.* Ann Arbor: University of Michigan Press.

Befu, H. 1986. "Gift-giving in Modern Japan." In *Japanese Culture and Behavior.* T. S. Lebra and W. P. Lebra, eds. Honolulu: University of Hawaii Press.

Belgrave, L., M. Wykle and J. Choi. 1993. "Health, Double Jeopardy, and Culture: The Use of Institutionalization by African-Americans." *The Gerontologist* 33:382.

Benedict, R. 1946. *The Chrysanthemum and the Sword.* Boston: Houghton Mifflin.

Benet, S. 1974. *Abkhasians: The Long-living People of the Caucasus.* New York: Holt, Rinehart and Winston.

Bengtson, V. 1996. "Continuities and Discontinuities in Intergenerational Relationships Over Time." In *Adulthood and Aging: Research on Continuities and Discontinuities.* V. Bengtson, ed. New York: Springer.

Bengtson, V. and L. Greenwell. Forthcoming. "Families, Poverty and the Changing Contract Between Generations." In *Changing Families and Childhood.* W. Edelstein et al., eds. Berlin: Walter de Gruyter and Co.

Bengtson, V. and L. Morgan. 1987. "Ethnicity and Aging: A Comparison of Three Ethnic Groups." In *Growing Old in Different Societies: Cross-Cultural Perspectives.* J. Sokolovsky, ed. Acton, MA: Copley.

Berardo, F. 1970. "Survivorship and Social Isolation: The Case of the Aged Widower." *Family Coordinator* 19:11–25.

Berkman, L. F. 1985. "The Relationship of Social Networks and Social Support to Morbidity and Mortality." In *Social Support and Health*. S. Cohen and S. L. Syme, eds. New York: Academic.

Bernardi, B. 1985. *Age Class Systems*. London: Cambridge.

Bethel, D. L. 1992. "Life on Obasuteteyama." In *Japanese Social Organization*. T. S. Lebra, ed. Honolulu: University of Hawaii Press.

Bever, E. 1982. "Old Age and Witchcraft in Early Modern Europe." In *Old Age in Preindustrial Society*. P. Sterns, ed. New York: Holmes and Meier.

Beyene, Y. 1989. *From Menarche to Menopause: Reproductive Lives of Peasant Women in Two Cultures*. Albany: State University of New York Press.

Bialik, R. 1992. "Family Care of the Elderly in Mexico." In *Family Care of the Elderly*. J. Kosberg, ed. Newbury Park, CA: Sage.

Biesele, M. and N. Howell. 1981. "The Old People Give You Life." In *Other Ways of Growing Old*. P. Amoss and S. Harrell, eds. Stanford, CA: Stanford University Press.

Billingsley, A. 1990. "Understanding African-American Family Diversity" In *The State of Black America 1990*. National Urban League, ed. New York: National Urban League.

Binstock, R. 1993. "Health Care Costs Around the World: Is Aging a Fiscal 'Black Hole'?" *Generations* (Winter): 37–42.

Binstock, R., L. Cluff and O. von Mering, eds. 1996. *The Future of Long-Term Care: Social and Policy Issues*. Baltimore: Johns Hopkins University Press.

Binstock, R. and L. K. George, eds. 1996. *Handbook of Aging and the Social Sciences*. San Diego: Academic Press.

Blakemore, K. 1989. "Does Age Matter? The Case of Old Age in Minority Groups." In *Becoming and Being Old: Sociological Approaches to Later Life*. B. Bytheway, T. Keil, P. Allat and A. Bryman, eds. Thousand Oaks, CA: Sage.

Blakemore, K. and M. Boneham, eds. 1994. *Age, Race and Ethnicity: A Comparative Approach*. Philadelphia: Open University Press.

Bleek, D. F. 1928. *The Naron: A Bushman Tribe of the Central Kalahari*. Cambridge, MA: Cambridge University Press.

Blieszner, R. and V. H. Bedford, eds. 1995. *Handbook of Aging and the Family*. Westport, CT: Greenwood Press.

Blume, L., N. Persily and J. Mintzer. 1992. "The Prevalence of Dementia: The Confusion of Numbers." *The American Journal of Alzheimer's Care and Related Disorders & Research* (May/June):3–11.

Blythe, R. 1979. *The View in Winter: Reflections on Old Age*. New York: Harcourt Brace Jovanovich.

Boise, L. 1991. "Family Care of the Aged in Sweden." *Viewpoint Sweden* 3:1–5. New York: Swedish Information Service.

Borman, L. 1983. "Self-Help Groups, Professionals, and the Redefinition of Pathological States." In *Clinical Anthropology: A New Approach to American Health Problems*. D. Shimkin and P. Golde, eds. Lanham, MD: University Press of America.

Borsch-Supan, A. 1994. "Aging in Germany and the United States: International Comparisons." In *Studies in the Economics of Aging*. D. A. Wise, ed. Chicago: University of Chicago Press.

Boserup, E. 1970. *Woman's Role in Economic Development*. New York: St. Martin's Press.

Bourdieu, Pierre. 1977. *Outline of a Theory of Practice*. Cambridge: Cambridge University Press.

Bowlby, J. 1980. *Attachment and Loss, III: Loss: Sadness and Depression*. New York: Basic.

Bowles, S., D. M. Gordon and T. E. Weiskopf. 1990. *After the Waste Land: A Democratic Economics for the Year 2000*. Armonk, NY: M. E. Sharpe, Inc.

Braun, K., J. Takamura and T. Mouget. 1996. "Perceptions of Dementia, Caregiving, and Help-seeking Among Recent Vietnamese Immigrants." *Journal of Cross-Cultural Gerontology* 11(1):213–228.

Bradsher, J. 1997. "Older Women and the Experience of Widowhood." In *Handbook on Women and Aging*. J. Coyle, ed. Westport, CT: Greenwood.

Bretall, R. 1951. *A Kierkegaard Anthology*. Princeton: Princeton University Press.

Brink, T., ed. 1992. "Hispanic Aged Mental Health." Special issue of *Clinical Gerontologist* 11(3/4).

Brinslow, P. 1995. *Alien Nation*. New York: Random House.

Brody, E. M. 1985. "Parent Care as a Normative Family Stress." *Gerontologist* 25(1): 19–29.

————. 1990. *Women in the Middle: Their Parent-Care Years*. New York: Springer.

Brody, E. M., P. T. Johnson, M. C. Fulcomer and A. M. Lang. 1983. "Women's Changing Roles and Help to Elderly Parents: Attitudes of Three Generations of Women." *Journal of Gerontology* 38(5):597–607.

Brody, E. M., M. H. Kleban, M. P. Lawton and H. Silverman. 1971. "Excess Disabilities of Mentally Impaired Aged: Impact of Individualized Treatment." *The Gerontologist* 11:124–132.

Brody, H. 1992. "Assisted Death: A Compassionate Response to a Medical Failure." *New England Journal of Medicine* 327:1384–1388.

Brody, J. A. 1982. "An Epidemiologist Views Senile Dementia: Facts and Fragments." *American Journal of Epidemiology* 115:155–162.

Brody, S. and G. Ruff, eds. 1986. *Aging and Rehabilitation*. New York: Springer.

Brown, J. 1982. "Cross-Cultural Perspectives on Middle-aged Women." *Current Anthropology* 23(2):143–148.

Brown, J., P. Subbaiah and S. Therese. 1994. "Being in Charge: Older Women and Their Younger Female Kin." *Journal of Cross-Cultural Gerontology* 9(2):231–254.

Brown, T. 1988. "Long-Term Care for the Elderly in Kyoto, Japan." *Journal of Cross-Cultural Gerontology* 3:323–348.

Brubaker, T. H. and C. M. Michael. 1987. "Amish Families in Later Life." In *Ethnic Dimensions of Aging*. D. E. Gelfand and C. M. Barresi, eds. New York: Springer.

Bryant, S. and W. Rakowski. 1992. "Predictors of Mortality Among Elderly African-Americans." *Research On Aging* 14(1):50–58.

Bryceson, D., ed. 1995. *Women Wielding the Hoe*. Herndon, VI: Berg.

Bulletin on Aging. 1994. Double issue, number 2/3.

Burger, J. 1990. *First Peoples*. New York: Anchor.

Burton, L. M. 1992. "Black Grandparents Rearing Children of Drug-Addicted Parents: Stressors, Outcomes and Social Service Needs." *Gerontologist* 32:744–751.

Burton, L. and V. Bengtson. 1985. "Black Grandmothers: Issues of Timing and Continuity in Roles." In *Grandparenthood*. V. Bengtson and J. Robinson, eds. Beverly Hills, CA: Sage.

Burton, L. and C. Devries. 1992. "Challenges and Rewards: African American Grandparents as Surrogate Parents." *Generations* (Summer):51–54.

Burton, L. and S. Sorenson. 1992. "Temporal Context and the Caregiver Role: Perspectives from Ethnographic Studies of Multigeneration African-American Families." In *Caregiving Systems: Informal and Formal Helpers*. S. Zarit, K. Perlin and K. W. Schaie, eds. Hillsdale, NJ: L. Erlbaum.

Buss, T. F., C. Beres, C. R. Hofstetter and A. Pomidor. 1994. "Health Status among Elderly Hungarians and Americans." *Journal of Cross-Cultural Gerontology* 9(3):301–322.

Butler, R. 1975. *Why Survive? Being Old in America*. New York: Harper & Row.

Byrne, S. W. 1974. "Arden, an Adult Community." In *Anthropologists in Cities*. G. Foster and R. Kemper, eds. Boston: Little Brown.

Cain, M. 1991. "Welfare, Institutions in Comparative Perspective, the Fate of the Elderly in Contemporary South Asia and Preindustrial Western Europe." In *Life, Death and the Elderly: Historical Perspectives*. Pelling and R. Smith, eds. London: Routledge.

Cairl, R., ed. 1995. *Somebody Tell Me Who I Am!: Reshaping Thoughts About Care and Management of Confused and Memory Impaired Older Adults*. St. Petersburg, FL: Caremor.

Callahan, D., R. Ter Meuken and E. Topinkova, eds. 1995. "Resource Allocation and Societal Responses to Old Age." Special issue of *Ageing and Society* 15(2).

Callahan, J. 1995. *Menopause: A Midlife Passage*. Bloomington: Indiana University Press.

Cambell, S. and P. Silverman. 1996. *Widower: When Men Are Left Alone*. Amityville, NY: Baywood.

Campbell, R. 1984. "Nursing Homes and Long-Term Care in Japan." *Pacific Affairs* 57(1):78–89.

Campbell, R. and E. Brody. 1985. "Women's Changing Roles and Help to the Elderly: Attitudes of Women in the United States and Japan." *The Gerontologist* 25(6):587–592.

Cancian, F. 1992. *The Decline of Community in Zinacantan*. Stanford, CA: Stanford University Press.

Cantor, M. 1979. "The Informal Support System of New York's Inner City Elderly: Is Ethnicity a Factor?" In *Ethnicity and Aging*. D. Gelfand and A. Kutzik, eds. New York: Springer.

————. 1992. "Families and Caregiving in an Aging Society." *Generations* (Summer): 67–70.

Cantor, M. and V. Little. 1985. "Aging and Social Care." In *Handbook of Aging and the Social Sciences*. R. Binstock and E. Shanas, eds. New York: Van Nostrand Reinhold.

Caplan, G. and M. Killilea, eds. 1976. *Support Systems and Mutual Help: Multidisciplinary Explorations*. New York: Grune and Stratton.

Carael, M. 1994. "The Impact of Marriage Change on the Risks of Exposure to Sexually

Transmitted Diseases in Africa.'' In *Nuptuality in Sub-Saharan Africa: Contemporary Anthropological and Demographic Perspectives*. C. Bledsoe and G. Pison, eds. Oxford: Clarendon.

Carrick, P. 1985. *Ethics in Antiquity: Philosophical Perspectives on Abortion and Euthanasia*. Boston: Dordrecht.

Carson, D. K. 1995. ''American Indian Elder Abuse: Risk and Protective Factors among the Oldest Americans.'' *Journal of Elder Abuse* 6(3/4):17–39.

Carstenen, L., B. Edelstein and L. Dornbrand, eds. 1996. *The Practical Handbook of Clinical Gerontology*. Thousand Oaks, CA: Sage.

Caselli, G., J. Vallin, J. Vaupel and A. Yashin. 1987. ''Age-Specific Mortality Trends in France and Italy Since 1900: Period and Cohort Effects.'' *European Journal of Population* 3:33–60.

Cassel, J. 1976. ''The Contribution of the Social Environment to Host Resistance—The Fourth Wade Hampton Frost Lecture.'' *American Journal of Epidemiology* 2(102):107–123.

Cattell, M. G. 1989a. ''Knowledge and Social Change in Samia, Western Kenya.'' *Journal of Cross-Cultural Gerontology* 4:225–244.

———. 1989b. ''Old Age in Rural Kenya: Gender, the Life Course and Social Change.'' Ph.D. diss. Bryn Mawr College.

———. 1990. ''Models of Old Age among the Samia of Kenya: Family Support of the Elderly.'' *Journal of Cross-Cultural Gerontology* 5:375–394.

———. 1992a. ''Informal Systems of Old Age Support in Developing Countries: Anthropological Perspectives.'' Unpublished background paper for The World Bank 1994, *Averting the Old Age Crisis*. New York: Oxford University Press.

———. 1992b. ''Praise the Lord and Say No to Men: Older Samia Women Empowering Themselves.'' *Journal of Cross-Cultural Gerontology* 7:307–330.

———. 1993. ''Caring for the Elderly in Sub-Saharan Africa.'' *Ageing International* XX(2):13–19.

———. 1994. '' 'Nowadays It Isn't Easy to Advise the Young': Grandmothers and Granddaughters among Abaluyia of Kenya.'' *Journal of Cross-Cultural Gerontology* 9:157–178.

———. 1995. ''Gender, Aging and Health: A Comparative Approach.'' In *Gender and Health: An International Perspective*. C. Sargent and C. Brettell, eds. Englewood Cliffs, NJ: Prentice-Hall.

———. 1996. ''Gender, Age and Power: Hierarchy and Liminality among Abaluyia Women of Kenya.'' East Lansing, MI: Michigan State University, Working Papers on Women in International Development.

———. 1997. ''The Discourse of Neglect: Family Support for Elderly in Samia.'' In *African Families and the Crisis of Social Change*. T. S. Weisner, C. Bradley and P. L. Kilbride, eds. Westport CT: Greenwood Press.

Cawley, M. 1979. ''Rural Industrialization and Social Change in Western Ireland.'' *Sociologia Ruralis* 19(1):43–57.

CeloCruz, M. 1992. ''Aid in Dying: Should We Decriminalize Physician-Assisted Suicide and Physician-Controlled Euthanasia.'' *American Journal of Law and Medicine* 18:369–394.

Chadiha, L., N. Morrow-Howell, O. Darkwa and J. McGillick. 1994. ''Targeting the Black Church and Clergy for Disseminating Knowledge About Alzheimer's Disease and Caregivers' Support Services.'' *American Journal of Alzheimer's Care and Related Disorders and Research* (May/June):1–4.

Chalfie, D. 1994. ''Going It Alone: A Closer Look at Grandparents Parenting Grandchildren.'' Monograph. Washington, DC: American Association of Retired Persons.

Chamie, M. 1992. ''Harmonization and Use of Health Expectancy Indices: Where We Stand, Where We Could be Going.'' Paper presented at the Fifth Meeting of the International Network on Health Expectancy (REVES-5), Ottawa.

Chan, C. 1993. ''Urban Neighborhood Mobilization and Community Care of the Elderly in the People's Republic of China.'' *Journal of Cross-Cultural Gerontology* 8(3): 253–270.

Chaney, E., ed. 1990. *Empowering Older Women: Cross-Cultural Views.* Washington, DC: American Association of Retired Persons.

Chapman, T. M. 1976. *The Decolonization Of Niue.* Wellington, New Zealand: Victoria University Press.

———. 1982. ''Modern times (Ko e magahala fakamui).'' In *Niue: A History Of The Island.* Niue/Suva, Fiji: Niue Government/Institute for Pacific Studies, University of the South Pacific.

Chappell, N. 1995. ''Informal Social Support.'' In *Promoting Successful and Productive Aging.* L. Bond, S. Cutler and A. Grams, eds. Thousand Oaks, CA: Sage.

Chatters, L. and R. Taylor. 1993. ''Intergenerational Support: The Provision of Assistance to Parents by Adult Children.'' In *Aging In Black America.* J. Jackson, L. Chatters and R. Taylor, eds. Newbury Park, CA: Sage.

Checkoway, B. 1994. ''Empowering the Elderly: Gerontological Health Promotion in Latin America.'' *Ageing and Society* 14:75–95.

Chee, P. and R. Kane. 1983. ''Cultural Factors Affecting Nursing Home Care for Minorities: A Study of Black American and Japanese-American Groups.'' *Journal of American Geriatrics Society* 31(2):109–112.

Chen, P., E. S. H. Yu, M. Zhang, W. T. Liu, R. Hill and R. Katzman. 1995. ''ADL Dependence and Medical Conditions in Chinese Older Persons: A Population-Based Survey in Shanghai, China.'' *Journal of the American Geriatrics Society* 43:378–383.

Chen, S. 1996. *Social Policy of the Economic State and Community Care in Chinese Culture.* Aldershot, UK: Avebury.

Cherlin, A. and F. Furstenberg. 1992. *The New American Grandparent: A Place in the Family a Life Apart.* Cambridge, MA: Harvard University Press.

Chester, B. and N. Holtan. 1992. ''Working with Refugee Survivors of Torture.'' *Cross-Cultural Medicine-A Decade Later* (Special Issue). *Western Journal of Medicine* 157:301–304.

Childs, M. 1980. *Sweden: The Middle Way on Trial.* New Haven, CT: Yale University Press.

Choe, E. H. 1989. *Population Aging in the Republic of Korea.* Asian Population Studies Series No. 97. New York: United Nations Economic and Social Commission for Asia and the Pacific.

Chopra, D. 1993. *Ageless Body, Timeless Mind: The Quantum Alternative to Growing Old.* Toronto: Harmony Books.

Christopher, C. and T. Inui (1993). ''When a House Is Not a Home: The Meaning of Shelter Among Chronically Homeless Older Men.'' *Gerontologist* 33:396–402.

Chung, R., C. Y. Lin and K. M. Lin. 1994. "Help-Seeking Behavior among Southeast Asian Refugees." *Journal of Community Psychology* 22:109–120.

Cicirelli, V. 1981. *Helping Elderly Parents: The Role of Adult Children*. Boston: Auburn Howe.

Clark, M. 1972. "Cultural Values and Dependency in Later Life." In *Aging and Modernization*. D. Cowgill and L. Holmes, eds. New York: Appleton-Century-Crofts.

Clark, N. 1997. *The Politics of Physician Assisted Suicide*. New York: Garland.

Clark, M. and B. Anderson. 1967. *Culture and Aging: An Anthropological Study of Older Americans*. Springfield, IL: Charles Thomas.

Climo, J. 1992. *Distant Parents*. New Brunswick: Rutgers University Press.

Coalition for the Homeless. 1984. *Crowded Out: Homelessness and the Elderly Poor in New York City*. New York: Coalition for the Homeless.

Cohen, C. 1996a. "The Elderly Homeless: A Conceptual Model." In *Psychosocial Needs of Special Populations of Elderly*. I. Szwabo and G. Grossberg, eds. New York: Springer.

———. 1996b. "The Effects of Poverty and Education on Temporoparietal Perfusion in Alzheimer's Disease: A Reconsideration of the Cerebral Reserve Hypothesis." *International Journal of Geriatric Psychiatry* 11.

Cohen, C., A. Alder and J. Mintz. 1983. "Assessing Social Network Interventions— Results of an Experimental Service Program Conducted in a Single-room Occupancy Hotel." In *Rediscovering Self-help: Professionals and Informal Care*. Parker and D. Pancoast, eds. Beverly Hills: Sage.

Cohen, C. and M. Crane. 1996. "Old and Homeless in London and New York City: A Cross-national Comparison." In *Homelessness and Mental Health*. D. Bhugra, ed. London: Cambridge University Press.

Cohen, C., H. Onserud and C. Monaco. 1992. "Project Rescue: Serving the Homeless and Marginally Housed Elderly," *Gerontologist* 32:466–471.

———. 1993. "Outcomes for the Mentally Ill in a Program for Older Homeless Persons." *Hospital and Community Psychiatry* 44:650–656.

Cohen, C. et al. 1997. "Predictors of Becoming Redomiciled Among Older Homeless Women." *The Gerontologist* 37:67–74.

Cohen, D. and C. Eisdorfer. 1988. "Depression in Family Members Caring for a Relative with Alzheimer's Disease." *Journal of the American Geriatrics Society* 36:885–889.

Cohen, D. et al. 1990. "Caring for Relatives with Alzheimer's Disease: The Mental Health Risks to Spouses, Children and other Family Caregivers." *Behavior, Health, and Aging* 1:171–182.

Cohen, L. 1992a. "No Aging in India." Ph.D. diss. Ann Arbor: UMI Dissertation Services.

———. 1992b. "No Aging in India: The Uses of Gerontology." *Culture, Medicine and Psychiatry* 16:123–161.

———. 1994. "Old Age: Cultural and Critical Perspectives." *Annual Review in Anthropology* 23:137–158.

———. 1995. "Toward an Anthropology of Senility: Anger, Weakness, and Alzheimer's in Banares, India." *Medical Anthropology Quarterly* 9(3):314–334.

Cohler, B. 1983. "Stress or Support: Relations Between Older Women from Three European Ethnic Groups and their Relatives." In *Minority Aging: Sociological and Social Psychological Issues*. R. Manuel, ed. Westport, CT: Greenwood Press.

Cohler, B. and H. Grunebaum. 1981. *Mothers, Grandmothers and Daughters: Personality and Child Care in Three Generation Families.* New York: Wiley.

Cohler, B. and M. Lieberman. 1980. "Social Relations and Mental Health." *Research on Aging* 2(4):445–469.

Cohler, B., M. Lieberman and L. Welch. 1977. "Social Relations and Interpersonal Resources among Middle-aged and Older Irish, Italian and Polish-American Men and Women." Chicago: The University of Chicago, Committee on Human Development.

Coke, M. and J. Twaite. 1995. *The Black Elderly: Satisfaction and Quality of Life.* Binghamton, NY: Haworth Press.

Cole, T. 1992. *The Journey of Life: A Cultural History of Aging in America.* Cambridge, MA: Cambridge University Press.

Colen, J. 1979. "Critical Issues in the Development of Environmental Support Systems for the Aged." *Allied Health and Behavioral Sciences* 2(1):74–90.

———. 1982. "Using Natural Helping Networks in Social Service Delivery Systems." In *Minority Aging.* R. Manuel, ed. Westport, CT: Greenwood Press.

Coles, C. 1990. "The Older Woman in Hausa Society: Power and Authority in Urban Nigeria." In *The Cultural Context of Aging: Worldwide Perspectives.* J. Sokolovsky, ed. Westport, CT: Bergin & Garvey.

Conference of European Ministers Responsible for Family Affairs. 1983. *National Replies to the Questionnaire: The Role of the Elderly in the Family in the Context of the Society of the 1980s, Sweden.* Strasbourg, France.

Conn, D. and N. Mace. 1996. *Quality of Life in Long-Term Care.* New York: Haworth Press.

Connell, J. 1983. *Migration, Employment and Development in the South Pacific.* Country Report Number 11—Niue. Noumea, New Caledonia: South Pacific Commission.

Conrad, C. 1992. "Old Age in the Modern and Postmodern Western World." In *Handbook of the Humanities and Aging.* T. R. Cole, D. D. van Tassel and R. Kastenbaum, eds. New York: Springer.

Contreras de Lehr, E. 1989. "Women and Old Age: Status of the Elderly Women in Mexico." In *Mid-life and Older Women in Latin America and the Caribbean.* Pan American Health Organization. Washington, DC: Pan American Health Organization.

———. 1992. "Ageing and Family Support in Mexico." In *Family Support for the Elderly: The International Experience.* H. Kendig, A. Hasimoto and L. Coppard, eds. New York: Oxford University Press.

Coogle, C. and R. Finley, eds. 1994. *Families Who Care: Assisting African-American and Rural Families Dealing with Dementia.* Richmond, VA: Virginia Center on Aging.

Cool, L. 1981. "Ethnic Identity: A Source of Community Esteem for the Elderly." *Anthropological Quarterly* 54:179–189.

———. 1987. "The Effects of Social Class and Ethnicity on the Aging Process." In *The Elderly as Modern Pioneers.* P. Silverman, ed. Bloomington: Indiana University Press.

Cool, L. and J. McCabe. 1987. "The 'Scheming Hag' and the 'Dear Old Thing': The Anthropology of Aging Women." In *Growing Old in Different Societies: Cross-Cultural Perspectives.* J. Sokolovsky, ed. Acton, MA: Copley.

Cooney, B. E. 1990. *Long-term care in Denmark.* Tampa, FL: International Exchange Center on Gerontology, University of South Florida.

Coplan, D. 1987. "Eloquent Knowledge: Lesotho Migrants' Songs and the Anthropology of Experience." *American Ethnologist* 21:413–433.

Corder, E. H. et al. 1993. "Gene Dose of Apolipoprotein E Type 4 Allele and the Risk of Alzheimer's Disease in Late-Onset Families." *Science* 261: 921–923.

———. 1995. "Apolipoprotein E and the Epidemiology of Alzheimer's Disease." In *Research Advances in Alzheimer's Disease and Related Disorders.* K. Iqbal, J. A. Mortimer, B. Winblad and H. M. Wisniewski, eds. New York: Wiley & Sons.

Council of Ethical and Judicial Affairs, American Medical Association. 1992. "Decisions Near the End of Life." *Journal of the American Medical Association* 264:369–372.

Counts, D. A. 1991. "Aging, Health and Women in West New Britain." *Journal of Cross-Cultural Gerontology* 6(3):277–286.

Counts, D. A. and D. R. Counts, eds. 1985a. *Aging and Its Transformations: Moving Toward Death in Pacific Societies.* New York: University Press Of America.

———. 1985b. "I'm Not Dead Yet!: Aging and Death: Process and Experience in Kaliai." In *Aging and Its Transformations: Moving Toward Death in Pacific Societies.* D. A. Counts and D. R. Counts, eds. New York: University Press Of America.

———. 1992. "They're My Family Now: The Creation of Community Among RVers." Anthropologica 34: 153–182.

Covey, H. C. 1993. "A Return to Infancy: Old Age and the Second Childhood in History." *International Journal of Aging and Human Development* 32(2):81–90.

Coward, R. T. 1979. "Planning Community Services for the Rural Elderly: Implications from Research." *The Gerontologist* 19:275–282.

Coward, R. T. and G. Lee, eds. 1985 *The Elderly in Rural Society: Every Fourth American.* New York: Springer.

Coward, R. T., G. Lee, J. Dwer and K. Seccombe. 1993. *Old and Alone in America.* Washington, DC: American Association of Retired Persons.

Cowgill, D. 1972. "A Theory of Aging in Cross-Cultural Perspective." In *Aging and Modernization.* D. Cowgill and L. Holmes, eds. New York: Appleton-Century-Crofts.

———. 1974. "The Aging of Populations and Society." *The Annals of the American Academy of Political and Social Sciences* 415:1–18.

———. 1986. *Aging Around the World.* Belmont, CA: Wadsworth.

Cowgill, D. and L. D. Holmes, eds. 1972. *Aging and Modernization.* New York: Appleton-Century-Crofts.

Crane, M. 1994. "The Mental Health Problems of Elderly People Living on London's Streets." *International Journal of Geriatric Psychiatry* 9: 87–95.

Crews, D. and R. Garruto, eds. 1994. *Biological Anthropology and Aging.* New York: Oxford University Press.

Crigger, B. 1995. Report: Assisted Suicide. *Hastings Center Report* 25:1–52.

Crohan, S. and T. Antonucci. 1989. "Friends as a Source of Social Support in Old Age." In *Older Adult Friendships.* R. Adams and R. Blieszner, eds. Berkeley: Sage.

Crystal, S. 1982. *America's Old Age Crisis: Public Policy and the Two Worlds of Aging.* New York: Basic Books.

Cuellar, J. 1978. "El Senior Citizens Club: The Older Mexican-American in the Voluntary Association." In *Life's Career Aging: Cultural Variations on Growing Old*. B. G. Myerhoff and A. Simic, eds. Beverly Hills: Sage.

Cuellar, J. and J. Weeks. 1980. "Minority Elderly Americans: A Prototype for Area Agencies on Aging." Executive Summary. San Diego: Allied Health Association.

Cumming, E. and W. Henry. 1961. *Growing Old: The Process of Disengagement*. New York: Basic Books.

Curtis, F. S. and M. Cyars. (n.d.). *Handbook for the Department of Women*. Church of God in Christ, Memphis: Church of God in Christ Publishing House.

Daatland, S. O. 1994. "Recent Trends and Future Prospects for the Elderly in Scandinavia." *Journal of Aging and Social Policy* 6(1/2):181–197.

Daly, M. 1981. *Social and Economic History of Ireland since 1800*. Dublin: Educational Company.

Damron-Rodriguez, J., S. Wallace and R. Kington. 1994. "Service Utilization and Minority Elderly: Appropriateness, Accessibility and Acceptability." In *Cultural Diversity and Geriatric Care: Challenges to the Health Professions*. D. Wieland, D. Benton, B. J. Kramer and G. D. Dawson, eds. Binghamton, NY: The Haworth Press.

Dandekar, K. 1996. *The Elderly in India*. Thousand Oaks, CA: Sage.

Das Gupta, M. 1995. "Life Course Perspectives on Women's Autonomy and Health Outcomes." *American Anthropologist* 97:481–491.

Datan, N. et al. 1970. "Climacterium In Three Culture Contexts." *Tropical and Geographical Medicine* 22:77–86.

Davies, D. 1975. *The Centenarians of the Andes*. Garden City, NY: Anchor Press.

Davis, D. 1997. "Inequality and Insecurity in Contemporary China." In *Aging: Asian Experiences Past and Present*. S. Formanek and S. Linhart, eds. Vienna: Verlag der Osterreichischen Akademie der Wissenschaften.

Davis, L. H. and B. F. McGadney. 1993. "Self-Care Practices of Black Elders." In *Ethnic Elderly and Long-Term Care*. C. M. Barresi and D. E. Stull, eds. New York: Springer.

Davis-Friedmann, D. 1991. *Long Lives: Chinese Elderly and the Communist Revolution*. N.p.

Decalmer, P. and F. Glendenning, eds. 1993. *The Mistreatment of Elderly People*. Thousand Oaks, CA: Sage.

DeHaney, W. T. 1987. "Romanticizing the Status of the Rural Elderly: Theory and Policy Implications." *The Gerontologist* 27:321–329.

del Valle, A. G., and M. Usher. 1982. "Group Therapy with Aged Latino Women: A Pilot Project and Study." *Clinical Gerontologist* 1:51–58.

Demos, J. 1982. *Entertaining Satan: Witchcraft and Culture of Early New England*. New York: Oxford University Press.

Detzner, D. F. 1992. "Life Histories: Conflict in Southeast Asian Refugee Families: A Life History Approach." In *Qualitative Methods in Family Research*. J. Gilgun, K. Daly and F. Handel, eds. Newbury Park, CA: Sage.

———. 1996. "No Place Without a Home: Southeast Asian Grandparents in Refugee Families." *Generations* 20(1):45–48.

DeVos, G. 1982. "Ethnic Pluralism: Conflict and Accommodation." In *Ethnic Identity: Cultural Continuities and Change*. G. DeVos and L. Romanucci-Ross, eds. Chicago: University of Chicago Press.

DHHS. 1992. "Special Issue on Alzheimer's Disease." *Aging Magazine*, 363–364. U.S. Department of Health and Human Services.

Diamond, T. 1992. *Making Gray Gold: Narratives of Nursing Home Care*. Chicago: University of Chicago Press.

Dickerson-Putman, J. 1994a. "Political Economy and Age." *The Aging Experience: Diversity and Commonality Across Cultures*. J. Keith, C. Fry, A. Glascock, C. Ikels, J. Dickerson-Putman, H. Harpending and P. Draper, eds. Thousand Oaks, CA: Sage.

———. 1994b. "Old Women at the Top—An Exploration of Age Stratification Among Bena Bena Women." *Journal of Cross-Cultural Gerontology* 9(2):193–205.

Dinh, K. T., B. R. Sarason and I. G. Sarason. 1994. "Parent-Child Relationships in Vietnamese Immigrant Families." *Journal of Family Psychology* 8:471–488.

Donner, W. W. 1987. "Compassion, Kinship and Fosterage: Contexts for the Care of the Childless Elderly in a Polynesian Community." *Journal of Cross-Cultural Gerontology* 2(1):43–60.

Dorfman, R. and K. Walsh. 1996. "Theoretical Dimensions of Successful Aging." *Journal of Aging and Identity* 1(3):165–176.

Doty, P. 1986a. "Health Status and Health Services Use Among Older Women: An International Perspective." In *Aging in the Third World*. K. G. Kinsella, ed. Washington, DC: Center for International Research, U.S. Bureau of the Census.

———. 1986b. "Family Care of the Elderly: The Role of Public Policy." *Milbank Memorial Fund Quarterly* 64:34–75.

———. 1993. "International Long-Term Care Reform: A Demographic, Economic, and Policy Overview." *Journal of Cross-Cultural Gerontology* 8:447–461.

Dougherty, M. 1978a. *Becoming a Woman in the Rural South*. New York: Holt, Rinehart & Winston.

———. 1978b. "An Anthropological Perspective On Aging and Women in the Middle Years." In *The Anthropology of Health*. E. Bauwens, ed. St. Louis, MO: C. V. Mosby.

Douglas, M. 1966. *Purity and Danger*. London: Routledge & Kegan Paul.

Dowd, J. 1975. "Aging as Exchange: A Preface to Theory." *Journal of Gerontology* 30(5):584–594.

———. 1980. *Stratification Among the Aged*. Monterey, CA: Brooks/Cole.

———. 1984. "Beneficence and Aged." *Journal of Gerontology* 39(2):102–108.

Dowd, J. and V. L. Bengtson. 1978. "Aging in Minority Populations: An Examination of the Double Jeopardy Hypothesis." *Journal of Gerontology* 33(3):427–436.

Draper, P. 1976. "Social and Economic Constraints on Child Life among the !Kung." In *Kalahari Hunter-Gatherers: Studies of the !Kung San and Their Neighbors*. R. B. Lee and I. DeVore, eds. Cambridge, MA: Harvard University Press.

———. 1992. "Room to Maneuver: !Kung Women Cope with Men." In *Sanctions and Sanctuary: Cultural Perspectives on the Beating of Wives*. D. A. Counts, J. K. Brown and J. C. Campbell, eds. Boulder, CO: Westview Press.

Draper, P. and A. Buchanan. 1992. "If You Have a Child You Have Life: Demographic and Cultural Perspectives on Fathering in Old Age in !Kung Society." In *Father-Child Relations: Cultural and Biosocial Contexts*. B. S. Hewlett, ed. New York: Aldine De Gruyter.

Draper, P. and H. Harpending. 1994. "Cultural Considerations in the Experience of Aging: Two African Cultures." In *Functional Performance in Older Adults*. B. R. Bonder and M. B. Wagner, eds. Philadelphia: F. A. Davis.

Draper, P. and J. Keith. 1992. "Cultural Contexts of Care: Family Caregiving for Elderly in America and Africa." *Journal of Aging Studies* 6:113–134.

Dreze, J. 1990. *Widows in Rural India*. London: Development Economics Research Programme.

Driver, H. 1969. *Indians of North America*. Chicago: University of Chicago Press.

Du Toit, B. 1990. *Aging and Menopause Among Indian South African Women*. Albany: State University of New York Press.

Durkheim, E. 1915. *The Elementary Forms of the Religious Life*. J. W. Swain, trans. New York: The Free Press, paperback edition 1965.

Dykstra, P. 1990. *Next of Non-Kin*. Amsterdam: Swets and Zetlinger.

Eagleton, T. 1983. *Literary Theory: An Introduction*. Oxford: Basil Blackwell.

Eaton, S. 1981 (1907). *The Roosevelt Bears Go to Washington*. New York: Dover.

Eckert, K. 1980. *The Unseen Elderly: A Study of Marginally Subsistant Hotel Dwellers*. San Diego: Campanile Press.

Edmonds, M. M. 1990. "The Health of the Black Aged Female." In *Black Aged: Understanding Diversity and Service Needs*. Z. Harel, E. A. McKinney and M. Williams, eds. Newbury Park, CA: Sage.

Eisdorfer, C. and V. Kumar, eds. Forthcoming. *Advances in the Diagnosis and Treatment of Alzheimer's Disease*. New York: Springer.

Eisenstadt, S. N. 1956. *From Generation to Generation*. New York: Free Press.

Elder, G. H., Jr., E. B. Robertson and R. D. Conger. 1995. "Fathers and Sons in Rural America: Occupational Choice and Intergenerational Ties Across the Life Course." In *Aging and Generational Relations over the Life Course*. T. Hareven, ed. Chicago: Aldine De Gruyter.

Ellickson, J. 1988. "Never the Twain Shall Meet: Aging Men and Women in Bangladesh." *Journal of Cross-Cultural Gerontology* 3(1):53–70.

Elliott, K. S. 1995. "Dementia, Outreach 'Inreach,' and Chinese Culture." *Association for Anthropology and Gerontology Newsletter* 16:4–6.

Elliott, K. S. and R. Campbell. 1993. "Changing Ideas About Family Care for the Elderly in Japan." *Journal of Cross-Cultural Gerontology* 8:119–135.

Elliott, K. S., M. Di Minno, D. Lam and A. M. Tu. 1996. "Working with Chinese Families in the Context of Dementia." In *Ethnicity and the Dementias*. G. Yeo and D. Gallagher-Thompson, eds. Washington, DC: Taylor and Francis.

Elliot, S. 1996. "Middle Age Catches Up with the Me Generation." *New York Times*, January 6, C4.

Elmendorf, W. and A. Kroeber. 1960. *The Structure of Twona Culture with Notes on Yurok Culture*. Pullman: Washington State University.

Emanuel, E. 1994. "The History of Euthanasia in the United States and Britain." *Annals of Internal Medicine* 121:793–802.

Erikson, E. 1963. *Childhood and Society*. New York: Norton.

Escobar, J. and E. Randolph. 1982. "The Hispanic and Social Networks." In *Mental Health and Hispanic Americans*. R. Becerra, M. Karno and J. Escobar, eds. New York: Grune & Stratton.

Estes, C. 1979. *The Aging Enterprise*. San Francisco: Jossey-Bass.

———. 1993. "The Aging Enterprise Revisited." *The Gerontologist* 33:292–298.

———. 1996. "The Political Economy of Aging." In *Handbook of Aging and Social Sciences*, 4th ed. R. Binstock and L. George, eds. New York: Academic Press.

Etienne, M. 1983. "Gender Relations and Conjugality among the Baule." In *Female and Male in West Africa*. C. Oppong, ed. London: George Allen & Unwin.

Evers, H. 1981. "Care or Custody? The Experience of Women Patients in Long-Stay Geriatric Wards." In *Controlling Women: The Normal and the Deviant*. B. Hutter and G. Williams, eds. London: Croom Helm.

Fabian, J. 1983. *Time and the Other: How Anthropology Makes Its Object*. New York: Columbia University Press.

Facio, E. 1996. *Understanding Older Chicanas*. Thousand Oaks, CA: Sage.

Fandetti, D. and D. Gelfand. 1976. "Care of the Aged: Attitudes of White Ethnic Families." *The Gerontologist* 16(6):544–549.

Farmer, B. 1996. *A Nursing Home and Its Organizational Climate: An Ethnography*. Westport, CT: Auburn House.

Featherstone, M. and A. Wernick, eds. 1995. *Images of Aging: Cultural Representations of Later Life*. New York: Routledge.

Federal Council on Aging. 1979. "Policy Issues Concerning Elderly Minorities." No. 80–20670. Washington, DC: Department of Health and Human Services.

———. 1981. *The Need for Long Term Care*. Washington, DC: U.S. Department of Health and Human Services.

Feil, N. 1993. *The Validation Breakthrough*. N.P.: MacLennan and Petty Pty., Ltd.

Fernow, N. 1992. "Swedish Elder Care in Transition." *Current Sweden* 392:1–5. Stockholm: Swedish Institute.

Field, K. L. 1993. Personal Communication.

Finau, S. A., I. A. M. Prior and J. G. Evans. 1982. "Ageing in the South Pacific." *Social Science and Medicine* 16:1539–1549.

Finch, J. and D. Groves, eds. 1983. *A Labour of Love: Women, Work and Caring*. London: Routledge & Kegan Paul.

Finley, G. E. 1982. "Modernization and Aging." In *Review of Human Development*. M. Fields et al., eds. New York: John Wiley and Sons.

Firth, R. 1936. *We, The Tikopia*. London: Allen & Unwin.

Fischer, D. H. 1978. *Growing Old in America*. Oxford, MA: Oxford University Press.

Fisher, M. F. K. 1983. *Sister Age*. New York: Knopf.

Fisk, E. K. 1978. *The Island of Niue: Development or Dependence for a Very Small Nation*. Canberra: Australian National University. Development Studies Centre Occasional Paper 9.

Fleming, S. and I. Brown. 1983. "The Impact of a Death Education Program for Nurses in a Long-Term Care Hospital." *Gerontologist* 23:192–195.

Flint, M. and R. Samil. 1990. "Cultural and Subcultural Meanings of the Menopause." *Annals of the New York Academy of Sciences* 592:134–148.

Folta, J. R. and E. S. Deck. 1987. "Elderly Black Widows in Rural Zimbabwe." *Journal of Cross-Cultural Gerontology* 2(4):321–344.

Foner, A. and D. I. Kertzer. 1978. "Transitions Over the Life Course: Lessons From Age-Set Societies." *American Journal of Sociology* 83:1081–1104.

Foner, N. 1984a. *Ages in Conflict: A Cross-Cultural Perspective on Inequality Between Old and Young*. New York: Columbia University Press.

———. 1984b. "Age and Social Change." In *Age and Anthropological Theory*. D. Kertzer and J. Keith, eds. Ithaca, NY: Cornell University Press.

———. 1985. "Old and Frail and Everywhere Unequal." *The Hastings Center Report* 15(2):27–31.

———. 1989. "Older Women in Nonindustrial Cultures: Consequences of Power and Privilege." *Women and Health* 14:227–237.

———. 1994. *The Caregiving Dilemma: Work in an American Nursing Home*. Berkeley: University of California Press.

Foreman, G. 1934. *The Five Civilized Tribes*. Norman: University of Oklahoma Press.

Fortes, M. 1978. "An Anthropologist's Apprenticeship." *Annual Review of Anthropology* 7:1–30.

———. 1984. "Age, Gender, and Social Structure." In *Age and Anthropological Theory*. D. Kertzer and J. Keith, eds. Ithaca: Cornell University Press.

Foster, G. and B. Anderson. 1978. *Medical Anthropology*. New York: John Wiley.

Francher, J. S. 1973. "It's the Pepsi Generation: Accelerated Aging and the Television Commercial." *International Journal of Aging and Human Development* 4(3):245–255.

Francis, D. 1984. *Will You Still Need Me, Will You Still Feed Me, When I'm 64?* Bloomington: Indiana University Press.

Frankovich, M. K. 1974. "Child-Rearing on Niue: An Ethnopsychological Analysis of Aspects Relevant to the Goals and Acquisition of a Contemporary Western Education." Master's thesis, Psychology Department, University of Waikato, New Zealand.

Frazier, E. F. 1939. *The Negro Family in the United States*. Chicago: University of Chicago Press.

Free, M. 1995. *The Private World of the Hermitage: Lifestyles of the Rich and Old in an Elite Retirement Home*. Westport, CT: Bergin and Garvey.

Freedman, V. et al. 1994. "Family Networks: Predictors of Nursing Home Entry." *American Journal of Public Health* 84(5):843–845.

Frenk, J., J. L. Bobadilla, C. Stern, T. Frejka and R. Lozano. 1991. "Elements for a Theory of the Health Transition." *Health Transition Review* 1:21–38.

Friedland, R. P. 1994. *Clinics in Geriatric Medicine: Alzheimer's Disease Update*. Philadelphia: W. B. Saunders Company.

Friedman, E. 1982. "The Myth of the Shiksa." In *Ethnicity and Family Therapy*. M. McGoldrick, J. Pearce and J. Giordano, eds. New York: Guilford.

Friedman, L., M. Daly and A. Lazur. 1995. "Burden Among White and Black Caregivers to Elderly Adults." *Journal of Gerontology* 50B:S110–118.

Friis, H. 1979. "The Aged in Denmark: Social Programmes." In *Reaching the Aged— Social Services in Forty-Four Countries*. M. I. Teicher, D. Thursz and J. L. Vigilante, eds. Beverly Hills: Sage.

Fry, C. 1977. "Community as Community: The Aged Graded Case." *Human Organization* 36:115–123.

———. 1980a. *Aging in Culture and Society, Comparative Viewpoints and Strategies*. Brooklyn: J. F. Bergin.

———. 1980b. "Cultural Dimensions of Age." In *Aging, Culture and Society: Comparative Perspectives and Strategies*. C. Fry, ed. New York: Praeger.

———. 1981. *Dimensions: Aging, Culture and Health*. Brooklyn, NY: J. F. Bergin.

———. 1988. "Comparative Research in Aging." In *Gerontology: Perspectives and Issues*. K. Ferraro, ed. New York: Springer.

———. 1994. "Kinship and Individuation." In *Adult Intergenerational Relations: Effects of Societal Change*. K. W. Schaie, V. Bengtson and L. Burton, eds. New York: Springer.

―――. 1995. "Commentary: Kindred and Kin: The First and Last Source of Support." In *Adult Intergenerational Relations: Effects of Societal Change*. V. Bengtson, K. Schaie and L. Burton, eds. New York: Springer.

―――. 1996. "Age, Aging and Culture." In *Handbook on Aging and the Social Sciences*, 4th ed. R. Binstock and L. George, eds. New York: Academic Press.

Fry, C. and J. Keith. 1982. "The Life Course as a Cultural Unit." In *Aging from Birth to Death*, vol. 2). M. Riley, ed. Boulder, CO: Westview Press.

―――. 1986. *New Methods for Old Age Research*. South Hadley, MA: Bergin & Garvey Publishers, Inc.

Gabriel, E. 1972. *20 years of Creativity: Senior Citizens of Tompkins County, Progress Report: 1952–1972*. Ithaca, NY: The Senior Citizens Council of Tompkins County, Inc.

Gaines, A. 1988–89. "Alzheimer's Disease in the Context of Black (Southern) Culture." *Health Matrix* 6(4):33–38.

Gallagher, D., J. Breckenridge, L. Thompson and J. Peterson. 1983. "Effects of Bereavement on Indicators of Mental Health in Elderly Widows and Widowers." *Journal of Gerontology* 38:565–571.

Gallagher, S. 1994. *Older People Giving Care*. Westport, CT: Auburn House.

Gallagher-Thompson, D., M. Talamantes, R. Ramirez and I. Valverde. 1996. "Service Delivery Issues and Recommendations for Working with Mexican-American Family Caregivers." In *Ethnicity and the Dementias*. G. Yeo and D. Gallagher-Thompson, eds. Washington, DC: Taylor and Francis.

Garcia, C. 1993. "What Do We Mean by Extended Family? A Closer Look at Hispanic Multigenerational Families." *Journal of Cross-Cultural Gerontology* 8(2):137–146.

Gelfand, D., ed. 1982. *Aging: The Ethnic Factor*. Boston: Little Brown.

―――. 1994. *Aging and Ethnicity: Knowledge and Services*. New York: Springer.

Gelfand, D. and C. M. Barresi, eds. 1987. *Ethnic Dimensions of Aging*. New York: Springer.

Gelfand, D. and D. Fandetti. 1980. "Suburban and Urban White Ethnics: Attitudes Towards Care of the Aged." *Gerontologist* 20:588–594.

Gelfand, D. and B. W. K. Yee. 1992. "Trends and Forces: Influence of Immigration, Migration, and Acculturation on the Fabric of Aging in America." *Generations* 15:7–10.

Genovese, E. 1974. *Roll, Jordan, Roll*. New York: Vintage Books.

German, P. 1995. "Prevention and Chronic Disease in Older Individuals." In *Promoting Successful and Productive Aging*. L. Bond, S. Cutler and A. Grams, eds. Thousand Oaks, CA: Sage.

Gerontological Society of America. 1994. *Minority Elders: Five Goals Toward Building a Public Policy Base*. Washington, DC: The Gerontological Society of America.

Ghiglione, Loren. 1990. *The American Journalist: Paradox of the Press*. Washington, DC: Library of Congress.

Gibbs, T. 1988. "Health-Seeking Behavior of Elderly Blacks." In *The Black American Elderly: Research on Physical and Psychosocial Health*. J. S. Jackson et al., eds. New York: Springer.

Gibson, M. J. 1984. "Family Support Patterns, Programs, and Policies." In *Innovative Aging Programs Abroad: Implications for the U.S.* C. Nusberg, with M. J. Gibson and S. Peace, eds. Westport, CT: Greenwood Press.

————. 1985. *Older Women Around the World.* Washington, DC: International Federation on Ageing.

Gibson, R. 1986. "Blacks in an Aging Society." *Daedalus* 115(1):349–371.

————. 1987. "Defining Retirement for Black Americans." In *Ethnic Dimensions of
Aging.* D. Gelfand and C. M. Barresi, eds. New York: Springer.

————. 1991. "Minority Families as Resources for their Elders." In *Diversity in an
Aging Society.* P. Stanford and F. Torres-Gil, eds. San Diego: National Resource
Center on Aging.

————. 1995. "Promoting Successful and Productive Aging in Minority Populations."
In *Promoting Successful and Productive Aging.* L. Bond, S. Cutler and A. Grams.
eds. Thousand Oaks, CA: Sage.

Giele, J. Z. 1982. "Family and Social Networks." In *International Perspectives on Aging: Population and Policy Challenges.* R. Binstock, W. S. Chow and J. Schultz,
eds. New York: United Nations Fund for Population Activities.

Gilkes, C. T. 1985. "Together and in Harness: Women's Traditions in the Sanctified
Church." *SIGNS* 10(4):678–699.

————. 1986. "The Role of Church and Community Mothers: Ambivalent American
Sexism or Fragmented African Familyhood?" *Journal of Feminist Studies in Religion* 2(1) (Spring).

Gill, D. and S. Ingman. 1994. *Eldercare, Distributive Justice, and the Welfare State:
Retrenchment or Expansion.* Albany: State University of New York Press.

Ginsberg, L. H., ed. 1976. *Social Work in Rural Communities: A Book of Readings.* New
York: Council on Social Work Education.

Glascock, A. P. 1982. "Decrepitude and Death-hastening: The Nature of Old Age in
Third World Societies." In *Aging and the Aged in the Third World: Part I.* J.
Sokolovsky, ed. Williamsburg, VA: College of William & Mary.

————. 1994. "Age, Health and Functionality." In *The Aging Experience: Diversity
and Commonality Across Cultures.* J. Keith, C. Fry, A. Glascock, C. Ikels, J.
Dickerson-Putman, H. Harpending and P. Draper, eds. Thousand Oaks, CA: Sage.

Glascock, A. P. and S. L. Feinman. 1980. "A Holocultural Analysis of Old Age." *Comparative Social Research* 3:311–333.

————. 1981. "Social Asset or Social Burden: Treatment of the Aged in Non-Industrial
Societies." In *Dimensions: Aging, Culture, and Health.* C. Fry, ed. South Hadley:
MA: Bergin & Garvey.

Glick, I., R. Weiss and C. Parkes. 1974. *The First Year of Bereavement.* New York:
Wiley.

Global Aging Report. 1996. "Growing Old in Better Health." *Global Aging Report* 1:
1:6.

Goebel, A. and M. Epprecht. 1995. "Women and Employment in Sub-Saharan Africa:
Testing the World Bank and WID Models with a Lesotho Case Study." *African
Studies Review* 38:1–22.

Goffman, E. 1961. *Asylums.* New York: Doubleday.

Golant, S., ed. 1992. *Housing America's Elderly.* Thousand Oaks, CA: Sage.

Gold, S. J. 1992. *Refugee Communities: A Comparative Field Study.* Newbury Park, CA:
Sage.

Golden, S. 1992. *The Woman Outside: Meanings and Myths of Homelessness.* Berkeley:
University of California Press.

Goldsmith, P. 1985. "Healing and Denominationalism on the Georgia Coast." *The Southern Quarterly* 23(3) (Spring).

Goldstein, M. and C. Beall. 1981. "Modernization and Aging in the Third and Fourth World: Views from the Rural Hinterland in Nepal." *Human Organization* 40(1): 48–55.

Goldstein, M., S. Schuler and J. Ross. 1983. "Social and Economic Forces Affecting Intergenerational Relations in Extended Families in a Third World Country: A Cautionary Tale from South Asia." *Journal of Gerontology* 38(6):716–724.

Goodale, J. 1971. *Tiwi Women*. Seattle: University of Washington Press.

Goodman, R. A. 1971. "Some *Aitu* Beliefs of Modern Samoans." *Journal of the Polynesian Society* 80:463–479.

Gornick, M. et al. 1996. "Effects of Race and Income on Mortality and Use of Services Among Medicare Beneficiaries." *New England Journal of Medicine* 335:791–799.

Gort, E., ed. 1988. *Aging in Cross-Cultural Perspective: Africa and the Americas*. New York: Phelps Stokes Institute.

Gouldner, A. W. 1960. "The Norm of Reciprocity." *American Sociological Review* 25(2):161–178.

Gozdziak, E. 1988. *Older Refugees in the United States: From Dignity to Despair*. Washington, DC: Refugee Policy Group.

Gratton, B. 1986. *Family, Work and Welfare Among Boston's Aged, 1890–1950*. Philadelphia: Temple University Press.

———. 1987. "Familism among the Black and Mexican-American Elderly: Myth or Reality." *Journal of Aging Studies* 1(1):19–32.

Gratton, B. and C. Haber. 1993. "Rethinking Industrialization: Old Age and the Family Economy." In *Voices and Visions of Aging*. T. R. Cole, W. A. Achenbaum, P. L. Jakobi and R. Kastenbaum, eds. New York: Springer.

Graves, A. et al. 1994. "Opportunities and Challenges in International Collaborative Epidemiologic Research of Dementia and Its Subtypes: Studies Between Japan and the U.S." *International Psychogeriatrics* 6(2):209–223.

Gray, R. F. 1964. "Introduction." In *The Family Estate in Africa: Studies in the Role of Property in Family Structure and Lineage Continuity*. Boston: Boston University Press.

Greeley, A. et al. 1980. *Ethnic Drinking Subcultures*. Brooklyn: J. F. Bergin (Praeger).

Green, B. 1993. *A Study in Discourse Analysis*. Hawthorne, NY: Aldine de Gruyter.

Greene, R. R. 1980. "Ageism and Death Anxiety as Related to Geriatric Social Work as a Career Choice." Ph.D. diss. University of Maryland School of Social Work.

Groger, L. 1994. "Limit of Support and Reaction to Illness: An Exploration of Black Elders' Pathway to Long-term Care Settings." *Journal of Cross-Cultural Gerontology* 9:369–387.

———. 1995. "A Nursing Home Can Be a Home." *Journal of Aging Studies* 9(2):137–153.

Gubrium, J. 1975. *Living and Dying at Murray Manor*. New York: St. Martin's Press.

———., ed. 1976. *Time, Roles and Self in Old Age*. New York: Human Sciences Press.

———. 1982. "Fictive Family: Everyday Usage, Analytic, and Human Service Considerations." *American Anthropologist* 84:878–185 885.

———. 1986. *Oldtimers and Alzheimer's: The Descriptive Organization of Senility*. Greenwich, CT: JAI Press.

————. 1987. "Organizational Embeddedness and Family Life." In *Aging, Health and Family: Long-Term Care*. T. Brubaker, ed. Newbury Park, CA: Sage.

————. 1992. "Qualitative Research Comes of Age in Gerontology." *Gerontologist* 32(5):581–582.

————., ed. 1993. "Contributions of Qualitative Research on Aging." Special issue of *Qualitative Research on Aging* 3:3.

Gubrium, J. and J. Holstein. 1997. *The New Language of Qualitative Method*. New York: Oxford University Press.

Gubrium, J. and A. Sanker, eds. 1990. *The Home Care Experience*. Newbury Park, CA: Sage.

Guemple, D. L. 1969. "Human Resource Management: The Dilemma of the Aging Eskimo." *Sociological Symposium* 2:59–4.

Guillemard, A. M., ed. 1983. *Old Age and the Welfare State*. Beverly Hills: Sage.

————. 1995. "Equity between Generations in Aging Societies: The Problem of Assessing Public Policies." In *Aging and Generational Relations over the Life Course*. T. Hareven, ed. Hawthorne, NY: Aldine de Gruyter.

Guralnik, J. et al. 1995. *The Women's Health and Aging Study: Health and Social Characteristics of Older Women with Disability*. Bethesda, MD: National Institute on Aging.

Gutierrez-Mayka, M. and J. N. Henderson. 1993. "Social Work for Non-Social Workers: An Example of Unplanned Role Expansion in a Community Health Intervention Project." *Journal of Gerontological Social Work* 20:135–146.

Gutmann, D. 1967. "Aging among the Highland Maya: A Comparative Study." *Journal of Personality and Social Psychology* 7(1):28–35.

————. 1987. *Reclaimed Powers: Toward a New Psychology of Men and Women in Later Life*. New York: Basic Books.

Guyer, J. I. 1986. "Beti Widow Inheritance and Marriage Law: A Social History." In *Widows in African Societies: Choices and Constraints*. B. Potash, ed. Stanford, CA: Stanford University Press.

Guzlow, Z. and G. Tracy. 1976. "The Role of Self-Help Clubs in Adaptation to Chronic Illness and Disability." *Social Science and Medicine* 10:407–414.

Haber, C. 1997. "Witches, Widows, Wives, and Workers: The Historiography of Older Women." In *Handbook on Women and Aging*. J. Coyle, ed. Westport, CT: Greenwood.

Habib, J., G. Sundstrom and K. Windmiller. 1993. "Understanding the Pattern of Support for the Elderly: A Comparison Between Israel and Sweden." *Journal of Aging and Social Policy* 5(1/2):187–206.

Hadenius, S. and A. Lindgren. 1992. *On Sweden*. Stockholm: Swedish Institute.

Hadjihristev, A. 1988. *Life-Styles for Longer Life: Longevity in Bulgaria*. G. Lesnoff-Caravaglia, trans. Springfield, IL: Charles C. Thomas.

Hahn, T. 1870. "Die Buschmäner." *Globus* 18(5):65–153.

Hakansson, N. T. 1994. "The Detachability of Women: Gender and Kinship in Processes of Socioeconomic Change among the Gusii of Kenya." *American Ethnologist* 21:516–538.

Halperin, R. 1984. "Age in Cultural Economics: An Evolutionary Approach." In *Age and Anthropological Theory*. D. Kertzer and J. Keith, eds. Ithaca, NY: Cornell University Press.

————. 1987. "Age in Cross-Cultural Perspective: An Evolutionary Approach." In *The*

Elderly as Modern Pioneers. P. Silverman, ed. Bloomington: Indiana University Press.

Halsell, G. 1976. *Los Viejos—Secrets of Long Life from the Sacred Valley.* Emmaus, PA: Rodale Press.

Hamilton, V. 1971. *A Study of Blessington, Co. Wicklow.* Manuscript.

Hannan, D. F. 1979. *Displacement and Development: Class, Kinship and Social Change in Ireland.* Institute Paper #96. Dublin: Economic and Social Research Council.

Hansen, J. D. 1994. "Hunter-Gatherer to Pastoral Way of Life: Effects of the Transition on Health, Growth, and Nutritional Status." *South African Journal of Science* 89: 559–564.

Hanson, A. R. 1970. *Rapan Lifeways: Society and History on a Polynesian Island.* Boston: Little, Brown.

Hardy, J. 1994. "Alzheimer's Disease: Clinical Molecular Genetics." In *Clinics in Geriatric Medicine.* R. Friedland, ed. Philadelphia: W. B. Saunders Company.

Hardy, M. and L. Hazelrigg. 1995. "Gender, Race/Ethnicity, and Poverty in Later Life." *Journal of Aging Studies* 9:43–63.

Hareven, T., ed. 1995a. *Aging and Generational Relations Over the Life Course: A Historical and Cross Cultural Perspective.* Berlin: Walter de Gruyter and Co.

———. 1995b. "Changing Images of Aging and the Social Construction of the Life Course." In *Images of Aging: Cultural Representations of Later Life.* M. Featherstone and A. Wernick, eds. New York: Routledge.

Harlan, W. H. 1968. "Social Status of the Aged in Three Indian Villages." In *Middle Age and Aging.* B. Neugarten, ed. Chicago: University of Chicago Press.

Hart, C. W. 1970. "Fieldwork among the Tiwi 1928–29." In *Being an Anthropologist: Fieldwork in Eleven Cultures.* G. Spindler, ed. New York: Holt, Rinehart & Winston.

Hart, C. W. and A. R. Pilling. 1961. *The Tiwi of North Australia.* New York: Holt, Rinehart & Winston.

Hart, V. et al. 1996. "Strategies for Increasing Participation of Ethnic Minorities in Alzheimer's Disease Diagnostic Centers: A Multifaceted Approach in California." *Gerontologist* 36(2):259–263.

Hashimoto, A. 1991. "Urbanization and Changes in Living Arrangements of the Elderly." In *Ageing and Urbanization.* New York: United Nations.

———. 1993. "Family Relations in Later Life: A Cross-Cultural Perspective." *Generations* (Winter) :24–26.

———. 1996. *The Gift of Generations: Japanese and American Perspectives on Aging and the Social Contract.* Cambridge, UK: Cambridge University Press.

Hatchett, S. and J. S. Jackson. 1993. "African American Extended Kin Systems: An Assessment." In *Family Ethnicity—Strength in Diversity.* H. P. McAdoo, ed. Newbury Park, CA: Sage.

Hay, M. J. and S. Stichter, eds. 1984. *African Women South of the Sahara.* London and New York: Longman.

Hayes, C., R. Kalish and D. Guttmann, eds. 1986. *European-American Elderly: A Guide For Practice.* New York: Springer.

Hazan, H. 1980. *The Limbo People: A Study of the Constitution of the Time Universe Among the Aged.* Boston: Routledge & Kegan Paul.

———. 1984. "Continuity and Transformation Among the Aged: A Study in the Anthropology of Time." *Current Anthropology* 25:567–578.

———. 1996. *From First Principles: An Experiment in Ageing.* Westport, CT: Greenwood.

Heckscher, E. F. 1954. *An Economic History of Sweden.* Cambridge, MA: Harvard University Press.

Heikkinen, E., W. E. Waters and Z. J. Brzezinski. 1983. *The Elderly in Eleven Countries.* Copenhagen: World Health Organization, Regional Office for Europe.

Heisel, M. A. 1985. "Aging in the Context of Population Policies in Developing Countries." *Population Bulletin of the United Nations.*

Hellebrandt, F. 1980. "Aging among the Advantaged: A New Look at the Stereotype of the Elderly." *The Gerontologist* 20(4):404–417.

Hemlock Society of the U.S.A. 1994. *Newsletter.* Eugene, OR: Hemlock Society of America.

Henderson, J. N. 1987. "Mental Disorders Among the Elderly: Dementia and Its Sociocultural Correlates." In *The Elderly as Modern Pioneers.* P. Silverman, ed. Bloomington: Indiana University Press.

———. 1990a. "Anthropology, Health and Aging." In *Anthropology and Aging: Comprehensive Reviews.* R. Rubinstein, ed. Norwell, MA: Kluwer.

———. 1990b. "Alzheimer's Disease in Cultural Context." In *The Cultural Context of Aging: Worldwide Perspectives.* J. Sokolovsky, ed. New York: Bergin & Garvey.

———. 1992. "The Power of Support: Alzheimer's Disease Support Groups for Minority Families." *Aging* (363–364) :24–28.

———. 1994a. "The Gerontology of American Indian Epidemiology." Paper presentation, American Public Health Association Annual Meeting, Washington, DC.

———. 1994b. "Caregiving Issues in Culturally Diverse Populations." *Seminars in Speech and Language* 15:216–225.

———. 1994c. "Race and Ethnicity." In *Qualitative Research in Elderly Populations.* J. Gubrium and A. Sankar, eds. New York: Sage.

———. 1996. "Cultural Dynamics of Dementia in a Cuban and Puerto Rican Population in the U.S." In *Ethnicity and the Dementias.* G. Yeo and D. Gallagher-Thompson, eds. Washington, DC: Taylor and Francis.

Henderson, J. N. and M. Gutierrez-Mayka. 1992. "Ethnocultural Themes in Caregiving to Alzheimer's Patients in Hispanic Families." *Clinical Gerontologist* 11:59–74.

Henderson, J. N., M. Gutierrez-Mayka, J. Garcia and S. Boyd. 1993. "A Model for Alzheimer's Disease Support Group Development in African American and Hispanic Populations." *The Gerontologist* 33:409–414.

Henderson, J. N. and M. Vesperi, eds. 1995. *The Culture of Long-Term Care: Nursing Home Ethnography.* Westport, CT: Greenwood.

Hendricks, J., ed. 1981. *In the Country of the Old.* Farmingdale, NY: Baywood.

———. 1995. "The Social Construction of Ageism." In *Promoting Successful and Productive Aging.* L. Bond, S. Cutler and A. Grams, eds. Thousand Oaks, CA: Sage.

Hendrie, H. et al. 1993. "Alzheimer's Disease Rare in Cree." *International Psychogeriatrics* 5 (1) :5–14.

Hennessy, C. H. and R. John. 1995. "The Interpretation of Burden among Pueblo Indian Caregivers." *Journal of Aging Studies* 9(3):231–244.

Henry, J. 1963. *Culture Against Man.* New York: McGraw-Hill.

Hermalin, A., M. Ofstedal and M. Chang. 1995. "Types of Supports for the Aged and Their Providers in Taiwan." In *Aging and Generational Relations over the Life Course.* T. Hareven, ed. Hawthorne, NY: Aldine de Gruyter.

Herskovits, E. 1995. "Struggling over Subjectivity: Debates about 'Self' and Alzheimer's Disease." *Medical Anthropology Quarterly* 9(2):146–164.

Hertz, R. 1960 (1907). *Death and The Right Hand.* Trans. R. Needham and C. Needham. Glencoe, IL: Free Press.

Herz, F. and E. Rosen. 1982. "Jewish Families." In *Ethnicity and Family Therapy.* M. McGoldrick, J. Pearce and J. Giordano, eds. New York: Guilford.

Hewitt, R. 1986. *Structure, Meaning and Ritual in the Narratives of the Southern San.* Hamburg: Helmut Burke Verlag.

Higuchi, K. 1992. "Rōjin kea o dō suru ka—ronten" [What to Do about Elder Care—a Discussion]. In *Nihon no Ronten.* Bungeishunju, ed. Tokyo: Bungeishunju.

Hill, R. et al. 1993. *Research on the African-American Family: A Holistic Perspective.* Westport, CT: Auburn House.

Hirsh, H. L. 1985. "Who May Eat and Who May Starve?" *Nursing Homes* (July/August):9–10.

Himes, C., D. Hogan and D. Eggebeen. 1996. "Living Arrangements of Minority Elders." *Journal of Gerontology* 51B(1):S42–48.

Ho, M. K. 1987. *Family Therapy with Ethnic Minorities.* Newbury Park, CA: Sage.

Hochschild, A. R. 1973. *The Unexpected Community: Portrait of an Old Age Subculture.* Berkeley: University of California Press.

Hockey, J. and A. James. 1993. *Growing Up and Growing Old: Ageing and Dependency in The Life Course.* London: Sage Publications.

Hoefler, J. 1994. *Deathright: Culture, Medicine, Politics, and the Right to Die.* Boulder, CO: Westview.

Holder, A. R. 1984. "Writing DNR Orders that Won't Get You Sued." *Medical Economics,* September 17:82–87.

Holmberg, A. 1969. *Nomads of the Long Bow.* Garden City, NY: Natural History Press.

Holmberg, A. R. 1961. "Age in the Andes." In *Aging and Leisure.* R. W. Kleemeier, ed. New York: Oxford University Press.

Holmes, D., M. Holmes and J. Terisi. 1983. "Differences among Black, Hispanic, and White People in Knowledge about Long-Term Care Services." *Health Care Financing Review* 5(2):51–66.

Holmes, E. 1986. "Aging in Modern and Traditional Societies." *The World and I* (9). Baltimore: The Washington Times.

Holmes, E. and L. D. Holmes. 1987. "Western Polynesia's Home for the Aged: Are Concept and Culture Compatible?" *Journal of Cross-Cultural Gerontology* 2(4): 359 376.

Holmes, L. D. 1972. "The Role and Status of the Aged in a Changing Samoa." In *Aging And Modernization.* D. O. Cowgill and L. D. Holmes, eds. New York: Appleton-Century-Crofts.

———. 1974. *Samoan Village.* New York: Holt, Rinehart & Winston.

———. 1987. "Cultural Values and Cultural Change." *Journal of Cross-Cultural Gerontology* 2:195–200.

Holmes, L. D. and E. Rhoads. 1987. "Aging and Change in Samoa." In *Growing Old in Different Societies: Cross-Cultural Perspectives.* J. Sokolovsky, ed. Acton, MA: Copley.

Holzberg, C. 1982. "Ethnicity and Aging: Anthropological Perspectives on More than Just the Minority Elderly." *Gerontologist* 22(3):249–257.

Hoover, S. L. and J. S. Siegel. 1986. "International Demographic Trends and Perspectives on Aging." *Journal of Cross-Cultural Gerontology* 1:5–30.

Hooyman, N. and Kiyak, H. 1993. *Social Gerontology*. Boston: Allyn and Bacon.

Hopper, K. and J. Hamburg. 1984. *The Making Of America's Homeless: From Skid Row To New Poor*. New York: Community Service Society.

Hopper, S. 1993. "The Influence of Ethnicity on the Health of Older Women." *Clinics in Geriatric Medicine: Care of the Older Woman* 9:231–257.

Hornum, B. 1987. "The Elderly in British New Towns: New Roles, New Networks." In *Growing Old in Different Societies*. J. Sokolovsky, ed. Acton, MA: Copley.

Hoskins, I. 1994a. "Working Women and Eldercare: A Six Nation Overview." *Ageing International* 11:58–62.

———. 1994b. *Combining Work and Eldercare: A Challenge for the 1990's and Beyond*. Geneva: International Labour Office.

Hostetler, J. and G. Huntington. 1971. *Children in Amish Society: Socialization*. New York: Holt, Rinehart & Winston.

Howe, N. 1995. "Why the Graying of the Welfare State Threatens to Flatten the American Dream—or Worse." *Generations* 19:15–19.

Howell, N. 1979. *Demography of the Dobe Area !Kung*. New York: Academic.

Hu, T. and W. S. Cartwright. 1986. "Evaluation of the Costs of Caring for the Senile Demented Elderly: A Pilot Study." *The Gerontologist* 26:158–163.

Hu, Y. H. 1995. "Elderly Suicide Risk in Family Contexts: A Critique of the Asian Family Care Model." *Journal of Cross-Cultural Gerontology* 10(3):199–217.

Human Resources Administration. 1987. *Comprehensive Homeless Assistance Plan*. Washington, DC: Human Resource Administration.

Humphry, D. 1991. *The Final Exit*. Eugene, OR: The Hemlock Society.

Huntsman, J. and A. Hooper. 1975. "Male and Female in Tokelau Culture." *Journal of the Polynesian Society* 84(4):415–430.

Hurston, Z. N. 1983. *The Sanctified Church*. Berkeley: Turtle Island.

Hurtado, A-D., D. Hayes-Bautista, R. Valdez and A. Hernandez. 1992. *Redefining California: Latino Social Engagement in a Multicultural Society*. Los Angeles: University of California, Chicano Studies Research Center.

Hurwicz, M.-L., ed. 1995. "Cultural Contexts of Aging and Health." Special Issue of *Medical Anthropology Quarterly* 9:2.

Huseby-Darvas, E. V. 1987. "Elderly Women in a Hungarian Village: Childlessness, Generativity, and Social Control." *Journal of Cross-Cultural Gerontology* 2(1): 15–42.

Hyden, M. 1994. *Woman Battering as Marital Act: The Construction of a Violent Marriage*. New York: Oxford University Press.

Hynson, L. M. 1975. "Rural-Urban Differences in Satisfaction Among the Elderly." *Rural Sociology* 40:64–65.

Ikels, C. 1983. *Aging and Adaptation: Chinese in Hong Kong and the United States*. Hamden, CT: Archon.

———. 1986. "Older Immigrants and Natural Helpers." *Journal of Cross-Cultural Gerontology* 1(2):209–222.

———. 1989. "Becoming a Human Being in Theory and in Practice: Chinese Views of Human Development." In *Social Structure and Aging: Comparative Perspectives on Age Structuring in Modern Societies*. D. Kertzer and K. W. Schaie, eds. Hillsdale, NJ: Erlbaum.

————. 1990. "Family Caregivers and the Elderly in China." In *Aging and Caregiving: Theory, Research, and Policy*. D. Biegel and A. Blum, eds. Newbury Park, CA: Sage.

————. 1991. "Aging and Disability in China: Cultural Issues in Measurement and Interpretation." *Social Science and Medicine* 32(6):649–655.

————. 1993. "Chinese Kinship and the State: Shaping of Policy for the Elderly." In *Annual Review of Gerontology and Geriatrics: Focus on Kinship, Aging and Social Change*. G. L. Maddox and M. P. Lawton, eds. New York: Springer.

————, ed. 1993. "Home Health Care and Elders: International Perspectives." Special Issue of *Journal of Cross-Cultural Gerontology* 8:4.

————. 1996. *The Return of the God of Wealth: The Transition to a Market Economy in Urban China*. Stanford, CA: Stanford University Press.

————. Forthcoming. "The Experience of Dementia in China." *Culture, Medicine and Psychiatry*.

Ikels, C., J. Keith and C. L. Fry. 1988. "The Use of Qualitative Methodologies in Large-Scale Cross-Cultural Research." In *Qualitative Gerontology*. S. Reinharz and G. Roles, eds. New York: Springer.

Inal-Ipa, S. D. 1982. "Changes in the Abkhazian Traditional Way of Life Since the Late 19th Century" (unpublished paper).

Ineichen, B. 1995. "Senile Dementia in Japan: Prevalence and Response." *Social Science and Medicine* 42:169–172.

Ingstad, B., F. Bruun, E. Sandberg and S. Tlou. 1992. "Care for the Elderly, Care by the Elderly: The Role of Elderly Women in a Changing Tswana Society." *Journal of Cross-Cultural Gerontology* 7:379–398.

Ingstad, B. and S. Reynolds, eds. 1995. *Disability and Culture*. Berkeley: University of California Press.

Interrante, J. 1987. "To Have without Holding: Memories of Life With a Person with AIDS." *Radical America* 2(6):55–62.

Jackson, J. J. 1972. "Comparative Life Styles and Family and Friend Relationships Among Older Black Women." *The Family Coordinator* 21:477–485.

————. 1980. *Minorities and Aging*. Belmont, CA.: Wadsworth.

————. 1985. "Race, National Origin, Ethnicity and Aging." In *Handbook of Aging and the Social Sciences*, 2d ed. R. Binstock and E. Shanas, eds. New York: Van Nostrand Reinhold.

Jackson, J. J. and D. Ensley. 1990–1991. "Ethnogerontology's Status and Complementarity and Conflicting Social and Cultural Concerns for American Minority Elders." *Journal of Minority Aging* 12:41–78.

Jackson, J. S., L. Chatters and R. Taylor, eds. 1993. *Aging in Black America*. Newbury Park, CA: Sage.

Jackson, J. S., R. Jayakody and T. C. Antonucci. 1995. "Exchanges within Black American Three-Generation Families: The Family Environment Context Model." In *Aging and Generational Relations over the Life Course*. T. Hareven, ed. Hawthorne, NY: Aldine de Gruyter.

Jackson, J. S., S. Lockery and F. Juster. 1996. "Introduction: Health and Retirement Among Ethnic and Racial Minority Groups." *Gerontologist* 36(3):282–284.

Jackson, J. S., P. Newton, A. Ostfield, D. Savage and E. L. Schneider, eds. 1988. *The Black American Elderly: Research on Physical and Psychosocial Health*. New York: Springer.

Jackson, M. and Z. Harel. 1983. "Ethnic Differences in Social Support Networks." *Urban Health* 9:35–38.

Jacobs, J. 1974. *Fun City: An Ethnographic Study of a Retirement Community.* New York: Holt, Rinehart & Winston.

Jacobson, D. 1987. "The Cultural Context of Social Support Networks." *Medical Anthropology Quarterly* 1:42–67.

Jecker, N. 1994. "Physician Assisted Suicide in the Netherlands and the United States." *Journal of the American Geriatrics Society* 42(6):672–678.

Jendrek, M. 1994. "Grandparents Who Parent Their Grandchildren: Circumstances and Decisions." *The Gerontologist* 34(2):206–216.

Jenike, B. R. n.d. "Learning to Volunteer: Women's Support Networks for the Care of the Elderly in Urban Japan." Paper presented at the 94th Annual Meeting of the American Anthropological Association, November 18, 1995.

Jerrome, D. 1981. "The Significance of Friendship for Women in Later Life." *Ageing and Society* 1(2):175–197.

―――. 1988. " 'That's What It's All About': Old People's Organization as a Context for Aging." *Journal of Aging Studies* 2(1):71–81.

―――. 1992. *Good Company: An Anthropological Study of Old People in Groups.* Edinburgh: University of Edinburgh Press.

Jochelson, V. 1933. *The Yakut.* New York: American Museum of Natural History.

Johansson, L. 1993. "Promoting Home-Based Elder Care: Some Swedish Experiences." *Journal of Cross-Cultural Gerontology* 8:391–406.

John, R. and D. Baldridge. 1996. *The NICOA Report: Health and Long Term Care for Indian Elders.* Washington, DC: National Indian Policy Center.

John, R., P. Blanchard and C. Hennessy. 1997. "Hidden lives: Aging and Contemporary American Indian Women." In *Handbook on Women and Aging.* J. Coyle, ed. Westport, CT: Greenwood.

Johns, S., I. Hydle and O. Aschjem. 1990. "The Act of Abuse: a Two Headed Monster of Injury and Offence." *Journal of Elder Abuse and Neglect* 3(1):53–64.

Johnson, C. 1983a. "A Cultural Analysis of Grandmother." *Research on Aging* 5:547–568.

―――. 1983b. "Fairweather Friends and Rainy Day Kin: An Anthropological Analysis of Old Age Friendships in the United States." *Urban Anthropology* 12:103–123.

―――. 1985. *Growing Up and Growing Old in Italian-American Families.* New Brunswick, NJ: Rutgers University Press.

―――. 1987. "The Institutional Segregation of the Aged." In *The Elderly as Modern Pioneers.* P. Silverman, ed. Bloomington: Indiana University Press.

―――. 1995. "Cultural Diversity in Late-Life Families." In *Handbook of Aging and the Family.* R. Blieszner and V. Bedford, eds. Westport, CT: Greenwood Press.

Johnson, C. and B. Barer. 1997. *Life Beyond 85 Years: The Aura of Survivorship.* New York: Springer.

Johnson, S. K. 1971. *Idle Haven: Community Building among the Working Class Retired.* Berkeley: University of California Press.

Jones, F. C. 1973. "The Lofty Role of the Black Grandmother." *Crisis* 80(1):19–21.

Jones, G. and B. Miesen, eds. 1992. *Care Giving in Dementia: Research and Applications.* London: Tavistock/Routledge.

Jonsson Gardens Document. 1983. Linkoping.

Jorm, A. F. 1990. *The Epidemiology of Alzheimer's Disease and Related Disorders.* New York: Chapman and Hall.

Journal of Housing for Elderly 11 (1). 1994. Special issue: "University Linked Retirement Communities: Student Visions of Eldercare." L. A. Pastalan and B. Schwarz, eds.

Juniper, A. B. 1922. "Native Dietry on Niue Island." *Journal of Home Economics* 14(11):612–614.

Jylha, M. and J. Jokela. 1990. "Individual Experiences as Cultural—A Cross-Cultural Study on Loneliness Among the Elderly." *Aging and Society* 10:295–315.

Kagan, D. 1980. "Activity and Aging in a Colombian Peasant Village." In *Aging in Culture and Society.* C. L. Fry, ed. New York: Bergin.

Kagawa-Singer, M. 1995. "Diverse Cultural Beliefs and Practices About Death and Dying in the Elderly." *Gerontological and Geriatric Education* 15:101–116.

Kahn, R. and T. Antonucci. 1980. "Convoys Over the Life Course: Attachment, Roles, and Social Support." In *Life-Span Development and Behavior*, vol. 3. P. B. Baltes and O. Brim, eds. New York: Academic Press.

———. 1981. "Convoys of Social Support: A Life-Course Approach." In *Aging: Social Change.* S. Kiesler, J. Morgan and V. K. Oppenheimer, eds. New York: Academic Press.

Kaiser, M. and S. Chawla. 1994. "Caregivers and Care Recipients: The Elderly in Developing Countries." *Ageing International* 11:42–49.

Kalish, R. and D. Reynolds. 1976. *Death and Ethnicity: A Psychocultural Study.* Los Angeles: Ethel Percy Andrus Gerontology Center, University of Southern California.

Kaminsky, M. 1993. "Definitional Ceremonies: Depoliticizing and the Reenchanting the Culture of Aging." In *Voices and Visions of Aging: Toward a Critical Gerontology.* T. Cole, A. Achenbaum, P. Jacobi and R. Kastenbaum, eds. New York: Springer.

Kaminsky, M., ed. 1992. *Remembered Lives: The Work of Ritual, Storytelling and Growing Older.* Ann Arbor: University of Michigan Press.

Kandel, R. and M. Heider. 1979. "Friendship and Factionalism in a Tri-Ethnic Housing Complex for the Elderly in North Miami." *Anthropological Quarterly* 52(1):49–60.

Kane, R. et al. 1991. "Adult Foster Care for the Elderly in Oregon: A Mainstream Alternative to Nursing Homes?" *American Journal of Public Health* 81:1113–1120.

Kane, R., G. Evans and D. Macfayden, eds. 1990. *Improving the Health of Older People: A World View.* Oxford: Oxford University Press.

Kart, C. S. 1993. "Community-Based, Noninstitutional Long-Term Care Service Utilization by Aged Blacks: Facts and Issues." In *Ethnic Elderly and Long-Term Care.* C. M. Barresi and D. E. Stull, eds. New York: Springer.

Kart, C. S. and C. F. Longino, Jr. 1987. "The Support Systems of Older People: A Test of the Exchange Paradigm." *Journal of Aging Studies* 1(3):253–264.

Kastenbaum, R. 1963. "Cognitive and Personal Futurity in Later Life." *Journal of Individual Psychology* 19:216–222.

———. 1966. "On the Meaning of Time in Later Life." *Journal of Genetic Psychology* 109:9–25.

Katz, R. 1982. *Boiling Energy: Community Healing Among the Kalahari Kung.* Cambridge, MA: Harvard University Press.

Katz, R. and M. Biesele. 1986. "!Kung Healing: The Symbolism of Sex Roles and Culture Change." In *The Past and Future of !Kung Ethnography: Critical Reflections and Symbolic Perspectives. Essays In Honor of Lorna Marshall.* M. Biesele, with R. Gordon and R. Lee, eds. Hamburg: Helmut Buske Verlag.

Katz, R., M. Biesele and V. St. Denis. 1995. *Healing Makes Our Hearts Happy: Spirituality and Transformation among the Ju/'hoansi of the Kalahari.* Rochester, VT: Inner Traditions.

Katz, S. 1995. "Imaging the Life-Span: From Premodern Miracles to Postmodern Fantasies." In *Images of Aging: Cultural Representations of Later Life.* M. Featherstone and A. Wernick, eds. London: Routledge.

Kaufert, J., P. Kaufert and D. Locker. 1987. "After the Epidemic: The Long-Term Impact of Poliomylitis." In *Health and Canadian Society.* D. Coburn et al., eds. Toronto: Fitzhenry.

Kaufert, J. and E. Shapiro. 1996. "Cultural, Linguistic and Contextual Factors in Validating the Mental Status Questionnaire." *Transcultural Psychiatric Research Review* 20:4.

Kaufert, P. and M. Lock. 1992. "What are Women For?: Cultural Construction of Menopausal Women in Japan and Canada." In *Her Prime: New Views of Middle-Aged Women.* V. Kerns and J. Brown, eds. Urbana: University of Illinois Press.

Kaufman, S. 1986. *The Ageless Self: Sources of Meaning in Late Life.* New York: Meridian.

————. 1988. "Stroke Rehabilitation and the Negotiation of Identity." In *Qualitative Gerontology.* S. Reinhart and G. Rowles, eds. New York: Springer.

Kayberry, P. 1939. *Aboriginal Women.* New York: Gordon Press.

Kaye, L. 1995. "Assessing the Efficacy of a Self-Help Support Group Program for Older Women." *Journal of Women and Aging* 7(4):11–30.

Kaye, L. and J. Applegate. 1994. "Older Men and the Family Caregiving Orientation." In *Older Men's Lives.* E. Thompson, ed. Thousand Oaks, CA: Sage.

Kayser-Jones, J. S. 1981. *Old, Alone, and Neglected: Care of the Aged in Scotland and the United States.* Berkeley: University of California Press.

Keesing, F. M. 1953. *Social Anthropology in Polynesia.* London: Oxford University Press.

Keigher, S. and F. Pratt. 1991. "Growing Housing Hardship Among the Elderly." In *Housing Risks and Homelessness Among the Urban Elderly.* S. Keigher, ed. New York: Haworth Press.

Keith, J. 1977. *Old People, New Lives: Community Creation in a Retirement Residence.* Chicago: University of Chicago Press.

————, ed. 1979. "The Ethnography of Old Age." Special issue of *Anthropological Quarterly* 52(1).

————. 1982. *Old People as People: Social and Cultural Influences on Aging and Old Age.* Boston: Little, Brown.

————. 1986. "Participant Observation." In *New Methods for Old Age Research.* C. Fry and J. Keith, eds. South Hadley, MA: Bergin and Garvey.

————. 1988. "A Modest Little Method Whose Presumptions May Amuse You." In *Methodological Issues in Aging.* W. Schaie, R. Cambell, W. Meredith and J. Nesselroade, eds. New York: Springer.

———. 1992. "Taking Care in Cultural Context: Anthropological Queries." In *Family Support for the Elderly: An International Experience*. H. Kendig, A. Hashimoto and L. Coppard, eds. New York: Oxford University Press.

———. 1994. "Old Age and Age Integration: An Anthropological Perspective." In *Age and Structural Lag: Essays on Changing Work, Retirement and Other Structures*. M. Riley, R. Kahn and A. Foner, eds. New York: John Wiley and Sons.

Keith, J., C. Fry, A. P. Glascock, C. Ikels, J. Dickerson-Putman, H. C. Harpending and P. Draper. 1994. *The Aging Experience: Diversity and Commonality Across Cultures*. Thousand Oaks, CA: Sage.

Kellogg, S. 1995. *Law and the Transformation of Aztec Culture, 1500–1700*. Norman, OK: University of Oklahoma Press.

Kelly, W. 1993a. "Japan's Debates about an Aging Society: The Later Years in the Land of the Rising Sun." In *Justice Across Generations: What Does It Mean?* L. Cohen, ed. Washington, DC: American Association of Retired Persons.

———. 1993b. Finding a Place in Metropolitan Japan: Ideologies, Institutions, and Everyday Life. In *Postwar Japan as History*. A. Gordon, ed. Berkeley: University of California Press.

Kemp, B., F. Staples and W. Lopez-Aquires. 1987. "Epidemiology of Depression and Dysphoria in our Elderly Hispanic Population." *Journal of the American Geriatrics Society* 35:920–926.

Kemper, P. and C. Murtaugh. 1991. "Lifetime Use of Nursing Home Care." *New England Journal of Medicine* 324:595–600.

Kendig, H., A. Hashimoto and L. Coppard, eds. 1992. *Family Support for the Elderly: An International Experience*. New York: Oxford University Press.

Kenya, Republic of. 1981. *Kenya Population Census, 1979*, vol. 1. Nairobi: Central Bureau of Statistics.

———. 1994. *Kenya Population Census, 1989*, vol. 1. Nairobi: Central Bureau of Statistics.

Kenyon, S. 1994. "Gender and Alliance in Central Sudan." *Journal of Cross-Cultural Gerontology* 9(2) 141–155.

Kent, S. and R. B. Lee. 1992. "A Hematological Study of !Kung Kalahari Foragers: An Eighteen-Year Comparison." In *Diet, Demography and Disease: Changing Perspectives on Anemia*. P. Stuart-Macadam and S. Kent, eds. New York: Aldine De Gruyter.

Kerns, V. 1983. *Woman and the Ancestors*. Urbana: University of Illinois Press.

Kerns, V. and J. K. Brown, eds. 1992. *In Her Prime: New Views of Middle-Aged Women*, 2d ed. Urbana: University of Illinois Press.

Kertzer, D. 1982. "Generation and Age in Cross Cultural Perspective." In *Aging from Birth to Death*, vol. 2. M. Riley, ed. Boulder, CO: Westview Press.

Kertzer, D. and J. Keith, eds. 1984. *Age and Anthropological Theory*. Ithaca, NY: Cornell University Press.

Kertzer, D. and P. Laslett, eds. 1994. *Demography Society and Old Age*. Berkeley: University of California Press.

Kertzer, D. and O. B. B. Madison. 1981. "Women's Age-Set Systems in Africa: The Latuka of Southern Sudan." In *Dimensions: Aging, Culture and Health*. C. Fry, ed. Brooklyn: J. F. Bergin.

Khasiani, S. 1985. *Adolescent Fertility in Kenya with Special Reference to High School Teenage Pregnancy*. Nairobi: The Pathfinder Fund.

Khoa, L. X. and D. D. Bui. 1985. "Southeast Asian Mutual Assistance Associations: An Approach for Community Development." In *Southeast Asian Mental Health: Treatment, Prevention, Services, Training, and Research*. T. C. Owan, ed. Washington DC: National Institute of Mental Health.

Khullar, G. S. and B. Reynolds. 1985. "Correlates of Religious Participation and Life Satisfaction." *Free Inquiry in Creative Sociology* 13(1):57–59.

Kiefer, C. 1974. "Lessons from the Issei." In *Late Life: Communities and Environmental Policy*. J. Gubrium, ed. Springfield, IL.: Charles Thomas.

———. 1987. "Care of the Aged in Japan." In *Health, Illness, and Medical Care in Japan*. E. Norbeck and M. Lock, eds. Honolulu: University of Hawaii Press.

———. 1990. "The Elderly in Modern Japan: Elite, Victims, or Plural Players?" In *The Cultural Context of Aging: Worldwide Perspectives*. J. Sokolovsky, ed. New York: Bergin and Garvey.

Kilbride, P. L. 1990. "Adolescent Premarital Pregnancies among Abaluyia of Kenya: The Grandparent Role." Paper presented at African Studies Association annual meeting, Baltimore.

Kilbride, P. L. and J. Kilbride. 1990. *Changing Family Life in East Africa: Women and Children at Risk*. University Park: Pennsylvania State University Press.

———. 1992. "Stigma, Role Overload, and the Delocalization of Family Tradition: Problems Facing the Contemporary Kenyan Woman." Paper presented at the Conference on Ecological and Cultural Change and Human Development in Western Kenya, Kakamega, Kenya.

King, V. and G. Elder. 1995. "American Children View Their Grandparents: Linked Lives Across Three Rural Generations." *Journal of Marriage and the Family* 57: 165–178.

Kinoshita, Y. and C. Kiefer. 1992. *Refuge of the Honored: Social Organization in a Japanese Retirement Community*. Berkeley, CA: University of California Press.

Kinsella, K. 1988. *Aging in the Third World*. Staff Paper No. 35. Washington, DC: U.S. Bureau of the Census, Center for International Research.

———. 1990. *Living Arrangements of the Elderly and Social Policy: A Cross-National Perspective*. Staff Paper No. 52. Washington, DC: U.S. Bureau of the Census, Center for International Research.

———. 1992a. *Population and Health Transitions*. Washington, DC: Center for International Research, U.S. Bureau of the Census.

———. 1992b. "Aging Trends: Kenya." *Journal of Cross-Cultural Gerontology* 7:259–268.

———. 1994. "Dimensiones Demograficas y de Salud en America Latina y el Caribe." In *La Atencion de los Ancianos: Un Desafio para los Años Noventa*. Scientific Publication No. 546. Washington, DC: Pan American Health Organization.

Kinsella, K. and Y. Gist. 1995. *Older Workers, Retirement, and Pensions: A Comparative International Chartbook*. Washington, DC: Bureau of the Census.

Kinsella, K. and C. Taeuber. 1993. *An Aging World II*. Washington, DC: U.S. Government Printing Office.

Kirkpatrick, J. 1985a. "*Ko'oua*: Aging in the Marquesas Islands." In *Aging And Its Transformations: Moving Toward Death in Pacific Societies*. D. A. Counts and D. R. Counts, eds. New York: University Press of America. (ASAO Monograph Number 10).

———. 1985b. "How Personal Differences Can Make a Difference." In *The Social*

Construction of the Person. K. J. Gergen and K. E. Davis, eds. New York: Springer.

Kirwen, M. C. 1979. *African Widows.* Maryknoll, NY: Orbis Books.

Kirwin, P. M. 1988. "The Challenge of Community Long Term Care: The Dependent Aged." *Journal of Aging Studies* 2(3):255–266.

Kitano, H. and R. Daniels. 1988. *Asian Americans.* Englewood Cliffs, NJ: Prentice-Hall.

Kitwood, T. 1993. "Towards a Theory of Dementia Care: The Interpersonal Process." *Ageing and Society* 13:51–67.

Kitwood, T. and K. Bredin. 1992. "Towards a Theory of Dementia Care: Personhood and Well-being." *Ageing and Society* 12:269–287.

Kivett, V. 1985. "Aging in Rural Society: Non-Kin Community Relations and Participation." In *The Elderly in Rural Society: Every Fourth American.* R. T. Coward and G. R. Lee, eds. New York: Springer.

Kivette, V. 1991. "Centrality of the Grandfather Role Among Rural Older Black and White Men." *Journal of Gerontology* 46:S250–258.

Klapper, J., S. Moss, M. Moss and R. Rubinstein. 1994. "The Social Context of Grief Among Adult Daughters Who Have Lost a Parent." *Journal of Aging Studies* 8: 29–43.

Knipscheer, C. et al., eds. 1995. *Living Arrangements and Social Networks of Older Adults.* Amsterdam, The Netherlands: VU University Press.

Knodel, J., N. Chayovan and S. Siriboon. 1995. "Familial Support and the Life Course of Thai Elderly and Their Children." In *Aging and Generational Relations over the Life Course.* T. Hareven, ed. Hawthorne, NY: Aldine de Gruyter.

Koblik, S. ed. 1975. *Sweden's Development from Poverty to Affluence 1750–1970.* Minneapolis: University of Minnesota Press.

Koenig, H. G. 1988. *Religion, Health, and Aging: A Review and Theoretical Integration.* New York: Greenwood Press.

Kohli, M. 1986. "The World We Forgot: A Historical Review of the Life Course." In *Later Life: The Social Psychology of Aging.* V. W. Marshall, ed. Beverly Hills: Sage.

Kongable, L., K. Buckwalter and J. Stolley. 1989. "The Effects of Pet Therapy on the Social Behavior of Institutionalized Alzheimer's Clients." *Archives of Psychiatric Nursing* 3(4):191–198.

Kopec, J. A. 1995. "Concepts of Disability: The Activity Space Model." *Social Science and Medicine* 40(5):649–656.

Kornhaber, A. 1996. *Contemporary Grandparenting.* Thousand Oaks, CA: Sage.

Korpi, W. 1978. *The Working Class in Welfare Capitalism: Work, Unions and Politics in Sweden.* London, Boston, and Henley: Routledge and Kegan Paul.

Korte, A. 1978. "Social Interaction and Morale of Spanish-Speaking Elderly." Unpublished Ph.D. diss. School of Social Welfare, Denver University.

Kosberg, J. 1992. *Family Care of the Elderly: Social and Cultural Changes.* Newbury Park, CA: Sage.

Kosberg, J. and J. Garcia, eds. 1995. *Elder Abuse: International and Cross-Cultural Perspectives.* Binghamton, NY: Haworth Press.

Koyano, W. 1989. "Japanese Attitudes Toward the Elderly: A Review of Research Findings." *Journal of Cross-Cultural Gerontology* 4(4):335–346.

Koyano, W. et al. 1994. "The Social Support System of the Japanese Elderly." *Journal of Cross-Cultural Gerontology* 9(3):323–333.

Kramer, B. 1991. "Urban American Indian Aging." *Journal of Cross-Cultural Geron-tology* 6(2):205–219.

Kramer, B. and J. Barker. 1996. "Homelessness Among Older Urban American Indians, Los Angeles, 1987–1989." *Human Organization* 55(4):396–408.

Krause, N. and E. Borawski-Clark. 1994. "Clarifying the Functions of Social Support in Later Life." *Research on Aging* 16(3):251–259.

Krause, N. and L. Goldenhar. 1992. "Acculturation and Psychological Distress in Three Groups of Elderly Hispanics." *Journal of Gerontology* 47:S279–288.

Krause, N. and J. Liang. 1992. "Cultural Variation in Depressive Symptoms in Later Life." *International Psychogeriatrics* 4(2):173–190.

Krieger, L. 1985. "Former Senator Pleads for Dignified Death." *American Medical News*, October 25:13–14.

Kroeber, A. 1939. *Cultural and Natural Areas of Native North America, Vol. 38*. University of California Publications in American Archaeology and Ethnology.

Krout, J. 1986. *The Aged in Rural America*. Westport, CT: Greenwood Press.

———. 1989. *Senior Centers in America*. Westport, CT: Greenwood Press.

———. 1993. *Community Based Services for the Rural Elderly*. Newbury Park, CA: Sage.

———. 1994. "Community Size Differences in Senior Center Resources, Programming, and Participation: A Longitudinal Study." *Research on Aging* 16(4):440–462.

———. 1995. "Senior Centers and Service for the Frail Elderly." *Journal of Aging and Social Policy* 7:59–76.

Krout, J. A. and D. L. Larson. 1980. "Self-Assessed Needs of the Rural Elderly." Paper presented at the annual meetings of the Rural Sociological Society, Ithaca, New York.

Kumajai, F. 1988. "Filial Violence in Japan." *Victimology* 8:173–194.

Kunitz, S. and J. Levy. 1989. "Aging and Health Among the Navaho Indians." In *Aging and Health*. K. Markides, ed. Thousand Oaks, CA: Sage.

———. 1991. *Navaho Aging: The Transition from Family to Institutional Support*. Tucson: University of Arizona Press.

Kunz, E. and K. Shannon. 1996. "PACE: Managed Care for the Frail Elderly." *American Journal of Managed Care* 2:301–304.

Kurtz, L. 1997. *Self-Help and Support Groups*. Thousand Oaks, CA: Sage.

La Fontaine, J. S. 1978. "Introduction." In *Sex and Age as Principles of Social Differentiation*. J. S. La Fontaine, ed. New York: Academic Press.

Laczko, F. and K. Payne, eds. 1994. *Older People in Eastern and Central Europe—The Price of Transition to a Market Economy*. London: HelpAge International.

Ladner, J. A. 1971. *Tomorrow's Tomorrow*. New York: Doubleday.

Ladner, S. 1992. "The Elderly Homeless." In *Homelessness: A National Perspective*. M. Robertson and M. Greenblatt, eds. New York: Plenum.

LaFargue, J. P. 1981. "Those You Can Count On: A Social Network Study of Family Organization in an Urban Black Population." Ph.D. diss. University of Washington.

Laird, C. 1979. *Limbo: A Memoir of Life in a Nursing Home by a Survivor*. Novato, CA: Chandler and Sharp.

Langness, L. L. and H. LeVine. 1986. *Culture and Retardation: Life Stories of Mildly Mentally Retarded Persons in American Society*. Dordrecht, The Netherlands: Reidel.

Laslett, P. 1976. "Societal Development and Aging." In *Handbook of Aging and the Social Sciences*. R. Binstock and E. Shanas, eds. New York: Van Nostrand Reinhold.

———. 1989. *A Fresh Map of Life*. London: Weidenfeld.

———. 1994a. "Necessary Knowledge: Age and Aging in Societies of the Past." In *Aging in the Past: Demography, Society and Old Age*. D. Kertzer and P. Laslett, eds. Berkeley: University of California Press.

———. 1994b. "The Third Age, The Fourth Age and the Future." *Ageing and Society* 14:436–447.

Lawton, M. P., M. Moss and E. Moles. 1984. "The Supra-Personal Neighborhood Context of Older People: Age Heterogeneity and Well-Being." *Environment and Behavior* 16(1):89–109.

Le, N. 1993. "The Case of the Southeast Asian Refugees: Policy for a Community 'At Risk'." In *The State of Asian Pacific America: Policy Issues to the Year 2020*. Leadership Education for Asian Pacifics and UCLA Asian American Studies Center. Los Angeles: LEAP Asian Pacifics and UCLA Asian American Studies Center.

Leaf, A. 1975. *Youth in Old Age*. New York: McGraw-Hill.

———. 1982. "Long-Lived Populations: Extreme Old Age." *Journal of the American Geriatrics Society* 38:485–487.

Lebra, T. 1984. *Japanese Women: Constraint and Fulfillment*. Honolulu: University of Hawaii Press.

———. 1986. "Compensative Justice and Moral Investment among Japanese, Chinese and Koreans." In *Japanese Culture and Behavior*. T. S. Lebra and W. P. Lebra, eds. Honolulu: University of Hawaii Press.

Lee, G. 1985. "Theoretical Perspective on Social Networks." In *Social Support Networks and the Care of the Elderly*. W. Sauer and R. Coward, eds. New York: Springer.

Lee, G. R. 1985. Kinship and Social Support of the Elderly: The Case of the United States. *Aging and Society* 5(1):19–38.

Lee, G. R. and M. C. Cassidy. 1981. "Kinship Systems and Extended Family Ties." In *The Family in Rural Society*. R. Coward and W. M. Smith, Jr., eds. Boulder, CO: Westview Press.

Lee, G. R. and M. L. Lassey. 1982. "The Elderly." In *Rural Society in the U.S.: Issues for the 1980's*. D. A. Dillman and D. A. Hobbs, eds. Boulder, CO: Westview Press.

Lee, G. R. and L. B. Whitbeck. 1987. "Residential Location and Social Relations among Older Persons." *Rural Sociology* 52:89–97.

Lee, R. 1968. "The Sociology of !Kung Bushman Trance Performances." In *Trance and Possession States*. R. Prince, ed. Montreal: Bucke Memorial Society.

———. 1969. "Eating Christmas in the Kalahari." *Natural History* (December): 14–22, 60–63.

———. 1979. *The !Kung San: Men, Women and Work in a Foraging Society*. Cambridge: Cambridge University Press.

———. 1984. *The Dobe !Kung*. New York: Holt, Rinehart & Winston.

———. 1985. "Work, Sexuality and Aging among !Kung Women." In *In Her Prime: A New View of Middle-Aged Women*. J. K. Brown and V. Kerns, eds. South Hadley MA: Bergin & Garvey.

Lee, R. and M. Biesele. 1991. "Dependency or Self-Reliance? The !Kung San Forty

Years On." Paper presented at the Symposium on "Theoretical and Methodological Flexibility in Long-term Fieldwork in Social Anthropology" at the American Anthropological Association Annual Meeting. Chicago: November 20–24, 1991.

Lee, R. and I. DeVore, eds. 1976. *Kalahari Hunter-Gatherers: Studies of the !Kung San and Their Neighbors.* Cambridge, MA: Harvard University Press.

Lee, R. and H. G. Rosenberg. 1993. "Fragments of the Future: Aspects of Social Reproduction among the Ju/hoansi." In *Hunters and Gatherers in the Modern Context: Proceedings of the Seventh International Conference on Hunting and Gathering Societies.* Institute of Ethnology and Anthropology, Russian Academy of Sciences, Moscow, 18–22 August, 1:413–424.

Leeson, G. and E. Tufte. 1994. "Concerns for Carers—Family Support in Denmark." *Aging International* (March): 49–53.

Legesse, A. R. 1973. *Gada.* New York: Free Press.

Lehman, D., J. Ellard and C. Wortman. 1986. "Social Support for the Bereaved: Recipients' and Providers Perspectives on What Is Helpful." *Journal of Consulting and Clinical Psychology* 54:438–446.

Le Navenec, C. and T. Vonhof. 1996. *One Day at a Time: How Families Manage the Experience of Dementia.* Westport, CT: Auburn House.

Lenke, L. 1990. *Alcohol and Criminal Violence: Time Series Analyses in a Comparative Context.* Stockholm: Almqvist & Wiksell.

Levi-Strauss, C. 1936. "Contributions a L'etude de L'organization Sociale des Indiens Bororo" (Contributions to the Study of the Social Organization of the Bororo Indians). *Societe des Americanistes de Paris* 28:269–304.

Levin, J., L. Chatters and R. Taylor. 1995. "Religious Effects on Health Status and Life Satisfaction Among Black Americans." *Gerontologist* 50B:S158–163.

Levine, R. 1965. "Intergenerational Tensions and Extended Family Structures in Africa." In *Social Structure and the Family.* E. Shanas and G. Strieb, eds. Englewood Cliffs, NJ: Prentice-Hall.

LeVine, S. and R. A. LeVine. 1985. "Age, Gender, and the Demographic Transition: The Life Course in Agrarian Societies." In *Gender and the Life Course.* A. S. Rossi, ed. New York: Aldine.

Levkoff, S., I. Macarthur and J. Bucknall. 1995. "Elderly Mental Health in the Developing World." *Social Science and Medicine* 41(7):983–1003.

Levy, R. 1973. *Tahitians: Mind and Experience in the Society Islands.* Chicago: University of Chicago Press.

Lew, L. S. 1991. "Elderly Cambodians in Long Beach: Creating Cultural Access to Health Care." *Journal of Cross-Cultural Gerontology* 6:199–203.

Lewis, O. 1963. *Life in a Mexican Village: Tepotzlan Restudied.* Urbana: University of Illinois Press.

Liem, N. D. and D. F. Kehmeier. 1979. "The Vietnamese." In *Peoples and Cultures of Hawaii.* J. F. McDermott, ed. Honolulu: University Press of Hawaii.

Li, G. et al. 1991. "A Three-Year Follow-up Study of Age-Related Dementia in an Urban Area of Beijing." *Acta Psychiatr. Scand.* 83:99–104.

Linn, M., B. Linn and R. Harris. 1981. "Stressful Life Events, Psychological Symptoms, and Psychosocial Adjustment in Anglo, Black, and Cuban Elderly." *Social Science and Medicine* 15:283–287.

Lipmann, B. 1995. *The Elderly Homeless: An Investigation of the Provision of Services for Frail, Elderly Homeless Men and Women in the United States of America, Britain, Sweden and Denmark.* Williamstown, Australia: Wintringham Hostels.

Little, V. 1982. *Open Care for the Aging: Comparative International Approaches.* New York: Springer.

———. 1983. "Introduction: Cross-National Reports on Elderly Care in Developing Countries." *Gerontologist* 23(6):573–575.

Litwak, E. 1985. *Helping the Elderly: The Complementary Roles of Informal Networks and Formal Systems.* New York: Guilford.

Litwin, H. 1995. *Uprooted in Old Age: Soviet Jews and Their Social Networks in Israel.* Westport, CT: Greenwood.

Lock, M. 1993a. "Ideology, Female Midlife, and the Greying of Japan." *Journal of Japanese Studies* 19:43–78.

———. 1993b. *Encounters With Aging: Mythologies of Menopause in Japan and North America.* Berkeley: University of California Press.

Loeb, E. M. 1926. *History and Traditions of Niue.* Honolulu: Bernice P. Bishop Museum. Bulletin Number 32. (New York: Kraus Reprints).

Lofgren, O. 1980. "Historical Perspectives on Scandinavian Peasantries." *Annual Review of Anthropology* 9:187–215.

Longhofer, J. 1994. "Nursing Home Utilization: a Comparative Study of the Hutterian Brethren, the Old Order Amish, and the Mennonites." *Journal of Aging Studies* 8:95–120.

Lopata, H. 1972. "Role Changes In Widowhood: A World Perspective." In *Aging and Modernization.* D. Cowgill and L. Holmes, eds. New York: Appleton-Century-Crofts.

———. 1979. *Women as Widows.* New York: Elsevier.

———, ed. 1987a. *Widows, Volume 1: The Middle East, Asia and the Pacific.* Durham, NC: Duke University Press.

———, ed. 1987b. *Widows: North America.* Durham, NC: Duke University Press.

———, ed. 1988. *Widows: Other Countries, Other Places.* Durham, NC: Duke University Press.

———. 1996. *Current Widowhood.* Thousand Oaks, CA: Sage.

Lozier, J. and R. Althouse. 1975. "Retirement to the Porch in Rural Appalachia." *International Journal of Aging and Human Development* 6(1):7–15.

Lubber, J. W. et al. 1988. "Health Promotion for the Rural Elderly." *The Journal of Rural Health* 4(3) 85–96

Luborsky, M. 1993. "Sociocultural Factors Shaping Technology Usage: Fulfilling the Promise." *Technology and Disability* 2(1):71–78.

———. 1994a. "The Cultural Adversity of Physical Disability: Erosion of Full Adult Personhood." *Journal of Aging Studies* 8(3):239–253.

———. 1994b. "The Identification and Analyses of Themes and Patterns." In *Qualitative Methods in Aging Research.* J. Gubrium and A. Sankar, eds. Thousand Oaks, CA: Sage.

———. 1995. "The Process of Self-report of Impairment in Clinical Research." *Social Science and Medicine* 40(11):1447–1459.

Luborsky, M. and R. Rubinstein. 1987. "Ethnicity and Lifetimes: Self-concepts and

Situational Contexts of Ethnic Identity in Late Life." In *Ethnic Dimensions of Aging.* D. Gelfand and C. Barresi, eds. New York: Springer.

―――. 1995. "Sampling in Qualitative Research: Rationale, Issues, and Methods." *Research on Aging* 17(1):89–113.

Luomala, K. 1978. "Symbolic Slaying in Niue: Post-European Changes in a Dramatic Ritual Complex." In *The Changing Pacific: Essays In Honor of H. E. Maude.* N. Gunson, ed. Melbourne, Australia: Oxford University Press.

Lyman, K. 1989. "Bringing the Social Back in: A Critique of the Biomedicalization of Dementia." *The Gerontologist* 29(5):597–605.

Lynch., A., D. R. Detzner and J. B. Eicher. 1995. "Hmong American New Year Rituals: Generational Bonds through Dress." *Clothing and Textiles Research Journal* 13: 111–120.

MacDonald, M., G. Remus and G. Laing. 1994. "Research Consideration: the Link between Housing and Health in the Elderly." *Journal of Gerontological Nursing* 20(7):5–10.

Mace, N. and P. Rabins. 1981. *The 36-Hour Day.* Baltimore: Johns Hopkins University Press.

MacManus, S. 1996. *Young Versus Old: Generational Combat in the 21st Century.* Boulder, CO: Westview.

Maddox, G. L. and M. P. Lawton, eds. 1993. *Annual Review of Gerontology and Geriatrics.* Focus on Kinship, Aging, and Social Change, vol. 13. New York: Springer.

Maeda, D. 1983. "Family Care in Japan." *Gerontologist* 23(6):579–583.

Maeda, D. and Y. Shimizu. 1992. "Family Support for Elderly People in Japan." In *Family Support for the Elderly: The International Experience.* H. Kendig, A. Hashimoto and L. Coppard, eds. Oxford: Oxford University Press.

Mahon, R. and R. Meidner. 1994. " 'System Shift'; or, What Is the Future of Swedish Social Democracy?" *Socialist Review* 23(4):57–77.

Main, A. 1994. "Reducing Morbidity in Stroke." In *Dementia and Cognitive Impairments.* L. J. Fitten, ed. Tokyo: Nankodo Publisher.

Makiesky-Barrow, S. and A. M. Lovell. 1987. "Homelessness and the Limited Options of Older Women." *Association for Anthropology and Gerontology Newsletter* 8(4):3–6.

Maldonado, D. 1975. "The Chicano Aged." *Social Work* 20:213–216.

―――. 1985. "The Hispanic Elderly: A Socio-Historical Framework for Public Policy." *Journal of Applied Gerontology* 4:18–27.

Malmberg, B. and S. H. Zarit. 1993. "Group Homes for People With Dementia: A Swedish Example." *The Gerontologist* 33(5):682–686.

Management and Coordination Agency (Sōmuchō). 1996. Rōdōryoku chōsa [Survey of the Labor Force]. In *Asahi Shimbun Japan Almanac 1997.* Tokyo: Asahi Shimbunsha.

Management and Coordination Agency. 1990. *International Comparative Survey on Elderly Peoples Lives and Attitudes (Rojin no seikatsu to ishiki ni kansuru kokusai hikaku chosa)* (in Japanese). Tokyo: Management and Coordination Agency.

Manton, K. G., L. S. Corder and E. Stallard. 1993. "Estimates of Change in Chronic Disability and Institutional Incidence and Prevalence Rates in the U.S. Elderly Population From the 1982, 1984 and 1989 National Long Term Care Survey." *Journal of Gerontology* 48:S153–166.

Manton, K. G., J. E. Dowd and M. A. Woodbury. 1986. "Conceptual and Measurement

Issues in Assessing Disability Cross-Nationally: Analysis of a WHO-Sponsored Survey of the Disablement Process in Indonesia.'' *Journal of Cross-Cultural Gerontology* 1(4):339–362.

Manton, K. G., G. Myers and G. Andrews. 1987. ''Morbidity and Disability Patterns in Four Developing Nations: The Implications for Social and Economic Integration of the Elderly.'' *Journal of Cross-Cultural Gerontology* 2:115.

Manton, K. G., E. Stallard and L. S. Corder. 1995. ''Changes in Morbidity and Chronic Disability in the U.S. Elderly Population: Evidence from the 1982, 1984, and 1989 National Long Term Care Surveys.'' *Journal of Gerontology: Social Sciences* 50B(4):194–204.

Manuel, R., ed. 1982. *Minority Aging: Sociological and Social Psychological Issues.* Westport, CT: Greenwood.

Margolick, D. 1994. ''Jurors Acquit Dr. Kevorkian in Suicide Case.'' *New York Times*, May 3: A1.

Markides, K. 1996. ''Race, Ethnicity and Aging: Impact of Inequality.'' In *Handbook of Aging and Social Sciences*, 4th ed. R. Binstock and L. George, eds. New York: Academic Press.

Markides, K., J. Boldt and L. Ray. 1986. ''Sources of Helping and Intergenerational Solidarity: A Three-Generation Study of Mexican Americans.'' *Journal of Gerontology* 41:506–511.

Markides, K., J. Liang and J. S. Jackson. 1990. Race, Ethnicity and Aging: Conceptual and Methodological Issues. In *Handbook of Aging and the Social Sciences*. R. Binstock and L. K. George, eds. San Diego: Academic Press.

Markides, K. and C. H. Mindel. 1987. *Aging and Ethnicity.* Beverly Hills: Sage.

Markides, K. and S. Vernon. 1984. ''Aging, Sex-role Orientation and Adjustment: A Three-generations Study of Mexican Americans.'' *Journal of Gerontology* 39(5): 586–591.

Markson, E. W. 1979. ''Ethnicity as a Factor in the Institutionalization of the Ethnic Elderly.'' In *Ethnicity and Aging: Theory, Research, and Policy.* D. Gelfand and A. Kutzik, eds. New York: Springer.

Markson, E. and M. Gognalons. 1992. In *Growing Old In America*, 4th ed. B. Hess and E. Markson, eds. New Brunswick, NJ: Transaction.

Marshall, L. 1961. ''Sharing, Talking and Giving: Relief of Social Tensions among the !Kung Bushmen.'' *Africa* 31:231–249.

———. 1976. *The !Kung of Nyae Nyae.* Cambridge, MA: Harvard University Press.

Martin, E. P. and J. M. Martin. 1978. *The Black Extended Family.* Chicago: University of Chicago Press.

Marx, K. 1963. *The Eighteenth Brumaire of Louis Bonaparte.* New York: International.

Mathers, C. 1991. *Health Expectancies in Australia 1981 and 1988.* Canberra: Australian Government Publishing Service.

Matthews, S. 1979. *The Social World of Old Women: Management of Self-Identity.* Beverly Hills: Sage.

Mauss, M. 1967. *The Gift: Forms and Functions of Exchange in Archaic Societies.* Ian Cunnison, trans. New York: W. W. Norton.

Maxwell, E. 1986. ''Fading Out: Resource Control and Cross-cultural Patterns of Deference.'' *Journal of Cross-Cultural Gerontology* 1:73–89.

Maxwell, E. and R. Maxwell. 1980. ''Contempt for the Elderly: A Cross-cultural Analysis.'' *Current Anthropology* 24:569–570.

————. 1992. "Insults to the Body Civil: Mistreatment of Elderly in Two Plains Indians Tribes." *Journal of Cross-Cultural Gerontology* 7:3–23.

Maxwell, R. 1970. "The Changing Status of Elders in a Polynesian Society." *Aging And Human Development* 1(2):137–146.

Maxwell, R., P. Silverman and E. K. Maxwell. 1982. "The Motive for Gerontocide." *Studies in Third World Societies* 22:67–84.

Mazess, R. and S. Forman. 1979. "Longevity and Age Exaggeration in Vilacabamba, Ecuador." *Journal of Gerontology* 34(1):94–98.

McAdoo, H. P. 1988. "Transgenerational Patterns of Upward Mobility in African-American Families." In *Black Families.* H. P. McAdoo, ed. Newbury Park, CA: Sage.

McArdle, J. and C. Yeracaris. 1981. "Respect for the Elderly in Preindustrial Societies as Related to Their Activity." *Behavior Science Research* 16(3/4):307–339.

McCallum, J. 1993. "Foreword: 'De-Constructing' Family Care Policy for the Elderly: A Note." *Journal of Aging and Social Policy* 5(1/2):1–5.

McCulloch, B. 1995. "The Relationship of Family Proximity and Social Support to the Mental Health of Older Rural Adults: the Appalachian Context." *Journal of Ageing and Society* 9:65–81.

McCulloch, B. and G. Roles, eds. 1993. "Poverty Among the Elderly of Rural America." Special Issue of *Journal of Applied Gerontology* 12:3.

McEwen, J. M. 1974. "Understanding Polynesians." In *Polynesian And Pakeha In New Zealand Education, Volume 2: Ethnic Differences And The School.* D. H. Bray and C. G. N. Hill, eds. Auckland, New Zealand: Heinemann Educational Books.

McGoldrick, M., J. Pearce and J. Giordano. 1982. *Ethnicity and Family Therapy.* New York: Guilford.

McLachlan, S. 1982. "Savage Island or Savage History? An Interpretation of Early European Contact with Niue." *Pacific Studies* 6:26–51.

McNeely, R. and J. Cohen, eds. 1983. *Aging in Minority Groups.* Beverly Hills: Sage.

McRae, J. M. 1975. *Elderly in the Environment—Northern Europe.* Gainesville, FL: College of Architecture and Center for Gerontological Studies and Programs.

Mead, M. 1928. *The Coming of Age in Samoa.* New York: William Morrow.

————. 1951. "Cultural Contexts of Aging." In *No Time to Grow Old, New York State Legislative Committee on Problems of Aging.* Legislative Document No. 12.

————. 1967. "Ethnological Aspects of Aging." *Psychosomatics* 8(4):33–37.

Medvedev, Z. A. 1974. "Caucasus and Altay Longevity: A Biological or Social Problem?" *The Gerontologist* 14:381–387.

Mercier, J. and E. Powers. 1984. "The Family and Friends of Rural Aged as a Natural Support System." *Journal of Community Psychology* 12:334–346.

Merry, S. 1996. "Urban Danger: Life in a Neighborhood of Strangers." In *Urban Life,* 3d ed. G. Gmelch and W. Zenner, eds. Prospect Heights, IL: Waveland Press.

Mexico D. F., DGE. 1970. *Integracion Territorial.* Direccion General de Estadistica.

————. 1973. "Special Tabulation." Direccion General de Estadistica (Typewritten).

Meyer, J. S., K. L. McClintoc, R. L. Rogers, R. Sims and K. F. Mortel. 1988. Aetiologic Considerations and Risk Factors for Multi-infarct Dementia. *Journal of Neurology, Neurosurgery and Psychiatry* 51:1489–1497.

Meyer, R., ed. 1988. *Bend the Trend: Meeting the Needs of the Rural Elderly.* Proceedings of a Conference on the Rural Elderly. Lawrence: Kansas University Press.

Michaels, D. and C. Levine. 1992. "Estimates of the Number of Motherless Youth

Orphaned by AIDS in the United States.'' *Journal of the American Medical Association* 268(24):3456–3461.

Migdale, J. 1974. *Peasants, Politics, and Revolution*. Princeton: Princeton University Press.

Millard, A. 1980. ''Corn, Cash and Population Genetics: Family Demography in Rural Mexico.'' Ph.D. diss. University of Texas at Austin.

Miller, B. et al. 1996. ''Minority Use of Community Long-Term Care Services: A Comparative Analysis.'' *Journal of Gerontology* 51B(3):S70–81.

Miller, C. M. 1996. ''Some Fear Reform Will Create a Crisis in Foster Care.'' *St. Petersburg Times*, November 3, 1B, 6B.

Miller, F., T. Quill, H. Brody, J. Fletcher, L. Gostin and D. Meier. 1994. ''Regulating Physician-Assisted Death.'' *New England Journal of Medicine* 331:119–123.

Miller, J. 1991. ''The On Lok Senior Health Services Consolidated Model of Long-term Care.'' In *Community Based Long-Term Care: Innovative Models*. J. Miller, ed. Newbury Park, CA: Sage.

Mindek, D. 1994. '' 'No Nos Sobra, Pero Gracias a Dios, Tampoco Nos Falta,' Crecimiento Demographico y Modernizacion en San Jeronimo Amanalco.'' Master's thesis. Iberoamericana University.

Ministry of Health and Welfare (Kōseishō), Prime Minister's Office for Health Welfare for the Elderly. 1992. *Netakiri Zero o Mezashite*, 2d ed. [Aiming for No Bedridden]. Tokyo: Chohōki Shuppan.

Ministry of Health and Welfare (Kōseishō). 1995. Kokumin Seikatsu Kiso Chōsa [Basic Survey of National Life]. In *Asahi Shimbun Japan Almanac 1996*. Tokyo: Asahi Shimbunsha.

———. 1996. *Kōsei Hakusho, Heisei 8 Nen han* [White Paper on Public Welfare, 1996 edition]. Tokyo: Kōseishō.

Minkler, M. 1990. ''Intergenerational Issues.'' In *Diversity in an Aging America: Challenges for the 1990's*. S. Schoenrock, J. Roberts and J. Hyde, eds. San Diego: National Resource Center on Minority Aging.

———. 1994. ''Grandparents as Parents.'' *Ageing International* (March): 24–28.

Minkler, M. and C. L. Estes, eds. 1984. *Readings in the Political Economy of Aging*. Farmingdale, NY: Baywood.

———, eds. 1991. *Critical Perspectives on Aging: The Political and Moral Economy of Growing Old*. Amityville, NY: Baywood.

Minkler, M. and K. Roe. 1993. *Grandmothers as Caregivers*. Newbury Park, CA.: Sage.

Minkler, M., K. Roe and M. Price. 1992. ''The Physical and Emotional Health of Grandmothers Raising Grandchildren in the Crack Cocaine Epidemic.'' *The Gerontologist* 32(6):752–761.

Mitchell, G. D. 1977. ''Village Agriculture in Niue: An Examination of Factors Influencing Participation and Productivity.'' Master's thesis. Geography Department, University of Canterbury, New Zealand.

Mitchner, J. 1994. *Recessional*. New York: Fawcett Crest.

Mollica, R. F., C. Y. Yacl, P. Bollini, T. Truong, S. Tor and J. Labelle. 1992. ''The Harvard Trauma Questionnaire: Validating a Cross-cultural Instrument for Measuring Torture, Trauma, and Posttraumatic Stress Disorder in Indochinese Refugees.'' *The Journal of Nervous and Mental Disease* 180:111–116.

Monk, A. and C. Cox. 1991. *Home Care for the Elderly*. Westport, CT: Auburn House.

Moon, J-H. and J. Pearl. 1991. ''Alienation of Elderly Korean American Immigrants as

Related to Place of Residence, Gender, Age, Years of Education, Time in the U.S., Living With or Without Children and Living With or Without Spouse." *International Journal of Aging and Human Development* 32:115–125.

Moore, A. 1973. *Life Cycles in Atchalan.* New York: Teachers College Press.

Moore, S. F. 1978. "Old Age in a Life-Term Social Arena." In *Life's Career-Aging: Cultural Variations on Growing Old.* B. Myerhoff and A. Simic., eds. Beverly Hills: Sage.

Moore, T. J. 1993. *Lifespan.* New York: Simon & Schuster.

Morgan, Henry. 1866. *Ned Nevins, the Newsboy; or Street Life in Boston.* Boston: Lee and Shepard.

Morgan, J. H., ed. 1985. *Aging in Developing Societies.* Scholastic Monograph Series. Bristol, IN: Wyndham Hall Press.

Morgan, L., K. Eckert and S. M. Lyon. 1995. *Small Board-and-Care Homes: Residential Care in Transition.* Baltimore: Johns Hopkins University Press.

Morris, R. 1994. "Public Policy for the Elderly: Are Priorities Shifting?: Unfamiliar Choices for Advocates in the 1990's." *Journal of Aging and Social Policy* 6(1/2).

Mortimer, J. A., 1995. "The Epidemiology of Alzheimer's Disease: Beyond Risk Factors." In *Research Advances in Alzheimer's Disease and Related Disorders.* K. Igbal, J. A. Mortimer, B. Winblad and H. Wisniewski, eds. New York: Wiley.

Mortimer, J. A. and A. B. Graves. 1993. "Education and Socioeconomic Determinants of Dementia and Alzheimer's Disease." *Neurology* 43(Suppl. 4):s39–s44.

Morycz, R. 1992. "Caregiving Families and Cross-Cultural Perspectives." In *Caregiving Systems: Informal and Formal Helpers.* S. Zarit, K. Perlin and K. W. Schaie, eds. Hillsdale, NJ: L. Erlbaum.

Moynihan, D. P. 1965. *The Case for National Action: The Negro Family.* Washington, DC: U.S. Department of Labor.

Mui, A. and D. Burnette. 1994. "Long-term Care Service Use by Frail Elders: Is Ethnicity a Factor?" *Gerontologist* 34(2):190–198.

Mullen, F. 1996. "Public Benefits: Grandparents, Grandchildren, and Welfare Reform." *Generations* 20(1):61–65.

Murdock, G. P. 1967. "Ethnographic Atlas: A Summary." *Ethnology* 6(2).

Murphy, R. 1987. *The Body Silent.* New York: Henry Holt and Company.

Murphy, R., J. Scheer, Y. Murphy and R. Mack. 1988. "Physical Disability and Social Liminality: A Study in the Rituals of Adversity." *Social Science and Medicine* 26(2):235–242.

Murray, A. W. 1863. *Missions In Western Polynesia.* London: J. Snow.

Myerhoff, B. 1978a. *Number Our Days.* New York: E. P. Dutton.

———. 1978b. "A Symbol Perfected in Death: Continuity and Ritual in the Life and Death of an Elderly Jew." In *Life's Career Aging: Cultural Variations on Growing Old.* B. Myerhoff and A. Simic, eds. Beverly Hills: Sage.

———. 1982. "Rites of Passage: Process and Paradox." In *Celebration: Studies in Festivity and Ritual.* V. Turner, ed. Washington, DC: Smithsonian Institution Press.

Myerhoff, B. and A. Simic, eds. 1978. *Life's Career-Aging: Cultural Variations on Growing Old.* Beverly Hills: Sage.

Myers, G. 1982. "The Aging of Populations." In *International Perspectives on Aging:*

Population and Policy Challenges. R. Binstock, W. S. Chow and J. Schulz, eds. New York: United Nations Fund for Population Activities.

————. 1985. "Demographic and Socio-Economic Aspects of Population Aging." *Research Project on Population Aging.* Initiating Meeting. Paris: Committee for International Cooperation in National Research in Demography.

————. 1990. "Demography and Aging." In *Handbook of Aging and the Social Sciences.* R. H. Binstock and L. K. George, eds. New York: Academic Press.

————. 1992. "Demographic Aging and Family Support for Older Persons." In *Family Support for the Elderly: The International Experience.* H. L. Kendig, A. Hashimoto and L. C. Coppard, eds. Oxford: Oxford University Press, for the World Health Organization.

Myers, G. and E. Agree. 1994. "The World Ages, the Family Changes." *Ageing International* 21(1):11–18.

Myers, L. W. 1978. "Elderly Black Women and Stress Resolution: An Exploratory Study." *The Black Sociologist* 8(1–4):29–37.

Myles, J. 1984. *Old Age in the Welfare State: The Political Economy of Public Pensions.* Boston and Toronto: Little, Brown.

Nadel, S. F. 1952. "Witchcraft in Four African Societies." *American Anthropologist* 54: 18–29.

Nahemow, N. 1987. "Grandparenthood Among the Baganda: Role Option in Old Age." In *Growing Old in Different Societies.* J. Sokolovsky, ed. Acton, MA: Copley.

Nanfang Ribao. October 4, 1991. "Liwan District Introduces Worker Contributory Pension Scheme."

Narduzzi, J. L. 1994. *Mental Health Among Elderly Native Americans.* New York: Garland.

Naroll, R., G. Michik and F. Naroll. 1976. *Worldwide Theory Testing.* New Haven, CT: Human Relation Area Files Press.

Nason, J. D. 1981. "Respected Elder or Old Person: Aging in a Micronesian Community." In *Other Ways of Growing Old.* P. T. Amoss and S. Harrell, eds. Stanford, CA: Stanford University Press.

National Center for Health Statistics. 1987. *Current Estimates from the National Health Interview Survey.* Vital and Health Statistics Series 10, No. 164. Washington, DC: U.S. Government Printing Office.

National Commission on Aging. 1982. *Just Another Age: A Swedish Report to the World Assembly on Aging.* Stockholm: Departementens Reprocentral.

National Council of the Aged. 1983. *Community Services for the Aged.* Dublin: National Council of the Aged.

————. 1984. *Incomes of the Elderly in Ireland.* Dublin: National Council of the Aged.

National Indian Council on Aging. 1979. *The Continuum of Life: Health Concerns of the Indian Elderly.* Final Report on the Second National Indian Conference on Aging, Billings, Montana, August 15–18, 1978. Albuquerque, NM: Adobe Press.

————. 1981. *American Indian Elderly: A National Profile.* Albuquerque, NM: Cordoba Printing.

Ncube, W. and J. Stewart. 1995. *Widowhood, Inheritance Laws, Customs & Practices.* Harare, Zimbabwe: Women and Law in Southern Africa Research Project.

Nelson, G. 1980. "Social Services to the Urban and Rural Aged: The Experience of New York State Senate Research Service." *The Gerontologist* 29(2):200–207.

Network News. 1992. "Older Women in Central and Eastern Europe: Caught in the

Transition.'' *Network News: A Newsletter of the Global Link for Midlife and Older Women* 7(1):1–6.

New Zealand Coalition For Trade And Development. 1982. *The Ebbing Tide: The Impact of Migration on Pacific Island Societies.* Wellington: New Zealand Coalition For Trade And Development.

Newman, S. A. 1991. ''Euthanasia: Orchestrating the Last Syllable of . . . Time.'' *University of Pittsburgh Law Review* 53:153–191.

Nihon Hōsō Kyokai (NHK). 1993. ''Obāchan no Omedetai'' [Blessed With Grandma]. TV broadcast.

Niue Government. 1982. *Niue: A History of the Island.* Niue/Suva, Fiji: Niue Government/Institue for Pacific Studies, University of the South Pacific.

———. 1985. *Report of a 1984 Mini-Census of Population.* Niue: Department of Economic Development.

———. 1988. *Census of Population and Dwellings 1986.* Statistics Unit, Administrative Department, Alofi, Niue.

Njiro, E. I. 1993. ''Labour Force Participation and the Women's Movement.'' In *The Women's Movement in Kenya.* S. A. Khasiani and E. I. Njiro, eds. Nairobi: Association of African Women for Research and Development.

Noguchi, P. H. 1983. ''Shiranai Station: Not a Destination but a Journey.'' In *Work and Lifecourse in Japan.* D. W. Plath, ed. Albany: State University of New York Press.

Nusberg, C. 1982. ''World Assembly Seeks to Alert Developing Countries About Their Aging Populations.'' *Aging International* 9(2):7–9.

Nusberg, C. and J. Sokolovsky, eds. 1994. *The International Directory of Research and Researchers in Comparative Gerontology.* 3rd ed. Washington, DC: American Association of Retired Persons.

Nusberg, C. with M. J. Gibson and S. Peace. 1984. *Innovative Aging Programs Abroad: Implication for the U.S.* Westport, CT: Greenwood Press.

Nyamwaya, D. 1992. *African Indigenous Medicine.* Nairobi: African Medical and Research Foundation.

Nydegger, C. 1983. ''Family Ties of the Aged in Cross-Cultural Perspective.'' *The Gerontologist* 23:26–32.

———, ed. 1984. ''Anthropological Approaches to Aging Research.'' Special issue, *Research on Aging.*

Oakley, R. 1992. *Old Age and Caregiving among the !Kung San.* Master's research paper. Department of Anthropology, University of Toronto.

Obeyesekere, G. 1982. ''Sinhalese-Buddhist Identity in Ceylon.'' In *Ethnic Identity: Cultural Continuities and Change.* G. DeVos and L. Romanucci-Ross, eds. Chicago: University of Chicago Press.

O'Brien, M. 1994. ''Vascular Disease and Dementia.'' In *Dementia and Cognitive Impairments.* L. J. Fitten, ed. Tokyo: Nankodo Publisher.

O'Connor, J. and M. Daly. 1983. *The West Limerick Study.* Limerick, Ireland: Social Research Center.

Ogawa, N. and R. Retherford. 1993. ''Care of the Elderly in Japan: Changing Norms and Expectations.'' *Journal of Marriage and the Family* 55:585–597.

Ogbu, J. U. 1973. ''Seasonal Hunger in Tropical Africa as a Cultural Phenomenon.'' *Africa* 43:317–332.

Okley, J., ed. 1990. ''Clubs for the Troisieme Age: Communitas or Conflict.'' In *An-*

thropology and the Riddle of the Sphinx: Paradoxes of Change in the Life Course. P. Spencer, ed. London and New York: Routledge.

Okojie, F. A. 1988. "Aging in Sub-Saharan Africa: Toward Redefinition of Needs Research and Policy Directions." *Journal of Cross-Cultural Gerontology* 3:3–20.

Oliver, D. L. 1961. *The Pacific Islands*, rev. ed. Honolulu: University of Hawaii Press.

Olson, L. 1993. *The Graying of the World: Who Will Care for the Frail Elderly.* Binghamton, NY: Haworth.

Olson, P. 1990. "The Elderly in the People's Republic of China." In *The Cultural Context of Aging: Worldwide Perspectives.* J. Sokolovsky, ed. Westport, CT: Bergin & Garvey.

Olsson, S. E. 1993. *Social Policy and the Welfare State in Sweden.* Lund, Sweden: Arkiv.

Olsson Hort, S. E. 1995. Personal Communication.

O'Nell, C. W. 1972. "Aging in a Zapotec Community." *Human Development* 15:294–309.

Osako, M. 1979. "Aging and Family Among Japanese-Americans: The Role of the Ethnic Tradition in the Adjustment to Old Age." *Gerontologist* 5:448–455.

Osuntokun, B. et al. 1992. "Cross-cultural Studies in Alzheimer's Disease." *Ethnicity and Disease* 2:352–357.

Padget, D., ed. 1995. *Handbook on Ethnicity, Aging, and Mental Health.* Westport, CT: Greenwood.

Pahl, R. E. 1965. "Class and Community in English Commuter Villages." *Sociologia Ruralis* 5:2–23.

Palmore, E. 1975a. *The Honorable Elders: A Cross-Cultural Analysis of Aging in Japan.* Durham, NC: Duke University Press.

———. 1975b. "The Status and Integration of the Aged in Japanese Society." *Journal of Gerontology* 30:199–208.

———. 1984. "Longevity in Abkhazia: A Reevaluation." *Gerontologist* 24:95–96.

———. 1987. "Cross-Cultural Perspectives on Widowhood." *Journal of Cross-Cultural Gerontology* 2(1):93–106.

Palmore, E. and D. Maeda. 1985. *The Honorable Elders Revisited: A Revised Cross-Cultural Analysis of Aging in Japan.* Durham, NC: Duke University Press.

Pan American Health Organization. 1989. *Mid-life and Older Women in Latin America and the Caribbean.* Washington, DC: Pan American Health Organization.

———. 1994. *Health Conditions in the Americas.* 1994 Edition, volume 1. Scientific Publication No. 549. Washington, DC: Pan American Health Organization.

Pang, P. 1990. "Hwabyung: The Construction of a Korean Popular Illness Among Korean Elderly Immigrant Women in the U.S." *Culture, Medicine and Psychiatry* 14(4):495–512.

Paradise, S. 1993. "Older Never Married Women: A Cross-Cultural Investigation." In *Faces of Women and Aging.* N. Davis, E. Cole and E. Rothblum, eds. Binghamton, NY: Harrington Press.

Parkes, C. and R. Weiss. 1983. *Recovery from Bereavement.* New York: Basic.

Parkin, D. and D. Nyamwaya, eds. 1987. *Transformations of African Marriage.* Manchester, UK: Manchester University Press.

Passarge, S. 1907. *Die Buschmänner der Kalahari.* Berlin: Dietrich Reimer.

Payne, B. and R. Cikovic. 1995. "An Empirical Examination of the Characteristics, Consequences, and Causes of Elder Abuse in Nursing Homes." *Journal of Elder Abuse and Neglect* 7(4):61–74.

Peace, S. M. 1981. *An International Perspective on the Status of Older Women.* Washington, DC: International Federation on Ageing.

Pearson, J. L. and C. Yeates, eds. 1995. Special issue of *International Psychogeriatrics* 7(2), "Suicide and Aging: International Perspectives."

Penrod, J. D., R. Kane, R. Kane and M. Finch. 1995. "Who Cares? The Size, Scope, and Composition of the Caregiver Support System." *The Gerontologist* 35:489–497.

Perez y Lizaur, M. 1970. "Asentamiento e Historia Demografica: Cuatro Comunidades." Master's thesis. Universidad Ibero Americana, Mexico, D. F.

Perkinson, M. 1980. "Alternate Roles For The Elderly: An Example From A Midwestern Retirement Community." *Human Organization* 39:219–226.

Perkinson, M. and D. Rockermann. Forthcoming. "Older Women Living in a Continuing Care Retirement Community: Marital Status and Friendship Formation." *Journal of Women and Aging.*

Peterson, J. W. 1990. "Age of Wisdom: Elderly Black Women in Family and Church." In *The Cultural Context of Aging.* J. Sokolovsky, ed. New York: Bergin & Garvey.

Peterson, P. 1996. *Will America Grow Up Before It Grows Old?* New York: Random House.

Peterson, S. A. and R. J. Maiden. 1993. *The Public Lives of Rural Older Americans.* Lanham, MD: University Press of America.

Pettitt, G. 1946. *Primitive Education in North America.* University of California Publications in American Archaeology and Ethnology 43:1–182.

Phillips, D., ed. 1992. *Ageing in Newly Industrializing Countries of East and Southeast Asia.* London: Edward Arnold.

Phillips, D. and H. P. Bartlett. 1995. "Aging Trends—Singapore." *Journal of Cross-Cultural Gerontology* 10(4):349–356.

Phillipson, C. 1996. "Interpretations of Aging Perspectives from Humanist Gerontology." *Aging and Society* 16:359–369.

Picot, S. et al. 1997. "Cultural Assessments and the Recruitment and Retention of African Americans into Alzheimers Disease Research." *Journal of Aging and Ethnicity* 1(1):5–18.

Pifer, A. 1994. "A Generation at Risk: Public Policy for the Third Age." *Ageing International* 21(2):67–68.

Pilisak, M. and M. Minkler. 1980. "Supportive Networks: Life Ties for the Elderly." *Journal of Social Issues* 36:95–116.

Plakans, A. 1989. "Stepping Down in Former Times: A Comparative Assessment of Retirement in Traditional Europe." In *Age Structuring in Comparative Perspective.* D. Kertzer and K. W. Schaie, eds. Hillsdale, NJ: Lawrence Erlbaum.

Plath, D. 1964. *The After Hours.* Berkeley: University of California Press.

———. 1972. "Japan: The After Years." In *Aging and Modernization.* D. Cowgill and L. D. Holmes, eds. New York: Appleton-Century-Crofts.

———. 1987. "Ecstasy Years—Old Age in Japan." In *Growing Old in Different Societies: Cross-Cultural Perspectives.* J. Sokolovsky, ed. Acton, MA: Copley Press.

Pollard, B. 1979. "The Problem of Aid-dependent Economy: The Case of Niue." In *South Pacific Dossier.* G. Woods, ed. Canberra: Australian Council for Overseas Aid.

Pollock, N. J. 1979. "Work, Wages, and Shifting Cultivation on Niue." *Pacific Studies* 2:132–143.

Pomar, J. B. 1941. *Relaciones de Texcoco y de la Nueva España*. Mexico, D. F.: S. Chavez Hayhoe.

Poon, L., ed. 1992. *The Georgia Centenarian Study*. Amityville, NY: Baywood.

Portes, A. and R. G. Rumbaut. 1990. *Immigrant American: A Portrait*. Berkeley: University of California Press.

Potash, B. 1986a. "Widows in Africa: An Introduction." In *Widows in African Soci Choices and Constraints*. B. Potash, ed. Stanford, CA: Stanford University Press.

———, ed. 1986b. *Widows in African Societies: Choices and Constraints*. Stanford, CA: Stanford University Press.

Powers, B. 1988a. "Social Networks, Social Support, and Elderly Institutionalized People." *Advances in Nursing Science* 10(2):40–58.

———. 1988b. "Self-Perceived Health of Elderly Institutionalized People." *Journal of Cross-Cultural Gerontology* 3(3):299–321.

Pratt, H. 1995. "Seniors' Organizations and Seniors' Empowerment: An International Perspective." In *Empowering Older People*. D. Thursz, C. Nusberg and J. Prather, eds. Westport, CT: Auburn House.

Press, I. 1967. "Maya Aging: Cross-Cultural Projective Techniques and the Dilemma of Interpretation." *Psychiatry* 30(2):197–202.

Press, I. and M. McKool. 1972. "Social Structure and Status of the Aged: Toward Some Valid Cross-Cultural Generalizations." *Aging and Human Development* 3(4):297–306.

Purdy J. and D. Arguello. 1992. "Hispanic Familism in Caretaking of Older Adults: Is It Functional?" *Journal of Gerontological Social Work* 19(2):29–43.

Pynoos, J. and S. P. Liebig. 1995. *Housing Frail Elders: International Policies, Perspectives, and Prospects*. Baltimore: Johns Hopkins Press.

Quadagno, J. 1982. *Aging in Early Industrial Society*. New York: Academic Press.

———. 1996. "Social Security and the Myth of the Entitlement 'Crisis'." *Gerontologist* 36:3:391–399.

Quill, T., C. Cassel and D. Meier. 1992. "Care of the Hopelessly Ill." *New England Journal of Medicine* 327:1380–1384.

Raboteau, A. J. 1995. *A Fire In The Bones*. Boston: Beacon Press.

Raffel, N. K. and M. W. Raffel. 1987. "Elderly Care: Similarities and Solutions in Denmark and the United States." *Public Health Reports* 102(5):494–500.

Ram-Prasad, C. 1995. "A Classical Indian Philosophical Perspective on Ageing and the Meaning of Life." *Ageing and Society* 15:1–36.

Range, E. C. F., Jr., ed. 1973. *Official Manual with the Doctrines and Discipline of the Church of God in Christ 1973*. Memphis: Church of God in Christ Publishing House.

Ratzel, F. 1894. *The History of Mankind*, vol. 11. London: Macmillan.

Redfield, R. 1930. *Tepotzlan: A Mexican Village*. Chicago: University of Chicago Press.

Regnier, V., J. Hamilton and S. Yatabe. 1995. *Assisted Living Housing for the Aged and Frail: Innovations in Design, Management, and Financing*. New York: Columbia University Press.

Reichel-Dolmatoff, G. and A. Reichel-Dolmatoff. 1961. *The People of Aritama*. Chicago: University of Chicago Press.

Reinharz, S. 1988. "Creating Utopia for the Elderly." *Society*, January/February.

Reischauer, E. 1977. *The Japanese.* Cambridge, MA: Harvard University Press.

Rempusheski, V. F. 1988. "Caring for Self and Others: Second Generation Polish American Elders in an Ethnic Club." *Journal of Cross-Cultural Gerontology* 3(3):223–271.

Rhoads, E. 1984. "The Impact of Modernization on the Aged in American Samoa." *Pacific Studies* 7:15–33.

Rhoads, E. and L. D. Holmes. 1995. *Other Cultures, Elder Years,* 2d ed. Thousand Oaks, CA: Sage.

Rich, D., T. Rich and L. Mullins, eds. 1995. *Old and Homeless—Double Jeopardy: An Overview of Current Practice and Policies.* Westport, CT: Greenwood.

Richlin-Klonsky, J. and V. Bengtson. 1996. "Pulling Together, Drifting Apart: A Longitudinal Case Study of a Four-Generation Family." *Journal of Aging Studies* 10: 255–279.

Rick, K. and J. Forward. 1992. "Acculturation and Perceived Intergenerational Differences Among Hmong Youth." *Journal of Cross-Cultural Psychology* 23(1):85–94.

Ritchie, J. and J. Ritchie. 1979. *Growing Up in Polynesia.* Sydney: Allen & Unwin.

———. 1981. "Child-Rearing and Child Abuse: The Polynesian Context." In *Child Abuse And Neglect: Cross-Cultural Perspectives.* J. E. Korbin, ed. Berkeley: University of California Press.

Rivers, W. H. R. 1926. *Psychology and Ethnology.* London: Kegan Paul.

Rivlin, A. M. and J. M. Wiener. 1988. *Caring for the Disabled Elderly: Who Will Pay?* Washington, DC: Brookings Institution.

Rix, S. E. 1991. "Older Women and Development." Paper presented at the Expert Group Meeting, Integration of Ageing and Elderly Women into Development, Vienna.

Robine, J. M. and I. Romieu. 1993. *Statistical World Yearbook on Health Expectancy.* Montpellier: Laboratoire d'Epidemiologie et d'Economie de la Sante.

Robertson, J. 1995. "Grandparenting in an Era of Rapid Change." In *Handbook of Aging and the Family.* R. Bleiszner and V. Bedford, eds. Westport, CT: Greenwood.

Robles, S. 1987. "Widowhood in Los Robles: Parent-Child Relations and Economic Survival in Old Age in Urban Mexico." *Journal of Cross-Cultural Gerontology* 1(3):223–237.

Roe, K., M. Minkler and R. Barwell. 1994. "The Assumption of Caregiving: Grandmothers Raising The Children of the Crack Cocaine Epidemic." *Qualitative Health Research* 4(3):281–303.

Roebuck, J. 1983. "Grandma as Revolutionary: Elderly Women and Some Modern Patterns of Social Change." *International Journal on Aging and Human Development* 17(4):249–266.

Rohner, R. P. et al. 1978. "Guidelines for Holocultural Research." *Current Anthropology* 19:128–129.

Romanucci-Ross, L. 1982. "Italian Ethnic Identity and Its Transformations." In *Ethnic Identity: Cultural Continuities and Change.* G. DeVos and L. Romanucci-Ross, eds. Chicago: University of Chicago Press.

Rose, A. M. 1962. "The Subculture of Aging: A Topic for Sociological Research." *Gerontologist* 2:123–127.

Rose, M. 1990. *Evolutionary Biology of Aging.* New York: Oxford University Press.

Rosenberg, R. 1996. "Genetic Factors for the Development of Alzheimer's Disease in the Cherokee Indian." *Archives of Neurology* 53:997–1000.

Rosenblatt, P. 1993. "Cross-Cultural Variation in the Experience, Expression and Understanding of Grief." In *Ethnic Variations in Dying, Death and Grief.* D. Irish, ed. Washington, DC: Taylor and Francis.

Rosow, I. 1967. *Social Integration of the Aged.* New York: Free Press.

Ross, J. 1977. *Old People, New Lives.* Chicago: University of Chicago Press.

Rossi, A. S., ed. 1985. *Gender and the Life Course.* New York: Aldine.

Roth, J. 1982. *Shopping Bag Ladies of New York.* New York: Pilgrim Press.

Rotunno, M. and M. McGoldrick. 1982. "Italian Families." In *Ethnicity and Family Therapy.* M. McGoldrick, J. Pearce and J. Giordano, eds. New York: Guilford.

Rubenstein, L. and B. J. Kramer. 1994. "Health Problems in Old Age: Cross-Cultural Comparisons." In *Cultural Diversity and Geriatric Care: Challenges to the Health Professions.* D. Wieland, D. Benton, B. J. Kramer and G. D. Dawson, eds. Binghamton, NY: The Haworth Press.

Rubin, V., ed. 1983. *Proceedings of the First Joint US-USSR Symposium on Aging and Longevity.* New York: International Research and Exchange Board.

Rubinstein, R. 1987. "Childless Elderly: Theoretical Perspectives and Practical Concerns." *Journal of Cross-Cultural Gerontology* 2(1):1–14.

———. 1990. "Nature, Culture, Gender, Age: A Critical Review." In *Anthropology and Aging: Comprehensive Reviews.* R. Rubinstein, ed. Dordrecht: Kluwer Academic.

———. 1992. "Anthropological Methods in Gerontological Research: Entering the Realm of Meaning." *Journal of Aging Studies* 6:57–66.

———. 1995a. "Narratives of Elder Parental Death: A Structural and Cultural Analyses." *Medical Anthropology Quarterly* 9(2):257–276.

———. 1995b. "The Engagement of Life History and Life Review among the Aged: A Research Case Study." *Journal of Aging Studies* 9(3):187–203.

Rubinstein, R. and P. T. Johnsen. 1982. "Toward A Comparative Perspective on Filial Response to Aging Populations." In *Aging and the Aged in the Third World: Part 1, Studies in Third World Societies* (No. 22). J. Sokolovsky, ed. Williamsburg, VA: College of William and Mary.

Ruggie, M. 1984. *The State and Working Women: A Comparative Study of Britain and Sweden.* Princeton: Princeton University Press.

Ryan, T. F. 1977. Prehistoric Niue: An Egalitarian Polynesian Society. Master's thesis. Anthropology Department, University of Auckland, New Zealand.

Ryan, T. F., comp. 1984. *Palagi Views Of Niue: Historical Literature 1774–1889.* Auckland: Auckland University.

Sahlins, M. 1965. "The Sociology of Primitive Exchange." In *The Relevance of Models in Social Anthropology* M. Banton, ed. *ASA Monographs*, No. 1. London: Tavistock.

———. 1972. *Stone Age Economics.* Chicago: Aldine.

Salmon, A. 1994. *Double Jeopardy: Resources and Minority Elders.* New York: Garland.

Samuelsson, K. 1975. "The Philosophy of Swedish Welfare Policies." In *Sweden's Development from Poverty to Affluence 1750–1970.* S. Koblik, ed. Minneapolis: University of Minnesota Press.

Sandberg, A., G. Broms, A. Grip, L. Sundstrom, J. Steen and P. Ullmark. 1992. *Technological Change and Co-Determination in Sweden.* Philadelphia: Temple University Press.

Sanderson, S., ed. 1995. *Civilizations and World Systems.* Thousand Oaks, CA: Altamira.

Sangree, W. H. 1986. "Role Flexibility and Status Continuity: Tiriki (Kenya) Age Groups Today." *Journal of Cross-Cultural Gerontology* 1(2):117–138.

———. 1987. "The Childless Elderly In Tiriki, Kenya, and Irigwe, Nigeria: A Comparative Analysis of the Relationship Between Beliefs About Childlessness and the Social Status of the Childless Elderly." *Journal of Cross-Cultural Gerontology* 2(3):201–223.

———. 1988. "Age and Power: Life Course Trajectories and Age Structuring of Power Relations in East and West Africa." In *Social Structure and Aging: Comparative Perspectives in Age Structuring in Modern Societies.* D. Kertzer, J. Meyer and K. W. Schaie, eds. Hillsdale, NJ: Erlbaum Associates.

Sankar, A. 1983. "Cultural Alternatives for the Vulnerable Elderly." In *Aging and the Aged in the Third World: Part II*, Regional and Ethnographic Perspectives. J. Sokolovsky, ed. Williamsburg, VA: College of William and Mary.

———. 1984. " 'It's Just Old Age': Old Age as a Diagnosis in American and Chinese Medicine." In *Age and Anthropological Theory.* D. Kertzer and J. Keith, eds. Ithaca, NY: Cornell University Press.

———. 1987. "The Living Dead: Cultural Constructions of the Oldest Old." In *The Elderly as Modern Pioneers.* P. Silverman, ed. Bloomington: Indiana University Press.

Sarton, M. 1982. *As We Are Now.* New York: Norton.

Sasaki, T. 1992. "Manpawā ni tyūkōnen jiko jitsugen katsu kase" [Self-Realization in Middle-Aged Manpower]. *Fukushi Shinbun* [Welfare Paper] (November 30):2.

Savishinsky, J. 1990. "The Defiance of Hope: Dementia Sufferers and Their Carers in a London Borough." In *The Home Care Experience.* J. Gubrium and A. Sanker, eds. Newbury Park, CA: Sage.

———. 1991. *The Ends of Time: Life and Work in a Nursing Home.* Westport, CT: Bergin & Garvey.

———. 1995. "The Unbearable Lightness of Retirement: Ritual and Support in a Modern Life Passage." *Research on Aging* 17(3):243–259.

Schapera, I. 1930. *The Khoisan People of South Africa.* London: Routledge.

Scharf, T. and C. Wenger. 1995. *International Perspectives on Community Care for Older People.* Aldershot, UK: Avebury.

Scheer, J. and M. Luborsky. 1991. "The Cultural Context of Polio Biographies." *Orthopedics* 14(11):1173–1181.

Scheper-Huges, N. 1979. *Saints, Scholars and Schizophrenics: Mental Illness in Rural Ireland.* Berkeley: University of California Press.

———. 1987. "Deposed Kings: The Demise of the Rural Irish Gerontocracy." In *Growing Old in Different Societies.* J. Sokolovsky, ed. Acton, MA: Copley.

Schildkrout, E. 1986. "Widows in Hausa Society: Ritual Phase or Social State?" In *Widows in African Societies: Choices and Constraints.* B. Potash, ed. Stanford, CA: Stanford University Press.

Schnitzer, M. 1970. *The Economy of Sweden: A Study of the Modern Welfare State.* New York and London: Praeger.

Schryer, F. 1993. "Ethnic Identity and Land Tenure Disputes in Modern Mexico." In *The Indian in Latin American History.* J. Kicza, ed. Wilmington, DE: Scholarly Resources.

Schulz, J. 1996. "Facts to Keep in Mind When You're Told Older Americans Are 'Better Off'." *NCOA Perspectives on Aging* (April-June):4–11.

Schulz, J. H. and D. Davis-Friedmann, eds. 1987. *Aging China: Family, Economics, and Government Policies in Transition*. Washington, DC: The Gerontological Society of America.

Schweitzer, M. 1987. "The Elders: Cultural Dimensions of Aging in Two American Indian Communities." In *Growing Old in Different Societies*. J. Sokolovsky, ed. Acton, MA.: Copley.

———. 1991. *Anthropology of Aging: A Partially Annotated Bibliography*. Westport, CT: Greenwood.

———. Forthcoming. *Bridging Generations: American Indian Grandmothers— Traditions and Transitions*. Albuquerque: University of New Mexico Press.

Scott-Maxwell, F. 1991. *The Measure of My Days*. New York: Penguin.

Seefeldt, C. 1982. "Paraguay and the United States: A Cross-Cultural Study of Children's Attitudes Toward The Elderly." *International Journal of Comparative Sociology* 23:235–242.

———. 1984. "Children's Attitudes Toward the Elderly: A Cross-Cultural Comparison." *International Journal of Aging and Human Development* 19(4):321–330.

Seitz, J. 1978. "A History of the Samia Location, 1890–1930." Ph.D. diss. West Virginia University.

Selby, P. and M. Schechter. 1982. *Aging 2000*. Lancaster, PA: MTP Press Limited.

Sen, K. 1994. *Ageing: Debates on Demographic Transition and Social Policy*. London: Zed Books.

Sennott-Miller, L. 1989. "The Health and Socioeconomic Situation of Midlife and Older Women in Latin America and the Caribbean." In *Midlife and Older Women in Latin America and the Caribbean*. Washington, DC: American Association of Retired Persons.

———. 1994. "Research on Latin America: Present Status and Future Directions." *Journal of Cross-Cultural Gerontology* 9(1):87–97.

Serby, M., J. Chou and E. Franssen. 1987. "Dementia in an American-Chinese Nursing Home Population." *American Journal of Psychiatry* 144(6):811–812.

Sered, S. S. 1987. "The Liberation of Widowhood." *Journal of Cross-Cultural Gerontology* 2(2):139–150.

Shanas, E. 1979. "Social Myth as Hypothesis: The Case of the Family Relations of Old People." *Gerontologist* 19:3–9.

Shanas, E. and M. Susmann. 1981. "The Family in Later Life: Social Structure and Social Policy." In *Aging: Social Change*. S. Kiesler, J. Morgan and V. Oppenheimer, eds. New York: Academic.

Shanas, E., P. Townsend, D. Wedderburn, H. Friis, P. Milhojano and J. Stehouwer. 1968. *Older People in Three Industrial Societies*. New York: Atherton Press.

Shantakumar, G. 1996. "Preparing for the Greying Century: Lessons from an Industrializing Country and Future Developments." *Ageing International* 23(1):52–66.

Sharp, L. 1981. "Old Age Among the Chipewyan." In *Other Ways of Growing Old: Anthropological Perspectives*. P. Amoss and S. Harrell, eds. Stanford, CA: Stanford University Press.

Shea, D., T. Miles and M. Hayward. 1996. "The Health-Wealth Connection." *Gerontologist* 36(3):342–349.

Sheehan, T. 1976. "Senior Esteem as a Factor of Societal Economic Complexity." *Gerontologist* 16:433–440.

Sheehy, G. 1995. *New Passages: Mapping Your Life Across Time*. New York: Random House.

Shenk, D. n.d. "Nursing Home as Focal Point for Services in a Rural Community: A Case Study from Denmark." Unpublished paper.

———. 1987. *Someone to Lend a Helping Hand—the Lives of Rural Older Women in Central Minnesota*. St. Cloud, MN: Central Minnesota Council on Aging.

———. 1991. "Older Rural Women as Recipients and Providers of Social Support." *Journal of Aging Studies* 5(4):347–358.

———. Forthcoming. *Someone to Lend a Helping Hand: Women Growing Older in Rural America*. Newark, NJ: Gordon and Breach.

Shenk, D. and A. Achenbaum, eds. 1994. *Changing Perspectives of Aging and the Aged*. New York: Springer.

Shenk, D. and K. Christiansen. 1993. "The Evolution of the System of Care for the Aged in Denmark." *Journal of Aging and Social Policy* 5(1–2):169–186.

Shenk, D. and J. Sokolovsky. 1997. *Teaching About Aging: Interdisciplinary and Cross-Cultural Perspectives*, 2nd ed. Providence, PA: Association for Anthropology and Gerontology.

Sheppard, H. L., B. E. Robinson and C. Cuervo, eds. 1988. *Geriatric Hypertension*. Tampa, Fl: International Exchange Center on Gerontology.

Shield, R. R. 1988. *Uneasy Endings: Daily Life in an American Nursing Home*. Ithaca, NY: Cornell University Press.

———. 1995. "Ethics in the Nursing Home: Cases, Choices, and Issues." In *The Culture of Long Term Care: Nursing Home Ethnography*. J. N. Henderson and M. D. Vesperi, eds. Westport CT: Greenwood Press.

———. 1996. "Managing the Care of Nursing Home Residents: The Challenge of Integration." In *Focus on Managed Care and Quality Assurance: Integrating Acute and Chronic Care*. R. Newcomer and A. Wilkinson, eds. NY: Springer.

———. Forthcoming. "Wary Partners: Certified Nursing Aassistants and Resident Family Members in Nursing Homes." In *Gray Areas: Anthropology and the Nursing Home*. P. Stafford, ed. Sante Fe, NM: School of American Research.

Shomaker, D. J. 1990. "Health Care, Cultural Expectations and Frail Elderly Navajo Grandmothers." *Journal of Cross-Cultural Gerontology* 5(1):21–34.

Shore, B. 1978. "Ghosts and Government: A Structural Analysis of Alternative Institutions for Conflict Management in Samoa." *Man* 13:175–199.

———. 1982. *Sala'ilua: A Samoan Mystery*. New York: Columbia University Press.

Shostak, M. 1981. *Nisa: The Life and Words of a !Kung Woman*. Cambridge, MA: Harvard University Press.

Siampos, G. 1990. "Trends and Future Prospects of the Female Over Life by Regions in Europe." *Statistical Journal of the United Nations Economic Commission for Europe* 7:13–25.

Silverman, P., ed. 1987a. *The Elderly as Modern Pioneers*. Bloomington: Indiana University Press.

———. 1987b. "Community Settings." In *The Elderly as Modern Pioneers*. P. Silverman, ed. Bloomington: Indiana University Press.

Silverman, P. and R. J. Maxwell. 1987. "The Significance of Information and Power in the Comparative Study of the Aged." In *Growing Old in Different Societies: Cross-Cultural Perspectives*. J. Sokolovsky, ed. Acton, MA: Copley.

Silverman, P. R. 1986. *Widow-To-Widow*. New York: Springer.

Silverstein, M., T. Parrott and V. Bengtson. 1995. "Factors that Predispose Middle-Aged Sons and Daughters to Provide Social Support to Older Parents." *Journal of Marriage and the Family* 57:465–475.

Simic, A. 1978a. "Introduction: Aging and the Aged in Cultural Perspectives." In *Life's Career Aging: Cultural Variations on Growing Old*. B. Myerhoff and A. Simic, eds. Beverly Hills, CA: Sage.

———. 1978b. "Winners and Losers: Aging Yugoslavs in a Changing World." In *Life's Career Aging: Cultural Variations on Growing Old*. B. Myerhoff and A. Simic, eds. Beverly Hills, CA: Sage.

———. 1990. "Aging, World View, and Intergenerational Relationships in America and Yugoslavia." In *The Cultural Context of Aging*. J. Sokolovsky, ed. Westport, CT: Bergin & Garvey.

Simmons, L. 1945 (1970). *The Role of the Aged in Primitive Society*. New Haven, CT: Archon Books.

———. 1946. "Attitudes Toward Aging and the Aged: Primitive Societies." *Journal of Gerontology* 1:72–95.

———. 1952. "Social Participation of the Aged in Different Cultures." *Annals of the American Academy of Political and Social Science* 279:43–51.

———. 1959. "Aging In Modern Society." In *Toward a Better Understanding of Aging*. Seminar on Aging, September 8–13, 1958, Aspen, Colorado. New York: Council on Social Work Education.

———. 1960. "Aging In Primitive Societies: A Comparative Survey of Family Life and Relationships." In *Handbook of Social Gerontology*. C. Tibbetts, ed. Chicago: University of Chicago Press.

Singh, A., B. Kinsey and J. Morton. 1991. "Informal Support Among the Elderly in Four Ethnic Cultural Settings in Canada and the U.S.A." *International Journal of Contemporary Sociology* 28(1–2):56–83.

Slorah, P. 1994. "Grandparents of Grandchildren at Risk for Abuse and Neglect: A Policy Analysis." Ph.D. diss. University of South Florida.

Smith, A. 1994. "African-American Grandmothers' War Against the Crack-Cocaine Epidemic." *Arete* (Journal of the College of Social Work, University of Southern California) 19(1):22–36.

Smith, R. 1961a. "Cultural Differences in the Life Cycle and the Concept of Time." In *Aging and Leisure*. R. Kleemeier, ed. New York: Oxford University Press.

———. 1961b. "Japan: The Later Years of Life and the Concept of Time." In *Aging and Leisure*. R. Kleemeier ed. New York: Oxford University Press.

Smith, S. P. 1983. *Niue: The Island and Its People*. Suva, Fiji: Institute for Pacific Studies, University of the South Pacific. [Reprinted from the Journal of the Polynesian Society, Volumes 11 and 12, 1902 and 1903.]

Smithers, J. 1985. *Determined Survivors: Community Life Among the Urban Elderly*. New Brunswick, NJ: Rutgers University Press.

Social Studies Course (SSC). 1982. *The Development of Blessington and the Surrounding Areas*. Blessington: St. Mark's Vocational School.

Sodei, T. 1995. "Tradition Impedes Organizational Empowerment in Japan." In *Empowering Older People*. D. Thursz, C. Nusberg and J. Prather, eds. Westport, CT: Auburn House.

Sokolovsky, J. 1982b. "Self-Help in an Aztec Village in Modern Mexico." In *Beliefs and Self-Help: Cross-Cultural Perspectives and Approaches.* G. Weber and L. Cohen, eds. New York: Human Science Press.

———. 1985. "Ethnicity, Culture and Aging: Do Differences Really Make a Difference?" *Journal of Applied Gerontology* 4:6–17.

———. 1986. "Network Methodologies in the Study of Aging." In *New Methods for Old Age Research*, 2d ed. C. Fry and J. Keith, eds. Boston Bergin and Garvey.

Sokolovsky, J., ed. 1982a. *Aging and the Aged in the Third World: Part I.* Williamsburg, VA: College of William and Mary.

———. 1987. *Growing Old in Different Societies: Cross-Cultural Perspectives.* Acton, MA: Copley.

———, ed. 1990. *The Cultural Context of Aging: World-Wide Perspectives.* Westport, CT: Bergin and Garvey.

———, ed. 1991. "Health, Aging and Development." Special issue of the *Journal of Cross-Cultural Gerontology* 6:3.

Sokolovsky, J. and C. Cohen. 1978. "The Cultural Meaning of Personal Networks for the Inner-City Elderly." *Urban Anthropology* 7:323–343.

———. 1981. "Measuring Social Interaction of the Urban Elderly: A Methodological Synthesis." *International Journal of Aging and Human Development* 13:233–244.

———. 1987. "Networks as Adaptation: The Cultural Meaning of Being a 'Loner' Among the Inner City Elderly." In *Growing Old in Different Societies: Cross-Cultural Perspectives.* J. Sokolovsky, ed. Acton, MA: Copley.

Sokolovsky, J., C. Cohen, D. Berger and J. Geiger. 1978. "Personal Networks of Ex-mental Patients in a Manhattan SRO Hotel." *Human Organization* 37(1):4–15.

Sokolovsky, J. and J. Sokolovsky, eds. 1983a. *Aging and the Aged in the Third World: Part II, Regional and Ethnographic Perspectives.* Williamsburg, VA: College of William and Mary.

———. 1983b. "Familial and Public Contexts for Aging: Growing Old in a Rapidly Changing Mexican Village." In *Aging and the Aged in the Third World: Part II, Regional and Ethnographic Perspectives.* Williamsburg, VA: College of William and Mary.

Sokolovsky, J., S. Sosic and G. Pavlekovic. 1991. "Self-Help Groups for the Aged in Yugoslavia: How Effective Are They?" *Journal of Cross-Cultural Gerontology* 6(3):319–330.

Soldo, B. J. 1980. "America's Elderly in the 1980's." *Population Bulletin* 35(4).

Soldo, B. J. and M. S. Hill. 1993. Intergenerational Transfers: Economic, Demographic, and Social Perspectives. *Annual Review of Gerontology and Geriatrics* 1(13):187–216.

Solomon, J. C. and J. Marx. 1995. " 'To Grandmother's House We Go': Health and School Adjustment of Children Raised Solely by Grandparents." *The Gerontologist* 35:3.

Somers, A. R. and N. L. Spears. 1992. *The Continuing Care Retirement Community, A Significant Option for Long-Term Care?* New York: Springer.

Sontag, S. 1972. "The Double Standard of Aging." *Saturday Review of the Society* 55(39):29–38.

Soper, R., ed. 1986. *Kenya Socio-Cultural Profiles: Busia District.* Nairobi: Ministry of Planning and National Development.

Sotomayor, M., ed. 1994. *In Triple Jeopardy, Aged Hispanic Women: Insights and Experiences.* Washington, DC: National Hispanic Council on Aging.

Sotomayor, M. and H. Curiel, eds. 1988. *Hispanic Elderly: A Cultural Signature*. Edinburgh, TX: Pan American University Press.

Sotomayor, M. and A. Garcia. 1993. *Elderly Latinos: Issues and Solutions for the 21st Century*. Washington DC: National Hispanic Council on Aging.

Soustelle, J. 1961. *Daily Life of Aztecs on the Eve of the Spanish Conquest*. Stanford, CA: Stanford University Press.

Sparks, D. 1975. "The Still Rebirth: Retirement and Role Discontinuity." *Journal of Asian and African Studies* 10:64–74.

Special Committee on Aging, United States Senate. 1989. *The American Indian Elderly: The Forgotten Population*. Washington, DC: U.S. Government Printing Office.

Special Issue on Ethnicity. 1994. *Journal of Aging Studies* 8:3.

Spence, S. A. 1993. "Rural Elderly African Americans and Service Delivery: A Study of Health and Social Service Needs and Service Accessibility." *Journal of Gerontological Social Work* 20(3–4):187–203.

Spencer, P. 1965. *The Samburu: A Study of Gerontocracy in a Nomadic Tribe*. Berkeley: University of California Press.

———, ed. 1990. *Anthropology and the Riddle of the Sphinx: Paradoxes of Change in the Life Course*. London and New York:Routledge.

———. 1996. "Age Sets, Age Grades, and Age Generation Systems." In *The Encyclopedia of Cultural Anthropology*. New York: Henry Holt and Company.

Springer, D. and T. Brubaker. 1984. *Family Caregivers and Dependent Elderly*. Beverly Hills: Sage.

St. Petersburg Times. 1995. "She's Oldest Person in History." *St. Petersburg Times*, October 18:2.

Stacey-Konnert, C. and J. Pynoos. 1992. "Friendship and Social Networks in a Continuing Care Retirement Community." *Journal of Applied Gerontology* 11(3):298–313.

Stack, C. 1974. *All Our Kin: Strategies for Survival in a Black Community*. New York: Harper & Row.

Stafford, P. B. 1991. "The Social Construction of Alzheimer's Disease." In *Biosemiotics: The Semiotic Web*. T. A. Sebeok and J. Umiker-Sebeok, eds. Berlin: Mouton de Gruyter.

Stahl, A. 1991. *Providing Transportation for the Elderly and Handicapped in Sweden: Experiences Gained and Future Trends*. Stockholm: Swedish Transport Research Board.

Stanford, E. and F. Torres-Gil. 1994. *Diversity: New Approaches to Ethnic Minority Aging*. Amityville, NY: Baywood.

Staples, R. 1973. *The Black Woman in America*. Chicago: Nelson Hall.

Statistics and Information Department. 1994. *Report on Comprehensive Survey of Living Condition of the People on Health and Welfare (Kokumin seikatsu kiso chosa)* (in Japanese). Tokyo: Ministry of Health and Welfare.

Steenberg, C., M. Ansak and J. Chin-Hansen. 1993. "On Lok's Model: Managed Long-Term Care." In *Ethnic Elderly and Long-Term Care*. C. Barresi and D. Stull, eds. New York: Springer.

Stein, H. 1979. "Rehabilitation and Chronic Illness in American Culture." *Ethos* 7:153–167.

Stephens, J. 1976. *Loners, Losers and Lovers: A Sociological Study of the Aged Tenants of a Slum Hotel*. Seattle: University of Washington Press.

Stephenson, H. and G. Renard. 1993. "Trusting Ole' Wise Owls: Therapeutic Use of

Cultural Strengths in African-American Families.'' *Professional Psychology: Research and Practice* 24(4):433–442.

Stevens, N. 1995. "Gender and Adaptation to Widowhood in Later Life.'' *Ageing and Society* 15:37–58.

Stewart, F. 1977. *Fundamentals of Age-Group Systems*. New York: Academic Press.

Steyn, H. P. 1994. "Role and Position of Elderly !Xu in the Schmidtsdrift Bushman Community.'' *South African Journal of Ethnology* 17(2):31–38.

Stokes, E. 1990. "Ethnography of a Social Border: The Case of an American Retirement Community in Mexico.'' *Journal of Cross-Cultural Gerontology* 5:169–182.

Stoller, E. 1992. "Gender Differences in the Experiences of Caregiving Spouses.'' In *Gender, Families, and Elder Care*. J. Dwyer and R. Coward, eds. London: Sage Publishing.

Stoller, E. and R. Gibson, eds. 1996. *Worlds of Difference: Inequality in the Aging Experience*. 2nd ed. Thousand Oaks, CA: Pine Forge.

Strange, H. and M. Teitelbaum. 1987. *Aging and Cultural Diversity*. South Hadley, MA: Bergin & Garvey.

Strawbridge, W. and M. Wallhagen. 1992. "Is All the Family Always Best.'' *Journal of Aging Studies* 4(1):81–92.

Streib, G. F., A. J. La Greca and W. E. Folts. 1986. "Retirement Communities: People, Planning, Prospects.'' In *Housing an Aging Society*. R. J. Newcomer, M. P. Lawton and T. O. Byers, eds. New York: Van Nostrand Reinhold.

Stroud, H. 1995. *The Promise of Paradise: Recreational and Retirement Communities in the United States Since 1950*. Baltimore: Johns Hopkins University Press.

Stucki, B. R. 1992. "The Long Voyage Home: Return Migration among Aging Cocoa Farmers of Ghana.'' *Journal of Cross-Cultural Gerontology* 7:363–378.

Suchman, E. 1964. "Sociomedical Variations Among Ethnic Groups.'' *American Journal of Sociology* 70:328–329.

Sue, D. W. and D. Sue. 1990. *Counseling the Culturally Different: Theory and Practice*, 2d ed. New York: John Wiley & Sons.

Sue, S. 1991. "Ethnicity and Culture in Psychological Research and Practice.'' In *Psychological Perspectives on Human Diversity in America*. J. D. Goodchilds, ed. Washington, DC: American Psychological Association.

Sussman, M. 1965. "The Isolated Nuclear Family: Fact or Fiction?'' *Social Problems* 6:333–340.

———. 1976. The Family Life of Old People. In *Handbook of Aging and the Social Sciences*. R. Binstock and E. Shanas, eds. New York: Van Nostrand Reinhold.

Suzman, R. M., D. P. Willis and K. G. Manton, eds. 1992. *The Oldest Old*. New York: Oxford University Press.

Sverdrup, H. 1938. *Hos Tundra-folke* (With the People of the Tundra). Oslo: Gyldendal Norsk Forlag.

Swedish Institute. 1986. "Old-Age Care in Sweden.'' Stockholm: Swedish Institute.

———. 1994. "The Care of the Elderly in Sweden.'' *Fact Sheets on Sweden* 8:1. Stockholm: Swedish Institute.

Taietz, P. 1976. "Two Conceptual Models of the Senior Center.'' *Journal of Gerontology* 31(2):219–222.

Taietz, P. and S. Milton. 1979. "Rural-urban Differences in the Structure of Services for the Elderly in Upstate New York Counties.'' *Journal of Gerontology* 34(3):429–437.

Talamantes, M. et al. 1996. "SES and Ethnic Differences in Perceived Caregiver Availability Among Young-Old Mexican Americans and Non-Hispanic Whites." *Gerontologist* 36(1):88–99.

Tanjasiri, S., S. Wallace and K. Shibata. 1995. "Picture Imperfect: Hidden Problems Among Asian Pacific Islander Elderly." *Gerontologist* 35(6):753–760.

Tate, N. 1983. "The Black Aging Experience." In *Aging in Minority Groups*. R. McNeely and J. Colen, eds. Beverly Hills: Sage.

Taylor, R., H. T. Nemaia and J. Connell. 1987. "Mortality in Niue, 1978–1982." *New Zealand Medical Journal* 100:477–481.

Taylor, R. J. 1986. "Religious Participation Among Elderly Blacks." *The Gerontologist* 26(6):630–636.

———. 1988. "Aging and Supportive Relationships among Black Americans." In *The Black American Elderly: Research on Physical and Psychosocial Health*. J. S. Jackson et al., eds. New York: Springer.

Taylor, R. J., V. M. Keith and M. B. Tucker. 1993. "Gender, Marital, Familial, and Friendship Roles." In *Aging in Black America*. J. J. Jackson, L. M. Chatters and R. J. Taylor, eds. Newbury Park, CA: Sage.

Tefft, S. 1968. "Intergenerational Value Differentials and Family Structure Among the Wind River Shoshone." *American Anthropologist* 70:330–333.

Teicher, M., D. Thursz and J. Vigilante. 1979. *Reaching the Aged: Social Services in Forty-Four Countries*. Beverly Hills: Sage.

Teitelbaum, M. 1987. "Old Age, Midwifery and Good Talk: Paths to Power in a West African Gerontocracy." In *Aging and Cultural Diversity: New Directions and Annotated Bibliography*. H. Strange and M. Teitlebaum, eds. South Hadley, MA: Bergin & Garvey.

Teski, M. 1981. "Living Together: An Ethnography of a Retirement Hotel." Washington, DC: University Press of America.

Teski, M. et al. 1983. *A City Revitalized: The Elderly Lose at Monopoly*. Lanham, MD: University Press of America.

Teski, M. and K. Teski. 1982. "Aging, Life Dissatisfaction and Perceptions of Distress in a Kalmuk Community." Presented at the Annual Meeting of the Gerontological Society.

The World Almanac. 1995. Mahwah, NJ: Funk & Wagnalls Corporation.

The Topeka Capital-Journal. 1986. "U.S. Loses in Study of Nations." December 9:36.

The Tampa Tribune. 1992. "Baylife" Section:1.

Thomas, F. R. 1990. *Americans in Denmark: Comparisons of the Two Cultures by Writers, Artists and Teachers*. Carbondale: Southern Illinois Press.

Thomas, L., M. Sokolovsky, R. Feinberg. 1996. "Ideology, Narrative, and Identity: The Case of Elderly Jewish Immigrants from the Former USSR." *Journal of Aging and Identity* 1(1):51–72.

Thomas, S. 1992. "Old Age in Meru, Kenya: Adaptive Reciprocity in a Changing Rural Community." Ph.D. diss. University of Florida.

———. 1995. "Shifting Meanings of Time, Productivity and Social Worth in the Life Course in Meru, Kenya." *Journal of Cross-Cultural Gerontology* 10(3):233–256.

Thomlinson, R. 1976. *Population Dynamics. Causes and Consequences of World Demographic Change*. New York: Random House.

Thompson, E., ed. 1994. *Older Men's Lives*. Thousand Oaks, CA: Sage.

Thompson, L. 1940. *Southern Lau, Fiji: An Ethnography*. Honolulu: Bernice P. Bishop Museum.

Thomson, J. 1885. *Through Masai Land*. London: Edward Arnold.

Thursz, D., C. Nusberg and J. Prather, eds. 1995. *Empowering Older People*. Westport, CT: Auburn House.

Tobin, S. and M. Lieberman. 1976. *Last Home for the Aged*. San Francisco: Jossey-Bass.

Tocqueville, A. 1945. *Democracy in America*. New York: Vintage Books.

Tokarev, S. A. and I. S. Gurvich. 1964. "The Yakuts." In *The Peoples of Siberia*. M. G. Levin and L. P. Potapov, eds. Chicago: University of Chicago Press.

Tomita, S. K. 1994. "The Consideration of Cultural Factors in the Research of Elder Mistreatment with an In-depth Look at the Japanese." *Journal of Cross-Cultural Gerontology* 9(1):39–52.

Topping, D. M. 1977. "The Pacific Islands: Part I: Polynesia." *American Universities Field Staff Reports*. South East Asia Series, volume XXV (2).

Torres-Gil, F. 1978. "Age, Health, and Culture: An Examination of Health Among Spanish Speaking Elderly." In *Hispanic Families*. M. Montiel, ed. Washington, DC: National Coalition of Spanish Speaking Mental Health Organizations.

———. 1987. "Aging in an Ethnic Society: Policy Issues for Aging Among Minority Groups." In *Ethnic Dimensions of Aging*. D. E. Gelfand and C. M. Barresi, eds. New York: Springer.

Toshiba Nichiyō Gekijyō, KSCI. 1992. "Son's Return Home." 60-minute drama.

Tout, K. 1989. *Ageing in Developing Countries*. Oxford: Oxford University Press.

Tout, K., ed. 1993. *Elderly Care: A World Perspective*. London, New York: Chapman and Hall.

Tracy, M. 1993. "Government Versus the Family: The False Dichotomy." *Generations* (Winter): 47–50.

Tracy, M. and P. Tracy. 1993. "Health Care and Family Support Systems of Functionally Impaired Rural Elderly Men and Women in Telengganu, Malaysia." *Journal of Cross-Cultural Gerontology* 8(1):35–68.

Tran, T. V. 1988. "Sex Differences in English Language Acculturation and Learning Strategies Among Vietnamese Adults Aged 40 and Over in the United States." *Sex Roles* 19:747–758.

———. 1991. "Family Living Arrangement and Social Adjustment Among Three Ethnic Groups of Elderly Indochinese Refugees." *International Journal of Aging and Human Development* 32:91–102.

Tran, T. V. et al. 1996. "Acculturation, Health, Stress and Distress Among Elderly Hispanics." *Journal of Cross-Cultural Gerontology* 11(2) 149–165.

Trela, J. and J. Sokolovsky. 1979. "Culture, Ethnicity, and Policy for the Aged." In *Ethnicity and Aging*. D. Gelfand and D. Fandetti, eds. New York: Springer.

Tripp-Reimer, T., B. Sorofman, G. Lauer, M. Martin and L. Afifi. 1988. "To Be Different from the World: Patterns of Elder Care Among Iowa Old Order Amish." *Journal of Cross-Cultural Gerontology* 3(3):185–195.

Troll, L. E., ed. 1986. *Family Issues in Current Gerontology*. New York: Springer.

Trusswell, A. S. and J. D. L. Hansen. 1976. "Medical Research among the !Kung." In *Kalahari Hunter-Gatherers*. R. B. Lee and I. DeVore, eds. Cambridge, MA: Harvard University Press.

Tsai, W. 1987. "Life After Retirement: Elderly Welfare in China." *Asian Survey* 27: 566–576.

Tsuji, Y. 1994. "Incense Money in Japan: Persistence and Change in Tradition." Paper presented at the 46th annual meeting of the Association for Asian Studies, Boston, March 24–27.

———. 1997. "Continuities and Changes in the Conceptions of Old Age in Japan." In *Aging: Asian Experiences Past and Present*. S. Formanek and S. Linhart, eds. Vienna: Verlag der Osterreichischen Akademie der Wissenschaften.

Turnbull, C. 1965. *Wayward Servants*. Garden City, NY: Natural History Press.

———. 1972. *The Mountain People*. New York: Simon & Schuster.

Turner, R. 1983. "Direct, Indirect, and Moderating Effects of Social Support on Psychological Distress and Associated Conditions." In *Psychological Stress: Trends in Theory and Research*. H. Kaplan, ed. Orlando, FL: Academic Press.

Turner, S. 1994. "The Continued Drama of Swedish Political Economy." *The Swedish Program Newsletter*. Stockholm: The Swedish Program.

Turner, V. 1957. *Schism and Continuity in an African Society: A Study of Ndembu Village Life*. Manchester, UK: Manchester University Press.

———. 1969. *The Ritual Process*. Ithaca, NY: Cornell University Press.

———. 1982. *Celebration: Studies in Festivity and Ritual*. Washington, DC: Smithsonian Institution Press.

Twigg, J. 1989. "Models of Carers: How Do Social Care Agencies Conceptualize Their Relationship with Informal Carers?" *The Journal of Social Policy* 18(1):53–66.

U.S. Bureau of the Census. 1991. "Global Aging: Comparative Indicators and Future Trends" (wall chart). Washington, DC: Department of Commerce.

———. 1993. *1990 Census Population: Asians and Pacific Islanders in the United States*. Washington, DC: Government Printing Office.

———. 1995. *Sixty-Five Plus in the U.S.* Washington, DC: Government Printing Office.

———. 1996. *World Population Profile*. Washington, DC: Center for International Research, U.S. Bureau of the Census.

———. 1997. *The State of the Nation*. Washington, DC: U.S. Government Printing Office.

U.S. Census of Population and Housing. 1990. Summary of Tape File 1, California. Sacramento, CA: State of California State Census Data Center.

U.S. Commission on Civil Rights. 1982. *Minority Elderly Services: New Programs, Old Problems*, Part 1. Washington, DC: Government Printing Office.

U.S. Congress Office of Technology Assessment. 1990. *Confused Minds, Burdened Families: Finding Help for People with Alzheimer's and Other Dementias*. OTA-BA-404. Washington, DC: U.S. Government Printing Office.

U.S. Department of Health and Human Services. 1982. *Social Security Programs Throughout the World, 1981*. Research Report No. 58. Washington, DC: U.S. Government Printing Office.

———. 1990. *Health Status of the Disadvantaged*. Public Health Service. Health Resources and Services Administration. Bureau of Health Professions. Washington, DC: U.S. Government Printing Office.

———. 1991. *Aging in America: Trends and Projections*. U.S. Bureau of the Census, "Money, Income & Poverty Status in the United States, 1989." Current Population Reports Series P-60, No. 181. Washington, DC: U.S. Government Printing Office.

U.S. Department of Housing and Urban Development. 1984. *A Report to the Secretary on the Homeless and Emergency Shelters*. Washington, DC: U.S. Government Printing Office.

U.S. Select Committee on Aging. 1987. *Exploding the Myths: Caregiving in America.* Comm. Pub. No. 99–611. Washington, DC: U.S. Government Printing Office.

U.S. Senate Special Committee on Aging. 1988. *Aging America: Trends and Projections.* Washington, DC: U.S. Department of Health and Human Services.

———. 1993. *Report on Developments in Aging: 1992*, vol. 1. Washington, DC: U.S. Government Printing Offices.

Udvardy, M. and M. G. Cattell. 1992a. "Gender, Aging and Power in Sub-Saharan Africa: Challenges and Puzzles." *Journal of Cross-Cultural Gerontology* 7:275–288.

———, eds. 1992b. "Gender, Aging and Power in Sub-Saharan Africa: Challenges and Puzzles." Special issue, *Journal of Cross-Cultural Gerontology* 7(4).

Uhlenberg, P. 1995. "Intergenerational Support in Sri Lanka: The Elderly and Their Children." In *Aging and Generational Relations over the Life Course.* T. Hareven, ed. Hawthorne, NY: Aldine de Gruyter.

Ujimoto, K. 1987. "Ethnic Identity Retention of the Aged Japanese-Canadians and Their Well-Being." In *Ethnic Dimensions of Aging: Current Perspectives.* D. Gelfand and C. Barresi, eds. New York: Springer.

United Nations. 1985. *The World Aging Situation: Strategies and Policies.* New York: United Nations.

———. 1993. *Demographic Yearbook: Population Ageing and the Situation of Elderly People.* New York: United Nations.

United Nations Department for Economic and Social Information and Policy Analysis. 1995. *World Population Prospects: The 1994 Revision.* Annex Tables. New York: United Nations.

United Nations Department of International Economic and Social Affairs. 1988. "Sex Differentials in Survivorship in the Developing World: Levels, Regional Patterns and Demographic Determinants." *Population Bulletin of the United Nations* 25:51–64.

———. 1991. *The Sex and Age Distributions of Population.* ST/ESA/SER.A/122. New York: United Nations.

Urban Institute. 1993. *Hunger Among the Elderly: Local and National Comparisons.* Washington, DC: The Urban Institute.

Valle, R. 1981. "Natural Support Systems, Minority Groups, and the Late Life Dementias: Implications for Service Delivery Research and Polity." In *Clinical Aspects of Alzheimer's Disease and Senile Dementia.* N. Miller and G. Cohen, eds. New York: Raven.

———. 1989. "Cultural and Ethnic Issues in Alzheimer's Disease Family Research." In *Alzheimer's Disease Treatment and Family Stress: Directions for Research.* E. Light and B. Lebowitz, eds. Bethesda, MD: National Institute on Mental Health.

Valle, R. and L. Mendoza. 1978. *The Elder Latino.* San Diego CA: Campanile.

Van Gennep, A. 1960 (1908). *The Rites of Passage.* Chicago: University of Chicago Press.

van Nostrand, J., R. Clark and T. Romøren. 1993. "Nursing Home Care in Five Nations." *Ageing International* (June).

van Willigen, J. 1989. *Getting Some Age on Me: Social Organization of Old People in a Rural American Community.* Lexington: University of Kentucky Press.

van Willigen, J., N. K. Chadha and S. Kedia. 1995. "Personal Networks and Personal Texts: Social Aging in Dehli India." *Journal of Cross-Cultural Gerontology* 10(3):175–198.

Vargas, L. 1992. "Diversity of Aging Experience in Latin America and the Caribbean." *Clinical Gerontologist* 11:5–19.

Vasa Hills Document. 1976. Stockholm.

Vatuk, S. 1980. "Withdrawal and Disengagement as a Cultural Response to Aging in India." In *Aging in Culture and Society: Comparative Viewpoints and Strategies.* C. Fry et al., eds. South Hadley, MA: Bergin & Garvey.

———. 1990. " 'To Be a Burden on Others': Dependency Anxiety Among the Elderly in India." In *Divine Passions: The Social Construction of Emotion in India.* O. Lynch, ed. Berkeley: University of California Press.

Velez, C. G. 1978. "Youth and Aging in Central Mexico: One Day in the Life of Four Families of Migrants." In *Life's Career Aging: Cultural Variations on Growing Old.* B. G. Myerhoff and A. Simic, eds. Beverly Hills: Sage.

Velkoff, V. and K. Kinsella. 1993. *Aging in Eastern Europe and the Former Soviet Union.* Washington, DC: U.S. Bureau of the Census, Center for International Research.

Vellenga, D. D. 1986. "The Widow among the Matrilineal Akan of Southern Ghana." In *Widows in African Societies: Choices and Constraints.* B. Potash, ed. Stanford, CA: Stanford University Press.

Verbrugge, L. 1989. "Recent, Present, and Future Health of American Adults." *Annual Review of Public Health* 10:333–361.

———. 1992. "Disability Transition for Older Persons With Arthritis." *Journal of Aging and Health* 4(2):212–243.

Verbrugge, L. and A. Jette. 1994. "The Disablement Process." *Social Science and Medicine* 38(1):1–14.

Vesperi, M. 1985. *City of Green Benches: Growing Old in a New Downtown.* Ithaca, NY: Cornell University Press.

———. 1987. "The Reluctant Consumer: Nursing Home Residents in the Post-Bergman Era." In *Growing Old In Different Societies: Cross-Cultural Perspectives* J. Sokolovsky, ed. Acton, MA: Copley.

———. 1995. "Nursing Home Research Comes of Age: Toward an Ethnological Perspective on Long Term Care." In *The Culture of Long Term Care: Nursing Home Ethnography.* N. Henderson and M. Vesperi, eds. Westport, CT: Greenwood.

Vincentnathan, S. G. and L. Vincentnathan. 1994. "Equality and Hierarchy in Untouchable Intergenerational Relations and Conflict Resolutions." *Journal of Cross-Cultural Gerontology* 9:1–19.

Virchow, R. 1959 (1849). *Disease, Life and Man: Selected Essays.* L. J. Rather, ed. Stanford, CA: Stanford University Press.

Vivelo, F. R. 1977. *The Herero of Western Botswana: Aspects of Change in a Group of Bantu-Speaking Cattle Herders.* St. Paul, MI: West.

von Mering, O. 1957. "A Family of Elders." In *Remotivating the Mental Patient.* O. von Mering and S. King, eds. New York: Russell Sage Foundation.

———. 1996. "American Culture and Long-Term Care." In *The Future of Long-Term Care: Social and Policy Issues.* R. Binstock, L. Cluff and O. von Mering, eds. Baltimore: Johns Hopkins University Press.

von Mering, O. and S. Gordon. 1993. "Buying into a New Community to Age Well: A U.S.A. Perspective." In *Elderly Care: A World Perspective.* K. Tout, ed. New York: Chapman and Hall.

von Mering, O. and L. Neff. 1993. "Joining a Life Care Community: An Alternative to 'Frailing' into a Nursing Home in the U.S.A." *Generations Review* 3:4.

Wada, S. 1995. "The Status and Image of the Elderly in Japan." In *Images of Aging: Cultural Representations of Later Life.* M. Featherstone and A. Wernick, eds. London: Routledge.

Wagner, D. 1995. "Special Report: Public Policy Focus on Grandparents Raising Grandchildren." *AAGE Newsletter* 16(4):5.

Walker, A. 1992. "Integration, Social Policy and Elderly Citizens: Towards a European Agenda on Ageing?" *Generations Review* 2(4):2–8.

Walker, A., ed. 1996. *The New Generational Contract: Intergenerational Relationships, Old Age, and Welfare.* London: UCL Press.

Wallace, S. and C. Lew-Ting. 1992. "Getting By at Home: Community Based Long-Term Care of Latino Elderly." *Western Journal of Medicine* 157:337–344.

Walls, C. T. 1992. "The Role of Church and Family Support in the Lives of Older African Americans." *Generations* 17(3) (Summer): 33–36.

Walls, C. T. and S. H. Zarit. 1991. "Informal Support from Black Churches and the Well-Being of Elderly Blacks." *Gerontologist* 31(4):490–496.

Walsh, A. C. and A. D. Trlin. 1973. "Niuean Migration: Niuean Socio-economic Background, Characteristics of Migrants, and Settlements in Auckland." *Journal of Polynesian Society* 82: 47–85.

Wang, L. and J. Schneider. 1993. "Home Care for the Chronically Ill Elderly in China: The Family Sickbed in Tianjin." *Journal of Cross-Cultural Gerontology* 8(4): 331–348.

Ward, R. 1984. "The Marginality and Salience of Being Old: When Is Age Relevant?" *Gerontologist* 24(3):227–232.

Warner, L. 1937. *A Black Civilization.* New York: Harper & Brothers.

Watson, W. 1990. "Family Care, Economics, and Health." In *Black Aged.* Z. Harel, E. A. McKinney and M. Williams, eds. Newbury Park, CA: Sage.

Watson, W. and R. J. Maxwell. 1977. *Human Aging and Dying: A Study in Sociocultural Gerontology.* New York: St. Martin's.

Wax, M. 1962. "The Changing Role of the Home for the Aged." *Gerontologist* 2:128–133.

Way, P. and K. Stanecki. 1994. *The Impact of HIV/AIDS on World Population.* Washington, DC: U.S. Government Printing Office.

Weeks, J. 1984. *Aging: Concepts and Social Issues.* Belmont, CA: Wadsworth.

Weeks, J. and J. Cuellar. 1981. "The Role of Family Members in the Helping Networks of Older People." *Gerontologist* 21:338–394.

Weibel-Orlando, J. 1987. *Final Report: Ethnicity, Continuity and Successful Aging.* Bethesda, MD: National Institute on Aging.

———. 1991. *Indian Country, L.A.: Maintaining Ethnic Community in Complex Society.* Urbana: University of Illinois Press.

Weinstein-Shr, G. and N. Z. Henkin. 1991. "Continuity and Change: Intergenerational Relations in Southeast Asian Refugee Families." *Marriage and Family Review* 16:351–367.

Wenger, C. 1984. *The Supportive Network: Coping With Old Age.* London: Allen & Unwin.

———. 1992. "Support Networks and Dementia: Aging in Liverpool." Working Paper

4, Bangor: University of Wales, Centre for Social Policy Research and Development.

———. 1993. "The Formation of Social Networks: Self-Help, Mutual Aid and Old People in Contemporary Britain." *Journal of Aging Studies* 7:25–40.

———. 1995. "A Comparison of Urban with Rural Support Networks: Liverpool and North Wales." *Ageing and Society* 15:59–81.

———. 1996. "Social Network Research in Gerontology: How Did We Get There and Where Do We Go Next?" In *Sociology of Ageing.* V. Minichiello, N. Chappell, A. Walker and H. Kendig, eds. Melbourne: International Sociological Association.

Wenger, C. and F. St. Leger. 1992. "Community Structure and Support Network Variations." *Ageing and Society* 12:213–236.

Wentowski, G. 1981. "Reciprocity and Coping Strategies of Older People: Cultural Dimensions of Network Building." *The Gerontologist* 21(6):600–610.

Westermeyer, J. 1986. "Migration and Psychopathology." In *Refugee Mental Health in Resettlement Countries.* C. L. Williams and J. Westermeyer, eds. Washington, DC: Hemisphere Publishing Corporation.

Westin, C. 1992. "Changes in Attitudes Toward Immigrants." Stockholm: Swedish Institute.

White, L. 1996. "Prevalence of Dementia in Older Japanese-American Men in Hawaii." *Journal of the American Medical Association* 276:955–960.

Whitehouse, P. J. and W. E. Dean. 1995. "Situated Beyond Maturity: Lessons for Alzheimer's Disease Research." *Journal of the American Geriatric Society* 43:1314–1315.

Whitfield, K. 1997. "Studying Cognition in Older African Americans: Some Conceptual Considerations." *Journal of Aging and Ethnicity* 1(1):41–52.

Wiessner, P. 1977. "Hxaro: A Regional System of Reciprocity for Reducing Risk Among the !Kung San." Ph.D. diss. University of Michigan.

———. 1983. "Social and Ceremonial Aspects of Death among the !Kung San." *Botswana Notes and Records* 15:1–15.

Wilder, D. et al. 1995. "Characteristics of Brief Screens for Dementia in a Multi-Cultural Population." *American Journal of Geriatric Psychiatry* 3(2):96–107.

Wilhite, B. 1994. "Outside Voices: The Daily Experiences of Japanese with Disabilities in Later Life." *Educational Gerontology* 20:783–796.

Williams, M. D. 1974. *Community in a Black Pentecostal Church: An Anthropological Study.* Prospect Heights, IL: Waveland.

Witter, W. 1994. "Some Women in Japan Sour on the Idea of Married Life." *Washington Times,* December 19.

Wolf, D. 1995. "Changes in Living Arrangements of Older Women: An International Study." *Gerontologist* 35(6):724–731.

Wolleson, A. M. 1989. "Koltgarden—from Idea to Reality." In *The Elderly in Denmark.* Copenhagen: The Danish Cultural Institute.

Wong, T., S. C. Ho and I. T. S. Yu. 1994. "Changing Health Needs and Emerging Health Problems." In *Guangdong: Survey of a Province Undergoing Rapid Change.* Y. M. Yeung and D. K. Y. Chu, eds. Hong Kong: Chinese University Press.

Wood, J. and R. Parham. 1990. "Coping with Perceived Burden: Ethnic and Cultural Issues in Alzheimer's Family Caregiving." *Journal of Applied Gerontology* 9(3):325–339.

Wood, J. and T. Wan. 1993. "Ethnicity and Minority Issues in Family Caregiving to

Rural Black Elders." *Ethnic Elderly and Long-Term Care*. C. M. Barresi and D. E. Stull, eds. New York: Springer.

Woodsong, C. 1994. "Old Farmers, Invisible Farmers: Age and Agriculture in Jamaica." *Journal of Cross-Cultural Gerontology* 9(3):277–299.

Woodworth, R. 1994. Presentation. Gerontological Society of America Annual Meetings, Atlanta, GA.

World Bank. 1980. *World Development Report*. New York: Oxford University Press.

———. 1985. *World Development Report*. Washington, DC: World Bank.

———. 1994. *Averting the Old Age Crisis*. New York: Oxford University Press.

World Health Organization. 1991. *World Health Statistics Annual 1990*. Geneva: World Health Organization.

———. 1995. *The World Health Report 1995*. Geneva: World Health Organization.

Wright, B. 1983. *Physical Disability: A Psychosocial Approach*. 2nd ed. New York: Harper.

Yale, R. 1995. *Developing Support Groups for Individuals with Early-Stage Alzheimer's Disease*. Baltimore, MD: Health Professions Press.

Yee, B. 1989. "Loss of One's Homeland and Culture During the Middle Years." In *Coping With the Losses of Middle Age*. R. A. Kalish, ed. Newbury Park, CA: Sage Publications.

———. 1992. "Markers of Successful Aging among Vietnamese Refugee Women." *Women and Therapy* 12:221–238.

———, ed. 1997. "Ethnogeriatrics: Impact of Cultural and Minority Experiences on Geriatric Rehabilitation." Special Issue of *Topics in Geriatric Rehabilitation* 12(4).

———. Forthcoming a. *Variations in Aging: Older Minorities*. Texas Consortium of Geriatric Education Centers, UTMB School of Allied Health Sciences, University of Texas Medical Branch at Galveston.

———. Forthcoming b. "Life-Span Development of Asian and Pacific Islanders: Impact of Gender and Age Roles." In *Developing Cultural Competence in Evaluation of Substance Abuse Prevention among Asian and Pacific Islander Communities*. B. Yee, N. Mokuau and S. Kim, eds. Center for Substance Abuse Prevention Cultural Competence Series V.

Yee, B., L. Huang and A. Lew. Forthcoming. "Asian and Pacific Islander Families: Life-Span Socialization in a Cultural Context." In *Handbook of Asian American Psychology, Vol. I*. L. Lee and N. Zane, eds. Newbury Park, CA: Sage.

Yee, B. and N. Thu. 1987. "Correlates of Drug Abuse and Abuse Among Indochinese Refugees: Mental Health Implications." *Journal of Psychoactive Drugs* 19:77–83.

Yee, B. and G. Weaver. 1994. "Ethnic Minorities and Health Promotion: Developing a 'Culturally Competent' Agenda." *Generations* (Spring): 39–44.

Yeo, G. and D. Gallagher-Thompson, eds. 1996. *Ethnicity and the Dementias*. New York: Taylor and Francis.

Yeo, G. et al. 1994. "Faculty Development in Ethnogeriatrics." Paper presented at the Gerontology Society of America Meetings, Atlanta.

Yomiuri Nenkan 1995 [Yomiuri Yearbook 1995]. 1995. Tokyo: Yomiuri Shinbun.

Yomiuri Nenkan 1997 [Yomiuri Yearbook 1997]. 1997. Tokyo: Yomiuri Shinbun.

Yomiuri Shinbun. 1995. "65 sai ijyō saita 1821 man-nin" [65 and Over Have Topped 18,210,000 Persons]. *Yomiuri Shinbun*, September 15:1.

Yoshida, S., ed. 1994. *Aging in Japan*. Tokyo: Japan Aging Research Center (JARC).

Young, R. and F. Ikeuchi. 1997. In *Aging: Asian Experiences Past and Present*. S. Formanek and S. Linhart, eds. Vienna: Verlag der Osterreichischen Akademie der Wissenschaften.

Young, R. and E. Kahana. 1995. "The Context of Caregiving and Well-Being Outcomes Among African and Caucasian Americans." *The Gerontologist* 35:225–232.

Young, R. and E. Olson, eds. 1991. *Health, Illness, and Disability in Later Life*. Newbury Park, CA: Sage.

Young, T. K. 1994. *The Health of Native Americans*. New York: Oxford University Press.

Yuzawa, Y. 1994. *About Japan Series: Japanese Families*. Tokyo: Foreign Press Center.

Yu, E. S. 1992. "U.S. National Health Data on Asian Americans and Pacific Islanders: A Research Agenda for the 1990's." *American Journal of Public Health* 82: 1645–1652.

Yu, L. 1992. "Intergenerational Transfer of Resources Within Policy and Cultural Contexts." In *Caregiving Systems: Informal and Formal Helpers*. S. Zarit, K. Perlin and K. W. Schaie, eds. Hillsdale, NJ: L. Erlbaum.

Yu, L., Y. Yu and P. Mansfield. 1990. "Gender and Changes in Support of Aged Parents in China." *Gender and Society* 4:83–89.

Zborowski, M. 1969. *People in Pain*. San Francisco: Jossey-Bass.

Zimmer, L. J. 1987. "Who Will Bury Me?: The Plight of Childless Elderly Among the Gende." *Journal of Cross-Cultural Gerontology* 2(1):61–78.

Zisselman, M. et al. 1996. "A Pet Therapy Intervention With Geriatric Psychiatry In-patients." *The American Journal of Occupational Therapy* 50(1):47–51.

Index

Abuse. *See* Elder abuse and neglect

Abandonment. *See* Elder abuse and neglect

African-American culture: age concepts in, 2; extended kinship network in, 267–68, 446, 447–48, 449; literature on, 277–80; religion and spirituality in, 279–80, 285–90, 291, 449–50; social support network in, 291, 446–50; value of children in, 277, 285

African-American elderly women, 276–91; as caregivers, 446; child raising and grandparenting by, 279, 281, 284–85; disability and, 443–51; as family historian, 284–85; health status of, 447; impoverishment of, 257–58; religious and spiritual roles of, 279–80, 285–90, 291; as wise women, 280, 281–85, 286, 289–90

African women elders: as grandmothers, 85–86; healing and religious roles of, 82–83; living arrangements of, 75–76, 90; quality of caregiving for, 90–95; reciprocal relationships of, 89–90; sociocultural contexts of aging and, 72; widowhood of, 72–96; wife inheritance and remarriage of, 74–75, 83–85; work and economic conditions of, 76

Age-based status: administrative/informational roles and, 7; in Asian cultures, 185–86, 225, 233–34, 296–97; dementia in Indian culture and, 457; social boundaries and, 127–28; support in traditional peasant societies and, 6–7

Age boundaries, 3–5; chronological demarcation of, 18; culture and, 392–93; linguistic markers of, 127, 198, 199–201 (*see also* Language and age terms); ritualization of, 2–3, 127–28

Age-grades 127–28

Ageism, 125–26, 245, 354–55

Age-segregated environments, quality of life in, 322, 354–55

Age-sets, 3, 127, 128

Aging: cultural context of, xiv–xvi, 350–51; global view of, 2–5; illness linked with, 393; myths, xxiv–xxv, 391–92

Aging and Modernization, xviii. *See also* Modernization

Aging Enterprise: in the United States, 104; in Sweden, 184

Aging in place, xxvi

AIDS epidemic, parentless children and, 160–61

Akiyama, Hiroko, 163

Alzheimer's disease, 268, 395–96, 427;

About the Editor and Contributors

HIROKO AKIYAMA, Ph.D., is Assistant Research Scientist in the Life Course Development program in the Institute for Social Research at the University of Michigan. Dr. Akiyama's research interests have focused on gender, culture, social relations, and health.

TONI C. ANTONUCCI, Ph.D., is Program Director in the Life Course Development Program in the Institute for Social Research and Professor of Psychology, both at the University of Michigan. She has been awarded a Fogarty International Senior Fellowship and has been a Chercheur Etrangere at the Institut National de la Sante et Recherche Medicale in Paris, France. Dr. Antonucci's research interests have focused, for more than twenty years, on social relationships across the life-span.

JUDITH C. BARKER, Ph.D., does research and teaches at the Medical Anthropology Program, University of California, San Francisco. She has published widely on how the elderly manage various chronic illnesses on a day-to-day basis, and has conducted fieldwork on this topic in the South Pacific and in the United States.

RUTH CAMPBELL, M.S.W., directs the social work department of Turner Geriatric Services, University of Michigan Medical Center. She is also a faculty associate for the University of Michigan's Institute of Gerontology. She has conducted research on outpatient programs for the elderly, innovative nursing home programs and cross-cultural and intergenerational studies of Japanese and American elderly.

MARIA G. CATTELL, Ph.D., is an anthropologist teaching at Millersville University in Pennsylvania and a research associate at the Field Museum of Natural History. She has been doing research on older people and social change in Kenya since 1982 and also among Zulus in South Africa and in a Philadelphia neighborhood. She is co-author of *Old Age in Global Perspective: Cross-Cultural and Cross-National Views* (1994).

CARL COHEN, M.D., is Professor of Psychiatry and Director of Geriatric Psychiatry at the SUNY Health Science Center at Brooklyn. He has published widely in the areas of social psychiatry and social gerontology and is co-author of *Old Men of the Bowery* (1989).

KITTER CHRISTIANSEN, M.A., is a psychologist and family counselor. She completed early work at the Lokken-Vra research site as a part of her graduate work at Aalborg University Center, Aalborg, Denmark.

MONIKA DEPPEN-WOOD, M.A., has taught Sociology of Aging and Social Problems at Rutgers University/Camden and lectured on ''Food, Culture and Aging'' and ''Cross-Cultural Communication'' at the University of Pennsylvania's Institute on Aging. She currently is employed by the Philadelphia Geriatric Center as project director for a federally-funded study, ''Polio Disabilities: Personal Meaning, Well-Being, and Age.''

JEANETTE DICKERSON-PUTMAN, Ph.D., is currently an associate professor of anthropology at Indiana University at Indianapolis. As a member of Project AGE, she carried out an ethnographic study of age in Blessington, Republic of Ireland. She has also explored various aspects of gender, age and development in Papua New Guinea and French Polynesia.

PATRICIA DRAPER, Ph.D., is a cultural anthropologist and professor appointed in anthropology and human development at Pennsylvania State University. Her research interests include southern African hunter gatherers, African cultures and human life course issues. Her fieldwork has been conducted in Botswana and Namibia and concerned the Ju/'hoansi peoples of the western Kalahari.

CHRISTINE L. FRY, Ph.D., is Professor of Anthropology at Loyola University of Chicago. She is co-director of Project AGE (with Jennie Keith). Her interests are in cross-cultural comparisons of aging and community studies of older adults. She has published on the life course, the anthropology of aging and on retirement communities.

ANTHONY P. GLASCOCK, Ph.D., is Professor of Anthropology and Head of the Department of Psychology, Sociology, and Anthropology at Drexel University. He has conducted research on aging and old age for the last fifteen years, publishing widely on gerontological issues, including research in Somalia and Ireland. His current research interests are on gerontological assessment and the development of a comprehensive case monitoring and management service.

HENRY C. HARPENDING, Ph.D., is Professor of Anthropology and Human Development at The Pennsylvania State University. He served as one of the members of "Project Age" and has conducted fieldwork with the !Kung Bushmen of the northern Kalahari and with Herero pastoralists of the same area. His interests include human population genetics, demography and the evolution of family organization.

J. NEIL HENDERSON, Ph.D., is an Associate Professor of Anthropology at the Department of Community and Family Health in the College of Public Health at the University of South Florida. He is co-editor of *The Culture of Long Term Care: Nursing Home Ethnography* (1995). He is also editor of the *Journal of Cross-Cultural Gerontology*.

CHARLOTTE IKELS, Ph.D., is an Associate Professor of Anthropology at Case Western Reserve University. She has published extensively on aging among Chinese populations in Hong Kong, the United States, and China. Her most recent book, *The Return of the God of Wealth: The Transition to a Market Economy in Urban China* (1996) analyzes the impact of the post-Mao economic reforms on the daily lives of China's urban residents.

JENNIE KEITH, Ph.D., is Professor of Anthropology and Provost at Swarthmore College. Her research has investigated the meaning of age in different cultural contexts and the creation of community in retirement residences. Her most recent publication is *The Aging Experience* (1994), written with six other members of "Project Age." This work examined the influence of social and cultural context on aging in seven communities in Africa, Ireland, Hong Kong and the United States.

KEVIN KINSELLA, Ph.D., is Chief of the Aging Studies Branch of the International Programs Center, U.S. Bureau of the Census. His professional activities have focussed on the roles of women in development, population projections for developing countries (particularly in Latin America), and the demography of aging internationally. Current research interests include retirement systems and pension coverage, and the nature of the epidemiologic transition in the Third World.

MARK R. LUBORSKY, Ph.D., is Senior Research Anthropologist and Assistant Director of Research at the Philadelphia Geriatric Center. Federal and foundation grants support his studies of cultural values and personal meanings, and how these relate to mental and physical health, and to disability and rehabilitation processes.

JANE W. PETERSON, Ph.D., is professor of nursing at Seattle University. She received a Ph.D. in anthropology from the University of Washington, Seattle. Her interests include organization of Black families, African-American women, and health care issues.

BRENDA ROBB JENIKE is a Ph.D. candidate in sociocultural anthropology at the University of California, Los Angeles. She is continuing her research on family caregiving to the elderly as a Japan Foundation dissertation fellow at Ochanomizu University in Tokyo.

HARRIET G. ROSENBERG, Ph.D., is an associate professor in the Division of Social Science at York University, Canada. Her research interests focus on social reproduction and social change. She is the author of *A Negotiated World: Three Centuries of Change in a French Alpine Village* (1988) and co-author of *Through the Kitchen Window: The Politics of Home and Family* (1990).

ROBERT L. RUBINSTEIN, Ph.D., is Senior Research Anthropologist and Director of Research at the Philadelphia Geriatric Center. He has conducted research in the United States and Vanuatu. His gerontological research interests include social relations of the elderly, childlessness in later life and the home environments of old people.

JOEL SAVISHINSKY is Professor of Anthropology at Ithaca College. He has done research in Turkey, England, the Bahamas, the Canadian North, and rural America. He is author of *The Ends of Time: Life and Work in a Nursing Home* (1991), which won the Gerontological Society of America's Kalish Award for Innovative Publishing.

JESSICA SCHEER, Ph.D., is a senior research associate at the National Rehabilitation Hospital Research Center in Washington, DC. Her interests and publications are in the areas of culture and disability, aging with disabilities (polio and spinal cord injury) and anthropological approaches to mental health problems.

DENA SHENK, Ph.D., is coordinator of the Gerontology Program and Professor of Anthropology at the University of North Carolina at Charlotte. Her primary research interests focus on diversity in the aging experience based on gender, culture, and environmental contexts. She has also published on the use of visual methodologies in aging research and is currently working on in-depth analyses of individual life histories and beginning a new project on ''Wise Older Women: Thriving in the African-American Community.''

RENÉE ROSE SHIELD, Ph.D., is a cultural anthropologist and clinical assistant professor of Community Health at Brown University. She is the author of *Uneasy Endings: Daily Life in an American Nursing Home* (1988) and other articles about nursing home culture.

JAY SOKOLOVSKY, Ph.D., is a Professor of Anthropology at the University of South Florida, St. Petersburg Campus. He has recently completed NIA-funded research on the help-seeking behavior of families trying to support a relative with dementia in the community. Dr. Sokolovsky specializes in cross-cultural, comparative gerontology and has written several books and authored over 20 articles dealing with this subject. In his research he has studied the elderly in a Mexican peasant village, Croatia, England, New York's inner-city, the new town of Columbia, Maryland and in Tampa, Florida. He has edited *Growing Old in Different Societies* (1987) and is co-author of *Old Men of the Bowery* (1989). He is co-founder and former President of the Association of Anthropology and Gerontology and the founder of the International Commission on Aging of the International Union of Anthropological and Ethnological Sciences.

YOHKO TSUJI, Ph.D., is a Japanese cultural anthropologist trained in the United States. She is currently a Research Associate at the East Asia Program of Cornell University. Her research primarily covers the United States and Japan and includes aging, the life course and the family as well as the impact of social change.

MARIA D. VESPERI, Ph.D., is an Associate Professor of Anthropology at New College, the honors campus of the Florida State University System. She is author of *City of Green Benches: Growing Old in a New Downtown* (1985) and co-editor of *The Culture of Long Term Care: Nursing Home Ethnography* (1995). Her current projects include a 150-year social history of a utopian community and a collection of essays that draw upon her experiences as a former journalist and editorial writer.

JOAN WEIBEL-ORLANDO, Ph.D., is an associate professor in the department of anthropology at the University of Southern California. She has worked with American Indians in both urban and rural communities since 1973 and has published widely in the areas of Indian alcohol use and abuse, aging and bi-cultural adaptation. Her book, *Indian Country, L.A.: Ethnic Community Maintenance in Complex Society*, was published in 1991. She is currently writing a book about intergenerational relations among Italian-Americans and their Tuscan relatives.

BARBARA W. K. YEE, Ph.D., is a life-span developmental psychologist who is of Chinese-Hawaiian heritage. Her research has examined adaptation and coping of Southeast Asian elders since 1975. Currently, she is studying the transmission of cultural health beliefs and practices across generations within Asian and Pacific Islander families.

BRUCE M. ZELKOVITZ, Ph.D., is Professor of Sociology at Washburn University and is an adviser to the Swedish Program at Stockhom University. He has a continuing interest in the political economy of Sweden and is currently doing research linking the sociology of sport, the sociology of opera, and aging.

ISBN 0-89789-452-9

HARDCOVER BAR CODE